# LINUX

## IN A NUTSHELL

*A Desktop Quick Reference*

# LINUX
## IN A NUTSHELL

*A Desktop Quick Reference*

Third Edition

*Ellen Siever, Stephen Spainhour,*
*Stephen Figgins & Jessica P. Hekman*

### O'REILLY®

*Beijing • Cambridge • Farnham • Köln • Paris • Sebastopol • Taipei • Tokyo*

## Linux in a Nutshell, Third Edition

by Ellen Siever, Stephen Spainhour, Stephen Figgins, and Jessica P. Hekman

Copyright © 2000, 1999, 1997 O'Reilly & Associates, Inc. All rights reserved.
Printed in the United States of America.

Published by O'Reilly & Associates, Inc., 101 Morris Street, Sebastopol, CA 95472.

**Editor:** Andy Oram

**Production Editor:** Darren Kelly

**Cover Designer:** Edie Freedman

**Printing History:**

| | |
|---|---|
| January 1997: | First Edition. |
| February 1999: | Second Edition. |
| August 2000: | Third Edition. |

### Library of Congress Cataloging-in-Publication Data

Linux in a nutshell : a desktop reference / Ellen Siever ... [et. al.].--3rd ed.
    p. cm.
  ISBN 0-596-00025-1
    1. Linux. 2. Operating systems (Computers) I. Siever, Ellen. II. Siever, Ellen. Linux in a nutshell.

  QA76.76.O63 L5459 2000
  005.4'69—dc21                       .           00-058456

# Table of Contents

# *Preface*

This is a book about Linux, a freely available clone of the Unix operating system for personal computers. Linux was first developed by Linus Torvalds, who built the first Linux kernel and continues to centrally coordinate improvements. The operating system continues to grow under the dedicated cultivation of a host of other programmers and hackers all over the world, all connected through the Internet. Beyond the kernel code, Linux includes utilities and commands from the Free Software Foundation's GNU project, Berkeley Unix (BSD), and a complete port of the X Window System (XFree86) from the X Consortium, in addition to many features written specifically for Linux. Even more recent projects extend Linux in exciting ways, some through changes to the kernel—such as real-time scheduling and RAID support—and some through libraries and applications that radically change the user's experience; the GNOME and KDE desktops briefly covered in this book are the most prominent examples.

This book is a quick reference for the basic commands and features of the Linux operating system. As with other books in O'Reilly's "In a Nutshell" series, this book is geared toward users who know what they want to do and have some idea how to do it, but just can't remember the correct command or option. We hope this guide will become an invaluable desktop reference for the Linux user.

## *Other Resources*

This book will not tell you how to install and maintain a Linux system. For that, you will probably want O'Reilly's *Learning Red Hat Linux* or *Learning Debian GNU/Linux*, by Bill McCarty, which contain Linux distributions on CD-ROM and provide help with installation and configuration. Alternatively, *Running Linux* by Matt Welsh, Matthias Kalle Dalheimer, and Lar Kaufman is an in-depth guide suitable for all major distributions. For networking information, check out *Linux Network Administrator's Guide* by Olaf Kirch and Terry Dawson. In addition to

O'Reilly's Linux titles, our wide range of Unix, X, Perl, and Java titles may also be of interest to the Linux user.

## Online Documentation

The Internet is also full of information about Linux. One of the best resources is the Linux Documentation Project at *http://www.linuxdoc.org*. It has numerous short guides called HOWTOs, along with some full manuals. For online information about the GNU utilities covered in this book, consult *http://www.gnu.org* (or one of the dozens of mirror sites around the world). The Free Software Foundation, which is in charge of GNU, publishes its documentation in a number of hardcopy books about various tools.

## *Linux Journal and Linux Magazine*

*Linux Journal* and *Linux Magazine* are monthly magazines for the Linux community, written and published by a number of Linux activists. They contain articles ranging from novice questions and answers to kernel programming internals. *Linux Journal* is the oldest magazine and is published by S.S.C. Incorporated, *http://www.ssc.com*. *Linux Magazine* is at *http://www.linuxmagazine.com*.

## *Linux Usenet Newsgroups*

If you have access to Usenet news, the following Linux-related newsgroups are available:

*comp.os.linux.announce*
> A moderated newsgroup containing announcements of new software, distributions, bug reports, and goings-on in the Linux community. All Linux users should read this group. Submissions may be mailed to *linux-announce@news.ornl.gov*.

*comp.os.linux.help*
> General questions and answers about installing or using Linux.

*comp.os.linux.admin*
> Discussions relating to systems administration under Linux.

*comp.os.linux.networking*
> Discussions relating to networking with Linux.

*comp.os.linux.development*
> Discussions about developing the Linux kernel and system itself.

*comp.os.linux.misc*
> A catch-all newsgroup for miscellaneous discussions that don't fall under the previous categories.

There are also several newsgroups devoted to Linux in languages other than English, such as *fr.comp.os.linux* in French and *de.comp.os.linux* in German.

## Online Linux Support

There are many ways of obtaining help online, where volunteers from around the world offer expertise and services to assist users with questions and problems.

The OpenProjects IRC Network is an IRC network devoted entirely to Open Projects—Open Source and Open Hardware alike. Some of its channels are designed to provide online Linux support services. IRC stands for Internet Relay Chat, and is a network service that allows you to talk interactively on the Internet to other users. IRC networks support multiple channels on which groups of people talk. Whatever you type in a channel is seen by all other users of that channel.

There are a number of active channels on the OpenProjects IRC network where you will find users 24 hours a day, 7 days a week who are willing and able to help you solve any Linux problems you may have, or just chat. You can use this service by installing an IRC client like *irc-II*, connecting to servername *irc.openprojects.org:6667*, and joining the `#linpeople` channel.

### Linux User Groups

Many Linux User Groups around the world offer direct support to users. Many Linux User Groups engage in activities such as installation days, talks and seminars, demonstration nights, and other completely social events. Linux User Groups are a great way of meeting other Linux users in your area. There are a number of published lists of Linux User Groups. Some of the better-known ones are:

*Groups of Linux Users Everywhere*
   *http://www.ssc.com/glue/groups*

*LUG list project*
   *http://www.nllgg.nl/lugww*

*LUG registry*
   *http://www.linux.org/users*

## Conventions

This desktop quick reference follows certain typographic conventions:

**Bold**
   is used for commands, programs, and options. All terms shown in bold are typed literally.

*Italic*
   is used to show arguments and variables that should be replaced with user-supplied values. Italic is also used to indicate filenames and directories and to highlight comments in examples.

`Constant Width`
   is used to show the contents of files or the output from commands.

**Constant Width Bold**

is used in examples and tables to show commands or other text that should be typed literally by the user.

*Constant Width Italic*

is used in examples and tables to show text that should be replaced with user-supplied values.

*%, $*

are used in some examples as the *tcsh* shell prompt (%) and as the Bourne or **bash** shell prompt ($).

[ ] surround optional elements in a description of syntax. (The brackets themselves should never be typed.) Note that many commands show the argument [*files*]. If a filename is omitted, standard input (e.g., the keyboard) is assumed. End with an end-of-file character.

*EOF*

indicates the end-of-file character (normally Ctrl-D).

| is used in syntax descriptions to separate items for which only one alternative may be chosen at a time.

→ is used at the bottom of a right-hand page to show that the current entry continues on the next page. The continuation is marked by a ←.

The owl icon designates a note, which is an important aside to its nearby text. For example . . .

 When you see the owl icon, you know the text beside it is a note, like this.

A final word about syntax. In many cases, the space between an option and its argument can be omitted. In other cases, the spacing (or lack of spacing) must be followed strictly. For example, **−w***n* (no intervening space) might be interpreted differently from **−w** *n*. It's important to notice the spacing used in option syntax.

## We'd Like to Hear from You

We have tested and verified all of the information in this book to the best of our ability, but you may find that features have changed (or even that we have made mistakes!). Please let us know about any errors you find, as well as your suggestions for future editions, by writing:

O'Reilly & Associates, Inc.
101 Morris Street
Sebastopol, CA 95472
800-998-9938 (in the U.S. or Canada)

707-829-0515 (international/local)
707-829-0104 (fax)

You can also send us messages electronically. To be put on the m
request a catalog, send email to:

*info@oreilly.com*

To ask technical questions or comment on the book, send email to:

*bookquestions@oreilly.com*

We have a web site for the book, where we list examples, errata, and any plans
for future editions. You can access this page at:

*http://www.oreilly.com/catalog/linuxnut3*

For more information about this book and others, see the O'Reilly web site:

*http://www.oreilly.com*

# Acknowledgments

This edition of *Linux in a Nutshell* is the result of the cooperative efforts of many
people. Thanks to Andy Oram for his editorial skills, to Val Quercia for her project
management skills, and to both of them for pitching in to check existing chapters
and update and write new material as needed. The CVS material that makes up the
bulk of Chapter 14 was written by Gregor N. Purdy.

For technical review, thanks go to Matt Welsh of *Running Linux* and *Installation
and Getting Started Guide* fame; Michael K. Johnson of Red Hat Software; Robert J.
Chassell, Phil Hughes, and Laurie Lynne Tucker of *Linux Journal*; Arnold Robbins,
Julian T. J. Midgley, Terry Dawson, Doug Moreen, Ron Passerini, and Mark Stone.

# CHAPTER 1

# *Introduction*

In just a few years, Linux has grown from a student/hacker playground to an upstart challenger in the server market to a well-respected system taking its rightful place in educational and corporate networks. A freely redistributable clone of the Unix operating system, Linux is turning up everywhere. People use it for web servers, file servers, and workstations instead of—or alongside—systems from traditional Unix vendors as well as Windows NT. In addition to its role in large networks (because it's a friendly fellow that fits in very nicely with other operating systems), Linux is popular among Windows users who just want to try something that gives them more speed, more power, and more control.

The historical impact of Linux goes even beyond its own penetration into the markets of proprietary operating systems. Its success has inspired countless other free software or open source (*http://opensource.org*) projects, including Samba, GNOME, and a mind-boggling collection of innovative projects that you can browse at numerous sites like SourceForge (*http://sourceforge.net*). As both a platform for other developers and a development model, Linux gave a tremendous boost to the Free Software Foundation's GNU project, which in turn had furnished key software that made the development of Linux possible. In short, Linux is a central participant in the most exciting and productive free software movement ever seen.

If you haven't obtained Linux yet or have it but don't know exactly how to get started using it, see the Preface.

## *The Excitement of Linux*

Linux is first of all free software: anyone can download the source from the Internet or buy it on a low-cost CD-ROM. But Linux is becoming well known because it's more than free software—it's unusually good software. You can get more from your hardware with Linux (particularly on Intel systems, where it was originally

1

developed) and be assured of fewer crashes; even its security is better than many commercial alternatives.

As free software, Linux revives the grand creativity and the community of sharing that Unix was long known for. The unprecedented flexibility and openness of Unix—which newcomers usually found confusing and frustrating but which they eventually found they couldn't live without—continually inspired extensions, new tools like Perl, and experiments in computer science that sometimes ended up in mainstream commercial computer systems.

Many fondly remember the days when AT&T provided universities with Unix source code at no charge, and the University of Berkeley started distributing its version in any manner that allowed people to get it. For these older hackers, Linux can bring back the spirit of working together—all the more so because the Internet is now widespread. And for the many who are too young to remember the first round of open systems (such as the hordes of students attracted to Linux) or whose prior experience has been woefully constricted by proprietary operating systems, now is the time to discover the wonders of freely distributable source code and infinitely adaptable interfaces.

The Linux kernel itself was originally designed by Linus Torvalds at the University of Helsinki in Finland and later developed through collaboration with countless volunteers worldwide. By "kernel," we mean the core of the operating system itself—not the applications (such as the compiler, shells, and so forth) that run on it. Today, the term "Linux" is often used to mean the kernel as well as the applications and complete system environment.

Most Linux systems cannot be technically referred to as a "version of Unix," as they have not been submitted to the required tests and licensed properly.* However, at least one Linux distribution has in fact been branded as POSIX.1. Linux offers all the common programming interfaces as standard Unix systems, and as you can see from this book, all the common Unix utilities have been reimplemented on Linux. It is a powerful, robust, fully usable system for those who like Unix.

The economic power behind Linux's popularity is its support for an enormous range of hardware used with IBM-compatible personal computers. People who are accustomed to MS-DOS and Microsoft Windows are often amazed at how much faster their hardware appears to work with Linux—it makes efficient use of its resources.

For the first several years, users were attracted to Linux for a variety of financial and political reasons, but soon they discovered an unexpected benefit: it works better than many commercial systems. With the Samba file and print server, for instance, Linux serves a large number of end-user PCs without crashing. With the Apache web server, it provides more of the useful features web administrators want than competing products do.

---

* Before an operating system can be called "Unix," it must be branded by X/Open.

## Distribution and Support

While it is convenient to download one or two new programs over the Internet and fairly feasible to download something as large as the Linux kernel, getting a whole working system over phone lines is an absurd proposition. Over the years, therefore, commercial and noncommercial packages called *distributions* have emerged. The first consisted of approximately 50 diskettes, at least one of which would usually turn out to be bad and have to be replaced. When CD-ROM drives became widespread, Linux really took off.

After getting Linux, the average user is concerned next with support. While Usenet newsgroups offer very quick response and meet the needs of many intrepid users, you can also buy support from the vendors of the major distributions and a number of independent experts. Linux is definitely supported at least as well as commercial software.

Intel is still by far the most common hardware running Linux, but Linux is also now commercially available on a number of other hardware systems, notably the PowerPC, the 64-bit Intel Itanium processor, the Alpha (created by Digital Equipment Corporation, now Compaq), the SPARC, and the MIPS chip.

## Commands on Linux

Linux commands are not the same as standard Unix ones. They're better! This is because most of them are provided by the GNU project run by the Free Software Foundation (FSF). GNU means "GNU's Not Unix"—the first word of the phrase is supposed to be expanded with infinite recursion.

Benefiting from years of experience with standard Unix utilities and advances in computer science, programmers on the GNU project have managed to create versions of standard tools that have more features, run faster and more efficiently, and lack the bugs or inconsistencies that persist in the original standard versions.

While GNU provided the programming utilities and standard commands like *grep*, most of the system and network administration tools on Linux came from the Berkeley Software Distribution (BSD). In addition, some people wrote tools specifically for Linux to deal with special issues such as filesystems that only Linux supports. This book documents all the standard Unix commands that are commonly available on most Linux distributions.

The third type of software most commonly run on Linux is the X Window System, ported by the XFree86 project to standard Intel chips. While this book cannot cover the wide range of utilities that run on X, we briefly cover some of the useful customizations you may want to make to your KDE, GNOME, or **fvwm** desktop.

## What This Book Offers

Based originally on the classic O'Reilly & Associates quick reference, *Unix in a Nutshell*, this book has been expanded to include much information that is specific to Linux. The current edition includes chapters on package managers (which make it easy to install, update, and remove related software files), on the KDE and

GNOME desktops, and on the **fvwm** window manager, as well as new commands and expanded discussions of several topics such as CVS and **bash**.

*Linux in a Nutshell* doesn't teach you Linux—it is, after all, a quick reference— but novices as well as highly experienced users will find it of great value. When you have some idea what command you want but aren't sure just how it works or what combinations of options give you the exact output required, this book is the place to turn. It is also an eye-opener: it can make you aware of options that you never knew about before.

Like computer systems from the age in which Unix was born (the early 1970s), Linux is mostly a command-driven system. Most versions of Linux provide a few graphical tools, and several commercial products are available, but none of these graphical utilities are central to Linux. That is why this book, like the traditional *Unix in a Nutshell* reference, focuses on the shell and on commands you run from the shell.

Of course, Linux offers a windowing system—a very rich and flexible one, as befits a rich and flexible operating system. But a lot of the time you'll just open a simulated VT100 terminal (the **xterm** program) and enter commands into that. You'll find yourself moving back and forth between graphical programs and the commands listed in this book.

So the first thing you've got to do, once you're over the hurdle of installing Linux, is get to know the common utilities run from the shell prompt. If you know absolutely nothing about Unix, we recommend you read a basic guide (introductory chapters in the O'Reilly books *Learning Red Hat Linux, Learning Debian GNU/ Linux,* and *Running Linux* can get you started). This book offers a context for understanding different kinds of commands (including commands for programming, system administration, and network administration) in Chapter 2, *System and Network Administration Overview,* followed by the command reference itself in Chapter 3, *Linux Commands.* Chapter 3 is obviously the central focus of the book, containing about one third its bulk.

The small chapters immediately following Chapter 3 help you get your system set up. Since most users do not want to completely abandon other operating systems (whether a Microsoft Windows system, OS/2, or some Unix flavor), Linux often resides on the same computer as other systems. The user can boot the system he needs for a particular job. Chapter 4, *Boot Methods,* lists the commonly used booting options on Intel systems, including LILO (Linux Loader) and Loadlin. The next chapter, Chapter 5, *Red Hat and Debian Package Managers,* covers the Red Hat package manager (**rpm**), which is supported by both the Red Hat and the SuSE distributions, and the Debian package manager (**dpkg**). Package managers are crucial for installing and updating software; they make sure you have all the files you need in the proper versions.

All commands are interpreted by the shell. The shell is simply a program that accepts commands from the user and executes them. Different shells sometimes use slightly different syntax to mean the same thing. Under Linux, two popular shells are **bash** and **tcsh**, and they differ in subtle ways. (One of the nice things about Linux, and other Unix systems is that you have a variety of shells to choose from, each with strengths and weaknesses.) We offer several chapters on shells.

You may decide to read these after you've used Linux for a while, because they mostly cover powerful, advanced features that you'll want when you're a steady user.

In order to get real work done, you'll have to learn some big, comprehensive utilities: notably an editor and some scripting tools. Two major editors are used on Linux: **vi** and Emacs. Both have chapters in this book. Following the editors come two chapters on classic Unix tools for manipulating text files on a line-by-line basis: **sed** and **gawk** (the GNU version of the traditional **awk**). O'Reilly also has a separate book about each of these topics that you may find valuable, because none is completely intuitive upon first use. (Emacs does have an excellent built-in tutorial, though; to invoke it, press **Ctrl-H** followed by **t** for "tutorial.")

CVS (Concurrent Versions System) and RCS (Revision Control System) manage files so you can retrieve old versions and maintain different versions simultaneously. Originally used by programmers who have complicated requirements for building and maintaining applications, these tools have turned out to be valuable for anyone who maintains files of any type, particularly when coordinating a team of people. CVS is a layer on top of RCS that makes it easier for multiple people to edit a file simultaneously. Chapter 14, *CVS and RCS*, presents CVS and RCS commands.

Every distribution of Linux is slightly different, but you'll find that the commands we document are what you use most of the time and that they work the same on all distributions. Basic commands, programming utilities, system administration, and network administration are all covered here. But some areas were so big that we had to leave them out. The many applications that depend on the X Window System didn't make the cut. Nor did TEX (a text-processing tool used extensively in academia and by Linux users in general), or the many useful programming languages like Perl, Tcl/Tk, and Python with which users vastly expand the capabilities of their systems. These subjects would stretch the book out of its binding.

Our goal in producing this book is to provide convenience, and that means keeping it small. It certainly doesn't have everything the manual pages have. But you'll find that it has what you need 95% of the time.

## Sources and Licenses

When you get Linux, you also get the source code. The same goes for all the utilities on Linux (unless your vendor offered a commercial application or library as a special enhancement). You may never bother looking at the source code, but it's key to Linux's strength. The source code has to be provided by the vendor, under the Linux license, and it permits those who are competent at such things to fix bugs, provide advice about the system's functioning, and submit improvements that benefit all of us. The license is the well-known General Public License, also known as the *GPL* or *copyleft*, invented and popularized by the Free Software Foundation.

The FSF, founded by Richard Stallman, is a phenomenon that many people would believe to be impossible if it did not exist. (The same goes for Linux, in fact—10 years ago, who would have imagined a robust operating system developed by collaborators over the Internet and made freely redistributable?) One of the most popular editors on Unix, GNU Emacs, comes from the FSF. So do **gcc** and **g++** (C and C++ compilers), which for a while used to set the standard for optimization and fast code. One of the largest projects within GNU is the GNOME desktop, which already encompasses several useful general-purpose libraries, window managers, and applications. The GNOME developers have big plans for providing an environment that integrates not only the applications on each user's system but also the services provided throughout a whole organization.

Dedicated to the sharing of software, the FSF provides all its code and documentation on the Internet and allows anyone with a whim for enhancements to alter the source code. One of its projects is the Debian distribution of Linux.

In order to prevent hoarding, the FSF requires that the source code for all enhancements be distributed under the same GPL that it uses. This encourages individuals or companies to make improvements and share them with others. The only thing someone cannot do is add enhancements and then try to sell the product as commercial software—that is, to withhold the source code. That would be taking advantage of the FSF and the users. You can find the GPL in any software covered by that license and online at *http://www.gnu.org/copyleft/gpl.html.*

As we said earlier, many tools on Linux come from BSD instead of GNU. BSD is also free software. The license is significantly different, but that doesn't have to concern you as a user. The effect of the difference is that companies are permitted to incorporate the software into their proprietary products, a practice that is severely limited by the GNU license.

# Beginner's Guide

If you're just beginning to work on a Linux system, the abundance of commands might prove daunting. To help orient you, the following lists present a sampling of commands on various topics.

## Communication

| | |
|---|---|
| **ftp** | File Transfer Protocol. |
| **login** | Sign on. |
| **rlogin** | Sign on to remote system. |
| **rsh** | Run shell or single command on remote system. |
| **talk** | Exchange messages interactively with other terminals. |
| **telnet** | Connect to another system. |
| **tftp** | Trivial file transfer protocol. |
| **uudecode** | Decode file prepared for mailing by **uuencode**. |
| **uuencode** | Encode file containing binary characters for mailing. |
| **vacation** | Respond to mail automatically. |

## Comparisons

| | |
|---|---|
| cmp | Compare two files, byte by byte. |
| comm | Compare items in two sorted files. |
| diff | Compare two files, line by line. |
| diff3 | Compare three files. |

## File Management

| | |
|---|---|
| cat | Concatenate files or display them. |
| chfn | Change user information for finger, email, etc. |
| cksum | Compute checksum. |
| chmod | Change access modes on files. |
| chsh | Change login shell. |
| cp | Copy files. |
| csplit | Break files at specific locations. |
| dd | Copy files in raw disk form. |
| file | Determine a file's type. |
| head | Show the first few lines of a file. |
| less | Display files by screenful. |
| ln | Create filename aliases. |
| ls | List files or directories. |
| merge | Merge changes from different files. |
| mkdir | Create a directory. |
| more | Display files by screenful. |
| mv | Move or rename files or directories. |
| newgrp | Change current group. |
| pwd | Print working directory. |
| rcp | Copy files to remote system. |
| rm | Remove files. |
| rmdir | Remove directories. |
| split | Split files evenly. |
| tail | Show the last few lines of a file. |
| wc | Count lines, words, and characters. |

## Printing

| | |
|---|---|
| lpq | Show status of print jobs. |
| lpr | Send to the printer. |
| lprm | Remove print job. |
| lpstat | Get printer status. |
| pr | Format and paginate for printing. |

## Programming

| | |
|---|---|
| ar | Create and update library files. |
| as | Generate object file. |
| bison | Generate parsing tables. |
| cpp | Preprocess C code. |
| flex | Lexical analyzer. |
| g++ | GNU C++ compiler. |
| gcc | GNU C compiler. |
| ld | Link editor. |
| m4 | Macro processor. |
| make | Create programs. |
| ranlib | Regenerate archive symbol table. |
| rpcgen | Translate RPC to C code. |
| yacc | Generate parsing tables. |

## Program Maintenance

| | |
|---|---|
| cvs | Manage different versions (revisions) of source files. |
| etags | Generate symbol list for use with the Emacs editor. |
| gctags | Generate symbol list for use with the vi editor. |
| gdb | GNU debugger. |
| gprof | Display object file's profile data. |
| imake | Generate makefiles for use with **make**. |
| make | Maintain, update, and regenerate related programs and files. |
| nm | Display object file's symbol table. |
| patch | Apply patches to source code. |
| rcs | Manage different versions (revisions) of source files. |
| size | Print the size of an object file in bytes. |
| strace | Trace system calls and signals. |
| strip | Strip symbols from an object file. |

## Searching

| | |
|---|---|
| apropos | Search manpages for topic. |
| egrep | Extended version of **grep**. |
| fgrep | Search files for literal words. |
| find | Search the system for filenames. |
| grep | Search files for text patterns. |
| strings | Search binary files for text patterns. |
| whereis | Find command. |

## Shell Programming

| | |
|---|---|
| echo | Repeat command-line arguments on the output. |
| expr | Perform arithmetic and comparisons. |
| printf | Format and print command-line arguments. |
| sleep | Pause during processing. |
| test | Test a condition. |

## Storage

| | |
|---|---|
| bzip2 | Compress files to free up space. |
| cpio | Create and unpack file archives. |
| gunzip | Expand compressed (*.gz* and *.Z*) files (preferred). |
| gzip | Compress files to free up space. |
| shar | Create shell archive. |
| tar | Copy files to or restore files from an archive medium. |
| zcat | Display contents of compressed files. |

## System Status

| | |
|---|---|
| at | Execute commands later. |
| atq | Show jobs queued by **at**. |
| atrm | Remove job queued by **at**. |
| chgrp | Change file group. |
| chown | Change file owner. |
| crontab | Automate commands. |
| date | Display or set date. |
| df | Show free disk space. |
| du | Show disk usage. |
| env | Show environment variables. |
| finger | Display information about users. |
| kill | Terminate a running command. |
| printenv | Show environment variables. |
| ps | Show processes. |
| stty | Set or display terminal settings. |
| who | Show who is logged on. |

## Text Processing

| | |
|---|---|
| col | Process control characters. |
| cut | Select columns for display. |
| ex | Line editor underlying **vi**. |
| expand | Convert tabs to spaces. |
| fmt | Produce roughly uniform line lengths. |

| fold | Break lines. |
| gawk | Process lines or records one by one. |
| ghostscript | Display PostScript or PDF file. |
| groff | Format **troff** input. |
| ispell | Interactively check spelling. |
| join | Merge different columns into a database. |
| paste | Merge columns or switch order. |
| rev | Prints each line of input, reversing it character by character. |
| sed | Noninteractive text editor. |
| sort | Sort or merge files. |
| tac | Print lines in reverse. |
| tr | Translate (redefine) characters. |
| uniq | Find repeated or unique lines in a file. |
| vi | Visual text editor. |
| xargs | Process many arguments in manageable portions. |

## *Miscellaneous*

| banner | Make posters from words. |
| bc | Arbitrary precision calculator. |
| cal | Display calendar. |
| clear | Clear the screen. |
| man | Get information on a command. |
| nice | Reduce a job's priority. |
| nohup | Preserve a running job after logging out. |
| passwd | Set your login password. |
| script | Produce a transcript of your login session. |
| su | Become a superuser. |
| tee | Simultaneously store output in file and send to screen. |
| which | Print pathname of a command. |

CHAPTER 2

# System and Network Administration Overview

## Common Commands

Following are lists of commonly used system administration commands.

### Clocks

| | |
|---|---|
| hwclock | Manage hardware clock. |
| netdate | Set clock according to *host*'s clock. |
| rdate | Manage time server. |
| zdump | Print list of time zones. |
| zic | Create time conversion information files. |

### Daemons

| | |
|---|---|
| apmd | Advanced Power Management daemon. |
| bootpd | Internet Boot Protocol daemon. |
| fingerd | Finger daemon. |
| ftpd | File Transfer Protocol daemon. |
| gated | Manage routing tables between networks. |
| identd | Identify user running TCP/IP process. |
| imapd | IMAP mailbox server daemon. |
| inetd | Internet services daemon. |
| kerneld | Provide automatic kernel module loading. |
| klogd | Manage **syslogd**. |
| lpd | Printer daemon. |
| mountd | NFS mount request server. |

| named | Internet domain name server. |
| nfsd | NFS daemon. |
| pop2d | POP server. |
| pop3d | POP server. |
| powerd | Monitor UPS connection. |
| pppd | Maintain Point-to-Point Protocol (PPP) network connections. |
| rdistd | Remote file distribution server. |
| rexecd | Remote execution server. |
| rlogind | **rlogin** server. |
| routed | Routing daemon. |
| rshd | Remote shell server. |
| rwhod | Remote who server. |
| syslogd | System logging daemon. |
| talkd | Talk daemon. |
| tcpd | TCP network daemon. |
| tftpd | Trivial File Transfer Protocol daemon. |
| update | Buffer flush daemon. |
| ypbind | NIS binder process. |
| yppasswdd | NIS password modification server. |
| ypserv | NIS server process. |

## *Hardware*

| agetty | Start user session at terminal. |
| arp | Manage the ARP cache. |
| cardctl | Control PCMCIA cards. |
| cardmgr | PCMCIA card manager daemon. |
| cfdisk | Maintain disk partitions (graphical interface). |
| fdisk | Maintain disk partitions. |
| getty | Start user session at terminal. |
| kbdrate | Manage the keyboard's repeat rate. |
| ramsize | Print information about RAM disk. |
| setserial | Set serial port information. |
| slattach | Attach serial lines as network interfaces. |

## *Host Information*

| arch | Print machine architecture. |
| dnsdomainname | Print DNS domain name. |
| domainname | Print NIS domain name. |
| free | Print memory usage. |
| host | Print host and zone information. |
| hostname | Print or set hostname. |

| nslookup | Query Internet domain name servers. |
| uname | Print host information. |

## Installation

| cpio | Copy file archives. |
| install | Copy files into locations providing user access and set permissions. |
| rdist | Distribute files to remote systems. |
| tar | Copy files to or restore files from an archive medium. |

## Mail

| fetchmail | Retrieve mail from remote servers. |
| formail | Convert input to mail format. |
| mailq | Print a summary of the mail queue. |
| makemap | Update **sendmail**'s database maps. |
| rmail | Handle **uucp** mail. |
| sendmail | Send and receive mail. |

## Managing Filesystems

To Unix systems, a *filesystem* is some device (such as a hard drive, floppy, or CD-ROM) that is formatted to store files. Filesystems can be found on hard drives, floppies, CD-ROMs, or other storage media that permit random access.

The exact format and means by which the files are stored are not important; the system provides a common interface for all *filesystem types* that it recognizes. Under Linux, filesystem types include the Second Extended Filesystem, or *ext2fs*, which you probably use to store Linux files. The second extended filesystem was developed primarily for Linux and supports 256-character filenames, 4-terabyte maximum filesystem size, and other useful features. (It is "second" because it is the successor to the extended filesystem type.) Other common filesystem types include the MS-DOS filesystem, which allows files on MS-DOS partitions and floppies to be accessed under Linux, and the ISO 9660 filesystem used by CD-ROMs.

| debugfs | Debug **extfs** filesystem. |
| dosfsck | Check and repair a DOS or VFAT filesystem. |
| dumpe2fs | Print information about superblock and blocks group. |
| e2fsck | Check and repair a second extended filesystem. |
| fdformat | Format floppy disk. |
| fsck | Check and repair filesystem. |
| fsck.minix | Check and repair a MINIX filesystem. |
| fuser | List processes using a filesystem. |
| mke2fs | Make new second extended filesystem. |
| mkfs | Make new filesystem. |

| | |
|---|---|
| mkfs.ext2 | Another name for **mke2fs**. |
| mkfs.minix | Make new MINIX filesystem. |
| mklost+found | Make *lost+found* directory. |
| mkraid | Set up a RAID device. |
| mkswap | Designate swap space. |
| mount | Mount a filesystem. |
| raidstart | Activate a RAID device. |
| raidstop | Turn off a RAID device. |
| rdev | Describe or change values for root filesystem. |
| rootflags | List or set flags to use in mounting root filesystem. |
| showmount | List exported directories. |
| swapdev | Display or set swap device information. |
| swapoff | Cease using device for swapping. |
| swapon | Begin using device for swapping. |
| sync | Write filesystem buffers to disk. |
| tune2fs | Manage second extended filesystem. |
| umount | Unmount a filesystem. |

## *Managing the Kernel*

| | |
|---|---|
| depmod | Create module dependency listing. |
| insmod | Install new kernel module. |
| lsmod | List kernel modules. |
| modprobe | Load new module and its dependent modules. |
| rmmod | Remove module. |

## *Networking*

| | |
|---|---|
| dip | Establish dial-up IP connections. |
| gdc | Administer **gated** routing daemon. |
| ifconfig | Manage network interfaces. |
| ipchains | Administer firewall facilities (2.2 kernel). |
| iptables | Administer firewall facilities (2.4 kernel). |
| named | Translate between domain names and IP addresses. |
| netstat | Print network status. |
| portmap | Map daemons to ports. |
| rarp | Manage RARP table. |
| route | Manage routing tables. |
| routed | Dynamically keep routing tables up-to-date. |
| rpcinfo | Report RPC information. |
| ruptime | Check how long remote system has been up. |
| rwho | Show who is logged in to remote system. |
| systat | Show status of remote systems. |
| traceroute | Trace network route to remote host. |

## NIS Administration

| | |
|---|---|
| domainname | Set or display name of current NIS domain. |
| makedbm | Rebuild NIS databases. |
| ypbind | Connect to NIS server. |
| ypcat | Print values in NIS database. |
| ypchfn | Change user information in NIS database for finger, email, etc. |
| ypchsh | Change user login shell in NIS database. |
| ypinit | Build new NIS databases. |
| ypmatch | Print value of one or more NIS keys. |
| yppasswd | Change user password in NIS database. |
| yppasswdd | Update NIS database in response to **yppasswd**. |
| yppoll | Determine version of NIS map at NIS server. |
| yppush | Propagate NIS map. |
| ypserv | NIS server daemon. |
| ypset | Point **ypbind** at a specific server. |
| ypwhich | Display name of NIS server or map master. |
| ypxfr | Transfer NIS database from server to local host. |

## Printing

| | |
|---|---|
| lpc | Control line printer. |
| tunelp | Tune the printer parameters. |

## Security and System Integrity

| | |
|---|---|
| badblocks | Search for bad blocks. |
| chroot | Change root directory. |

## Starting and Stopping the System

| | |
|---|---|
| bootpd | Internet Boot Protocol daemon. |
| bootpgw | Internet Boot Protocol gateway. |
| bootptest | Test **bootpd**. |
| halt | Stop or shut down system. |
| init | Change runlevel. |
| reboot | Shut down, then reboot system. |
| runlevel | Print system runlevel. |
| shutdown | Shut down system. |
| telinit | Change the current runlevel. |
| uptime | Display uptimes of local machines. |

## System Activity and Process Management

A number of additional commands in Chapter 3, *Linux Commands*, are particularly useful in controlling processes, including **kill**, **killall**, **killall5**, **pidof**, **ps**, and **who**.

| | |
|---|---|
| fuser | Identify processes using file or filesystem. |
| psupdate | Update */boot/psupdate*. |
| renice | Change the priority of running processes. |
| top | Show most CPU-intensive processes. |

## Users

| | |
|---|---|
| chpasswd | Change multiple passwords. |
| groupadd | Add a new group. |
| groupdel | Delete a group. |
| groupmod | Modify groups. |
| grpck | Check the integrity of group system files. |
| grpconv | Convert group file to shadow group file. |
| lastlog | Generate report of last user login times. |
| newusers | Add new users in a batch. |
| pwck | Check the integrity of password system files. |
| pwconv | Convert password file to shadow passwords. |
| rusers | Print **who**-style information on remote machines. |
| rwall | Print a message to remote users. |
| useradd | Add a new user. |
| userdel | Delete a user and her home directory. |
| usermod | Modify a user's information. |
| w | List logged-in users. |
| wall | Write to all users. |
| whoami | Show how you are currently logged in. |

## Miscellaneous

| | |
|---|---|
| cron | Schedule commands for specific times. |
| dmesg | Print bootup messages after the system is up. |
| ldconfig | Update library links and do caching. |
| logger | Send messages to the system logger. |
| logrotate | Compress and rotate system logs. |
| rstat | Display *host*'s system status. |
| run-parts | Run all scripts in a directory. |

# Overview of Networking

Networks connect computers so that the different systems can share information. For users and system administrators, Unix systems have traditionally provided a set of simple but valuable network services, which let you check whether systems are running, refer to files residing on remote systems, communicate via electronic mail, and so on.

For most commands to work over a network, each system must be continuously running a server process in the background, silently waiting to handle the user's request. This kind of process is called a *daemon*; common examples, on which you rely for the most basic functions of your Linux system, are **named** (which translates numeric IP addresses into the alphanumeric names that humans are so fond of), **lpd** (which sends documents to a printer, possibly over a network), and **ftpd** (which allows you to connect to another machine via **ftp**).

Most Unix networking commands are based on Internet protocols. These are standardized ways of communicating across a network on hierarchical layers. The protocols range from addressing and packet routing at a relatively low layer to finding users and executing user commands at a higher layer.

The basic user commands that most systems support over Internet protocols are generally called TCP/IP commands, named after the two most common protocols. You can use all of these commands to communicate with other Unix systems besides Linux systems. Many can also be used to communicate with non-Unix systems, because a wide variety of systems support TCP/IP.

This section also covers NFS and NIS, which allow for transparent file and information sharing across networks, and **sendmail**.

## TCP/IP Administration

| | |
|---|---|
| ftpd | Server for file transfers. |
| gated | Manage routing tables between networks. |
| host | Print host and zone information. |
| ifconfig | Configure network interface parameters. |
| named | Translate between domain names and IP addresses. |
| netstat | Print network status. |
| nslookup | Query domain name servers. |
| ping | Check that a remote host is online and responding. |
| pppd | Create PPP serial connection. |
| rdate | Notify time server that date has changed. |
| route | Manage routing tables. |
| routed | Dynamically keep routing tables up to date. |
| slattach | Attach serial lines as network interfaces. |
| telnetd | Server for Telnet sessions from remote hosts. |
| tftpd | Server for restricted set of file transfers. |

## NFS and NIS Administration

| | |
|---|---|
| domainname | Set or display name of current NIS domain. |
| makedbm | Rebuild NIS databases. |
| portmap | DARPA port to RPC program number mapper. |
| rpcinfo | Report RPC information. |
| ypbind | Connect to NIS server. |
| ypcat | Print values in NIS database. |
| ypinit | Build new NIS databases. |
| ypmatch | Print value of one or more NIS keys. |
| yppasswd | Change user password in NIS database. |
| yppasswdd | Update NIS database in response to **yppasswd**. |
| yppoll | Determine version of NIS map at NIS server. |
| yppush | Propagate NIS map. |
| ypserv | NIS server daemon. |
| ypset | Point **ypbind** at a specific server. |
| ypwhich | Display name of NIS server or map master. |
| ypxfr | Transfer NIS database from server to local host. |

# Overview of TCP/IP

TCP/IP is a set of communications protocols that define how different types of computers talk to one another. It's named for its two most common protocols, the Transmission Control Protocol and the Internet Protocol. The Internet Protocol moves data between hosts: it splits data into packets, which are then forwarded to machines via the network. The Transmission Control Protocol ensures that the packets in a message are reassembled in the correct order at their final destination and that any missing datagrams are resent until they are correctly received. Other protocols provided as part of TCP/IP include:

*Address Resolution Protocol (ARP)*
    Translates between Internet and local hardware addresses (Ethernet et al.)

*Internet Control Message Protocol (ICMP)*
    Error-message and control protocol

*Point-to-Point Protocol (PPP)*
    Enables TCP/IP (and other protocols) to be carried across both synchronous and asynchronous point-to-point serial links

*Reverse Address Resolution Protocol (RARP)*
    Translates between local hardware and Internet addresses (opposite of ARP)

*Serial Line Internet Protocol (SLIP)*
    Carries IP over serial lines

*Simple Mail Transport Protocol (SMTP)*
    Used by **sendmail** to send mail via TCP/IP

---

*Simple Network Management Protocol (SNMP)*
Performs distributed network management functions via TCP/IP

*User Datagram Protocol (UDP)*
Provides data transfer, without the reliable delivery capabilities of TCP

Background about TCP/IP is described in the three-volume set *Internetworking with TCP/IP* by Douglas R. Comer, published by Prentice-Hall. The commands in this chapter and the next are described in more detail in *TCP/IP Network Administration*, 2d ed., by Craig Hunt and *Linux Network Administrator's Guide* by Olaf Kirch and Terry Dawson, both published by O'Reilly & Associates.

In the architecture of TCP/IP protocols, data is passed down the stack (toward the Network Access Layer) when it is being sent to the network and up the stack when it is being received from the network (see Figure 2-1).

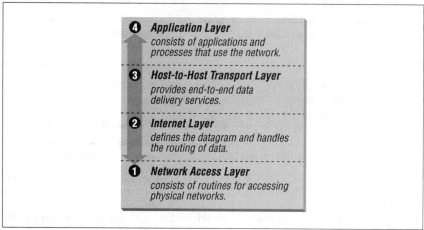

*Figure 2–1. Layers in the TCP/IP protocol architecture*

## IP Addresses

The IP (Internet) address is a 32-bit binary number that differentiates your machine from all others on the network. Each machine must have a unique IP address. An IP address contains two parts: a network part and a host part. The number of address bits used to identify the network and host differ according to the class of the address. There are three main address classes: A, B, and C (see Figure 2-2). The leftmost bits indicate what class each address is.

A more recent standard called Classless Inter-Domain Routing (CIDR) extends the class system's idea of using initial bits to identify where packets should be routed. Under CIDR, a new domain can be created with any number of fixed leftmost bits (not just a multiple of 8).

Another new standard called IPv6 changes the method of addressing and increases the number of fields, but it will be a while before anyone uses it.

If you wish to connect to the Internet, contact the Network Information Center and have them assign you a network address. If you are not connecting to an outside

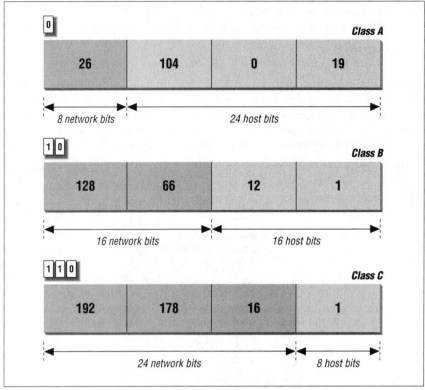

*Figure 2–2. IP address structure*

network, you can choose your own network address, as long as it conforms to the IP address syntax. You should use special reserved addresses provided for in RFC 1597, which lists IP network numbers for private networks that don't have to be registered with the IANA (Internet Assigned Numbers Authority). An IP address is different from an Ethernet address, which is assigned by the manufacturer of the physical Ethernet card.

## Gateways and Routing

Gateways are hosts responsible for exchanging routing information and forwarding data from one network to another. Each portion of a network that is under a separate local administration is called an autonomous system (AS). Autonomous systems connect to each other via exterior gateways. An AS also may contain its own system of networks, linked via interior gateways.

### Gateway protocols

Gateway protocols include:

*EGP (Exterior Gateway Protocol)*

*BGP (Border Gateway Protocol)*
    Protocols for exterior gateways to exchange information

*RIP (Routing Information Protocol)*
    Interior gateway protocol; most popular for LANs

*Hello Protocol*

*OSPF (Open Shortest Path First)*
    Interior gateway protocol

### Routing daemons

**gated** and **routed**, the routing daemons, can be run on a host to make it function as a gateway. Only one of them can run on a host at any given time. **gated** is the gateway routing daemon and allows a host to function as both an exterior and interior gateway. It simplifies the routing configuration by combining the protocols RIP, Hello, BGP, EGP, and OSPF into a single package.

**routed**, a network routing daemon that uses RIP, allows a host to function as an interior gateway only. **routed** manages the Internet routing tables. For more details on **gated** and **routed**, see Chapter 3.

### Routing tables

Routing tables provide information needed to route packets to their destinations. This information includes destination network, gateway to use, route status, and number of packets transmitted. Routing tables can be displayed with the **netstat** command.

## Name Service

Each host on a network has a name that points to information about the host. Hostnames can be assigned to any device that has an IP address. Name service translates the hostnames (easy for people to remember) to IP addresses (the numbers the computer deals with).

### DNS and BIND

The Domain Name System (DNS) is a distributed database of information about hosts on a network. Its structure is similar to that of the Unix filesystem—an inverted tree, with the root at the top. The branches of the tree are called *domains* (or *subdomains*) and correspond to IP addresses. The most popular implementation of DNS is the BIND (Berkeley Internet Name Domain) software.

DNS works as a client/server application. The *resolver* is the client, the software that asks questions about host information. The *name server* is the process that answers the questions. The server side of BIND is the **named** daemon. You can interactively query name servers for host information with the **nslookup** command. For more details on **named** and **nslookup**, see Chapter 3.

As the name server of its domain, your machine would be responsible for keeping (and providing on request) the names of the machines in its domain. Other name servers on the network would forward requests for these machines to it.

### Domain names

The full domain name is the sequence of names, starting from the current domain and going back to the root, with a period separating the names. For instance, *oreilly.com* indicates the domain *oreilly* (for O'Reilly & Associates), which is under the domain *com* (for commercial). One machine under this domain is *www.oreilly.com*. Top-level domains include:

*com*
> Commercial organizations

*edu*
> Educational organizations

*gov*
> Government organizations

*mil*
> Military departments

*net*
> Commercial Internet organizations, usually Internet service providers

*org*
> Miscellaneous organizations

Countries also have top-level domains.

## Configuring TCP/IP

### ifconfig

The network interface represents the way that the networking software uses the hardware—the driver, the IP address, and so forth. To configure a network interface, use the **ifconfig** command. With **ifconfig**, you can assign an address to a network interface, setting the netmask, broadcast address, and IP address at boot time. You can also set network interface parameters, including the use of ARP, the use of driver-dependent debugging code, the use of one-packet mode, and the address of the correspondent on the other end of a point-to-point link. For more information on **ifconfig**, see the Chapter 3.

### Serial-line communication

There are two protocols for serial-line communication: Serial Line IP (SLIP) and Point-to-Point Protocol (PPP). These protocols let computers transfer information using the serial port instead of a network card and a serial cable in place of an Ethernet cable.

Under Linux, the SLIP driver is installed in the kernel. To convert a serial line to SLIP mode, use the **slattach** program (details on **slattach** are available in Chapter 3). Don't forget that after putting the line in SLIP mode, you still have to run **ifconfig** to configure the network interface. For example, if your machine is named **tanuki** and you have dialed in to **ruby**:

```
# ifconfig sl0 tanuki pointopoint ruby
# route add ruby
# route add default gw ruby
```

This configures the interface as a point-to-point link to **ruby**, adds the route to **ruby**, and makes it a default route, specifying **ruby** as the gateway.

PPP was intended to remedy some of SLIP's failings; it can hold packets from non-Internet protocols, it implements client authorization and error detection/correction, and it dynamically configures each network protocol that passes through it. Under Linux, PPP exists as a driver in the kernel and as the daemon **pppd**. For more information on **pppd**, see Chapter 3.

## Troubleshooting TCP/IP

The following commands can be used to troubleshoot TCP/IP. For more details on these commands, see Chapter 3.

*ifconfig*
Provide information about the basic configuration of the network interface.

*netstat*
Display network status.

*ping*
Indicate whether a remote host can be reached.

*nslookup*
Query the DNS name service.

*traceroute*
Trace route taken by packets to reach network host.

# Overview of Firewalls and Masquerading

A firewall computer is a secure system that sits between an internal network and an external network (i.e., the Internet). It is configured with a set of rules that it uses to determine what traffic is allowed to pass and what traffic is barred. While a firewall is generally intended to protect the network from malicious or even accidentally harmful traffic from the outside, it can also be configured to monitor traffic leaving the network. As the sole entry point into the system, the firewall makes it easier to construct defenses and monitor activity.

The firewall can also be set up to present a single IP address to the outside world, even though it may use multiple IP addresses internally. This is known as *masquerading*. Masquerading can act as additional protection hiding the very existence of a network. It also saves the trouble and expense of obtaining multiple IP addresses.

---

 The discussion of **iptables** applies to Version 2.4 Linux kernels. As this book was being written, both **iptables** and the 2.4 kernel were still in development. The final product may differ slightly from what we describe here. See the O'Reilly book *Linux Network Administrator's Guide* by Olaf Kirch and Terry Dawson or the the "Linux IPTABLES-HOWTO" for more information. This HOWTO, and a myriad of others, can be obtained from the the Linux Documentation Project web sites (see the Preface).

---

IP firewalling and masquerading are implemented in Linux Version 2.2 with the **ipchains** utility and in Linux Version 2.4 with the **iptables** facility. The 2.0 kernels used a command called **ipfwadm**, which is included in the command section for older systems but will not be covered here. The two newer commands are very similar, but some of the organization of the rules they use is different. The firewalling facilities built into the 2.4 kernel are also designed to be extensible. If there is some function missing from the implementation, you could add it. See the "Linux netfilter Hacking HOWTO" for details on how to do this.

Most distributions come with all the firewall support already built into the kernel, but if it is not built into yours, you need to compile firewall support into the kernel by running **make config** with the 2.2 kernel and selecting all of the following networking options:

* Network firewalls

* TCP/IP networking

* IP: firewalling

If you want to support a transparent proxy service on your firewall, select the following option:

* IP: transparent proxy support

If you want your firewall to support masquerading, select the following options as well:

* IP: masquerading

* IP: ICMP masquerading

With the 2.4 kernel, you will need to select these options:

- Network packet filtering (replaces **ipchains**)

- IP tables support (required for filtering/masq/NAT)

- Packet filtering

There are several extended target and matching rule modules you may wish to compile as well. The behavior of those extension modules is described under the **iptables** command. If you have an existing firewall designed for the 2.2 kernel, or the 2.0 kernel, you can compile support for these older-style commands and use them with your new kernel instead of the newer **iptables** style of netfiltering.

The firewalling facility provides built-in rule sets, or chains, against which each network packet is checked. In the 2.4 kernel, these chains are also organized into tables that separate out filtering functions from masquerading and packet mangling functions. In either kernel, if a match is found, the counters on that rule are incremented and any target for that rule is applied. A target might accept, reject, or masquerade a packet or even pass it along to another chain for processing. Details on the chains provided in both **iptables** and **ipchains** can be found under the description of the appropriate command.

In addition to these chains, you can create your own user-defined chains. You might want a special chain for your PPP interfaces or for packets from a particular site. To call a user-defined chain, you just make it the target for a match.

It is possible to make it through a chain without matching any rules that have a target. If no rule matches the packet in a user-defined chain, control returns to the chain from which it was called, and the next rule in that chain is checked. If no rule matches the packet in a built-in chain a default policy for that chain is used. The default policy can be any of the special targets that determine what is done with a packet. The valid targets for each command are detailed in the commands section.

In the 2.2 kernel, you use the **ipchains** command to define the rules. Once you have the rules defined, you can use **ipchains-save** to create a file with all the rule definitions and **ipchains-restore** to restore those definitions when you reboot. The equivalent 2.4 kernel command for defining rules is **iptables**. **iptables-save** and **iptables-restore** were not completed at the time of this writing but should work similarly to their **ipchains** counterparts.

For more information on the kinds of decisions you need to make and the considerations that go into defining the rules, see a general book on firewalls such as the O'Reilly book *Building Internet Firewalls* by D. Brent Chapman and Elizabeth D. Zwicky. For more details on **ipchains** or **iptables**, consult the *Linux Network Administrator's Guide*, 2d ed. by Olaf Kirch and Terry Dawson, or consult one of the relevant HOW-TOs, such as the "Linux IPCHAINS HOW-TO" or the "Linux IPTABLES HOW-TO."

# Overview of NFS

The Network File System (NFS) is a distributed filesystem that allows users to mount remote filesystems as if they were local. NFS uses a client-server model, in which a server exports directories to be shared, and clients mount the directories to access the files in them. NFS eliminates the need to keep copies of files on several machines by letting the clients all share a single copy of a file on the server. NFS is an RPC-based application-level protocol. For more information on the architecture of network protocols, see the section "Overview of TCP/IP" earlier in this chapter.

## Administering NFS

Setting up NFS clients and servers involves starting the NFS daemons, exporting filesystems from the NFS servers, and mounting them on the clients. The */etc/exports* file is the NFS server configuration file; it controls which files and directories are exported and what kinds of access are allowed. Names and addresses for clients receiving services are kept in the */etc/hosts* file.

## Daemons

NFS server daemons, called *nfsd daemons*, run on the server and accept RPC calls from clients. NFS servers also run the **mountd** daemon to handle mount requests. On the client, caching and buffering are handled by **biod**, the block I/O daemon. The **portmap** daemon maps RPC program numbers to the appropriate TCP/IP port numbers.

## Exporting Filesystems

To set up an NFS server, first check that all the hosts that will mount your filesystem can reach your host. Next, edit the */etc/exports* file to include the mount-point pathname of the filesystem to be exported. If you are running **mountd**, the files will be exported as the permissions in */etc/exports* allow.

## Mounting Filesystems

To enable an NFS client, mount a remote filesystem after NFS is started, either by using the **mount** command or by specifying default remote filesystems in */etc/fstab*. A **mount** request calls the server's **mountd** daemon, which checks the access permissions of the client and returns a pointer to a filesystem. Once a directory is mounted, it remains attached to the local filesystem until it is dismounted with the **umount** command or until the local system is rebooted.

Usually, only a privileged user can mount filesystems with NFS. However, you can enable users to mount and unmount selected filesystems using the **mount** and **umount** commands if the **user** option is set in */etc/fstab*. This can reduce traffic by having filesystems mounted only when needed. To enable user mounting, create an entry in */etc/fstab* for each filesystem to be mounted.

# Overview of NIS

The Network Information System (NIS) refers to the service formerly known as Sun Yellow Pages (YP). It is used to make configuration information consistent on all machines in a network. It does this by designating a single host as the master of all the system administration files and databases and distributing this information to all other hosts on the network. The information is compiled into databases called *maps*. NIS is built on the RPC protocol. There are currently two NIS servers freely available for Linux, **yps** and **ypserv**.

## Servers

In NIS, there are two types of servers—master and slave servers. Master servers are responsible for maintaining the maps and distributing them to the slave servers. The files are then available locally to requesting processes.

## Domains

An NIS domain is a group of hosts that use the same set of maps. The maps are contained in a subdirectory of */var/yp* having the same name as the domain. The machines in a domain share password, hosts, and group file information. NIS domain names are set with the **domainname** command.

## NIS Maps

NIS stores information in database files called maps. Each map consists of a pair of **dbm** database files, one containing a directory of keys (a bitmap of indices), and the other containing data values. The non-ASCII structure of **dbm** files necessitates using NIS tools such as **yppush** to move maps between machines.

The file */var/yp/YP_MAP_X_LATE* contains a complete listing of active NIS maps as well as NIS aliases for NIS maps. All maps must be listed here in order for NIS to serve them.

## Map Manipulation Utilities

The following utilities are used to administer NIS maps:

*makedbm*
> Make **dbm** files. Modify only *ypservers* map and any nondefault maps.

*ypinit*
> Build and install NIS databases. Manipulate maps when NIS is being initialized. Should not be used when NIS is already running.

*yppush*
> Transfer updated maps from the master server.

# Administering NIS

NIS is enabled by setting up NIS servers and NIS clients. The descriptions given here describe NIS setup using **ypserv**, which does not support a master/slave server configuration. All NIS commands depend on the RPC **portmap** program, so make sure it is installed and running before setting up NIS.

## Setting up an NIS server

Setting up an NIS server involves:

1. Setting a domain name for NIS using **domainname**

2. Editing the *ypMakefile*, which identifies which databases to build and what sources to use in building them

3. Copying the *ypMakefile* to */var/yp/Makefile*

4. Running **make** from the */var/yp* directory, which builds the databases and initializes the server

5. Starting **ypserv**, the NIS server daemon

## Setting up an NIS client

Setting up an NIS client involves setting the domain name for NIS using **domainname**, which should be the same name used by the NIS server, and running **ypbind**.

## NIS User Accounts

NIS networks have two kinds of user accounts: distributed and local. Distributed accounts must be administered from the master machine; they provide information that is uniform on each machine in an NIS domain. Changes made to distributed accounts are distributed via NIS maps. Local accounts are administered from the local computer; they provide account information unique to a specific machine. They are not affected by NIS maps, and changes made to local accounts do not affect NIS. When NIS is installed, preexisting accounts default to local accounts.

# RPC and XDR

RPC (Remote Procedure Call) is the session protocol used by both NFS and NIS. It allows a host to make a procedure call that appears to be local but is really executed remotely on another machine on the network. 11 RPC is implemented as a library of procedures, plus a network standard for ordering bytes and data structures called XDR (eXternal Data Representation).

CHAPTER 3

# *Linux Commands*

This chapter presents the Linux user, programmer, and system administration commands. Each entry is labeled with the command name on the outer edge of the page. The syntax line is followed by a brief description and a list of available options. Many commands come with examples at the end of the entry. If you need only a quick reminder or suggestion about a command, you can skip directly to the examples.

Typographic conventions for describing command syntax are listed in the Preface. For help in locating commands, see the index at the back of this book.

We've tried to be as thorough as possible in listing options. The basic command information and most options should be correct; however, there are many Linux distributions and many versions of commands. New options are added and sometimes old options are dropped. You may, therefore, find some differences between the options you find described here and the ones on your system. When there seems to be a discrepancy, check the manpage. For most commands you can also use the option −−**help** to get a brief usage message. (Even when it isn't a valid option, it will usually result in an "invalid option" error along with the usage message.)

Traditionally, commands take single-letter options preceded by a single hyphen, like −**d**. A more recent convention allows long options preceded by two hyphens, like −−**debug**. Often, a feature can be invoked through either the old style or the new style of options.

# Alphabetical Summary of Commands

agetty

**agetty** [*options*] *port baudrate* [*term*]

System administration command. The Linux version of **getty**. Set terminal type, modes, speed, and line discipline. **agetty** is invoked by **init**. It is the second process in the series **init-getty-login-shell**, which ultimately connects a user with the Linux system. **agetty** reads the user's login name and invokes the **login** command with the user's name as an argument. While reading the name, **agetty** attempts to adapt the system to the speed and type of device being used.

You must specify a port, which **agetty** will search for in the */dev* directory. You may use −, in which case **agetty** reads from standard input. You must also specify *baudrate*, which may be a comma-separated list of rates, through which **agetty** will step. Optionally, you may specify the *term*, which is used to override the TERM environment variable.

*Options*

−h  Specify hardware, not software, flow control.

−i  Suppress printing of */etc/issue* before printing the login prompt.

−l *program*
    Specify the use of *program* instead of */bin/login*.

−m  Attempt to guess the appropriate baud rate.

−t *timeout*
    Specify that **agetty** should exit if the **open** on the line succeeds and there is no response to the login prompt in *timeout* seconds.

−L  Do not require carrier detect; operate locally only. Use this when connecting terminals.

apmd

**apmd** [*options*]

System administration command. **apmd** handles events reported by the Advanced Power Management BIOS driver. The driver reports on battery level and requests to enter sleep or suspend mode. **apmd** will log any reports it gets via **syslogd** and take steps to make sure that basic sleep and suspend requests are handled gracefully. You can fine-tune the behavior of **apmd** by specifying an **apmd_proxy** command to run when it receives an event.

**−c** *n*, **−−check** *n*

> Set the number of seconds to wait for an event before
> rechecking the power level. Default is to wait indefi-
> nitely. Setting this causes the battery levels to be
> checked more frequently.

**−P** *command*, **−−apmd_prxy** *command*

> Specify the **apmd_proxy** command to run when APM
> driver events are reported. This is generally a shell
> script. The *command* will be invoked with parameters
> indicating what kind of event was received. The param-
> eters are in the next list.

**−p** *n*, **−−percentage** *n*

> Log information whenever the power changes by *n*
> percent. The default is 5. Values greater than 100 will
> disable logging of power changes.

**−V**, **−−version**

> Print version and exit.

**−v**, **−−version**

> Verbose mode; all events are logged.

**−W**, **−−wall**

> Use **wall** to alert all users of a low battery status.

**−w** *n*, **−−warn** *n*

> Log a warning at ALERT level when the battery charge
> drops below *n* percent. The default is 10. Negative val-
> ues disable low battery level warnings.

**−q**, **−−quiet**

> Disable low battery level warnings.

**−?**, **−−help**

> Print help summary and exit.

*Parameters*

The apmd proxy script will be invoked with the following
parameters:

**start**

> Invoked when the daemon starts.

**stop**

> Invoked when the daemon stops.

$\rightarrow$

| | |
|---|---|
| **apmd**<br>← | **suspend** [ **system** ∣ **user** ]<br>Invoked when a suspend request has been made. The second parameter indicates whether the request was made by the system or by the user.<br><br>**standby** [ **system** ∣ **user** ]<br>Invoked when a standby request has been made. The second parameter indicates whether the request was made by the system or by the user.<br><br>**resume** [ **suspend** ∣ **standby** ∣ **critical** ]<br>Invoked when the system resumes normal operation. The second parameter indicates the mode the system was in before resuming. (**critical** suspends indicate an emergency shutdown. After a **critical** suspend the system may be unstable and you can use the **resume** command to help you recover from the suspension.<br><br>**change power**<br>Invoked when system power is changed from AC to battery or from battery to AC.<br><br>**change battery**<br>Invoked when the APM BIOS driver reports that the battery is low.<br><br>**change capability**<br>Invoked when the APM BIOS driver reports some hardware that affects its capability has been added or removed. |
| **apropos** | **apropos** *string* . . .<br><br>Search the short manual page descriptions in the **whatis** database for occurrences of each *string* and display the result on the standard output. Like **whatis**, except that it searches for strings instead of words. Equivalent to **man –k**. |
| **ar** | **ar** [**–V**] *key* [*args*] [*posname*] *archive* [*files*]<br><br>Maintain a group of *files* that are combined into a file *archive*. Used most commonly to create and update library files as used by the link editor (**ld**). Only one key letter may be used, but each can be combined with additional *args* (with no separations between). *posname* is the name of a file in *archive*. When moving or replacing *files*, you can specify that they be placed before or after *posname*. **–V** prints the version number of **ar** on standard error. |

*Key*

**d**    Delete *files* from *archive*.

**m**    Move *files* to end of *archive*.

**p**    Print *files* in *archive*.

**q**    Append *files* to *archive*.

**r**    Replace *files* in *archive*.

**t**    List the contents of *archive* or list the named *files*.

**x**    Extract contents from *archive* or only the named *files*.

*Arguments*

**a**    Use with **r** or **m** key to place *files* in the archive after *posname*.

**b**    Same as **a** but before *posname*.

**c**    Create *archive* silently.

**f**    Truncate long filenames.

**i**    Same as **b**.

**l**    For backward compatibility; meaningless in Linux.

**o**    Preserve original timestamps.

**s**    Force regeneration of *archive* symbol table (useful after running **strip**).

**S**    Do not regenerate symbol table.

**u**    Use with **r** to replace only *files* that have changed since being put in *archive*.

**v**    Verbose; print a description of actions taken.

*Example*

Replace **mylib.a** with object files from the current directory:

```
ar r mylib.a `ls *.o`
```

## arch

Print machine architecture type to standard output. Equivalent to **uname −m**.

| | |
|---|---|
| **arp** | **arp** [*options*] |
| | TCP/IP command. Clear, add to, or dump the kernel's ARP cache (*/proc/net/arp*). |
| | *Options* |
| | −**v**  Verbose mode. |
| | −**t** *type* |
| | Search for *type* entries when examining the ARP cache. *type* must be **ether** (Ethernet) or **ax25** (AX.25 packet radio); **ether** is the default. |
| | −**a** [*hosts*] |
| | Display *hosts'* entries or, if none are specified, all entries. |
| | −**d** *host* |
| | Remove *host*'s entry. |
| | −**s** *host hardware-address* |
| | Add the entry *host hardware-address*, where **ether** class addresses are 6 hexadecimal bytes, colon-separated. |
| | −**f** *file* |
| | Read entries from *file* and add them. |
| **as** | **as** [*options*] *files* |
| | Generate an object file from each specified assembly language source *file*. Object files have the same root name as source files but replace the .s suffix with .o. There may be some additional system-specific options. |
| | *Options* |
| | −− [ | *files*] |
| | Read input files from standard input, or from *files* if the pipe is used. |
| | −**a**[dhlns][=*file*] |
| | With only the −**a** option, list source code, assembler listing, and symbol table. The other options specify additional things to list or omit: |
| | −**ad** |
| | Omit debugging directives. |

**−ah**
> Include the high-level source code, if available.

**−al**  Include an assembly listing.

**−an**
> Suppress forms processing.

**−as**  Include a symbol listing.

**=*file***
> Set the listing filename to *file*.

**−defsym** *symbol=value*
> Define the *symbol* to have the value *value*, which must be an integer.

**−f**  Skip preprocessing.

**−−gstabs**
> Generate stabs debugging information.

**−o** *objfile*
> Place output in object file *objfile* (default is *file*.o).

**−v**  Display the version number of the assembler.

**−I** *path*
> Include *path* when searching for .**include** directives.

**−K**  Warn before altering difference tables.

**−L**  Do not remove local symbols, which begin with **L**.

**−R**  Combine both data and text in text section.

**−W**
> Quiet mode.

---

**at** [*options*] *time*

Execute commands at a specified *time* and optional *date*. The commands are read from standard input or from a file. (See also **batch**.) End input with *EOF*. *time* can be formed either as a numeric hour (with optional minutes and modifiers) or as a keyword. It can contain an optional *date*, formed as a month and date, a day of the week, or a special keyword (*today* or *tomorrow*). An increment can also be specified.

The **at** command can always be issued by a privileged user. Other users must be listed in the file */etc/at.allow* if it exists; otherwise, they must not be listed in */etc/at.deny*. If neither file exists, only a privileged user can issue the command.

→

## Options

**−c** *job* [*job*...]
Display the specified jobs on the standard output. This option does not take a time specification.

**−d** *job* [*job*...]
Delete the specified jobs. Same as **atrm**.

**−f** *file*
Read job from *file*, not standard input.

**−l**  Report all jobs that are scheduled for the invoking user. Same as **atq**.

**−m**  Mail user when job has completed, regardless of whether output was created.

**−q** *letter*
Place job in queue denoted by *letter*, where *letter* is any single letter from a−z or A−Z. Default queue is **a**. (The batch queue defaults to **b**.) Higher-lettered queues run at a lower priority.

**−V**  Display the version number.

## Time

*hh:mm* [*modifiers*]
Hours can have one digit or two (a 24-hour clock is assumed by default); optional minutes can be given as one or two digits; the colon can be omitted if the format is *h*, *hh*, or *hhmm*; (e.g., valid times are 5, 5:30, 0530, 19:45). If modifier **am** or **pm** is added, *time* is based on a 12-hour clock. If the keyword **zulu** is added, times correspond to Greenwich Mean Time.

**midnight** | **noon** | **teatime** | **now**
Use any one of these keywords in place of a numeric time. **teatime** translates to 4:00 p.m.; **now** must be followed by an *increment*.

## Date

*month num*[, *year*]
*month* is one of the 12 months, spelled out or abbreviated to its first three letters; *num* is the calendar date of the month; *year* is the four-digit year. If the given *month* occurs before the current month, **at** schedules that month next year.

*day*
> One of the seven days of the week, spelled out or abbreviated to its first three letters.

**today | tomorrow**
> Indicate the current day or the next day. If *date* is omitted, **at** schedules **today** when the specified *time* occurs later than the current time; otherwise, **at** schedules **tomorrow**.

*Increment*

Supply a numeric increment if you want to specify an execution time or day *relative* to the current time. The number should precede any of the keywords **minute**, **hour**, **day**, **week**, **month**, or **year** (or their plural forms). The keyword **next** can be used as a synonym of **+ 1**.

*Examples*

Note that the first two commands are equivalent:

```
at 1945 pm December 9
at 7:45pm Dec 9
at 3 am Saturday
at now + 5 hours
at noon next day
```

## atq [*options*]

List the user's pending jobs, unless the user is a privileged user; in that case, everybody's jobs are listed. Same as **at** −l.

*Options*

−q *queue*
> Query only the specified queue and ignore all other queues.

−v  Show jobs that have completed but not yet been deleted.

−V  Print the version number.

## atrm [*options*] *job* [*job* . . . ]

Delete jobs that have been queued for future execution. Same as **at** −d.

→

| | |
|---|---|
| **atrm**<br>← | *Options*<br><br>**−q** *queue*<br>    Remove job from the specified queue.<br><br>**−V** Print the version number and then exit. |
| **badblocks** | **badblocks** [*options*] *device block-count*<br><br>System administration command. Search *device* for bad blocks. You must specify the number of blocks on the device (*block-count*).<br><br>*Options*<br><br>**−b** *blocksize*<br>    Expect *blocksize*-byte blocks.<br><br>**−o** *file*<br>    Direct output to *file*.<br><br>**−v** Verbose mode.<br><br>**−w** Test by writing to each block and then reading back from it. |
| **banner** | **banner** [*option*] [*characters*]<br><br>Print *characters* as a poster. If no *characters* are supplied, **banner** prompts for them and reads an input line from standard input. By default, the results go to standard output, but they are intended to be sent to a printer.<br><br>*Option*<br><br>**−w** *width*<br>    Set width to *width* characters. Note that if your banner is in all lowercase, it will be narrower than *width* characters. If *−w* is not specified, the default width is 132. If *−w* is specified but *width* is not provided, the default is 80.<br><br>*Example*<br><br>`/usr/games/banner -w50 Happy Birthday! |lpr` |

**basename** *name* [*suffix*]
**basename** *option*

Remove leading directory components from a path. If *suffix* is given, remove that also. The result is printed to standard output.

*Options*

**--help**
> Print help message and then exit.

**--version**
> Print the version number and then exit.

*Examples*

```
% basename /usr/lib/libm.a
libm.a

% basename /usr/lib/libm.a .a
libm
```

**batch** [*options*] [*time*]

Execute commands entered on standard input. If time is omitted, execute them when the system load permits (when the load average falls below 0.8). Very similar to **at**, but does not insist that the execution time be entered on the command line. See **at** for details.

*Options*

**-f** *file*
> Read job from *file*, not standard input.

**-m** Mail user when job has completed, regardless of whether output was created.

**-q** *letter*
> Place job in queue denoted by *letter*, where *letter* is one letter from a–z or A–Z. The default queue is **a**. (The batch queue defaults to **b**.) Higher-lettered queues run at a lower priority.

**-V** Print the version number and then exit.

**-v** Display the time a job will be executed.

| | |
|---|---|
| **bash** | **bash** [*options*] [*file* [*arguments*]]<br>**sh** [*options*] [*file* [*arguments*]]<br><br>Standard Linux shell, a command interpreter into which all other commands are entered. For more information, see Chapter 7, *bash: The Bourne-Again Shell*. |
| **bc** | **bc** [*options*] [*files*]<br><br>**bc** is a language (and compiler) whose syntax resembles that of C, but with unlimited-precision arithmetic. **bc** consists of identifiers, keywords, and symbols, which are briefly described in the following entries. Examples are given at the end.<br><br>Interactively perform arbitrary-precision arithmetic or convert numbers from one base to another. Input can be taken from *files* or read from the standard input. To exit, type **quit** or **EOF**.<br><br>*Options*<br><br>−l, −−mathlib<br>    Make functions from the math library available.<br><br>−s, −−standard<br>    Ignore all extensions, and process exactly as in POSIX.<br><br>−w, −−warn<br>    When extensions to POSIX **bc** are used, print a warning.<br><br>−q, −−quiet<br>    Do not display welcome message.<br><br>−v, −−version<br>    Print version number.<br><br>*Identifiers*<br><br>An identifier is a series of one or more characters. It must begin with a lowercase letter but may also contain digits and underscores. No uppercase letters are allowed. Identifiers are used as names for variables, arrays, and functions. Variables normally store arbitrary-precision numbers. Within the same program you may name a variable, an array, and a function using the same letter. The following identifiers would not conflict: |

*x*  Variable *x*.

*x*[*i*]  Element *i* of array *x*. *i* can range from 0 to 2047 and can also be an expression.

*x*(*y*,*z*)
>   Call function *x* with parameters *y* and *z*.

### Input-output keywords

**ibase**, **obase**, **scale**, and **last** store a value. Typing them on a line by themselves displays their current value. You can also change their values through assignment. The letters A–F are treated as digits whose values are 10–15.

**ibase** = *n*
>   Numbers that are input (e.g., typed) are read as base *n* (default is 10).

**obase** = *n*
>   Numbers that are displayed are in base *n* (default is 10). Note: Once **ibase** has been changed from 10, use A to restore **ibase** or **obase** to decimal.

**scale** = *n*
>   Display computations using *n* decimal places (default is 0, meaning that results are truncated to integers). **scale** is normally used only for base-10 computations.

**last**  Value of last printed number.

### Statement keywords

A semicolon or a newline separates one statement from another. Curly braces are needed when grouping multiple statements.

**if** (*rel-expr*) {*statements*} [**else** {*statements*}]
>   Do one or more *statements* if relational expression *rel-expr* is true. Otherwise, do nothing, or if *else* (an extension) is specified, do alternative *statements*. For example:

>   ```
>   if(x==y) {i = i + 1} else {i = i - 1}
>   ```

**while** (*rel-expr*) {*statements*}
>   Repeat one or more *statements* while *rel-expr* is true; for example:

>   ```
>   while(i>0) {p = p*n; q = a/b; i = i-1}
>   ```

→

**for** (*expr1*; *rel-expr*; *expr2*) {*statements*}

Similar to **while**; for example, to print the first 10 multiples of 5, you could type:

```
for(i=1; i<=10; i++) i*5
```

GNU **bf** does not require three arguments to **for**. A missing argument 1 or 3 means that those expressions will never be evaluated. A missing argument 2 evaluates to the value 1.

**break**

Terminate a **while** or **for** statement.

**print** *list*

GNU extension. It provides an alternate means of output. *list* consists of a series of comma-separated strings and expressions; **print** displays these entities in the order of the list. It does not print a newline when it terminates. Expressions are evaluated, printed, and assigned to the special variable *last*. Strings (which may contain special characters, i.e., characters beginning with \) are simply printed. Special characters can be:

a    Alert or bell

b    Backspace

f    Form feed

n    Newline

r    Carriage return

q    Double quote

t    Tab

\    Backslash

**continue**

GNU extension. When within a **for** statement, jump to the next iteration.

**halt**

GNU extension. Cause the **bc** processor to quit.

**limits**

GNU extension. Print the limits enforced by the local version of **bc**.

## Function keywords

**define** *f*(*args*) {

> Begin the definition of function *f* having the arguments *args*. The arguments are separated by commas. Statements follow on successive lines. End with a }.

**auto** *x, y*

> Set up *x* and *y* as variables local to a function definition, initialized to 0 and meaningless outside the function. Must appear first.

**return**(*expr*)

> Pass the value of expression *expr* back to the program. Return 0 if (*expr*) is left off. Used in function definitions.

**sqrt**(*expr*)

> Compute the square root of expression *expr*.

**length**(*expr*)

> Compute how many significant digits are in *expr*.

**scale**(*expr*)

> Same as **length**, but count only digits to the right of the decimal point.

**read**( )

> GNU extension. Read a number from standard input. Return value is the number read, converted via the value of **ibase**.

## Math library functions

These are available when **bc** is invoked with −l. Library functions set **scale** to 20.

**s**(*angle*)

> Compute the sine of *angle*, a constant or expression in radians.

**c**(*angle*)

> Compute the cosine of *angle*, a constant or expression in radians.

**a**(*n*)

> Compute the arctangent of *n*, returning an angle in radians.

**e**(*expr*)

> Compute **e** to the power of *expr*.

l(*expr*)

Compute the natural log of *expr*.

j(*n*, *x*)

Compute the Bessel function of integer order *n*.

### Operators

These consist of operators and other symbols. Operators can be arithmetic, unary, assignment, or relational:

**arithmetic**

    +  –  *  /  %  ^

**unary**

    –  ++  ––

**assignment**

    =+  =-  =*  =/  =%  =^  =

**relational**

    <  <=  >  >=  ==  !=

### Other symbols

**/\* \*/**

Enclose comments.

( )   Control the evaluation of expressions (change precedence). Can also be used around assignment statements to force the result to print.

{ }   Use to group statements.

[ ]   Indicate array index.

**"*text*"**

Use as a statement to print *text*.

### Examples

Note in these examples that when you type some quantity (a number or expression), it is evaluated and printed, but assignment statements produce no display.

| | |
|---|---|
| **ibase = 8** | *Octal input* |
| 20 | *Evaluate this octal number* |
| 16 | *Terminal displays decimal value* |
| **obase = 2** | *Display output in base 2 instead of base 10* |
| 20 | *Octal input* |
| 10000 | *Terminal now displays binary value* |
| **ibase = A** | *Restore base-10 input* |
| **scale = 3** | *Truncate results to 3 decimal places* |
| 8/7 | *Evaluate a division* |
| 1.001001000 | *Oops! Forgot to reset output base to 10* |
| **obase=10** | *Input is decimal now, so A isn't needed* |
| 8/7 | |

The following lines show the use of functions:

```
define p(r,n){    Function p uses two arguments
auto v            v is a local variable
v = r^n           r raised to the n power
return(v)}        Value returned

scale=5
x=p(2.5,2)        x = 2.5 ^ 2
x                 Print value of x
6.25
length(x)         Number of digits
3
scale(x)          Number of places right of decimal point
2
```

---

## biff [*arguments*]                                           **biff**

Notify user of mail arrival and sender's name. **biff** operates asynchronously. Mail notification works only if your system is running the **comsat(8)** server. The command **biff y** enables notification, and the command **biff n** disables notification. With no arguments, **biff** reports **biff**'s current status.

---

## bison [*options*] *file*                                       **bison**

Given a *file* containing context-free grammar, convert into tables for subsequent parsing while sending output to *file.c.* This utility is both to a large extent compatible with **yacc** and named for it. All input files should use the suffix *.y*; output files will use the original prefix. All long options (those preceded by --) may instead be preceded by +.

### *Options*

−b *prefix*, −−**file-prefix**=*prefix*
    Use *prefix* for all output files.

−d, −−**defines**
    Generate *file.h*, producing **#define** statements that relate **bison**'s token codes to the token names declared by the user.

−r, −−**raw**
    Use **bison** token numbers, not **yacc**-compatible translations, in *file.h*.

$\rightarrow$

| | |
|---|---|
| **bison**<br>← | **−k, −−token-table**<br>Include token names and values of YYNTOKENS, YYN-NTS, YYNRULES, and YYNSTATES in *file.c*.<br><br>**−l, −−no-lines**<br>Exclude **#line** constructs from code produced in *file.c*. (Use after debugging is complete.)<br><br>**−n, −−no-parser**<br>Suppress parser code in output, allowing only declarations. Assemble all translations into a switch statement body and print it to *file.act*.<br><br>**−o** *file*, **−−output-file=***file*<br>Output to *file*.<br><br>**−p** *prefix*, **−−name-prefix=***prefix*<br>Substitute *prefix* for **yy** in all external symbols.<br><br>**−t, −−debug**<br>Compile runtime debugging code.<br><br>**−v, −−verbose**<br>Verbose mode. Print diagnostics and notes about parsing tables to *file.output*.<br><br>**−V, −−version**<br>Display version number.<br><br>**−y, −−yacc, −−fixed-output-files**<br>Duplicate **yacc**'s conventions for naming output files. |
| **bootpd** | **bootpd** [*options*] [*configfile* [*dumpfile*] ]<br><br>TCP/IP command. Internet Boot Protocol server. **bootpd** normally is run by */etc/inetd* by including the following line in the file */etc/inetd.conf*:<br><br>`bootps dgram udp wait root /etc/bootpd bootpd`<br><br>This causes **bootpd** to be started only when a boot request arrives. It may also be started in standalone mode, from the command line. Upon startup, **bootpd** first reads its configuration file, */etc/bootptab* (or the *configfile* listed on the command line), then begins listening for BOOTREQUEST packets.<br><br>**bootpd** looks in */etc/services* to find the port numbers it should use. Two entries are extracted: **bootps**—the **bootp** server listening port—and **bootpc**—the destination port used to reply to clients. |

If **bootpd** is compiled with the –DDEBUG option, receipt of a SIGUSR1 signal causes it to dump its memory-resident database to the file */etc/bootpd.dump* or the command-line specified *dumpfile*.

*Options*

−c *directory*
> Force **bootpd** to work in *directory*.

−d *level*
> Specify the debugging level. Omitting *level* will increment the level by 1.

−t *timeout*
> Specify a timeout value in minutes. A timeout value of 0 means wait forever.

*Configuration file*

The **bootpd** configuration file has a format in which two-character, case-sensitive tag symbols are used to represent host parameters. These parameter declarations are separated by colons. The general format is:

`hostname: tg=value: tg=value: tg=value`

where *hostname* is the name of a bootp client and *tg* is a tag symbol. The currently recognized tags are listed next.

*Tags*

| Tag | Meaning |
| --- | --- |
| **bf** | Bootfile |
| **bs** | Bootfile size in 512-octet blocks |
| **cs** | Cookie server address list |
| **ds** | Domain name server address list |
| **gw** | Gateway address list |
| **ha** | Host hardware address |
| **hd** | Bootfile home directory |
| **hn** | Send hostname |
| **ht** | Host hardware type (see Assigned Numbers RFC) |
| **im** | Impress server address list |
| **ip** | Host IP address |
| **lg** | Log server address list |
| **lp** | **lpr** server address list |
| **ns** | IEN-116 name server address list |
| **rl** | Resource location protocol server address list |
| **sm** | Host subnet mask |
| **tc** | Table continuation |

→

| bootpd ← | Tag | Meaning |
| --- | --- | --- |
| | to | Time offset in seconds from UTC |
| | ts | Time server address list |
| | vm | Vendor magic cookie selector |

There is also a generic tag, T*n*, where *n* is an RFC 1048 vendor field tag number. Generic data may be represented as either a stream of hexadecimal numbers or as a quoted string of ASCII characters.

---

**bootpgw**

**bootpgw** [*options*] *server*

Internet Boot Protocol Gateway. Maintain a gateway that forwards **bootpd** requests to *server*. In addition to dealing with BOOTREPLY packets, also deal with BOOTREQUEST packets. **bootpgw** is normally run by */etc/inetd* by including the following line in the file */etc/inetd.conf:*

```
bootps dgram udp wait root /etc/bootpgw bootpgw
```

This causes **bootpgw** to be started only when a boot request arrives. **bootpgw** takes all the same options as **bootpd**, except **-c**.

---

**bootptest**

**bootptest** [*options*] *server* [*template*]

TCP/IP command. Test *server*'s **bootpd** daemon by sending requests every second for 10 seconds or until the server responds. Read options from the *template* file, if provided.

*Options*

**-f** *file*
Read the boot filename from *file*.

**-h** Identify client by hardware, not IP, address.

**-m** *magic-number*
Provide *magic-number* as the first word of the vendor options field.

---

**bzip2**

**bzip2** [*options*] *filenames*
**bunzip2** [*options*] *filenames*

bzcat [*option*] *filenames*
bzip2recover *filenames*

File compression and decompression utility similar to **gzip**,
but uses a different algorithm and encoding method to get
better compression. **bzip2** replaces each file in *filenames*
with a compressed version of the file and with a *.bz2* extension appended. **bunzip2** decompresses each file compressed by **bzip2** (ignoring other files, except to print a
warning). **bzcat** decompresses all specified files to standard
output, and **bzip2recover** is used to try to recover data from
damaged files.

*Options*

−−  End of options; treat all subsequent arguments as file-
    names.

−*dig*

Set block size to *dig* × 100KB when compressing,
where *dig* is a single digit from 1 to 9.

−c, −−stdout

Compress or decompress to standard output.

−d, −−decompress

Force decompression.

−f, −−force

Force overwrite of output files. Default is not to overwrite. Also forces breaking of hard links to files.

−k, −−keep

Keep input files; don't delete them.

−L, −−license, −V, −−version

Print license and version information and exit.

−q, −−quiet

Quiet. Print only critical messages.

−s, −−small

Use less memory, at the expense of speed.

−t, −−test

Check the integrity of the files, but don't actually compress them.

−v, −−verbose

Verbose. Show the compression ratio for each file processed. Add more −v's to increase the verbosity.

→

| | |
|---|---|
| **bzip2**<br>← | **−z, −−compress**<br>Forces compression, even if invoked as **bunzip2** or **bzcat**.<br><br>**−−repetitive-fast, −−repetitive-best**<br>Sometimes useful in versions earlier than 0.9.5 (which has an improved sorting algorithm) for providing some control over the algorithm. |
| **c++** | **c++** [*options*] *files*<br><br>See **g++**. |
| **cal** | **cal** [*−jy*] [[*month*] *year*]<br><br>Print a 12-month calendar (beginning with January) for the given *year* or a one-month calendar of the given *month* and *year. month* ranges from 1 to 12. *year* ranges from 1 to 9999. With no arguments, print a calendar for the current month.<br><br>*Options*<br><br>−j   Display Julian dates (days numbered 1 to 365, starting from January 1).<br><br>−m  Display Monday as the first day of the week.<br><br>−y   Display entire year.<br><br>*Examples*<br><br>`cal 12 1995`<br>`cal 1994 > year_file` |
| **cardctl** | **cardctl** [*options*] *command*<br><br>System administration command. Control PCMCIA sockets or select the current scheme. The current scheme is sent along with the address of any inserted cards to configuration scripts (by default located in */etc/pcmcia*). The **scheme** command displays or changes the scheme. The other commands operate on a named card socket number or, if no number is given, all sockets.<br><br>*Commands* |

**config** [*socket*]
    Display current socket configuration.

**eject** [*socket*]
    Prepare the system for the card(s) to be ejected.

**ident** [*socket*]
    Display card identification information.

**insert** [*socket*]
    Notify system that a card has been inserted.

**reset** [*socket*]
    Send reset signal to card.

**resume** [*socket*]
    Restore power to socket and reconfigure for use.

**scheme** [*name*]
    Display current scheme or change to specified scheme *name*.

**status** [*socket*]
    Display current socket status.

**suspend** [*socket*]
    Shut down device and cut power to socket.

### Options

**−c** *directory*
    Look for card configuration information in *directory* instead of */etc/pcmcia*.

**−f** *file*
    Use *file* to keep track of the current scheme instead of */var/run/pcmcia-scheme*.

**−s** *file*
    Look for current socket information in *file* instead of */var/run/stab*.

---

**cardmgr** [*options*]

System administration command. The PCMCIA card daemon. **cardmgr** monitors PCMCIA sockets for devices that have been added or removed. When a card is detected, it attempts to get the card's ID and configure it according to the card configuration database (usually stored in */etc/pcmcia/config*). By default, **cardmgr** both creates a system log entry when it detects cards and beeps. Two high beeps mean it successfully identified and configured a device. One

→

| | |
|---|---|
| **cardmgr** ← | high beep followed by one low beep means it identified the device, but was unable to configure it successfully. One low beep means it could not identify the inserted card. Information on the currently configured cards can be found in */var/run/stab*. |

**Options**

**−c***directory*
> Look in *directory* for the card configuration database instead of */etc/pcmcia*.

**−d** use **modprobe** instead of **insmod** to load the PCMCIA device driver.

**−f** Run in the foreground to process the current cards, then run as a daemon.

**−m***directory*
> Look in *directory* for card device modules instead of */lib/modules/* `uname -r`.

**−o** Configure the cards present in one pass, then exit.

**−p***file*
> Write **cardmgr**'s process ID to *file* instead of */var/run/cardmgr.pid*.

**−q** Run in quiet mode. No beeps.

**−s***file*
> Write current socket information to *file* instead of */var/run/stab*.

**−v** Verbose mode.

**−V** Print version number and exit.

---

| | |
|---|---|
| **cat** | **cat** [*options*] [*files*] |

Read (concatenates) one or more *files* and print them on standard output. Read standard input if no *files* are specified or if − is specified as one of the files; input ends with EOF. You can use the > operator to combine several files into a new file or >> to append files to an existing file.

**Options**

**−A, −−show-all**
> Same as **−vET**.

**−b, −−number-nonblank**
 Number all nonblank output lines, starting with 1.

**−e** Same as −vE.

**−E, −−show-ends**
 Print $ at the end of each line.

**−n, −−number**
 Number all output lines, starting with 1.

**−s, −−squeeze-blank**
 Squeeze down multiple blank lines to one blank line.

**−t** Same as −vT.

**−T, −−show-tabs**
 Print TAB characters as ^I.

**−u** Ignored; retained for Unix compatibility.

**−v, −−show-nonprinting**
 Display control and nonprinting characters, with the exception of LINEFEED and TAB.

*Examples*

| | |
|---|---|
| `cat ch1` | *Display a file* |
| `cat ch1 ch2 ch3 > all` | *Combine files* |
| `cat note5 >> notes` | *Append to a file* |
| `cat > temp1` | *Create file at terminal; end with EOF* |
| `cat > temp2 << STOP` | *Create file at terminal; end with* **STOP** |

---

cc [*options*] *files*

See **gcc**.

---

cpp [*options*] [ *ifile* [ *ofile* ] ]

GNU C language preprocessor. **cpp** is invoked as the first pass of any C compilation by the **gcc** command. The output of **cpp** is a form acceptable as input to the next pass of the C compiler, and **cpp** normally invokes **gcc** after it finishes processing. *ifile* and *ofile* are, respectively, the input and output for the preprocessor; they default to standard input and standard output.

*Options*

**−$** Do not allow $ in identifiers.

→

**–dM**

Suppress normal output. Print series of **#defines** that create the macros used in the source file.

**–dD**

Similar to **–dM** but exclude predefined macros and include results of preprocessing.

**–idirafter** *dir*

Search *dir* for header files when a header file is not found in any of the included directories.

**–imacros** *file*

Process macros in *file* before processing main files.

**–include** *file*

Process *file* before main file.

**–iprefix** *prefix*

When adding directories with **–iwithprefix**, prepend *prefix* to the directory's name.

**–iwithprefix** *dir*

Append *dir* to the list of directories to be searched when a header file cannot be found in the main include path. If **–iprefix** has been set, prepend that prefix to the directory's name.

**–lang-c**, **–lang-c++**, **–lang-objc**, **–lang-objc++**

Expect the source to be in C, C++, Objective C, or Objective C++, respectively.

**–lint**

Display all lint commands in comments as **#pragma lint** *command*.

**–nostdinc**

Search only specified, not standard, directories for header files.

**–nostdinc++**

Suppress searching of directories believed to contain C++-specific header files.

**–pedantic**

Warn verbosely.

**–pedantic-errors**

Produce a fatal error in every case in which **–pedantic** would have produced a warning.

**−traditional**

Behave like traditional C, not ANSI.

**−undef**

Suppress definition of all nonstandard macros.

**−A***name[=def]*

Assert *name* with value *def* as if defined by a **#assert**.

**−C** Pass along all comments (except those found on **cpp** directive lines). By default, **cpp** strips C-style comments.

**−D***name[=def]*

Define *name* with value *def* as if by a **#define**. If no *=def* is given, *name* is defined with value 1. **−D** has lower precedence than **−U**.

**−H** Print pathnames of included files, one per line, on standard error.

**−I***dir*

Search in directory *dir* for **#include** files whose names do not begin with **/** before looking in directories on standard list. **#include** files whose names are enclosed in double quotes and do not begin with **/** will be searched for first in the current directory, then in directories named on **−I** options, and last in directories on the standard list.

**−M [−MG]**

Suppress normal output. Print a rule for **make** that describes the main source file's dependencies. If **−MG** is specified, assume that missing header files are actually generated files, and look for them in the source file's directory.

**−MD** *file*

Similar to **−M**, but output to *file*; also compile the source.

**−MM**

Similar to **−M**. Describe only those files included as a result of **#include "***file***"**.

**−MMD** *file*

Similar to **−MD**, but describe only the user's header files.

**−P** Preprocess input without producing line-control information used by next pass of C compiler.

→

**−U**_name_
> Remove any initial definition of _name_, where _name_ is a reserved symbol predefined by the preprocessor or a name defined on a **−D** option. Names predefined by **cpp** are **unix** and **i386** (for Intel systems).

**−Wcomment, −Wcomments**
> Warn when encountering the beginning of a nested comment.

**−Wtraditional**
> Warn when encountering constructs that are interpreted differently in ANSI from traditional C.

*Special names*

**cpp** understands various special names, some of which are:

**_ _DATE_ _**
> Current date (e.g., Oct 10 1999)

**_ _FILE_ _**
> Current filename (as a C string)

**_ _LINE_ _**
> Current source line number (as a decimal integer)

**_ _TIME_ _**
> Current time (e.g., 12:00:00)

These special names can be used anywhere, including macros, just like any other defined names. **cpp**'s understanding of the line number and filename may be changed using a **#line** directive.

*Directives*

All **cpp** directive lines start with # in column 1. Any number of blanks and tabs is allowed between the # and the directive. The directives are:

**#assert** _name (string)_
> Define a question called _name_, with an answer of _string_. Assertions can be tested with **#if** directives. The predefined assertions for **#system**, **#cpu**, and **#machine** can be used for architecture-dependent changes.

**#unassert** _name_
> Remove assertion for question _name_.

**#define** _name token-string_
> Define a macro called _name_, with a value of _token-string_. Subsequent instances of _name_ are replaced with _token-string_.

**#define** *name( arg, ... , arg ) token-string*

This allows substitution of a macro with arguments. *token-string* will be substituted for *name* in the input file. Each call to *name* in the source file includes arguments that are plugged into the corresponding *args* in *token-string*.

**#undef** *name*

Remove definition of the macro *name*. No additional tokens are permitted on the directive line after *name*.

**#ident** *string*

Put *string* into the comment section of an object file.

**#include** *"filename"*, **#include<***filename***>**

Include contents of *filename* at this point in the program. No additional tokens are permitted on the directive line after the final " or >.

**#line** *integer-constant "filename"*

Cause **cpp** to generate line-control information for the next pass of the C compiler. The compiler behaves as if *integer-constant* is the line number of the next line of source code and *filename* (if present) is the name of the input file. No additional tokens are permitted on the directive line after the optional *filename*.

**#endif**

End a section of lines begun by a test directive (**#if**, **#ifdef**, or **#ifndef**). No additional tokens are permitted on the directive line.

**#ifdef** *name*

Lines following this directive and up to matching **#endif** or next **#else** or **#elif** will appear in the output if *name* is currently defined. No additional tokens are permitted on the directive line after *name*.

**#ifndef** *name*

Lines following this directive and up to matching **#endif** or next **#else** or **#elif** will appear in the output if *name* is not currently defined. No additional tokens are permitted on the directive line after *name*.

**#if** *constant-expression*

Lines following this directive and up to matching **#endif** or next **#else** or **#elif** will appear in the output if *constant-expression* evaluates to nonzero.

→

| | |
|---|---|
| **cpp** ← | **#elif** *constant-expression* |

An arbitrary number of **#elif** directives are allowed between an **#if**, **#ifdef**, or **#ifndef** directive and an **#else** or **#endif** directive. The lines following the **#elif** and up to the next **#else**, **#elif**, or **#endif** directive will appear in the output if the preceding test directive and all intervening **#elif** directives evaluate to zero, and the *constant-expression* evaluates to nonzero. If *constant-expression* evaluates to nonzero, all succeeding **#elif** and **#else** directives will be ignored.

**#else**

Lines following this directive and up to the matching **#endif** will appear in the output if the preceding test directive evaluates to 0, and all intervening **#elif** directives evaluate to 0. No additional tokens are permitted on the directive line.

**#error**

Report fatal errors.

**#warning**

Report warnings, but then continue processing.

---

**cfdisk**

**cfdisk** [*options*] [*device*]

System administration command. Partition a hard disk. *device* may be */dev/hda* (default), */dev/hdb*, */dev/sda*, */dev/sdb*, */dev/sdc*, or */dev/sdd*. See also **fdisk**.

*Options*

−a Highlight the current partition with a cursor, not reverse video.

−c *cylinders*
　　Specify the number of cylinders.

−h *heads*
　　Specify the number of heads.

−s *sectors*
　　Specify the number of sectors per track.

−z Do not read the partition table; partition from scratch.

−P *format*
　　Display the partition table in *format*, which must be **r** (raw data), **s** (sector order), or **t** (raw format).

**up arrow, down arrow**
> Move among partitions.

**b**   Toggle partition's bootable flag.

**d**   Delete partition (allow other partitions to use its space).

**g**   Alter the disk's geometry. Prompt for what to change: cylinders, heads, or sectors (**c**, **h**, or **s**, respectively).

**h**   Help.

**m**   Attempt to ensure maximum usage of disk space in the partition.

**n**   Create a new partition. Prompt for more information.

**p**   Display the partition table.

**q**   Quit without saving information.

**t**   Prompt for a new filesystem type, and change to that type.

**u**   Change the partition size units, rotating from megabytes to sectors to cylinders and back.

**W**   Save information. Note that this letter must be upper-case.

---

**chattr** [*options*] *mode files*      **chattr**

Modify file attributes. Specific to Linux Second Extended Filesystem. Behaves similarly to symbolic **chmod**, using **+**, **−**, and **=**. *mode* is in the form *opcode attribute*. See also **lsattr**.

*Options*

**−R**   Modify directories and their contents recursively.

**−V**   Print modes of attributes after changing them.

**−v** *version*
> Set the file's version.

*Opcodes*

**+**   Add attribute.

**−**   Remove attribute.

| chattr ← | = | Assign attributes (removing unspecified attributes). |
|---|---|---|

**Attributes**

A    Don't update access time on modify.

a    Append only for writing. Can be set or cleared only by a privileged user.

c    Compressed.

d    No dump.

i    Immutable. Can be set or cleared only by a privileged user.

s    Secure deletion; the contents are zeroed on deletion.

u    Undeletable.

S    Synchronous updates.

**Examples**

`chattr +a myfile`    *As superuser*

---

**chfn**

**chfn** [*options*] [*username*]

Change the information that is stored in */etc/passwd* and displayed when a user is fingered. Without *options*, **chfn** enters interactive mode and prompts for changes. To make a field blank, enter the keyword **none**. Only a privileged user can change information for another user. For regular users, **chfn** prompts for the user's password before making the change.

**Options**

−f, −−full-name
    Specify new full name.

−h, −−home-phone
    Specify new home phone number.

−o, −−office
    Specify new office number.

−p, −−office-phone
    Specify new office phone number.

−u, −−help
    Print help message and then exit.

−v, −−version
 Print version information and then exit.

*Example*

```
chfn -f "Ellen Siever" ellen
```

**chgrp** [*options*] *newgroup files*
**chgrp** [*options*]

Change the group of one or more *files* to *newgroup. newgroup* is either a group ID number or a group name located in */etc/group*. Only the owner of a file or a privileged user may change its group.

*Options*

−c, −−changes
 Print information about those files that are changed.

−f, −−silent, −−quiet
 Do not print error messages about files that cannot be changed.

−−help
 Print help message and then exit.

−R, −−recursive
 Traverse subdirectories recursively, applying changes.

−−reference=*filename*
 Change the group to that associated with *filename*. In this case, *newgroup* is not specified.

−v, −−verbose
 Verbosely describe ownership changes.

−−version
 Print version information and then exit.

**chmod** [*options*] *mode files*
**chmod** [*options*] − −reference=*filename files*

Change the access *mode* (permissions) of one or more *files*. Only the owner of a file or a privileged user may change its mode. *mode* can be numeric or an expression in the form of *who opcode permission. who* is optional (if omitted, default is **a**); choose only one *opcode*. Multiple modes may be specified, separated by commas.

→

| chmod | *Options* |
| ← | |

**chmod**
←

*Options*

**−c, −−changes**
Print information about files that are changed.

**−f, −−silent, −−quiet**
Do not notify user of files that **chmod** cannot change.

**−−help**
Print help message and then exit.

**−R, −−recursive**
Traverse subdirectories recursively, applying changes.

**−−reference=***filename*
Change permissions to those associated with *filename*.

**−v, −−verbose**
Print information about each file, whether changed or not.

**−−version**
Print version information and then exit.

*Who*

u    User

g    Group

o    Other

a    All (default)

*Opcode*

+    Add permission.

−    Remove permission.

=    Assign permission (and remove permission of the unspecified fields).

*Permissions*

r    Read.

w    Write.

x    Execute.

s    Set user (or group) ID.

t    Sticky bit; save text (file) mode or prevent removal of files by nonowners (directory).

u   User's present permission.

g   Group's present permission.

o   Other's present permission.

Alternatively, specify permissions by a three-digit octal number. The first digit designates owner permission; the second, group permission; and the third, other's permission. Permissions are calculated by adding the following octal values:

4   Read.

2   Write.

1   Execute.

Note: A fourth digit may precede this sequence. This digit assigns the following modes:

4   Set user ID on execution to grant permissions to process based on file's owner, not on permissions of user who created the process.

2   Set group ID on execution to grant permissions to process based on the file's group, not on permissions of user who created the process.

1   Set sticky bit.

### Examples

Add execute-by-user permission to *file*:

```
chmod u+x file
```

Either of the following will assign read/write/execute permission by owner (7), read/execute permission by group (5), and execute-only permission by others (1) to *file*:

```
chmod 751 file
chmod u=rwx,g=rx,o=x file
```

Any one of the following will assign read-only permission to *file* for everyone:

```
chmod =r file
chmod 444 file
chmod a-wx,a+r file
```

Set the user ID, assign read/write/execute permission by owner, and assign read/execute permission by group and others:

```
chmod 4755 file
```

| | |
|---|---|
| chown | chown [*options*] *newowner files*<br>chown [*options*] −−reference=*filename files*<br><br>Change the ownership of one or more *files* to *newowner.* *newowner* is either a user ID number or a login name located in */etc/passwd.* **chown** also accepts users in the form *newowner: newgroup* or *newowner.newgroup.* The last two forms change the group ownership as well. If no owner is specified, the owner is unchanged. With a period or colon but no group, the group is changed to that of the new owner. Only the current owner of a file or a privileged user may change its owner.<br><br>*Options*<br><br>−c, −−changes<br>    Print information about those files that are changed.<br><br>−−dereference<br>    Follow symbolic links.<br><br>−f, −−silent, −−quiet<br>    Do not print error messages about files that cannot be changed.<br><br>−h, −−no-dereference<br>    Change the ownership of each symbolic link (on systems that allow it), rather than the referenced file.<br><br>−v, −−verbose<br>    Print information about all files that **chown** attempts to change, whether or not they are actually changed.<br><br>−R, −−recursive<br>    Traverse subdirectories recursively, applying changes.<br><br>−−reference=*filename*<br>    Change owner to the owner of *filename* instead of specifying a new owner explicitly.<br><br>−−help<br>    Print help message and then exit.<br><br>−−version<br>    Print version information and then exit. |
| chpasswd | chpasswd [*option*]<br><br>System administration command. Change user passwords in a batch. **chpasswd** accepts input in the form of one *username:password* pair per line. If the −e option is not |

specified, *password* will be encrypted before being stored.

*Option*

−e   Passwords given are already encrypted.

---

**chroot** *newroot* [*command*]

System administration command. Change root directory for *command* or, if none is specified, for a new copy of the user's shell. This command or shell is executed relative to the new root. The meaning of any initial / in pathnames is changed to *newroot* for a command and any of its children. In addition, the initial working directory is *newroot*. This command is restricted to privileged users.

---

**chsh** [*options*] [*username*]

Change your login shell, interactively or on the command line. Warn if *shell* does not exist in */etc/shells*. Specify the full path to the shell. **chsh** prompts for your password. Only a privileged user can change another user's shell.

*Options*

−l, −−list-shells
    Print valid shells, as listed in */etc/shells*, and then exit.

−s *shell*, −−shell *shell*
    Specify new login shell.

−u, −−help
    Print help message and then exit.

−v, −−version
    Print version information and then exit.

*Example*

```
chsh -s /bin/tcsh
```

---

**cksum** [*files*]

Compute a cyclic redundancy check (CRC) checksum for all *files*; used to ensure that a file was not corrupted during transfer. Read from standard input if the character − or no files are given. Display the resulting checksum, the number

→

| | |
|---|---|
| **cksum**<br>← | of bytes in the file, and (unless reading from standard input) the filename. |

| | |
|---|---|
| **clear** | **clear**<br><br>Clear the terminal display. |

| | |
|---|---|
| **cmp** | **cmp** [*options*] *file1 file2* [*skip1* [*skip2*]]<br><br>Compare *file1* with *file2*. Use standard input if *file1* is − or missing. See also **comm** and **diff**. Files can be of any type. *skip1* and *skip2* are optional offsets in the files at which the comparison is to start. |

*Options*

**−c, −−print-chars**
  Print differing bytes as characters.

**−i** *num*, **−−ignore-initial=***num*
  Ignore the first *num* bytes of input.

**−l, −−verbose**
  Print offsets and codes of all differing bytes.

**−s, −−quiet, −−silent**
  Work silently; print nothing, but return exit codes:

  0   Files are identical.

  1   Files are different.

  2   Files are inaccessible.

*Example*

Print a message if two files are the same (exit code is 0):

```
cmp -s old new && echo 'no changes'
```

| | |
|---|---|
| **col** | **col** [*options*]<br><br>A postprocessing filter that handles reverse linefeeds and escape characters, allowing output from **tbl** or **nroff** to appear in reasonable form on a terminal. |

*Options*

**−b** Ignore backspace characters; helpful when printing manpages.

**−f**   Process half-line vertical motions, but not reverse line motion. (Normally, half-line input motion is displayed on the next full line.)

**−l** *n*

   Buffer at least *n* lines in memory. The default buffer size is 128 lines.

**−x**   Normally, **col** saves printing time by converting sequences of spaces to tabs. Use **−x** to suppress this conversion.

### Examples

Run *myfile* through **tbl** and **nroff**, then capture output on screen by filtering through **col** and **more**:

```
tbl myfile | nroff | col | more
```

Save manpage output for the **ls** command in *out.print*, stripping out backspaces (which would otherwise appear as ^H):

```
man ls | col -b > out.print
```

## colcrt [*options*] [*files*]

A postprocessing filter that handles reverse linefeeds and escape characters, allowing output from **tbl** or **nroff** to appear in reasonable form on a terminal. Put half-line characters (e.g., subscripts or superscripts) and underlining (changed to dashes) on a new line between output lines.

### Options

**−**    Do not underline.

**−2**   Double space by printing all half-lines.

## colrm [*start* [*stop*]]

Remove specified columns from a file, where a column is a single character in a line. Read from standard input and write to standard output. Columns are numbered starting with 1; begin deleting columns at (including) the *start* column, and stop at (including) the *stop* column. Entering a tab increments the column count to the next multiple of either the *start* or *stop* column; entering a backspace decrements it by 1.

→

| | |
|---|---|
| colrm<br>← | *Example*<br><br>`colrm 3 5 < test1 > test2` |
| column | **column** [*options*] [*files*]<br><br>Format input from one or more *files* into columns, filling rows first. Read from standard input if no files are specified.<br><br>*Options*<br><br>**−c** *num*<br>   Format output into *num* columns.<br><br>**−s** *char*<br>   Delimit table columns with *char*. Meaningful only with **−t**.<br><br>**−t**   Format input into a table. Delimit with whitespace, unless an alternate delimiter has been provided with **−s**.<br><br>**−x**   Fill columns before filling rows. |
| comm | **comm** [*options*] *file1 file2*<br><br>Compare lines common to the sorted files *file1* and *file2*. Three-column output is produced: lines unique to *file1*, lines unique to *file2*, and lines common to both files. **comm** is similar to **diff** in that both commands compare two files. But **comm** can also be used like **uniq**; that is, **comm** selects duplicate or unique lines between *two* sorted files, whereas **uniq** selects duplicate or unique lines within the *same* sorted file.<br><br>*Options*<br><br>**−**   Read the standard input.<br><br>**−***num*<br>   Suppress printing of column *num*. Multiple columns may be specified and should not be space-separated.<br><br>**−−help**<br>   Print help message and exit.<br><br>**−−version**<br>   Print version information and exit. |

Compare two lists of top-10 movies, and display items that appear in both lists:

```
comm -12 siskel_top10 ebert_top10
```

---

**compress** [*options*] *files*

Compress one or more *files*, replacing each with the compressed file of the same name with *.Z* appended. If no file is specified, compress standard input. Each file specified is compressed separately. **compress** ignores files that are symbolic links. See also **gzip**.

*Options*

**−b** *maxbits*
  Limit the maximum number of bits.

**−c**  Write output to standard output, not to a *.Z* file.

**−d**  Decompress instead of compressing. Same as **uncompress**.

**−f**  Force generation of an output file even if one already exists.

**−r**  If any of the specified files is a directory, compress recursively.

**−v**  Print compression statistics.

**−V**  Print version and compilation information and then exit.

---

**cp** [*options*] *file1 file2*
**cp** [*options* ] *files directory*

Copy *file1* to *file2*, or copy one or more *files* to the same names under *directory*. If the destination is an existing file, the file is overwritten; if the destination is an existing directory, the file is copied into the directory (the directory is *not* overwritten).

*Options*

**−a**, **−−archive**
  Preserve attributes of original files where possible. Same as **−dpR**.

$\rightarrow$

**cp**
←

**−b, −−backup**
Back up files that would otherwise be overwritten.

**−d, −−no-dereference**
Do not dereference symbolic links; preserve hard link relationships between source and copy.

**−f, −−force**
Remove existing files in the destination.

**−i, −−interactive**
Prompt before overwriting destination files.

**−l, −−link**
Make hard links, not copies, of nondirectories.

**−p, −−preserve**
Preserve all information, including owner, group, permissions, and timestamps.

**−P, −−parents**
Preserve intermediate directories in source. The last argument must be the name of an existing directory. For example, the command:

```
cp --parents jphekman/book/ch1 newdir
```

copies the file *jphekman/book/ch1* to the file *newdir/jphekman/book/ch1*, creating intermediate directories as necessary.

**−r, −R, −−recursive**
Copy directories recursively.

**−S** *backup-suffix*, **−−suffix=***backup-suffix*
Set suffix to be appended to backup files. This may also be set with the SIMPLE_BACKUP_SUFFIX environment variable. The default is ˜. You need to explicitly include a period if you want one before the suffix (e.g., specify *.bak*, not *bak*).

**−s, −−symbolic-link**
Make symbolic links instead of copying. Source filenames must be absolute.

**−u, −−update**
Do not copy a file to an existing destination with the same or newer modification time.

**−v, −−verbose**
Before copying, print the name of each file.

**–V** *type*, **– –version-control=***type*

Set the type of backups made. You may also use the VERSION_CONTROL environment variable. The default is **existing**. Valid arguments are:

**t, numbered**

Always make numbered backups.

**nil, existing**

Make numbered backups of files that already have them; otherwise, make simple backups.

**never, simple**

Always make simple backups.

**–x, – –one-file-system**

Ignore subdirectories on other filesystems.

---

## cpio *flags* [*options*]

Copy file archives in from or out to tape or disk, or to another location on the local machine. Each of the three flags **–i**, **–o**, or **–p** accepts different options.

### Flags

**–i, – –extract** [*options*] [*patterns*]

Copy in (extract) from an archive files whose names match selected *patterns*. Each pattern can include Bourne shell filename metacharacters. (Patterns should be quoted or escaped so they are interpreted by **cpio**, not by the shell.) If *pattern* is omitted, all files are copied in. Existing files are not overwritten by older versions from the archive unless **–u** is specified.

**–o, – –create** [*options*]

Copy out to an archive a list of files whose names are given on the standard input.

**–p, – –pass-through** [*options*] *directory*

Copy (pass) files to another directory on the same system. Destination pathnames are interpreted relative to the named *directory*.

### Comparison of valid options

Options available to the **–i**, **–o**, and **–p** flags are shown here. (The **–** is omitted for clarity):

```
i:  bcdf mnrtsuv B SVCEHMR IF
o: 0a c          vABL VC HM O F
p: 0a  d lm    uv    L V    R
```

→

cpio
←

*Options*

**−0, −−null**
　Expect list of filenames to be terminated with null, not newline. This allows files with a newline in their names to be included.

**−a, −−reset-access-time**
　Reset access times of input files after reading them.

**−A, −−append**
　Append files to an existing archive, which must be a disk file. Specify this archive with −O or −F.

**−b, −−swap**
　Swap bytes and half-words to convert between big-endian and little-endian 32-bit integers.

**−B**　Block input or output using 5120 bytes per record (default is 512 bytes per record).

**−−blocksize=***size*
　Set input or output blocksize to *size* × 512 bytes.

**−c**　Read or write header information as ASCII characters; useful when source and destination machines are different types.

**−C** *n*, **−−io-size=***n*
　Like −B, but blocksize can be any positive integer *n*.

**−d, −−make-directories**
　Create directories as needed.

**−E** *file*, **−−pattern-file=***file*
　Extract filenames from the archives that match patterns in *file*.

**−f, −−nonmatching**
　Reverse the sense of copying; copy all files *except* those that match *patterns*.

**−F** *file*, **−−file=***file*
　Use *file* as the archive, not **stdin** or **stdout**. *file* can reside on another machine, if given in the form *user@hostname:file* (where *user@* is optional).

**−−force-local**
　Assume that *file* (provided by −F, −I, or −O) is a local file, even if it contains a colon (:) indicating a remote file.

**−H** *type*, **−−format=***type*
Use *type* format. Default for copy-out is **bin**; for copy-in the default is autodetection of the format. Valid formats (all caps also accepted) are:

**bin** Binary

**odc**
Old (POSIX.1) portable format

**newc**
New (SVR4) portable format

**crc** New (SVR4) portable format with checksum added

**tar** Tar

**ustar**
POSIX.1 tar (also recognizes GNU tar archives)

**hpbin**
HP-UX's binary (obsolete)

**hpodc**
HP-UX's portable format

**−I** *file*
Read *file* as an input archive. May be on a remote machine (see **−F**).

**−k** Ignored. For backward compatibility.

**−l**, **−−link**
Link files instead of copying.

**−L**, **−−dereference**
Follow symbolic links.

**−m**, **−−preserve-modification-time**
Retain previous file modification time.

**−M** *msg*, **−−message=***msg*
Print *msg* when switching media, as a prompt before switching to new media. Use variable **%d** in the message as a numeric ID for the next medium. **−M** is valid only with **−I** or **−O**.

**−n**, **−−numeric-uid-gid**
When verbosely listing contents, show user ID and group ID numerically.

**−−no-absolute-filenames**
Create all copied-in files relative to the current directory.

→

**--no-preserve-owner**
> Make all copied files owned by yourself, instead of the owner of the original. Useful only if you are a privileged user.

**-O** *file*
> Archive the output to *file*, which may be a file on another machine (see **-F**).

**--only-verify-crc**
> For a CRC-format archive, verify the CRC of each file; don't actually copy the files in.

**--quiet**
> Don't print the number of blocks copied.

**-r** Rename files interactively.

**-R** [*user*][*:group*], **--owner** [*user*][*:group*]
> Reassign file ownership and group information to the user's login ID (privileged users only).

**-s, --swap-bytes**
> Swap bytes of each two-byte half-word.

**-S, --swap-half-words**
> Swap half-words of each four-byte word.

**--sparse**
> For copy-out and copy-pass, write files that have large blocks of zeros as sparse files.

**-t, --list**
> Print a table of contents of the input (create no files). When used with the **-v** option, resembles output of **ls -l**.

**-u, --unconditional**
> Unconditional copy; old files can overwrite new ones.

**-v, --verbose**
> Print a list of filenames processed.

**-V, --dot**
> Print a dot for each file read or written (this shows **cpio** at work without cluttering the screen).

**--version**
> Print version number and then exit.

*Examples*

Generate a list of files whose names end in *.old* using **find**; use list as input to **cpio**:

```
find . -name "*.old" -print | cpio -ocBv > /dev/rst8
```

Restore from a tape drive all files whose names contain **save** (subdirectories are created if needed):

```
cpio -icdv "*save*" < /dev/rst8
```

Move a directory tree:

```
find . -depth -print | cpio -padm /mydir
```

## cron

System administration command. Normally started in a system startup file. Execute commands at scheduled times, as specified in users' files in */var/cron/tabs*. Each file shares its name with the user who owns it. The files are controlled via the command **crontab**.

## crontab [*options*] [*file*]

View, install, or uninstall your current *crontab* file. A privileged user can run **crontab** for another user by supplying **-u** *user*. A *crontab* file is a list of commands, one per line, that will execute automatically at a given time. Numbers are supplied before each command to specify the execution time. The numbers appear in five fields, as follows:

| | |
|---|---|
| *Minute* | 0-59 |
| *Hour* | 0-23 |
| *Day of month* | 1-31 |
| *Month* | 1-12 |
| | Jan, Feb, Mar, ... |
| *Day of week* | 0-6, with 0 = Sunday |
| | Sun, Mon, Tue, ... |

Use a comma between multiple values, a hyphen to indicate a range, and an asterisk to indicate all possible values. For example, assuming these *crontab* entries:

```
59 3 * * 5      find / -print | backup_program
0 0 1,15 * *    echo "Timesheets due" | mail user
```

The first command backs up the system files every Friday at 3:59 a.m., and the second command mails a reminder on the 1st and 15th of each month.

The superuser can always issue the **crontab** command. Other users must be listed in the file */etc/cron.allow* if it exists; otherwise, they must not be listed in */etc/cron.deny*. If neither file exists, only the superuser can issue the command.

→

| | |
|---|---|
| **crontab**<br>← | *Options*<br><br>The −e, −l, and −r options are not valid if any *files* are specified.<br><br>−e Edit the user's current *crontab* file (or create one).<br><br>−l Display the user's *crontab* file on standard output.<br><br>−r Delete the user's *crontab* file.<br><br>−u *user*<br>Indicates which *user*'s *crontab* file will be acted upon. |
| **csh** | **csh** [*options*] [*file* [*arguments*]]<br><br>C shell, a command interpreter into which all other commands are entered. For more information, see Chapter 8, *csh and tcsh*. |
| **csplit** | **csplit** [*options*] *file arguments*<br><br>Separate *file* into context-based sections and place sections in files named xx00 through xx*n* (*n* < 100), breaking *file* at each pattern specified in *arguments*. See also **split**.<br><br>*Options*<br><br>− Read from standard input.<br><br>−b *suffix*, −−suffix-format=*suffix*<br>Append *suffix* to output filename. This option causes −n to be ignored. *suffix* must specify how to convert the binary integer to readable form by including exactly one of the following: %d, %i, %u, %o, %x, or %X. The value of *suffix* determines the format for numbers as follows:<br><br>%d Signed decimal<br><br>%i Same as %d<br><br>%u Unsigned decimal<br><br>%o Octal<br><br>%x Hexadecimal<br><br>%X Same as %x. |

-f *prefix*, --**prefix**=*prefix*
> Name new files *prefix*00 through *prefixn* (default is **xx**00 through **xx***n*).

-k, --**keep-files**
> Keep newly created files, even when an error occurs (which would normally remove these files). This is useful when you need to specify an arbitrarily large repeat argument, {*n*}, and you don't want an out-of-range error to cause removal of the new files.

-n *num*, --**digits**=*num*
> Use output filenames with numbers *num* digits long. The default is 2.

-s, -q, --**silent**, --**quiet**
> Suppress all character counts.

-z, --**elide-empty-files**
> Do not create empty output files. However, number as if those files had been created.

### Arguments

Any one or a combination of the following expressions may be specified as arguments. Arguments containing blanks or other special characters should be surrounded by single quotes.

/*expr*/[*offset*]
> Create file from the current line up to the line containing the regular expression *expr*. *offset* should be of the form +*n* or −*n*, where *n* is the number of lines below or above *expr*.

%*expr*%[*offset*]
> Same as /*expr*/ except no file is created for lines previous to line containing *expr*.

*num*
> Create file from current line up to (but not including) line number *num*. When followed by a repeat count (number inside { }), put the next *num* lines of input into another output file.

{*n*} Repeat argument *n* times. May follow any of the preceding arguments. Files will split at instances of *expr* or in blocks of *num* lines. If * is given instead of *n*, repeat argument until input is exhausted.

→

| csplit ← | *Examples*

Create up to 20 chapter files from the file *novel*:

```
csplit -k -f chap. novel '/CHAPTER/' '{20}'
```

Create up to 100 address files (xx00 through xx99), each four lines long, from a database named *address_list*:

```
csplit -k address_list 4 {99}
```
|
| ctags | **ctags** [*options*] *files*

Create a list of function and macro names that are defined in the specified C, C++, FORTRAN, Java, Perl, **yacc**, or other source *files*. The output list (named *tags* by default) contains lines of the form:

```
name       file       context
```

where *name* is the function or macro name, *file* is the source file in which *name* is defined, and *context* is a search pattern that shows the line of code containing *name*. After the list of tags is created, you can invoke **vi** on any file and type:

```
:set tags=tagsfile
:tag name
```

This switches the **vi** editor to the source file associated with the *name* listed in *tagsfile* (which you specify with −t).

**etags** produces an equivalent file for tags to be used with Emacs.

*Options*

−a, −−append
  Append tag output to existing list of tags.

−d, −−defines
  Include tag entries for C preprocessor definitions.

−i *file*, −−include=*file*
  Add a note to the tags file that *file* should be consulted in addition to the normal input file.

−l *language*, −−language=*language*
  Consider the files that follow this option to be written in *language*. Use the −h option for a list of languages and their default filename extensions. |

−o *file*, −−output=*file*
> Write to *file*.

−r*regexp*, −−regex=*regexp*
> Include a tag for each line that matches *regexp* in the files following this option.

−R, −−no-regex
> Don't include tags based on regular-expression matching for the files that follow this option.

−t, −−typedefs
> Include tag entries for **typedefs**.

−u, −−update
> Update tags file to reflect new locations of functions (e.g., when functions are moved to a different source file). Old tags are deleted; new tags are appended.

−v, −−vgrind
> Print to standard output a listing (index) of each function, source file, and page number (1 page = 64 lines).

−w, −−no-warn
> Suppress warning messages.

−x, −−cxref
> Produce a listing of each function, and its line number, source file, and context.

−B, −−backward-search
> Search for tags backward through files.

−C, −−c++
> Expect *.c* and *.h* files to contain C++, not C, code.

−H, −h, −−help
> Print usage information and exit.

−S, −−ignore-indentation
> Normally **ctags** uses indentation to parse the tag file; this option tells it to rely on it less.

−T, −−typedefs-and-c++
> Include tag entries for typedefs, structs, enums, unions, and C++ member functions.

−V, −−version
> Print the version number and exit.

| | |
|---|---|
| **cut** | **cut** *options* [*files*]

Cut out selected columns or fields from one or more *files*. In the following options, *list* is a sequence of integers. Use a comma between separate values and a hyphen to specify a range (e.g., **1-10,15,20** or **50–**). See also **paste** and **join**.

*Options*

**–b** *list*, **––bytes** *list*
  Specify *list* of positions; only bytes in these positions will be printed.

**–c** *list*, **––characters** *list*
  Cut the column positions identified in *list*.

**–d** *c*, **––delimiter** *c*
  Use with **–f** to specify field delimiter as character *c* (default is tab); special characters (e.g., a space) must be quoted.

**–f** *list*, **––fields** *list*
  Cut the fields identified in *list*.

**–n**  Don't split multibyte characters.

**–s**, **––only-delimited**
  Use with **–f** to suppress lines without delimiters.

**––output-delimiter=***string*
  Use *string* as the output delimiter. By default, the output delimiter is the same as the input delimiter.

**––help**
  Print help message and then exit.

**––version**
  Print version information and then exit.

*Examples*

Extract usernames and real names from */etc/passwd*:

`cut -d: -f1,5 /etc/passwd`

Find out who is logged on, but list only login names:

`who | cut -d" " -f1`

Cut characters in the fourth column of *file*, and paste them back as the first column in the same file:

`cut -c4 file | paste - file` |

Print the current date and time. You may specify a display *format*. *format* can consist of literal text strings (blanks must be quoted) as well as field descriptors, whose values will appear as described in the following entries (the listing shows some logical groupings). A privileged user can change the system's date and time.

### Options

**+*format***

> Display current date in a nonstandard format. For example:

```
% date +"%A %j %n%k %p"
Tuesday 248
15 PM
```

> The default is %a %b %e %T %Z %Y—e.g., Tue Sep 5 14:59:37 EDT 2000.

**−d** *date*, **−−date** *date*

> Display *date*, which should be in quotes and may be in the format *d* **days** or *m* **months** *d* **days** to print a date in the future. Specify **ago** to print a date in the past. You may include formatting (see the "Format" section that follows).

**−f** *datefile*, **−−file=***datefile*

> Like −d but printed once for each line of *datefile*.

**−I** [*timespec*], **−−iso-8601**[=*timespec*]

> Display in ISO-8601 format. If specified, *timespec* can have one of the values **date** (for date only), **hours**, **minutes**, or **seconds** to get the indicated precision.

**−r** *file*, **−−reference=***file*

> Display the time *file* was last modified.

**−R, −−rfc-822**

> Display the date in RFC 822 format.

**−−help**

> Print help message and exit.

**−−version**

> Print version information and exit.

**−s** *date*, **−−set** *date*

> Set the date.

→

**date**
←

-u, --universal
    Set the date to Greenwich Mean Time, not local time.

*Format*

%   Literal %.

–   Do not pad fields (default: pad fields with zeros).

_   Pad fields with space (default: zeros).

%a  Abbreviated weekday.

%b  Abbreviated month name.

%c  Country-specific date and time format.

%d  Day of month (01–31).

%h  Same as %b.

%j  Julian day of year (001–366).

%k  Hour in 24-hour format, without leading zeros (0–23).

%l  Hour in 12-hour format, without leading zeros (1–12).

%m
    Month of year (01–12).

%n  Insert a new line.

%p  String to indicate AM or PM.

%r  Time in %I:%M:%S %p (12-hour) format.

%s  Seconds since "The Epoch," 1970-01-01 00:00:00 UTC
    (a nonstandard extension).

%t  Insert a tab.

%w  Day of week (Sunday = 0).

%x  Country-specific date format.

%y  Last two digits of year (00–99).

%z  RFC 822–style numeric time zone.

%A  Full weekday.

%B  Full month name.

%D  Date in %m/%d/%y format.

%H  Hour in 24-hour format (00–23).

**%I**   Hour in 12-hour format (01–12).

**%M**   Minutes (00–59).

**%S**   Seconds (00–59).

**%T**   Time in %H:%M:%S format.

**%U**   Week number in year (00–53); start week on Sunday.

**%V**   Week number in year (01–52); start week on Monday.

**%W**

Week number in year (00–53); start week on Monday.

**%X**   Country-specific time format.

**%Y**   Four-digit year (e.g., 1996).

**%Z**   Time zone name.

### Strings for setting date

Strings for setting the date may be numeric or nonnumeric. Numeric strings consist of time, day, and year in the format *MMDDhhmm[[CC]YY][.ss]*. Nonnumeric strings may include month strings, time zones, a.m., and p.m.

*time*

A two-digit hour and two-digit minute (*hhmm*); *hh* uses 24-hour format.

*day*

A two-digit month and two-digit day of month (*MMDD*); default is current day and month.

*year*

The year specified as either the full four-digit century and year or just the two-digit year; the default is the current year.

### Examples

Set the date to July 1 (**0701**), 4 a.m. (**0400**), 1995 (**95**):

```
date 0701040095
```

The command:

```
date +"Hello%t Date is %D %n%t Time is %T"
```

produces a formatted date as follows:

```
Hello     Date is 05/09/93
     Time is 17:53:39
```

| | |
|---|---|
| **dd** | **dd** *options* |

Make a copy of an input file (**if**) using the specified conditions, and send the results to the output file (or standard
output if **of** is not specified). Any number of options can be
supplied, although **if** and **of** are the most common and are
usually specified first. Because **dd** can handle arbitrary
blocksizes, it is useful when converting between raw physical devices.

### Options

**bs=***n*

    Set input and output blocksize to *n* bytes; this option
    overrides **ibs** and **obs**.

**cbs=***n*

    Set the size of the conversion buffer (logical record
    length) to *n* bytes. Use only if the conversion *flag* is
    **ascii**, **ebcdic**, **ibm**, **block**, or **unblock**.

**conv=***flags*

    Convert the input according to one or more (comma-
    separated) *flags* listed next. The first five *flags* are
    mutually exclusive.

    **ascii**

        EBCDIC to ASCII.

    **ebcdic**

        ASCII to EBCDIC.

    **ibm**

        ASCII to EBCDIC with IBM conventions.

    **block**

        Variable-length records (i.e., those terminated by a
        newline) to fixed-length records.

    **unblock**

        Fixed-length records to variable-length.

    **lcase**

        Uppercase to lowercase.

    **ucase**

        Lowercase to uppercase.

    **noerror**

        Continue processing after read errors.

**notrunc**
> Don't truncate output file.

**swab**
> Swap each pair of input bytes.

**sync**
> Pad input blocks to **ibs** with trailing zeros.

**count=**$n$
> Copy only $n$ input blocks.

**ibs=**$n$
> Set input blocksize to $n$ bytes (default is 512).

**if=***file*
> Read input from *file* (default is standard input).

**obs=**$n$
> Set output blocksize to $n$ bytes (default is 512).

**of=***file*
> Write output to *file* (default is standard output).

**seek=**$n$
> Skip $n$ output-sized blocks from start of output file.

**skip=**$n$
> Skip $n$ input-sized blocks from start of input file.

**--help**
> Print help message and then exit.

**--version**
> Print the version number and then exit.

You can multiply size values ($n$) by a factor of 1024, 512, or 2 by appending the letter **k**, **b**, or **w**, respectively. You can use the letter **x** as a multiplication operator between two numbers.

*Examples*

Convert an input file to all lowercase:

```
dd if=caps_file of=small_file conv=lcase
```

Retrieve variable-length data; write it as fixed-length to **out**:

```
data_retrieval_cmd | dd of=out conv=sync,block
```

---

## debugfs [[*option*] *device*]

System administration command. Debug an **ext2** filesystem. *device* is the special file corresponding to the device

$\rightarrow$

**debugfs**
←

containing the **ext2** filesystem (e.g., */dev/hda3*).

*Option*

**−w** Open the filesystem read-write.

*Commands*

**cat** *file*
> Dump the contents of an inode to standard output.

**cd** *directory*
> Change the current working directory to *directory.*

**chroot** *directory*
> Change the root directory to be the specified inode.

**close**
> Close the currently open filesystem.

**clri** *file*
> Clear the contents of the inode corresponding to *file.*

**dump** *file out_file*
> Dump the contents of an inode to *out_file.*

**expand_dir** *directory*
> Expand *directory.*

**find_free_block** [*goal*]
> Find first free block starting from *goal* (if specified) and allocate it.

**find_free_inode** [*dir* [*mode*]]
> Find a free inode and allocate it.

**freeb** *block*
> Mark *block* as not allocated.

**freei** *file*
> Free the inode corresponding to *file.*

**help**
> Print a list of commands understood by **debugfs**.

**icheck** *block*
> Do block-to-inode translation.

**initialize** *device blocksize*
> Create an **ext2** filesystem on *device.*

**kill_file** *file*
> Remove *file* and deallocate its blocks.

**ln** *source_file dest_file*
>   Create a link.

**ls** [*pathname*]
>   Emulate the **ls** command.

**modify_inode** *file*
>   Modify the contents of the inode corresponding to *file*.

**mkdir** *directory*
>   Make *directory*.

**mknod** *file* [p | [[c | b] *major minor*]]
>   Create a special device file.

**ncheck** *inode*
>   Do inode-to-name translation.

**open** [–w] *device*
>   Open a filesystem.

**pwd**
>   Print the current working directory.

**quit**
>   Quit **debugfs**.

**rm** *file*
>   Remove *file*.

**rmdir** *directory*
>   Remove *directory*.

**setb** *block*
>   Mark *block* as allocated.

**seti** *file*
>   Mark in use the inode corresponding to *file*.

**show_super_stats**
>   List the contents of the super block.

**stat** *file*
>   Dump the contents of the inode corresponding to *file*.

**testb** *block*
>   Test whether *block* is marked as allocated.

**testi** *file*
>   Test whether the inode corresponding to *file* is marked as allocated.

**unlink** *file*
>   Remove a link.

$\rightarrow$

| | |
|---|---|
| **debugfs** ← | **write** *source_file file* |
| | Create a file in the filesystem named *file*, and copy the contents of *source_file* into the destination file. |
| **depmod** | **depmod** [*options*] *modules* |
| | System administration command. Create a dependency file for the modules given on the command line. This dependency file can be used by **modprobe** to automatically load the relevant *modules*. The normal use of **depmod** is to include the line **/sbin/depmod –a** in one of the files in */etc/rc.d* so the correct module dependencies will be available after booting the system. |
| | *Options* |
| | **–a** Create dependencies for all modules listed in */etc/conf.modules*. |
| | **–d** Debug mode. Show all commands being issued. |
| | **–e** Print a list of all unresolved symbols. |
| | **–v** Print a list of all processed modules. |
| | *Files* |
| | */etc/conf.modules* |
| | Information about modules: which ones depend on others, and which directories correspond to particular types of modules. |
| | */sbin/insmod, /sbin/rmmod* |
| | Programs that **depmod** relies on. |
| **df** | **df** [*options*] [*name*] |
| | Report the amount of free disk space available on all mounted filesystems or on the given *name*. (**df** cannot report on unmounted filesystems.) Disk space is shown in 1KB blocks (default) or 512-byte blocks (if the environment variable POSIXLY_CORRECT is set). *name* can be a device name (e.g., */dev/hd\**), the directory name of a mounting point (e.g., */usr*), or a directory name (in which case **df** reports on the entire filesystem in which that directory is mounted). |

*Options*

**−a, −−all**
> Include empty filesystems (those with 0 blocks).

**−−block-size=***n*
> Show space as *n*-byte blocks.

**−h, −−human-readable**
> Print sizes in a format friendly to human readers (e.g., 1.9G instead of 1967156).

**−H, −−si**
> Like −h, but show as power of 1000 rather than 1024.

**−i, −−inodes**
> Report free, used, and percent-used inodes.

**−k, −−kilobytes**
> Print sizes in kilobytes.

**−l, −−local**
> Show local filesystems only.

**−m, −−megabytes**
> Print sizes in megabytes.

**−−no-sync**
> Show results without invoking **sync** first (i.e., without flushing the buffers). This is the default.

**−P, −−portability**
> Use POSIX output format (i.e., print information about each filesystem on exactly one line).

**−−sync**
> Invoke **sync** (flush buffers) before getting and showing sizes.

**−t** *type*, **−−type=***type*
> Show only *type* filesystems.

**−T, −−print-type**
> Print the type of each filesystem in addition to the sizes.

**−x** *type*, **−−exclude-type=***type*
> Show only filesystems that are not of type *type*.

**−−help**
> Print help message and then exit.

→

| | |
|---|---|
| **df** <br> ← | **--version** <br> Print the version and then exit. |
| **diff** | **diff** [*options*] [*diroptions*] *file1 file2* <br><br> Compare two text files. **diff** reports lines that differ between *file1* and *file2.* Output consists of lines of context from each file, with *file1* text flagged by a < symbol and *file2* text by a > symbol. Context lines are preceded by the **ed** command (**a, c,** or **d**) that would be used to convert *file1* to *file2.* If one of the files is –, standard input is read. If one of the files is a directory, **diff** locates the filename in that directory corresponding to the other argument (e.g., **diff my_dir junk** is the same as **diff my_dir/junk junk**). If both arguments are directories, **diff** reports lines that differ between all pairs of files having equivalent names (e.g., *olddir/program* and *newdir/program*); in addition, **diff** lists filenames unique to one directory, as well as subdirectories common to both. See also **cmp**. |

*Options*

**–a, --text**
> Treat all files as text files. Useful for checking to see if binary files are identical.

**–b, --ignore-space-change**
> Ignore repeating blanks and end-of-line blanks; treat successive blanks as one.

**–B, --ignore-blank-lines**
> Ignore blank lines in files.

**–c**  Context **diff**: print 3 lines surrounding each changed line.

**–C** *n,* --context[=*n*]
> Context **diff**: print *n* lines surrounding each changed line. The default context is 3 lines.

**–d, --minimal**
> To speed up comparison, ignore segments of numerous changes and output a smaller set of changes.

**–D***symbol,* --ifdef=*symbol*
> When handling C files, create an output file that contains all the contents of both input files, including **#ifdef** and **#ifndef** directives that reflect the directives in both files.

**−e, −−ed**

Produce a script of commands (**a**, **c**, **d**) to re-create *file2* from *file1* using the **ed** editor.

**−F** *regexp*, **−−show-function-line**[=*regexp*]

For context and unified **diff**, show the most recent line containing *regexp* before each block of changed lines.

**−H** Speed output of large files by scanning for scattered small changes; long stretches with many changes may not show up.

**−−help**

Print brief usage message.

**−−horizon-lines=***n*

In an attempt to find a more compact listing, keep *n* lines on both sides of the changed lines when performing the comparison.

**−i, −−ignore-case**

Ignore case in text comparison. Uppercase and lowercase are considered the same.

**−I** *regexp*, **−−ignore-matching-lines=***regexp*

Ignore lines in files that match the regular expression *regexp*.

**−l, −−paginate**

Paginate output by passing it to **pr**.

**−L** *label*, **−−label** *label*, **−−label=***label*

For context and unified **diff**, print *label* in place of the filename being compared. The first such option applies to the first filename and the second option to the second filename.

**−−left-column**

For two-column output (**−y**), show only left column of common lines.

**−n, −−rcs**

Produce output in RCS **diff** format.

**−N, −−new-file**

Treat nonexistent files as empty.

**−p, −−show-c-function**

When handling files in C or C-like languages such as Java, show the function containing each block of changed lines. Assumes **−c** but can also be used with a unified **diff**.

→

**−P, −−unidirectional-new-file**
> If two directories are being compared and the first lacks a file that is in the second, pretend that an empty file of that name exists in the first directory.

**−q, −−brief**
> Output only whether files differ.

**−r, −−recursive**
> Compare subdirectories recursively.

**−s, −−report-identical-files**
> Indicate when files do not differ.

**−S** *filename*, **−−starting-file=***filename*
> For directory comparisons, begin with the file *filename*, skipping files that come earlier in the standard list order.

**−−suppress-common-lines**
> For two-column output (−y), do not show common lines.

**−t, −−expand-tabs**
> Produce output with tabs expanded to spaces.

**−T, −−initial-tab**
> Insert initial tabs into output to line up tabs properly.

**−u** Unified **diff**: print old and new versions of lines in a single block, with 3 lines surrounding each block of changed lines.

**−U** *n*, **−−unified[=***n*]
> Unified **diff**: print old and new versions of lines in a single block, with *n* lines surrounding each block of changed lines. The default context is 3 lines.

**−v, −−version**
> Print version number of this version of **diff**.

**−w, −−ignore-all-space**
> Ignore all whitespace in files for comparisons.

**−W** *n*, **−−width=***n*
> For two-column output (−y), produce columns with a maximum width of *n* characters. Default is 130.

**−x** *regexp*, **−−exclude=***regexp*
> Do not compare files in a directory whose names match *regexp*.

–X *filename*, **––exclude-from=***filename*
> Do not compare files in a directory whose names match patterns described in the file *filename*.

**–y, ––side-by-side**
> Produce two-column output.

–*n* For context and unified **diff**, print *n* lines of context. Same as specifying a number with –C or –U.

---

**diff3** [*options*] *file1 file2 file3*

Compare 3 files and report the differences. No more than one of the files may be given as – (indicating that it is to be read from standard input). The output is displayed with the following codes:

**====**
> All three files differ.

**====1**
> *file1* is different.

**====2**
> *file2* is different.

**====3**
> *file3* is different.

**diff3** is also designed to merge changes in two differing files based on a common ancestor file (i.e., when two people have made their own set of changes to the same file). **diff3** can find changes between the ancestor and one of the newer files and generate output that adds those differences to the other new file. Unmerged changes are places where both of the newer files differ from each other and at least one of them from the ancestor. Changes from the ancestor that are the same in both of the newer files are called *merged changes*. If all three files differ in the same place, it is called an *overlapping change*.

This scheme is used on the command line with the ancestor being *file2*, the second filename. Comparison is made between *file2* and *file3*, with those differences then applied to *file1*.

*Options*

→

**diff3**

←

**-3, --easy-only**
Create an **ed** script to incorporate into *file1* unmerged, nonoverlapping differences between *file1* and *file3*.

**-a, --text**
Treat files as text.

**-A, --show-all**
Create an **ed** script to incorporate all changes, showing conflicts in bracketed format.

**-e, --ed**
Create an **ed** script to incorporate into *file1* all unmerged differences between *file2* and *file3*.

**-E, --show-overlap**
Create an **ed** script to incorporate unmerged changes, showing conflicts in bracketed format.

**-x, --overlap-only**
Create an **ed** script to incorporate into *file1* all differences where all three files differ (overlapping changes).

**-X** Same as **-x**, but show only overlapping changes, in bracketed format.

**-m, --merge**
Create file with changes merged (not an **ed** script).

**-L** *label*, **--label=***label*
Use *label* to replace filename in output.

**-i** Append the **w** (save) and **q** (quit) commands to **ed** script output.

**-T, --initial-tab**
Begin lines with a tab instead of two spaces in output to line tabs up properly.

**-v, --version**
Print version information and then exit.

---

**dip**

**dip** [*options*] [*chat scriptfile*]

System administration command. Set up or initiate dial-up Internet connections. **dip** can be used to establish connections for users dialing out or dialing in. Commands can be used in interactive mode or placed in a script file for use in dial-out connections. To establish dial-in connections, **dip** is often is used as a shell and may be executed using the commands **diplogin** or **diplogini**.

−a   In dial-in mode, prompt for username and password. Same as the **diplogini** command.

−i   Initiate a login shell for a dial-in connection. Same as the **diplogin** command.

−k   Kill the most recent **dip** process or the process running on the device specified by the −l option.

−l *device*
    Used with the −k option. Specifies a tty *device*.

−m *mtu*
    Maximum Transfer Unit. The default is 296.

−p *protocol*
    The *protocol* to use: SLIP, CSLIP, PPP, or TERM.

−t   Command mode. This is usually done for testing.

−v   Verbose mode.

*Commands*

Most of these commands can be used either in interactive mode or in a script file.

**beep** *times*
    Beep the terminal the specified number of *times*.

**bootp**
    Retrieve local and remote IP addresses using the BOOTP protocol.

**break**
    Send a BREAK.

**chatkey** *keyword code*
    Map a modem response keyword to a numeric code.

**config** [interface|routing] [pre|up|down|post] *arguments*
    Modify **interface** characteristics or the **routing** table, before the link comes up, when it is up, when it goes down, or after it is down. The syntax for *arguments* is the same as arguments for the **ifconfig** or **route** commands.

**databits** 7|8
    Set the number of data bits.

**dec** *$variable* [*value*]
    Decrement *$variable* by *value*. The default is 1.

→

**default**

Set default route to the IP address of the host connected to.

**dial** *phonenumber* [*timeout*]

Dial *phonenumber*. Abort if remote modem doesn't answer within *timeout* seconds. Set **$errlvl** according to the modem response.

**echo on|off**

Enable or disable the display of modem commands.

**exit** [*n*]

Exit the script. Optionally return the number *n* as the exit status.

**flush**

Clear the input buffer.

**get** *$variable* [ask|remote [*timeout*]] *value*

Set *$variable* to *value*. If **ask** is specified, prompt the user for a value. If **remote** is specified, retrieve the value from the remote system. Abort after *timeout* seconds.

**goto** *label*

Jump to the section identified by *label*.

**help**

List available commands.

**if** *expr* goto *label*

Jump to the section identified by *label* if the expression evaluates to true. An expression compares a variable to a constant using one of these operators: =, !=, <, >, <=, or >=.

**inc** *$variable* [*value*]

Increment *$variable* by *value*. The default is 1.

**init** *string*

Set the *string* used to initialize the modem. The default is ATE0 Q0 V1 X1.

**mode** *protocol*

Set the connection *protocol*. Valid values are SLIP, CSLIP, PPP, and TERM. The default is SLIP.

**netmask** *mask*

Set the subnet mask.

**parity E|O|N**

Set the line parity to even, odd, or none.

**password**

Prompt user for password.

**proxyarp**

Install a proxy ARP entry in the local ARP table.

**print** *$variable*

Display the content of *$variable*.

**psend** *command*

Execute *command* in a shell, and send output to the serial device. Commands are executed using the user's real UID.

**port** *device*

Specify the serial device the modem is attached to.

**quit**

Exit with a nonzero exit status. Abort the connection.

**reset**

Reset the modem.

**securid**

Prompt user for the variable part of an ACE System SecureID password and send it together with the stored prefix to the remote system.

**securidf** *prefix*

Store the fixed part of an ACE System SecureID password.

**send** *string*

Send *string* to the serial device.

**shell** *command*

Execute command in a shell using the user's real UID.

**skey** [*timeout*]

Wait for an S/Key challenge, then prompt user for the secret key. Generate and send the response. Abort if challenge is not received within *timeout* seconds. S/Key support must be compiled into **dip**.

**sleep** *time*

Wait *time* seconds.

**speed** *bits-per-second*

Set the port speed. Default is 38400.

→

Linux
Commands

| | |
|---|---|
| **dip**<br>← | **stopbits 1 | 2**<br>　　Set the number of stop bits.<br><br>**term**<br>　　Enable terminal mode. Pass keyboard input directly to the serial device.<br><br>**timeout** *time*<br>　　Set the number of seconds the line can be inactive before the link is closed.<br><br>**wait** *text* [*timeout*]<br>　　Wait *timeout* seconds for *text* to arrive from the remote system. If *timeout* is not specified, wait forever. |
| **dirname** | **dirname** *pathname*<br><br>Print *pathname* excluding the last level. Useful for stripping the actual filename from a pathname. If there are no slashes (no directory levels) in *pathname*, **dirname** prints . to indicate the current directory. See also **basename**. |
| **dmesg** | **dmesg** [*options*]<br><br>System administration command. Display the system control messages from the kernel ring buffer. This buffer stores all messages since the last system boot or the most recent ones, if the buffer has been filled.<br><br>*Options*<br><br>−c　Clear buffer after printing messages.<br><br>−n *level*<br>　　Set the level of system message that will display on console. |
| **dnsdomainname** | **dnsdomainname**<br><br>TCP/IP command. Print the system's DNS domain name. See also **hostname**. |
| **domainname** | **domainname** [*name*]<br><br>NFS/NIS command. Set or display name of current NIS domain. With no argument, **domainname** displays the name of the current NIS domain. Only a privileged user can set |

the domain name by giving an argument; this is usually done in a startup script.

**dosfsck** [*options*] *device*
**fsck.ext2** [*options*] *device*

System administration command. Similar to **fsck**, but specifically intended for MS-DOS filesystems. When checking an MS-DOS filesystem, **fsck** calls this command. Normally **dosfsck** stores all changes in memory, then writes them when checks are complete.

*Options*

-a  Automatically repair the system; do not prompt the user.

-A  Use the Atari version of the MS-DOS filesystem.

-d *file*
Drop the named file from the file allocation table. Force checking, even if kernel has already marked the filesystem as valid. **dosfsck** will normally exit without checking if the system appears to be clean.

-l *file*
Consult *file* for a list of bad blocks, in addition to checking for others.

-n  Ensure that no changes are made to the filesystem. When queried, answer "no."

-p  "Preen." Repair all bad blocks noninteractively.

-t  Display timing statistics.

-v  Verbose.

-y  When queried, answer "yes."

-B *size*
Expect to find the superblock at *size*; if it's not there, exit.

-F  Flush buffer caches before checking.

-L *file*
Consult *file* for list of bad blocks instead of checking filesystem for them.

**du**

du [*options*] [*directories*]

Print disk usage (as the number of 1KB blocks used by each named directory and its subdirectories; default is current directory).

*Options*

−a, −−all
    Print usage for all files, not just subdirectories.

−b, −−bytes
    Print sizes in bytes.

−c, −−total
    In addition to normal output, print grand total of all arguments.

−D, −−dereference-args
    Follow symbolic links, but only if they are command-line arguments.

−h, −−human-readable
    Print sizes in human-reader-friendly format.

−H, −−si
    Like −h, but show as power of 1000 rather than 1024.

−k, −−kilobytes
    Print sizes in kilobytes (this is the default).

−l, −−count-links
    Count the size of all files, whether or not they have already appeared (i.e., via a hard link).

−L, −−dereference
    Follow symbolic links.

−−exclude=*pattern*
    Exclude files that match *pattern*.

−−max-depth=*num*
    Report sizes for directories only down to *num* levels below the starting point (which is level 0).

−m, −−megabytes
    Print sizes in megabytes.

−s, −−summarize
    Print only the grand total for each named directory.

−S, −−separate-dirs
    Do not include the sizes of subdirectories when totaling the size of parent directories.

**−x, −−one-file-system**
Display usage of files in current filesystem only.

**−X, −−exclude-from=**_file_
Exclude files that match any pattern in _file_.

**−−help**
Print help message and then exit.

**−−version**
Print the version and then exit.

---

**dumpe2fs** _device_

System administration command. Print information about _device_'s superblock and blocks group.

---

**dumpkeys** [_options_]

Print information about the keyboard driver's translation tables to standard output. Further information is available in the manual pages under _keytables_.

*Options*

**−1, −−separate-lines**
Print one line for each modifier/keycode pair and prefix **plain** to each unmodified keycode.

**−c**_charset_, **−−charset=**_charset_
Specify character set with which to interpret character code values. The default character set is **iso-8859-1**. The full list of valid character sets is available with the **−−help** option.

**−−compose-only**
Print compose key combinations only. Requires compose key support in the kernel.

**−f, −−full-table**
Output in canonical, not short, form: for each key, print a row with modifier combinations divided into columns.

**−−funcs-only**
Print function key string definitions only; do not print key bindings or string definitions.

→

| | |
|---|---|
| dumpkeys ← | **−h, −−help**<br>Print help message and the version.<br><br>**−i, −−short-info**<br>Print in short-info format, including information about acceptable keycode keywords in the keytable files; the number of actions that can be bound to a key; a list of the ranges of action codes (the values to the right of a key definition); and the number of function keys that the kernel supports.<br><br>**−−keys-only**<br>Print key bindings only; do not print string definitions.<br><br>**−l, −−long-info**<br>Print the same information as in **−−short-info**, plus a list of the supported action symbols and their numeric values.<br><br>**−n, −−numeric**<br>Print action code values in hexadecimal notation; do not attempt to convert them to symbolic notation.<br><br>**−S** *num*, **−−shape**=*num*<br>Print using *num* to determine table shape. Values of *num* are:<br><br>0   Default<br><br>1   Same as **−−full-table**<br><br>2   Same as **−−separate-lines**<br><br>3   One line for each keycode up to the first hole, then one line per modifier/keycode pair |
| **e2fsck** | **e2fsck** [*options*] *device*<br>**fsck.ext2** [*options*] *device*<br><br>System administration command. Similar to **fsck**, but specifically intended for Linux Second Extended Filesystems. When checking a second extended filesystem, **fsck** calls this command.<br><br>*Options*<br><br>**−b** *superblock*<br>Use *superblock* instead of default superblock. |

−d   Debugging mode.

−f   Force checking, even if kernel has already marked the filesystem as valid. **e2fsck** will normally exit without checking if the system appears to be clean.

−l *file*
> Consult *file* for a list of bad blocks, in addition to checking for others.

−n   Ensure that no changes are made to the filesystem. When queried, answer "no."

−p   "Preen." Repair all bad blocks noninteractively.

−t   Display timing statistics.

−v   Verbose.

−y   When queried, answer "yes."

−B *size*
> Expect to find the superblock at *size*; if it's not there, exit.

−F   Flush buffer caches before checking.

−L *file*
> Consult *file* for list of bad blocks instead of checking filesystem for them.

---

## echo [−n] [*string*]

This is the **/bin/echo** command. **echo** also exists as a command built into the C shell and **bash**. The following character sequences have special meanings:

\a   Alert (bell)

\b   Backspace

\c   Suppress trailing newline

\f   Form feed

\n   Newline

\r   Carriage return

\t   Horizontal tab

\v   Vertical tab

$\rightarrow$

**echo**
←

\\    Literal backslash

*\nnn*
    The octal character whose ASCII code is *nnn*.

*Options*

−e  Enable character sequences with special meaning. (In some versions, this option is not required in order to make the sequences work.)

−E  Disable character sequences with special meaning.

−n  Suppress printing of newline after text.

−−help
    Print help message and then exit.

−−version
    Print version information and then exit.

*Examples*

```
/bin/echo "testing printer" | lp
/bin/echo "TITLE\nTITLE" > file ; cat doc1 doc2 >> file
/bin/echo "Warning: ringing bell \a"
```

---

**egrep**

**egrep** [*options*] [*regexp*] [*files*]

Search one or more *files* for lines that match an extended regular expression *regexp*. **egrep** doesn't support the regular expressions \(, \), \n, \<, \>, \{, or \} but does support the other expressions, as well as the extended set +, ?, |, and ( ). Remember to enclose these characters in quotes. Regular expressions are described in Chapter 9, *Pattern Matching*. Exit status is 0 if any lines match, 1 if none match, and 2 for errors.

See **grep** for the list of available options. Also see **fgrep**. **egrep** typically runs faster than those commands.

*Examples*

Search for occurrences of *Victor* or *Victoria* in *file*:

```
egrep 'Victor(ia)*' file
egrep '(Victor|Victoria)' file
```

Find and print strings such as *old.doc1* or *new.doc2* in *files*, and include their line numbers:

```
egrep -n '(old|new)\.doc?' files
```

**emacs** [*options*] [*files*]

A text editor and all-purpose work environment. For more information, see Chapter 10, *The Emacs Editor.*

**env** [*option*] [*variable=value* ... ] [*command*]

Display the current environment or, if an environment *variable* is specified, set it to a new *value* and display the modified environment. If *command* is specified, execute it under the modified environment.

*Options*

**–, –i, ––ignore-environment**
Ignore current environment entirely.

**–u** *name,* **––unset** *name*
Unset the specified variable.

**––help**
Print help message and then exit.

**––version**
Print version information and then exit.

**etags** [*options*] *files*

Create a list of function and macro names that are defined in the specified C, Pascal, FORTRAN, **yacc**, or **flex** source *files*. The output list (named *tags* by default) contains lines of the form:

```
name    file    context
```

where *name* is the function or macro name, *file* is the source file in which *name* is defined, and *context* is a search pattern that shows the line of code containing *name*. After the list of tags is created, you can invoke Emacs on any file and type:

```
ESC-x visit-tags-table
```

You will be prompted for the name of the tag table; the default is TAGS. To switch to the source file associated with the *name* listed in *tagsfile*, type:

```
ESC-x find-tag
```

You will be prompted for the tag you would like Emacs to search for. **ctags** produces an equivalent tags file for use

→

| etags ← | with **vi**. |
|---|---|

**Options**

−a, −−append
Append tag output to existing list of tags.

−d, −−defines
Include tag entries for C preprocessor definitions.

−i *file*, −−include=*file*
Add a note to the tags file that *file* should be consulted in addition to the normal input file.

−l *language*, −−language=*language*
Consider the files that follow this option to be written in *language*. Use the −h option for a list of languages and their default filename extensions.

−o *file*, −−output=*file*
Write to *file*.

−r *regexp*, −−regex=*regexp*
Include a tag for each line that matches *regexp* in the files following this option.

−C, −−c++
Expect *.c* and *.h* files to contain C++, not C, code.

−D, −−no-defines
Do not include tag entries for C preprocessor definitions.

−H, −h, −−help
Print usage information.

−R, −−noregex
Don't include tags based on regular-expression matching for the files that follow this option.

−S, −−ignore-indentation
Normally **etags** uses indentation to parse the tag file; this option tells it to rely on it less.

−V, −−version
Print the version number.

| ex | **ex** [*options*] *file* |
|---|---|

An interactive command-based editor. For more informa-

**expand** [*options*] *files*

Convert tabs in given files (or standard input, if the file is named –) to appropriate number of spaces; write results to standard output.

*Options*

–*tabs*, –t, ––tabs *tabs*
  *tabs* is a comma-separated list of integers that specify the placement of tab stops. If exactly one integer is provided, the tab stops are set to every *integer* spaces. By default, tab stops are 8 spaces apart. With –t and ––tabs, the list may be separated by whitespace instead of commas.

–i, ––initial
  Convert tabs only at the beginning of lines.

––help
  Print help message and then exit.

––version
  Print version information and then exit.

**expr** *arg1 operator arg2* [ *operator arg3* ... ]

Evaluate arguments as expressions and print the result. Arguments and operators must be separated by spaces. In most cases, an argument is an integer, typed literally or represented by a shell variable. There are three types of operators: arithmetic, relational, and logical, as well as keyword expressions. Exit status for **expr** is **0** (expression is nonzero and nonnull), **1** (expression is 0 or null), or **2** (expression is invalid).

*Arithmetic operators*

Use these to produce mathematical expressions whose results are printed:

+  Add *arg2* to *arg1*.

–  Subtract *arg2* from *arg1*.

*  Multiply the arguments.

→

/     Divide *arg1* by *arg2*.

%     Take the remainder when *arg1* is divided by *arg2*.

Addition and subtraction are evaluated last, unless they are grouped inside parentheses. The symbols *, (, and ) have meaning to the shell, so they must be escaped (preceded by a backslash or enclosed in single quotes).

### Relational operators

Use these to compare two arguments. Arguments can also be words, in which case comparisons are defined by the locale. If the comparison statement is true, the result is 1; if false, the result is 0. Symbols > and < must be escaped.

=, ==
    Are the arguments equal?

!=     Are the arguments different?

>     Is *arg1* greater than *arg2*?

>=     Is *arg1* greater than or equal to *arg2*?

<     Is *arg1* less than *arg2*?

<=     Is *arg1* less than or equal to *arg2*?

### Logical operators

Use these to compare two arguments. Depending on the values, the result can be *arg1* (or some portion of it), *arg2*, or 0. Symbols | and & must be escaped.

|     Logical OR; if *arg1* has a nonzero (and nonnull) value, the result is *arg1*; otherwise, the result is *arg2*.

&     Logical AND; if both *arg1* and *arg2* have a nonzero (and nonnull) value, the result is *arg1*; otherwise, the result is 0.

:     Like **grep**; *arg2* is a pattern to search for in *arg1*. *arg2* must be a regular expression. If part of the *arg2* pattern is enclosed in \( \), the result is the portion of *arg1* that matches; otherwise, the result is simply the number of characters that match. By default, a pattern match always applies to the beginning of the first argument (the search string implicitly begins with a ^). Start the search string with .* to match other parts of the string.

**index** *string character-list*
> Return the first position in *string* that matches the first possible character in *character-list*. Continue through *character-list* until a match is found, or return 0.

**length** *string*
> Return the length of *string*.

**match** *string regex*
> Same as *string* : *regex*.

**quote** *token*
> Treat *token* as a string, even if it would normally be a keyword or an operator.

**substr** *string start length*
> Return a section of *string*, beginning with *start*, with a maximum length of *length* characters. Return **null** when given a negative or nonnumeric *start* or *length*.

*Examples*

Division happens first; result is 10:

`expr 5 + 10 / 2`

Addition happens first; result is 7 (truncated from 7.5):

`expr \( 5 + 10 \) / 2`

Add 1 to variable *i*. This is how variables are incremented in shell scripts:

`i=`expr $i + 1``

Print 1 (true) if variable **a** is the string "hello":

`expr $a = hello`

Print 1 (true) if **b** plus 5 equals 10 or more:

`expr $b + 5 \>= 10`

Find the 5th, 6th, and 7th letters of the word *character*.

`expr substr character 5 3`

In the examples that follow, variable **p** is the string "version.100". This command prints the number of characters in **p**:

`expr $p : '.*'`        *Result is 11*

→

| | |
|---|---|
| **expr**<br>← | Match all characters and print them:<br><br>**expr $p : '\(.*\)'**    *Result is "version.100"*<br><br>Print the number of lowercase letters at the beginning of **p**:<br><br>**expr $p : '[a-z]*'**    *Result is 7*<br><br>Match the lowercase letters at the beginning of **p**:<br><br>**expr $p : '\([a-z]*\)'**    *Result is "version"*<br><br>Truncate **$x** if it contains five or more characters; if not, just print **$x**. (Logical OR uses the second argument when the first one is 0 or null; i.e., when the match fails.)<br><br>**expr $x : '\(.....\)' \| $x**<br><br>In a shell script, rename files to their first five letters:<br><br>**mv $x `expr $x : '\(.....\)' \| $x`**<br><br>(To avoid overwriting files with similar names, use **mv −i**.) |

| | |
|---|---|
| **false** | **false**<br><br>A null command that returns an unsuccessful (nonzero) exit status. Normally used in **bash** scripts. See also **true**. |

| | |
|---|---|
| **fdformat** | **fdformat** [*options*] *device*<br><br>Low-level format of a floppy disk. The device for a standard format is usually **/dev/fd0** or **/dev/fd1**.<br><br>*Option*<br><br>**−n**  Do not verify format after completion. |

| | |
|---|---|
| **fdisk** | **fdisk** [*options*] [*device*]<br><br>System administration command. Maintain disk partitions via a menu. **fdisk** displays information about disk partitions, creates and deletes disk partitions, and changes the active partition. It is possible to assign a different operating system to each of the four partitions, though only one partition is active at any given time. You can also divide a physical partition into several logical partitions. The minimum recommended size for a Linux system partition is 40MB. Normally, *device* will be */dev/hda*, */dev/hdb*, */dev/sda*, */dev/sdb*, */dev/hdc*, */dev/hdd*, and so on. See also **cfdisk**. |

**-l**   List partition tables and exit.

**-s**partition
   Display the size of *partition*, unless it is a DOS partition.

**Commands**

**a**   Toggle a bootable flag on current partition.

**d**   Delete current partition.

**l**   List all partition types.

**m**   Main menu.

**n**   Create a new partition; prompt for more information.

**p**   Print a list of all partitions and information about each.

**q**   Quit; do not save.

**t**   Replace the type of the current partition.

**u**   Modify the display/entry units, which must be cylinders or sectors.

**v**   Verify: check for errors; display a summary of the number of unallocated sectors.

**w**   Save changes; exit.

---

fetchmail [*options*] [*servers* . . .]

fetchmail

System administration command. Retrieve mail from mail servers and forward it to the local mail delivery system. **fetchmail** retrieves mail from servers that support the common mail protocols POP2, POP3, IMAP2bis, and IMAP4. Messages are delivered via SMTP through port 25 on the local host and through your system's mail delivery agent (such as *sendmail*), where they can be read through the user's mail client. **fetchmail** settings are stored in the ~/.fetchmailrc file. Parameters and servers can also be set on the command line, which will override settings in the *.fetchmailrc* file. **fetchmail** is compatible with the **popclient** program, and users can use both without having to adjust file settings.

→

**fetchmail**
←

*Options*

**−a, −−all**
> Retrieve all messages from server, even ones that have already been seen but left on the server. The default is to only retrieve new messages.

**−A** *type*, **−−auth** *type*
> Specify the type of authentication. *type* may be: **password**, **kerberos_v5**, or **kerberos**. Authentication type is usually established by **fetchmail** by default, so this option isn't very useful.

**−B** *n*, **−−fetchlimit** *n*
> Set the maximum number of messages (*n*) accepted from a server per query.

**−b** *n*, **−−batchlimit** *n*
> Set the maximum number of messages sent to an SMTP listener per connection. When this limit is reached, the connection will be broken and reestablished. The default of 0 means no limit.

**−c, −−check**
> Check for mail on a single server without retrieving or deleting messages. Works with IMAP but not well with other protocols, if at all.

**−D** [*domain*], **−−smtpaddress** [*domain*]
> Specify the *domain* name placed in RCPT TO lines sent to SMTP. The default is the local host.

**−E** *header*, **−−envelope** *header*
> Change the header assumed to contain the mail's envelope address (usually "X-Envelope-to:") to *header*.

**−e** *n*, **−−expunge** *n*
> Tell an IMAP server to EXPUNGE (i.e., purge messages marked for deletion) after *n* deletes. A setting of 0 indicates expunging only at the end of the session. Normally, an **expunge** occurs after each delete.

**−F, −−flush**
> For POP3 and IMAP servers, remove previously retrieved messages from the server before retrieving new ones.

**−f** *file*, **−−fetchmailrc** *file*
> Specify a nondefault name for the **fetchmail** configuration file.

**−I** *specification*, **−−interface** *specification*

Require that the mail server machine is up and running at a specified IP address (or range) before polling. The *specification* is given as *interface/ipaddress/mask*. The first part indicates the type of TCP connection expected (*sl0*, *ppp0*, etc.), the second is the IP address, and the third is the bit mask for the IP, assumed to be 255.255.255.255.

**−K, −−nokeep**

Delete all retrieved messages from the mail server.

**−k, −−keep**

Keep copies of all retrieved messages on the mail server.

**−l** *size*, **−−limit** *size*

Set the maximum message size that will be retrieved from a server. Messages larger than this size will be left on the server and marked unread.

**−M** *interface*, **−−monitor** *interface*

In daemon mode, monitor the specified TCP/IP *interface* for any activity besides itself, and skip the poll if there is no other activity. Useful for PPP connections that automatically time out with no activity.

**−m** *command*, **−−mda** *command*

Pass mail directly to mail delivery agent, rather than send to port 25. The *command* is the path and options for the mailer, such as **/usr/lib/sendmail -oem**. A %T in the command will be replaced with the local delivery address, and an %F will be replaced with the message's **From** address.

**−n, −−norewrite**

Do not expand local mail IDs to full addresses. This option will disable expected addressing and should only be used to find problems.

**−P** *n*, **−−port** *n*

Specify a port to connect to on the mail server. The default port numbers for supported protocols are usually sufficient.

**−p** *proto*, **−−protocol** *proto*

Specify the protocol to use when polling a mail server. *proto* can be:

POP2

Post Office Protocol 2.

→

**POP3**

> Post Office Protocol 3.

**APOP**

> POP3 with MD5 authentication.

**RPOP**

> POP3 with RPOP authentication.

**KPOP**

> POP3 with Kerberos v4 authentication on port 1109.

**IMAP**

> IMAP2bis, IMAP4, or IMAP4rev1. **fetchmail** autodetects their capabilities.

**IMAP-K4**

> IMAP4 or IMAP4rev1 with Kerberos v4 authentication.

**IMAP-GSS**

> IMAP4 or IMAP4rev1 with GSSAPI authentication.

**ETRN**
> ESMTP.

**−Q** *string*, **−−qvirtual** *string*

> Remove the prefix *string*, which is the local user's hostid, from the address in the envelope header (such as "Delivered-To:").

**−r** *folder*, **−−folder** *folder*

> Retrieve the specified mail *folder* from the mail server.

**−s**, **−−silent**

> Suppress status messages during a **fetch**.

**−U**, **−−uidl**

> For POP3, track the age of kept messages via unique ID listing.

**−u** *name*, **−−username** *name*

> Specify the user *name* to use when logging into the mail server.

**−V**, **−−version**

> Print the version information for **fetchmail** and display the options set for each mail server. Performs no **fetch**.

**−v**, **−−verbose**

> Display all status messages during a **fetch**.

| | |
|---|---|
| **–Z** *nnn*, **––antispam** *nnn*<br>    Specify the SMTP error *nnn* to signal a spam block<br>    from the client. If *nnn* is –1, this option is disabled. | fetchmail |

---

**fgrep** [*options*] *pattern* [*files*]

Search one or more *files* for lines that match a literal text string *pattern*. Exit status is 0 if any lines match, 1 if not, and 2 for errors.

See **grep** for the list of available options. Also see **egrep**.

*Examples*

Print lines in *file* that don't contain any spaces:

```
fgrep -v ' ' file
```

Print lines in *file* that contain the words in **spell_list**:

```
fgrep -f spell_list file
```

fgrep

---

**file** [*options*] *files*

Classify the named *files* according to the type of data they contain. **file** checks the magic file (usually */usr/share/magic*) to identify some file types.

*Options*

**–b**  Brief mode; do not prepend filenames to output lines.

**–c**  Check the format of the magic file (*files* argument is invalid with **–c**). Usually used with **–m**.

**–f** *file*<br>    Read the names of files to be checked from *file*.

**–L**  Follow symbolic links. By default, symbolic links are not followed.

**–m** *file*<br>    Search for file types in *file* instead of */usr/share/magic*.

**–n**  Flush standard output after checking a file.

**–s**  Check files that are block or character special files in addition to checking ordinary files.

**–v**  Print the version.

file

→

**file**
←

−z  Attempt checking of compressed files.

Many file types are understood. Output lists each filename, followed by a brief classification such as:

```
ascii text
c program text
c-shell commands
data
empty
iAPX 386 executable
directory
[nt]roff, tbl, or eqn input text
shell commands
symbolic link to ../usr/etc/arp
```

*Example*

List all files that are deemed to be troff/nroff input:

```
file * | grep roff
```

---

**find**

**find** [*pathnames*] [*conditions*]

An extremely useful command for finding particular groups of files (numerous examples follow this description). **find** descends the directory tree beginning at each *pathname* and locates files that meet the specified *conditions*. The default pathname is the current directory. The most useful conditions include **−print** (which is the default if no other expression is given), **−name** and **−type** (for general use), **−exec** and **−size** (for advanced users), and **−mtime** and **−user** (for administrators).

Conditions may be grouped by enclosing them in \( \) (escaped parentheses), negated with ! (use \! in the C shell), given as alternatives by separating them with **−o**, or repeated (adding restrictions to the match; usually only for **−name**, **−type**, **−perm**). Modification refers to editing of a file's contents. Change refers to modification, permission or ownership changes, and so on; therefore, for example, **−ctime** is more inclusive than **−atime** or **−mtime**.

*Conditions and actions*

**−atime** +*n* | −*n* | *n*
  Find files that were last accessed more than *n* (+*n*), less than *n* (−*n*), or exactly *n* days ago. Note that **find** changes the access time of directories supplied as *path-names*.

**−ctime** +*n* | −*n* | *n*

 Find files that were changed more than *n* (+*n*), less
 than *n* (−*n*), or exactly *n* days ago. A change is anything that changes the directory entry for the file, such
 as a **chmod**.

**−depth**

 Descend the directory tree, skipping directories and
 working on actual files first (and *then* the parent directories). Useful when files reside in unwritable directories (e.g., when using **find** with **cpio**).

**−exec** *command* { } \;

 Run the Linux *command*, from the starting directory on
 each file matched by **find** (provided *command* executes successfully on that file; i.e., returns a 0 exit status). When *command* runs, the argument { } substitutes
 the current file. Follow the entire sequence with an
 escaped semicolon (\;).

**−follow**

 Follow symbolic links and track the directories visited
 (don't use this with **−type l**).

**−group** *gname*

 Find files belonging to group *gname*. *gname* can be a
 group name or a group ID number.

**−inum** *n*

 Find files whose inode number is *n*.

**−links** *n*

 Find files having *n* links.

**−mount, −xdev**

 Search for files that reside only on the same filesystem
 as *pathname*.

**−mtime** +*n* | −*n* | *n*

 Find files that were last modified more than *n* (+*n*),
 less than *n* (−*n*), or exactly *n* days ago. A modification
 is a change to a file's data.

**−name** *pattern*

 Find files whose names match *pattern*. Filename
 metacharacters may be used but should be escaped or
 quoted.

**−newer** *file*

 Find files that have been modified more recently than
 *file*; similar to **−mtime**. Affected by **−follow** only if it
 occurs after **−follow** on the command line.

→

−ok *command* { } \;

Same as **−exec** but prompts user to respond with **y** before *command* is executed.

**−perm** *nnn*

Find files whose permission flags (e.g., **rwx**) match octal number *nnn* exactly (e.g., 664 matches −rw−rw−r−−). Use a minus sign before *nnn* to make a "wildcard" match of any unspecified octal digit (e.g., −perm −600 matches −rw−******, where * can be any mode).

**−print**

Print the matching files and directories, using their full pathnames. Return true.

**−regex** *pattern*

Like **−path** but uses **grep**-style regular expressions instead of the shell-like globbing used in **−name** and **−path**.

**−size** *n*[c]

Find files containing *n* blocks, or if **c** is specified, *n* characters long.

**−type** *c*

Find files whose type is *c*. *c* can be **b** (block special file), **c** (character special file), **d** (directory), **p** (fifo or named pipe), **l** (symbolic link), **s** (socket), or **f** (plain file).

**−user** *user*

Find files belonging to *user* (name or ID).

**−daystart**

Calculate times from the start of the day today, not 24 hours ago.

**−maxdepth** *num*

Do not descend more than *num* levels of directories.

**−mindepth** *num*

Begin applying tests and actions only at levels deeper than *num* levels.

**−noleaf**

Normally, **find** assumes that each directory has at least two hard links that should be ignored (a hard link for its name and one for "."; i.e., two fewer "real" directories than its hard link count indicates). **−noleaf** turns off this assumption, a useful practice when **find** runs on non-Unix-style filesystems. This forces **find** to examine all entries, assuming that some might prove to be directories into which it must descend (a time-waster on Unix).

**−amin +***n* | **−***n* | *n*

Find files last accessed more than *n* (+*n*), less than *n* (−*n*), or exactly *n* minutes ago.

**−anewer** *file*

Find files that were accessed after *file* was last modified. Affected by **−follow** when after **−follow** on the command line.

**−cmin +***n* | **−***n* | *n*

Find files last changed more than *n* (+*n*), less than *n* (−*n*), or exactly *n* minutes ago.

**−cnewer** *file*

Find files that were changed after they were last modified. Affected by **−follow** when after **−follow** on the command line.

**−empty**

Continue if file is empty. Applies to regular files and directories.

**−false**

Return false value for each file encountered.

**−fstype** *type*

Match files only on *type* filesystems. Acceptable types include **minix**, **ext**, **ext2**, **xia**, **msdos**, **umsdos**, **vfat**, **proc**, **nfs**, **iso9660**, **hpfs**, **sysv**, **smb**, and **ncpfs**.

**−gid** *num*

Find files with numeric group ID of *num*.

**−ilname** *pattern*

A case-insensitive version of **−lname**.

**−iname** *pattern*

A case-insensitive version of **−name**.

**−ipath** *pattern*

A case-insensitive version of **−path**.

**−iregex** *pattern*

A case-insensitive version of **−regex**.

**−lname** *pattern*

Search for files that are symbolic links, pointing to files named *pattern*. *pattern* can include shell metacharacters and does not treat **/** or **.** specially. The match is case-insensitive.

→

−mmin +*n* | −*n* | *n*

> Find files last modified more than *n* (+*n*), less than *n* (−*n*), or exactly *n* minutes ago.

−nouser

> The file's user ID does not correspond to any user.

−nogroup

> The file's group ID does not correspond to any group.

−path *pattern*

> Find files whose names match *pattern*. Expect full pathnames relative to the starting pathname (i.e., do not treat / or . specially).

*Examples*

List all files (and subdirectories) in your home directory:

`find $HOME -print`

List all files named *chapter1* in the /work directory:

`find /work -name chapter1 -print`

List all files beginning with *memo* owned by *ann*:

`find /work -name 'memo*' -user ann -print`

Search the filesystem (begin at root) for manpage directories:

`find / -type d -name 'man*' -print`

Search the current directory, look for filenames that *don't* begin with a capital letter, and send them to the printer:

`find . \! -name '[A-Z]*' -exec lpr {} \;`

Find and compress files whose names *don't* end with *.gz*:

`gzip `find . \! -name '*.gz' -print``

Remove all empty files on the system (prompting first):

`find / -size 0 -ok rm {} \;`

Search the system for files that were modified within the last two days (good candidates for backing up):

`find / -mtime -2 -print`

Recursively **grep** for a pattern down a directory tree:

`find /book -print | xargs grep '[Nn]utshell'`

If the files *kt1* and *kt2* exist in the current directory, their names can be printed with the command:

```
$ find . -name 'kt[0-9]'
./kt1
./kt2
```

Since the command prints these names with an initial ./ path, you need to specify the ./ when using the **-path** option:

```
$ find . -path './kt[0-9]'
./kt1
./kt2
```

The **-regex** option uses a complete pathname, like **-path**, but treats the following argument as a regular expression rather than a glob pattern (although in this case the result is the same):

```
$ find . -regex './kt[0-9]'
./kt1
./kt2
```

**finger** [*options*] *users*

Display data about one or more *users*, including information listed in the files *.plan* and *.project* in each *user*'s home directory. You can specify each *user* either as a login name (exact match) or as a first or last name (display information on all matching names). Networked environments recognize arguments of the form *user@host* and *@host*.

### Options

-l  Force long format (default): everything included by the **-s** option and home directory, home phone, login shell, mail status, *.plan, .project,* and *.forward*.

-m  Suppress matching of users' "real" names.

-p  Omit *.plan* and *.project* files from display.

-s  Show short format: login name, real name, terminal name, write status, idle time, office location, and office phone number.

**in.fingerd** [*option*]

TCP/IP command. Remote user information server. **fingerd** provides a network interface to the **finger** program. It listens for TCP connections on the **finger** port and, for each connection, reads a single input line, passes the line to **finger**, and copies the output of **finger** to the user on the client

→

| | |
|---|---|
| **fingerd**<br>← | machine. **fingerd** is started by **inetd** and must have an entry in **inetd**'s configuration file, */etc/inetd.conf.*<br><br>*Option*<br><br>−w Include additional information, such as uptime and the name of the operating system. |
| **flex** | **flex** [*options*] [*file*]<br><br>**flex** (Fast Lexical Analyzer Generator) is a faster variant of **lex**. It generates a lexical analysis program (named *lex.yy.c*) based on the regular expressions and C statements contained in one or more input *files*. See also **bison**, **yacc**, and the O'Reilly book *lex & yacc* by John Levine, Tony Mason, and Doug Brown.<br><br>*Options*<br><br>−b  Generate backup information to *lex.backup.*<br><br>−d  Debug mode.<br><br>−f  Use faster compilation (limited to small programs).<br><br>−h  Help summary.<br><br>−i  Scan case-insensitively.<br><br>−l  Maximum **lex** compatibility.<br><br>−o *file*<br>     Write output to *file* instead of *lex.yy.c.*<br><br>−p  Print performance report.<br><br>−s  Exit if the scanner encounters input that does not match any of its rules.<br><br>−t  Print to standard out. (By default, **flex** prints to *lex.yy.c.*)<br><br>−v  Print a summary of statistics.<br><br>−w  Suppress warning messages.<br><br>−B  Generate batch (noninteractive) scanner.<br><br>−F  Use the fast scanner table representation.<br><br>−I  Generate an interactive scanner (default).<br><br>−L  Suppress **#line** directives in *lex.yy.c.* |

−P *prefix*
> Change default **yy** prefix to *prefix* for all globally visible variable and function names.

−V  Print version number.

−7  Generate a 7-bit scanner.

−8  Generate an 8-bit scanner (default).

−+  Generate a C++ scanner class.

−C  Compress scanner tables but do not use equivalence classes.

−Ca
> Align tables for memory access and computation. This creates larger tables but gives faster performance.

−Ce
> Construct equivalence classes. This creates smaller tables and sacrifices little performance (default).

−Cf
> Generate full scanner tables, not compressed.

−CF
> Generate faster scanner tables, like −**F**.

−Cm
> Construct metaequivalence classes (default).

−Cr
> Bypass use of the standard I/O library. Instead use **read( )** system calls.

---

fmt [*options*] [*files*]

Convert text to specified width by filling lines and removing newlines. Concatenate files on the command line, or read text from standard input if − (or no file) is specified. By default, preserve blank lines, spacing, and indentation. **fmt** attempts to break lines at the end of sentences and to avoid breaking lines after a sentence's first word or before its last.

*Options*

−c, −−crown-margin
> Crown margin mode. Do not change each paragraph's first two lines' indentation. Use the second line's indentation as the default for subsequent lines.

→

| | |
|---|---|
| **fmt**<br>← | **-p** *prefix*, **--prefix=***prefix*<br>Format only lines beginning with *prefix*.<br><br>**-s, --split-only**<br>Suppress line-joining.<br><br>**-t, --tagged-paragraph**<br>Tagged paragraph mode. Same as crown mode when the indentation of the first and second lines differs. If the indentation is the same, treat the first line as its own separate paragraph.<br><br>**-u, --uniform-spacing**<br>Print exactly one space between words and two between sentences.<br><br>**-w** *width*, **--width=***width*<br>Set output width to *width*. The default is 75.<br><br>**--help**<br>Print help message and then exit.<br><br>**--version**<br>Print version information and then exit. |
| **fold** | **fold** [*option*] [*files*]<br><br>Break the lines of the named *files* so that they are no wider than the specified width (default is 80). **fold** breaks lines exactly at the specified width, even in the middle of a word. Reads from standard input when given − as a file.<br><br>*Options*<br><br>**-b, --bytes**<br>Count bytes, not columns (i.e., consider tabs, backspaces, and carriage returns to be one column).<br><br>**-s, --spaces**<br>Break at spaces only, if possible.<br><br>**-w, --width** *width*<br>Set the maximum line width to *width*. Default is 80. |
| **formail** | **formail** [*options*]<br><br>Filter standard input into mailbox format. If no sender is apparent, provide the sender *foo@bar*. By default, escape bogus **From** lines with >. |

*+skip*

Do not split first *skip* messages.

*–total*

Stop after splitting *total* messages.

**–a** *headerfield*

Append *headerfield* to header, unless it already exists. If *headerfield* is **Message-ID** or **Resent-Message-ID** with no contents, generate a unique message ID.

**–b**  Do not escape bogus **From** lines.

**–c**  When header fields are more than one line long, concatenate the lines.

**–d**  Do not assume that input must be in strict mailbox format.

**–e**  Allow messages to begin one immediately after the other; do not require empty space between them.

**–f**  Do not edit non-mailbox-format lines. By default, formail prepends **From** to such lines.

**–i** *headerfield*

Append *headerfield* whether or not it already exists. Rename each existing *headerfield* to **Old-***headerfield*, unless they are empty.

**–k**  For use only with **–r**. Keep the body as well as the fields specified by **–r**.

**–m** *minfields*

Require at least *minfields* before recognizing the beginning of a new message. Default is 2.

**–n**  Allow simultaneous **formail** processes to run.

**–p** *prefix*

Escape lines with *prefix* instead of **>**.

**–q**  Do not display write errors, duplicate messages, and mismatched **Content-Length** fields. This is the default; use **–q–** to turn it off.

**–r**  Throw away all existing fields, retaining only **X-Loop**, and generate autoreply header instead. You can preserve particular fields with the **–i** option.

→

| | |
|---|---|
| formail<br>← | **−s**   Must be the last option; everything following it will be assumed to be its arguments. Divide input to separate mail messages, and pipe them to the program specified or concatenate them to standard output (by default). |
| | **−t**   Assume sender's return address to be valid. (By default, **formail** favors machine-generated addresses.) |

**−u** *headerfield*
Delete all but the first occurrence of *headerfield*.

**−x** *headerfield*
Display the contents of *headerfield* on a single line.

**−z**   When necessary, add a space between field names and contents. Remove ("zap") empty fields.

**−A** *headerfield*
Append *headerfield* whether or not it already exists.

**−B**   Assume that input is in BABYL **rmail** format.

**−D** *maxlen idcache*
Remember old message IDs (in *idcache*, which will grow no larger than approximately *maxlen*). When splitting, refuse to output duplicate messages. Otherwise, return true on discovering a duplicate. With **−r**, look at the sender's mail address instead of the message ID.

**−I** *headerfield*
Append *headerfield* whether or not it already exists. Remove existing fields.

**−R** *oldfield newfield*
Change all fields named *oldfield* to *newfield*.

**−U** *headerfield*
Delete all but the last occurrence of *headerfield*.

**−Y**   Format in traditional Berkeley style (i.e., ignore **Content-Length** fields).

**−X** *headerfield*
Display the field name and contents of *headerfield* on a single line.

| | |
|---|---|
| **free** | **free** [*options*]<br><br>Display statistics about memory usage: total free, used, physical, swap, shared, and buffers used by the kernel. |

**−b**  Calculate memory in bytes.

**−k**  Default. Calculate memory in kilobytes.

**−m**  Calculate memory in megabytes.

**−o**  Do not display "buffer adjusted" line. The −o switch disables the display "−/+ buffers" line.

**−s** *time*

Check memory usage every *time* seconds.

**−t**  Display all totals on one line at the bottom of output.

**−V**  Display version information.

---

**fsck** [*options*] [*filesystem*] . . .

fsck

System administration command. Call the filesystem checker for the appropriate system type, to check and repair filesystems. If a filesystem is consistent, the number of files, number of blocks used, and number of blocks free are reported. If a filesystem is inconsistent, **fsck** prompts before each correction is attempted. **fsck**'s exit code can be interpreted as the sum of all of those conditions that apply:

**1**   Errors were found and corrected.

**2**   Reboot suggested.

**4**   Errors were found but not corrected.

**8**   **fsck** encountered an operational error.

**16**  **fsck** was called incorrectly.

**128**

A shared library error was detected.

*Options*

**−−**  Pass all subsequent options to filesystem-specific checker. All options that **fsck** doesn't recognize will also be passed.

**−r**  Interactive mode; prompt before making any repairs.

**−s**  Serial mode.

**−t** *fstype*

Specify the filesystem type. Do not check filesystems of any other type.

→

| | |
|---|---|
| **fsck**<br>← | **−A**   Check all filesystems listed in */etc/fstab*.<br><br>**−N**   Suppress normal execution; just display what would be done.<br><br>**−R**   Meaningful only with **−A**: check all filesystems listed in */etc/fstab* except the root filesystem.<br><br>**−T**   Suppress printing of title.<br><br>**−V**   Verbose mode. |
| **fsck.minix** | **fsck.minix** [*options*] *device*<br><br>System administration command. Similar to **fsck**, but specifically intended for Linux MINIX filesystems.<br><br>*Options*<br><br>**−a**   Automatic mode; repair without prompting.<br><br>**−f**   Force checking, even if kernel has already marked the filesystem. **fsck.minix** will normally exit without checking if the system appears to be clean.<br><br>**−l**   List filesystems.<br><br>**−m**   Enable MINIX-like "mode not cleared" warnings.<br><br>**−r**   Interactive mode; prompt before making any repairs.<br><br>**−s**   Display information about superblocks.<br><br>**−v**   Verbose mode. |
| **ftp** | **ftp** [*options*] [*hostname*]<br><br>Transfer files to and from remote network site *hostname*. **ftp** prompts the user for a command. The commands are listed after the options. Some of the commands are toggles, meaning they turn on a feature when it is off and vice versa.<br><br>*Options*<br><br>**−d**   Enable debugging.<br><br>**−g**   Disable filename globbing.<br><br>**−i**   Turn off interactive prompting. |

**−n**   No autologin upon initial connection.

**−v**   Verbose. Show all responses from remote server.

*Commands*

**![*command* [*args*]]**
> Invoke an interactive shell on the local machine. If arguments are given, the first is taken as a command to execute directly, with the rest of the arguments as that command's arguments.

**$ *macro-name* [*args*]**
> Execute the macro *macro-name* that was defined with the **macdef** command. Arguments are passed to the macro unglobbed.

**account** [*passwd*]
> Supply a supplemental password that will be required by a remote system for access to resources once a login has been successfully completed. If no argument is given, the user will be prompted for an account password in a nonechoing mode.

**append** *local-file* [*remote-file*]
> Append a local file to a file on the remote machine. If *remote-file* is not given, the local filename is used after being altered by any **ntrans** or **nmap** setting. File transfer uses the current settings for *type, format, mode,* and *structure.*

**ascii**
> Set the file transfer type to network ASCII (default).

**bell**
> Sound a bell after each file transfer command is completed.

**binary**
> Set file transfer type to support binary image transfer.

**bye**
> Terminate FTP session and then exit **ftp**.

**case**
> Toggle remote computer filename case mapping during **mget**. The default is off. When **case** is on, files on the remote machine with all-uppercase names will be copied to the local machine with all-lowercase names.

**cd** *remote-directory*
> Change working directory on remote machine to *remote-directory.*

→

**cdup**

> Change working directory of remote machine to its parent directory.

**chmod** [*mode*] [*remote-file*]

> Change file permissions of *remote-file*. If options are omitted, the command prompts for them.

**close**

> Terminate FTP session and return to command interpreter.

**cr**  Toggle carriage return stripping during ASCII-type file retrieval.

**delete** *remote-file*

> Delete file *remote-file* on remote machine.

**debug** [*debug-value*]

> Toggle debugging mode. If *debug-value* is specified, it is used to set the debugging level.

**dir** [*remote-directory*] [*local-file*]

> Print a listing of the contents in the directory *remote-directory*, and, optionally, place the output in *local-file*. If no directory is specified, the current working directory on the remote machine is used. If no local file is specified or − is given instead of the filename, output comes to the terminal.

**disconnect**

> Synonym for **close**.

**form** *format*

> Set the file transfer form to *format*. Default format is *file*.

**get** *remote-file* [*local-file*]

> Retrieve the *remote-file* and store it on the local machine. If the local filename is not specified, it is given the same name it has on the remote machine, subject to alteration by the current **case**, **ntrans**, and **nmap** settings. If local file is −, output comes to the terminal.

**glob**

> Toggle filename expansion for **mdelete**, **mget**, and **mput**. If globbing is turned off, the filename arguments are taken literally and not expanded.

**hash**

> Toggle hash-sign (#) printing for each data block transferred.

**help** [*command*]

> Print help information for *command*. With no argument, **ftp** prints a list of commands.

**idle** [*seconds*]

> Get/set idle timer on remote machine. *seconds* specifies the length of the idle timer; if omitted, the current idle timer is displayed.

**image**

> Same as **binary**.

**lcd** [*directory*]

> Change working directory on local machine. If *directory* is not specified, the user's home directory is used.

**ls** [*remote-directory*] [*local-file*]

> Print listing of contents of directory on remote machine, in a format chosen by the remote machine. If *remote-directory* is not specified, current working directory is used.

**macdef** *macro-name*

> Define a macro. Subsequent lines are stored as the macro *macro-name*; a null line terminates macro input mode. When **$i** is included in the macro, loop through arguments, substituting the current argument for **$i** on each pass. Escape **$** with \.

**mdelete** *remote-files*

> Delete the *remote-files* on the remote machine.

**mdir** *remote-files local-file*

> Like **dir**, except multiple remote files may be specified.

**mget** *remote-files*

> Expand the wildcard expression *remote-files* on the remote machine and do a **get** for each filename thus produced.

**mkdir** *directory-name*

> Make a directory on the remote machine.

**mls** *remote-files local-file*

> Like **nlist**, except multiple remote files may be specified, and the local file must be specified.

$\rightarrow$

**mode** [*mode-name*]

Set file transfer mode to *mode-name*. Default mode is stream mode.

**modtime** [*file-name*]

Show last modification time of the file on the remote machine.

**mput** [*local-files*]

Expand wildcards in *local-files* given as arguments and do a **put** for each file in the resulting list.

**newer** *remote-file* [*local-file*]

Get file if remote file is newer than local file.

**nlist** [*remote-directory*] [*local-file*]

Print list of files of a directory on the remote machine to *local-file* (or the screen if *local-file* is not specified). If *remote-directory* is unspecified, the current working directory is used.

**nmap** [*inpattern outpattern*]

Set or unset the filename mapping mechanism. The mapping follows the pattern set by *inpattern*, a template for incoming filenames, and *outpattern*, which determines the resulting mapped filename. The sequences **$1** through **$9** are treated as variables, for example, the *inpattern* **$1.$2**, along with the input file *readme.txt*, would set **$1** to **readme** and **$2** to **txt**. An *outpattern* of **$1.data** would result in an output file of *readme.data*. **$0** corresponds to the complete filename. [*string1*, *string2*] is replaced by *string1*, unless that string is null, in which case it's replaced by *string2*.

**ntrans** [*inchars* [*outchars*]]

Set or unset the filename character translation mechanism. Characters in a filename matching a character in *inchars* are replaced with the corresponding character in *outchars*. If no arguments are specified, the filename mapping mechanism is unset. If arguments are specified:

• Characters in remote filenames are translated during **mput** and **put** commands issued without a specified remote target filename.

• Characters in local filenames are translated during **mget** and **get** commands issued without a specified local target filename.

**open** *host* [*port*]

Establish a connection to the specified *host* FTP server. An optional *port* number may be supplied, in which case **ftp** will attempt to contact an FTP server at that port.

**prompt**

Toggle interactive prompting.

**proxy** *ftp-command*

Execute an FTP command on a secondary control connection (i.e., send commands to two separate remote hosts simultaneously).

**put** *local-file* [*remote-file*]

Store a local file on the remote machine. If *remote-file* is left unspecified, the local filename is used after processing according to any **ntrans** or **nmap** settings in naming the remote file. File transfer uses the current settings for *type*, *file*, *structure*, and *transfer mode*.

**pwd**

Print name of the current working directory on the remote machine.

**quit**

Synonym for **bye**.

**quote** *arg1 arg2...*

Send the arguments specified, verbatim, to the remote FTP server.

**recv** *remote-file* [*local-file*]

Synonym for **get**.

**reget** *remote-file* [*local-file*]

Retrieve a file (like **get**), but restart at the end of *local-file*. Useful for restarting a dropped transfer.

**remotehelp** [*command-name*]

Request help from the remote FTP server. If *command-name* is specified, remote help for that command is returned.

**remotestatus** [*filename*]

Show status of the remote machine, or, if *filename* is specified, *filename* on remote machine.

**rename** [*from*] [*to*]

Rename file *from* on remote machine to *to*.

→

**reset**

Clear reply queue.

**restart** *marker*

Restart the transfer of a file from a particular byte count.

**rmdir** [*directory-name*]

Delete a directory on the remote machine.

**runique**

Toggle storing of files on the local system with unique filenames. When this option is on, rename files as .**1** or .**2**, and soon, as appropriate, to preserve unique file-names, and report each such action. Default value is off.

**send** *local-file* [*remote-file*]

Synonym for **put**.

**sendport**

Toggle the use of PORT commands.

**site** [*command*]

Get/set site-specific information from/on remote machine.

**size** *filename*

Return size of *filename* on remote machine.

**status**

Show current status of **ftp**.

**struct** [*struct-name*]

Set the file transfer structure to *struct-name*. By default, **stream** structure is used.

**sunique**

Toggle storing of files on remote machine under unique filenames.

**system**

Show type of operating system running on remote machine.

**tenex**

Set file transfer type to that needed to talk to TENEX machines.

**trace**

Toggle packet tracing.

**type** [*type-name*]

Set file transfer **type** to *type-name*. If no type is specified, the current type is printed. The default type is network ASCII.

**umask** [*mask*]

Set user file-creation mode mask on the remote site. If mask is omitted, the current value of the mask is printed.

**user** *username* [*password*] [*account*]

Identify yourself to the remote FTP server. **ftp** will prompt the user for the password, if not specified and the server requires it, and the account field.

**verbose**

Toggle verbose mode.

**?** [*command*]

Same as **help**.

---

**in.ftpd** [*options*]

TCP/IP command. Internet File Transfer Protocol server. The server uses the TCP protocol and listens at the port specified in the **ftp** service specification. **ftpd** is started by **inetd** and must have an entry in **inetd**'s configuration file, */etc/inetd.conf.*

*Options*

**−d**  Write debugging information to the syslog.

**−l**  Log each FTP session in the syslog.

**−T***maxtimeout*

Set maximum timeout period in seconds. Default limit is 15 minutes.

**−t***timeout*

Set timeout period to *timeout* seconds.

---

**fuser** [*options*] [*files* | *filesystems*]

Identify processes that are using a file or filesystem. **fuser** outputs the process IDs of the processes that are using the *files* or local *filesystems*. Each process ID is followed by a letter code: **c** if process is using file as current directory, **e** if executable, **f** if an open file, **m** if a shared library, and **r** if the root directory. Any user with permission to read */dev/*

$\rightarrow$

| | |
|---|---|
| **fuser**<br>← | *kmem* and */dev/mem* can use **fuser**, but only a privileged user can terminate another user's process. **fuser** does not work on remote (NFS) files.<br><br>If more than one group of files is specified, the options may be respecified for each additional group of files. A lone dash (–) cancels the options currently in force, and the new set of options applies to the next group of files.<br><br>*Options*<br><br>–   Return all options to defaults.<br><br>*–signal*<br>     Send *signal* instead of SIGKILL.<br><br>–a  Display information on all specified files, even if they are not being accessed by any processes.<br><br>–i  Request user confirmation to kill a process. Ignored if –**k** is not also specified.<br><br>–k  Send SIGKILL signal to each process.<br><br>–l  List signal names.<br><br>–m  Expect *files* to exist on a mounted filesystem; include all files accessing that filesystem.<br><br>–s  Silent.<br><br>–u  User login name, in parentheses, also follows process ID.<br><br>–v  Verbose.<br><br>–V  Display version information. |
| **g++** | **g++** [*options*] *files*<br><br>Invoke **gcc** with the options necessary to make it recognize C++. **g++** recognizes all the file extensions **gcc** does, in addition to C++ source files (*.C*, *.cc*, or *.cxx* files) and C++ preprocessed files (*.ii* files). See also **gcc**. |
| **gated** | **gated** [*options*]<br><br>TCP/IP command. Gateway routing daemon. **gated** handles multiple routing protocols and replaces **routed** and any routing daemons that speak the Hello, EGP, or BGP routing protocols. **gated** currently handles the RIP, BGP, EGP, Hello, |

and OSPF routing protocols and can be configured to perform all or any combination of the five.

*Options*

−c  Parse configuration file for syntax errors, then exit **gated**, leaving a dump file in */usr/tmp/gated_dump*.

−f *config_file*
   Use alternate configuration file, *config_file*. Default is */etc/gated.conf*.

−n  Do not modify kernel's routing table.

−t [*trace_options*]
   Start **gated** with the specified tracing options enabled. If no flags are specified, assume **general**. The trace flags are:

   **adv** Management of policy blocks.

   **all** Includes **normal**, **policy**, **route**, **state**, **task**, and **timer**.

   **general**
      Includes **normal** and **route**.

   **iflist**
      The kernel interface list.

   **normal**
      Normal protocols instances.

   **parse**
      Lexical analyzer and parser.

   **policy**
      Instances in which policy is applied to imported and exported routes.

   **route**
      Any changes to routing table.

   **state**
      State machine transitions.

   **symbols**
      Symbols read from kernel—note that they are read before the configuration file is parsed, so this option must be specified on the command line.

   **task**
      System tasks and interfaces.

→

| | |
|---|---|
| **gated**<br>← | **timer**<br>    Timer usage.<br><br>−**C** Parse configuration file for errors and set exit code to indicate if there were any (1) or not (0), then exit.<br><br>−**N** Do not daemonize. |
| **gawk** | **gawk** [*options*] '*script*' [*var=value . . .*] [*files*]<br>**gawk** [*options*] −**f** *scriptfile* [*var=value . . .*] [*files*]<br><br>The GNU version of **awk**, a program that does pattern matching, record processing, and other forms of text manipulation. For more information, see Chapter 13, *The gawk Scripting Language*. |
| **gcc** | **gcc** [*options*] *files*<br><br>Compile one or more C source files (*file.c*), assembler source files (*file.s*), or preprocessed C source files (*file.i*). If the file suffix is not recognizable, assume that the file is an object file or library. **gcc** automatically invokes the link editor **ld** (unless −**c**, −**S**, or −**E** is supplied). In some cases, **gcc** generates an object file having a *.o* suffix and a corresponding root name. By default, output is placed in *a.out.* **gcc** accepts many system-specific options not covered here.<br><br>Note: **gcc** is the GNU form of **cc**; on most Linux systems, the command **cc** will invoke **gcc**. The command **g++** will invoke **gcc** with the appropriate options for interpreting C++.<br><br>*Options*<br><br>−**a**  Provide profile information for basic blocks.<br><br>−**ansi**<br>    Enforce full ANSI conformance.<br><br>−**b** *machine*<br>    Compile for use on *machine* type.<br><br>−**c**  Create linkable object file for each source file, but do not call linker.<br><br>−**dD**<br>    Print #**defines**. |

**–dM**

Suppress normal output. Print series of **#defines** that are in effect at the end of preprocessing.

**–dN**

Print **#defines** with macro names only, not arguments or values.

**–fno-asm**

Do not recognize **asm, inline,** or **typeof** as keywords. Implied by **–ansi.**

**–fno-builtin**

Do not recognize built-in functions unless they begin with two underscores.

**–fno-gnu-keywords**

Do not recognize **classof, headof, signature, sigof,** or **typeof** as keywords.

**–fno-ident**

Do not respond to **#ident** commands.

**–fsigned-bitfields**

**–funsigned-bitfields**

**–fno-signed-bitfields**

**–fno-unsigned-bitfields**

Set default control of bitfields to signed or unsigned if not explicitly declared.

**–fsigned-char**

Cause the type **char** to be signed.

**–fsyntax-only**

Check for syntax errors. Do not attempt to actually compile.

**–funsigned-char**

Cause the type **char** to be unsigned.

**–g** Include debugging information for use with **gdb.**

**–g***level*

Provide *level* amount of debugging information. *level* must be 1, 2, or 3, with 1 providing the least amount of information. The default is 2.

**–idirafter** *dir*

Include *dir* in the list of directories to search when an include file is not found in the normal include path.

$\rightarrow$

Linux
Commands

**−include** *file*
> Process *file* before proceeding to the normal input file.

**−imacros** *file*
> Process the macros in *file* before proceeding to the normal input file.

**−iprefix** *prefix*
> When adding directories with **−iwithprefix**, prepend *prefix* to the directory's name.

**−isystem** *dir*
> Add *dir* to the list of directories to be searched when a system file cannot be found in the main include path.

**−iwithprefix** *dir*
> Append *dir* to the list of directories to be searched when a header file cannot be found in the main include path. If **−iprefix** has been set, prepend that prefix to the directory's name.

**−l***lib*
> Link to *lib*.

**−nostartfiles**
> Force linker to ignore standard system startup files.

**−nostdinc**
> Search only specified, not standard, directories for header files.

**−nostdinc++**
> Suppress searching of directories believed to contain C++-specific header files.

**−nostdlib**
> Suppress linking to standard library files.

**−o** *file*
> Specify output file as *file*. Default is *a.out*.

**−p**  Provide profile information for use with **prof**.

**−pedantic**
> Warn verbosely.

**−pedantic-errors**
> Err in every case in which **−pedantic** would have produced a warning.

**−pg**
> Provide profile information for use with **gprof**.

**–pipe**
> Transfer information between stages of compiler by pipes instead of temporary files.

**–s** Remove all symbol table and relocation information from the executable.

**–save-temps**
> Save temporary files in the current directory when compiling.

**–static**
> Suppress linking to shared libraries.

**–traditional**
> Attempt to behave like a traditional C compiler.

**–traditional-cpp**
> Cause the preprocessor to attempt to behave like a traditional C preprocessor.

**–trigraphs**
> Include trigraph support.

**–u** *symbol*
> Force the linker to search libraries for a definition of *symbol* and to link to them, if found.

**–undef**
> Define only those constants required by the language standard, not system-specific constants like **unix**.

**–v** Verbose mode. Display commands as they are executed, **gcc** version number, and preprocessor version number.

**–w** Suppress warnings.

**–x** *language*
> Expect input file to be written in *language*, which may be **c**, **objective-c**, **c-header**, **c++**, **cpp-output**, **assembler**, or **assembler-with-cpp**. If **none** is specified as *language*, guess the language by filename extension.

**–A***question*(*answer*)
> If the preprocessor encounters a conditional such as **#if** *question*, assert *answer* in response. To turn off standard assertions, use **–A–**.

**–B***path*
> Specify the *path* directory in which the compiler files are located.

$\rightarrow$

**−C** Retain comments during preprocessing. Meaningful only with **−E**.

**−D***name*[*=def*]

Define *name* with value *def* as if by a **#define**. If no *=def* is given, *name* is defined with value 1. **−D** has lower precedence than **−U**.

**−E** Preprocess the source files, but do not compile. Print result to standard output.

**−I***dir*

Include *dir* in list of directories to search for include files. If *dir* is **−**, search those directories that were specified by **−I** *before* the **−I−** only when **#include** "*file*" is specified, not **#include** <*file*>.

**−L***dir*

Search *dir* in addition to standard directories.

**−M** Instead of compiling, print a rule suitable for inclusion in a makefile that describes dependencies of the source file based on its **#include** directives. Implies **−E**.

**−MD**

Similar to **−M**, but sends dependency information to files ending in *.d* in addition to ordinary compilation.

**−MG**

Used with **−M** or **−MM**. Suppress error messages if an included file does not exist; useful if the included file is automatically generated by a build.

**−MMD**

Similar to **−MD**, but record only user header file information, not system header file information.

**−MM**

Similar to **−M**, but limit the rule to non-standard **#include** files; that is, only files declared through **#include** "*file*" and not those declared through **#include** <*file*>.

**−H** Print pathnames of included files, one per line, on standard error.

**−O**[*level*]

Optimize. *level* should be 1, 2, 3, or 0. The default is 1. 0 turns off optimization; 3 optimizes the most.

**−P** Preprocess input without producing line-control information used by next pass of C compiler. Meaningful only with **-E**.

**−S**  Compile source files into assembler code, but do not assemble.

**−U***name*

Remove any initial definition of *name*, where *name* is a reserved symbol predefined by the preprocessor or a name defined on a **−D** option. Names predefined by cpp are **unix** and **i386**.

**−V** *version*

Attempt to run **gcc** version *version*.

**−W**

Warn more verbosely than normal.

**−Wl,***option*

Invoke linker with *option*, which may be a comma-separated list.

**−Wa,***option*

Call assembler with *option*, which may be a comma-separated list.

**−Waggregate-return**

Warn if any functions return structures or unions are defined or called.

**−Wall**

Enable **−W**, **−Wchar-subscripts**, **−Wcomment**, **−Wformat**, **−Wimplicit**, **−Wparentheses**, **−Wreturn-type**, **−Wswitch**, **−Wtemplate-debugging**, **−Wtrigraphs**, **−Wuninitialized**, and **−Wunused**.

**−Wcast-align**

Warn when encountering instances in which pointers are cast to types that increase the required alignment of the target from its original definition.

**−Wcast-qual**

Warn when encountering instances in which pointers are cast to types that lack the type qualifier with which the pointer was originally defined.

**−Wchar-subscripts**

Warn when encountering arrays with subscripts of type **char**.

**−Wcomment**

Warn when encountering the beginning of a nested comment.

→

**−Wconversion**

Warn in particular cases of type conversions.

**−Werror**

Exit at the first error.

**−Wformat**

Warn about inappropriately formatted **printf**s and **scanf**s.

**−Wimplicit**

Warn when encountering implicit function or parameter declarations.

**−Winline**

Warn about illegal inline functions.

**−Wmissing-declarations**

Warn if a global function is defined without a previous declaration.

**−Wmissing-prototypes**

Warn when encountering global function definitions without previous prototype declarations.

**−Wnested-externs**

Warn if an **extern** declaration is encountered within a function.

**−Wno-import**

Don't warn about use of **#import**.

**−Wp,***options*

Pass *options* to the preprocessor. Multiple options are separated by commas. Not a warning parameter.

**−Wparentheses**

Enable more verbose warnings about omitted parentheses.

**−Wpointer-arith**

Warn when encountering code that attempts to determine the size of a function or void.

**−Wredundant-decls**

Warn if anything is declared more than once in the same scope.

**−Wreturn-type**

Warn about functions defined without return types or with improper return types.

**−Wshadow**
> Warn when a local variable shadows another local variable.

**−Wstrict-prototypes**
> Insist that argument types be specified in function declarations and definitions.

**−Wswitch**
> Warn about switches that skip the index for one of their enumerated types.

**−Wtemplate-debugging**
> Warn if debugging is not available for C++ templates.

**−Wtraditional**
> Warn when encountering code that produces different results in ANSI C and traditional C.

**−Wtrigraphs**
> Warn when encountering trigraphs.

**−Wuninitialized**
> Warn when encountering uninitialized automatic variables.

**−Wunused**
> Warn about unused variables and functions.

**−Xlinker** *option*
> Pass an *option* to the linker. A linker option with an argument requires two −Xs, the first specifying the option and the second specifying the argument.

*Pragma directives*

**#pragma interface** [*header-file*]
> Used in header files to force object files to provide definition information via references, instead of including it locally in each file. C++-specific.

**#pragma implementation** [*header-file*]
> Used in main input files to force generation of full output from *header-file* (or, if it is not specified, from the header file with the same base name as the file containing the pragma directive). This information will be globally visible. Normally the specified header file contains a **#pragma interface** directive.

| gdb | **gdb** [*options*] [*program* [*core* |*pid*]] |
|---|---|

GDB (GNU DeBugger) allows you to step through C, C++, and Modula-2 programs in order to find the point at which they break. The program to be debugged is normally specified on the command line; you can also specify a core or, if you want to investigate a running program, a process ID.

*Options*

**−s** *file*, **−symbols=***file*
> Consult *file* for symbol table. With **−e**, also uses *file* as the executable.

**−e** *file*, **−exec=***file*
> Use *file* as executable, to be read in conjunction with source code. May be used in conjunction with **−s** to read symbol table from the executable.

**−c** *file*, **−core=***file*
> Consult *file* for information provided by a core dump.

**−x** *file*, **−command=***file*
> Read **gdb** commands from *file*.

**−d** *directory*, **−directory=***directory*
> Include *directory* in path that is searched for source files.

**−n**, **−nx**
> Ignore *.gdbinit* file.

**−q**, **−quiet**
> Suppress introductory and copyright messages.

**−batch**
> Exit after executing all the commands specified in *.gdbinit* and **-x** files. Print no startup messages.

**−cd=***directory*
> Use *directory* as **gdb**'s working directory.

**−f**, **−fullname**
> Show full filename and line number for each stack frame.

**−b** *bps*
> Set line speed of serial device used by GDB to *bps*.

**−tty=***device*
> Set standard in and standard out to *device*.

These are just some of the more common **gdb** commands; there are too many commands to list all of them here:

**bt**    Print the current location within the program and a stack trace showing how the current location was reached. (**where** does the same thing.)

**break**
Set a breakpoint in the program.

**cd**    Change the current working directory.

**clear**
Delete the breakpoint where you just stopped.

**commands**
List commands to be executed when breakpoint is hit.

**c**    Continue execution from a breakpoint.

**delete**
Delete a breakpoint or a watchpoint; also used in conjunction with other commands.

**display**
Cause variables or expressions to be displayed when program stops.

**down**
Move down one stack frame to make another function the current one.

**frame**
Select a frame for the next **continue** command.

**info**
Show a variety of information about the program. For instance, **info breakpoints** shows all outstanding breakpoints and watchpoints.

**jump**
Start execution at another point in the source file.

**kill**    Abort the process running under **gdb**'s control.

**list**    List the contents of the source file corresponding to the program being executed.

**next**
Execute the next source line, executing a function in its entirety.

→

*Linux Commands*

| | |
|---|---|
| **gdb**<br>← | **print**<br>Print the value of a variable or expression.<br><br>**pwd**<br>Show the current working directory.<br><br>**ptype**<br>Show the contents of a datatype, such as a structure or C++ class.<br><br>**quit**<br>Exit **gdb**.<br><br>**reverse-search**<br>Search backward for a regular expression in the source file.<br><br>**run**  Execute the program.<br><br>**search**<br>Search for a regular expression in the source file.<br><br>**set variable**<br>Assign a value to a variable.<br><br>**signal**<br>Send a signal to the running process.<br><br>**step**<br>Execute the next source line, stepping into a function if necessary.<br><br>**undisplay**<br>Reverse the effect of the **display** command; keep expressions from being displayed.<br><br>**until**<br>Finish the current loop.<br><br>**up**  Move up one stack frame to make another function the current one.<br><br>**watch**<br>Set a watchpoint (i.e., a data breakpoint) in the program.<br><br>**whatis**<br>Print the type of a variable or function. |
| **gdc** | **gdc** [*options*] *command*<br><br>TCP/IP command. Administer **gated**. Various commands start and stop the daemon, send signals to it, maintain the |

configuration files, and manage state and core dumps.

*Options*

**−c** *size*
> Specify maximum core dump size.

**−f** *size*
> Specify maximum file dump size.

**−m** *size*
> Specify maximum data segment size.

**−n** Suppress editing of the kernel forwarding table.

**−q** Quiet mode: suppress warnings and log errors to **syslogd** instead of standard error.

**−s** *size*
> Specify maximum stack size.

**−t** *seconds*
> Wait *seconds* seconds (default is 10) for **gated** to complete specified operations at start and stop time.

*Commands*

**BACKOUT**
> Restore */etc/gated.conf* from */etc/gated.conf−*, whether or not the latter exists.

**backout**
> Restore */etc/gated.conf* from */etc/gated.conf−*, assuming the latter exists.

**checkconf**
> Report any syntax errors in */etc/gated.conf.*

**checknew**
> Report any syntax errors in */etc/gated.conf+.*

**COREDUMP**
> Force **gated** to core dump and exit.

**createconf**
> Create an empty */etc/gated.conf+* if one does not already exist, and set it to mode 664, owner **root**, group **gdmaint**.

**dump**
> Force **gated** to dump to */usr/tmp/gated_dump* and then continue normal operation.

→

gdc
←

**interface**

Reload interface configuration.

**KILL**

Terminate immediately (ungracefully).

**modeconf**

Set all configuration files to mode 664, owner **root**, group **gdmaint**.

**newconf**

Make sure that */etc/gated.conf+* exists and move it to */etc/gated.conf.* Save the old */etc/gated.conf* as */etc/gated.conf-*.

**reconfig**

Reload configuration file.

**restart**

Stop and restart **gated**.

**rmcore**

Remove any **gated** core files.

**rmdmp**

Remove any **gated** state dump files.

**rmparse**

Remove any **gated** files that report on parse errors. These are generated by the **checkconf** and **checknew** commands.

**running**

Exit with zero status if **gated** is running and nonzero if it is not.

**start**

Start **gated**, unless it is already running, in which case return an error.

**stop**

Stop **gated** as gracefully as possible.

**term**

Terminate gracefully.

**toggletrace**

Toggle tracing.

*Files*

*/etc/gcd.conf+*

The test configuration file. Once you're satisfied that it works, you should run *gated newconf* to install it as */etc/gated.conf.*

*/etc/gated.conf–*
A backup of the old configuration file.

*/etc/gated.conf– –*
A backup of the backup of the old configuration file.

*/etc/gated.conf*
The actual configuration file.

*/etc/gated.pid*
**gated**'s process ID.

*/usr/tmp/gated_dump*
The state dump file.

*/usr/tmp/gated_parse*
A list of the parse errors generated by reading the configuration file.

---

**getkeycodes**

Print the kernel's scancode-to-keycode mapping table.

---

**getty** [*options*] *port* [*speed* [*term* [*lined*]]]

System administration command. Set terminal type, modes, speed, and line discipline. Linux systems may use **agetty** instead, which uses a different syntax. **getty** is invoked by **init**. It is the second process in the series **init-getty-login-shell**, which ultimately connects a user with the Linux system. **getty** reads the user's login name and invokes the **login** command with the user's name as an argument. While reading the name, **getty** attempts to adapt the system to the speed and type of device being used.

You must specify a *port* argument, which **getty** will use to attach itself to the device */dev/port*. **getty** will then scan the defaults file, usually */etc/default/getty*, for runtime values and parameters. These may also be specified, for the most part, on the command line, but the values in the defaults file take precedence. The *speed* argument is used to point to an entry in the file */etc/gettydefs*, which contains the initial baud rate, tty settings, and login prompt and final speed and settings for the connection. The first entry is the default in */etc/gettydefs*. *term* specifies the type of terminal, with *lined* the optional line discipline to use.

→

| | |
|---|---|
| **getty**<br>← | *Options*<br><br>−c *file*<br>    Check the *gettydefs* file. *file* is the name of the *gettydefs* file. Produces the files' values and reports parsing errors to standard output.<br><br>−d *file*<br>    Use a different default file.<br><br>−h  Do not force a hangup on the port when initializing.<br><br>−r *delay*<br>    Wait for single character from port, then wait *delay* seconds before proceeding.<br><br>−t *timeout*<br>    If no username is accepted within *timeout* seconds, close connection.<br><br>−w *string*<br>    Wait for *string* characters from port before proceeding. |
| **gprof** | **gprof** [*options*] [*object_file*]<br><br>Display the profile data for an object file. The file's symbol table is compared with the call graph profile file *gmon.out* (previously created by compiling with **gcc -pg**).<br><br>*Options*<br><br>−a  Do not display statically declared functions. Since their information might still be relevant, append it to the information about the functions loaded immediately before.<br><br>−b  Do not display information about each field in the profile.<br><br>−c  Consult the object file's text area to attempt to determine the program's static call graph. Display static-only parents and children with call counts of 0.<br><br>−e *routine*<br>    Do not display entries for *routine* and its descendants.<br><br>−f *routine*<br>    Print only *routine*, but include time spent in all routines. |

**-k** *from to*
>    Remove arcs between the routines *from* and *to*.

**-s**    Summarize profile information in the file *gmon.sum*.

**-v**    Print version and exit.

**-z**    Include zero-usage calls.

**-E** *routine*
>    Do not display entries for *routine* and its descendants or include time spent on them in calculations for total time.

**-F** *routine*
>    Print only information about *routine*. Do not include time spent in other routines.

---

**grep** [*options*] *pattern* [*files*]

Search one or more *files* for lines that match a regular expression *pattern*. Regular expressions are described in Chapter 9. Exit status is 0 if any lines match, 1 if none match, and 2 for errors. See also **egrep** and **fgrep**.

*Options*

**-a, --text**
>    Don't suppress output lines with binary data; treat as text.

**-b, --byte-offset**
>    Print the byte offset within the input file before each line of output.

**-b, --byte-offset**
>    Print the byte offset within the input file before each line of output.

**-c, --count**
>    Print only a count of matched lines. With **-v** or **--revert-match** option, count nonmatching lines.

**-d** *action*, **--directories=**_action_
>    Define an *action* for processing directories. Possible actions are:

>    **read**
>>        Read directories like ordinary files (default).

→

skip
> Skip directories.

**recurse**
> Recursively read all files under each directory. Same as –r.

–e *pattern*, **––regexp**=*pattern*
> Search for *pattern*. Same as specifying a pattern as an argument, but useful in protecting patterns beginning with –.

–f *file*, **––file**=*file*
> Take a list of patterns from *file*, one per line.

–h, **––no-filename**
> Print matched lines but not filenames (inverse of –l).

–i, **––ignore-case**
> Ignore uppercase and lowercase distinctions.

–l, **––files-with-matches**
> List the names of files with matches but not individual matched lines; scanning per file stops on the first match.

–n, **––line-number**
> Print lines and their line numbers.

–q, **––quiet**, **––silent**
> Suppress normal output in favor of quiet mode; the scanning stops on the first match.

–r, **––recursive**
> Recursively read all files under each directory. Same as –d recurse.

–s, **––no-messages**
> Suppress error messages about nonexistent or unreadable files.

–v, **––revert-match**
> Print all lines that *don't* match *pattern*.

–w, **––word-regexp**
> Match on whole words only. Words are divided by characters that are not letters, digits, or underscores.

–x, **––line-regexp**
> Print lines only if *pattern* matches the entire line.

–A *num*, **––after-context**=*num*
> Print *num* lines of text that occur after the matching line.

**−B** *num*, **−−before-context=***num*
> Print *num* lines of text that occur before the matching line.

**−C[***num***]**, **−−context=[***num***]**, **−***num*
> Print *num* lines of leading and trailing context. Default context is 2 lines.

**−L**, **−−files-without-match**
> List files that contain no matching lines.

**−V**, **−−version**
> Print the version number and then exit.

*Examples*

List the number of users who use **tcsh**:

```
grep -c /bin/tcsh /etc/passwd
```

List header files that have at least one **#include** directive:

```
grep -l '^#include' /usr/include/*
```

List files that don't contain *pattern*:

```
grep -c pattern files | grep :0
```

**groff** [*options*] [*files*]
**troff** [*options*] [*files*]

Frontend to the **groff** document-formatting system, which normally runs **troff** along with a postprocessor appropriate for the selected output device. Options without arguments can be grouped after a single dash (−). A filename of − denotes standard input.

*Options*

**−a** Generate an ASCII approximation of the typeset output.

**−b** Print a backtrace.

**−C** Enable compatibility mode.

**−d***cs*, **−d***name=s*
> Define the character *c* or string *name* to be the string *s*.

**−e** Preprocess with **eqn**.

**−E** Don't print any error messages.

grep

groff

Linux
Commands

−f*fam*
   Use *fam* as the default font family.

−F*dir*
   Search *dir* for subdirectories with *DESC* and font files before the default */usr/lib/groff/font.*

−h   Print a help message.

−i   Read standard input after all *files* have been processed.

−l   Send the output to a printer (as specified by the print command in the device description file).

−L*arg*
   Pass *arg* to the spooler. Each argument should be passed with a separate −L option.

−m*name*
   Read the macro file *tmac.name.*

−M*dir*
   Search directory *dir* for macro files before the default directory */usr/lib/groff/tmac.*

−n*num*
   Set the first page number to *num.*

−N   Don't allow newlines with **eqn** delimiters; equivalent to **eqn**'s −N option.

−o*list*
   Output only pages specified in *list*, which is a comma-separated list of page ranges.

−p   Preprocess with **pic.**

−P*arg*
   Pass *arg* to the postprocessor. Each argument should be passed with a separate −P option.

−r*cn*, −*name=n*
   Set the number register *c* or *name* to *n. c* is a single character and *n* is any **troff** numeric expression.

−R   Preprocess with **refer.**

−s   Preprocess with **soelim.**

−S   Use safer mode (i.e., pass the −S option to **pic** and use the −msafer macros with **troff**).

−t   Preprocess with **tbl.**

–T*dev*

    Prepare output for device *dev*; the default is **ps**.

–v  Make programs run by **groff** print out their version number.

–V  Print the pipeline on stdout instead of executing it.

–w*name*

    Enable warning *name*. You can specify multiple –**w** options. See the **troff** manpage for a list of warnings.

–W*name*

    Disable warning *name*. You can specify multiple –**W** options. See the **troff** manpage for a list of warnings.

–z  Suppress **troff** output (except error messages).

–Z  Do not postprocess **troff** output. Normally **groff** automatically runs the appropriate postprocessor.

### *Devices*

**ascii**

    Typewriter-like device

**dvi**  TEX dvi format

**latin1**

    Typewriter-like devices using the ISO Latin-1 character set

**ps**  PostScript

**X75**

    75-dpi X11 previewer

**X100**

    100-dpi X11 previewer

**lj4**  HP LaserJet4-compatible (or other PCL5-compatible) printer

### *Environment variables*

**GROFF_COMMAND_PREFIX**

    If set to be X, **groff** will run **Xtroff** instead of **troff**.

**GROFF_FONT_PATH**

    Colon-separated list of directories in which to search for the *devname* directory.

**GROFF_TMAC_PATH**

    Colon-separated list of directories in which to search for the macro files.

→

| | |
|---|---|
| groff<br>← | **GROFF_TMPDIR**<br>If set, temporary files will be created in this directory; otherwise, they will be created in TMPDIR (if set) or */tmp* (if TMPDIR is not set).<br><br>**GROFF_TYPESETTER**<br>Default device.<br><br>**PATH**<br>Search path for commands that **groff** executes. |
| **groupadd** | **groupadd** [*options*] *group*<br><br>System administration command. Create new group account *group*.<br><br>*Options*<br><br>−g*gid*<br>Assign numerical group ID. (By default, the first available number above 500 is used.) The value must be unique unless the −o option is used.<br><br>−o   Accept a nonunique *gid* with the −g option. |
| **groupdel** | **groupdel** *group*<br><br>System administration command. Remove *group* from system account files. You may still need to find and change permissions on files that belong to the removed group. |
| **groupmod** | **groupmod** [*options*] *group*<br><br>System administration command. Modify group information for *group*.<br><br>*Options*<br><br>−g *gid*<br>Change the numerical value of the group ID. Any files that have the old *gid* will have to be changed manually. The new *gid* must be unique unless the −o option is used. |

−n *name*
   Change the group name to *name*.

−o Override. Accept a nonunique *gid*.

---

**groups** [*options*] [*users*]

Show the groups that each *user* belongs to (default user is the owner of the current group). Groups are listed in */etc/passwd* and */etc/group*.

*Options*

−−**help**
   Print help message.

−−**version**
   Print version information.

---

**grpck** [*option*] [*files*]

System administration command. Remove corrupt or duplicate entries in the */etc/group* and */etc/gshadow* files. Generate warnings for other errors found. **grpck** will prompt for a "yes" or "no" before deleting entries. If the user replies "no," the program will exit. If run in a noninteractive mode, the reply to all prompts is "no." Alternate group and gshadow *files* can be checked. If other errors are found, the user will be encouraged to run the **groupmod** command.

*Option*

−n Noninteractive mode.

*Exit codes*

0   Success.

1   Syntax error.

2   One or more bad group entries found.

3   Could not open group files.

4   Could not lock group files.

5   Could not write group files.

| | |
|---|---|
| **grpconv** | **grpconv**<br>**grpunconv**<br><br>System administration command. Like **pwconv**, the **grpconv** command creates a shadowed group file to keep your encrypted group passwords safe from password cracking programs. **grpconv** creates the */etc/gshadow* file based on your existing */etc/groups* file and replaces your encrypted password entries with **x**. If you add new entries to the */etc/groups* file, you can run **grpconv** again to transfer the new information to */etc/gshadow*. It will ignore entries that already have a password of **x** and convert those that do not. **grpunconv** restores the encrypted passwords to your */etc/groups* file and removes the */etc/gshadow* file. |
| **gs** | **gs** [*options*] [*files*]<br><br>An interpreter for Adobe Systems' PostScript and PDF (Portable Document Format) languages; used for document processing. With – in place of *files*, standard input is used.<br><br>*Options*<br><br>*– – filename arg1* ...<br>    Take the next argument as a filename, but use all remaining arguments to define ARGUMENTS in userdict (not systemdict) as an array of those strings, before running the file.<br><br>–g*number1*x*number2*<br>    Specify width and height of device; intended for systems like the X Window System.<br><br>–q  Quiet startup.<br><br>–r*number*, –r*number1*x*number2*<br>    Specify X and Y resolutions (for the benefit of devices, such as printers, that support multiple X and Y resolutions). If only one number is given, it is used for both X and Y resolutions.<br><br>–D*name*=*token*, –d*name*=*token*<br>    Define a name in systemdict with the given definition. The token must be exactly one token (as defined by the token operator) and must not contain any whitespace.<br><br>–D*name*, –d*name*<br>    Define a name in systemdict with a null value. |

**–I***directories*

Adds the designated list of directories at the head of the search path for library files.

**–S***name=string*, **–s***name=string*

Define a name in systemdict with a given string as value.

***Special names***

**–dDISKFONTS**

Causes individual character outlines to be loaded from the disk the first time they are encountered.

**–dNOBIND**

Disables the **bind** operator. Useful only for debugging.

**–dNOCACHE**

Disables character caching. Useful only for debugging.

**–dNODISPLAY**

Suppresses the normal initialization of the output device. May be useful when debugging.

**–dNOPAUSE**

Disables the prompt and pause at the end of each page.

**–dNOPLATFONTS**

Disables the use of fonts supplied by the underlying platform (e.g., the X Window System).

**–dSAFER**

Disables the **deletefile** and **renamefile** operators and the ability to open files in any mode other than read-only.

**–dWRITESYSTEMDICT**

Leaves systemdict writable.

**–sDEVICE=***device*

Selects an alternate initial output device.

**–sOUTPUTFILE=***filename*

Selects an alternate output file (or pipe) for the initial output device.

| | |
|---|---|
| **gunzip** | **gunzip** [*options*] [*files*] |
| | Uncompress *files* compressed by **gzip**. See **gzip** for a list of options. |
| **gzexe** | **gzexe** [*option*] [*files*] |
| | Compress executables. When run, these files automatically uncompress, thus trading time for space. **gzexe** creates backup files (*filename˜*), which should be removed after testing the original. |
| | *Option* |
| | −d Decompress files. |
| **gzip** | **gzip** [*options*] [*files*] <br> **gunzip** [*options*] [*files*] <br> **zcat** [*options*] [*files*] |
| | Compress specified files (or read from standard input) with Lempel-Ziv coding (LZ77). Rename compressed file to *filename.gz*; keep ownership modes and access/modification times. Ignore symbolic links. Uncompress with **gunzip**, which takes all of **gzip**'s options, except those specified. **zcat** is identical to **gunzip** −c and takes the options −fhLV, described here. Files compressed with the **compress** command can be decompressed using these commands. |
| | *Options* |
| | −*n*, −−fast, −−best <br> Regulate the speed of compression using the specified digit *n*, where −1 or −−fast indicates the fastest compression method (less compression) and −9 or −−best indicates the slowest compression method (most compression). The default compression level is −6. |
| | −a, −−ascii <br> ASCII text mode: convert end-of-lines using local conventions. This option is supported only on some non-Unix systems. |
| | −c, −−stdout, −−to-stdout <br> Print output to standard output, and do not change input files. |

**-d, --decompress, --uncompress**

Same as **gunzip**.

**-f, --force**

Force compression. **gzip** would normally prompt for permission to continue when the file has multiple links, its *.gz* version already exists, or it is reading compressed data to or from a terminal.

**-h --help**

Display a help screen and then exit.

**-l, --list**

Expects to be given compressed files as arguments. Files may be compressed by any of the following methods: **gzip**, **deflate**, **compress**, **lzh**, and **pack**. For each file, list uncompressed and compressed sizes (the latter being always -1 for files compressed by programs other than **gzip**), compression ratio, and uncompressed name. With **-v**, also print compression method, the 32-bit CRC of the uncompressed data, and the timestamp. With **-N**, look inside the file for the uncompressed name and timestamp.

**-L, --license**

Display the **gzip** license and quit.

**-n, --no-name**

When compressing, do not save the original filename and timestamp by default. When decompressing, do not restore the original filename if present, and do not restore the original timestamp if present. This option is the default when decompressing.

**-N, --name**

Default. Save original name and timestamp. When decompressing, restore original name and timestamp.

**-q, --quiet**

Print no warnings.

**-r, --recursive**

When given a directory as an argument, recursively compress or decompress files within it.

**-S** *suffix*, **--suffix** *suffix*

Append *.suffix*. Default is **gz**. A null suffix while decompressing causes **gunzip** to attempt to decompress all specified files, regardless of suffix.

→

| | |
|---|---|
| gzip<br>← | **−t, −−test**<br>Test compressed file integrity.<br><br>**−v, −−verbose**<br>Print name and percent size reduction for each file.<br><br>**−V, −−version**<br>Display the version number and compilation options. |
| halt | **halt** [*options*]<br><br>System administration command. Insert a note in the file */var/log/wtmp*; if the system is in runlevel 0 or 6, stop all processes; otherwise, call **shutdown −nf**.<br><br>*Options*<br><br>**−d**  Suppress writing to */var/log/wtmp*.<br><br>**−f**  Call **halt** even when **shutdown −nf** would normally be called (i.e., force a call to **halt**, even when not in runlevel 0 or 6).<br><br>**−n**  Suppress normal call to **sync**.<br><br>**−w**  Suppress normal execution; simply write to */var/log/wtmp*. |
| head | **head** [*options*] [*files*]<br><br>Print the first few lines (default is 10) of one or more *files*. If *files* is missing or −, read from standard input. With more than one file, print a header for each file.<br><br>*Options*<br><br>**−c** *num*[bkm], **−−bytes** *num*<br>Print first *num* bytes or, if *num* is followed by **b**, **k**, or **m**, first *num* 512-byte blocks, 1-kilobyte blocks, or 1-megabyte blocks.<br><br>**−−help**<br>Display help and then exit.<br><br>**−n** *num*, **−−lines** *num*, **−***num*<br>Print first *num* lines. Default is 10.<br><br>**−q, −−quiet, −−silent**<br>Quiet mode; never print headers giving filenames. |

**−v, −−verbose**
> Print filename headers, even for only one file.

**−−version**
> Output version information and then exit.

*Examples*

Display the first 20 lines of **phone_list**:

```
head -20 phone_list
```

Display the first 10 phone numbers having a 202 area code:

```
grep '(202)' phone_list | head
```

---

host [*options*] *host* [*server*]
host [*options*] *zone* [*server*]

System administration command. Print information about specified hosts or zones in DNS. Hosts may be IP addresses or hostnames; **host** converts IP addresses to hostnames by default and appends the local domain to hosts without a trailing dot. Default servers are determined in */etc/resolv.conf.* For more information about hosts and zones, try Chapters 1 and 2 of *DNS and BIND* by Paul Albitz and Cricket Liu, published by O'Reilly & Associates.

*Options*

**−a**  Same as **−t ANY**.

**−c** *class*
> Search for specified resource record class (IN, INTERNET, CS, CSNET, CH, CHAOS, HS, HESIOD, ANY, or *). Default is IN.

**−d**  Debugging mode. **−dd** is a more verbose version.

**−e**  Do not print information about domains outside of specified zone. For hostname queries, do not print "additional information" or "authoritative nameserver."

**−f** *file*
> Output to *file* as well as standard out.

**−i**  Given an IP address, return the corresponding *in-addr.arpa* address, class (always PTR), and hostname.

**−l** *zone*
> List all machines in *zone*.

→

**host**
←

**−m** Print only MR, MG, and MB records; recursively expand MR (renamed mail box) and MG (mail group) records to MB (mail box) records.

**−o** Do not print output to standard out.

**−p** [*server*]
For use with −l. Query only the zone's primary name-server (or *server*) for zone transfers, instead of those authoritative servers that respond. Useful for testing unregistered zones.

**−q** Quiet. Suppress warning, but not error, messages.

**−r** Do not ask contacted server to query other servers, but require only the information that it has cached.

**−t** *type*
Look for *type* entries in the resource record. *type* may be A, NS, PTR, ANY, or * (all).

**−u** Use TCP, not UDP.

**−v** Verbose. Include all fields from resource record, even time-to-live and class, as well as "additional information" and "authoritative nameservers" (provided by the remote nameserver).

**−vv**
Very verbose. Include information about *host*'s defaults.

**−w** Never give up on queried server.

**−x** Allow multiple hosts or zones to be specified. If a server is also specified, the argument must be preceded by **−X**.

**−A** For hostnames, look up the associated IP address, and then reverse look up the hostname, to see if a match occurs. For IP addresses, look up the associated host-name, and determine whether the host recognizes that address as its own. For zones, check IP addresses for all hosts. Exit silently if no incongruities are discovered.

**−C** Similar to −l, but also check to see if the zone's name servers are really authoritative. The zone's SOA (start of authority) records specify authoritative name servers (in NS fields). Those servers are queried; if they do not have SOA records, host reports a lame delegation. Other checks are made as well.

**−D** Similar to **−H** but include the names of hosts with more than one address per defined name.

**−E** Similar to **−H** but do not treat extra-zone hosts as errors. Extra-zone hosts are hosts in an undefined subdomain.

**−F** *file*

Redirect standard out to *file*, and print extra resource record output only on standard out.

**−G** *zone*

Similar to **−H** but include the names of gateway hosts.

**−H** *zone*

Print the number of unique hosts within *zone*. Do not include aliases. Also list all errors found (extra-zone names, duplicate hosts).

**−I** *chars*

Do not print warnings about domain names containing illegal characters *chars*, such as _.

**−L** *level*

For use with **−l**. List all delegated zones within this zone, up to *level* deep, recursively.

**−P** *servers*

For use with **−l**. *servers* should be a comma-separated list. Specify preferred hosts for secondary servers to use when copying over zone data. Highest priority is given to those servers that match the most domain components in a given part of *servers*.

**−R** Treat non-fully-qualified hostnames as BIND does, searching each component of the local domain.

**−S** For use with **−l**. Print all hosts within the zone to standard out. Do not print hosts within subzones. Include class and IP address. Print warning messages (illegal names, lame delegations, missing records, etc.) to standard error.

**−T** Print time-to-live values (how long information about each host will remain cached before the nameserver refreshes it).

**−X** *server*

Specify a server to query, and allow multiple hosts or zones to be specified.

→

| | |
|---|---|
| host<br>← | **−Z** When printing recource records, include trailing dot in domain names, and print time-to-live value and class name. |
| hostid | **hostid**<br><br>Print the ID number in hexadecimal of the current host. |
| hostname | **hostname** [*option*] [*nameofhost*]<br><br>Set or print name of current host system. A privileged user can set the hostname with the *nameofhost* argument.<br><br>*Option*<br><br>**−a, −−alias**<br>Display the alias name of the host (if used).<br><br>**−d, −−domain**<br>Print DNS domain name.<br><br>**−f, −−fqdn, −−long**<br>Print fully qualified domain name.<br><br>**−F** *file*, **−−file** *file*<br>Consult *file* for hostname.<br><br>**−h, −−help**<br>Print a help message and then exit.<br><br>**−i, −−ip-address**<br>Display the IP address(es) of the host.<br><br>**−s, −−short**<br>Trim domain information from the printed name.<br><br>**−v, −−verbose**<br>Verbose mode.<br><br>**−V, −−version**<br>Print version information and then exit.<br><br>**−y, −−yp, −−nis**<br>Display the NIS domain name. A privileged user can set a new NIS domain name with *nameofhost*. |
| hwclock | **hwclock** [*options*]<br><br>System administration command. Read or set the hardware clock. This command maintains change information in */etc/* |

*adjtime*, which can be used to adjust the clock based on how much it drifts over time. **hwclock** replaces the **clock** command. The single-letter options are included for compatibility with the older command.

*Options*

You may specify only one of the following options:

-a   Adjust the hardware clock based on information in */etc/ adjtime* and set the system clock to the new time.

--adjust

Adjust the hardware clock based on information in */etc/ adjtime*.

--date *date*

Meaningful only with the --set option. *date* is a string appropriate for use with the **date** command.

--debug

Print information about what **hwclock** is doing.

-r, --show

Print the current time stored in the hardware clock.

-s, --hctosys

Set the system time in accordance with the hardware clock.

--set

Set the hardware clock according to the time given in the --**date** parameter.

--test

Do not actually change anything. This is good for checking syntax.

-u, --utc

The hardware clock is stored in Universal Coordinated Time.

--version

Print version and exit.

-w, --systohc

Set the hardware clock in accordance with the system time.

---

icmpinfo [*options*]

TCP/IP command. Intercept and interpret ICMP packets. Print the address and name of the message's sender, the

$\rightarrow$

| | |
|---|---|
| **icmpinfo**<br>← | source port, the destination port, the sequence, and the packet size. By default, provide information only about packets that are behaving oddly.<br><br>*Options*<br><br>−k  Kill the **syslogd** process begun by −l.<br><br>−l  Record via **syslogd**. Only a privileged user may use this option.<br><br>−n  Use IP addresses instead of hostnames.<br><br>−p  Suppress decoding of port number: do not attempt to guess the name of the service that is listening at that port.<br><br>−s  Include IP address of interface that received the packet, in case there are several interfaces on the host machine.<br><br>−v  Verbose. Include information about normal ICMP packets. You may also specify -vv and -vvv for extra verbosity. |
| **id** | **id** [*options*] [*username*]<br><br>Display information about yourself or another user: user ID, group ID, effective user ID and group ID if relevant, and additional group IDs.<br><br>*Options*<br><br>−g, −−group<br>    Print group ID only.<br><br>−G, −−groups<br>    Print supplementary groups only.<br><br>−n, −−name<br>    With −u, −g, or −G, print user or group name, not number.<br><br>−r, −−real<br>    With −u, −g, or −G, print real, not effective, user ID or group ID.<br><br>−u, −−user<br>    Print user ID only. |

**−−help**
> Print help message and then exit.

**−−version**
> Print version information.

---

**in.identd** [*options*] [*kernelfile* [*kmemfile*]]

TCP/IP command. Provide the name of the user whose process is running a specified TCP/IP connection. You may specify the kernel and its memory space.

*Options*

**−a** *ip_address*
> Bind to *ip_address*. Useful only with **−b**. By default, bind to the INADDR_ANY address.

**−b**  Run standalone; not for use with **inetd**.

**−d**  Allow debugging requests.

**−g***gid*
> Attempt to run in the group *gid*. Useful only with **−b**.

**−i**  Run as a daemon, one process per request.

**−l**  Log via **syslogd**.

**−m**  Allow multiple requests per session.

**−n**  Return user IDs instead of usernames.

**−N**  Do not provide a user's name or user ID if the file *.noident* exists in the user's home directory.

**−o**  When queried for the type of operating system, always return OTHER.

**−p***port*
> Listen at *port* instead of the default, port 113.

**−t***seconds*
> Exit if no new requests have been received before *seconds* seconds have passed. Note that, with **−i** or **−w**, the next new request will result in **identd** being restarted. Default is infinity (never exit).

**−u***uid*
> Attempt to run as *uid*. Useful only with **−b**.

→

| | |
|---|---|
| identd<br>← | **-V**  Print version and exit.<br><br>**-w**  Run as a daemon, one process for all requests. |
| ifconfig | **ifconfig** [*interface*]<br>**ifconfig** [*interface address_family parameters addresses*]<br><br>TCP/IP command. Assign an address to a network interface and/or configure network interface parameters. **ifconfig** is typically used at boot time to define the network address of each interface on a machine. It may be used at a later time to redefine an interface's address or other parameters. Without arguments, **ifconfig** displays the current configuration for a network interface. Used with a single *interface* argument, **ifconfig** displays that particular interface's current configuration.<br><br>***Arguments***<br><br>*interface*<br>    String of the form *name unit*, for example, **en0**.<br><br>*address_family*<br>    Since an interface may receive transmissions in differing protocols, each of which may require separate naming schemes, you can specify the *address_family* to change the interpretation of the remaining parameters. You may specify **inet** (the default; for TCP/IP), **ax25** (AX.25 Packet Radio), **ddp** (Appletalk Phase 2), or **ipx** (Novell).<br><br>*Parameters*<br>    The following parameters may be set with **ifconfig**:<br><br>**allmulti/-allmulti**<br>    Enable/disable sending of incoming frames to the kernel's network layer.<br><br>**arp/-arp**<br>    Enable/disable use of the Address Resolution Protocol in mapping between network-level addresses and link-level addresses.<br><br>**broadcast**<br>    (**inet** only.) Specify address to use to represent broadcasts to the network. Default is the address with a host part of all 1s (i.e., x.y.z.255 for a class C network). |

**debug/–debug**
> Enable/disable driver-dependent debugging code.

**dest_address**
> Specify the address of the correspondent on the other end of a point-to-point link.

**down**
> Mark an interface "down" (unresponsive).

**hw** *class address*
> Set the interface's hardware class and address. *class* may be **ether** (Ethernet), **ax25** (AX.25 Packet Radio), or **ARCnet**.

**irq** *addr*
> Set the device's interrupt line.

**metric** *n*
> Set routing metric of the interface to *n*. Default is 0.

**mtu** *num*
> Set the interface's Maximum Transfer Unit (MTU).

**multicast**
> Set the multicast flag.

**netmask** *mask*
> (**inet** only.) Specify how much of the address to reserve for subdividing networks into subnetworks. *mask* can be specified as a single hexadecimal number with a leading 0x, with a dot notation Internet address, or with a pseudonetwork name listed in the network table */etc/networks*.

**pointopoint/–pointopoint** [*address*]
> Enable/disable point-to-point interfacing, so that the connection between the two machines is dedicated.

**up** Mark an interface "up" (ready to send and receive).

**trailers/–trailers**
> Request/disable use of a "trailer" link-level encapsulation when sending.

*address*
> Either a hostname present in the hostname database (*/etc/hosts*), or an Internet address expressed in the Internet standard dot notation.

| | |
|---|---|
| imake | imake *options* |

C preprocessor (**cpp**) interface to the **make** utility. **imake** (for *include make*) solves the portability problem of **make** by allowing machine dependencies to be kept in a central set of configuration files, separate from the descriptions of the various items to be built. The targets are contained in the *Imakefile*, a machine-independent description of the targets to be built, written as **cpp** macros. **imake** uses **cpp** to process the configuration files and the *Imakefile*, and to generate machine-specific *Makefiles*, which can then be used by **make**.

One of the configuration files is a template file, a master file for **imake**. This template file (default is *Imake.tmpl*) #**include**s the other configuration files that contain machine dependencies such as variable assignments, site definitions, and **cpp** macros, and directs the order in which the files are processed. Each file affects the interpretation of later files and sections of *Imake.tmpl*. Comments may be included in **imake** configuration files, but the initial # needs to be preceded with an empty C comment:

```
/**/#
```

For more information, see **cpp** and **make**. Also check out the Nutshell Handbook *Software Portability with imake*, by Paul DuBois.

*Options*

−D*define*
> Set directory-specific variables. This option is passed directly to **cpp**.

−e
> Execute the generated *Makefile*. Default is to leave this to the user.

−f *filename*
> Name of per-directory input file. Default is *Imakefile*.

−I*directory*
> Directory in which **imake** template and configuration files may be found. This option is passed directly to **cpp**.

−s *filename*
> Name of **make** description file to be generated. If *filename* is a —, the output is written to **stdout**. The default is to generate, but not execute, a *Makefile*.

**–T***template*
> Name of master template file used by **cpp**. This file is usually located in the directory specified with the –I option. The default file is *Imake.tmpl*.

**–v** Print the **cpp** command line used to generate the *Makefile*.

*Tools*

Following is a list of tools used with **imake**:

**makedepend** [*options*] *files*
> Create header file dependencies in *Makefiles*. **make-depend** reads the named input source *files* in sequence and parses them to process #**include**, #**define**, #**undef**, #**ifdef**, #**ifndef**, #**endif**, #**if**, and #**else** directives so it can tell which #**include** directives would be used in a compilation. **makedepend** determines the dependencies and writes them to the *Makefile*. **make** then knows which object files must be recompiled when a dependency has changed. **makedepend** has the following options:

> **– –** *options* **– –**
>> Ignore any unrecognized options following a double hyphen. A second double hyphen terminates this action. Recognized options between the hyphens are processed normally.

> **–a** Append dependencies to any existing ones instead of replacing existing ones.

> **–f***filename*
>> Write dependencies to *filename* instead of to *Makefile*.

> **–m** Print a warning when encountering a multiple inclusion.

> **–s***string*
>> Use *string* as delimiter in file, instead of # **DO NOT DELETE THIS LINE** — **make depend depends on it**.

> **–v** Verbose. List all files included by main source file.

> **–D***name*
>> Define *name* with the given value (first form) or with value 1 (second form).

> **–I***dir*
>> Add directory *dir* to the list of directories searched.

→

−Y *dir*

Search only *dir* for include files. Ignore standard
include directories.

**mkdirhier** *dir*...

Create directory *dir* and all missing parent directories
during file installation operations.

**xmkmf** [*option*] [*topdir*] [*curdir*]

Bootstrap a *Makefile* from an *Imakefile*. *topdir* specifies
the location of the project root directory. *curdir* (usually omitted) is specified as a relative pathname from
the top of the build tree to the current directory. The
−a option is equivalent to the following command
sequence:

```
% xmkmf
% make Makefiles
% make includes
% make depend
```

*Configuration files*

Following is a list of the **imake** configuration files:

*Imake.tmpl*

Master template for **imake**. *Imake.tmpl* includes all the
other configuration files, plus the *Imakefile* in the current directory.

*Imake.params*

Contains definitions that apply across sites and vendors.

*Imake.rules*

Contains **cpp** macro definitions that are configured for
the current platform. The macro definitions are fed into
**imake**, which runs **cpp** to process the macros. Newlines
(line continuations) are indicated by the string @@\
(double at sign, backslash).

*site.def*

Contains site-specific (as opposed to vendor-specific)
information, such as installation directories, what set of
programs to build, and any special versions of programs to use during the build. The *site.def* file changes
from machine to machine.

*Project.tmpl*

File containing X-specific variables.

*Library.tmpl*
> File containing library rules.

*Server.tmpl*
> File containing server-specific rules.

*.cf* The *.cf* files are the vendor-specific *VendorFiles* that live in *Imake.vb*. A *.cf* file contains platform-specific definitions, such as version numbers of the operating system and the compiler and workarounds for missing commands. The definitions in *.cf* files override the defaults, defined in *Imake.params*.

### The Imakefile

The *Imakefile* is a per-directory file that indicates targets to be built and installed and rules to be applied. **imake** reads the *Imakefile* and expands the rules into *Makefile* target entries. An *Imakefile* may also include definitions of **make** variables and list the dependencies of the targets. The dependencies are expressed as **cpp** macros, defined in *Imake.rules*. Whenever you change an *Imakefile*, you need to rebuild the *Makefile* and regenerate header file dependencies. For more information on **imake**, see *Software Portability with imake* by Paul DuBois.

---

## imapd

TCP/IP command. The Interactive Mail Access Protocol (IMAP) server daemon. **imapd** is invoked by **inetd** and listens on port 143 for requests from IMAP clients. IMAP allows mail programs to access remote mailboxes as if they were local. IMAP is a richer protocol than POP because it allows a client to retrieve message-level information from a server mailbox instead of the entire mailbox. IMAP can be used for online and offline reading. The popular Pine mail client contains support for IMAP.

---

## inetd [*option*] [*configuration_file*]

TCP/IP command. Internet services daemon. **inetd** listens on multiple ports for incoming connection requests. When it receives one, it spawns the appropriate server. When started, **inetd** reads its configuration information from either *configuration_file*, or from the default configuration file */etc/inetd.conf*. It then issues a call to **getservbyname**, creates a socket for each server, and binds each socket to the port for that server. It does a **listen** on all connection-based

$\rightarrow$

sockets, then waits, using **select** for a connection or data-gram.

When a connection request is received on a listening socket, **inetd** does an **accept**, creating a new socket. It then forks, dups, and execs the appropriate server. The invoked server has I/O to **stdin**, **stdout**, and **stderr** done to the new socket, connecting the server to the client process.

When there is data waiting on a datagram socket, **inetd** forks, dups, and execs the appropriate server, passing it any server program arguments. A datagram server has I/O to **stdin**, **stdout**, and **stderr** done to the original socket. If the datagram socket is marked as **wait**, the invoked server must process the message before **inetd** considers the socket available for new connections. If the socket is marked **nowait**, **inetd** continues to process incoming messages on that port.

The following servers may be started by **inetd**: bootpd, bootpgw, fingerd, ftpd, imapd, popd, rexecd, rlogind, rshd, talkd, telnetd, and tftpd. Do not arrange for **inetd** to start **named, routed, rwhod, sendmail, listen,** or any NFS server.

**inetd** rereads its configuration file when it receives a hangup signal, SIGHUP. Services may be added, deleted, or modified when the configuration file is reread.

### Option

−**d** Turn on socket-level debugging and print debugging information to stdout.

### Files

*/etc/inetd.conf*
    Default configuration file.

*/var/run/inetd.pid*
    **inetd**'s process ID.

---

**info**

info [*options*] [*topics*]

GNU hypertext reader: display online documentation previ-ously built from Texinfo input. Info files are arranged in a hierarchy and can contain menus for subtopics. When entered without options, the command displays the top-level info file (usually */usr/local/info/dir*). When *topics* are specified, find a subtopic by choosing the first *topic* from the menu in the top-level info file, the next *topic* from the new menu specified by the first *topic*, and so on. The initial display can also be controlled by the −**f** and −**n** options.

*Options*

−d *directories,* −−**directory** *directories*
> Search *directories,* a colon-separated list, for info files. If this option is not specified, use the INFOPATH environment variable or the default directory (usually */usr/ local/info*).

−−**dribble** *file*
> Store each keystroke in *file,* which can be used in a future session with the −−**restore** option to return to this place in **info**.

−f *file,* −−**file** *file*
> Display specified info file.

−n *node,* −−**node** *node*
> Display specified node in the info file.

−o *file,* −−**output** *file*
> Copy output to *file* instead of displaying it at the screen.

−−**help**
> Display brief help.

−−**restore** *file*
> When starting, execute keystrokes in *file.*

−−**subnodes**
> Display subtopics.

−−**version**
> Display version.

−−**vi-keys**
> Use **vi**-like key bindings.

---

init [*option*] [*runlevel*]

System administration command.

*Option*

−t *seconds*
> When changing runlevels, send SIGKILL *seconds* after SIGTERM. Default is 20.

*Files*

**init** is the first process run by any Unix machine at boot time. It verifies the integrity of all filesystems and then creates other processes, using **fork** and **exec**, as specified by

→

| init | /etc/inittab. Which processes may be run are controlled by |
|---|---|
| ← | *runlevel*. All process terminations are recorded in */var/run/* |

*utmp* and */var/log/wtmp*. When the runlevel changes, **init** sends SIGTERM and then, after 20 seconds, SIGKILL to all processes that cannot be run in the new runlevel.

### Runlevels

The current runlevel may be changed by **telinit**, which is often just a link to **init**. The default runlevels vary from distribution to distribution, but these are standard:

0    Halt the system.

**1, s, S**
   Single-user mode.

6    Reboot the system.

**q, Q**
   Reread */etc/inittab*.

Check the */etc/inittab* file for runlevels on your system.

---

**insmod**

**insmod** [*options*] *file* [*symbol=value* ... ]

System administration command. Load the module *file* into the kernel, changing any symbols that are defined on the command line. If the module file is named *file.o* or *file.mod*, the module will be named *file*.

### Options

**−f**   Force loading of module, even if some problems are encountered.

**−m**  Output a load map.

**−o** *name*
   Name module *name* instead of attempting to name it from the object file's name.

**−x**   Do not export: do not add any external symbols from the module to the kernel's symbol table.

---

**install**

**install** [*options*] [*file*] *directories*

System administration command. Used primarily in makefiles to update files. **install** copies files into user-specified directories. It will not overwrite a file. Similar to **cp** but attempts to set permission modes, owner, and group.

*Options*

**–d, ––directory**
> Create any missing directories.

**–g** *group,* **––group** *group*
> Set group ID of new file to *group* (privileged users only).

**–m** *mode,* **––mode** *mode*
> Set permissions of new file to *mode* (octal or symbolic). By default, the mode is **0755**.

**–o** [*owner*], **––owner** [*owner*]
> Set ownership to *owner* or, if unspecified, to root (privileged users only).

**–s, ––strip**
> Strip symbol tables.

**ipchains** *command* [*options*]

System administration command. Edit IP firewall rules in the 2.2 Linux kernel. A 2.2 Linux kernel compiled with firewall support will examine the headers of all network packets and compare them to matching rules to see what it should do with the packet. A firewall rule consists of some matching criteria and a target, a result to be applied if the packet matches the criteria. The rules are organized into chains. You can use these rules to build a firewall or just reject certain kinds of network connections.

Firewall rules are organized into chains, an ordered checklist that the kernel works through looking for matches. There are three built-in chains **input, output,** and **forward.** Packets entering the system are tested against the **input** chain. Those exiting the system are checked against the **output** chain. If an incoming packet is destined for some other system, it is checked against the **forward** chain. Each of these chains has a default target, a policy, in case no match is found. User-defined chains can be created and used as targets for packets, but they have no default policies. If no match can be found in a user-defined chain, the packet is returned to the chain from which it was called and tested against the next rule in that chain.

**ipchains** only changes the rules in the running kernel. When the system is powered off, all those changes are lost. You can use the **ipchains-save** command to make a script you can later run with **ipchains-restore** to restore your

→

firewall settings. Such a script is often called at boot up and many distributions have an **ipchains** initialization script that uses the output from **ipchains-save**.

### Commands

**ipchains** is always invoked with one of the following commands:

**–A** *chain rules*, **––append** *chain rules*
> Append new *rules* to *chain*.

**–I** *chain number rules*, **––insert** <*chain number rules*
> Insert *rules* into *chain* at the ordinal position given by *number*.

**–D** *chain rules*, **––delete** *chain rules*
> Delete *rules* from *chain*. Rules can be specified by their ordinal number in the chain as well as by a general rule description.

**–R** *chain number rule*, **––replace** *chain number rule*
> Replace a rule in *chain*. The rule to be replaced is specified by its ordinal *number*.

**–C** *chain rule*, **––check** *chain rules*
> Construct a network packet that matches the given *rule* and check how *chain* will handle it. The rule must describe the source, destination, protocol, and interface of the packet to be constructed.

**–L** [*chain*], **––list** *$PARAMETER*
> List the rules in *chain*. If no chain is specified, list the rules in all chains.

**–ML**, **––masquerading ––list**
> List masquerading connections.

**–MS** *tcp tcpfin udp*, **––masquerading ––set** *tcp tcpfin udp*
> Set timeout value in seconds for masquerading connections. **–MS** always takes three parameters specifying the timeout values for TCP sessions, TCP sessions that have received a FIN packet, and UDP packets.

**–F** *chain*, **––flush** *chain*
> Remove all rules from *chain*.

**–Z** [*chain*], **––zero** [*chain*]
> Reset the packet and byte counters in *chain*. If no chain is specified, all chains will be reset. When used without specifying a chain and combined with the **–L** command, it lists the current counter values before they are reset.

**−N** *chain,* **−−new-chain** *chain*

Create a new *chain*. The chain's name must be unique.

**−X** [*chain*], **−−delete-chain** *chain*

Delete *chain*. Only user-defined chains can be deleted, and there can be no references to the chain to be deleted. If no argument is given, all user-defined chains will be deleted.

**−P** *chain target,* **−−policy** *chain target*

Set the policy for a built-in *chain*; the target itself cannot be a chain.

**−h** [**icmp**]

Print a brief help message. If the option **icmp** is given, print a list of valid ICMP types.

*Targets*

A target can be the name of a chain or one of the following special values:

**ACCEPT**

Let the packet through.

**DENY**

Drop the packet.

**MASQ**

Masquerade the packet so it appears that it originated from the current system. Reverse packets from masqueraded connections are unmasqueraded automatically. This is a legal target for only the **forward** chain, or user-defined chains used in forwarding packets. To use this target, the kernel must be compiled with support for IP masquerading.

**REDIRECT** [*port*]

Redirect incoming packets to a local *port* on which you are running a transparent proxy program. If the specified port is 0 or is not given, the destination port of the packet is used as the redirection port. **REDIRECT** is only a legal target for the **input** chain or user-defined chains used in handling incoming packets. The kernel must be compiled with support for transparent proxies.

**REJECT**

Drop the packet and send an ICMP message back to the sender indicating the packet was dropped.

→

RETURN

Return to the chain from which this chain was called and check the next rule. If **RETURN** is the target of a rule in a built-in chain, then the built-in chain's default policy is applied.

### Rule specification parameters

These options are used to create rules for use with the preceding commands. Rules consist of some matching criteria and usually a target to jump to (–j) if the match is made. Many of the parameters for these matching rules can be expressed as a negative with an exclamation point (!) meaning "not." Those rules will match everything except the given parameter.

**–p** [!] *name*, **––protocol** [!] *$PARAMETER*

Match packets of protocol *name*. The value of *name* can be given as a name or number as found in the file */etc/protocols*. The most common values are **tcp**, **udp**, **icmp**, or the special value **all**. The number 0 is equivalent to **all**, and this is the default value when this option is not used.

**–s** [!] *address[/mask]* [!] *[port]*, **––source** [!] *address[/mask]* [!] *[port]*

Specifies the source *address* and *port* of the packet that will match this rule. The address may be supplied as a hostname, a network name, or an IP address. The optional mask is the netmask to use and may be supplied either in the traditional form (e.g., /255.255.255.0) or in the modern form (e.g., /24). The optional port specifies the TCP, UDP, or ICMP type that will match. You may supply a port specification only if you've supplied the –p parameter with one of the **tcp**, **udp** or **icmp** protocols. A colon can be used to indicate an inclusive range of ports or ICMP values to be used. (e.g., 20:25 for ports 20 through 25). If the first *port* parameter is missing, the default value is 0. If the second is omitted, the default value is 65535.

**–d** [!] *address[/mask]* [!] *[port]*, **––destination** [!] *address[/mask]* [port]*

Match packets with the destination *address*. The syntax for this command's parameters is the same as for the –s option.

**–j** *target*, **––jump** *target*

Jump to a special target or a user-defined chain. If this option is not specified for a rule, matching the rule only increases the rule's counters and the packet is tested against the next rule.

**−i [!]** *name*, **−−interface** *name*
Match packets from interface *name*[+]. *name* is the network interface used by your system (e.g., **eth0** or **ppp0**). A + can be used as a wildcard, so **ppp+** would match any interface name beginning with **ppp**.

**[!] −f, [!]−−fragment** *$PARAMETER*
The rule applies to everything but the first fragment of a fragmented packet.

**−−source-port [!]** *port*
Match packets from the source *port*. The syntax for specifying ports can be found in the preceding description of the −s option.

**−−destination-port [!]** *port*
Match packets with the destination *port*. The syntax for specifying ports can be found in the preceding description of the −s option.

**−−icmp-type [!]** *type*
Match packets with ICMP type name or number of *type*.

*Options*

**−b, −−bidirectional**
Put rule in both the input and output chain so packets will be matched in both directions.

**−v, −−verbose**
Verbose mode.

**−n, −−numeric**
Print all IP address and port numbers in numeric form. By default, names are displayed when possible.

**−l, −−log**
Log information for the matching packet to the system log.

**−t** *andmask xormask*, **−−TOS** *andmask xormask*
Change the Type of Service field in the packet's header. The TOS field is first ANDed with the 8-bit hexadecimal mask *andmask*, then XORed with the 8-bit hexadecimal mask *xormask*. Rules that would affect the least significant bit (LSB) portion of the TOS field are rejected.

→

| | |
|---|---|
| ipchains<br>← | **−x, −−exact**<br>　　Expand all numbers in a listing (−L). Display the exact value of the packet and byte counters instead of rounded figures.<br><br>**[!] −y, −−syn**<br>　　Match only incoming TCP connection requests, those with the SYN bit set and the ACK and FIN bits cleared. This blocks incoming TCP connections but leaves outgoing connections unaffected.<br><br>**−−line-numbers**<br>　　Used with the −L command. Add the line number to the beginning of each rule in a listing indicating its position in the chain.<br><br>**−−no-warnings**<br>　　Disable all warnings |
| ipchains-restore | **ipchains-restore** [*options*]<br><br>System administration command. Restore firewall rules. **ipchains-restore** takes commands generated by **ipchains-save** and uses them to restore the firewall rules for each chain. Often used by initialization scripts to restore firewall settings on boot.<br><br>*Options*<br><br>**−f**　Force updates of existing chains without asking.<br><br>**−v**　Print rules as they are being restored.<br><br>**−p**　If a nonexisting chain is targeted by a rule, create it. |
| ipchains-save | **ipchains-save** [*chain*] [*option*]<br><br>System administration command. Print the IP firewall rules currently stored in the kernel to **stdout**. If no *chain* is given, all chains will be printed. Output is usually redirected to a file, which can later be used by **ipchains-restore** to restore the firewall.<br><br>*Option*<br><br>**−v**　Print out rules to stderr as well as stdout, making them easier to see when redirecting output. |

ipfwadm *category command parameters* [*options*]
ipfwadm  −M [ −*l* | −*s* ] [*options*]

Administer a firewall and its rules, firewall accounting, and IP masquerading in the 2.0 Linux kernel. This command is replaced with **ipchains** in the 2.2 kernel, and **ipchains** is replaced by **iptables** in the 2.4 kernel.

There are four categories of rules: IP packet accounting, IP input firewall, IP output firewall, and IP forwarding firewall. The rules are maintained in lists, with a separate list for each category. See the manpage for **ipfw**(4) for a more detailed description of how the lists work.

Each **ipfwadm** command specifies only one category and one rule. To create a secure firewall, you issue multiple **ipfwadm** commands; the combination of their rules work together to ensure that your firewall operates as you intend it to. The second form of the command is for masquerading. The commands −l and −s described in the later list are the only ones that can be used with the masquerading category, −**M**.

*Categories*

One of the following flags is required to indicate the category of rules to which the command that follows the category applies.

−**A** [*direction*]
    IP accounting rules. Optionally, a direction can be specified:

    **in**   Count only incoming packets.

    **out** Count only outgoing packets.

    **both**
        Count both incoming and outgoing packets; this is the default.

−**F** IP forwarding firewall rules.

−**I** IP input firewall rules.

−**M** IP masquerading administration. Can be used only with the −l or −s command.

−**O** IP output firewall rules.

→

**ipfwadm**
←

*Commands*

The category is followed by a command indicating the specific action to be taken. Unless otherwise specified, only one action can be given on a command line. For the commands that can include a policy, the valid policies are:

**accept**
> Allow matching packets to be received, sent, or forwarded.

**deny**
> Block matching packets from being received, sent, or forwarded.

**reject**
> Block matching packets from being received, sent, or forwarded and also return an ICMP error message to the sending host.

The commands are:

**−a** [*policy*]
> Append one or more rules to the end of the rules for the category. No policy is specified for accounting rules. For firewall rules, a policy is required. When the source and/or destination names resolve to more than one address, a rule is added for each possible address combination.

**−c** Check whether this IP packet would be accepted, denied, or rejected by the type of firewall represented by this category. Valid only when the category is −I, −O, or −F. Requires the −V parameter to be specified (see "Parameters," later).

**−d** [*policy*]
> Delete one or more entries from the list of rules for the category. No policy is specified for accounting rules. The parameters specified with this command must exactly match the parameters from an append or insert command, or no match will be found and the rule will not be removed. Only the first matching rule in the list of rules is deleted.

**−f** Remove (flush) all rules for the category.

**−h** Display a help message with a brief description of the command syntax. Specified with no category:

```
% ipfwadm -h
```

**−i** [*policy*]

Insert a new rule at the beginning of the selected list for the category. No policy is specified for accounting rules. For firewall rules, a policy is required. When the source and/or destination names resolve to more than one address, a rule is added for each possible address combination.

**−l**　List all rules for the category. This option may be combined with the **−z** option to reset the packet and byte counters after listing their current values. Unless the **−x** option is also specified, the packet and byte counters are shown as *number***K** or *number***M**, rounded to the nearest integer. See also the **−e** option described under "Options" later.

**−p** *policy*

Change the default policy for the selected type of firewall to *policy*. The default policy is used when no matching rule is found. Valid only with **−I**, **−O**, or **−F**.

**−s** *tcp tcpfin udp*

Set the masquerading timeout values; valid only with **−M**. The three parameters are required and represent the timeout value in seconds for TCP sessions, TCP sessions after receiving a FIN packet, and UDP packets, respectively. A timeout value of 0 preserves the current timeout value of the corresponding entry.

**−z**　Reset the packet and byte counters for all rules in the category. This command may be combined with the **−l** command.

### Parameters

The following parameters can be specified with the **−a**, **−i**, **−d**, or **−c** commands, except as noted. Multiple parameters can be specified on a single **ipfwadm** command line.

**−D** *address*[/*mask*] [*port* . . . ]

The destination specification (optional). See the description of **−S** for the syntax, default values, and other requirements. ICMP types cannot be specified with **−D**.

**−P** *protocol*

The protocol of the rule or packet; possible values are **tcp**, **udp**, **icmp**, or **all**. Defaults to **all**, which matches all protocols. **−P** cannot be specified with the **−c** command.

$\rightarrow$

−S address[*/mask*] [*port* . . .]

The source IP address, specified as a hostname, a net-work name, or an IP address. The source address and mask default to 0.0.0.0/0. If −S is specified, −P must also be specified. The optional mask is specified as a network mask or as the number of 1s on the left of the network mask (e.g., a mask of 24 is equivalent to 255.255.255.0). The mask defaults to 32. One or more values of *port* may optionally be specified, indicating what ports or ICMP types the rule applies to. The default is **all**. Ports may be specified by their */etc/ services* entry. The syntax for indicating a range of ports is:

```
lowport:highport
```

For example:

```
-S 172.29.16.1/24 ftp:ftp-data
```

−V *address*

The address of the network interface the packet is received from (if category is −I) or is being sent to (if category is −O). *address* can be a hostname or an IP address, and defaults to 0.0.0.0, which matches any interface address. −V is required with the −c command:

```
-V 172.29.16.1
```

−W *name*

Identical to −V but takes a device name instead of its address:

```
-W ppp0
```

*Options*

−b  Bidirectional mode. The rule matches IP packets in both directions. This option is valid only with the −a, −i, and −d commands.

−e  Extended output. Used with the −l command to also show the interface address and any rule options. When listing firewall rules, also shows the packet and byte counters and the TOS (Type of Service) masks. When used with −M, also shows information related to delta sequence numbers.

−k  Match TCP acknowledgment packets (i.e., only TCP packets with the ACK bit set). This option is ignored for all other protocols and is valid only with the −a, −i, and −d commands.

-m  Accept masquerade packets for forwarding, making them appear to have originated from the local host. Recognizes reverse packets and automatically demasquerades them, bypassing the forwarding firewall. This option is valid only in forwarding firewall rules with policy **accept**. The kernel must have been compiled with CONFIG_IP_MASQUERADE defined.

-n  Numeric output. Print IP addresses and port numbers in numeric format.

-o  Log packets that match this rule to the kernel log. This option is valid only with the −a, −i, and −d commands. The kernel must have been compiled with CONFIG_IP_FIREWALL_VERBOSE defined.

−r [*port*]

Redirect packets to a local socket, even if they were sent to a remote host. If *port* is 0 (the default), the packet's destination port is used. This option is valid only in input firewall rules with policy **accept**. The kernel must have been compiled with CONFIG_IP_TRANSPARENT_ PROXY defined.

−t *andmask xormask*

Specify masks used for modifying the TOS field in the IP header. When a packet is accepted (with or without masquerading) by a firewall rule, its TOS field is bitwise ANDed with *andmask*, and the result is bitwise XORed with *xormask*. The masks are specified as 8-bit hexadecimal values. This option is valid only with the −a, −i, and −d commands and has no effect when used with accounting rules or with firewall rules for rejecting or denying a packet.

−v  Verbose output. Print detailed information about the rule or packet to be added, deleted, or checked. This option is valid only with the −a, −i, −d, and −c commands.

−x  Expand numbers. Display the exact value of the packet and byte counters, instead of a rounded value. This option is valid only when the counters are being listed anyway (see also the −e option).

−y  Match TCP packets with the SYN bit set and the ACK bit cleared. This option is ignored for packets of other protocols and is valid only with the −a, −i, and −d commands.

| iptables | **iptables** *command* [*options*] |
| :--- | :--- |

System administration command. Configure *netfilter* filtering rules. In the 2.4 kernel, the **ipchains** firewall capabilities are replaced with the *netfilter* kernel module. *netfilter* can be configured to work just like **ipchains**, but it also comes with the module **iptables**, which is similar to **ipchains** but extensible. *iptables* rules consist of some matching criteria and a target, a result to be applied if the packet matches the criteria. The rules are organized into chains. You can use these rules to build a firewall, masquerade your local area network, or just reject certain kinds of network connections.

There are three built-in tables for **iptables**, one for network filtering (**filter**), one for Network Address Translation (**nat**), and the last for specialized packet alterations (**mangle**). Firewall rules are organized into chains, ordered check lists of rules that the kernel works through looking for matches. The **filter** table has three built-in chains: **INPUT**, **OUTPUT**, and **FORWARD**. The **INPUT** and **OUTPUT** chains handle packets originating from or destined for the host system. The **FORWARD** chain handles mail just passing through the host system. The **nat** table also has three built-in chains: **PREROUTING**, **POSTROUTING**, and **OUTPUT**. **mangle** has only two chains: **PREROUTING** and **OUTPUT**.

*netfilter* checks packets entering the system. After applying any **PREROUTING** rules it passes them to the **INPUT** chain or to the **FORWARD** chain if the packet is just passing through. Upon leaving, the system packets are passed to the **OUTPUT** chain and then on to any **POSTROUTING** rules. Each of these chains has a default target, a policy, in case no match is found. User-defined chains can also be created and used as targets for packets but do not have default policies. If no match can be found in a user-defined chain, the packet is returned to the chain from which it was called and tested against the next rule in that chain.

**iptables** only changes the rules in the running kernel. When the system is powered off, all changes are lost. You can use the **iptables-save** command to make a script you can run with **iptables-restore** to restore your firewall settings. Such a script is often called at bootup. Many distributions will have an **iptables** initialization script that uses the output from **iptables-save**.

*Commands*

**iptables** is always invoked with one of the following commands:

**−A** *chain rules,* **−−append** *chain rules*
Append new *rules* to *chain.*

**−I** *chain number rules,* **−−insert** *chain number rules*
Insert *rules* into *chain* at the ordinal position given by *number.*

**−D** *chain rules,* **−−delete** *chain rules*
Delete *rules* from *chain.* Rules can be specified by their ordinal number in the chain as well as by a general rule description.

**−R** *chain number rule,* **−−replace** *chain number rule*
Replace a rule in *chain.* The rule to be replaced is specified by its ordinal *number.*

**−C** *chain rule,* **−−check** *chain rules*
Check how *chain* will handle a network packet that matches the given *rule.* The rule must describe the source, destination, protocol, and interface of the packet to be constructed.

**−L** [*chain*], **−−list** *$PARAMETER*
List the rules in *chain* or all chains if *chain* is not specified.

**−F** [*chain*], **−−flush** *chain*
Remove all rules from *chain* or from all chains if *chain* is not specified.

**−Z** [*chain*], **−−zero** *chain*
Zero the packet and byte counters in *chain.* If no chain is specified, all chains will be reset. When used without specifying a chain and combined with the **−L** command, it lists the current counter values before they are reset *chain.*

**−N** *chain,* **−−new-chain** *chain*
Create a new *chain.* The chain's name must be unique. This is how user-defined chains are created.

**−X** [*chain*], **−−delete-chain** *chain*
Delete the specified user-defined *chain* or all user-defined chains if no chain is specified.

**−P** *chain target,* **−−policy** *chain target*
Set the default policy for a built-in *chain*; the target itself cannot be a chain.

**−E** *old-chain new-chain,* **−−rename-chain** *old-chain new-chain*
Rename *old-chain* to *new-chain.*

→

**iptables**
←

**−h** [icmp]
> Print a brief help message. If the option **icmp** is given, print a list of valid ICMP types.

### Targets

A target may be the name of a chain or one of the following special values.

**ACCEPT**
> Let the packet through.

**DROP**
> Drop the packet.

**QUEUE**
> Send packets to the user space for processing.

**RETURN**
> Stop traversing the current chain and return to the point in the previous chain from which this one was called. If **RETURN** is the target of a rule in a built-in chain, the built-in chain's default policy is applied.

### Rule specification parameters

These options are used to create rules for use with the preceding commands. Rules consist of some matching criteria and usually a target to jump to (**−j**) if the match is made. Many of the parameters for these matching rules can be expressed as a negative with an exclamation point (!) meaning "not." Those rules will match everything except the given parameter.

**−p** [!] *name,* **−−protocol** [!] *$PARAMETER*
> Match packets of protocol *name.* The value of *name* can be given as a name or number as found in the file */etc/protocols.* The most common values are **tcp**, **udp**, **icmp**, or the special value **all**. The number 0 is equivalent to **all** and this is the default value when this option is not used. If there are extended matching rules associated with the specified protocol, they will be loaded automatically. You need not use the **−m** option to load them.

**−s** [!] *address*[/*mask*] [!] [*port*], **−−source** [!] *address*[/*mask*] [!] [*port*]
> Match packets with the source *address.* The address may be supplied as a hostname, a network name, or an IP address. The optional mask is the netmask to use and may be supplied either in the traditional form (e.g., /255.255.255.0) or in the modern form (e.g., /24).

**–d** [!] *address*[/*mask*] [!] [*port*], **––destination** [!]
   *address*[/*mask*] [*port*]
   Match packets from the destination *address*. See the
   description of **–s** for the syntax of this option.

**–j** *target*, **––jump** *target*
   Jump to a special target or a user-defined chain. If this
   option is not specified for a rule, matching the rule
   only increases the rule's counters, and the packet is
   tested against the next rule.

**–i** [!] *name*[+], **––in-interface** *name*[+]
   Match packets being received from interface *name*.
   *name* is the network interface used by your system
   (e.g., **eth0** or **ppp0**). A **+** can be used as a wildcard, so
   **ppp+** would match any interface name beginning with
   **ppp**

**–o** [!] *name*[+], **––out-interface** *name*[+]
   Match packets being sent from interface *name*. See the
   description of **–i** for the syntax for *name*.

[!] **–f**, [!]**––fragment** *$PARAMETER*
   The rule applies only to the second or further frag-
   ments of a fragmented packet.

*Options*

**–v**, **––verbose**
   Verbose mode.

**–n**, **––numeric**
   Print all IP address and port numbers in numeric form.
   By default, text names are displayed when possible.

**–x**, **––exact**
   Expand all numbers in a listing (**–L**). Display the exact
   value of the packet and byte counters instead of
   rounded figures.

**–m** *module*, **––match**
   Explicitly load matching rule extensions associated with
   *module*. See the following section, "Match Extensions."

**–h** [icmp], **––help** [icmp]
   Print help message. If **icmp** is specified, a list of valid
   ICMP type names will be printed. **–h** can also be used
   with the **–m** option to get help on an extension module.

$\rightarrow$

**iptables**
←

−−line-numbers
> Used with the −L command. Add the line number to the beginning of each rule in a listing, indicating its position in the chain.

### Match extensions

Several kernel modules come with netfilter to extend matching capabilities of rules. Those associated with particular protocols are loaded automatically when the −p option is used to specify the protocol. Others need to be loaded explicitly with the −m option.

**tcp** Loaded when −p tcp is the only protocol specified.

−−source-port [!] [*port*][:*port*], −−sport [!] [*port*][:*port*]
> Match the specified source ports. Using the colon specifies an inclusive range of services to match. If the first port is omitted, 0 is the default. If the second port is omitted, 65535 is the default. You can also use a dash instead of a colon to specify the range.

−−destination-port [!] [*port*][:*port*], −−dport [!] [*port*][:*port*]
> Match the specified destination ports. The syntax is the same as for −−source-port.

−−tcp-flags [!] *mask comp*
> Match the packets with the TCP flags specified by *mask* and *comp*. *mask* is a comma-separated list of flags that should be examined. *comp* is a comma-separated list of flags that must be set for the rule to match. Valid flags are SYN, ACK, FIN, RST, URG, PSH, ALL, and NONE.

[!] −−syn
> Match packets with the SYN bit set and the ACK and FIN bits cleared. These are packets that request TCP connections; blocking them prevents incoming connections. Shorthand for −−tcp-flags SYN,RST,ACK SYN.

**udp**
> Loaded when −p udp is the only protocol specified.

−−source-port [!] [*port*][:*port*], −−sport [!] [*port*][:*port*]
> Match the specified source ports. The syntax is the same as for the −−source-port option of the TCP extension.

**--destination-port** [!] [*port*][:*port*], **--dport** [!]
[*port*][:*port*]
> Match the specified destination ports. The syntax is
> the same as for **--source-port** option of the TCP
> extension.

**icmp**
> Loaded when **-p icmp** is the only protocol specified.

**--icmp-type** [!] *type*
> Match the specified icmp *type*. *type* may be a
> numeric ICMP type or one of the ICMP type names
> shown by the command **iptables -p icmp -h**.

**mac**
> Loaded explicitly with the **-m** option.

**--mac-source** [!] *address*
> Match the source *address* that transmitted the
> packet. *address* must be given in colon-separated
> hexbyte notation (for example, **--mac-source
> 00:60:08:91:CC:B7**.

**limit**
> Loaded explicitly with the **-m** option. The **limit** exten-
> sions are used to limit the number of packets matched.
> This is useful when combined with the **LOG** target.
> Rules using this extension match until the specified
> limit is reached.

**--limit** *rate*
> Match addresses at the given *rate*. *rate* is specified
> as a number with an optional **/second**, **/minute**,
> **hour**, or **/day** suffix. When this option is not set,
> the default is '3/hour'.

**--limit-burst** [*number*]
> Set the maximum *number* of packets to match in a
> burst. Once the number has been reached, no
> more packets are matched for this rule until the
> number has recharged. It recharges at the rate set
> by the **--limit** option. When not specified, the
> default is 5.

**multiport**
> Loaded explicitly with the **-m** option. The **multiport**
> extensions match sets of source or destination ports.
> These rules can be used only in conjunction with **-p
> tcp** and **-p udp**. Up to 15 ports can be specified in a
> comma-separated list.

→

**--source-port** [*ports*]
> Match the given source *ports*.

**--destination-port** [*ports*]
> Match the given destination *ports*.

**--port** [*ports*]
> Match if the packet has the same source and destination port and that port is one of the given *ports*.

**mark**
> Loaded explicitly with the **-m** option. This module works with the **MARK** extension target:
>
> **--mark** *value*[/*mask*]
> > Match the given unsigned mark value. If a mask is specified, it is logically ANDed with the mark before comparison.

**owner**
> Loaded explicitly with the **-m** option. The **owner** extensions match a local packet's creator's user, group process, and session IDs. This makes sense only as a part of the **OUTPUT** chain.
>
> **--uid-owner** *userid*
> > Match packets created by a process owned by *userid*.
>
> **--gid-owner** *groupid*
> > Match packets created by a process owned by *groupid*.
>
> **--pid-owner** *processid*
> > Match packets created by process ID *processid*.
>
> **--sid-owner** *sessionid*
> > Match packets created by a process in the session *sessionid*.

**state**
> Loaded explicitly with the **-m** option. This module matches the connection state of a packet.
>
> **--state** *states*
> > Match the packet if it has one of the states in the comma-separated list *states*. Valid states are **INVALID, ESTABLISHED, NEW,** and **RELATED**.

**tos** Loaded explicitly with the **-m** option. This module matches the Type of Service field in a packet's header.

--tos *value*
> Match the packet if it has a TOS of *value. value* can be a numeric value or a Type of Service name. **iptables -m tos -h** will give you a list of valid TOS values.

### Target extensions

Extension targets are optional additional targets supported by separate kernel modules. They have their own associated options.

### LOG

Log the packet's information in the system log.

--log-level *level*
> Set the syslog level by name or number (as defined by *syslog.conf*).

--log-prefix *prefix*
> Begin each log entry with the string *prefix*. The prefix string may be up to 30 characters long.

--log-tcp-sequence
> Log the TCP sequence numbers. This is a security risk if your log is readable by users.

--log-tcp-options
> Log options from the TCP packet header.

--log-ip-options
> Log options from the IP packet header.

### MARK

Used to mark packets with an unsigned integer value you can use later with the **mark** matching extension. Valid only with the **mangle** table.

--set-mark *value*
> Mark the packet with *value.*

### REJECT

Drop the packet and, if appropriate, send an ICMP message back to the sender indicating the packet was dropped. If the packet was an ICMP error message, an unknown ICMP type, or a nonhead fragment, or if too many ICMP messages have already been sent to this address, no message is sent.

--reject-with *type*
> Send the specified ICMP message type. Valid values are **icmp-net-unreachable**, **icmp-host-unreachable**, **icmp-port-unreachable**, or **icmp-proto-**

→

unreachable. If the packet was an ICMP ping packet, *type* may also be **echo-reply**.

## TOS

Set the Type of Service field in the IP header. **TOS** is a valid target only for rules in the **mangle** table.

**--set-tos** *value*

Set the TOS field to *value*. You can specify this as an 8-bit value or as a TOS name. You can get a list of valid names using **iptables –j TOS –h**.

## SNAT

Modify the source address of the packet and all future packets in the current connection. **SNAT** is valid only as a part of the **POSTROUTING** chain in the **nat** table.

**--to-source** *address[– address][port–port]*

Specify the new source address or range of addresses. If a **tcp** or **udp** protocol has been specified with the **–p** option, source ports may also be specified. If none is specified, map the new source to the same port if possible. If not, map ports below 512 to other ports below 512, those between 512 and 1024 to other ports below 1024, and ports above 1024 to other ports above 1024.

## DNAT

Modify the destination address of the packet and all future packets in the current connection. **DNAT** is valid only as a part of the **POSTROUTING** chain in the **nat** table.

**--to-destination** *address[– address][port–port]*

Specify the new destination address or range of addresses. The arguments for this option are the same as the **--to-source** argument for the **SNAT** extension target.

## MASQUERADE

Masquerade the packet so it appears that it originated from the current system. Reverse packets from masqueraded connections are unmasqueraded automatically. This is a legal target only for chains in the *nat* table that handle incoming packets and should be used only with dynamic IP addresses (like dial-up.) For static addresses use **DNAT**.

**--to-ports** *port[–port]*

Specify the port or range of ports to use when masquerading. This option is only valid if a **tcp** or udp protocol has been specified with the −p option. If this option is not used, the masqueraded packet's port will not be changed.

REDIRECT [−−to-port *port*]

Redirect the packet to a local *port*. This is useful for creating transparent proxies.

−−to-ports *port*[-*port*]

Specify the port or range of ports on the local system to which the packet should be redirected. This option is valid only if a **tcp** or **udp** protocol has been specified with the −p option. If this option is not used, the redirected packet's port will not be changed.

---

**iptables-restore** [*file*]

System administration command. Restore firewall rules. **iptables-restore** takes commands generated by **iptables-save** and uses them to restore the firewall rules for each chain. Often used by initialization scripts to restore firewall settings on boot. *file* is the name of a file whose contents were generated by **iptables-save**. If not specified, the command takes its input from stdin. This command was not completed at the time this book went to print. There may be options not listed here.

---

**iptables-save** [*chain*]

System administration command. Print the IP firewall rules currently stored in the kernel to stdout. If no *chain* is given, all chains will be printed. Output may be redirected to a file that can later be used by **iptables-restore** to restore the firewall. This command was not completed at the time this book went to print. There may be options not listed here.

---

**ispell** [*options*] [*files*]

Compare the words of one or more named *files* with the system dictionary. Display unrecognized words on the top of the screen, accompanied by possible correct spellings, and allow editing, via a series of commands.

→

**ispell**
←

*Options*

**−b**  Back up original file in *filename*.bak.

**−d** *file*
Search *file* instead of standard dictionary file.

**−m**  Suggest different root/affix combinations.

**−n**  Expect nroff or troff input file.

**−p** *file*
Search *file* instead of personal dictionary file.

**−t**  Expect TEX or LATEX input file.

**−w** *chars*
Consider *chars* to be legal, in addition to a−z and A−Z.

**−x**  Do not back up original file.

**−B**  Search for missing blanks (resulting in concatenated words) in addition to ordinary misspellings.

**−C**  Do not produce error messages in response to concatenated words.

**−L** *number*
Show *number* lines of context.

**−M**  List interactive commands at bottom of screen.

**−N**  Suppress printing of interactive commands.

**−P**  Do not attempt to suggest more root/affix combinations.

**−S**  Sort suggested replacements by likelihood that each is correct.

**−T** *type*
Expect all files to be formatted by *type*.

**−W** *n*
Never consider words that are *n* characters or less to be misspelled.

**−V**  Use hat notation (^L) to display control characters and M− to display characters with the high bit set.

*Interactive Commands*

**?**  Display help screen.

**space character**
Accept the word in this instance.

*number*
> Replace with suggested word that corresponds to *number*.

!*command*
> Invoke shell and execute *command* in it. Prompt before exiting.

a   Accept word as correctly spelled, but do not add it to personal dictionary.

i   Accept word and add it (capitalized, if so in file) to personal dictionary.

l   Search system dictionary for words.

q   Exit without saving.

r   Replace word.

u   Accept word and add lowercase version of it to personal dictionary.

x   Skip to the next file, saving changes.

^L   Redraw screen.

^Z   Suspend **ispell**.

---

## join [*options*] *file1 file2*

Join lines of two sorted files by matching on a common field. If either *file1* or *file2* is –, read from standard input.

### Options

−a *filenum*
> Print a line for each unpairable line in file *filenum*, in addition to the normal output.

−e *string*
> Replace missing input fields with *string*.

−i, −−ignore-case
> Ignore case differences when comparing keys.

−1 *fieldnum1*
> Join field in *file1* is *fieldnum1*. Default is the first field.

−2 *fieldnum2*
> Join field in *file2* is *fieldnum2*. Default is the first field.

→

| | |
|---|---|
| join<br>← | **-o** *fieldlist*<br>　Order the output fields according to *fieldlist*, where each entry in the list is in the form *filenum.fieldnum.* Entries are separated by commas or blanks.<br><br>**-t** *char*<br>　Specifies the field-separator character (default is white-space ).<br><br>**-v** *filenum*<br>　Print only unpairable lines from file *filenum.*<br><br>**--help**<br>　Print help message and then exit.<br><br>**--version**<br>　Print the version number and then exit. |
| **kbd_mode** | **kbd_mode** [*option*]<br><br>Print or set the current keyboard mode, which may be RAW, MEDIUMRAW, or XLATE.<br><br>*Options*<br><br>**-a**　Set mode to XLATE (ASCII mode).<br><br>**-k**　Set mode to MEDIUMRAW (keycode mode).<br><br>**-s**　Set mode to RAW (scancode mode).<br><br>**-u**　Set mode to UNICODE (UTF-8 mode). |
| **kbdrate** | **kbdrate** [*options*]<br><br>System administration command. Control the rate at which the keyboard repeats characters, as well as its delay time. Using this command without options sets a repeat rate of 10.9 characters per second; the default delay is 250 milliseconds. When Linux boots, however, it sets the keyboard rate to 30 characters per second.<br><br>*Options*<br><br>**-s**　Suppress printing of messages.<br><br>**-r** *rate*<br>　Specify the repeat rate, which must be one of the following numbers (all in characters per second): 2.0, 2.1, 2.3, 2.5, 2.7, 3.0, 3.3, 3.7, 4.0, 4.3, 4.6, 5.0, 5.5, 6.0, |

6.7, 7.5, 8.0, 8.6, 9.2, 10.0, 10.9, 12.0, 13.3, 15.0, 16.0, 17.1, 18.5, 20.0, 21.8, 24.0, 26.7, or 30.0.

**−d** *delay*

> Specify the delay, which must be one of the following (in milliseconds): 250, 500, 750, or 1000.

## kerneld

System administration command. **kerneld** automatically loads kernel modules when they are needed, thereby reducing kernel memory usage from unused loaded modules and replacing manual loading of modules with **modprobe** or **insmod**. If a module has not been used for more than one minute, **kerneld** automatically removes it.

**kerneld** comes with the modules-utilities package and is set up during kernel configuration; its functionality is provided by interactions between that package and the kernel. **kerneld** is aware of most common types of modules. When more than one possible module can be used for a device (such as a network driver), **kerneld** uses the configuration file */etc/conf.modules*, which contains path information and aliases for all loadable modules, to determine the correct module choice.

**kerneld** can also be used to implement dial-on-demand networking, such as SLIP or PPP connections. The network connection request can be processed by **kerneld** to load the proper modules and set up the connection to the server.

## kill [*option*] *IDs*

This is the **/bin/kill** command; there is also a shell command of the same name. Send a signal to terminate one or more process *IDs*. You must own the process or be a privileged user. If no signal is specified, TERM is sent.

### Options

**−l**   List all signals.

**−p**   Print the process ID of the named process, but don't send it a signal. To use this option, specify the full path (e.g., **/bin/kill −p**).

$\rightarrow$

| | |
|---|---|
| **kill** ← | *—signal* <br><br> The signal number (from */usr/include/sys/signal.h*) or name (from **kill** —l). With a signal number of 9 (HUP), the kill cannot be caught by the process; use this to kill a process that a plain **kill** doesn't terminate. The default is TERM. |
| **killall** | **killall** [*options*] *names* <br><br> Kill processes by command name. If more than one process is running the specified command, kill all of them. Treat command names that contain a / as files; kill all processes that are executing that file. <br><br> *Options* <br><br> *—signal* <br>      Send *signal* to process (default is TERM). *signal* may be a name or number. <br><br> **—e**   Require an exact match to kill very long names (i.e., longer than 15 characters). Normally, **killall** kills everything that matches within the first 15 characters. With —e, such entries are skipped. (Use —v to print a message for each skipped entry.) <br><br> **—g**   Kill the process group to which the process belongs. <br><br> **—i**   Prompt for confirmation before killing processes. <br><br> **—l**   List known signal names. <br><br> **—q**   Quiet; do not complain of processes not killed. <br><br> **—v**   Verbose: after killing process, report success and process ID. <br><br> **—V**   Print version information. <br><br> **—w**   Wait for all killed processes to die. Note that **killall** may wait forever if the signal was ignored or had no effect, or if the process stays in zombie state. |

## killall5

The System V equivalent of **killall**, this command kills all processes except those on which it depends.

## klogd [*options*]

System administration command. Control which kernel messages are displayed on the console; prioritize all messages, and log them through **syslogd**. On many operating systems, **syslogd** performs all the work of **klogd**, but on Linux the features are separated. Kernel messages are gleaned from the */proc* filesystem and from system calls to **syslogd**. By default, no messages appear on the console. Messages are sorted into 8 levels, 0–7, and the level number is prepended to each message.

### Priority levels

0   Emergency situation (**KERN_EMERG**).

1   A crucial error has occurred (**KERN_ALERT**).

2   A serious error has occurred (**KERN_CRIT**).

3   An error has occurred (**KERN_ERR**).

4   A warning message (**KERN_WARNING**).

5   The situation is normal but should be checked (**KERN_NOTICE**).

6   Information only (**KERN_INFO**).

7   Debugging messages (**KERN_DEBUG**).

### Options

−c *level*
Print all messages of a higher priority (lower number) than *level* to the console.

−d   Debugging mode.

−f *file*
Print all messages to *file*; suppress normal logging.

−k *file*
Use *file* as source of kernel symbols.

−n   Avoid autobackgrounding. This is needed when **klogd** is started from **init**.

→

Linux
Commands

| klogd ← | **-o**   One-shot mode. Prioritize and log all current messages, then immediately exit. |
|---|---|

**-s**   Suppress reading of messages from the */proc* filesystem.

*Files*

*/usr/include/linux/kernel.h, /usr/include/sys/syslog.h*
   Sources for definitions of each logging level

*/proc/kmsg*
   A file examined by **klogd** for messages

*/var/run/klogd.pid*
   **klogd**'s process ID

---

**ksyms**

**ksyms** [*options*]

System administration command. Print a list of all exported kernel symbols (name, address, and defining module, if applicable).

*Options*

**-a**   Include symbols from unloaded modules.

**-h**   Suppress header message.

**-m**   Include starting address and size. Useful only for symbols in loaded modules.

*File*

*/proc/ksyms*
   Another source of the same information

---

**lastlog**

**lastlog** [*options*]

System administration command. Print the last login times for system accounts. Login information is read from the file */var/log/lastlog*.

*Options*

**-t***n*
   Print only logins more recent than *n* days ago.

**-u***name*
   Print only login information for user *name*.

**ld** [*options*] *objfiles*                                                  **ld**

Combine several *objfiles*, in the specified order, into a single
executable object module (*a.out* by default). **ld** is the link
editor and is often invoked automatically by compiler commands.

*Options*

−c *file*
> Consult *file* for commands.

−d, −dc, −dp
> Force the assignment of space to common symbols.

−defsym *symbol*=*expression*
> Create the global *symbol* with the value *expression*.

−e *symbol*
> Set *symbol* as the address of the output file's entry
> point.

−i  Produce a linkable output file; attempt to set its magic
> number to OMAGIC.

−l*arch*
> Include the archive file *arch* in the list of files to link.

−m *linker*
> Emulate *linker*.

−n  Make text read-only; attempt to set NMAGIC.

−noinhibit-exec
> Produce output file even if errors are encountered.

−o *output*
> Place output in *output*, instead of *a.out*.

−oformat *format*
> Specify output format.

−r  Produce a linkable output file; attempt to set its magic
> number to OMAGIC.

−s  Do not include any symbol information in output.

−shared
> Create a shared library.

−sort-common
> Do not sort global common symbols by size.

→

**−t**  Announce each input file's name as it is processed.

**−u** *symbol*
Force *symbol* to be undefined.

**−v, −−version**
Show version number.

**−−verbose**
Print information about **ld**; print the names of input files while attempting to open them.

**−warn-common**
Warn when encountering common symbols combined with other constructs.

**−warn-once**
Provide only one warning per undefined symbol.

**−x**  With −s or −S, delete all local symbols that begin with **L**.

**−L** *dir*
Search directory *dir* before standard search directories (this option must precede the −l option that searches that directory).

**−M**  Display a link map on standard out.

**−Map** *file*
Print a link map to *file*.

**−N**  Allow reading of and writing to both data and text; mark ouput if it supports Unix magic numbers; do not page-align data.

**−R** *file*
Obtain symbol names and addresses from *file*, but suppress relocation of *file* and its inclusion in output.

**−S**  Do not include debugger symbol information in output.

**−Tbss** *address*
Begin bss segment of output at *address*.

**−Tdata** *address*
Begin data segment of output at *address*.

**−Ttext** *address*
Begin text segment of output at *address*.

**−Ur**
Synonymous with −r except when linking C++ programs, where it resolves constructor references.

**−X**  With −s or −S, delete local symbols beginning with **L**.

**−V**  Show version number and emulation linkers for **−m** option.

---

**ldconfig** [*options*] *directories*

System administration command. Examine the libraries in the given *directories*, */etc/ld.so.conf*, */usr/lib*, and */lib*; update links and cache where necessary. Usually run in startup files or after the installation of new shared libraries.

*Options*

**−D**  Debug. Suppress all normal operations.

**−l**  Library mode. Expect libraries as arguments, not directories. Manually link specified libraries.

**−n**  Suppress examination of */usr/lib* and */lib* and reading of */etc/ld.so.conf*; do not cache.

**−N**  Do not cache; only link.

**−p**  Print all directories and candidate libraries in the cache. Expects no arguments.

**−v**  Verbose. Include version number, and announce each directory as it is scanned and links as they are created.

**−X**  Do not link; only rebuild cache.

*Files*

*/lib/ld.so*
> Linker and loader.

*/etc/ld.so.conf*
> List of directories that contain libraries.

*/etc/ld.so.cache*
> List of the libraries found in those libraries mentioned in */etc/ld.so.conf*.

| | |
|---|---|
| ldd | **ldd** [*options*] *programs* |
| | Display a list of the shared libraries each *program* requires. |
| | **Options** |
| | **−v**   Display **ldd**'s version. |
| | **−V**   Display the linker's version. |
| less | **less** [*options*] [*filename*] |
| | **less** is a program for paging through files or other output. It was written in reaction to the perceived primitiveness of **more** (hence its name). Some commands may be preceded by a number. |
| | **Options** |
| | **−[z]** *num* |
| | Set number of lines to scroll to *num*. Default is one screenful. A negative *num* sets the number to *num* lines less than the current number. |
| | **+[+]** *command* |
| | Run *command* on startup. If *command* is a number, jump to that line. The option ++ applies this command to each file in the command-line list. |
| | **−?**   Print help screen. Ignore all other options; do not page through file. |
| | **−a**   When searching, begin after last line displayed. (Default is to search from second line displayed.) |
| | **−b** *buffers* |
| | Use *buffers* buffers for each file (default is 10). Buffers are 1 kilobyte in size. |
| | **−c**   Redraw screen from top, not bottom. |
| | **−d**   Suppress dumb-terminal error messages. |
| | **−e**   Automatically exit after reaching EOF twice. |
| | **−f**   Force opening of directories and devices; do not print warning when opening binaries. |
| | **−g**   Highlight only string found by past search command, not all matching strings. |

**–h***num*
>    Never scroll backward more than *num* lines at once.

**–i**    Make searches case-insensitive, unless the search string contains uppercase letters.

**–j***num*
>    Position target line on line *num* of screen. Target line can be the result of a search or a jump. Count lines beginning from 1 (top line). A negative *num* is counted back from bottom of screen.

**–k***file*
>    Read *file* to define special key bindings.

**–m**    Display **more**-like prompt, including percent of file read.

**–n**    Do not calculate line numbers. Affects **–m** and **–M** options and = and **v** commands (disables passing of line number to editor).

**–o***file*
>    When input is from a pipe, copy output to *file* as well as to screen. (Prompt for overwrite authority if *file* exists.)

**–p***pattern*
>    At startup, search for first occurrence of *pattern*.

>    **m**    Set medium prompt (specified by **–m**).

>    **M**    Set long prompt (specified by **–M**).

>    **=**    Set message printed by = command.

**–q**    Disable ringing of bell on attempts to scroll past EOF or before beginning of file. Attempt to use visual bell instead.

**–r**    Display "raw" control characters, instead of using ^*x* notation. Sometimes leads to display problems.

**–s**    Print successive blank lines as one line.

**–t***tag*
>    Edit file containing *tag*. Consult *./tags* (constructed by **ctags**).

**–u**    Treat backspaces and carriage returns as printable input.

$\rightarrow$

**−w**  Print lines after EOF as blanks instead of tildes (˜).

**−x***n*
     Set tab stops to every *n* characters. Default is 8.

**−y***n*
     Never scroll forward more than *n* lines at once.

**−B**  Do not automatically allocate buffers for data read from a pipe. If **−b** specifies a number of buffers, allocate that many. If necessary, allow information from previous screens to be lost.

**−C**  Redraw screen by clearing it and then redrawing from top.

**−E**  Automatically exit after reaching EOF once.

**−G**  Never highlight matching search strings.

**−I**  Make searches case-insensitive, even when the search string contains uppercase letters.

**−M**  Prompt more verbosely than with **−m**, including percentage, line number, and total lines.

**−N**  Print line number before each line.

**−O***file*
     Similar to **−o** but does not prompt when overwriting file.

**−P**[m,M,=]*prompt*
     Set *prompt* (as defined by **−m**, **−M**, or **=**). Default is short prompt (**−m**).

**−Q**  Never ring terminal bell.

**−S**  Cut, do not fold, long lines.

**−T***file*
     With the **−t** option or **:t** command, read *file* instead of *./tags*.

**−U**  Treat backspaces and carriage returns as control characters.

**−X**  Do not send initialization and deinitialization strings from termcap to terminal.

### Commands

Many commands can be preceded by a numeric argument, referred to as *number* in the command descriptions.

**SPACE, ^V, f, ^F**
> Scroll forward the default number of lines (usually one windowful).

**z**   Similar to SPACE but allows the number of lines to be specified, in which case it resets the default to that number.

**RETURN, ^N, e, ^E, j, ^J**
> Scroll forward. Default is one line. Display all lines, even if the default is more lines than the screen size.

**d, ^D**
> Scroll forward. Default is one-half the screen size. The number of lines may be specified, in which case the default is reset.

**b, ^B, ESC-v**
> Scroll backward. Default is one windowful.

**w**   Like **b** but allows the number of lines to be specified, in which case it resets the default to that number.

**y, ^Y, ^P, k, ^K**
> Scroll backward. Default is one line. Display all lines, even if the default is more lines than the screen size.

**u, ^U**
> Scroll backward. Default is one-half the screen size. The number of lines may be specified, in which case the default is reset.

**r, ^R, ^L**
> Redraw screen.

**R**   Like **r** but discard buffered input.

**F**   Scroll forward. When an EOF is reached, continue trying to find more output, behaving similarly to **tail −f**.

**g, <, ESC-<**
> Skip to a line. Default is 1.

**G, >, ESC->**
> Skip to a line. Default is the last one.

**p, %**
> Skip to a position *number* percent of the way into the file.

**{**   If the top line on the screen includes a {, find its matching }. If the top line contains multiple {s, use *number* to determine which one to use in finding a match.

→

} If the bottom line on the screen includes a }, find its matching {. If the bottom line contains multiple }s, use *number* to determine which one to use in finding a match.

( If the top line on the screen includes a (, find its matching ). If the top line contains multiple (s, use *number* to determine which one to use in finding a match.

) If the bottom line on the screen includes a ), find its matching (. If the bottom line contains multiple )s, use *number* to determine which one to use in finding a match.

[ If the top line on the screen includes a [, find its matching ]. If the top line contains multiple [s, use *number* to determine which one to use in finding a match.

] If the bottom line on the screen includes a ], find its matching [. If the bottom line contains multiple ]s, use *number* to determine which one to use in finding a match.

**ESC-^F**

Behave like { but prompt for two characters, which it substitutes for { and } in its search.

**ESC-^B**

Behave like } but prompt for two characters, which it substitutes for { and } in its search.

**m** Prompt for a lowercase letter and then use that letter to mark the current position.

' Prompt for a lowercase letter and then go to the position marked by that letter. There are some special characters:

    ' Return to position before last "large movement."

    ^ Beginning of file.

    $ End of file.

**^X^X**

Same as '.

*/pattern*

Find next occurrence of *pattern*, starting at second line displayed. Some special characters can be entered before *pattern*:

!     Find lines that do not contain *pattern*.

*     If current file does not contain *pattern*, continue through the rest of the files in the command line list.

@     Search from the first line in the first file specified on the command line, no matter what the screen currently displays.

**?pattern**

Search backward, beginning at the line before the top line. Treats !, *, and @ as special characters when they begin *pattern*, as / does.

**ESC-/pattern**

Same as /*.

**ESC-?pattern**

Same as ?*.

**n**     Repeat last *pattern* search.

**N**     Repeat last *pattern* search, in the reverse direction.

**ESC-n**

Repeat previous search command but as though it were prefaced by *.

**ESC-N**

Repeat previous search command but as though it were prefaced by * and in the opposite direction.

**ESC-u**

Toggle search highlighting.

**:e** [*filename*]

Read in *filename* and insert it into the command-line list of filenames. Without *filename*, reread the current file. *filename* may contain special characters:

%     Name of current file

#     Name of previous file

**^X^V, E**

Same as :e.

**:n**     Read in next file in command-line list.

**:p**     Read in previous file in command-line list.

**:x**     Read in first file in command-line list.

→

:f, =, ^G

Print filename, position in command-line list, line number on top of window, total lines, byte number, and total bytes.

– Expects to be followed by a command-line option letter. Toggles the value of that option or, if appropriate, prompts for its new value.

–+ Expects to be followed by a command-line option letter. Resets that option to its default.

–– Expects to be followed by a command-line option letter. Resets that option to the opposite of its default, where the opposite can be determined.

_ Expects to be followed by a command-line option letter. Display that option's current setting.

+*command*

Execute *command* each time a new file is read in.

**q, :q, :Q, ZZ**

Exit.

v Not valid for all versions. Invoke editor specified by $VISUAL or $EDITOR, or **vi** if neither is set.

! [*command*]

Not valid for all versions. Invoke $SHELL or **sh**. If *command* is given, run it and then exit. Special characters:

% Name of current file

# Name of previous file

!! Last shell command

| *mark-letter* **command**

Not valid for all versions. Pipe fragment of file (from first line on screen to *mark-letter*) to *command. mark-letter* may also be:

^ Beginning of file.

$ End of file.

., **newline**

Current screen is piped.

*Prompts*

The prompt interprets certain sequences specially. Those beginning with % are always evaluated. Those beginning with ? are evaluated if certain conditions are true. Some prompts determine the position of particular lines on the screen. These sequences require that a method of determining that line be specified. See the **–P** option and the manpage for more information.

---

**ln** [*options*] *sourcename* [*destname*]
**ln** [*options*] *sourcenames destdirectory*

Create pseudonyms (links) for files, allowing them to be accessed by different names. In the first form, link *sourcename* to *destname*, where *destname* is usually a new filename, or (by default) the current directory. If *destname* is an existing file, it is overwritten; if *destname* is an existing directory, a link named *sourcename* is created in that directory. In the second form, create links in *destdirectory*, each link having the same name as the file specified.

### Options

**–b, ––backup**
  Back up files before removing the originals.

**–d, –F, ––directory**
  Allow hard links to directories. Available to privileged users.

**–f, ––force**
  Force the link (don't prompt for overwrite permission).

**––help**
  Print a help message and then exit.

**–i, ––interactive**
  Prompt for permission before removing files.

**–n, ––no-dereference**
  Replace symbolic links to directories instead of dereferencing them. **––force** is useful with this option.

**–s, ––symbolic**
  Create a symbolic link. This lets you link across filesystems and also see the name of the link when you run **ls** **–l** (otherwise, there's no way to know the name that a file is linked to).

**–S** *suffix*, **––suffix** *suffix*
  Append *suffix* to files when making backups, instead of the default ˜.

**–v, ––verbose**
  Verbose mode.

$\rightarrow$

*Linux
Commands*

| | |
|---|---|
| ln<br>← | **--version**<br>Print version information and then exit.<br><br>**-V, --version-control** *value*<br>Control the types of backups made. The acceptable values for version-control are:<br><br>**t, numbered**<br>Numbered.<br><br>**nil, existing**<br>Simple (˜) unless a numbered backup exists; then make a numbered backup.<br><br>**never, simple**<br>Simple. |
| locate | locate [*options*] *pattern*<br><br>Search database(s) of filenames and print matches. *, ?, [, and ] are treated specially; / and . are not. Matches include all files that contain *pattern*, unless *pattern* includes metacharacters, in which case **locate** requires an exact match.<br><br>*Options*<br><br>**-d** *path*, **--database=***path*<br>Search databases in *path*. *path* must be a colon-separated list.<br><br>**-h, --help**<br>Print a help message and then exit.<br><br>**--version**<br>Print version information and then exit. |
| **lockfile** | lockfile [*options*] *filenames*<br><br>Create semaphore file(s), used to limit access to a file. When **lockfile** fails to create some of the specified files, it pauses for 8 seconds and retries the last one on which it failed. The command processes flags as they are encountered (i.e., a flag that is specified after a file will not affect that file). |

*Options*

−*sleeptime*
> Time **lockfile** waits before retrying after a failed creation attempt. Default is 8 seconds.

−! Invert return value. Useful in shell scripts.

−l *lockout_time*
> Time (in seconds) after a lockfile was last modified at which it will be removed by force. See also **−s**.

−ml, −mu
> If the permissions on the system mail spool directory allow it or if **lockfile** is suitably setgid, it can lock and unlock your system mailbox with the options **−ml** and **−mu**, respectively.

−r *retries*
> Stop trying to create *files* after *retries* retries. The default is −1 (never stop trying). When giving up, remove all created files.

−s *suspend_time*
> After a lockfile has been removed by force (see **−l**), a suspension of 16 seconds takes place by default. (This is intended to prevent the inadvertent immediate removal of any lockfile newly created by another program.) Use **−s** to change the default 16 seconds.

**logger** [*options*] [*message* . . . ]

TCP/IP command. Add entries to the system log (via **syslogd**). A message can be given on the command line, or standard input is logged.

*Options*

−f *file*
> Read *message* from *file*.

−i Include the process ID of the **logger** process.

−p *pri*
> Enter message with the specified priority *pri*. Default is **user.notice**.

−t *tag*
> Mark every line in the log with the specified *tag*.

| | |
|---|---|
| login | **login** [*name* | *option*]<br><br>Log in to the system. **login** asks for a username (*name* can be supplied on the command line) and password (if appropriate).<br><br>If successful, **login** updates accounting files, sets various environment variables, notifies users if they have mail, and executes startup shell files.<br><br>Only the root user can log in when */etc/nologin* exists. That file is displayed before the connection is terminated. Furthermore, root may connect only on a tty that is listed in */etc/securetty*. If *˜/.hushlogin* exists, execute a quiet login. If */var/adm/lastlog* exists, print the time of the last login.<br><br>*Options*<br><br>**−f**   Suppress second login authentication.<br><br>**−h** *host*<br>        Specify name of remote host. Normally used by servers, not humans; may be used only by root.<br><br>**−p**   Preserve previous environment. |
| logname | **logname** [*option*]<br><br>Consult */var/run/utmp* for user's login name. If found, print it; otherwise, exit with an error message.<br><br>*Options*<br><br>**−−help**<br>        Print a help message and then exit.<br><br>**−−version**<br>        Print version information and then exit. |
| logrotate | **logrotate** [*options*] *config_files*<br><br>System administration command. Manipulate log files according to commands given in *config_files*.<br><br>*Options*<br><br>**−d**   Debug mode. No changes will be made to log files. |

**−s, −−state** *file*
> Save state information in *file*. The default is */var/lib/ logrotate.status*.

**−−usage**
> Usage version and copyright information.

### Commands

**compress**
> Compress old versions of log files with **gzip**.

**copytruncate**
> Copy log file, then truncate it in place. For use with programs whose logging cannot be temporarily halted.

**create** [*permissions*] [*owner*] [*group*]
> After rotation, re-create log file with the specified *permissions, owner,* and *group. permissions* must be in octal. If any of these parameters is missing, the log file's original attributes will be used.

**daily**
> Rotate log files every day.

**delaycompress**
> Don't compress log file until the next rotation.

**errors** *address*
> Mail any errors to the given *address*.

**endscript**
> End a **postrotate** or **prerotate** script.

**ifempty**
> Rotate log file even if it is empty. Overrides the default **notifempty** option.

**include** *file*
> Read the *file* into current file. If *file* is a directory, read all files in that directory into the current file.

**mail** *address*
> Mail any deleted logs to *address*.

**monthly**
> Rotate log files only the first time **logrotate** is run in a month.

**nocompress**
> Override **compress**.

$\rightarrow$

| | |
|---|---|
| **logrotate**<br>← | **nocopytruncate**<br>Override **copytruncate**. |

**nocreate**
Override **create**.

**nodelaycompress**
Override **delaycompress**.

**noolddir**
Override **olddir**.

**notifempty**
Override **ifempty**.

**olddir** *directory*
Move logs into *directory* for rotation. *directory* must be on the same physical device as the original log files.

**postrotate**
Begin a script of directives to apply after the log file is rotated. The script ends when the **endscript** directive is read.

**prerotate**
Begin a script of directives to apply before a log file is rotated. The script ends when the **endscript** directive is read.

**rotate** *number*
The *number* of times to rotate a log file before removing it.

**size** *n*[k | M]
Rotate log file when it is greater than *n* bytes. *n* can optionally be followed by **k** for kilobytes or **M** for megabytes.

---

**look**

look.[*options*] *string* [*file*]

Search for lines in *file* (*/usr/dict/words* by default) that begin with *string*.

*Options*

−**a**  Use alternate dictionary */usr/dict/web2*.

−**d**  Compare only alphanumeric characters.

−**f**  Search is not case-sensitive.

−t *character*
    Stop checking after the first occurrence of *character.*

---

**lpc** [*command*]

System administration command. Control line printer. If executed without a command, **lpc** will accept commands from standard input.

### Commands

**?, help** [*commands*]
    Get a list of commands or help on specific commands.

**abort all** | *printer*
    Terminate current printer daemon and disable printing for the specified *printer.*

**clean all** | *printer*
    Remove files that cannot be printed from the specified printer queues.

**disable all** | *printer*
    Disable specified printer queues.

**down all** | *printer message*
    Disable specified printer queues and put *message* in the printer status file.

**enable all** | *printer*
    Enable the specified printer queues.

**exit, quit**
    Exit **lpc.**

**restart all** | *printer*
    Try to restart printer daemons for the specified printers.

**start all** | *printer*
    Enable the printer queues and start printing daemons for the specified printers.

**status all** | *printer*
    Return the status of the specified printers.

**stop all** | *printer*
    Disable the specified printer daemons after any current jobs are completed.

**topq printer** [*jobnumbers*] [*users*]
    Put the specifed jobs at the top of the printer's queue in the order the jobs are listed.

→

| | |
|---|---|
| **lpc** ← | **up all**\|*printer* |
| | Enable print queues and restart daemons for the specified printers. |
| **lpd** | **lpd** [*option*] [*port*] |
| | TCP/IP command. Line printer daemon. **lpd** is usually invoked at boot time from the *rc2* file. It makes a single pass through the printer configuration file (traditionally */etc/printcap*) to find out about the existing printers and prints any files left after a crash. It then accepts requests to print files in a queue, transfer files to a spooling area, display a queue's status, or remove jobs from a queue. In each case, it forks a child process for each request, then continues to listen for subsequent requests. If *port* is specified, **lpd** listens on that port; otherwise, it uses the **getservbyname** call to ascertain the correct port. |
| | The file *lock* in each spool directory prevents multiple daemons from becoming active simultaneously. After the daemon has set the lock, it scans the directory for files beginning wth *cf*. Lines in each *cf* file specify files to be printed or nonprinting actions to be performed. Each line begins with a key character, which specifies information about the print job or what to do with the remainder of the line. Key characters are: |

C    Classification—string to be used for the classification line on the burst page.

c    **cifplot** file.

f    Formatted file—name of a file to print that is already formatted.

g    Graph file.

H    Hostname—name of machine where **lpd** was invoked.

J    Job name—string to be used for the jobname on the burst page.

L    Literal—this line contains identification information from the password file and causes the banner page to be printed.

l    Formatted file, but suppress page breaks and printing of control characters.

**M**    Mail—send mail to the specified user when the current print job completes.

**n**    **ditroff** file.

**P**    Person—login name of person who invoked **lpd**.

**r**    DVI file.

**T**    Title—string to be used as the title for **pr**.

**t**    **troff** file.

**U**    Unlink—name of file to remove upon completion of printing.

*Option*

−l    Enable logging of all valid requests.

*Files*

*/etc/printcap*
    Printer description file

*/var/spool/\**
    Spool directories

*/var/spool/\*/minfree*
    Minimum free space to leave

*/dev/lp\**
    Printer devices

*/etc/hosts.equiv*
    Machine names allowed printer access

*/etc/hosts.lpd*
    Machine names allowed printer access, but not under same administrative control

---

**lpq** [*options*] [*user*]

Check the print spool queue for status of print jobs. For each job, display username, rank in the queue, filenames, job number, and total file size (in bytes). If *user* is specified, display information only for that user.

*Options*

−l    Print information about each file comprising a job.

→

| | |
|---|---|
| lpq ← | **–P***printer*<br>Specify which printer to query. Without this option, **lpq** uses the printer set in the PRINTER environment variable or the default system printer.<br><br>*num*<br>Check status for job number *num*. |
| lpr | **lpr** [*options*] *files*<br><br>Send *files* to the printer spool queue.<br><br>***Options***<br><br>**–c**  Expect data produced by **cifplot**.<br><br>**–d**  Expect data produced by TEX in the DVI (device-independent) format.<br><br>**–f**  Use a filter that interprets the first character of each line as a standard carriage control character.<br><br>**–g**  Expect standard plot data as produced by the **plot** routines.<br><br>**–l**  Use a filter that allows control characters to be printed and suppresses page breaks.<br><br>**–n**  Expect data from **ditroff** (device-independent **troff**).<br><br>**–p**  Use **pr** to format the files.<br><br>**–t**  Expect data from **troff** (phototypesetter commands).<br><br>**–v**  Expect a raster image for devices like the Benson Varian.<br><br>**–P***printer*<br>Output to *printer* instead of the printer specified in the PRINTER environment variable or the system default.<br><br>**–h**  Do not print the burst page.<br><br>**–m**  Send mail to notify of completion.<br><br>**–r**  Remove the file upon completion of spooling. Cannot be used with the **–s** option.<br><br>**–s**  Use symbolic links instead of copying files to the spool directory. This can save time and disk space for large files. Files should not be modified or removed until they have been printed. |

**–#***num*
> Print *num* copies of each listed file.

**–C** *string*
> Replace system name on the burst page with *string*.

**–J** *name*
> Replace the job name on the burst page with *name*. If omitted, uses the first file's name.

**–T** *title*
> Use *title* as the title when using **pr**.

**–i** [*cols*]
> Indent the output. Default is 8 columns. Specify number of columns to indent with the *cols* argument.

**–w** *num*
> Set *num* characters as the page width for **pr**.

---

**lprm** [*options*] [*jobnum*] [*user*]

Remove a print job from the print spool queue. You must specify a job number or numbers, which can be obtained from **lpq**. A privileged user may use the *user* parameter to remove all files belonging to a particular user or users.

*Options*

**–P***printer*
> Specify printer name. Normally, the default printer or printer specified in the PRINTER environment variable is used.

**–**
> Remove all jobs in the spool owned by *user*.

---

**lpstat** [*options*]

Show the status of the print queue. With options that take a *list* argument, omitting the list produces all information for that option. *list* can be separated by commas or, if enclosed in double quotes, by spaces.

*Options*

**–a** [*list*]
> Show whether the *list* of printer or class names is accepting requests.

$\rightarrow$

| lpstat | -c [*list*] |
| --- | --- |
| ← |     Show information about printer classes named in *list*. |

-c [*list*]
    Show information about printer classes named in *list*.

-d   Show the default printer destination.

-f [*list*]
    Verify that the *list* of forms is known to **lp**.

-l   Use after -f to describe available forms, after -p to show printer configurations, or after -s to describe printers appropriate for the specified character set or print wheel.

-o [*list*]
    Show the status of output requests. *list* contains printer names, class names, or request IDs.

-p [*list*]
    Show the status of printers named in *list*.

-r   Show whether the print scheduler is on or off.

-R   Show the job's position in the print queue.

-s   Summarize the print status (shows almost everything).

-t   Show all status information (reports everything).

-u [*list*]
    Show request status for users on *list*. *list* can be **all** to show information on all users.

-v [*list*]
    Show device associated with each printer named in *list*.

---

**lptest**

**lptest** [*length*] [*count*]

Generate a lineprinter test pattern on standard output. Prints a standard ripple pattern of all printable ASCII characters, offset by one position on each succeeding line.

*Parameters*

*length*
    Specify the output line length (default is 79).

*count*
    Specify the number of lines to print (default is 200).

**ls** [*options*] [*names*]

List contents of directories. If no *names* are given, list the files in the current directory. With one or more *names*, list files contained in a directory *name* or that match a file *name. names* can include filename metacharacters. The options let you display a variety of information in different formats. The most useful options include −F, −R, −l, and −s. Some options don't make sense together (e.g., −u and −c).

*Options*

−1, −−format=single-column
Print one entry per line of output.

−a List all files, including the normally hidden files whose names begin with a period.

−b, −−escape
Display nonprinting characters in octal and alphabetic format.

−c, −−time-ctime, −−time=status
List files by status change time (not creation/modification time).

−−color, −−colour, −−color=yes, −−colour=yes
Colorize the names of files depending on the type of file.

−−color=no, −−colour=no
Disables colorization. This is the default. Provided to override a previous color option.

−−color=tty, −−colour=tty
Same as −−color, but only if standard output is a terminal. Very useful for shell scripts and command aliases, especially if your favorite pager does not support color control codes.

−d, −−directory
Report only on the directory, not its contents.

−f Print directory contents in exactly the order in which they are stored, without attempting to sort them.

−−full-time
List times in full, rather than use the standard abbreviations.

−−help
Print a help message and then exit.

→

**−i, −−inode**
List the inode for each file.

**−k, −−kilobytes**
If file sizes are being listed, print them in kilobytes. This option overrides the environment variable POSIXLY_CORRECT.

**−l, −−format=long, −−format=verbose**
Long format listing (includes permissions, owner, size, modification time, etc.).

**−m, −−format=commas**
Merge the list into a comma-separated series of names.

**−n, −−numeric-uid-gid**
Like −l, but use group-ID and user-ID numbers instead of owner and group names.

**−p**   Mark directories by appending / to them.

**−q, −−hide-control-chars**
Show nonprinting characters as **?**.

**−r, −−reverse**
List files in reverse order (by name or by time).

**−s, −−size**
Print size of the files in blocks.

**−t, −−sort=time**
Sort files according to modification time (newest first).

**−u, −−time=atime, −−time=access, −−time=use**
Sort files according to the file access time.

**−−version**
Print version information on standard output, then exit.

**−x, −−format=across, −−format=horizontal**
List files in rows going across the screen.

**−A, −−almost-all**
List all files, including the normally hidden files whose names begin with a period. Does not include the . and . directories.

**−B, −−ignore-backups**
Do not list files ending in ˜, unless given as arguments.

**−C, −−format=vertical**
List files in columns (the default format).

**−F, −−classify**

Flag filenames by appending / to directories, * to executable files, @ to symbolic links, | to FIFOs, and = to sockets.

**−G, −−no-group**

In long format, do not display group name.

**−I, −−ignore** *pattern*

Do not list files whose names match the shell pattern *pattern*, unless they are given on the command line.

**−L, −−dereference**

List the file or directory referenced by a symbolic link rather than the link itself.

**−N, −−literal**

Do not list filenames.

**−Q, −−quote-name**

Quote filenames with "; quote nongraphic characters with alphabetic and octal backslash sequences.

**−R, −−recursive**

Recursively list subdirectories as well as the specified (or current) directory.

**−S, −−sort=size**

Sort by file size, largest to smallest.

**−T, −−tabsize** *n_cols*

Assume that each tabstop is *n_cols* columns wide. The default is 8.

**−U, −−sort=none**

Do not sort files. Similar to −f but display in long format.

**−X, −−sort=extension**

Sort by file extension.

### Examples

List all files in the current directory and their sizes; use multiple columns and mark special files:

```
ls -asCF
```

List the status of directories */bin* and */etc*:

```
ls -ld /bin /etc
```

List C source files in the current directory, the oldest first:

```
ls -rt *.c
```

$\rightarrow$

| | |
|---|---|
| ls<br>← | Count the nonhidden files in the current directory:<br><br>`ls | wc -l` |
| lsattr | **lsattr** [*options*] [*files*]<br><br>Print attributes of files on a Linux Second Extended File System. See also **chattr**.<br><br>*Options*<br><br>**−a**  List all files in specified directories.<br><br>**−d**  List directories' attributes, not the attributes of the contents.<br><br>**−R**  List directories and their contents recursively.<br><br>**−v**  List version of files.<br><br>**−V**  List version and then exit. |
| lsmod | **lsmod**<br><br>System administration command. List all loaded modules: their name, size (in 4KB units) and, if appropriate, a list of referring modules.<br><br>*File*<br><br>*/proc/modules*<br>    Source of the same information. |
| m4 | **m4** [*options*] [*macros*] [*files*]<br><br>Macro processor for C and other files.<br><br>*Options*<br><br>**−e, −−interactive**<br>    Operate interactively, ignoring interrupts.<br><br>**−d***flags*, **−−debug=***flags*<br>    Specify *flag*-level debugging.<br><br>**−l***n*, **−−arglength=***n*<br>    Specify the length of debugging output. |

−o *file*, −−error-output=*file*
> Place output in *file*. Despite the name, print error messages on standard error.

−p, −−prefix-built-ins
> Prepend **m4_** to all built-in macro names.

−s, −−synclines
> Insert **#line** directives for the C preprocessor.

−B*n*
> Set the size of the push-back and argument collection buffers to *n* (default is 4096).

−D*name*[=*value*], −−define=*name*[=*value*]
> Define *name* as *value* or, if *value* is not specified, define *name* as null.

−E, −−fatal-warnings
> Consider all warnings to be fatal, and exit after the first of them.

−F*file*, −−freeze-state *file*
> Record **m4**'s frozen state in *file*, for later reloading.

−G, −−traditional
> Behave like traditional **m4**, ignoring GNU extensions.

−H*n*, −−hashsize=*n*
> Set symbol-table hash array to *n* (default is 509).

−I*directory*, −−include=*directory*
> Search *directory* for include files.

−Q, −−quiet, −−silent
> Suppress warning messages.

−R*file*, −−reload-state *file*
> Load state from *file* before starting execution.

−U*name*, −−undefine=*name*
> Undefine *name*.

---

**mail** [*options*] [*users*]

Read mail or send mail to other *users*. The **mail** utility allows you to compose, send, receive, forward, and reply to mail. **mail** has two main modes: compose mode, in which you create a message, and command mode, in which you manage your mail.

While **mail** is a powerful utility, it can be tricky for a novice user. Most Linux distributions include **pine** and **elm**, which

$\rightarrow$

**mail**
←

are much easier to use.

This section presents **mail** commands, options, and files. To get you started, here are two of the most basic commands.

To enter interactive mail-reading mode, type:

`mail`

To begin writing a message to *user*, type:

`mail` *user*

Enter the text of the message, one line at a time, pressing Enter at the end of each line. To end the message, enter a single period (.) in the first column of a new line, and press Enter.

### Command-line options

**−b** *list*
  Set blind carbon copy field to comma-separated *list*.

**−c** *list*
  Set carbon copy field to comma-separated *list*.

**−d**  Print debugging information.

**−f** [*file*]
  Process contents of *file*, instead of */var/spool/mail/$user*. If *file* is omitted, process *mbox* in the user's home directory.

**−i**  Do not respond to tty interrupt signals.

**−n**  Do not consult */etc/mail.rc* when starting up.

**−p**  Read mail in POP mode.

**−s** *subject*
  Set subject to *subject*.

**−u**  Process contents of */var/spool/mail/$user*. Default.

**−v**  Verbose. Print information about mail delivery to standard out.

**−I**  Interactive—even when standard input has been redirected from the terminal.

**−N**  When printing a mail message or entering a mail folder, do not display message headers.

**−P**  Disable POP mode.

~!   Execute a shell escape from compose mode.

~?   List compose mode escapes.

~b *names*
    Add names to or edit the *Bcc:* header.

~c *names*
    Add names to or edit the *Cc:* header.

~d   Read in the *dead.letter* file.

~e   Invoke text editor.

~f *messages*
    Insert *messages* into message being composed.

~F *messages*
    Similar to ~f, but include message headers.

~h   Add to or change all the headers interactively.

~m *messages*
    Similar to ~f, but indent with a tab.

~M *messages*
    Similar to ~m, but include message headers.

~p   Print message header fields and message being sent.

~q   Abort current message composition.

~r *filename*
    Append file to current message.

~s *string*
    Change *Subject:* header to *string.*

~t *names*
    Add names to or edit the **To** list.

~v   Invoke editor specified with the VISUAL environment variable.

~| *command*
    Pipe message through *command.*

~: *mail-command*
    Execute *mail-command.*

~~ *string*
    Insert *string* in text of message, prefaced by a single tilde (~). If string contains a ~, it must be escaped with a \.

→

*Linux Commands*

**mail**
←

| Command-mode commands | |
|---|---|
| ? | List summary of commands (help screen). |
| ! | Execute a shell command. |
| – *num* | Print *num*th previous message; defaults to immediately previous. |
| alias (a) | Print or create alias lists. |
| alternates (alt) | Specify remote accounts on remote machines that are yours. Tell mail not to reply to them. |
| chdir (c) | **cd** to home or specified directory. |
| copy (co) | Similar to **save**, but do not mark message for deletion. |
| delete (d) | Delete message. |
| dp | Delete current message and display next one. |
| edit (e) | Edit message. |
| exit (ex, x) | Exit **mail** without updating folder. |
| file (fi) | Switch folders. |
| folder (fold) | Read messages saved in a file. Files can be: |
| | #         Previous |
| | %         System mailbox |
| | %*user*    *user*'s system mailbox |
| | &          *mbox* |
| | +*folder*   File in *folder* directory. |
| folders | List folders. |
| headers (h) | List message headers at current prompt. |
| headers+ (h+) | Move forward one window of headers. |
| headers– (h–) | Move back one window of headers. |
| help | Same as ?. |
| hold (ho) | Hold messages in system mailbox. |
| ignore | Append list of fields to ignored fields. |
| mail *user* (m) | Compose message to *user*. |
| mbox | Default. Move specified messages to *mbox* on exiting. |
| next (n) | Type next message or next message that matches argument. |
| preserve (pr) | Synonym for **hold**. |
| print [*list*] (p) | Display each message in *list*. |
| Print [*list*] (P) | Similar to **print**, but include header fields. |
| quit (q) | Exit **mail** and update folder. |
| reply (r) | Send mail to all on distribution list. |
| Reply (R) | Send mail to author only. |
| respond | Same as **reply**. |

| retain | Always include this list of header fields when printing messages. With no arguments, list retained fields. |
|---|---|
| save (s) | Save message to folder. |
| saveignore | Remove ignored fields when saving. |
| saveretain | Override **saveignore** to retain specified fields. |
| set (se) | Set or print **mail** options. |
| shell (sh) | Enter a new shell. |
| size | Print size of each specified message. |
| source | Read commands from specified file. |
| top | Print first few lines of each specified message. |
| type (t) | Same as **print**. |
| Type (T) | Same as **Print**. |
| unalias | Discard previously defined aliases. |
| undelete (u) | Restore deleted message. |
| unread (U) | Mark specified messages as unread. |
| unset (uns) | Unset **mail** options. |
| visual (v) | Edit message with editor specified by the VISUAL environment variable. |
| write (w) | Write message, without header, to file. |
| xit (x) | Same as **exit**. |
| z | Move **mail**'s attention to next windowful of text. Use **z–** to move it back. |

### *mail options*

These options are used inside of the *.mailrc* file. The syntax is **set** *option* or **unset** *option*.

| append | Append (do not prepend) messages to *mbox*. |
|---|---|
| ask | Prompt for subject. |
| askbcc | Prompt for blind carbon copy recipients. |
| askcc | Prompt for carbon copy recipients. |
| asksub | Prompt for **Subject** line. |
| autoprint | Print next message after a delete. |
| chron | Display messages in chronological order, most recent last. |
| debug | Same as **–d** on command line. |
| dot | Interpret a solitary . as an EOF. |
| folder | Define directory to hold mail folders. |
| hold | Keep message in system mailbox upon quitting. |

→

| mail ← | ignore | Ignore interrupt signals from terminal. Print them as @. |
|---|---|---|
| | ignoreeof | Do not treat ˆD as an EOF. |
| | metoo | Do not remove sender from groups when mailing to them. |
| | noheader | Same as −N on command line. |
| | nokerberos | Retrieve POP mail via POP3, not KPOP, protocol. |
| | nosave | Do not save aborted letters to *dead.letter*. |
| | pop-mail | Retrieve mail with POP3 protocol, and save it in *mbox.pop*. |
| | prompt | Set prompt to a different string. |
| | Replyall | Switch roles of **Reply** and **reply**. |
| | quiet | Do not print version at startup. |
| | searchheaders | When given the specifier */x:y*, expand all messages that contain the string *y* in the *x* header field. |
| | verbose | Same as −v on command line. |
| | verbose-pop | Display status while retrieving POP mail. |

*Special files*

| | *calendar* | Contains reminders that the operating system mails to you. |
|---|---|---|
| | *.maildelivery* | Mail delivery configuration file. |
| | *.mailrc* | Mail configuration file. |
| | *triplog* | Keeps track of your automatic response recipients. |
| | *tripnote* | Contains automatic message. |

| mailq | **mailq** [*option*] |
|---|---|
| | System administration command. List all messages in the **sendmail** mail queue. Equivalent to **sendmail −bp**. |
| | *Option* |
| | −v   Verbose mode. |

| mailstats | **mailstats** [*options*] |
|---|---|
| | System administration command. Display a formatted report of the current **sendmail** mail statistics. |

*Options*

−C *file*
> Use **sendmail** configuration file *file* instead of the default *sendmail.cf* file.

−f *file*
> Use **sendmail** statistics file *file* instead of the file specified in the **sendmail** configuration file.

−o  Don't show the name of the mailer in the report.

---

**make** [*options*] [*targets*] [*macro definitions*]

Update one or more *targets* according to dependency instructions in a description file in the current directory. By default, this file is called *makefile* or *Makefile*. Options, targets, and macro definitions can be in any order. Macros definitions are typed as:

`name=string`

For more information on **make**, see *Managing Projects with make* by Andrew Oram and Steve Talbott.

*Options*

−d, −−debug
> Print detailed debugging information.

−e, −−environment-overrides
> Override **makefile** macro definitions with environment variables.

−f *makefile*, −−file=*makefile*, −−makefile=*makefile*
> Use *makefile* as the description file; a filename of − denotes standard input.

−h, −−help
> Print options to **make** command.

−i, −−ignore-errors
> Ignore command error codes (same as **.IGNORE**).

−j [*jobs*], −−jobs [=*jobs*]
> Attempt to execute *jobs* jobs simultaneously, or, if no number is specified, as many jobs as possible.

−k, −−keep-going
> Abandon the current target when it fails, but keep working with unrelated targets.

→

**make**
←

−l [*load*], −−load-average [=*load*], −−max-load [=*load*]
Attempt to keep load below *load*, which should be a floating-point number. Used with −j.

−n, −−just-print, −−dry-run, −−recon
Print commands but don't execute (used for testing).

−o *file*, −−old-file=*file*, −−assume-old=*file*
Never remake *file* or cause other files to be remade on account of it.

−p, −−print-data-base
Print rules and variables in addition to normal execution.

−q, −−question
Query; return 0 if file is up-to-date; nonzero otherwise.

−r, −−no-built-in-rules
Do not use default rules.

−s, −−silent, −−quiet
Do not display command lines (same as .SILENT).

−t, −−touch
Touch the target files, without remaking them.

−v, −−version
Show version of **make**.

−w, −−print-directory
Display the current working directory before and after execution.

−−warn -undefined -variables
Print warning if a macro is used without being defined.

−C *directory*, −−directory *directory*
cd to *directory* before beginning **make** operations. A subsequent −C directive will cause **make** to attempt to cd into a directory relative to the current working directory.

−I *directory*, −−include-dir *directory*
Include *directory* in list of directories that contain included files.

−S, −−no-keep-going, −−stop
Cancel previous −k options. Useful in recursive **make**s.

−W *file*, −−what-if *file*, −−new-file *file*, −−assume-new *file*
Behave as though *file* has been recently updated.

Instructions in the description file are interpreted as single lines. If an instruction must span more than one input line, use a backslash (\) at the end of the line so that the next line is considered as a continuation. The description file may contain any of the following types of lines:

*Blank lines*

Blank lines are ignored.

*Comment lines*

A pound sign (#) can be used at the beginning of a line or anywhere in the middle. **make** ignores everything after the #.

*Dependency lines*

Depending on one or more targets, certain commands that follow will be executed. Possible formats include:

```
targets : dependencies
targets : dependencies ; command
```

Subsequent commands are executed if *dependency* files (the names of which may contain wildcards) do not exist or are newer than a target. If no prerequisites are supplied, then subsequent commands are *always* executed (whenever any of the targets are specified). No tab should precede any *targets*.

*Suffix rules*

These specify that files ending with the first suffix can be prerequisites for files ending with the second suffix (assuming the root filenames are the same). Either of these formats can be used:

```
.suffix.suffix:
.suffix:
```

The second form means that the root filename depends on the filename with the corresponding suffix.

*Commands*

Commands are grouped below the dependency line and are typed on lines that begin with a tab. If a command is preceded by a hyphen (−), **make** ignores any error returned. If a command is preceded by an at sign (@), the command line won't echo on the display (unless **make** is called with −n).

→

**make**
←

*macro definitions*

These have the following form:

```
name = string
```

or

```
define name
string
endef
```

Blank space is optional around the =.

*include statements*

Similar to the C include directive, these have the form:

```
include files
```

### Internal macros

**$?** The list of prerequisites that have been changed more recently than the current target. Can be used only in normal description file entries—not suffix rules.

**$@** The name of the current target, except in description file entries for making libraries, where it becomes the library name. Can be used both in normal description file entries and in suffix rules.

**$<** The name of the current prerequisite that has been modified more recently than the current target.

**$*** The name—without the suffix—of the current prerequisite that has been modified more recently than the current target. Can be used only in suffix rules.

**$%** The name of the corresponding .o file when the current target is a library module. Can be used both in normal description file entries and in suffix rules.

**$^** A space-separated list of all dependencies, with no duplications.

**$+** A space-separated list of all dependencies, including duplications.

### Pattern rules

These are a more general application of the idea behind suffix rules. If a target and a dependency both contain %, GNU **make** will substitute any part of an existing filename. For instance, the standard suffix rule:

```
$(cc) -o $@ $<
```

can be written as the following pattern rule:

```
%.o : %.c
$(cc) -o $@ $<
```

## Macro modifiers

**D**   The directory portion of any internal macro name except $?. Valid uses are:

```
$(*D)    $$(@D)    $(?D)    $(<D)
$(%D)    $(@D)     $(^D)
```

**F**   The file portion of any internal macro name except $?. Valid uses are:

```
$(*F)    $$(@F)    $(?F)    $(<F)
$(%F)    $(@F)     $(^F)
```

## Functions

**$(subst** *from*, *to*, *string***)**
Replace all occurrences of *from* with *to* in *string*.

**$(patsubst** *pattern*, *to*, *string***)**
Similar to **subst**, but treat % as a wildcard within *pattern*. Substitute *to* for any word in *string* that matches *pattern*.

**$(strip** *string***)**
Remove all extraneous whitespace.

**$(findstring** *substring*, *mainstring***)**
Return *substring* if it exists within *mainstring*; otherwise, return null.

**$(filter** *pattern*, *string***)**
Return those words in *string* that match at least one word in *pattern*. *pattern*s may include the wildcard %.

**$(filter-out** *pattern*, *string***)**
Remove those words in *string* that match at least one word in *pattern*. *pattern*s may include the wildcard %.

**$(sort** *list***)**
Return *list*, sorted in lexical order.

**$(dir** *list***)**
Return the directory part (everything up to the last slash) of each filename in *list*.

**$(notdir** *list***)**
Return the nondirectory part (everything after the last slash) of each filename in *list*.

→

**$(suffix** *list*)
> Return the suffix part (everything after the last period) of each filename in *list.*

**$(basename** *list*)
> Return everything but the suffix part (everything up to the last period) of each filename in *list.*

**$(addsuffix** *suffix,list*)
> Return each filename given in *list* with *suffix* appended.

**$(addprefix** *prefix,list*)
> Return each filename given in *list* with *prefix* prepended.

**$(join** *list1,list2*)
> Return a list formed by concatenating the two arguments, word by word (e.g., **$(join a b,.c .o)** becomes **a.c b.o**).

**$(word** *n,string*)
> Return the *n*th word of *string.*

**$(words** *string*)
> Return the number of words in *string.*

**$(firstword** *list*)
> Return the first word in the list *list.*

**$(wildcard** *pattern*)
> Return a list of existing files in the current directory that match *pattern.*

**$(origin** *variable*)
> Return one of the following strings that describes how *variable* was defined: **undefined**, **default**, **environment**, **environment override**, **file**, **command line**, **override**, or **automatic**.

**$(shell** *command*)
> Return the results of *command*. Any newlines in the result are to be converted to spaces. This function works similarly to backquotes in most shells.

***Macro string substitution***

**$(** *macro:s1=s2* )
> Evaluates to the current definition of **$(**macro**)**, after substituting the string *s2* for every occurrence of *s1* that occurs either immediately before a blank or tab or at the end of the macro definition.

*Special target names*

**.DEFAULT:**

Commands associated with this target are executed if **make** can't find any description file entries or suffix rules with which to build a requested target.

**.EXPORT_ALL_VARIABLES:**

If this target exists, export all macros to all child processes.

**.IGNORE:**

Ignore error codes. Same as the **–i** option.

**.PHONY:**

Always execute commands under a target, even if it is an existing, up-to-date file.

**.PRECIOUS:**

Files you specify for this target are not removed when you send a signal (such as an interrupt) that aborts **make** or when a command line in your description file returns an error.

**.SILENT:**

Execute commands, but do not echo them. Same as the **–s** option.

**.SUFFIXES:**

Suffixes associated with this target are meaningful in suffix rules. If no suffixes are listed, the existing list of suffix rules is effectively "turned off."

---

**makedbm** [*options*] *infile outfile*

NFS/NIS command. Make NIS **dbm** file. **makedbm** takes *infile* and converts it to a pair of files in **ndbm** format, namely *outfile.pag* and *outfile.dir*. Each line of the input file is converted to a single **dbm** record. All characters up to the first TAB or SPACE form the key, and the rest of the line is the data. If line ends with **\&**, the data for that record is continued on to the next line. It is left for the NIS clients to interpret #; **makedbm** does not treat it as a comment character. *infile* can be –, in which case the standard input is read.

**makedbm** generates a special entry with the key *yp_last_modified*, which is the date of infile (or the current time, if infile is –).

→

| | |
|---|---|
| **makedbm**<br>← | *Options* |

-b  Interdomain. Propagate a map to all servers using the interdomain name server **named**.

-d yp_*domain_name*
   Create a special entry with the key **yp_***domain_name*.

-i yp_*input_file*
   Create a special entry with the key **yp_***input_file*.

-l  Convert keys of the given map to lowercase.

-m yp_*master_name*
   Create a special entry with the key **yp_***master_name*. If no master hostname is specified, **yp_***master_name* is set to the local hostname.

-o yp_*output_file*
   Create a special entry with the key **yp_***output_name*.

-s  Secure map. Accept connections from secure NIS networks only.

-u dbm *filename*
   Undo a **dbm** file—print out a **dbm** file, one entry per line, with a single space separating keys from values.

*Example*

It is easy to write shell scripts to convert standard files such as */etc/passwd* to the key value form used by **makedbm**. For example, the **awk** program:

```
BEGIN { FS =":";OFS = "\t";}
{ print $1, $0}
```

takes the */etc/passwd* file and converts it to a form that can be read by **makedbm** to make the NIS file *passwd.byname*. That is, the key is a username and the value is the remaining line in the */etc/passwd* file.

---

**makemap**

**makemap** [*options*] *type name*

System administration command. Transfer from standard input to **sendmail**'s database maps. Input should be formatted as:

*key value*

You may comment lines with **#**, may substitute parameters with **%n**, and must escape literal % by entering it as **%%**. The *type* must be **dbm**, **btree**, or **hash**. The *name* is a filename to which **makemap** appends standard suffixes.

**−d** Allow duplicate entries. Valid only with **btree** type maps.

**−f** Suppress conversion of uppercase to lowercase.

**−N** Append a zero byte to each key.

**−o** Append to existing file instead of replacing it.

**−r** If some keys already exist, replace them. (By default, **makemap** will exit when encountering a duplicated key.)

**−s** Ignore safety checks.

**−v** Verbose mode.

---

**man** [*options*] [*section*] [*title*]

Display information from the online reference manuals. **man** locates and prints the named *title* from the designated reference *section*.

*Options*

**−7, −−ascii**
Expect a pure ASCII file, and format it for a 7-bit terminal or terminal emulator.

**−a, −−all**
Show all pages matching *title*.

**−b** Leave blank lines in output.

**−d, −−debug**
Display debugging information. Suppress actual printing of manual pages.

**−f, −−whatis**
Same as **whatis** command.

**−k, −−apropos**
Same as **apropos** command.

**−l, −−local-file**
Search local files, not system files, for manual pages. If i is given as *filename*, search standard input.

**−m** *systems*, **−−systems=***systems*
Search *systems'* manual pages. *systems* should be a comma-separated list.

→

**man**
←

−p *preprocessors*, −−preprocessor=*preprocessors*
Preprocess manual pages with *preprocessors* before turning them over to **nroff**, **troff**, or **groff**. Always runs **soelim** first.

−r *prompt*, −−prompt=*prompt*
Set prompt if **less** is used as pager.

−t, −−troff
Format the manual page with */usr/bin/groff -Tgv -man-doc*. Implied by −T and −Z.

−u, −−update
Perform a consistency check between manual page cache and filesystem.

−w, −−where, −−location
Print pathnames of entries on standard output.

−D, −−default
Reset all options to their defaults.

−L *locale*, −−locale=*locale*
Assume current locale to be *locale*; do not consult the **setlocale()** function.

−M *path*, −−manpath=*path*
Search for manual pages in *path*. Ignore −m option.

−P*pager*, −−pager=*pager*
Select paging program *pager* to display the entry.

−T *device*, −−troff-device[=*device*]
Format **groff** or **troff** output for *device*, such as **dvi**, **latin1**, **X75**, and **X100**.

−Z, −−ditroff
Do not allow postprocessing of manual page after **groff** has finished formatting it.

### Section names

Manual pages are divided into sections, depending on their intended audience:

1    Executable programs or shell commands

2    System calls (functions provided by the kernel)

3    Library calls (functions within system libraries)

4    Special files (usually found in */dev*)

5   File formats and conventions (e.g., */etc/passwd*)

6   Games

7   Macro packages and conventions

8   System administration commands (usually only for a privileged user)

9   Kernel routines (nonstandard)

---

## manpath [*options*]

Attempt to determine path to manual pages. Check $MAN-PATH first; if that is not set, consult */etc/man.conf*, user environment variables, and the current working directory. The **manpath** command is a symbolic link to **man**, but most of the options are ignored for **manpath**.

### Options

−d, −−debug
    Print debugging information.

−h   Print help message and then exit.

---

## merge [*options*] *file1 file2 file3*

Perform a three-way file merge. **merge** incorporates all changes that lead from *file2* to *file3* and puts the results into *file1*. **merge** is useful for combining separate changes to an original. Suppose *file2* is the original, and both *file1* and *file3* are modifications of *file2*. Then **merge** combines both changes. A conflict occurs if both *file1* and *file3* have changes in a common segment of lines. If a conflict is found, **merge** normally outputs a warning and puts brackets around the conflict, with lines preceded by <<<<<<< and >>>>>>>. A typical conflict looks like this:

```
<<<<<<< file1
relevant lines from file1
=======
relevant lines from file3
>>>>>>> file3
```

If there are conflicts, the user should edit the result and delete one of the alternatives.

| | |
|---|---|
| **merge**<br>← | **Options**<br><br>**−e**  Don't warn about conflicts.<br><br>**−p**  Send results to standard output instead of overwriting *file1*.<br><br>**−q**  Quiet; do not warn about conflicts.<br><br>**−A**  Output conflicts using the **−A** style of **diff3**. This merges all changes leading from *file2* to *file3* into *file1* and generates the most verbose output.<br><br>**−E**  Output conflict information in a less verbose style than **−A**; this is the default.<br><br>**−L** *label*<br>    Specify up to three labels to be used in place of the corresponding filenames in conflict reports. That is:<br><br>`merge -L x -L y -L z file_a file_b file_c`<br><br>    generates output that looks as if it came from *x*, *y*, and *z* instead of from *file_a*, *file_b*, and *file_c*.<br><br>**−V**  Print version number. |
| **mesg** | **mesg** [*option*]<br><br>Change the ability of other users to send **write** messages to your terminal. With no options, display the permission status.<br><br>**Options**<br><br>**n**    Forbid **write** messages.<br><br>**y**    Allow **write** messages (the default). |
| **mimencode** | **mimencode** [*options* ] [*filename* ] [−o *output_file* ]<br>**mimencode** [*options*] [*filename*] [-o *output_file*]<br><br>Translate to and from MIME encoding formats, the proposed standard for Internet multimedia mail formats. By default, **mimencode** reads standard input and sends a base64-encoded version of the input to standard output. |

**–b**  Use the (default) base64 encoding.

**–o** *output_file*
> Send output to the named file rather than to standard output.

**–p**  Translate decoded CRLF sequences into the local new-line convention during decoding and do the reverse during encoding; meaningful only when the default base64 encoding is in effect.

**–q**  Use the quoted-printable encoding instead of base64.

**–u**  Decode the standard input rather than encode it.

---

**mkdir** [*options*] *directories*                                            mkdir

Create one or more *directories*. You must have write permission in the parent directory in order to create a directory. See also **rmdir**. The default mode of the new directory is 0777, modified by the system or user's **umask**.

*Options*

**–m, ––mode** *mode*
> Set the access *mode* for new directories. See **chmod** for an explanation of acceptable formats for *mode*.

**–p, ––parents**
> Create intervening parent directories if they don't exist.

**––verbose**
> Print a message for each directory created.

**––help**
> Print help message and then exit.

**––version**
> Print version number and then exit.

*Examples*

Create a read-only directory named **personal**:

```
mkdir -m 444 personal
```

The following sequence:

```
mkdir work; cd work
mkdir junk; cd junk
mkdir questions; cd ../..
```

→

| | |
|---|---|
| mkdir<br>← | can be accomplished by typing this:<br><br>`mkdir -p work/junk/questions` |
| mke2fs | mke2fs [*options*] *device* [*blocks*]<br>mkfs.ext2 [*options*] *device* [*blocks*]<br><br>System administration command. Format *device* as a Linux Second Extended Filesystem. You may specify the number of blocks on the device or allow **mke2fs** to guess.<br><br>*Options*<br><br>−b *block-size*<br>    Specify block size in bytes.<br><br>−c  Scan *device* for bad blocks before execution.<br><br>−f *fragment-size*<br>    Specify fragment size in bytes.<br><br>−i *bytes-per-inode*<br>    Create an inode for each *bytes-per-inode* of space. *bytes-per-inode* must be 1024 or greater; it is 4096 by default.<br><br>−l *filename*<br>    Consult *filename* for a list of bad blocks.<br><br>−m *percentage*<br>    Reserve *percentage* percent of the blocks for use by privileged users.<br><br>−q  Quiet mode.<br><br>−v  Verbose mode.<br><br>−S  Write only superblock and group descriptors; suppress writing of inode table and block and inode bitmaps. Useful only when attempting to salvage damaged systems. |
| mkfs | mkfs [*options*] [*fs-options*] *filesys* [*blocks*]<br><br>System administration command. Construct a filesystem on a device (such as a hard disk partition). *filesys* is either the name of the device or the mountpoint. **mkfs** is actually a frontend that invokes the appropriate version of **mkfs** according to a filesystem type specified by the −t option. For example, a Linux Second Extended Filesystem uses **mkfs.ext2** (which is the same as **mke2fs**); MS-DOS |

filesystems use **mkfs.msdos**. *fs-options* are options specific to the filesystem type. *blocks* is the size of the filesystem in 1024-byte blocks.

*Options*

−V Produce verbose output, including all commands executed to create the specific filesystem.

−t *fs-type*
  Tells **mkfs** what type of filesystem to construct.

**filesystem-specific options**
  These options must follow generic options and not be combined with them. Most filesystem builders support these three options:

  −c Check for bad blocks on the device before building the filesystem.

  −l *file*
    Read the file *file* for the list of bad blocks on the device.

  −v Produce verbose ouput.

---

**mkfs.minix** [*options*] *device size*

System administration command. Creates a MINIX filesystem. See **mkfs**.

---

**mklost+found**

System administration command. Create a *lost+found* directory in the current working directory. Intended for Linux Second Extended Filesystems.

---

**mkraid** [*options*] *devices*

System administration command. Set up RAID array *devices* as defined in the */etc/raidtab* configuration file. **mkraid** can be used to initialize a new array or upgrade older RAID device arrays for the new kernel. Initialization will destroy any data on the disk devices used to create the array.

→

| | |
|---|---|
| **mkraid**<br>← | *Options*<br><br>−c *file*, −−configfile *file*<br>    Use *file* instead of */etc/raidtab*.<br><br>−f, −−force<br>    Initialize the devices used to create the RAID array even if they currently have data.<br><br>−h, −−help<br>    Print a usage message and then exit.<br><br>−o, −−upgrade<br>    Upgrade an older array to the current kernel's RAID version. Preserve data on the old array.<br><br>−V, −−version<br>    Print version information and then exit. |
| **mkswap** | **mkswap** [*option*] *device* [*size*]<br><br>System administration command. Create swap space on *device*. You may specify its *size* in blocks; each block is a page of about 4KB.<br><br>*Option*<br><br>−c  Check for bad blocks before creating the swap space. |
| **modprobe** | **modprobe** [*options*] [*modules*]<br><br>System administration command. With no options, attempt to load the specified module, as well as all modules on which it depends. If more than one module is specified, attempt to load further modules only if the previous module failed to load.<br><br>*Options*<br><br>−a  Load all listed modules, not just the first one.<br><br>−l [*pattern*]<br>    List all existing modules. This option may be combined with −t to specify a type of module, or you may include a *pattern* to search for.<br><br>−r  Remove the specified modules, as well as the modules on which they depend. |

−t *type*
> Load only a specific type of module. Consult */etc/ conf.modules* for the directories in which all modules of that type reside.

**Files**

*/etc/conf.modules*
> Information about modules: which ones depend on others, which directories correspond to particular types of modules.

*/sbin/insmod, /sbin/rmmod, /sbin/depmod*
> Programs that **modprobe** relies on.

---

more [*options*] [*files*]

Display the named *files* on a terminal, one screenful at a time. See **less** for an alternative to **more**. Some commands can be preceded by a number.

**Options**

+*num*
> Begin displaying at line number *num*.

−**num** *number*
> Set screen size to *number* lines.

+/*pattern*
> Begin displaying two lines before *pattern*.

−c  Repaint screen from top instead of scrolling.

−d  Display the prompt "Hit space to continue, Del to abort" in response to illegal commands; disable bell.

−f  Count logical rather than screen lines. Useful when long lines wrap past the width of the screen.

−l  Ignore form-feed (Ctrl-L) characters.

−p  Page through the file by clearing each window instead of scrolling. This is sometimes faster.

−r  Force display of control characters, in the form ^*x*.

−s  Squeeze; display multiple blank lines as one.

−u  Suppress underline characters.

→

**more**
←

## Commands

All commands in **more** are based on **vi** commands. An argument can precede many commands.

**SPACE**
Display next screen of text.

**z**     Display next *lines* of text, and redefine a screenful to *lines* lines. Default is one screenful.

**RETURN**
Display next *lines* of text, and redefine a screenful to *lines* lines. Default is one line.

**d, ˆD**
Scroll *lines* of text, and redefine scroll size to *lines* lines. Default is one line.

**q, Q, INTERRUPT**
Quit.

**s**     Skip forward one line of text.

**f**     Skip forward one screen of text.

**b, ˆB**
Skip backward one screen of text.

**'**     Return to point where previous search began.

**=**     Print number of current line.

*/pattern*
Search for *pattern*, skipping to *num*th occurrence if an argument is specified.

**n**     Repeat last search, skipping to *num*th occurrence if an argument is specified.

*!cmd, :!cmd*
Invoke shell and execute *cmd* in it.

**v**     Invoke **vi** editor on the file, at the current line.

**ˆL**    Redraw screen.

**:n**    Skip to next file.

**:p**    Skip to previous file.

**:f**    Print current filename and line number.

**.**     Reexecute previous command.

*Examples*

Page through *file* in "clear" mode, and display prompts:

**more -cd** `file`

Format *doc* to the screen, removing underlines:

**nroff doc | more -u**

View the manpage for the **grep** command; begin near the word "BUGS" and compress extra whitespace:

**man grep | more +/BUGS -s**

---

**mount** [*options*] [*special-device*] [*directory*]

System administration command. Mount a file structure. **mount** announces to the system that a removable file structure is present on *special-device*. The file structure is mounted on *directory*, which must already exist and should be empty; it then becomes the name of the root of the newly mounted file structure. If **mount** is invoked with no arguments, it displays the name of each mounted device, the directory on which it is mounted, whether the file structure is read-only, and the date it was mounted. Only a privileged user can use the **mount** command.

*Options*

−a  Mount all filesystems listed in */etc/fstab*. Note: this is the only option that cannot take a *special-device* or *node* argument.

−f  Fake mount. Go through the motions of checking the device and directory, but do not actually mount the filesystem.

−n  Do not record the mount in */etc/mtab*.

−o *option*
    Note: this is the only option to **mount** that requires a *special-device* or *node* argument. Qualify the mount with one of the specified *options*:

    **async**
        Read input and output to the device asynchronously.

    **auto**
        Allow mounting with the −a option.

→

**mount**
←

**defaults**

Use all options' default values (**async**, **auto**, **dev**, **exec**, **nouser**, **rw**, **suid**).

**dev**

Interpret any special devices that exist on the filesystem.

**exec**

Allow binaries to be executed.

**noauto**

Do not allow mounting via the −**a** option.

**nodev**

Do not interpret any special devices that exist on the filesystem.

**noexec**

Do not allow the execution of binaries on the filesystem.

**nosuid**

Do not acknowledge any **suid** or **sgid** bits.

**nouser**

Only privileged users will have access to the filesystem.

**remount**

Expect the filesystem to have already been mounted, and remount it.

**ro**    Allow read-only access to the filesystem.

**rw**    Allow read/write access to the filesystem.

**suid**

Acknowledge **suid** and **sgid** bits.

**sync**

Read input and output to the device synchronously.

**user**

Allow unprivileged users to mount the filesystem. Note that the defaults on such a system will be **nodev**, **noexec**, and **nosuid**, unless otherwise specified.

**check=relaxed|normal|strict**

Specify how strictly to regulate the integration of an MS-DOS filesystem when mounting it.

conv=binary|text|auto
> Specify method by which to convert files on MS-DOS and ISO 9660 filesystems.

**debug**
> Turn debugging on for MS-DOS and **ext2fs** filesystems.

**errors=continue|remount|ro|panic**
> Specify action to take when encountering an error. **ext2fs** filesystems only.

**−r**   Mount filesystem read-only.

**−t** *type*
> Specify the filesystem type. Possible values are: **minix**, **ext**, **ext2**, **xiafs**, **hpfs**, **msdos**, **umsdos**, **vfat**, **proc**, **nfs**, **iso9660**, **smbfs**, **ncpfs**, **affs**, **ufs**, **romfs**, **sysv**, **xenix**, and **coherent**. Note that **ext** and **xiafs** are valid only for kernels older than 2.1.21 and that **sysv** should be used instead of **xenix** and **coherent**.

**−v**   Display mount information verbosely.

**−w**   Mount filesystem read/write. This is the default.

*Files*

*/etc/fstab*
> List of filesystems to be mounted and options to use when mounting them.

*/etc/mtab*
> List of filesystems that are currently mounted and the options with which they were mounted.

---

rpc.mountd [*options*]

NFS/NIS command. NFS mount request server. **mountd** reads the file */etc/exports* to determine which filesystems are available for mounting by which machines. It also provides information as to what filesystems are mounted by which clients. See also **nfsd**.

*Options*

**−d, −−debug**
> Debug mode. Output all debugging information via **syslogd**.

| | |
|---|---|
| **mountd** <br> ← | **–f** *file*, **––exports-file** *file* <br>     Read the export permissions from *file* instead of */etc/ exports.* <br><br> **–n**, **––allow-non-root** <br>     Accept even those mount requests that enter via a non-reserved port. <br><br> **–p**, **––promiscuous** <br>     Accept requests from any host that sends them. <br><br> **–r**, **––re-export** <br>     Allow re-exportation of imported filesystems. <br><br> **–v**, **––version** <br>     Print the version number. <br><br> *File* <br><br> */etc/exports* <br>     Information about mount permissions. |
| **mv** | **mv** [*option*] *sources target* <br><br> Move or rename files and directories. The source (first column) and target (second column) determine the result (third column): |

| Source | Target | Result |
|---|---|---|
| File | *name* (nonexistent) | Rename file to *name.* |
| File | Existing file | Overwrite existing file with source file. |
| Directory | *name* (nonexistent) | Rename directory to *name.* |
| Directory | Existing directory | Move directory to be a subdirectory of existing directory. |
| One or more files | Existing directory | Move files to directory. |

*Options*

**–b**, **––backup**
    Back up files before removing.

–f, – –force

Force the move, even if *target* file exists; suppress messages about restricted access modes.

– –help

Print a help message and then exit.

–i, – –interactive

Query user before removing files.

–u, – –update

Do not remove a file or link if its modification date is the same as or newer than that of its replacement.

–v, – –verbose

Print the name of each file before moving it.

– –version

Print version information and then exit.

–S *suffix*, – –suffix=*suffix*

Override the SIMPLE_BACKUP_SUFFIX environment variable, which determines the suffix used for making simple backup files. If the suffix is not set either way, the default is a tilde (˜).

–V *value*, – –version-control=*value*

Override the VERSION_CONTROL environment variable, which determines the type of backups made. The acceptable values for version control are:

t, numbered
> Always make numbered backups.

nil, existing
> Make numbered backups of files that already have them, simple backups of the others. The default.

never, simple
> Always make simple backups.

---

named [*options*]

TCP/IP command. Internet domain name server. **named** is used by resolver libraries to provide access to the Internet distributed naming database. With no arguments, **named** reads */etc/named.boot* for any initial data and listens for queries on a privileged port. See RFC 1034 and RFC 1035 for more details.

There are several **named** binaries available at different Linux archives, displaying various behaviors. If your version

→

| named | doesn't behave like the one described here, never fear—it should have come with documentation. |
| :--- | :--- |
| ← | |

**Options**

**−d** *debuglevel*
> Print debugging information. *debuglevel* is a number indicating the level of messages printed.

**−p** *port*
> Use *port* as the port number. Default is 42.

[**−b**] *bootfile*
> File to use instead of *named.boot*. The **−b** is optional and allows you to specify a filename that begins with a leading dash.

**File**

*/etc/named.boot*
> Read when **named** starts up.

---

**namei**

**namei** [*options*] *pathname* [*pathname* . . .]

Follow a pathname until a terminal point is found (e.g., a file, directory, char device, etc.). If **namei** finds a symbolic link, it shows the link and starts following it, indenting the output to show the context. **namei** prints an informative message when the maximum number of symbolic links this system can have has been exceeded.

**Options**

**−m** Show the mode bits of each file type in the style of **ls**; for example: "rwxr-xr-x".

**−x** Show mountpoint directories with a **D**, rather than a **d**.

**File type characters**

For each line of output, **namei** prints the following characters to identify the file types found:

−  A regular file

?  An error of some kind

b  A block device

c  A character device

**d**  A directory

**f:**  The pathname **namei** is currently trying to resolve

**l**  A symbolic link (both the link and its contents are output)

**s**  A socket

---

**netdate** [*options*] [*protocol*] *hostname . . .*

TCP/IP command. Set the system time according to the time provided by one of the hosts in the list *hostname*. **netdate** tries to ascertain which host is the most reliable source. When run by an unprivileged user, **netdate** reports the current time, without attempting to set the system clock. You may specify the *protocol*—**udp** (the default) or **tcp**—once, or several times for various hosts.

*Options*

**−l** *time*

The most reliable host is chosen from the list by sorting the hosts into groups based on the times they return when questioned. The first host from the largest group is then polled a second time. The differences between its time and the local host's time on each poll are recorded. These two differences are then compared. If the gap between them is greater than *time* (the default is five seconds), the host is rejected as inaccurate.

**−v**  Display the groups into which hosts are sorted.

---

**netstat** [*options*]

TCP/IP command. Show network status. For all active sockets, print the protocol, the number of bytes waiting to be received, the number of bytes to be sent, the port number, the remote address and port, and the state of the socket.

*Options*

**−a**  Show the state of all sockets, not just active ones.

**−c**  Display information continuously, refreshing once every second.

→

| | |
|---|---|
| **netstat**<br>← | **−i** Include statistics for network devices. |
| | **−n** Show network addresses as numbers. |
| | **−o** Include additional information such as username. |
| | **−r** Show routing tables. |
| | **−t** List only TCP sockets. |
| | **−u** List only UDP sockets. |
| | **−v** Print the version number and exit. |
| | **−w** List only raw sockets. |
| | **−x** List only Unix domain sockets. |
| **newgrp** | **newgrp** [*group*]<br><br>Change user's group identification to the specified group. If no group is specified, change to the user's login group. The new group is then used for checking permissions. |
| **newusers** | **newusers** *file*<br><br>System administration command. Create or update system users from entries in *file*. Each line in *file* has the same format as an entry in */etc/passwd*, except passwords are unencrypted, and group IDs can be given as a name or number. During an update, the password age field is ignored if the user already exists in the */etc/shadow* password file. If a group name or ID does not already exist, it will be created. If a home directory does not exist, it will be created. |
| **nfsd** | **rpc.nfsd** [*options*]<br><br>System administration command. Daemon that starts the NFS server daemons that handle client filesystem requests. These daemons are user-level processes. The options are exactly the same as in **mountd**. |
| **nice** | **nice** [*option*] [*command* [*arguments*]]<br><br>Execute a *command* (with its *arguments*) with lower priority (i.e., be "nice" to other users). With no arguments, **nice** prints the default scheduling priority (niceness). If **nice** is a child process, it prints the parent process's scheduling prior- |

ity. Niceness has a range of −20 (highest priority) to 19 (lowest priority).

### Options

**−−help**
> Print a help message and then exit.

**−n** *adjustment,* **−***adjustment,* **−−adjustment=***adjustment*
> Run *command* with niceness incremented by *adjustment* (1–19); default is 10. A privileged user can raise priority by specifying a negative *adjustment* (e.g., −5).

**−−version**
> Print version information and then exit.

---

## nm [*options*] [*objfiles*]

Print the symbol table (name list) in alphabetical order for one or more object files. If no object files are specified, perform operations on *a.out.* Output includes each symbol's value, type, size, name, and so on. A key letter categorizing the symbol can also be displayed. If no object file is given, use *a.out.*

### Options

**−a, −−debug-syms**
> Print debugger symbols.

**−f** *format*
> Specify output format (**bsd, sysv,** or **posix**). Default is **bsd.**

**−g, −−extern-only**
> Print external symbols only.

**−n, -v, −−numeric-sort**
> Sort the external symbols by address.

**−p, −−no-sort**
> Don't sort the symbols at all.

**−r, −−reverse-sort**
> Sort in reverse, alphabetically or numerically.

**−−size-sort**
> Sort by size.

**−u, −−undefined-only**
> Report only the undefined symbols.

→

| | |
|---|---|
| nm<br>← | **−A, -o, −print-file-name**<br>Print input filenames before each symbol.<br><br>**−C, −−demangle**<br>Translate low-level symbol names into readable versions.<br><br>**−D, −−dynamic**<br>Print dynamic, not normal, symbols. Useful only when working with dynamic objects (some kinds of shared libraries, for example).<br><br>**−P, −−portability**<br>Same as **−f posix**.<br><br>**−V, −−version**<br>Print **nm**'s version number on standard error. |
| **nohup** | **nohup** *command* [*arguments*]<br><br>Run the named *command* with its optional command *arguments*, continuing to run it even after you log out (make *command* immune to hangups; i.e., **no hangup**). TTY output is appended to the file *nohup.out* by default. Modern shells preserve background commands by default; this command is necessary only in the original Bourne shell. |
| **nslookup** | **nslookup** [−*option* . . .] [*host_to_find* \| − [*server*]]<br><br>TCP/IP command. Query Internet domain name servers. **nslookup** has two modes: interactive and noninteractive. Interactive mode allows the user to query name servers for information about various hosts and domains or to print a list of hosts in a domain. It is entered either when no arguments are given (default name server will be used) or when the first argument is a hyphen and the second argument is the hostname or Internet address of a name server. Noninteractive mode is used to print just the name and requested information for a host or domain. It is used when the name of the host to be looked up is given as the first argument. Any of the *keyword=value* pairs listed under the interactive **set** command can be used as an option on the command line by prefacing the keyword with a −. The optional second argument specifies a name server.<br><br>*Options*<br><br>All of the options under the **set** interactive command can be entered on the command line, with the syntax |

−*keyword*[=*value*].

## Interactive commands

**exit**
Exit **nslookup**.

**finger** [*name*] [> | >>*filename*]
Connect with finger server on current host, optionally creating or appending to *filename*.

**help, ?**
Print a brief summary of commands.

*host* [*server*]
Look up information for *host* using the current default server or using *server* if specified.

**ls** −[ahd] *domain* [> | >>*filename*]
List information available for *domain*, optionally creating or appending to *filename*. The −a option lists aliases of hosts in the domain. −h lists CPU and operating system information for the domain. −d lists all contents of a zone transfer.

**lserver** *domain*
Change the default server to *domain*. Use the initial server to look up information about *domain*.

**root**
Change default server to the server for the root of the domain namespace.

**server** *domain*
Change the default server to *domain*. Use the current default server to look up information about *domain*.

**set** *keyword*[=*value*]
Change state information affecting the lookups. Valid keywords are:

**all** Print the current values of the frequently used options to **set**.

class= *name*
Set query class to IN (Internet), CHAOS, HESIOD, or ANY. Default is IN.

domain= *name*
Change default domain name to *name*.

**nslookup**
←

**[no]debug**
Turn debugging mode on or off.

**[no]d2**
Turn exhaustive debugging mode on or off.

**[no]defname**
Append default domain name to every lookup.

**[no]ignoretc**
Ignore truncate error.

**[no]recurse**
Tell name server to query or not query other servers if it does not have the information.

**[no]search**
With *defname*, search for each name in parent domains of current domain.

**[no]vc**
Always use a virtual circuit when sending requests to the server.

**port=***port*
Connect to name server using *port*.

**querytype=***value*
See **type=***value*.

**retry=***number*
Set number of retries to *number*.

**root=***host*
Change name of root server to *host*.

**srchlist=***domain*
Set search list to *domain*.

**timeout=***number*
Change timeout interval for waiting for a reply to *number* seconds.

**type=***value*
Change type of information returned from a query to one of:

| | |
|---|---|
| **A** | Host's Internet address |
| **ANY** | Any available information |
| **CNAME** | Canonical name for an alias |
| **HINFO** | Host CPU and operating system type |
| **MD** | Mail destination |

| | |
|---|---|
| **MG** | Mail group member |
| **MINFO** | Mailbox or mail list information |
| **MR** | Mail rename domain name |
| **MX** | Mail exchanger |
| **NS** | Nameserver for the named zone |
| **PTR** | Hostname or pointer to other information |
| **SOA** | Domain start-of-authority |
| **TXT** | Text information |
| **UINFO** | User information |
| **WKS** | Supported well-known services |

*view filename*
Sort and list output of previous **ls** command(s) with **more**.

---

**passwd** [*user*]

Create or change a password associated with a *user* name. Only the owner or a privileged user may change a password. Owners need not specify their *user* name.

---

**paste** [*options*] *files*

Merge corresponding lines of one or more *files* into tab-separated vertical columns. See also **cut**, **join**, and **pr**.

*Options*

**−**  Replace a filename with the standard input.

**−d***char*, **−−delimiters=***char*
Separate columns with *char* instead of a tab. Note: you can separate columns with different characters by supplying more than one *char*.

**−−help**
Print a help message and then exit.

**−−version**
Print version information and then exit.

**−s, −−serial**
Merge lines from one file at a time.

→

| paste | **Examples** |
| :--- | :--- |
| ← | Create a three-column *file* from files *x*, *y*, and *z*: |

```
paste x y z > file
```

List users in two columns:

```
who | paste - -
```

Merge each pair of lines into one line:

```
paste -s -d"\t\n" list
```

---

**patch**

patch [*options*] [*original* [*patchfile*]]

Apply the patches specified in *patchfile* to *original*. Replace the original with the new, patched version; move the original to *original.orig* or *original˜*.

**Options**

+ [*options*] [*original2*]
  Apply patches again, with different options or a different original file.

−b, −−backup
  Back up the original file.

−z *suffix*, −−suffix=*suffix*
  Back up the original file in *original.suffix*.

−B *prefix*, −−prefix=*prefix*
  Prepend *prefix* to the backup filename.

−c, −−context
  Interpret *patchfile* as a context diff.

−d *dir*, −−directory=*dir*
  cd to *directory* before beginning **patch** operations.

−D *string*, −−ifdef=*string*
  Mark all changes with:

```
#ifdef
string
#endif
```

−e, −−ed
  Treat the contents of *patchfile* as **ed** commands.

−E, −−remove-empty-files
  If **patch** creates any empty files, delete them.

**−f, −−force**

Force all changes, even those that look incorrect. Skip patches if the original file does not exist; force patches for files with the wrong version specified; assume patches are never reversed.

**−i** *file*, **−−input=***file*

Read patch from *file* instead of **stdin**.

**−t, −−batch**

Skip patches if the original file does not exist.

**−F** *num*, **−−fuzz=***num*

Specify the maximum number of lines that may be ignored (fuzzed over) when deciding where to install a hunk of code. The default is 2. Meaningful only with context diffs.

**−l, −−ignore-whitespace**

Ignore whitespace while pattern matching.

**−n, −−normal**

Interpret patch file as a normal diff.

**−N, −−forward**

Ignore patches that appear to be reversed or to have already been applied.

**−o** *file*, **−−output=***file*

Print output to *file*.

**−p**[*num*], **−−strip**[**=***num*]

Specify how much of preceding pathname to strip. A *num* of 0 strips everything, leaving just the filename. 1 strips the leading /; each higher number after that strips another directory from the left.

**−r** *file*, **−−reject-file=***file*

Place rejects (hunks of the patch file that **patch** fails to place within the original file) in *file*. Default is *original.rej*.

**−R, −−reverse**

Do a reverse patch: attempt to undo the damage done by patching with the old and new files reversed.

**−s, −−silent, −−quiet**

Suppress commentary.

**−u, −−unified**

Interpret patch file as a unified context diff.

→

| | |
|---|---|
| patch<br>← | **−V** *method*, **−−version-control=***method*<br>Specify method for creating backup files (overridden by **−B**):<br><br>**t, numbered**<br>Make numbered backups.<br><br>**nil, existing**<br>Back up files according to preexisting backup schemes, with simple backups as the default. This is **patch**'s default behavior.<br><br>**never, simple**<br>Make simple backups.<br><br>*Environment variables*<br><br>**TMPDIR**<br>Specify the directory for temporary files, */tmp* by default.<br><br>**SIMPLE_BACKUP_SUFFIX**<br>Suffix to append to backup files instead of *.orig* or ˜.<br><br>**VERSION_CONTROL**<br>Specify what method to use in naming backups (see **−V**). |
| pathchk | **pathchk** [ *option* ] *filenames*<br><br>Determine validity and portability of *filenames*. Specifically, determine if all directories within the path are searchable and if the length of the *filenames* is acceptable.<br><br>*Options*<br><br>**−p, −−portability**<br>Check portability for all POSIX systems.<br><br>**−−help**<br>Print a help message and then exit.<br><br>**−−version**<br>Print version information and then exit. |
| pcnfsd | **/usr/sbin/rpc.pcnfsd**<br><br>NFS/NIS command. NFS authentication and print request server. **pcnfsd** is an RPC server that supports ONC clients on PC systems. **pcnfsd** reads the configuration file */etc/* |

*pcnfsd.conf*, if present, then services RPC requests directed to program number 150001. This current release of the **pcnfsd** daemon (as of this printing) supports both Version 1 and Version 2 of the **pcnfsd** protocol. Requests serviced by **pcnfsd** fall into three categories: authentication, printing, and other. Only the authentication and printing services have administrative significance.

### Authentication

When **pcnfsd** receives a PCNFSD_AUTH or PCN-FSD2_AUTH request, it will log in the user by validating the username and password, returning the corresponding user ID, group IDs, home directory, and **umask**. At this time, **pcnfsd** will also append a record to the *wtmp* database. If you do not want to record PC logins in this way, add the line:

**wtmp off**

to the */etc/pcnfsd.conf* file.

### Printing

**pcnfsd** supports a printing model based on the use of NFS to transfer the actual print data from the client to the server. The client system issues a PCNFSD_PR_INIT or PCN-FSD2_PR_INIT request, and the server returns the path to a spool directory that the client may use and that is exported by NFS. **pcnfsd** creates a subdirectory for each of its clients; the parent directory is normally */usr/spool/pcnfs* and the subdirectory is the hostname of the client system. If you want to use a different parent directory, add the line:

**spooldir** *path*

to the */etc/pcnfsd.conf* file. Once a client has mounted the spool directory and has transferred print data to a file in this directory, **pcnfsd** will issue a PCNFSD_PR_START or PCN-FSD2_PR_START request. **pcnfsd** constructs a command based on the printing services of the server operating system and executes the command using the identity of the PC user. Every print request includes the name of the printer to be used. **pcnfsd** interprets a printer as either a destination serviced by the system print spooler or as a virtual printer. Virtual printers are defined by the following line in the */etc/pcnfsd.conf* file:

**printer** *name alias-for command*

where *name* is the name of the printer you want to define, *alias-for* is the name of a real printer that corresponds to

→

| | |
|---|---|
| pcnfsd<br>← | this printer, and *command* is a command that will be executed whenever a file is printed on *name*. |
| perl | **perl**<br><br>A powerful text-processing language that combines many of the most useful features of shell programs, C, **awk**, and **sed**, as well as adding extended features of its own. For more information, see *Learning Perl* by Randal L. Schwartz and *Programming Perl*, 2d ed., by Larry Wall, Tom Christiansen, and Randal L. Schwartz. |
| pidof | **pidof** [*options*] *programs*<br><br>Display the process IDs of the listed program or programs. **pidof** is actually a symbolic link to **killall5**.<br><br>*Options*<br><br>−o *pids*<br>    Omit all processes with the specified process ID. You may list several process IDs.<br><br>−s  Return a single process ID.<br><br>−x  Also return process IDs of shells running the named scripts. |
| ping | **ping** [*options*] *host*<br><br>System administration command. Confirm that a remote host is online and responding. **ping** is intended for use in network testing, measurement, and management. Because of the load it can impose on the network, it is unwise to use **ping** during normal operations or from automated scripts.<br><br>*Options*<br><br>−c *count*<br>    Stop after sending (and receiving) *count* ECHO_RESPONSE packets.<br><br>−d  Set SO_DEBUG option on socket being used.<br><br>−f  Flood **ping**-output packets as fast as they come back or 100 times per second, whichever is more. This can be very hard on a network and should be used with caution; only a privileged user may use this option. |

−i *wait*

 Wait *wait* seconds between sending each packet. Default is to wait 1 second between each packet. This option is incompatible with the −f option.

−l *preload*

 Send *preload* number of packets as fast as possible before falling into normal mode of behavior.

−n Numeric output only. No attempt will be made to look up symbolic names for host addresses.

−p *digits*

 Specify up to 16 pad bytes to fill out packet sent. This is useful for diagnosing data-dependent problems in a network. *digits* are in hex. For example, −p ff will cause the sent packet to be filled with all 1s.

−q Quiet output—nothing is displayed except the summary lines at startup time and when finished.

−r Bypass the normal routing tables and send directly to a host on an attached network.

−s *packetsize*

 Specify number of data bytes to be sent. Default is 56, which translates into 64 ICMP data bytes when combined with the 8 bytes of ICMP header data.

−v Verbose—list ICMP packets received other than ECHO_RESPONSE.

−R Set the IP record route option, which will store the route of the packet inside the IP header. The contents of the record route will be printed if the −v option is given, and will be set on return packets if the target host preserves the record route option across echoes or the −l option is given.

## in.pop2d

System administration command. Allow users to connect to port 109 and request the contents of their mailbox in */var/spool/mail*. **pop2d** requires a username and password before providing mail and can serve individual messages. See also **pop3d**.

### Commands

Each command must be entered on a separate line.

→

| pop2d | **HELO** |
| ← | Prompt for username and password. |
| | **FOLD** |
| | Open */var/spool/mail/$USER*. |
| | **HOST** |
| | Open */var/spool/pop/$USER*. |
| | **READ** |
| | Read a message. |
| | **RETR** |
| | Retrieve a message. |
| | **ACKS** |
| | Save the last message retrieved and move to next message. |
| | **ACKD** |
| | Delete the last message retrieved and move to next message. |
| | **NACK** |
| | Save the last message retrieved and expect to resend it. |
| | **QUIT** |
| | Exit. |

| pop3d | **in.pop3d** |
| | System administration command. **pop3d** is a more recent version of **pop2d**. It behaves similarly but accepts a slightly different list of commands. |
| | *Commands* |
| | **USER** |
| | Prompt for name. |
| | **PASS** |
| | Prompt for password. |
| | **STAT** |
| | Display the number of messages in the mailbox and its total size. |
| | **LIST** |
| | Display individual messages' sizes. |

## DELE

Delete a message.

## NOOP

Perform a null operation.

## LAST

Print the number of the most recently received message that has been read.

## RSET

Reset: clear all deletion marks.

## TOP

Print the first part of a message.

## QUIT

Exit.

---

## rpc.portmap [*option*]

NFS/NIS command. RPC program number to IP port mapper. **portmap** is a server that converts RPC program numbers to IP port numbers. It must be running in order to make RPC calls. When an RPC server is started, it tells **portmap** what port number it is listening to and what RPC program numbers it is prepared to serve. When a client wishes to make an RPC call to a given program number, it first contacts **portmap** on the server machine to determine the port number where RPC packets should be sent. **portmap** must be the first RPC server started.

### *Option*

−d  Run **portmap** in debugging mode. Does not allow **portmap** to run as a daemon.

---

## powerd *device*

System administration command. Monitor the connection to an uninterruptible power supply, which the user must specify via *device*. When power goes low, signal **init** to run its **powerwait** and **powerfail** entries; when full power is restored, signal **init** to run its **powerokwait** entries.

**pppd**

**pppd** [*options*] [*tty*] [*speed*]

System administration command. PPP stands for the Point-to-Point Protocol; it allows datagram transmission over a serial connection. **pppd** attempts to configure *tty* for PPP (searching in */dev*) or, by default, the controlling terminal. You can also specify a baud rate of *speed*.

*Options*

**asyncmap** *map*

Specify which control characters cannot pass over the line. *map* should be a 32-bit hex number, where each bit represents a character to escape. For example, bit 00000001 represents the character 0x00; bit 80000000 represents the character 0x1f or _. You may specify multiple characters.

**auth**

Require self-authentication by peers before allowing packets to move.

**connect** *command*

Connect as specified by *command*, which may be a binary or shell command.

**debug, –d**

Increment the debugging level.

**defaultroute**

Add a new default route in which the peer is the gateway. When the connection shuts down, remove the route.

**–detach**

Operate in the foreground. By default, **pppd** forks and operates in the background.

**disconnect** *command*

Close the connection as specified by *command*, which may be a binary or shell command.

**domain** *d*

Specify a domain name of *d*.

**escape** *character-list*

Escape all characters in *character-list*, which should be a comma-separated list of hex numbers. You cannot escape 0x20–0x3f or 0x5e.

**file** *file*

    Consult *file* for options.

**lock**

    Allow only **pppd** to access the device.

**mru** *bytes*

    Refuse packets of more than *bytes* bytes.

**name** *name*

    Specify a machine name for the local system.

**netmask** *mask*

    Specify netmask (for example, 255.255.255.0).

**passive, −p**

    Do not exit if peer does not respond to attempts to initiate a connection. Instead, wait for a valid packet from the peer.

**silent**

    Send no packets until after receiving one.

[*local_IP_address*]:[*remote_IP_address*]

    Specify the local and/or remote interface IP addresses, as hostnames or numeric addresses.

### Files

*/var/run/pppn.pid*

    **pppd**'s process ID. The *n* in *pppn.pid* is the number of the PPP interface unit corresponding to this **pppd** process.

*/etc/ppp/ip-up*

    Binary or script to be executed when the PPP link becomes active.

*/etc/ppp/ip-down*

    Binary or script to be executed when the PPP link goes down.

*/etc/ppp/pap-secrets*

    Contains usernames, passwords, and IP addresses for use in PAP authentication.

*/etc/ppp/options*

    System defaults. Options in this file are set *before* the command-line options.

*~/.ppprc*

    The user's default options. These are read before command-line options but after the system defaults.

→

| | |
|---|---|
| **pppd**<br>← | */etc/ppp/options.ttyname*<br>    Name of the default serial port. |
| **pr** | **pr** [*files*]<br><br>Convert a text file or files to a paginated, columned version, with headers. If – is provided as the filename, read from standard input.<br><br>*Options*<br><br>+*beg_pag*[:*end-pag*], −−**pages**=[*beg_pag*[:*end-pag*]<br>    Begin printing on page *beg_pag* and end on *end-pag* if specified.<br><br>−*num_cols*, −−**columns**=*num_cols*<br>    Print in *num_cols* number of columns, balancing the number of lines in the columns on each page.<br><br>−**a**, −−**across**<br>    Print columns horizontally, not vertically.<br><br>−**c**, −−**show-control-chars**<br>    Convert control characters to hat notation (such as ^C) and other unprintable characters to octal backslash format.<br><br>−**d**, −−**double-space**<br>    Double space.<br><br>−**e**[*tab-char*[*width*]], −−**expand-tabs**=[*tab-char*[*width*]]<br>    Convert tabs (or *tab-chars*) to spaces. If *width* is specified, convert tabs to *width* characters (default is 8).<br><br>−**f**, −**F**, −−**form-feed**<br>    Separate pages with form feeds, not newlines.<br><br>−**h** *header*, −−**header**=*header*<br>    Use *header* for the header instead of the filename.<br><br>−**i**[*out-tab-char*[*out-tab-width*]],<br>    −−**output-tabs**[=*out-tab-char*[*out-tab-width*]]<br>    Replace spaces with tabs on output. Can specify alternative tab character (default is tab) and width (default is 8).<br><br>−**J**, −−**join-lines**<br>    Merge full lines; ignore −**W** if set. |

**−l** *lines*, **−−length=***lines*
> Set page length to *lines* (default 66). If *lines* is less than 10, omit headers and footers.

**−m, −−merge**
> Print all files, one file per column.

**−n[***delimiter*[*digits*]], **−−number-lines[=***delimiter*[*digits*]]
> Number columns, or, with the **−m** option, number lines. Append *delimiter* to each number (default is a tab) and limit the size of numbers to *digits* (default is 5).

**−o** *width*, **−−indent=***width*
> Set left margin to *width*.

**−r, −−no-file-warnings**
> Continue silently when unable to open an input file.

**−s[***delimiter*], **−−separator[=***delimiter*]
> Separate columns with *delimiter* (default is a tab) instead of spaces.

**−S[***string*], **−−sep-string[=***string*]
> Separate columns with *string*. Default is a tab with **−J** and a space otherwise.

**−t, −−omit-header**
> Suppress headers, footers, and fills at end of pages.

**−T, −−omit-pagination**
> Like **−t** but also suppress form feeds.

**−v, −−show-non-printing**
> Convert unprintable characters to octal backslash format.

**−w** *page_width*, **−−width=***page_width*
> Set the page width to *page_width* characters for multi-column output. Default is 72.

**−W** *page_width*, **−−page-width=***page_width*
> Set the page width to always be *page_width* characters. Default is 72.

**−−help**
> Print a help message and then exit.

**−−version**
> Print version information and then exit.

| | |
|---|---|
| praliases | **praliases** [*option*]<br><br>System administration command. **praliases** prints the current **sendmail** mail aliases. (Usually defined in the */etc/aliases* or */etc/aliases.db* file.)<br><br>*Option*<br><br>**−f** *file*<br>    Read the aliases from the specified file instead of send-mail's default alias files. |
| printenv | **printenv** [*variables*]<br><br>Print values of all environment variables or, optionally, only the specified *variables*. |
| printf | **printf** *formats* [*strings*]<br><br>Print *strings* using the specified *formats*. *formats* can be ordinary text characters, C-language escape characters, or more commonly, a set of conversion arguments listed here.<br><br>*Arguments*<br><br>**%s**  Print the next *string*.<br><br>**%*n*$s**<br>    Print the *n*th *string*.<br><br>**%[-]** *m*[.*n*]**s**<br>    Print the next *string*, using a field that is *m* characters wide. Optionally, limit the field to print only the first *n* characters of *string*. Strings are right-adjusted unless the left-adjustment flag, −, is specified.<br><br>*Examples*<br><br>```
printf '%s %s\n' "My files are in" $HOME
printf '%-25.15s %s\n' "My files are in" $HOME
``` |
| ps | **ps** [*options*]<br><br>Report on active processes. Note that you do not need to include a − before options. In options, *list* arguments should either be separated by commas or be put in double quotes. In comparing the amount of output produced, note that **e** prints more than **a** and **l** prints more than **f**. |
```

*pids*
> Include only specified processes, which are given in a comma-delimited list.

a    List all processes.

c    Consult **task_struct** for command name.

e    Include environment.

f    "Forest" family tree format.

h    Suppress header.

j    Jobs format.

l    Produce a long listing.

m    Memory format.

n    Print user IDs and WCHAN numerically.

r    Exclude processes that are not running.

s    Signal format.

−−sort*delimiter*[+ | −]*key*[,[+ | −]*key*[, . . .]]
> Similar to **O**, but designed to protect multiletter sort keys. See the later list, "Sort keys".

t*tty*  Display only processes running on *tty*.

u    Include username and start time.

v    **vm** format.

w    Wide format. Don't truncate long lines.

x    Include processes without an associated terminal.

O[+ | −]*key*[,[+ | −]*key*[, . . .]]
> Sort processes. (See the following list, "Sort keys.")

> +    Return key to default direction.

> −    Reverse default direction on key.

S    Include child processes' CPU time and page faults.

*Sort keys*

**c, cmd**
> Name of executable.

→

**C, cmdline**
> Whole command line.

**f, flags**
> Flags.

**g, pgrp**
> Group ID of process.

**G, tpgid**
> Group ID of associated tty.

**j, cutime**
> Cumulative user time.

**J, cstime**
> Cumulative system time.

**k, utime**
> User time.

**K, stime**
> System time.

**m, min_flt**
> Number of minor page faults.

**M, maj_flt**
> Amount of major page faults.

**n, cmin_flt**
> Total minor page faults.

**N, cmaj_flt**
> Total major page faults.

**o, session**
> Session ID.

**p, pid**
> Process ID.

**P, ppid**
> Parent's process ID.

**r, rss**
> Resident set size.

**R, resident**
> Resident pages.

**s, size**
> Kilobytes of memory used.

**S, share**

Number of shared pages.

**t, tty**

tty.

**T, start_time**

Process's start time.

**U, uid**

User ID.

**u, user**

User's name.

**v, vsize**

Bytes of VM used.

**y, priority**

Kernel's scheduling priority.

## Fields

**PRI**  Process's scheduling priority. A higher number indicates lower priority.

**NI**  Process's **nice** value. A higher number indicates less CPU time.

**SIZE**

Size of virtual image.

**RSS**

Resident set size (amount of physical memory), in kilobytes.

**WCHAN**

Kernel function in which process resides.

**STAT**

Status:

| | |
|---|---|
| R | Runnable |
| T | Stopped |
| D | Asleep and not interruptible |
| S | Asleep |
| Z | Zombie |
| W | No resident pages (second field) |

→

| | |
|---|---|
| **ps**<br>← | N   Positive **nice** value (third field)<br><br>TT  Associated tty.<br><br>**PAGEIN**<br>    Number of major page faults.<br><br>**TRS**<br>    Size of resident text.<br><br>**SWAP**<br>    Amount of swap used, in kilobytes.<br><br>**SHARE**<br>    Shared memory. |
| **psupdate** | **psupdate** [*mapfile*]<br><br>System administration command. Update the **psupdate** database (on some systems */boot/psupdate*; on others, */etc/psdatabase*), which contains information about the kernel image system map file. If no *mapfile* is specified, **psupdate** uses the default (which is either */usr/src/linux/vmlinux* or */usr/src/linux/tools/zSystem*, depending on the distribution). |
| **pwck** | **pwck** [*option*] [*files*]<br><br>System administration command. Remove corrupt or duplicate entries in the */etc/passwd* and */etc/shadow* files. **pwck** will prompt for a "yes" or "no" before deleting entries. If the user replies "no," the program will exit. Alternate passwd and shadow *files* can be checked. If correctable errors are found, the user will be encouraged to run the **usermod** command.<br><br>*Option*<br><br>−n  Noninteractive mode. Don't prompt for input, and delete no entries. Return appropriate exit status.<br><br>*Exit status*<br><br>0   Success.<br><br>1   Syntax error.<br><br>2   One or more bad password entries found.<br><br>3   Could not open password files. |

4    Could not lock password files.

5    Could not write password files.

## pwconv
## pwunconv

System administration command. Convert unshadowed entries in */etc/passwd* into shadowed entries in the */etc/ shadow* file. Replace the encrypted password in */etc/password* with an x. Shadowing passwords keeps them safe from password cracking programs. **pwconv** creates additional expiration information for the */etc/shadow* file from entries in your */etc/login.defs* file. If you add new entries to the */etc/passwd* file, you can run **pwconv** again to transfer the new information to */etc/shadow*. Already shadowed entries are ignored. **pwunconv** restores the encrypted passwords to your */etc/passwd* file and removes the */etc/shadow* file. Some expiration information is lost in the conversion.

## pwd

Print the full pathname of the current working directory. See also the **dirs** shell command, built in to both **bash** and **csh/ tcsh**.

## quota [*options*] [*user* | *group*]

Display disk usage and total space allowed for a designated user or group. With no argument, the quota for the current user is displayed. This command reports quotas for all filesystems listed in */etc/fstab*.

### Options

−g   Given with a *user* argument, display the quotas for the groups of which the user is a member, instead of the user's quotas.

−q   Display information only for filesystems in which the user is over quota.

−u   The default behavior. When used with −g, display both user and group quota information.

−v   Display quotas for filesystems even if no storage is currently allocated.

| | |
|---|---|
| raidstart | **raidstart** [*options*] [*devices*]<br>**raidstop** [*options*] [*devices*]<br><br>System administration command. Start or stop RAID *devices* as defined in the RAID configuration file, */etc/raidtab*. If option −a (or −−all) is used, no *devices* need to be given; the command will be applied to all the devices defined in the configuration file.<br><br>*Options*<br><br>−a, −−all<br>    Apply command to all devices defined in the RAID configuration file.<br><br>−c *file*, −−configfile *file*<br>    Use *file* instead of */etc/raidtab*.<br><br>−h, −−help<br>    Print usage message and exit.<br><br>−V, −−version<br>    Print version and exit. |
| ramsize | **ramsize** [*option*] [*image* [*size* [*offset*]]]<br><br>System administration command. If no options are specified, print usage information for the RAM disk. The pair of bytes at offset 504 in the kernel image normally specify the RAM size; with a kernel *image* argument, print the information found at that offset. To change that information, specify a new *size* (in kilobytes). You may also specify a different *offset*. Note that **rdev −r** is the same as **ramsize**.<br><br>*Option*<br><br>−o *offset*<br>    Same as specifying an *offset* as an argument. |
| ranlib | **ranlib** *filename*<br><br>Generate an index for archive file *filename*. Same as running **ar -s**. |
| rarp | **rarp** [*options*]<br><br>System administration command. Administer the Reverse Address Resolution Protocol table (usually */proc/net/rarp*). |

*Options*

−a [*hostname*]

Show all entries. If *hostname* is specified, show only the entries relevant to *hostname*, which may be a list.

−d *hostname*

Remove the entries relevant to *hostname*, which may be a list.

−s *hostname hw_addr*

Add a new entry for *hostname*, with the hardware address *hw_addr*.

−t *type*

Check only for *type* entries when consulting or changing the table. *type* may be **ether** (the default) or **ax25**.

−v Verbose mode.

---

**rcp** [*options*] *file1 file2*
**rcp** [*options*] *file . . . directory*

Copy files between two machines. Each *file* or *directory* is either a remote filename of the form *rname@rhost:path* or a local filename.

*Options*

−k Attempt to get tickets for remote host; query **krb_real-mofhost** to determine realm.

−p Preserve modification times and modes of the source files.

−r If any of the source files are directories, **rcp** copies each subtree rooted at that name. The destination must be a directory.

−x Turns on DES encryption for all data passed by **rcp**.

---

**rdate** [*options*] [*host . . .*]

TCP/IP command. Retrieve the date and time from a host or hosts on the network and optionally set the local system time.

→

| | |
|---|---|
| **rdate**<br>← | *Options*<br><br>−p  Print the retrieved dates.<br><br>−s  Set the local system time from the host; must be specified by root. |
| **rdev** | **rdev** [*options*] [*image* [*value* [*offset*]]]<br><br>System administration command. If no arguments are specified, display a line, in */etc/mtab* syntax, that describes the root filesystem. Otherwise, change the values of the bytes in the kernel image that describe the RAM disk size (by default located at decimal byte offset 504 in the kernel), VGA mode (default 506), and root device (default 508). You must specify the kernel *image* to change and may specify a new *value* and a different *offset*.<br><br>*Options*<br><br>−o *offset*<br>    Same as specifying an *offset* as an argument. The offset is given in decimal.<br><br>−r  Behave like **ramsize**.<br><br>−s  Behave like **swapdev**.<br><br>−v  Behave like **vidmode**.<br><br>−R  Behave like **rootflags**. |
| **rdist** | **rdist** [*options*] [*names*]<br><br>System administration command. Remote file distribution client program. **rdist** maintains identical copies of files over multiple hosts. It reads commands from a file named *distfile* to direct the updating of files and/or directories. An alternative *distfile* can be specified with the −f option or the −c option.<br><br>*Options*<br><br>−a *num*<br>    Do not update filesystems with fewer than *num* bytes free.<br><br>−c *name* [*login@*]*host*[:*dest*]<br>    Interpret the arguments as a small *distfile*, where *login* is the user to log in as, *host* is the destination host, |

*name* is the local file to transfer, and *dest* is the remote name where the file should be installed.

**–d** *var=value*

Define *var* to have *value*. This option defines or overrides variable definitions in the *distfile*. Set the variable *var* to *value*.

**–f** *file*

Read input from *file* (by default, *distfile*). If *file* is –, read from standard input.

**–l** *options*

Specify logging options on the local machine.

**–m** *machine*

Update only *machine*. May be specified multiple times for multiple machines.

**–n** Suppress normal execution. Instead, print the commands that would have been executed.

**–o***options*

Specify one or more *options*, which must be comma-separated.

**chknfs**

Suppress operations on files that reside on NFS filesystems.

**chkreadonly**

Check filesystem to be sure it is not read-only before attempting to perform updates.

**chksym**

Do not update files that exist on the local host but are symbolic links on the remote host.

**compare**

Compare files; use this comparison rather than age as the criteria for determining which files should be updated.

**follow**

Interpret symbolic links, copying the file to which the link points instead of creating a link on the remote machine.

**ignlnks**

Ignore links that appear to be unresolvable.

→

**rdist**

←

**nochkgroup**

Do not update a file's group ownership unless the entire file needs updating.

**nochkmode**

Do not update file mode unless the entire file needs updating.

**nochkowner**

Do not update file ownership unless the entire file needs updating.

**nodescend**

Suppress recursive descent into directories.

**noexec**

Suppress **rdist** of executables that are in *a.out* format.

**numchkgroup**

Check group ownership by group ID instead of by name.

**numchkowner**

Check file ownership by user ID instead of by name.

**quiet**

Quiet mode; do not print commands as they execute.

**remove**

Remove files that exist on the remote host but not the local host.

**savetargets**

Save updated files in *name.old*.

**verify**

Print a list of all files on the remote machine that are out of date, but do not update them.

**whole**

Preserve directory structure by creating subdirectories on the remote machine. For example, if you **rdist** the file */foo/bar* into the directory */baz*, it would produce the file */baz/foo/bar*, instead of the default, */baz/bar*.

**younger**

Do not update files that are younger than the master files.

−p *path*

Specify the path to search for **rdistd** on the remote machine.

−t *seconds*

Specify the timeout period (default 900 seconds) after which **rdist** will sever the connection if the remote server has not yet responded.

−A *num*

Specify the minimum number of inodes that **rdist** requires.

−D  Debugging mode.

−F  Execute all commands sequentially, without forking.

−L *options*

Specify logging options on the remote machine.

−M *num*

Do not allow more than *num* child **rdist** processes to run simultaneously. Default is 4.

−P *path*

Specify path to **rsh** on the local machine.

---

**rdistd** *options*

System administration command. Start the **rdist** server. Note that you *must* specify the −S option, unless you are simply querying for version information with −V.

*Options*

−D  Debugging mode.

−S  Start the server.

−V  Display the version number and exit immediately.

---

**reboot** [*options*]

System administration command. Close out filesystems, shut down the system, then reboot the system. Because this command immediately stops all processes, it should be run only in single-user mode. If the system is not in runlevel 0 or 6, **reboot** calls **shutdown −nf**.

→

| | |
|---|---|
| reboot<br>← | *Options*<br><br>**-d** Suppress writing to */var/log/wtmp*.<br><br>**-f** Call **reboot** even when **shutdown** would normally be called.<br><br>**-n** Suppress normal call to **sync**.<br><br>**-w** Suppress normal execution; simply write to */var/log/ wtmp*. |
| renice | **renice** [*priority*] [*options*] [*target*]<br><br>Control the scheduling priority of various processes as they run. May be applied to a process, process group, or user (*target*). A privileged user may alter the priority of other users' processes. *priority* must, for ordinary users, lie between 0 and the environment variable PRIO_MAX (normally 20), with a higher number indicating increased niceness. A privileged user may set a negative priority, as low as PRIO_MIN, to speed up processes.<br><br>*Options*<br><br>+*num*<br>    Specify number by which to increase current priority of process, rather than an absolute priority number.<br><br>-*num*<br>    Specify number by which to decrease current priority of process, rather than an absolute priority number.<br><br>**-g** Interpret *target* parameters as process group IDs.<br><br>**-p** Interpret *target* parameters as process IDs (default).<br><br>**-u** Interpret *target* parameters as usernames. |
| reset | **reset**<br><br>Clear screen (reset terminal). |
| rev | **rev** [*file*]<br><br>Reverse the lines of a file onto standard output. The order of characters on each line is also reversed. If no file is speci- |

fied, **rev** reads from standard input.

**rexecd** *command-line*

TCP/IP command. Server for the **rexec** routine, providing remote execution facilities with authentication based on usernames and passwords. **rexecd** is started by **inetd** and must have an entry in **inetd**'s configuration file, */etc/inetd.conf*. When **rexecd** receives a service request, the following protocol is initiated:

1.  The server reads characters from the socket up to a null byte. The resulting string is interpreted as an ASCII number, base 10.

2.  If the number received in step 1 is nonzero, it is interpreted as the port number of a secondary stream to be used for stderr. A second connection is then created to the specified port on the client's machine.

3.  A null-terminated username of at most 16 characters is retrieved on the initial socket.

4.  A null-terminated, unencrypted password of at most 16 characters is retrieved on the initial socket.

5.  A null-terminated command to be passed to a shell is retrieved on the initial socket. The length of the command is limited by the upper bound on the size of the system's argument list.

6.  **rexecd** then validates the user, as is done at login time and, if the authentication was successful, changes to the user's home directory and establishes the user and group protections of the user.

7.  A null byte is returned on the connection associated with stderr, and the command line is passed to the normal login shell of the user. The shell inherits the network connections established by **rexecd**.

*Diagnostics*

**Username too long**
   Name is longer than 16 characters.

**Password too long**
   Password is longer than 16 characters.

→

*Linux Commands*

**rexecd**

← 

**Command too long**
Command passed is too long.

**Login incorrect**
No password file entry for the username exists.

**Password incorrect**
Wrong password was supplied.

**No remote directory**
**chdir** to home directory failed.

**Try again**
**fork** by server failed.

**<shellname>:** . . .
**fork** by server failed. User's login shell could not be started.

---

**rlogin**

**rlogin** *rhost* [*options*]

Remote login. **rlogin** connects the terminal on the current local host system to the remote host system *rhost*. The remote terminal type is the same as your local terminal type. The terminal or window size is also copied to the remote system if the server supports it.

*Options*

−8  Allow an 8-bit input data path at all times.

−e*c*
Specify escape character *c* (default is ˜).

−d  Debugging mode.

−k  Attempt to get tickets from remote host, requesting them in the realm as determined by **krb_realm-ofhost**.

−l *username*
Specify a different *username* for the remote login. Default is the same as your local username.

−x  Turns on DES encryption for all data passed via the **rlogin** session.

−E  Do not interpret any character as an escape character.

−K  Suppress all Kerberos authentication.

−L  Allow **rlogin** session to be run without any output post-processing (i.e., run in **litout** mode).

## rlogind [*options*]

TCP/IP command. Server for the **rlogin** program, providing a remote login facility, with authentication based on privileged port numbers from trusted hosts. **rlogind** is invoked by **inetd** when a remote login connection is requested and executes the following protocol:

- The server checks the client's source port. If the port is not in the range 0–023, the server aborts the connection.

- The server checks the client's source address and requests the corresponding hostname. If the hostname cannot be determined, the dot-notation representation of the host address is used.

The login process propagates the client terminal's baud rate and terminal type, as found in the environment variable, TERM.

### Options

−a  Verify hostname.

−l  Do not authenticate hosts via a nonroot *.rhosts* file.

−n  Suppress keep-alive messages.

## rm [*options*] *files*

Delete one or more *files*. To remove a file, you must have write permission in the directory that contains the file, but you need not have permission on the file itself. If you do not have write permission on the file, you will be prompted (**y** or **n**) to override.

### Options

−d, −−directory
> Remove directories, even if they are not empty. Available only to a privileged user.

−f, −−force
> Remove write-protected files without prompting.

−−help
> Print a help message and then exit.

→

| | |
|---|---|
| **rm**<br>← | **−i, −−interactive**<br>Prompt for **y** (remove the file) or **n** (do not remove the file).<br><br>**−r, −R, −−recursive**<br>If *file* is a directory, remove the entire directory and all its contents, including subdirectories. Be forewarned: use of this option can be dangerous.<br><br>**−v, −−verbose**<br>Turn on verbose mode. (**rm** prints the name of each file before removing it.)<br><br>**−−version**<br>Print version information and then exit.<br><br>**−−** Mark the end of options. Use this when you need to supply a filename beginning with −. |
| **rmail** | **rmail** *user . . .*<br><br>TCP/IP command. Handle remote mail received via **uucp**, collapsing **From** lines in the form generated by **mail** into a single line of the form **return-path!sender** and passing the processed mail onto **sendmail**. **rmail** is explicitly designed for use with **uucp** and **sendmail**. |
| **rmdir** | **rmdir** [*options*] *directories*<br><br>Delete the named *directories* (not the contents). *directories* are deleted from the parent directory and must be empty (if not, **rm −r** can be used instead). See also **mkdir**.<br><br>*Options*<br><br>**−−help**<br>Print a help message and then exit.<br><br>**−−ignore-fail-on-non-empty**<br>Ignore failure to remove directories that are not empty.<br><br>**−p, −−parents**<br>Remove *directories* and any intervening parent directories that become empty as a result; useful for removing subdirectory trees.<br><br>**−−verbose**<br>Turn on verbose mode; print message for each directory as it is processed. |

**−−version**
> Print version information and then exit.

---

**rmmod** [*option*] *modules*

System administration command. Unload a module or list of modules from the kernel. This command is successful only if the specified modules are not in use and no other modules are dependent on them.

*Option*

**−r**  Recursively remove stacked modules (all modules that use the specified module).

---

**rootflags** [*option*] *image* [*flags* [*offset*]]

System administration command. Sets *flags* for a kernel *image*. If no arguments are specified, print *flags* for the kernel image. *flags* is a 2-byte integer located at offset 498 in a kernel *image*. Currently the only effect of *flags* is to mount the root filesystem in read-only mode if *flags* is non-zero. You may change *flags* by specifying the kernel *image* to change, the new *flags*, and the byte-offset at which to place the new information (the default is 498). Note that **rdev −R** is a synonym for **rootflags**. If LILO is used, **rootflags** is not needed. *flags* can be set from the LILO prompt during a boot.

*Option*

**−o** *offset*
> Same as specifying an *offset* as an argument.

---

**route** [*option*] [*command*]

TCP/IP command. Manually manipulate the routing tables normally maintained by **routed**. **route** accepts two commands: **add**, to add a route, and **del**, to delete a route. The two commands have the following syntax:

> **add** [-net | -host] *address* [**gw** *gateway*]
> > [**netmask** *mask*] [**mss** *tcp-mss*] [**dev** *device*]
> > **del** *address*

*address* is treated as a plain route unless **−net** is specified or *address* is found in */etc/networks*. **−host** can be used to

→

| | |
|---|---|
| **route** ← | specify that *address* is a plain route whether or not it is found in */etc/networks*. The keyword *default* means to use this route for all requests if no other route is known. You can specify the *gateway* through which to route packets headed for that address, its *netmask*, TCP *mss*, and the *device* with which to associate the route. Only a privileged user may modify the routing tables. |
| | If no command is specified, **route** prints the routing tables. |
| | ***Option*** |
| | −n  Show numerical addresses; do not look up hostnames. (Useful if DNS is not functioning properly.) |
| | |
| **routed** | **routed** [*options*] [*logfile*] |
| | TCP/IP command. Network routing daemon. **routed** is invoked by a privileged user at boot time to manage the Internet routing tables. The routing daemon uses a variant of the Xerox NS Routing Information Protocol in maintaining up-to-date kernel routing-table entries. When **routed** is started, it uses the SIOCGIFCONF **ioctl** call to find those directly connected interfaces configured into the system and marked up. **routed** transmits a REQUEST packet on each interface, then enters a loop, listening for REQUEST and RESPONSE packets from other hosts. When a REQUEST packet is received, **routed** formulates a reply based on the information maintained in its internal tables. The generated RESPONSE packet contains a list of known routes. Any RESPONSE packets received are used to update the routing tables as appropriate. |
| | When an update is applied, **routed** records the change in its internal tables, updates the kernel routing table, and generates a RESPONSE packet reflecting these changes to all directly connected hosts and networks. |
| | ***Options*** |
| | −d  Debugging mode. Log additional information to the *logfile*. |
| | −g  Offer a route to the default destination. |
| | −q  Opposite of −s option. |
| | −s  Force **routed** to supply routing information, whether it is acting as an internetwork router or not. |

−t Stop **routed** from going into background and releasing itself from the controlling terminal, so that interrupts from the keyboard will kill the process.

---

**rpcgen** [*options*] *file*

Parse *file*, which should be written in the RPC language, and produce a program written in C that implements the RPC code. Place header code generated from *file.x* in *file.h*, XDR routines in *file_xdr.c*, server code in *file_svc.c*, and client code in *file_clnt.c*. Lines preceded by % are not parsed. By default, **rpcgen** produces SunOS 4.1-compatible code.

−a Produce all files (client and server).

−5 Produce SVR4-compatible code.

−c Create XDR routines. Cannot be used with other options.

−C Produce ANSI C code (default).

−D*name*[=*value*]
 Define the symbol *name*, and set it equal to *value* or 1.

−h Produce a header file. With −T, make the file support RPC dispatch tables. Cannot be used with other options.

−I Produce an **inetd**-compatible server.

−K *secs*
 Specify amount of time that the server should wait after replying to a request and before exiting. Default is 120. A *secs* of −1 prevents the program from ever exiting.

−l Produce client code. Cannot be used with other options.

−m Produce server code only, suppressing creation of a "main" routine. Cannot be used with other options.

−N New style. Allow multiple arguments for procedures. Not necessarily backward compatible.

−o [*file*]
 Print output to *file* or standard output.

−Ss Create skeleton server code only.

→

| | |
|---|---|
| **rpcgen**<br>← | **−t** Create RPC dispatch table. Cannot be used with other options.<br><br>**−T** Include support for RPC dispatch tables. |
| **rpcinfo** | *rpcinfo [options] [host] [program] [version]*<br><br>NFS/NIS command. Report RPC information. *program* can be either a name or a number. If a *version* is specified, **rpcinfo** attempts to call that version of the specified *program*. Otherwise, it attempts to find all the registered version numbers for the specified *program* by calling Version 0, and it attempts to call each registered version. |

*Options*

**−b** *program version*
Make an RPC broadcast to the specified *program* and *version*, using UDP, and report all hosts that respond.

**−d** *program version*
Delete the specified *version* of *program*'s registration. Can be executed only by the user who added the registration or a privileged user.

**−n** *portnum*
Use *portnum* as the port number for the −t and −u options, instead of the port number given by the portmapper.

**−p** [*host*]
Probe the portmapper on host and print a list of all registered RPC programs. If *host* is not specified, it defaults to the value returned by **hostname**.

**−t** *host program* [*version*]
Make an RPC call to *program* on the specified *host*, using TCP, and report whether a response was received.

**−u** *host program* [*version*]
Make an RPC call to *program* on the specified *host*, using UDP, and report whether a response was received.

*Examples*

To show all of the RPC services registered on the local machine, use:

```
$ rpcinfo -p
```

To show all of the RPC services registered on the machine named **klaxon**, use:

```
$ rpcinfo -p klaxon
```

To show all machines on the local net that are running the Network Information Service (NIS), use:

```
$ rpcinfo -b ypserv version | uniq
```

where *version* is the current NIS version obtained from the results of the −p switch earlier in this list.

## rpm [*options*]

The Red Hat Package Manager. A freely available packaging system for software distribution and installation. RPM packages are built, installed, and queried with the **rpm** command. For detailed information on **rpm**, see Chapter 5, *Red Hat and Debian Package Managers*.

## rsh [*options*] *host* [*command*]

Execute *command* on remote host, or, if no command is specified, begin an interactive shell on the remote host using **rlogin**.

### Options

−d Enable socket debugging.

−k Cause **rsh** to obtain tickets for the remote host in realm instead of the remote host's realm as determined by krb_realmofhost(3).

−l *username*
   Attempt to log in as *username*. By default, the name of the user executing **rsh** is used.

−n Redirects the input to **rsh** from the special device */dev/ null*. (This should be done when backgrounding **rsh** from a shell prompt, to direct the input away from the terminal.)

−x Turns on DES encryption for all data exchange.

−K Suppress Kerberos authentication.

| | |
|---|---|
| **rshd** | **rshd** [*options*]

TCP/IP command. Remote shell server for programs such as **rcmd** and **rcp**, which need to execute a noninteractive shell on remote machines. **rshd** is started by **inetd** and must have an entry in **inetd**'s configuration file, */etc/inetd.conf.*

All options are exactly the same as those in **rlogind**, except for −L, which is unique to **rshd**.

*Option*

−L  Log all successful connections and failed attempts via syslogd. |
| **rstat** | **rstat** *host*

TCP/IP command. Summarize *host*'s system status: the current time, uptime, and load averages—the average number of jobs in the run queue. Queries the remote host's **rstat_svc** daemon. |
| **run-parts** | **run-parts** [*options*] [*directory*]

System administration command. Run, in lexical order, all scripts found in *directory*. Exclude scripts whose filenames include nonalphanumeric characters (besides underscores and hyphens).

*Options*

−−  Interpret all subsequent arguments as filenames, not options.

−−test
    Print information listing which scripts would be run, but suppress actual execution of them.

−−umask=*umask*
    Specify *umask*. The default is 022. |

**runlevel**

System administration command. Display the previous and current system runlevels.

**ruptime** [*options*]

TCP/IP command. Provide information on how long each machine on the local network has been up and which users are logged in to each. If a machine has not reported in for 11 minutes, assume it is down. The listing is sorted by host-name.

*Options*

−a   Include users who have been idle for more than one hour.

−l   Sort machines by load average.

−r   Reverse the normal sort order.

−t   Sort machines by uptime.

−u   Sort machines by the number of users logged in.

**rusers** [*options*] [*host*]

TCP/IP command. List the users logged on to *host*, or to all local machines, in **who** format (hostname, usernames).

*Options*

−a   Include machines with no users logged in.

−l   Include more information: tty, date, time, idle time, remote host.

**rwall** *host* [*file*]

TCP/IP command. Print a message to all users logged on to *host*. If *file* is specified, read the message from it; otherwise, read from standard input.

**rwho** [*option*]

Report who is logged on for all machines on the local network (similar to **who**).

→

| | |
|---|---|
| rwho<br>← | *Option*<br><br>−a  List users even if they've been idle for more than one hour. |
| rwhod | **rwhod**<br><br>TCP/IP command. System status server that maintains the database used by the **rwho** and **ruptime** programs. Its operation is predicated on the ability to broadcast messages on a network. As a producer of information, **rwhod** periodically queries the state of the system and constructs status messages, which are broadcast on a network. As a consumer of information, it listens for other **rwhod** servers' status messages, validates them, then records them in a collection of files located in the directory */var/spool/rwho*. Messages received by the **rwhod** server are discarded unless they originated at an **rwhod** server's port. Status messages are generated approximately once every 3 minutes. |
| script | **script** [*option*] [*file*]<br><br>Fork the current shell and make a typescript of a terminal session. The typescript is written to *file*. If no *file* is given, the typescript is saved in the file *typescript*. The script ends when the forked shell exits, usually with Ctrl-D or **exit**.<br><br>*Option*<br><br>−a  Append to *file* or *typescript* instead of overwriting the previous contents. |
| sed | **sed** [*options*] [*command*] [*files*]<br><br>Stream editor—edit one or more *files* without user interaction. See Chapter 12, *The sed Editor*, for more information. |
| sendmail | **sendmail** [*flags*] [*address* . . . ]<br><br>System administration command. **sendmail** is a mail transfer agent (MTA) or, more simply, a mail router. It accepts mail from a user's mail program, interprets the mail address, rewrites the address into the proper form for the delivery program, and routes the mail to the correct delivery program. |

**–b***x*

Set operation mode to *x*. Operation modes are:

a   Run in ARPAnet mode.

d   Run as a daemon.

i   Initialize the alias database.

m   Deliver mail (default).

p   Print the mail queue.

s   Speak SMTP on input side.

t   Run in test mode.

v   Verify addresses; do not collect or deliver.

**–C** *file*

Use configuration file *file*.

**–d** *level*

Set debugging level.

**–F** *name*

Set full name of user to *name*.

**–f** *name*

Sender's name is *name*.

**–h** *cnt*

Set hop count (number of times message has been processed by **sendmail**) to *cnt*.

**–n**   Do not alias or forward.

**–o** *x value*

Set option *x* to value *value*. Options are described below.

**–p** *protocol*

Receive messages via the *protocol* protocol.

**–q** [*time*]

Process queued messages immediately, or at intervals indicated by *time* (for example, **–q30m** for every half hour).

**–r** *name*

Obsolete form of **–f**.

→

**sendmail**
←

-t   Read head for **To:**, **Cc:**, and **Bcc:** lines, and send to everyone on those lists.

-v   Verbose.

-X *file*
> Log all traffic to *file*. Not to be used for normal logging.

*Configuration options*

The following options can be set with the −o flag on the command line or the **O** line in the configuration file:

7   Format all incoming messages in 7 bits.

a*min*
> If the D option is set, wait *min* minutes for the *aliases* file to be rebuilt before returning an alias database out-of-date warning.

A*file*
> Use alternate alias file.

b*minblocks*[/*maxsize*]
> Require at least *minblocks* to be free, and optionally set the maximum message size to *maxsize*. If *maxsize* is omitted, the slash is optional.

B*char*
> Set unquoted space replacement character.

c   On mailers that are considered "expensive" to connect to, don't initiate immediate connection.

C*num*
> Checkpoint the queue when mailing to multiple recipients. **sendmail** will rewrite the list of recipients after each group of *num* recipients has been processed.

d*x*   Set the delivery mode to *x*. Delivery modes are **d** for deferred delivery, **i** for interactive (synchronous) delivery, **b** for background (asynchronous) delivery, and **q** for queue only—i.e., deliver the next time the queue is run.

D   Try to automatically rebuild the alias database if necessary.

e*x*   Set error processing to mode *x*. Valid modes are **m** to mail back the error message, **w** to write back the error message, **p** to print the errors on the terminal (default), **q** to throw away error messages, and **e** to do special processing for the BerkNet.

*Etext*

    Set error message header. *text* is either text to add to an error message or the name of a file. A filename must include its full path and begin with a /.

**f**    Save Unix-style **From** lines at the front of messages.

*Fmode*

    Set default file permissions for temporary files. If this option is missing, default permissions are 0644.

**G**    Compare local mail names to the GECOS section in the password file.

**g** *n*  Default group ID to use when calling mailers.

*Hfile*

    SMTP help file.

**h** *num*

    Allow a maximum of *num* hops per message.

**i**    Do not take dots on a line by themselves as a message terminator.

**I** *arg*

    Use DNS lookups and tune them. Queue messages on connection refused. The *arg* arguments are identical to resolver flags without the RES_ prefix. Each flag can be preceded by a plus or minus to enable or disable the corresponding name server option. There must be a whitespace between the I and the first flag.

**j**    Use MIME format for error messages.

*Jpath*

    Set an alternative *.forward* search path.

**k***num*

    Specify size of the connection cache.

**K***time*

    Time out connections after *time*.

**l**    Do not ignore **Errors-To** header.

**L***n*  Specify log level.

**m**    Send to **me** (the sender) also if I am in an alias expansion.

**M***Xvalue*

    Define a macro's value in command line. Assign *value* to macro *X*.

→

n    When running **newaliases**, validate the right side of aliases.

o    If set, this message may have old-style headers. If not set, this message is guaranteed to have new-style headers (i.e., commas instead of spaces between addresses).

p*what,what,* . . .
    Tune how private you want the SMTP daemon. The *what* arguments should be separated from one another by commas. The *what* arguments may be any of the following:

**public**
    Make SMTP fully public (default).

**needmailhelo**
    Require site to send HELO or ELHO before sending mail.

**needexpnhelo**
    Require site to send HELO or ELHO before answering an address expansion request.

**needvrfyhelo**
    Like preceding argument but for verification requests.

**noexpn**
    Deny all expansion requests.

**novrfy**
    Deny all verification requests.

**authwarnings**
    Insert special headers in mail messages advising recipients that the message may not be authentic.

**goaway**
    Set all of the previous arguments (except **public**).

**restrictmailq**
    Allow only users of the same group as the owner of the queue directory to examine the mail queue.

**restrictqrun**
    Limit queue processing to root and the owner of the queue directory.

P*user*
    Send copies of all failed mail to *user* (usually postmaster).

q*fact*
> Multiplier (factor) for high-load queuing.

Q*queuedir*
> Select the directory in which to queue messages.

R   Don't prune route addresses.

S*file*
> Save statistics in the named file.

s   Always instantiate the queue file, even under circum-
> stances in which it is not strictly necessary.

T*time*
> Set the timeout on undelivered messages in the queue
> to the specified time.

t*stz, dtz*
> Set name of the time zone.

U*database*
> Consult the user database *database* for forwarding
> information.

u*N*  Set default user ID for mailers.

v   Run in verbose mode.

V*host*
> Fall-back MX host. *host* should be the fully qualified
> domain name of the fallback host.

w   Use a record for an ambiguous MX.

x*load*
> Queues messages when load level is higher than *load.*

X*load*
> Refuse SMTP connections when load is higher than
> *load.*

y*factor*
> Penalize large recipient lists by *factor.*

Y   Deliver each job that is run from the queue in a sepa-
> rate process. This helps limit the size of running pro-
> cesses on systems with very low amounts of memory.

z*factor*
> Multiplier for priority increments. This determines how
> much weight to give to a message's precedence header.
> **sendmail**'s default is 1800.

$\rightarrow$

**sendmail**

←

*Zinc*

Increment priority of items remaining in queue by *inc* after each job is processed. **sendmail** uses 90,000 by default.

### sendmail support files

*/usr/lib/sendmail*

Binary of **sendmail**.

*/usr/bin/newaliases*

Link to */usr/lib/sendmail*; causes the alias database to be rebuilt.

*/usr/bin/mailq*

Prints a listing of the mail queue.

*/etc/sendmail.cf*

Configuration file, in text form.

*/etc/sendmail.hf*

SMTP help file.

*/usr/lib/sendmail.st*

Statistics file. Doesn't need to be present.

*/etc/aliases*

Alias file, in text form.

*/etc/aliases.{pag,dir}*

Alias file in **dbm** format.

*/var/spool/mqueue*

Directory in which the mail queue and temporary files reside.

*/var/spool/mqueue/qf*

Control (queue) files for messages.

*/var/spool/mqueue/df*

Data files.

*/var/spool/mqueue/lf*

Lockfiles.

*/var/spool/mqueue/tf*

Temporary versions of *qf* files, used during queue-file rebuild.

*/var/spool/mqueue/nf*

Used when creating a unique ID.

    Transcript of current session.

---

**setfdprm** [*options*] *device* [*name*]

Load disk parameters used when autoconfiguring floppy devices.

### Options

−c *device*
    Clear parameters of *device*.

−n *device*
    Disable format-detection messages for *device*.

−p *device* [*name* | *parameter*]
    Permanently reset parameters for *device*. You can use *name* to specify a configuration, or you can specify individual parameters. The parameters that can be specified are **dev**, **size**, **sect**, **heads**, **tracks**, **stretch**, **gap**, **rate**, **spec1**, or **fmt_gap**. Consult */etc/fdprm* for the original values.

−y *device*
    Enable format-detection messages for *device*.

---

**setsid** *command* [*arguments*]

System administration command. Execute the named command and optional command *arguments* in a new session.

---

**sh** [*options*] [*file* [*arguments*]]

The standard Unix shell, a command interpreter into which all other commands are entered. On Linux, this is just another name for the **bash** shell. For more information, see Chapter 7, *bash: The Bourne Again Shell*.

---

**shar** [*options*] *files*
**shar** −S [*options*]

Create shell archives (or shar files) that are in text format and can be mailed. These files may be unpacked later by executing them with */bin/sh*. Other commands may be required on the recipient's system, such as **compress**, **gzip**, and **uudecode**. The resulting archive is sent to standard

$\rightarrow$

*Linux Commands*

output, unless the –o option is given.

*Options*

**–a, – –net-headers**
Allows automatic generation of headers. The **–n** option is required if the **–a** option is used.

**–b** *bits*, **– –bits-per-code=***bits*
Use **–b** *bits* as a parameter to **compress** (when doing compression). Default value is 12. The **–b** option automatically turns on **–Z**.

**–c, – –cut-mark**
Start the shar file with a line that says "Cut here."

**–d** *delimiter*, **– –here-delimiter=***delimiter*
Use *delimiter* for the files in the shar instead of SHAR_EOF.

**–f, – –basename**
Causes only simple filenames to be used when restoring, which is useful when building a shar from several directories or another directory. (If a directory name is passed to **shar**, the substructure of that directory will be restored whether or not **–f** is used.)

**–g** *level*, **– –level-for-gzip=***level*
Use *–level* as a parameter to **gzip** (when doing compression). Default is 9. The **–g** option turns on the **–z** option by default.

**– –help**
Print a help summary on standard output, then exit.

**–l** *nn*, **– –whole-size-limit=***nn*
Limit the output file size to *nn* kilobytes but don't split input files. Requires use of **–o**.

**–m, – –no-timestamp**
Don't generate **touch** commands to restore the file modification dates when unpacking files from the archive.

**–n** *name*, **– –archive-name=***name*
Name of archive to be included in the header of the shar files. Required if the **–a** option is used.

**– –no-i18n**
Do not produce internationalized shell archives; use default English messages. By default, **shar** produces archives that will try to output messages in the unpacker's preferred language (as determined by LANG/LC_MESSAGES).

**−o** *prefix,* **−−output-prefix**=*prefix*

Save the archive to files *prefix*.01 through *prefix.nn* (instead of sending it to standard output). This option must be used when either **−l** or **−L** is used.

**−p, −−intermix-type**

Allow positional parameter options. The options **−B**, **−T**, **−z**, and **−Z** may be embedded, and files to the right of the option will be processed in the specified mode.

**−−print-text-domain-dir**

Print the directory **shar** looks in to find messages files for different languages, then immediately exit.

**−q, −−quiet, −−silent**

Turn off verbose mode.

**−s** *who@where,* **−−submitter**=*who@where*

Supply submitter name and address, instead of allowing **shar** to determine it automatically.

**−−version**

Print the version number of the program on standard output, then exit.

**−w, −−no-character-count**

Do *not* check each file with **wc −c** after unpacking. The default is to check.

**−x, −−no-check-existing**

Overwrite existing files without checking. Default is to check and not overwrite existing files. If **−c** is passed as a parameter to the script when unpacking (**sh** *archive* **−c**), existing files will be overwritten unconditionally. See also **−X**.

**−z, −−gzip**

**gzip** and **uuencode** all files prior to packing. Must be unpacked with **uudecode** and **gunzip** (or **zcat**).

**−B, −−uuencode**

Treat all files as binary; use **uuencode** prior to packing. This increases the size of the archive, and it must be unpacked with **uudecode**.

**−D, −−no-md5-digest**

Do *not* use md5sum digest to verify the unpacked files. The default is to check.

**−F, −−force-prefix**

Force the prefix character to be prepended to every line even if not required. May slightly increase the size of the archive, especially if **−B** or **−Z** is used.

→

| shar ← | **−L** *nn*, **−−split-size-limit=***nn*<br>Limit output file size to *nn* kilobytes and split files if necessary. The archive parts created with this option must be unpacked in correct order. Requires use of **−o**. |
|---|---|

**−M**, **−−mixed-uuencode**
Pack files in mixed mode (the default). Distinguishes files as either text or binary; binaries are uuencoded prior to packing.

**−P**, **−−no-piping**
Use temporary files instead of pipes in the shar file.

**−Q**, **−−quiet-unshar**
Disable verbose mode.

**−S**, **−−stdin-file-list**
Read list of files to be packed from standard input rather than from the command line. Input must be in a form similar to that generated by the **find** command, with one filename per line.

**−T**, **−−text-files**
Treat all files as text.

**−V**, **−−vanilla-operation**
Produce shars that rely only upon the existence of **sed** and **echo** in the unsharing environment.

**−X**, **−−query-user**
Prompt user to ask if files should be overwritten when unpacking.

**−Z**, **−−compress**
Compress and uuencode all files prior to packing.

---

**showmount**

**showmount** [*options*] [*host*]

NFS/NIS command. Show information about an NFS server. This information is maintained by the **mountd** server on *host*. The default value for *host* is the value returned by **hostname**. With no options, show the clients that have mounted directories from the host. **showmount** is usually found in */usr/sbin*, which is not in the default search path.

*Options*

**−a, −−all**
Print all remote mounts in the format:

*hostname:directory*

where *hostname* is the name of the client and *directory* is the root of the filesystem that has been mounted.

**−d, −−directories**
List directories that have been remotely mounted by clients.

**−e, −−exports**
Print the list of exported filesystems.

**−h, −−help**
Provide a short help summary.

**−−no-headers**
Do not print headers.

**−v, −−version**
Report the current version number of the program.

---

**shutdown** [*options*] *when* [*message*]

System administration command. Terminate all processing. *when* may be a specific time (in *hh:mm* format), a number of minutes to wait (in +*m* format), or **now**. A broadcast *message* notifies all users to log off the system. Processes are signaled with SIGTERM, to allow them to exit gracefully. */etc/init* is called to perform the actual shutdown, which consists of placing the system in runlevel 1. Only privileged users can execute the **shutdown** command. Broadcast messages, default or defined, are displayed at regular intervals during the grace period; the closer the shutdown time, the more frequent the message.

*Options*

**−c** Cancel a shutdown that is in progress.

**−f** Reboot fast, by suppressing the normal call to **fsck** when rebooting.

**−h** Halt the system when shutdown is complete.

→

| | |
|---|---|
| **shutdown**<br>← | **−k**  Print the warning message, but suppress actual shut-down. |
| | **−n**  Perform shutdown without a call to **init**. |
| | **−r**  Reboot the system when shutdown is complete. |
| | **−t** *sec*<br>    Ensure a *sec*-second delay between killing processes and changing the runlevel. |
| | |
| **size** | **size** [*options*] [*objfile* . . . ] |
| | Print the number of bytes of each section of *objfile* and its total size. If *objfile* is not specified, *a.out* is used. |
| | *Options* |
| | **−d**  Display the size in decimal and hexadecimal. |
| | **−−format** *format*<br>    Imitate the **size** command from either System V (**−−format sysv**) or BSD (**−−format berkeley**). |
| | **−o**  Display the size in octal and hexadecimal. |
| | **−−radix** *num*<br>    Specify how to display the size: in hexadecimal and decimal (if *num* is **10** or **16**) or hexadecimal and octal (if *num* is **8**). |
| | **−x**  Display the size in hexadecimal and decimal. |
| | **−A**  Imitate System V's **size** command. |
| | **−B**  Imitate BSD's **size** command. |
| | |
| **slattach** | **slattach** [*options*] [*tty*] |
| | TCP/IP command. Attach serial lines as network interfaces, thereby preparing them for use as point-to-point connec-tions. Only a privileged user may attach or detach a net-work interface. |
| | *Options* |
| | **−c** *command*<br>    Run *command* when the connection is severed. |

**−d**  Debugging mode.

**−e**  Exit immediately after initializing the line.

**−h**  Exit when the connection is severed.

**−l**  Create UUCP-style lockfile in */var/spool/uucp*.

**−L**  Enable 3-wire operation.

**−m**  Suppress initialization of the line to 8 bits raw mode.

**−n**  Similar to **mesg −n**.

**−p** *protocol*
> Specify *protocol*, which may be **slip**, **adaptive**, **ppp**, or **kiss**.

**−q**  Quiet mode; suppress messages.

**−s** *speed*
> Specify line speed.

---

## sleep *amount*[*units*]

Wait a specified *amount* of time before executing another command. The default for *units* is seconds.

| Time | Units |
|------|---------|
| *s*  | seconds |
| *m*  | minutes |
| *h*  | hours |
| *d*  | days |

---

## sort [*options*] [*files*]

Sort the lines of the named *files*. Compare specified fields for each pair of lines, or, if no fields are specified, compare them by byte, in machine collating sequence. See also **uniq**, **comm**, and **join**.

### Options

**−b**  Ignore leading spaces and tabs.

**−c**  Check whether *files* are already sorted, and, if so, produce no output.

**−d**  Sort in dictionary order.

$\rightarrow$

**sort**
←

-f   Fold—ignore uppercase/lowercase differences.

--**help**
    Print a help message and then exit.

-i   Ignore nonprinting characters (those outside ASCII range 040–176).

-m  Merge (i.e., sort as a group) input files.

-n   Sort in arithmetic order.

-o*file*
    Put output in *file*.

-r   Reverse the order of the sort.

-t*c*  Separate fields with *c* (default is a tab).

-u   Identical lines in input file appear only one (unique) time in output.

-z*recsz*
    Provide *recsz* bytes for any one line in the file. This option prevents abnormal termination of **sort** in certain cases.

+*n* [-*m*]
    Skip *n* fields before sorting, and sort up to field position *m*. If *m* is missing, sort to end of line. Positions take the form *a.b*, which means character *b* of field *a*. If *.b* is missing, sort at the first character of the field.

-k *n*[,*m*]
    Similar to +. Skip *n*–1 fields and stop at *m*–1 fields (i.e., start sorting at the *n*th field, where the fields are numbered beginning with 1).

--**version**
    Print version information and then exit.

-M  Attempt to treat the first three characters as a month designation (JAN, FEB, etc.). In comparisons, treat JAN < FEB and any valid month as less than an invalid name for a month.

-T *tempdir*
    Directory pathname to be used for temporary files.

***Examples***

List files by decreasing number of lines:

```
wc -l * | sort -r
```

Alphabetize a list of words, remove duplicates, and print the frequency of each word:

```
sort -fd wordlist | uniq -c
```

Sort the password file numerically by the third field (user ID):

```
sort +2n -t: /etc/passwd
```

---

**split** [*option*] [*infile*] [*outfile*]

Split *infile* into equal-sized segments. *infile* remains unchanged, and the results are written to *outfile*aa, *outfile*ab, and so on. (default is **xaa**, **xab**, etc.). If *infile* is – (or missing), standard input is read. See also **csplit**.

*Options*

**–n, –l** *n*, **––lines=***n*
  Split *infile* into *n*-line segments (default is 1000).

**–b** *n*[bkm], **––bytes=***n*[bkm]
  Split *infile* into *n*-byte segments. Alternate blocksizes may be specified:

  **b**  512 bytes

  **k**  1 kilobyte

  **m**  1 megabyte

**–C** *bytes*[bkm], **––line-bytes=***bytes*[bkm]
  Put a maximum of *bytes* into file; insist on adding complete lines.

**––help**
  Print a help message and then exit.

**––verbose**
  Print a message for each output file.

**––version**
  Print version information and then exit.

**–**  Take input from the standard input.

*Examples*

Break *bigfile* into 1000-line segments:

```
split bigfile
```

Join four files, then split them into 10-line files named *new.aa*, *new.ab*, and so on. Note that without the –, **new.**

→

| | |
|---|---|
| split<br>← | would be treated as a nonexistent input file:<br><br>`cat list[1-4] | split -10 - new.` |
| stat | ## stat *filename* [*filenames* . . . ]<br><br>Print out the contents of an inode as they appear to the **stat** system call in a human-readable format. The error messages "Can't stat file" or "Can't lstat file" usually mean the file doesn't exist. "Can't readlink file" generally indicates that something is wrong with a symbolic link.<br><br>*Output*<br><br>Sample output from the command:<br><br>`stat /`<br><br>```<br> File: "/"<br> Size: 1024       Filetype: Directory<br> Mode: (0755/drwxr-xr-x)  Uid: (  0/  root) Gid: (  0/  system)<br>Device: 3,3   Inode: 2        Links: 21<br>Access: Tue Apr 11 04:02:01 2000(00000.11:47:35)<br>Modify: Wed Nov 17 11:46:38 1999(00146.03:02:58)<br>Change: Wed Nov 17 11:46:38 1999(00146.03:02:58)<br>``` |
| strace | ## strace [*options*] *command* [*arguments*]<br><br>Trace the system calls and signals for *command* and *arguments*. **strace** shows you how data is passed between the program and the system kernel. With no options, **strace** prints a line to **stderr** for each system call. It shows the call name, arguments given, the return value, and any error messages generated. A signal is printed with both its signal symbol and a descriptive string.<br><br>*Options*<br><br>−a *n*<br>    Align the return values in column *n*.<br><br>−c  Count all calls and signals and create a summary report when the program has ended.<br><br>−d  Debug mode. Print debugging information for **strace** on **stderr**.<br><br>−e *keyword*[=[!]*values*<br>    Pass an expression to **strace** to limit the types of calls or signals that are traced or change how they are displayed. The values for these expressions can be given as a comma-separated list. Preceding the list with an |

exclamation mark (!) negates the list. The special *values* of **all** and **none** are valid, as are the *values* listed with the following *keywords*.

**abbrev=** *names*
> Abbreviate output from large structures for system calls listed in *names*.

**read=** *descriptors*
> Print all data read from the given file *descriptors*.

**signal=** *symbols*
> Trace the listed signal *symbols* (for example, **signal**=SIGIO,SIGHUP).

**trace=** *values*
> Trace the listed *values*. *values* may be a list of system call names or one of the following sets of system calls:

> | | |
> |---|---|
> | **file** | Calls that take a filename as an argument |
> | **ipc** | Interprocess communication |
> | **network** | Network-related |
> | **process** | Process management |
> | **signal** | Signal-related |

**verbose=** *names*
> Unabbreviate structures for the given system call *names*. Default is **none**.

**write=** *descriptors*
> Print all data written to the given file *descriptors*.

**−f**   Trace forked processes.

**−ff**  Write system calls for forked processes to separate files named *filename.pid* when using the **−o** option.

**−h**   Print help and exit.

**−i**   Print instruction pointer with each system call.

**−o** *filename*
> Write output to *filename* instead of **stderr**. If *filename* starts with the pipe symbol |, treat the rest of the name as a command to which output should be piped.

**−O** *n*
> Override **strace**'s built-in timing estimates, and just subtract *n* microseconds from the timing of each system call to adjust for the time it takes to measure the call.

$\rightarrow$

| | |
|---|---|
| **strace**<br>← | **−p** *pid*<br>    Attach to the given process ID and begin tracking.<br>    **strace** can track more than one process if more than<br>    one option **−p** is given. Type Ctrl-c to end the trace.<br><br>**−q**  Quiet mode. Suppress attach and detach messages from<br>    **strace**.<br><br>**−r**  Relative timestamp. Print time in microseconds between<br>    system calls.<br><br>**−s** *n*<br>    Print only the first *n* characters of a string. Default<br>    value is 32.<br><br>**−S** *value*<br>    Sort output of **−c** option by the given *value. value* may<br>    be **calls**, **name**, **time**, or **nothing**. By default it is sorted<br>    by **time**.<br><br>**−T** Print time spent in each system call.<br><br>**−t**  Print time of day on each line of output.<br><br>**−tt** Print time of day with microseconds on each line of<br>    output.<br><br>**−ttt**<br>    Print timestamp on each line as number of seconds<br>    since the Epoch.<br><br>**−u** *username*<br>    Run command as *username*. Needed when tracing<br>    **setuid** and **setgid** programs.<br><br>**−V** Print version and exit.<br><br>**−v**  Verbose. Do not abbreviate structure information.<br><br>**−x**  Print all non-ASCII strings in hexadecimal.<br><br>**−xx**<br>    Print all strings in hexadecimal. |
| **strfile** | **strfile** [*options*] *input_file* [*output_file*]<br>**unstr** [**−c** *delimiter*] *input_file*[.*ext*] [*output_file*]<br><br>**strfile** creates a random-access file for storing strings. The<br>input file should be a file containing groups of lines sepa-<br>rated by a line containing a single percent sign (or other<br>specified delimiter character). **strfile** creates an output file<br>that contains a header structure and a table of file offsets for<br>each group of lines, allowing random access of the strings. |

The output file, if not specified on the command line, is
named *sourcefile.dat.* **unstr** undoes the work of **strfile**, printing out the strings contained in the input file in the order
that they are listed in the header file data. If no output file is
specified, **unstr** prints to standard output; otherwise, it
prints to the file specified. **unstr** can also globally change
the delimiter character in a strings file.

**strfile**

*Options*

Of the following options, only **−c** can be used with **unstr**.
All other options apply to **strfile** alone.

**−c** *delimiter*
Change the delimiting character from the percent sign
to *delimiter.* Valid for both **strfile** and **unstr**.

**−i**  Ignore case when ordering the strings.

**−o**  Order the strings alphabetically.

**−r**  Randomize access to the strings.

**−s**  Run silently; don't give a summary message when finished.

**−x**  Set the STR_ROTATED bit in the header *str_flags* field.

---

**strings** [*options*] *files*

**strings**

Search each *file* specified and print any printable character
strings found that are at least four characters long and followed by an unprintable character.

*Options*

**−, −a, −−all**
Scan entire object files; default is to scan only the initialized and loaded sections for object files.

**−f, −−print-file-name**
Print the name of the file before each string.

**−***min-len*, **−n** *min-len*, **−−bytes=***min-len*
Print only strings that are at least *min-len* characters.

**−t** *base*, **−−radix=***base*
Print the offset within the file before each string, in the
format specified by *base*:

→

| | |
|---|---|
| **strings** ← | **d**    Decimal |
| | **o**    Octal |
| | **x**    Hexadecimal |
| | **——target=**_format_ <br> Specify an alternative object code format to the system default. |
| | **—o**   Same as —t o. |
| | **——help** <br> Print help message and then exit. |
| | **—v, ——version** <br> Print version information and then exit. |
| **strip** | **strip** [_options_] _files_ <br><br> Remove symbols from object _files_, thereby reducing file sizes and freeing disk space. <br><br> **_Options_** <br><br> **—F** _format_, **——target=**_format_ <br> Expect the input file to be in the format _format_. <br><br> **—O** _format_, **——output-target=**_format_ <br> Write output file in _format_. <br><br> **—R** _section_, **——remove-section=**_section_ <br> Delete _section_. <br><br> **—s, ——strip-all** <br> Strip all symbols. <br><br> **—S, -g, ——strip-debug** <br> Strip debugging symbols. <br><br> **—x, ——discard-all** <br> Strip nonglobal symbols. <br><br> **—X, ——discard-locals** <br> Strip local symbols that were generated by the compiler. <br><br> **—v, ——verbose** <br> Verbose mode. |

**stty** [*options*] [*modes*]

Set terminal I/O options for the current standard input device. Without options, **stty** reports the terminal settings that differ from those set by running **stty sane**, where a ^ indicates the Ctrl key and ^` indicates a null value. Most modes can be negated using an optional – (shown in brackets). The corresponding description is also shown in brackets. Some arguments use non-POSIX extensions; these are marked with a *.

*Options*

**–a, – –all**
> Report all option settings.

**–g**  Report settings in hex.

*Control modes*

*n*  Set terminal baud rate to *n* (e.g., 2400).

**[–]clocal**
> [Enable] disable modem control.

**[–]cread**
> [Disable] enable the receiver.

**cs***bits*
> Set character size to *bits*, which must be 5, 6, 7, or 8.

**[–]cstopb**
> [1] 2 stop bits per character.

**[–]hup**
> [Do not] hang up connection on last close.

**[–]hupcl**
> Same as previous.

**ispeed** *n*
> Set terminal input baud rate to *n*.

**ospeed** *n*
> Set terminal output baud rate to *n*.

**[–]parenb**
> [Disable] enable parity generation and detection.

**[–]parodd**
> Use [even] odd parity.

→

**[–]crtscts***

> [Disable]enable RTS/CTS handshaking.

### Flow control modes

The following flow control modes are available by combining the *ortsfl*, *ctsflow*, and *rtsflow* flags:

| Flag Settings | Flow Control Mode |
|---|---|
| *ortsfl rtsflow ctsflow* | Enable unidirectional flow control. |
| *ortsfl rtsflow –ctsflow* | Assert RTS when ready to send. |
| *ortsfl –rtsflow ctsflow* | No effect. |
| *ortsfl –rtsflow –ctsflow* | Enable bidirectional flow control. |
| *–ortsfl rtsflow ctsflow* | Enable bidirectional flow control. |
| *–ortsfl rtsflow –ctsflow* | No effect. |
| *–ortsfl –rtsflow ctsflow* | Stop transmission when CTS drops. |
| *–ortsfl –rtsflow –ctsflow* | Disable hardware flow control. |

### Input modes

**[–]brkint**

> [Do not] signal INTR on break.

**[–]icrnl**

> [Do not] map CR to NL on input.

**[–]ignbrk**

> [Do not] ignore break on input.

**[–]igncr**

> [Do not] ignore CR on input.

**[–]ignpar**

> [Do not] ignore parity errors.

**[–]inlcr**

> [Do not] map NL to CR on input.

**[–]inpck**

> [Disable] enable input parity checking.

**[–]istrip**

> [Do not] strip input characters to 7 bits.

**[–]iuclc***

> [Do not] map uppercase to lowercase on input.

**[–]ixany***

> Allow [XON] any character to restart output.

**[–]ixoff [–]tandem**

[Do not] send START/STOP characters when queue is nearly empty/full.

**[–]ixon**

[Disable] enable START/STOP output control.

**[–]parmrk**

[Do not] mark parity errors.

**[–]imaxbel***

When input buffer is too full to accept a new character, [flush the input buffer] beep without flushing the input buffer.

### Output modes

**bs*n***

Select style of delay for backspaces (0 or 1).

**cr*n*** Select style of delay for carriage returns (0–3).

**ff*n*** Select style of delay for formfeeds (0 or 1).

**nl*n*** Select style of delay for linefeeds (0 or 1).

**tab*n***

Select style of delay for horizontal tabs (0–3).

**vt*n*** Select style of delay for vertical tabs (0 or 1).

**[–]ocrnl***

[Do not] map CR to NL on output.

**[–]ofdel***

Set fill character to [NULL] DEL.

**[–]ofill***

Delay output with [timing] fill characters.

**[–]olcuc***

[Do not] map lowercase to uppercase on output.

**[–]onlcr***

[Do not] map NL to CR-NL on output.

**[–]onlret***

On the terminal, NL performs [does not perform] the CR function.

**[–]onocr***

Do not [do] output CRs at column 0.

→

[–]opost
>[Do not] postprocess output.

### Local modes

[–]echo
>[Do not] echo every character typed.

[–]echoe, [–]crterase
>[Do not] echo ERASE character as BS-space-BS string.

[–]echok
>[Do not] echo NL after KILL character.

[–]echonl
>[Do not] echo NL.

[–]icanon
>[Disable] enable canonical input (ERASE, KILL, WERASE, and RPRINT processing).

[–]iexten
>[Disable] enable extended functions for input data.

[–]isig
>[Disable] enable checking of characters against INTR, SUSPEND, and QUIT.

[–]noflsh
>[Enable] disable flush after INTR or QUIT.

[–]tostop*
>[Do not] send SIGTTOU when background processes write to the terminal.

[–]xcase*
>[Do not] change case on local output.

[–]echoprt, [–]prterase*
>When erasing characters, echo them backward, enclosed in \ and /.

[–]echoctl. [–]ctlecho*
>Do not echo control characters literally. Use hat notation (e.g., ^Z).

[–]echoke [–]crtkill*
>Erase characters as specified by the **echoprt** and **echoe** settings (default is **echoctl** and **echok** settings).

*ctrl-char c*

> Set control character to *c*. *ctrl-char* is **dsusp** (flush input and then send stop), **eof**, **eol**, **eol2** (alternate end-of-line), **erase**, **intr**, **lnext** (treat next character literally), **kill**, **rprnt** (redraw line), **quit**, **start**, **stop**, **susp**, **swtch**, or **werase** (erase previous word). *c* can be a literal control character, a character in hat notation (e.g., ^**Z**), in hex (must begin with 0x), in octal (must begin with 0), or in decimal. Disable the control character with values of ^– or **undef**.

**min** *n*

> Set the minimum number of characters that will satisfy a read until the time value has expired when **–icanon** is set.

**time** *n*

> Set the number of tenths of a second before reads time out if the **min** number of characters have not been read when **–icanon** is set.

**line** *i*

> Set line discipline to *i* (1–126).

*Combination modes*

**cooked**

> Same as **–raw**.

**[–]evenp** **[–]parity**

> Same as **[– ]parenb** and **cs[8 ]7**.

**[–]parity**

> Same as **[– ]parenb** and **cs[8 ]7**.

**ek**　Reset ERASE and KILL characters to Ctrl-h and Ctrl-u, their defaults.

**[–]lcase**

> [Un] set **xcase**, **iuclc**, and **olcuc**.

**[–]LCASE**

> Same as **[– ]lcase**.

**[–]nl**

> [Un] set **icrnl** and **onlcr**. **–nl** also unsets **inlcr**, **igncr**, **ocrnl**, and **onlret**, **icrnl**, **onlcr**.

**[–]oddp**

> Same as **[– ]parenb**, **[– ]parodd**, and **cs7[8 ]**.

→

*Linux Commands*

**stty**
←

[–]raw
   [Disable] enable raw input and output (no ERASE, KILL, INTR, QUIT, EOT, SWITCH, or output postprocessing).

sane
   Reset all modes to reasonable values.

[–]tabs*
   [Expand to spaces] preserve output tabs.

[–]cbreak
   Same as –icanon.

[–]pass8
   Same as –parenb –istrip cs8.

[–]litout
   Same as –parenb –istrip cs8.

[–]decctlq*
   Same as –ixany.

crt   Same as **echoe echoctl echoke**.

dec
   Same as **echoe echoctl echoke –ixany**. Additionally, set INTERRUPT to ^C, ERASE to DEL, and KILL to ^U.

*Special settings*

ispeed *speed*
   Specify input speed.

ospeed *speed*
   Specify output speed.

rows *rows**
   Specify number of rows.

cols *columns*, columns *columns**
   Specify number of columns.

size*
   Display current row and column settings.

line *discipline**
   Specify line discipline.

speed
   Display terminal speed.

**su** [*option*] [*user*] [*shell_args*]

Create a shell with the effective user-ID *user*. If no *user* is specified, create a shell for a privileged user (that is, become a superuser). Enter *EOF* to terminate. You can run the shell with particular options by passing them as *shell_args* (e.g., if the shell runs **sh**, you can specify **−c** *command* to execute *command* via **sh** or **−r** to create a restricted shell).

*Options*

**−, −l, −−login**
> Go through the entire login sequence (i.e., change to *user*'s environment).

**−c** *command,* **−−command=***command*
> Execute *command* in the new shell and then exit immediately. If *command* is more than one word, it should be enclosed in quotes—for example:

> su -c 'find / -name \*.c -print' nobody

**−f, −−fast**
> Start shell with **−f** option. In **csh** and **tcsh**, this suppresses the reading of the *.cshrc* file. In **bash**, this suppresses filename pattern expansion.

**−m, −p, −−preserve-environment**
> Do not reset environment variables.

**−s** *shell,* **−−shell=***shell*
> Execute *shell*, not the shell specified in */etc/passwd*, unless *shell* is restricted.

**−−help**
> Print a help message and then exit.

**−−version**
> Print version information and then exit.

**sum** [*options*] *files*

Calculate and print a checksum and the number of (1KB) blocks for *file*. Useful for verifying data transmission.

*Options*

**−r**  The default setting. Use the BSD checksum algorithm.

→

| | |
|---|---|
| sum<br>← | **−s, −−sysv**<br>    Use alternate checksum algorithm as used on System V.<br>    The blocksize is 512 bytes.<br><br>**−−help**<br>    Print a help message and then exit.<br><br>**−−version**<br>    Print the version number and then exit. |
| **swapdev** | **swapdev** [*option*] [*image* [*swapdevice* [*offset*]]]<br><br>System administration command. If no arguments are given, display usage information about the swap device. If just the location of the kernel *image* is specified, print the information found there. To change that information, specify the new *swapdevice*. You may also specify the *offset* in the kernel image to change. Note that **rdev −s** is a synonym for **swapdev**.<br><br>*Option*<br><br>**−o** *offset*<br>    Synonymous to specifying an *offset* as an argument. |
| **swapoff** | **swapoff −a**  \|  *device* . . .<br><br>System administration command. Stop making the listed *devices* available for swapping and paging.<br><br>*Option*<br><br>**−a**  Consult */etc/fstab* for devices marked **sw**. Use those in<br>    place of the *device* argument. |
| **swapon** | **swapon** [*options*] *device* . . .<br><br>System administration command. Make the listed *devices* available for swapping and paging.<br><br>*Options*<br><br>**−a**  Consult */etc/fstab* for devices marked **sw**. Use those in<br>    place of the *device* argument. |

−p *priority*
> Specify a *priority* for the swap area. Higher priority areas will be used up before lower priority areas are used.

---

## sync

System administration command. Write filesystem buffers to disk. **sync** executes the **sync()** system call. If the system is to be stopped, **sync** must be called to ensure filesystem integrity. Note that **shutdown** automatically calls **sync** before shutting down the system. **sync** may take several seconds to complete, so the system should be told to **sleep** briefly if you are about to manually call **halt** or **reboot**. Note that **shutdown** is the preferred way to halt or reboot your system, since it takes care of **sync**-ing and other housekeeping for you.

---

## sysklogd

System administration command. **sysklogd**, the Linux program that provides **syslogd** functionality, behaves exactly like the BSD version of **syslogd**. The difference should be completely transparent to the user. However, **sysklogd** is coded very differently and supports a slightly extended syntax. It is invoked as **syslogd**. See also **klogd**.

*Options*

−d  Turn on debugging.

−f *configfile*
> Specify alternate configuration file.

−h  Forward messages from remote hosts to forwarding hosts.

−l *hostlist*
> Specify hostnames that should be logged with just their hostname, not their fully qualified domain name. Multiple hosts should be separated with a colon (:).

−m *markinterval*
> Select number of minutes between mark messages.

−n  Avoid autobackgrounding. This is needed when starting **syslogd** from **init**.

→

| | |
|---|---|
| syslogd<br>← | **−p** *socket*<br>    Send log to *socket* instead of */dev/log*.<br><br>**−r**  Receive messages from the network using an Internet domain socket with the **syslog** service.<br><br>**−s** *domainlist*<br>    Strip off domain names specified in *domainlist* before logging. Multiple domain names should be separated by a colon (:). |
| syslogd | **syslogd**<br><br>TCP/IP command. Log system messages into a set of files described by the configuration file */etc/syslog.conf.* Each message is one line. A message can contain a priority code, marked by a number in angle braces at the beginning of the line. Priorities are defined in *<sys/syslog.h>.* **syslogd** reads from an Internet domain socket specified in */etc/services.* To bring **syslogd** down, send it a terminate signal. |
| systat | **systat** [*options*] *host*<br><br>System administration command. Get information about the network or system status of a remote host by querying its **netstat**, **systat**, or **daytime** service.<br><br>*Options*<br><br>**−n, −−netstat**<br>    Specifically query the host's **netstat** service.<br><br>**−p** *port,* **−−port** *port*<br>    Specify port to query.<br><br>**−s, −−systat**<br>    Specifically query the host's **systat** service.<br><br>**−t, −−time**<br>    Specifically query the host's **daytime** service. |
| tac | **tac** [*options*] [*file*]<br><br>Named for the common command **cat**, **tac** prints files in reverse. Without a filename or with −, it reads from standard input. By default, it reverses the order of the lines, printing the last line first. |

## Options

**−b, −−before**
Print separator (by default a newline) before string that it delimits.

**−r, −−regex**
Expect separator to be a regular expression.

**−s** *string,* **−−separator=***string*
Specify alternate separator (default is newline).

**−−help**
Print a help message and then exit.

**−−version**
Print version information and then exit.

---

**tail** [*options*] [*file*]

Print the last 10 lines of the named *file* (or standard input if − is specified) on standard output.

## Options

**−***n*[*k*]
Begin printing at *n*th item from end-of-file. *k* specifies the item to count: **l** (lines, the default), **b** (blocks), or **c** (characters).

**−***k*  Same as **−***n*, but use the default count of 10.

**+***n*[*k*]
Like **−***n*, but start at *n*th item from beginning of file.

**+***k*  Like **−***k*, but count from beginning of file.

**−c** *num*{bkm}, **−−bytes** *num*{bkm}
Print last *num* bytes. An alternate blocksize may be specified:

**b**  512 bytes

**k**  1 kilobyte

**m**  1 megabyte

**−f**  Don't quit at the end of file; "follow" file as it grows. End when user presses Ctrl-C.

**−n** *num,* **−−lines** *num*
Print last *num* lines.

→

| | |
|---|---|
| tail<br>← | -q, --quiet, --silent<br>    Suppress filename headers.<br><br>--version<br>    Print version information and then exit.<br><br>*Examples*<br><br>Show the last 20 lines containing instances of .Ah:<br><br>`grep '\.Ah' `*file*` | tail -20`<br><br>Show the last 10 characters of variable **name**:<br><br>`echo "$name" | tail -c`<br><br>Print the last two blocks of **bigfile**:<br><br>`tail -2b bigfile` |
| talk | **talk** *person* [*ttyname*]<br><br>Talk to another user. *person* is either the login name of someone on your own machine or *user@host* on another host. To talk to a user who is logged in more than once, use *ttyname* to indicate the appropriate terminal name. Once communication has been established, the two parties may type simultaneously, with their output appearing in separate windows. To redraw the screen, type Ctrl-L. To exit, type your interrupt character; **talk** then moves the cursor to the bottom of the screen and restores the terminal. |
| talkd | **talkd** [*option*]<br><br>TCP/IP command. Remote user communication server. **talkd** notifies a user that somebody else wants to initiate a conversation. A **talk** client initiates a rendezvous by sending a CTL_MSG of type LOOK_UP to the server. This causes the server to search its invitation tables for an existing invitation for the client. If the lookup fails, the caller sends an ANNOUNCE message, causing the server to broadcast an announcement on the callee's login ports requesting contact. When the callee responds, the local server responds with the rendezvous address, and a stream connection is established through which the conversation takes place. |

−d  Write debugging information to the **syslogd** log file.

---

**tar** [*options*] [*tarfile*] [*other-files*]

Copy *files* to or restore *files* from an archive medium. If any *files* are directories, **tar** acts on the entire subtree. Options need not be preceded by − (though they may be). The exception to this rule is when you are using a long-style option (such as --**modification-time**). In that case, the exact syntax is:

```
tar --long-option -function-options files
```

For example:

```
tar --modification-time -xvf tarfile.tar
```

*Function options*

You must use exactly one of these, and it must come before any other options:

−c, −−**create**
    Create a new archive.

−d, −−**compare**
    Compare the files stored in *tarfile* with *other-files*. Report any differences: missing files, different sizes, different file attributes (such as permissions or modification time).

−r, −−**append**
    Append *other-files* to the end of an existing archive.

−t, −−**list**
    Print the names of *other-files* if they are stored on the archive (if *other-files* are not specified, print names of all files).

−u, −−**update**
    Add files if not in the archive or if modified.

−x, −−**extract**, −−**get**
    Extract *other-files* from an archive (if *other-files* are not specified, extract all files).

−A, −−**catenate**, −−**concatenate**
    Concatenate a second tar file on to the end of the first.

→

**tar**
←

*Options*

**n**     Select device *n*, where *n* is 0, . . . ,9999. The default is
         found in */etc/default/tar*.

**[*drive*][*density*]**
         Set drive (0–7) and storage density (**l**, **m**, or **h**, corre-
         sponding to low, medium, or high).

**−−atime-preserve**
         Preserve original access time on extracted files.

**−b, −−block-size=***n*
         Set block size to *n* × 512 bytes.

**−−checkpoint**
         List directory names encountered.

**−−exclude=***file*
         Remove *file* from any list of files.

**−f** *arch*, **−−file=***filename*
         Store files in or extract files from archive *arch*. Note
         that *filename* may take the form *hostname:filename*.

**−−force-local**
         Interpret filenames in the form *hostname:filename* as
         local files.

**−g, −−listed-incremental**
         Create new-style incremental backup.

**−h, −−dereference**
         Dereference symbolic links.

**−i, −−ignore-zeros**
         Ignore zero-sized blocks (i.e., EOFs).

**−−ignore-failed-read**
         Ignore unreadable files to be archived. Default behav-
         ior is to exit when encountering these.

**−k, −−keep-old-files**
         When extracting files, do not overwrite files with simi-
         lar names. Instead, print an error message.

**−l, −−one-file-system**
         Do not archive files from other file systems.

**−m, −−modification-time**
         Do not restore file modification times; update them to
         the time of extraction.

**−−null**

Allow filenames to be null-terminated with **−T**. Override **−C**.

**−−old, −−portability, −−preserve**

Equivalent to invoking both the **−p** and **−s** options.

**−p, −−same-permissions, −−preserve-permissions**

Keep ownership of extracted files same as that of original permissions.

**−−remove-files**

Remove originals after inclusion in archive.

**−−rsh-command=**_command_

Do not connect to remote host with **rsh**; instead, use _command_.

**−s, −−same-order, −−preserve-order**

When extracting, sort filenames to correspond to the order in the archive.

**−−totals**

Print byte totals.

**−−use-compress-program=**_program_

Compress archived files with _program_, or uncompress extracted files with _program_.

**−v, −−verbose**

Verbose. Print filenames as they are added or extracted.

**−w, −−interactive**

Wait for user confirmation (**y**) before taking any actions.

**−z, −−gzip, −−ungzip**

Compress files with **gzip** before archiving them, or uncompress them with **gunzip** before extracting them.

**−C, −−directory=**_directory_

**cd** to _directory_ before beginning **tar** operation.

**−F, −−info-script, −−new-volume-script=**_script_

Implies **−M** (multiple archive files). Run _script_ at the end of each file.

**−G, −−incremental**

Create old-style incremental backup.

**−K** _file_, **−−starting-file** _file_

Begin **tar** operation at file _file_ in archive.

→

**−L, −−tape-length=**_length_
Write a maximum of _length_ × 1024 bytes to each tape.

**−M, −−multivolume**
Expect archive to multivolume. With −c, create such an archive.

**−N** _date_, **−−after-date** _date_
Ignore files older than _date_.

**−O, −−to-stdout**
Print extracted files on standard out.

**−P, −−absolute-paths**
Do not remove initial slashes (/) from input filenames.

**−R, −−record-number**
Display archive's record number.

**−S, −−sparse**
Treat short file specially and more efficiently.

**−T** _filename_, **−−files-from** _filename_
Consult _filename_ for files to extract or create.

**−V** _name_, **−−label=**_name_
Name this volume _name_.

**−W, −−verify**
Check archive for corruption after creation.

**−X** _file_, **−−exclude** _file_
Consult _file_ for list of files to exclude.

**−Z, −−compress, −−uncompress**
Compress files with **compress** before archiving them, or uncompress them with **uncompress** before extracting them.

### Examples

Create an archive of _/bin_ and _/usr/bin_ (**c**), show the command working (**v**), and store on the tape in _/dev/rmt0_:

```
tar cvf /dev/rmt0 /bin /usr/bin
```

List the tape's contents in a format like **ls −l**:

```
tar tvf /dev/rmt0
```

Extract the _/bin_ directory:

```
tar xvf /dev/rmt0 /bin
```

Create an archive of the current directory and store it in a file _backup.tar_:

```
tar cvf - `find . -print` > backup.tar
```

(The – tells **tar** to store the archive on standard output, which is then redirected.)

## tcpd

TCP/IP command. Monitor incoming TCP/IP requests (such as those for **telnet**, **ftp**, **finger**, **exec**, **rlogin**). Provide checking and logging services; then pass the request to the appropriate daemon.

## tcpdchk [*options*]

TCP/IP command. Consult the TCP wrapper configuration (in */etc/hosts.allow* and */etc/hosts.deny*); display a list of all possible problems with it; attempt to suggest possible fixes.

### Options

–a   Include a list of rules; do not require an ALLOW keyword before allowing sites to access the local host.

–d   Consult *./hosts.allow* and *./hosts.deny* instead of */etc/hosts.allow* and */etc/hosts.deny*.

–i *conf-file*
> Specify location of *inetd.conf* or *tlid.conf* file. These are files that **tcpdchk** automatically uses in its evaluation of TCP wrapper files.

–v   Verbose mode.

## tcpdmatch [*options*] *daemon client*

TCP/IP command. Predict the TCP wrapper's response to a specific request. You must specify which *daemon* the request is made to (the syntax may be *daemon@host* for requests to remote machines) and the *client* from which the request originates (the syntax may be *user@client* for a specific user or a wildcard). Consult */etc/hosts.allow* and */etc/hosts.deny* to determine the TCP wrapper's actions.

### Options

–d   Consult *./hosts.allow* and *./hosts.deny* instead of */etc/hosts.allow* and */etc/hosts.deny*.

→

| | |
|---|---|
| **tcpdmatch** ← | **−i** *conf-file*<br>Specify location of *inetd.conf* or *tlid.conf* file. These are files that **tcpdmatch** automatically uses in its evaluation of TCP wrapper files. |
| **tcsh** | **tcsh** [*options*] [*file* [*arguments*]]<br><br>An extended version of the C shell, a command interpreter into which all other commands are entered. For more information, see Chapter 8. |
| **tee** | **tee** [*options*] *files*<br><br>Accept output from another command and send it both to the standard output and to *files* (like a T or fork in a road).<br><br>***Options***<br><br>**−a, −−append**<br>Append to *files*; do not overwrite.<br><br>**−i, −−ignore-interrupts**<br>Ignore interrupt signals.<br><br>**−−help**<br>Print a help message and then exit.<br><br>**−−version**<br>Print version information and then exit.<br><br>***Example***<br><br>`ls -l | tee savefile`    *View listing and save for later* |
| **telinit** | **telinit** [*option*] [*runlevel*]<br><br>System administration command. Signal **init** to change the system's runlevel. **telinit** is actually just a link to **init**, the ancestor of all processes.<br><br>***Option***<br><br>**−t** *seconds*<br>Send SIGKILL *seconds* after SIGTERM. Default is 20.<br><br>***Runlevels***<br><br>The default runlevels vary from distribution to distribution, but these are standard: |

0    Halt the system.

**1, s, S**
   Single user.

6    Reboot the system.

**a, b, c**
   Process only entries in */etc/inittab* that are marked with run level **a**, **b**, or **c**.

**q, Q**
   Reread */etc/inittab*.

Check the */etc/inittab* file for runlevels on your system.

---

**telnet** [*options*] [*host* [*port*]]

Access remote systems. **telnet** is the user interface that communicates with another host using the Telnet protocol. If **telnet** is invoked without *host*, it enters command mode, indicated by its prompt, **telnet>**, and accepts and executes the commands listed after the following options. If invoked with arguments, **telnet** performs an **open** command (shown in the following list) with those arguments. *host* indicates the host's official name. *port* indicates a port number (default is the Telnet port).

*Options*

−a   Automatic login into the remote system.

−d   Turn on socket-level debugging.

−e [*escape_char*]
   Set initial **telnet** escape character to *escape_char*. If *escape_char* is omitted, there will be no predefined escape character.

−l *user*
   When connecting to remote system and if remote system understands ENVIRON, send *user* to the remote system as the value for variable USER.

−n *tracefile*
   Open *tracefile* for recording the trace information.

−r   Emulate **rlogin**: the default escape character is a tilde (˜); an escape character followed by a dot causes **telnet** to disconnect from the remote host; a **^Z** instead of a dot suspends **telnet**; and a ] (the default **telnet** escape character) generates a normal **telnet** prompt. These codes are accepted only at the beginning of a line.

→

| | |
|---|---|
| **telnet**<br>← | **−8**   Request 8-bit operation. |

**−8**   Request 8-bit operation.

**−E**   Disable the escape character functionality.

**−L**   Specify an 8-bit data path on output.

**−S** *tos*
> Set the IP type-of-service (TOS) option for the Telnet connection to the value *tos*.

***Commands***

**CTRL-Z**
> Suspend **telnet**.

**!** [*command*]
> Execute a single command in a subshell on the local system. If *command* is omitted, an interactive subshell will be invoked.

**?** [*command*]
> Get help. With no arguments, print a help summary. If a command is specified, print the help information for just that command.

**close**
> Close a Telnet session and return to command mode.

**display** *argument* . . .
> Display all, or some, of the **set** and **toggle** values.

**environ** [*arguments* [ . . . ]]
> Manipulate variables that may be sent through the TEL-NET ENVIRON option. Valid arguments for **environ** are:

> *?*   Get help for the **environ** command.

> **define** *variable value*
> > Define *variable* to have a value of *value*.

> **undefine** *variable*
> > Remove *variable* from the list of environment variables.

> **export** *variable*
> > Mark *variable* to have its value exported to the remote side.

**unexport** *variable*

Mark *variable* to not be exported unless explicitly requested by the remote side.

**list**  Display current variable values.

**logout**

If the remote host supports the **logout** command, close the **telnet** session.

**mode** [*type*]

Depending on state of Telnet session, *type* is one of several options:

**?**  Print out help information for the **mode** command.

**character**

Disable TELNET LINEMODE option, or, if remote side does not understand the option, enter "character-at-a-time" mode.

**[–]edit**

Attempt to [disable] enable the EDIT mode of the TELNET LINEMODE option.

**[–]isig**

Attempt to [disable]enable the TRAPSIG mode of the LINEMODE option.

**line**

Enable LINEMODE option, or, if remote side does not understand the option, attempt to enter "old line-by-line" mode.

**[–]softtabs**

Attempt to [disable] enable the SOFT_TAB mode of the LINEMODE option.

**[–]litecho**

[Disable]enable LIT_ECHO mode.

**open**[**–l** *user*] *host* [*port*]

Open a connection to the named *host*. If no *port* number is specified, attempt to contact a Telnet server at the default port.

**quit**

Close any open Telnet session and then exit **telnet**.

**status**

Show current status of **telnet**. This includes the peer one is connected to as well as the current mode.

→

Linux
Commands

**telnet**
←

**send** *arguments*

>Send one or more special character sequences to the remote host. Following are the arguments that may be specified:

? Print out help information for **send** command.

**abort**
>Send Telnet ABORT sequence.

**ao** Send Telnet AO sequence, which should cause the remote system to flush all output from the remote system to the user's terminal.

**ayt** Send Telnet AYT (Are You There) sequence.

**brk** Send Telnet BRK (Break) sequence.

**do** *cmd*

**dont** *cmd*

**will** *cmd*

**wont** *cmd*
>Send Telnet DO *cmd* sequence, where *cmd* is a number between 0 and 255 or a symbolic name for a specific **telnet** command. If *cmd* is ? or **help**, this command prints out help (including a list of symbolic names).

**ec** Send Telnet EC (Erase Character) sequence, which causes the remote system to erase the last character entered.

**el** Send Telnet EL (Erase Line) sequence, which causes the remote system to erase the last line entered.

**eof** Send Telnet EOF (End Of File) sequence.

**eor** Send Telnet EOR (End Of Record) sequence.

**escape**
>Send current Telnet escape character (initially ^).

**ga** Send Telnet GA (Go Ahead) sequence.

**getstatus**
>If the remote side supports the Telnet STATUS command, **getstatus** sends the subnegotiation request that the server send its current option status.

> **ip**  Send Telnet IP (Interrupt process) sequence, which causes the remote system to abort the currently running process.

**nop**
> Send Telnet NOP (No operation) sequence.

**susp**
> Send Telnet SUSP (Suspend process) sequence.

**synch**
> Send Telnet SYNCH sequence, which causes the remote system to discard all previously typed (but not read) input.

**set** *argument value*

**unset** *argument value*
> Set any one of a number of **telnet** variables to a specific value or to **TRUE**. The special value **off** disables the function associated with the variable. **unset** disables any of the specified functions. The values of variables may be interrogated with the aid of the **display** command. The variables that may be specified are:

> **?**  Display legal **set** and **unset** commands.

> **ayt**  If **telnet** is in LOCALCHARS mode, this character is taken to be the alternate AYT character.

**echo**
> This is the value (initially ^E) which, when in "line-by-line" mode, toggles between doing local echoing of entered characters and suppressing echoing of entered characters.

> **eof**  If **telnet** is operating in LINEMODE or in the old "line-by-line" mode, entering this character as the first character on a line will cause the character to be sent to the remote system.

**erase**
> If **telnet** is in LOCALCHARS mode and operating in the "character-at-a-time" mode, then when this character is entered, a Telnet EC sequence will be sent to the remote system.

**escape**
> This is the Telnet escape character (initially ^[), which causes entry into the Telnet command mode when connected to a remote system.

→

**telnet**
←

**flushoutput**

If **telnet** is in LOCALCHARS mode and the flushoutput character is entered, a Telnet AO sequence is sent to the remote host.

**forw1**

If Telnet is in LOCALCHARS mode, this character is taken to be an alternate end-of-line character.

**forw2**

If Telnet is in LOCALCHARS mode, this character is taken to be an alternate end-of-line character.

**interrupt**

If Telnet AO is in LOCALCHARS mode and the **interrupt** character is entered, a Telnet IP sequence is sent to the remote host.

**kill** If Telnet IP is in LOCALCHARS mode and operating in the "character-at-a-time" mode, then when this character is entered, a Telnet EL sequence is sent to the remote system.

**lnext**

If Telnet EL is in LINEMODE or in the old "line-by-line" mode, then this character is taken to be the terminal's **lnext** character.

**quit**

If Telnet EL is in LOCALCHARS mode and the **quit** character is entered, a Telnet BRK sequence is sent to the remote host.

**reprint**

If Telnet BRK is in LINEMODE or in the old "line-by-line" mode, this character is taken to be the terminal's **reprint** character.

**rlogin**

Enable **rlogin** mode. Same as using −r command-line option.

**start**

If the Telnet TOGGLE-FLOW-CONTROL option has been enabled, this character is taken to be the terminal's **start** character.

**stop**

If the Telnet TOGGLE-FLOW-CONTROL option has been enabled, this character is taken to be the terminal's **stop** character.

**susp**

> If Telnet is in LOCALCHARS mode, or if the LINEMODE is enabled and the **suspend** character is entered, a Telnet SUSP sequence is sent to the remote host.

**tracefile**

> File to which output generated by **netdata** is written.

**worderase**

> If Telnet BRK is in LINEMODE or in the old "line-by-line" mode, this character is taken to be the terminal's **worderase** character. Defaults for these are the terminal's defaults.

slc [*state*]

> Set state of special characters when Telnet LINEMODE option has been enabled.

? List help on the **slc** command.

**check**

> Verify current settings for current special characters. If discrepancies are discovered, convert local settings to match remote ones.

**export**

> Switch to local defaults for the special characters.

**import**

> Switch to remote defaults for the special characters.

toggle *arguments* [ . . . ]

> Toggle various flags that control how Telnet responds to events. The flags may be set explicitly to **true** or **false** using the **set** and **unset** commands listed previously. The valid arguments are:

? Display legal **toggle** commands.

**autoflush**

> If **autoflush** and LOCALCHARS are both **true**, then when the **ao** or **quit** characters are recognized, Telnet refuses to display any data on the user's terminal until the remote system acknowledges that it has processed those Telnet sequences.

**autosynch**

> If **autosynch** and LOCALCHARS are both **true**, then when the **intr** or **quit** character is entered, the resulting Telnet sequence sent is followed by the

→

Linux
Commands

**telnet**
←

Telnet SYNCH sequence. Initial value for this **toggle** is **false**.

**binary**

Enable or disable the Telnet BINARY option on both the input and the output.

**inbinary**

Enable or disable the Telnet BINARY option on the input.

**outbinary**

Enable or disable the Telnet BINARY option on the output.

**crlf**

If this **toggle** value is **true**, carriage returns are sent as **CR-LF**. If **false**, carriage returns are sent as **CR-NUL**. Initial value is **false**.

**crmod**

Toggle carriage return mode. Initial value is **false**.

**debug**

Toggle socket level debugging mode. Initial value is **false**.

**localchars**

If the value is **true**, **flush**, **interrupt**, **quit**, **erase**, and **kill** characters are recognized locally, then transformed into appropriate Telnet control sequences. Initial value is **true**.

**netdata**

Toggle display of all network data. Initial value is **false**.

**options**

Toggle display of some internal **telnet** protocol processing pertaining to Telnet options. Initial value is **false**.

**prettydump**

When **netdata** is enabled, and if **prettydump** is enabled, the output from the **netdata** command is reorganized into a more user-friendly format, spaces are put between each character in the output, and an asterisk precedes any Telnet escape sequence.

**skiprc**

> Toggle whether to process *~/.telnetrc* file. Initial value is **false**, meaning the file is processed.

**termdata**

> Toggle printing of hexadecimal terminal data. Initial value is **false**.

z  Suspend **telnet**; works only for the **csh**.

---

**telnetd** [*options*]

TCP/IP command. Telnet protocol server. **telnetd** is invoked by the Internet server for requests to connect to the Telnet port (port 23 by default). **telnetd** allocates a pseudoterminal device for a client, thereby creating a login process that has the slave side of the pseudoterminal serving as **stdin**, **stdout**, and **stderr**. **telnetd** manipulates the master side of the pseudoterminal by implementing the Telnet protocol and by passing characters between the remote client and the login process.

*Options*

**−debug** [*port*]

> Start **telnetd** manually instead of through **inetd**. *port* may be specified as an alternate TCP port number on which to run **telnetd**.

**−D** *modifier(s)*

> Debugging mode. This allows **telnet** to print out debugging information to the connection, enabling the user to see what **telnet** is doing. Several modifiers are available for the debugging mode:

> **exercise**
> > Has not been implemented yet.

> **netdata**
> > Display data stream received by **telnetd**.

> **options**
> > Print information about the negotiation of the Telnet options.

> **ptydata**
> > Display data written to the pseudo terminal device.

→

Linux
Commands

| telnetd | report |
|---|---|
| ← | Print **options** information, as well as some additional information about what processing is going on. |

| test | test *expression*<br>[ *expression* ]<br><br>Also exists as a built-in in most shells.<br><br>Evaluate an *expression* and, if its value is **true**, return a zero exit status; otherwise, return a nonzero exit status. In shell scripts, you can use the alternate form [*expression*]. This command is generally used with conditional constructs in shell programs.<br><br>***File testers***<br><br>The syntax for all of these options is **test** *option file*. If the specified file does not exist, they return **false**. Otherwise, they will test the file as specified in the option description.<br><br>−b  Is the file block special?<br><br>−c  Is the file character special?<br><br>−d  Is the file a directory?<br><br>−e  Does the file exist?<br><br>−f  Is the file a regular file?<br><br>−g  Does the file have the set-group-ID bit set?<br><br>−k  Does the file have the sticky bit set?<br><br>−L  Is the file a symbolic link?<br><br>−p  Is the file a named pipe?<br><br>−r  Is the file readable by the current user?<br><br>−s  Is the file nonempty?<br><br>−S  Is the file a socket?<br><br>−t [*file-descriptor*]<br>    Is the file associated with *file-descriptor* (or 1, standard output, by default) connected to a terminal?<br><br>−u  Does the file have the set-user-ID bit set? |
|---|---|

**−w**  Is the file writable by the current user?

**−x**  Is the file executable?

**−O**  Is the file owned by the process's effective user ID?

**−G**  Is the file owned by the process's effective group ID?

### File comparisons

The syntax for file comparisons is **test** *file1 option file2*. A string by itself, without options, returns **true** if it's at least one character long.

**−nt**  Is *file1* newer than *file2*? Check modification, not creation, date.

**−ot**  Is *file1* older than *file2*? Check modification, not creation, date.

**−ef**  Do the files have identical device and inode numbers?

### String tests

The syntax for string tests is **test** *option string*.

**−z**  Is the string 0 characters long?

**−n**  Is the string at least 1 character long?

**= *string***
  Are the two strings equal?

**!= *string***
  Are the strings unequal?

### Expression tests

Note that an expression can consist of any of the previous tests.

**! *expression***
  Is the expression false?

***expression* −a *expression***
  Are the expressions both true?

***expression* −o *expression***
  Is either expression true?

### Integer tests

The syntax for integer tests is **test** *integer1 option integer2*. You may substitute **−l** *string* for an integer; this evaluates to *string*'s length.

→

| | |
|---|---|
| test<br>← | **−eq**<br>    Are the two integers equal?<br><br>**−ne**<br>    Are the two integers unequal?<br><br>**−lt**  Is *integer1* less than *integer2*?<br><br>**−le**  Is *integer1* less than or equal to *integer2*?<br><br>**−gt**  Is *integer1* greater than *integer2*?<br><br>**−ge**<br>    Is *integer1* greater than or equal to *integer2*? |
| tftp | **tftp** [*host* [*port*]]<br><br>User interface to the TFTP (Trivial File Transfer Protocol), which allows users to transfer files to and from a remote machine. The remote *host* may be specified, in which case **tftp** uses *host* as the default host for future transfers.<br><br>***Commands***<br><br>Once **tftp** is running, it issues the prompt:<br><br>`tftp>`<br><br>and recognizes the following commands:<br><br>**?** [*command-name* . . . ]<br>    Print help information.<br><br>**ascii**<br>    Shorthand for **mode ASCII**.<br><br>**binary**<br>    Shorthand for **mode binary**.<br><br>**connect** *hostname* [*port*]<br>    Set the *hostname*, and optionally the *port*, for transfers.<br><br>**get** *filename*<br>**get** *remotename localname*<br>**get** *filename1 filename2 filename3* . . . *filenameN*<br>    Get a file or set of files from the specified remote sources.<br><br>**mode** *transfer-mode*<br>    Set the mode for transfers. *transfer-mode* may be **ASCII** or **binary**. The default is **ASCII**. |

put *filename*
put *localfile remotefile*
put *filename1 filename2 . . . filenameN remote-directory*
> Transfer a file or set of files to the specified remote file or directory.

quit
> Exit **tftp**.

rexmt *retransmission-timeout*
> Set the per-packet retransmission timeout, in seconds.

status
> Print status information: whether **tftp** is connected to a remote host (i.e., whether a host has been specified for the next connection), the current mode, whether verbose and tracing modes are on, and the values for **retransmission timeout** and **total transmission timeout**.

timeout *total-transmission-timeout*
> Set the total transmission timeout, in seconds.

trace
> Toggle packet tracing.

verbose
> Toggle verbose mode.

---

**tftpd** [*homedir*]

TCP/IP command. Trivial File Transfer Protocol server. **tftpd** is normally started by **inetd** and operates at the port indicated in the **tftp** Internet service description in the */etc/ inetd.conf* file. By default, the entry for **tftpd** in */etc/ inetd.conf* is commented out; the comment character must be deleted to make **tfptd** operational. Before responding to a request, the server attempts to change its current directory to *homedir*; the default value is **tftpboot**.

---

**tload** [*options*] [*tty*]

Display system load average in graph format. If *tty* is specified, print it to that tty.

*Options*

−d *delay*
> Specify the delay, in seconds, between updates.

→

| | |
|---|---|
| tload<br>← | −s *scale*<br>  Specify scale (number of characters between each graph tick). A smaller number results in a larger scale. |
| top | **top** [*options*]<br><br>Provide information (frequently refreshed) about the most CPU-intensive processes currently running. See **ps** for explanations of the field descriptors. |

### top [*options*]

Provide information (frequently refreshed) about the most CPU-intensive processes currently running. See **ps** for explanations of the field descriptors.

#### Options

**−b**  Run in batch mode; don't accept command-line input. Useful for sending output to another command or to a file.

**−c**  Show command line in display instead of just command name.

**−d** *delay*
  Specify delay between refreshes.

**−i**  Suppress display of idle and zombie processes.

**−n** *num*
  Update display *num* times, then exit.

**−p** *pid*
  Monitor only processes with the specified process ID.

**−q**  Refresh without any delay. If user is privileged, run with highest priority.

**−s**  Secure mode. Disable some (dangerous) interactive commands.

**−S**  Cumulative mode. Print total CPU time of each process, including dead child processes.

#### Interactive commands

**space**
  Update display immediately.

**c**  Toggle display of command name or full command line.

**f, F**  Add fields to display or remove fields from the display.

**h, ?**  Display help about commands and the status of secure and cumulative modes.

**k**    Prompt for process ID to kill and signal to send (default is 15) to kill it.

**i**    Toggle suppression of idle and zombie processes.

**l**    Toggle display of load average and uptime information.

**m**   Toggle display of memory information.

**n, #**

Prompt for number of processes to show. If 0 is entered, show as many as will fit on the screen (default).

**o, O**

Change order of displayed fields.

**q**    Exit.

**r**    Apply **renice** to a process. Prompt for PID and **renice** value. Suppressed in secure mode.

**s**    Change delay between refreshes. Prompt for new delay time, which should be in seconds. Suppressed in secure mode.

**t**    Toggle display of processes and CPU states information.

**A**    Sort by age, with newest first.

**^L**  Redraw screen.

**M**   Sort tasks by resident memory usage.

**N**   Sort numerically by process ID.

**P**   Sort tasks by CPU usage (default).

**S**   Toggle cumulative mode. (See the −S option.)

**T**   Sort tasks by time/cumulative time.

**W**   Write current setup to ˜/.toprc. This is the recommended way to write a **top** configuration file.

---

**touch** [*options*] *files*

For one or more *files*, update the access time and modification time (and dates) to the current time and date. **touch** is useful in forcing other commands to handle files a certain way; e.g., the operation of **make**, and sometimes **find**, relies on a file's access and modification time. If a file doesn't exist, **touch** creates it with a filesize of 0.

→

| | |
|---|---|
| touch<br>← | *Options*<br><br>**−a, −−time=atime, −−time=access, −−time=use**<br>Update only the access time.<br><br>**−c, −−no-create**<br>Do not create any file that doesn't already exist.<br><br>**−d** *time*, **−−date** *time*<br>Change the time value to the specified *time* instead of the current time. *time* can use several formats and may contain month names, time zones, a.m. and p.m. strings, as well as others.<br><br>**−m, −−time=mtime, −−time=modify**<br>Update only the modification time.<br><br>**−r** *file*, **−−reference** *file*<br>Change times to be the same as those of the specified *file*, instead of the current time.<br><br>**−t** *time*<br>Use the time specified in *time* instead of the current time. This argument must be of the format: *[[cc]yy]mmddhhmm[.ss]*, indicating optional century and year, month, date, hours, minutes, and optional seconds.<br><br>**−−help**<br>Print help message and then exit.<br><br>**−−version**<br>Print the version number and then exit. |
| tr | **tr** [*options*] [*string1* [*string2*]]<br><br>Translate characters—copy standard input to standard output, substituting characters from *string1* to *string2* or deleting characters in *string1*.<br><br>*Options*<br><br>**−c, −−complement**<br>Complement characters in *string1* with respect to ASCII 001–377.<br><br>**−d, −−delete**<br>Delete characters in *string1* from output. |

**–s, ––squeeze-repeats**

Squeeze out repeated output characters in *string2*.

**–t, ––truncate-set1**

Truncate *string1* to the length of *string2* before translating.

**––help**

Print help message and then exit.

**––version**

Print the version number and then exit.

***Special characters***

Include brackets ([ ]) where shown.

\a    ^G (bell)

\b    ^H (backspace)

\f    ^L (form feed)

\n    ^J (newline)

\r    ^M (carriage return)

\t    ^I (tab)

\v    ^K (vertical tab)

*\nnn*

Character with octal value *nnn*.

\\    Literal backslash.

*char1–char2*

All characters in the range *char1* through *char2*. If *char1* does not sort before *char2*, produce an error.

[*char1–char2*]

Same as *char1–char2* if both strings use this.

[*char**]

In *string2*, expand *char* to the length of *string1*.

[*char**number*]

Expand *char* to number occurrences. [**x*4**] expands to **xxxx**, for instance.

[:*class*:]

Expand to all characters in *class*, where *class* can be:

**alnum**

Letters and digits

$\rightarrow$

**alpha**
Letters

**blank**
Whitespace

**cntrl**
Control characters

**digit**
Digits

**graph**
Printable characters except space

**lower**
Lowercase letters

**print**
Printable characters

**punct**
Punctuation

**space**
Whitespace (horizontal or vertical)

**upper**
Uppercase letters

**xdigit**
Hexadecimal digits

[=*char*=]
The class of characters in which *char* belongs.

*Examples*

Change uppercase to lowercase in a file:

```
cat file | tr '[A-Z]' '[a-z]'
```

Turn spaces into newlines (ASCII code 012):

```
tr ' ' '\012' < file
```

Strip blank lines from **file** and save in **new.file** (or use **011** to change successive tabs into one tab):

```
cat file | tr -s "" "\012" > new.file
```

Delete colons from **file**; save result in **new.file**:

```
tr -d : < file > new.file
```

TCP/IP command. Trace route taken by packets to reach network host. **traceroute** attempts tracing by launching UDP probe packets with a small TTL (time to live), then listening for an ICMP "time exceeded" reply from a gateway. *host* is the destination hostname or the IP number of host to reach. *packetsize* is the packet size in bytes of the probe datagram. Default is 38 bytes.

*Options*

−d  Turn on socket-level debugging.

−g *addr*

Enable the IP LSRR (Loose Source Record Route) option in addition to the TTL tests, to ask how someone at IP address *addr* can reach a particular target.

−l  Include the time-to-live value for each packet received.

−m *max_ttl*

Set maximum time-to-live used in outgoing probe packets to *max-ttl* hops. Default is 30 hops.

−n  Show numerical addresses; do not look up hostnames. (Useful if DNS is not functioning properly.)

−p *port*

Set base UDP port number used for probe packets to *port*. Default is (decimal) 33434.

−q *n*

Set number of probe packets for each time-to-live setting to the value *n*. Default is 3.

−r  Bypass normal routing tables and send directly to a host on an attached network.

−s *src_addr*

Use *src_addr* as the IP address that will serve as the source address in outgoing probe packets.

−t *tos*

Set the type-of-service in probe packets to *tos* (default 0). The value must be a decimal integer in the range 0 to 255.

−v  Verbose—received ICMP packets (other than TIME_EXCEEDED and PORT_UNREACHABLE) will be listed.

→

| | |
|---|---|
| traceroute<br>← | **−w** *wait*<br>Set time to wait for a response to an outgoing probe packet to *wait* seconds (default is 3 seconds). |
| troff | **troff**<br>See **groff**. |
| true | **true**<br>A null command that returns a successful (0) exit status. See also **false**. |
| tune2fs | **tune2fs** [*options*] *device*<br><br>System administration command. Tune the parameters of a Linux Second Extended Filesystem by adjusting various parameters. You must specify the *device* on which the filesystem resides; it must not be mounted read/write when you change its parameters.<br><br>*Options*<br><br>**−c** *mount-counts*<br>Specify the maximum number of mount counts between two checks on the filesystem.<br><br>**−e** *behavior*<br>Specify the kernel's behavior when encountering errors. *behavior* must be one of:<br><br>**continue**<br>Continue as usual.<br><br>**remount-ro**<br>Remount the offending filesystem in read-only mode.<br><br>**panic**<br>Cause a kernel panic.<br><br>**−g** *group*<br>Allow *group* (a group ID or name) to use reserved blocks.<br><br>**−i** *interval*[d | w | m]<br>Specify the maximum interval between filesystem checks. Units may be in days (**d**), weeks (**w**), or |

months (**m**). If *interval* is 0, checking will not be time-dependent.

**–l**   Display a list of the superblock's contents.

**–m** *percentage*
Specify the percentage of blocks that will be reserved for use by privileged users.

**–r** *num*
Specify the number of blocks that will be reserved for use by privileged users.

**–u** *user*
Allow *user* (a user ID or name) to use reserved blocks.

**tunelp** *device* [*options*]

System administration command. Control a lineprinter's device parameters. Without options, print information about device(s).

*Options*

**–a** [on | off]
Specify whether or not to abort if the printer encounters an error. By default, do not abort.

**–c** *n*
Retry device *n* times if it refuses a character. (Default is 250.) After exhausting *n*, sleep before retrying.

**–i** *irq*
Use *irq* for specified parallel port. Ignore **–t** and **–c**. If 0, restore noninterrupt driven (polling) action.

**–o** [on | off]
Specify whether to abort if device is not online or is out of paper.

**–q** [on | off]
Specify whether to print current IRQ setting.

**–r**   Reset port.

**–s**   Display printer's current status.

**–t** *time*
Specify a delay of *time* in jiffies to sleep before resending a refused character to the device. A jiffy is defined as either one tick of the system clock or one AC cycle time; it should be approximately 1/100th of a second.

→

| | |
|---|---|
| **tunelp**<br>← | **−w** *time*<br>Specify a delay of *time* in jiffies to sleep before resending a strobe signal.<br><br>**−C** [on\|off]<br>Specify whether to be extremely careful in checking for printer error. |
| **ul** | **ul** [*options*] [*names*]<br><br>Translate underscores to underlining. The correct sequence with which to do this will vary by terminal type. Some terminals are unable to handle underlining.<br><br>**Options**<br><br>**−i** Translate −, when on a separate line, to underline, instead of translating underscores.<br><br>**−t** *terminal-type*<br>Specify terminal type. By default, TERM is consulted. |
| **umount** | **umount** [*options*] [*special-device/directory*]<br><br>System administration command. Unmount a filesystem. **umount** announces to the system that the removable file structure previously mounted on device *special-device* is to be removed. **umount** also works by specifying the directory. Any pending I/O for the filesystem is completed, and the file structure is flagged as clean.<br><br>**Options**<br><br>**−a** Unmount all filesystems that are listed in */etc/mtab*.<br><br>**−n** Unmount, but do not record changes in */etc/mtab*.<br><br>**−t** *type*<br>Unmount only filesystems of type *type*. |
| **uname** | **uname** [*options*]<br><br>Print information about the machine and operating system. Without options, print the name of the operating system (Linux). |

*Options*

**−a, −−all**
> Combine all the system information from the other options.

**−m, −−machine**
> Print the hardware the system is running on.

**−n, −−nodename**
> Print the machine's hostname.

**−r, −−release**
> Print the release number of the kernel.

**−s, −−sysname**
> Print the name of the operating system (Linux).

**−p, −−processor**
> Print the type of processor (not available on all versions).

**−v**  Print build information about the kernel.

**−−help**
> Display a help message and then exit.

**−−version**
> Print version information and then exit.

---

**uncompress** [*options*] *files*

Uncompress files that were **compress**ed (i.e., whose names end in *.Z*). See **compress** for the available options; **uncompress** takes all the same options except −**r** and −**b**.

---

**unexpand** [*options*] [*files*]

Convert strings of initial whitespace, consisting of at least two spaces and/or tabs to tabs. Read from standard input if given no file or a file named −.

*Options*

**−a, −−all**
> Convert all, not just initial, strings of spaces and tabs.

**−***nums*, **−t** *nums*, **−−tabs** *nums*
> *nums* is a comma-separated list of integers that specify the placement of tab stops. If a single integer is provided, the tab stops are set to every *integer* spaces. By default, tab stops are 8 spaces apart. With −**t** and

→

| | |
|---|---|
| **unexpand**<br>← | —**tabs**, the list may be separated by whitespace instead of commas. This option implies −**a**.<br><br>−**help**<br>    Print help message and then exit.<br><br>−**version**<br>    Print the version number and then exit. |
| **uniq** | **uniq** [*options*] [*file1* [*file2*]]<br><br>Remove duplicate adjacent lines from sorted *file1*, sending one copy of each line to *file2* (or to standard output). Often used as a filter. Specify only one of −**d** or −**u**. See also **comm** and **sort**.<br><br>*Options*<br><br>−*n*, −**f** *n*, −−**skip-fields**=*n*<br>    Ignore first *n* fields of a line. Fields are separated by spaces or by tabs.<br><br>+*n*, −**s** *n*, −−**skip-chars**=*n*<br>    Ignore first *n* characters of a field.<br><br>−**c**, −−**count**<br>    Print each line once, prefixing number of instances.<br><br>−**d**, −−**repeated**<br>    Print duplicate lines once but no unique lines.<br><br>−**i**, −−**ignore-case**<br>    Ignore case differences when checking for duplicates.<br><br>−**u**, −−**unique**<br>    Print only unique lines (no copy of duplicate entries is kept).<br><br>−**w** *n*, −−**check-chars**=*n*<br>    Compare only first *n* characters per line (beginning after skipped fields and characters).<br><br>−−**help**<br>    Print a help message and then exit.<br><br>−−**version**<br>    Print version information and then exit.<br><br>*Examples*<br><br>Send one copy of each line from **list** to output file **list.new**:<br><br>`uniq list list.new` |

Show which names appear more than once:

```
sort names | uniq -d
```

---

unshar [*options*] [*files*]

Unpack a shell archive (shar file). **unshar** scans mail messages looking for the start of a shell archive. It then passes the archive through a copy of the shell to unpack it. **unshar** accepts multiple files. If no files are given, standard input is used.

*Options*

−c, −−overwrite
    Overwrite existing files.

−d *directory*, −−directory=*directory*
    Change to *directory* before unpacking any files.

−e, −−exit-0
    Sequentially unpack multiple archives stored in same file; uses clue that many **shar** files are terminated by an exit 0 at the beginning of a line. (Equivalent to −E "exit 0".)

−E *string*, −−split-at=*string*
    Like −e, but allows you to specify the string that separates archives.

−f, −−force
    Same as −c.

−−help
    Print help message and then exit.

−−version
    Print the version number and then exit.

---

update [*options*]

System administration command. **update** is a daemon that controls how often the kernel's disk buffers are flushed to disk. **update** is also known as **bdflush**. The daemon forks a couple of processes to call system functions *flush()* and *sync()*. When called by an unprivileged user, no daemon is created. Instead, **update** calls *sync()* and then exits. By default, update will wake up every 5 seconds and *flush()* some dirty buffers. If that doesn't work, it will try waking up every 30 seconds to *sync()* the buffers to disk. Not all of

→

| | |
|---|---|
| **update**<br>← | the listed options are available in every version of **update**.<br><br>***Options***<br><br>**-d**  Display the kernel parameters. This does not start the **update** daemon.<br><br>**-f** *seconds*<br>    Call *flush()* at this interval. Default is 5.<br><br>**-h**  Help. Print a command summary.<br><br>**-s** *seconds*<br>    Call *sync()* at this interval. Default is 30.<br><br>**-S**  Always use *sync()* instead of flush.<br><br>**-0** *percent*<br>    Flush buffers when the specified *percent* of the buffer cache is dirty.<br><br>**-1** *blocks*<br>    The maximum number of dirty blocks to write out per wake cycle.<br><br>**-2** *buffers*<br>    The number of clean buffers to try to obtain each time the free buffers are refilled.<br><br>**-3** *blocks*<br>    Flush buffers if dirty blocks exceed *blocks* when trying to refill the buffers.<br><br>**-4** *percent*<br>    Percent of buffer cache to scan when looking for free clusters.<br><br>**-5** *seconds*<br>    Time for a data buffer to age before being flushed.<br><br>**-6** *seconds*<br>    Time for a nondata buffer to age before being flushed.<br><br>**-7** *constant*<br>    The time constant to use for load average.<br><br>**-8** *ratio*<br>    How low the load average can be before trimming back the number of buffers. |
| **uptime** | **uptime**<br><br>Print the current time, amount of time logged in, number of users currently logged in (which may include the same user |

multiple times), and system load averages. This output is also produced by the first line of the **w** command.

---

useradd [*options*] [*user*]

System administration command. Create new user accounts or update default account information. Unless invoked with the −D option, *user* must be given. **useradd** will create new entries in system files. Home directories and initial files may also be created as needed.

*Options*

−c *comment*
    Comment field.

−d *dir*
    Home directory. The default is to use *user* as the directory name under the *home* directory specified with the −D option.

−e *date*
    Account expiration *date*. *date* is in the format MM/DD/YYYY. Two-digit year fields are also accepted. The value is stored as the number of days since January 1, 1970. This option requires the use of shadow passwords.

−f *days*
    Permanently disable account this many *days* after the password has expired. A value of −1 disables this feature. This option requires the use of shadow passwords.

−g *group*
    Initial *group* name or ID number. If a different default group has not been specified using the −D option, the default group is 1.

−G *groups*
    Supplementary *groups* given by name or number in a comma-separated list with no whitespace.

−k [*dir*]
    Copy default files to user's home directory. Meaningful only when used with the −m option. Default files are copied from */etc/skel/* unless an alternate *dir* is specified.

→

Linux
Commands

| | |
|---|---|
| **useradd**<br>← | **−m** Make user's home directory if it does not exist. The default is not to make the home directory. |
| | **−o** Override. Accept a nonunique *uid* with the **−u** option. (Probably a bad idea.) |
| | **−s** *shell*<br>Login *shell.* |
| | **−u** *uid*<br>Numerical user ID. The value must be unique unless the **−o** option is used. The default value is the smallest ID value greater than 99 and greater than every other *uid.* |
| | **−D** [*options*]<br>Set or display defaults. If *options* are specified, set them. If no options are specified, display current defaults. The options are: |
| | *−b dir*<br>Home directory prefix to be used in creating home directories. If the **−d** option is not used when creating an account, the *user* name will be appended to *dir.* |
| | *−e date*<br>Expire *date.* Requires the use of shadow passwords. |
| | *−f days*<br>Number of *days* after a password expires to disable an account. Requires the use of shadow passwords. |
| | *−g group*<br>Initial *group* name or ID number. |
| | *−s shell*<br>Default login *shell.* |
| **userdel** | **userdel** [*option*] *user*<br><br>System administration command. Delete all entries for *user* in system account files.<br><br>**Option**<br><br>**−r** Remove the home directory of *user* and any files contained in it. |

System administration command. Modify *user* account information.

### Options

**-c** *comment*
  Comment field.

**-d** *dir*
  Home directory.

**-e** *date*
  Account expiration *date*. *date* is in the format MM/DD/
  YYYY. Two-digit year fields are also accepted, but the
  value is stored as the number of days since January 1,
  1970. This option requires the use of shadow passwords.

**-f** *days*
  Permanently disable account this many *days* after the
  password has expired. A value of −1 disables this feature. This option requires the use of shadow passwords.

**-g** *group*
  Initial *group* name or number.

**-G** *groups*
  Supplementary *groups* given by name or number in a
  comma-separated list with no whitespace. *user* will be
  removed from any groups to which they currently
  belong that are not included in *groups*.

**-l** *name*
  Login *name*. This cannot be changed while the user is
  logged in.

**-o**  Override. Accept a nonunique *uid* with the **−u** option.

**-s** *shell*
  Login *shell*.

**-u** *uid*
  Numerical user ID. The value must be unique unless
  the −o option is used. Any files owned by *user* in the
  user's home directory will have their user ID changed
  automatically. Files outside of the home directory will
  not be changed. *user* should not be executing any processes while this is changed.

| | |
|---|---|
| users | **users** [*file*]<br><br>Print a space-separated list of each login session on the host. Note that this may include the same user multiple times. Consult *file* or, by default, */etc/utmp*. |
| usleep | **usleep** [*microseconds*]<br>**usleep** [*options*]<br><br>Sleep some number of microseconds (default is 1).<br><br>**Options**<br><br>**--help**<br>  Print help information and then exit.<br><br>**--usage**<br>  Print usage message and then exit.<br><br>**-v, --version**<br>  Print version information. |
| uudecode | **uudecode** [−o *outfile*] [*file*]<br><br>Read a uuencoded file and re-create the original file with the permissions and name set in the file (see **uuencode**). The −o option specifies an alternate output file. |
| uuencode | **uuencode** [−m] [*file*] *name*<br><br>Encode a binary *file*. The encoding uses only printable ASCII characters and includes the permissions and *name* of the file. When *file* is reconverted via **uudecode**, the output is saved as *name*. If the *file* argument is omitted, **uuencode** can take standard input, so a single argument is taken as the name to be given to the file when it is decoded. With the **−m** option, base64 encoding is used.<br><br>**Example**<br><br>It's common to encode a file and save it with an identifying extension, such as *.uue*. This example encodes the binary file *flower12.jpg*, names it *rose.jpg*, and saves it to a *.uue* file:<br><br>`% uuencode flower12.jpg rose.jpg > rose.uue` |

Encode *flower12.jpg* and mail it:

```
% uuencode flower12.jpg flower12.jpg | mail ellen@oreilly.com
```

---

**vacation**
**vacation** [*options*] [*user*]

Automatically return a mail message to the sender announcing that you are on vacation.

Use **vacation** with no options to initialize the vacation mechanism. The process performs several steps.

1.  Creates a *.forward* file in your home directory. The *.forward* file contains:

    ```
    \user, "|/usr/bin/vacation user"
    ```

    *user* is your login name. The action of this file is to actually deliver the mail to *user* (i.e., you) and to run the incoming mail through **vacation**.

2.  Creates the *.vacation.pag* and *.vacation.dir* files. These files keep track of who has sent you messages, so that they receive only one "I'm on vacation" message from you per week.

3.  Starts an editor to edit the contents of *.vacation.msg*. The contents of this file are mailed back to whomever sends you mail. Within its body, **$subject** is replaced with the contents of the incoming message's **Subject** line.

Remove or rename the *.forward* file to disable vacation processing.

***Options***

The **−a** and **−r** options are used within a *.forward* file; see the example.

**−a** *alias*
   Mail addressed to *alias* is actually mail for the *user* and should produce an automatic reply.

**−i** Reinitialize the *.vacation.pag* and *.vacation.dir* files. Use this right before leaving for your next vacation.

**−r** *interval*
   By default, no more than one message per week is sent to any sender. This option changes that interval. *interval* is a number with a trailing **s**, **m**, **h**, **d**, or **w** indicating seconds, minutes, hours, days, or weeks,

→

| | |
|---|---|
| **vacation**<br>← | respectively. If *interval* is **infinite**, only one reply is sent to each sender.<br><br>*Example*<br><br>Send no more than one reply every three weeks to any given sender:<br><br>```<br>$ cd<br>$ vacation -I<br>$ cat .forward<br>\jp, "|/usr/bin/vacation -r3w jp"<br>$ cat .vacation.msg<br>From: jp@wizard-corp.com (J. Programmer, via the vacation program)<br>Subject: I'm out of the office ...<br><br>Hi. I'm off on a well-deserved vacation after finishing<br>up whizprog 1.0. I will read and reply to your mail<br>regarding "$SUBJECT" when I return.<br><br>Have a nice day.<br>``` |
| **vi** | **vi** [*options*] [*files*]<br><br>A screen-oriented text editor based on **ex**. For more information on **vi**, see Chapter 11. |
| **vidmode** | **vidmode** [*option*] *image* [*mode* [*offset*]]<br><br>System administration command. Sets the video mode for a kernel *image*. If no arguments are specified, print current *mode* value. *mode* is a 1-byte value located at offset 506 in a kernel image. You may change the *mode* by specifying the kernel *image* to change, the new *mode*, and the byte offset at which to place the new information (the default is 506). Note that **rdev −v** is a synonym for **vidmode**. If **LILO** is used, **vidmode** is not needed. The video mode can be set from the LILO prompt during a boot.<br><br>*Modes*<br><br>−3  Prompt<br><br>−2  Extended VGA<br><br>−1  Normal VGA<br><br> 0  Same as entering 0 at the prompt<br><br> 1  Same as entering 1 at the prompt |

2 Same as entering **2** at the prompt

3 Same as entering **3** at the prompt

n Same as entering **n** at the prompt

*Option*

**−o** *offset*
 Same as specifying an *offset* as an argument.

---

**w** [*options*] [*user*]

Print summaries of system usage, currently logged-in users, and what they are doing. **w** is essentially a combination of **uptime, who**, and **ps −a**. Display output for one user by specifying *user*.

*Options*

**−f** Toggle printing the from (remote hostname) field.

**−h** Suppress headings and **uptime** information.

**−s** Use the short format.

**−u** Ignore the username while figuring out the current process and CPU times.

**−V** Display version information.

*File*

*/var/run/utmp*
 List of users currently logged on.

---

**wall** [*file*]

System administration command. Write to all users. **wall** reads a message from the standard input until an end-of-file. It then sends this message to all users currently logged in, preceded by "Broadcast Message from . . . " If *file* is specified, read input from that, rather than from standard input.

---

**wc** [*options*] [*files*]

Print character, word, and line counts for each file. Print a total line for multiple *files*. If no *files* are given, read standard input. See other examples under **ls** and **sort**.

→

| | |
|---|---|
| wc<br>← | *Options*<br><br>**–c, –bytes, ––chars**<br>    Print character count only.<br><br>**–l, ––lines**<br>    Print line count only.<br><br>**–w, ––words**<br>    Print word count only.<br><br>**––help**<br>    Print help message and then exit.<br><br>**––version**<br>    Print the version number and then exit.<br><br>*Examples*<br><br>Count the number of users logged in:<br><br>`who | wc -l`<br><br>Count the words in three essay files:<br><br>`wc -w essay.[123]`<br><br>Count lines in the file named by variable **$file** (don't display filename):<br><br>`wc -l < $file` |
| **whatis** | **whatis** *keywords*<br><br>Search the short manual page descriptions in the *whatis* database for each *keyword* and print a one-line description to standard output for each match. Like **apropos**, except that it only searches for complete words. Equivalent to **man –f**. |
| **whereis** | **whereis** [*options*] *files*<br><br>Locate the binary, source, and manual page files for specified commands/files. The supplied filenames are first stripped of leading pathname components and any (single) trailing extension of the form *.ext* (for example, *.c*). Prefixes of *s.* resulting from use of source code control are also dealt with. **whereis** then attempts to locate the desired program in a list of standard Linux directories (e.g., */bin, /etc, /usr/bin, /usr/local/bin/*, etc.). |

*Options*

−b   Search only for binaries.

−f   Terminate the last directory list and signal the start of filenames; required when any of the −B, −M, or −S options are used.

−m   Search only for manual sections.

−s   Search only for sources.

−u   Search for unusual entries, that is, files that do not have one entry of each requested type. Thus, the command **whereis −m −u *** asks for those files in the current directory that have no documentation.

−B *directories*
   Change or otherwise limit the directories to search for binaries.

−M *directory*
   Change or otherwise limit the directories to search for manual sections.

−S *directory*
   Change or otherwise limit the directories to search for sources.

*Example*

Find all files in */usr/bin* that are not documented in */usr/ man/man1* but that have source in */usr/src*:

```
% cd /usr/bin
% whereis -u -M /usr/man/man1 -S /usr/src -f *
```

---

## which [*options*] [−−] [*command*] [ . . . ]

List the full pathnames of the files that would be executed if the named *commands* had been run. **which** searches the user's $PATH environment variable. The C shell and **tcsh** have a built-in **which** command that has no options. To use the options, specify the full pathname (e.g., */usr/bin/which*).

*Options*

−a, −−all
   Print all matches, not just the first.

−i, −−read-alias
   Read aliases from standard input and write matches to standard output. Useful for using an alias for **which**.

→

| | |
|---|---|
| **which**<br>← | **−−skip-alias**<br>Ignore **−−read-alias** if present. Useful for finding normal binaries while using **−−read-alias** in an alias for **which**.<br><br>**−−skip-dot**<br>Skip directories that start with a dot.<br><br>**−−skip-tilde**<br>Skip directories that start with a tilde (~) and executables in $HOME.<br><br>**−−show-dot**<br>If a matching command is found in a directory that starts with a dot, print *./cmdname* instead of the full pathname.<br><br>**−−show-tilde**<br>Print a tilde (~) to indicate the user's home directory. Ignored if the user is root.<br><br>**−−tty-only**<br>Stop processing options on the right if not on a tty.<br><br>**−v, −V, −−version**<br>Print version information and then exit.<br><br>*Example*<br><br>```\n$ which cc ls\n/usr/bin/cc\nls:      aliased to ls -sFC\n```|
| **who** | **who** [*options*] [*file*]<br>**who am i**<br><br>Show who is logged in to the system. With no options, list the names of users currently logged in, their terminal, the time they have been logged in, and the name of the host from which they have logged on. An optional system *file* (default is */etc/utmp*) can be supplied to give additional information.<br><br>*Options*<br><br>**am i**<br>Print the username of the invoking user.<br><br>**−−help**<br>Print a help message and then exit. |

**−i, −u, −−idle**

Include idle times. An idle time of . indicates activity within the last minute; one of **old** indicates no activity in more than a day.

**−l, −−lookup**

Attempt to include canonical hostnames via DNS.

**−m** Same as **who am i**.

**−q, −−count**

"Quick." Display only the usernames and total number of users.

**−−version**

Print version information and then exit.

**−w, −T, −−mesg, −−message, −−writable**

Include user's message status:

+ **mesg y** (**write** messages allowed)

− **mesg n** (**write** messages refused)

? Cannot find terminal device

**−H, −−heading**

Print headings.

*Example*

This sample output was produced at 8 a.m. on April 17:

```
$ who -uH
NAME    LINE   TIME           IDLE   PID   COMMENTS
Earvin  ttyp3  Apr 16 08:14   16:25  2240
Larry   ttyp0  Apr 17 07:33   .      15182
```

Since Earvin has been idle since yesterday afternoon (16 hours), it appears that he isn't at work yet. He simply left himself logged in. Larry's terminal is currently in use.

---

## whoami

Print current user ID. Equivalent to **id −un**.

---

## write *user* [*tty*] *message*

Initiate or respond to an interactive conversation with *user*. A **write** session is terminated with *EOF*. If the user is logged in to more than one terminal, specify a *tty* number. See also

→

| | |
|---|---|
| **write**<br>← | **talk**; use **mesg** to keep other users from writing to your terminal. |
| **xargs** | **xargs** [*options*] [*command*]<br><br>Execute *command* (with any initial arguments), but read remaining arguments from standard input instead of specifying them directly. **xargs** passes these arguments in several bundles to *command*, allowing *command* to process more arguments than it could normally handle at once. The arguments are typically a long list of filenames (generated by **ls** or **find**, for example) that get passed to **xargs** via a pipe.<br><br>*Options*<br><br>−0, −−null<br>    Expect filenames to be terminated by NULL instead of whitespace. Do not treat quotes or backslashes specially.<br><br>−e[*string*], −−eof[=*string*]<br>    Set EOF to _ or, if specified, to *string*.<br><br>−−help<br>    Print a summary of the options to **xargs** and then exit.<br><br>−i[*string*], −−replace[=*string*]<br>    Edit all occurrences of {}, or *string*, to the names read in on standard input. Unquoted blanks are not considered argument terminators. Implies −x and −l 1.<br><br>−l[*lines*], −−max-lines[=*lines*]<br>    Allow no more than 1, or *lines*, nonblank input lines on the command line. Implies −x.<br><br>−n *args*, −−max-args=*args*<br>    Allow no more than *args* arguments on the command line. May be overridden by −s.<br><br>−p, −−interactive<br>    Prompt for confirmation before running each command line. Implies −t.<br><br>−P *max*, −−max-procs=*max*<br>    Allow no more than *max* processes to run at once. The default is 1. A maximum of 0 allows as many as possible to run at once.<br><br>−r, −−no-run-if-empty<br>    Do not run command if standard input contains only blanks. |

**–s** *max*, **––max-chars=***max*
> Allow no more than *max* characters per command line.

**–t**, **––verbose**
> Verbose mode. Print command line on standard error before executing.

**–x**, **––exit**
> If the maximum size (as specified by **–s**) is exceeded, exit.

**––version**
> Print the version number of **xargs** and then exit.

### Examples

**grep** for *pattern* in all files on the system:

```
find / -print | xargs grep pattern > out &
```

Run **diff** on file pairs (e.g., **f1.a** and **f1.b**, **f2.a** and **f2.b** . . . ):

```
echo $* | xargs -n2 diff
```

The previous line would be invoked as a shell script, specifying filenames as arguments. Display *file*, one word per line (same as **deroff –w**):

```
cat file | xargs -n1
```

Move files in *olddir* to *newdir*, showing each command:

```
ls olddir | xargs -i -t mv olddir/{} newdir/{}
```

---

**yacc** [*options*] *file*

Given a *file* containing context-free grammar, convert *file* into tables for subsequent parsing and send output to *y.tab.c*. This command name stands for yet another compiler-compiler. See also **flex**, **bison**, and *lex & yacc* by John Levine, Tony Mason, and Doug Brown.

### Options

**–b** *prefix*
> Prepend *prefix*, instead of *y*, to the output file.

**–d** Generate *y.tab.h*, producing **#define** statements that relate **yacc**'s token codes to the token names declared by the user.

→

| | |
|---|---|
| yacc<br>← | –l  Exclude **#line** constructs from code produced in *y.tab.c.* (Use after debugging is complete.)<br><br>–t  Compile runtime debugging code.<br><br>–v  Generate *y.output*, a file containing diagnostics and notes about the parsing tables. |
| yes | **yes** [*strings*]<br>**yes** [*option*]<br><br>Print the command-line arguments, separated by spaces and followed by a newline, until killed. If no arguments are given, print **y** followed by a newline until killed. Useful in scripts and in the background; its output can be piped to a program that issues prompts.<br><br>*Options*<br><br>**––help**<br>    Print a help message and then exit.<br><br>**––version**<br>    Print version information and then exit. |
| ypbind | **ypbind** [*options*]<br><br>NFS/NIS command. NIS binder process. **ypbind** is a daemon process typically activated at system startup time. Its function is to remember information that lets client processes on a single node communicate with some **ypserv** process. The information **ypbind** remembers is called a *binding*—the association of a domain name with the Internet address of the NIS server and the port on that host at which the **ypserv** process is listening for service requests. This information is cached in the file */var/yp/bindings/domainname.version.*<br><br>*Options*<br><br>**–ypset**<br>    May be used to change the binding. This option is very dangerous and should be used only for debugging the network from a remote machine.<br><br>**–ypsetme**<br>    **ypset** requests may be issued from this machine only. Security is based on IP address checking, which can be defeated on networks on which untrusted individuals may inject packets. This option is not recommended. |

**ypcat** [*options*] *mname*

NFS/NIS command. Print values in an NIS database specified by *mname*, which may be either a map name or a map
nickname.

*Options*

**−d** *domain*
  Specify *domain* other than default domain.

**−k**  Display keys for maps in which values are null or key
  is not part of value.

**−t**  Do not translate *mname* to map name.

**−x**  Display map nickname table listing the nicknames
  (*mnames*) known and map name associated with each
  nickname. Do not require an *mname* argument.

**ypchfn** [*option*] [*user*]

NFS/NIS command. Change your information stored in */etc/
passwd* and displayed when you are fingered; distribute the
change over NIS. Without options, **ypchfn** enters interactive
mode and prompts for changes. To make a field blank,
enter the keyword **none**. The superuser can change the
information for any *user*. See also **yppasswd** and **ypchsh**.

*Options*

**−f**  Behave like **ypchfn** (default).

**−l**  Behave like **ypchsh**.

**−p**  Behave like **yppasswd**.

**ypchsh** [*option*] [*user*]

NFS/NIS command. Change your login shell and distribute
this information over NIS. Warn if *shell* does not exist in
*/etc/shells*. The superuser can change the shell for any *user*.
See also **yppasswd** and **ypchfn**.

*Options*

**−f**  Behave like **ypchfn**.

→

| | |
|---|---|
| **ypchsh**<br>← | −l  Behave like **ypchsh** (default). |
| | −p  Behave like **yppasswd**. |

| | |
|---|---|
| **ypinit** | **ypinit** [*options*]<br><br>NFS/NIS command. Build and install an NIS database on an NIS server. **ypinit** can be used to set up a master or a slave server or slave copier. Only a privileged user can run **ypinit**.<br><br>***Options***<br><br>−c *master_name*<br>    Set up a slave copier database. *master_name* should be the hostname of an NIS server, either the master server for all the maps or a server on which the database is up-to-date and stable.<br><br>−m  Indicates that the local host is to be the NIS server.<br><br>−s *master_name*<br>    Set up a slave server database. *master_name* should be the hostname of an NIS server, either the master server for all the maps or a server on which the database is up-to-date and stable. |

| | |
|---|---|
| **ypmatch** | **ypmatch** [*options*] *key . . . mname*<br><br>NFS/NIS command. Print value of one or more *key*s from an NIS map specified by *mname*. *mname* may be either a map name or a map nickname.<br><br>***Options***<br><br>−d *domain*<br>    Specify *domain* other than default domain.<br><br>−k  Before printing value of a key, print key itself, followed by a colon (:).<br><br>−t  Do not translate nickname to map name.<br><br>−x  Display map nickname table listing the nicknames (*mnames*) known, and map name associated with each nickname. Do not require an *mname* argument. |

yppasswd [*option*] [*name*]

NFS/NIS command. Change login password in Network Information Service. Create or change your password, and distribute the new password over NIS. The superuser can change the password for any *user*. See also **ypchfn** and **ypchsh**.

*Options*

−f  Behave like **ypchfn**.

−l  Behave like **ypchsh**.

−p  Behave like **yppasswd** (default).

---

rpc.yppasswdd [*option*]

NFS/NIS command. Server for modifying the NIS password file. **yppasswdd** handles password change requests from **yppasswd**. It changes a password entry only if the password represented by **yppasswd** matches the encrypted password of that entry and if the user ID and group ID match those in the server's */etc/passwd* file. Then it updates */etc/passwd* and the password maps on the local server.

*Option*

−s  Support shadow password functions.

---

yppoll [*options*] *mapname*

NFS/NIS command. Determine version of NIS map at NIS server. **yppoll** asks a **ypserv** process for the order number and the hostname of the master NIS server for the named map.

*Options*

−h *host*
> Ask the **ypserv** process at *host* about the map parameters. If *host* is not specified, the hostname of the NIS server for the local host (the one returned by **ypwhich**) is used.

−d *domain*
> Use *domain* instead of the default domain.

| | |
|---|---|
| **yppush** | **yppush** [*options*] *mapnames* |
| | NFS/NIS command. Force propagation of changed NIS map. **yppush** copies a new version of an NIS map, *mapname*, from the master NIS server to the slave NIS servers. It first constructs a list of NIS server hosts by reading the NIS map **ypservers** with the **–d** option's *domain* argument. Keys within this map are the ASCII names of the machines on which the NIS servers run. A "transfer map" request is sent to the NIS server at each host, along with the information needed by the transfer agent to call back the **yppush**. When the attempt has been completed and the transfer agent has sent **yppush** a status message, the results may be printed to **stdout**. Normally invoked by */var/yp/Makefile*. |
| | *Options* |
| | **–d** *domain*<br>    Specify a *domain*. |
| | **–v**  Verbose—print message when each server is called and for each response. |
| **ypserv** | **ypserv** [*options*] |
| | NFS/NIS command. NIS server process. **ypserv** is a daemon process typically activated at system startup time. It runs only on NIS server machines with a complete NIS database. Its primary function is to look up information in its local database of NIS maps. The operations performed by **ypserv** are defined for the implementor by the NIS protocol specification and for the programmer by the header file *<rpcvc/yp_prot.h>*. Communication to and from **ypserv** is by means of RPC calls. |
| | *Options* |
| | **–d**  NIS service should go to the DNS for more host information. |
| | **–localonly**<br>    Indicates **ypserv** should not respond to outside requests. |
| | *Files and directories* |
| | */var/yp/[domainname]/*<br>    Location of NIS databases. |

| | |
|---|---|
| */var/yp/Makefile*<br>    Makefile that is responsible for creating NIS databases. | **ypserv** |
| **ypset** [*options*] *server*<br><br>NFS/NIS command. Point **ypbind** at a particular server. **ypset** tells **ypbind** to get NIS services for the specified domain from the **ypserv** process running on *server. server* indicates the NIS server to bind to and can be specified as a name or an IP address.<br><br>*Options*<br><br>**−d** *domain*<br>    Use *domain* instead of the default domain.<br><br>**−h** *host*<br>    Set **ypbind**'s binding on *host*, instead of locally. *host* can be specified as a name or an IP address. | **ypset** |
| **ypwhich** [*options*] [*host*]<br><br>NFS/NIS command. Return hostname of NIS server or map master. Without arguments, **ypwhich** cites the NIS server for the local machine. If *host* is specified, that machine is queried to find out which NIS master it is using.<br><br>*Options*<br><br>**−d** *domain*<br>    Use *domain* instead of the default domain.<br><br>**−m** *map*<br>    Find master NIS server for a map. No host can be specified with **−m**. *map* may be a map name or a nickname for a map.<br><br>**−t** *mapname*<br>    Inhibit nickname translation.<br><br>**−x**  Display map nickname table.  Do not allow any other options. | **ypwhich** |
| **ypxfr** [*options*] *mapname*<br><br>NFS/NIS command. Transfer an NIS map from the server to the local host by making use of normal NIS services. **ypxfr** creates a temporary map in the directory */etc/yp/domain* | **ypxfr** |
| | → |

**ypxfr**
←

(where *domain* is the default domain for the local host), fills it by enumerating the map's entries, and fetches the map parameters and loads them. If run interactively, **ypxfr** writes its output to the terminal. However, if it is invoked without a controlling terminal, and if the log file */usr/ admin/nislog* exists, it appends all its output to that file.

*Options*

−b  Preserve the resolver flag in the map during the transfer.

−C *tid prog ipadd port*
This option is for use only by **ypserv**. When **ypserv** invokes **ypxfr**, it specifies that **ypxfr** should call back a **yppush** process at the host with IP address *ipadd*, registered as program number *prog*, listening on port *port*, and waiting for a response to transaction *tid*.

−c  Do not send a "Clear current map" request to the local **ypserv** process.

−d *domain*
Specify a domain other than the default domain.

−f  Force the transfer to occur even if the version at the master is older than the local version.

−h *host*
Get the map from *host*, regardless of what the map says the master is. If host is not specified, **ypxfr** asks the NIS service for the name of the master and tries to get the map from there. *host* may be a name or an Internet address in the form *h.h.h.h*.

−S  Use only NIS servers running as **root** and using a reserved port.

−s *domain*
Specify a source *domain* from which to transfer a map that should be the same across domains (such as the *services.byname* map).

---

**zcat**

zcat [*options*] [*files*]

Read one or more *files* that have been compressed with **gzip** or **compress** and write them to standard output. Read standard input if no *files* are specified or if − is specified as one of the files; end input with *EOF*. **zcat** is identical to **gun-**

zip **–c** and takes the options **–fhLV** described for **gzip/gun-zip**.

---

**zcmp** [*options*] *files*

Read compressed files and pass them, uncompressed, to the **cmp** command, along with any command-line options. If a second file is not specified for comparison, look for a file called *file.gz*.

---

**zdiff** [*options*] *files*

Read compressed files and pass them, uncompressed, to the **diff** command, along with any command-line options. If a second file is not specified for comparison, look for a file called *file*.**gz**.

---

**zdump** [*options*] [*zones*]

System administration command. Dump a list of all known time zones or, if an argument is provided, a specific zone or list of zones. Include each zone's current time with its name.

*Options*

**–c** *year*
> Specify a cutoff year to limit verbose output. Meaningful only with **–v**.

**–v** Verbose mode. Include additional information about each zone.

---

**zforce** [*names*]

Rename all **gzip**ped files to *filename*.**gz**, unless file already has a .**gz** extension.

---

**zgrep** [*options*] [*files*]

Uncompress files and pass to **grep**, along with any command-line arguments. If no files are provided, read from (and attempt to uncompress) standard input. May be

$\rightarrow$

| | |
|---|---|
| **zgrep**<br>← | invoked as **zegrep** or **zfgrep** and will in those cases invoke **egrep** or **fgrep**. |
| **zic** | **zic** [*options*] [*files*]<br><br>System administration command. Create time conversion information files from the file or files specified. If the specified file is −, read information from standard input.<br><br>*Options*<br><br>**−d** *directory*<br>Place the newly created files in *directory*. Default is */usr/local/etc/zoneinfo*.<br><br>**−l** *timezone*<br>Specify a *timezone* to use for local time. **zic** links the zone information for *timezone* with the zone **localtime**.<br><br>**−p** *timezone*<br>Set the default rules for handling POSIX-format environment variables to the zone name specified by *timezone*.<br><br>**−s** Store time values only if they are the same when signed as when unsigned.<br><br>**−v** Verbose mode. Include extra error checking and warnings.<br><br>**−y** *command*<br>Check year types with *command*. Default is **yearistype**.<br><br>**−L** *file*<br>Consult *file* for information about leap seconds.<br><br>The source file(s) for **zic** should be formatted as a sequence of rule lines, zone lines, and link lines. An optional file containing leap second rules can be specified on the command line. Rule lines describe how time should be calculated. They describe changes in time, daylight savings time, war time, and any other changes that might affect a particular time zone. Zone lines specify which rules apply to a given zone. Link lines link similar zones together. Leap lines describe the exact time when leap seconds should be added or subtracted. Each of these lines is made up of fields. Fields are separated from one another by any number of whitespace characters. Comment lines are preceded by a #. The fields used in each line are listed next. |

The format of a rule line is:

```
Rule NAME FROM TO TYPE IN ON AT SAVE LETTERS
```

**NAME**
Name this set of rules.

**FROM**
Specify the first year to which this rule applies. Gregorian calendar dates are assumed. Instead of specifying an actual year, you may specify *minimum* or *maximum* for the minimum or maximum year representable as an integer.

**TO** Specify the last year to which this rule applies. Syntax is the same as for the FROM field.

**TYPE**
Specify the type of year to which this rule should be applied. The wildcard – instructs that all years be included. Any given year's type will be checked with the command given with the –**y** option or the default **yearistype** *year type*. An exit status of 0 is taken to mean the year is of the given type; an exit status of 1 means that it is not of the given type (see –**y** option).

**IN** Specify month in which this rule should be applied.

**ON** Specify day in which this rule should be applied. Whitespace is not allowed. For example:

1    The 1st

**firstSun**
The first Sunday

**Sun>=3**
The first Sunday to occur before or on the 3rd

**AT** Specify the time after which the rule is in effect. For example, you may use **13**, **13:00**, or **13:00:00** for 1:00 p.m.. You may include one of several suffixes (without whitespace between):

.  **s**    Local standard time.

**u, g, z**
Universal time.

w    Wall clock time (default).

**SAVE**

Add this amount of time to the local standard time. Formatted like **AT**, without suffixes.

**LETTERS**

Specify letter or letters to be used in time zone abbreviations (for example, S for EST). For no abbreviation,
enter –.

### Zone line fields

The format of a zone line is:

```
Zone NAME GMTOFF RULES/SAVE FORMAT [UNTIL]
```

**NAME**

Time zone name.

**GMTOFF**

The amount of hours by which this time zone differs
from GMT. Formatted like AT. Negative times are sub-
tracted from GMT; by default, times are added to it.

**RULES/SAVE**

Either the name of the rule to apply to this zone or the
amount of time to add to local standard time. To make
the zone the same as local standard time, specify –.

**FORMAT**

How to format time zone abbreviations. Specify the
variable part with %s.

**UNTIL**

Change the rule for the zone at this date. The next line
must specify the new zone information and therefore
must omit the string "Zone" and the NAME field.

### Link line fields

The format of a link line is:

```
Link LINK-FROM LINK-TO
```

**LINK-FROM**

The name of the zone that is being linked.

**LINK-TO**

An alternate name for the zone that was specified as
LINK-FROM.

***Leap line fields***

The format of a leap line is:

Leap YEAR MONTH DAY HH:MM:SS CORR R/S

**YEAR MONTH DAY HH:MM:SS**

Specify when the leap second happened.

**CORR**

Uses a + or a – to show whether the second was added or skipped.

**R/S** An abbreviation of Rolling or Stationary to describe whether the leap second should be applied to local wall clock time or to GMT.

zmore [*files*]

Similar to **more**. Uncompress files and print them, one screenful at a time. Works on files compressed with **compress**, **gzip**, or **pack** and with uncompressed files.

***Commands***

**space**

Print next screenful.

*i*[*number*]

Print next screenful, or *number* lines. Set *i* to *number* lines.

**d, ˆD**

Print next *i*, or 11, lines.

*i***z** Print next *i* lines or a screenful.

*i***s** Skip *i* lines. Print next screenful.

*i***f** Skip *i* screens. Print next screenful.

**q, Q, :q, :Q**

Go to next file, or, if current file is the last, exit **zmore**.

**e, q**

Exit **zmore** when the prompt "--More--(Next file: *file*)" is displayed.

**s** Skip next file and continue.

**=** Print line number.

→

| | |
|---|---|
| **zmore**<br>← | *i/expr*<br>      Search forward for *i*th occurrence (in all files) of *expr*,<br>      which should be a regular expression. Display occur-<br>      rence, including the two previous lines of context.<br><br>*in*   Search forward for the *i*th occurrence of the last regular<br>      expression searched for.<br><br>*!command*<br>      Execute *command* in shell. If *command* is not speci-<br>      fied, execute last shell command. To invoke a shell<br>      without passing it a command, enter \!.<br><br>.     Repeat the previous command. |
| **znew** | **znew** [*options*] [*files*]<br><br>Uncompress .Z files and recompress them in .gz format.<br><br>*Options*<br><br>−9   Optimal (and slowest) compression method.<br><br>−f   Recompress even if *filename*.**gz** already exists.<br><br>−t   Test new .**gz** files before removing .**Z** files.<br><br>−v   Verbose mode.<br><br>−K   If the original .**Z** file is smaller than the .**gz** file, keep it.<br><br>−P   Pipe data to conversion program. This saves disk<br>      space. |

CHAPTER 4

# *Boot Methods*

This chapter describes some techniques for booting your Linux system. Depending on your hardware and whether you want to run any other operating systems, you can configure the system to boot Linux automatically or to provide a choice between several operating systems. Choosing between operating systems is generally referred to as *dual booting*, but you can boot more than two (e.g., Linux and Windows 95/98/NT/2000). This chapter covers the following topics:

- The boot process

- LILO: the Linux loader

- Loadlin: booting from MS-DOS

- Dual booting Linux and Windows NT/2000

- Boot-time kernel options

- **initrd**: using a RAM disk

## *The Boot Process*

Once your Linux system is up and running, booting the system generally is pretty straightforward. But with the wide variety of hardware and software in use, there are many possibilities for configuring your boot process. The three most common choices are:

- Boot Linux from a floppy, leaving any other operating system to boot from the hard drive.

- Use the Linux Loader, LILO.* This is probably the most common method of booting and lets you boot both Linux and other operating systems.

- Run Loadlin, which is an MS-DOS program that boots Linux from within DOS.

Other boot managers that can load Linux are available, but we don't discuss them in this chapter. We also won't talk further about booting from a floppy except to say that whatever method you choose for booting, you should be sure to have a working boot floppy available for emergency use. In particular, don't experiment with the files and options in this chapter unless you have a boot floppy, because any error could leave you unable to boot from the hard disk.

On an Intel-based PC, the first sector of every hard disk is known as the *boot sector* and contains the partition table for that disk and possibly also code for booting an operating system. The boot sector of the first hard disk is known as the *master boot record* (MBR), because when you boot the system, the BIOS transfers control to a program that lives on that sector along with the partition table. That code is the *boot loader*, the code that initiates an operating system. When you add Linux to the system, you need to modify the boot loader, replace it, or boot from a floppy disk to start Linux.

In Linux, each disk and each partition on the disk is treated as a device. So, for example, the entire first hard disk is known as */dev/hda* and the entire second hard disk, if there is one, is */dev/hdb*. The first partition of the first hard drive is */dev/hda1*, and the second partition is */dev/hda2*; the first partition of the second hard drive is */dev/hdb1*; and so on. If your drives are SCSI instead of IDE, the naming works the same way except that the devices are */dev/sda, /dev/sda1*, and so on. Thus, if you want to specify that the Linux partition is the second partition of the first hard drive (as in the examples in this chapter), you refer to it as */dev/hda2*.

The rest of the chapter describes the various techniques for booting Linux and the options that you can specify to configure both the boot loader that you use and the Linux kernel. Both LILO and Loadlin let you pass options to the loader and they also let you specify options for the kernel.

## LILO: The Linux Loader

Once you've made the decision to install LILO, you still need to decide how it should be configured. If you want your system to dual boot Linux and Windows 95/98, you can install LILO on the master boot record (MBR) and set it up to let you select the system to boot. Dual booting Linux and Windows NT is not quite as straightforward, because Windows NT has its own loader on the MBR, and it expects to be the one in charge. Therefore, you need to make Linux an option in the NT loader and install LILO in the Linux partition as a secondary boot loader. The result is that the Windows NT loader transfers control to LILO, which then

---

* LILO is the standard boot program for i386-architecture machines. On the Alpha, the equivalent boot program is called MILO (Mini Loader), and on the SPARC, it is SILO.

boots Linux. The same applies to Windows 2000, which uses the NT loader. See the section "Dual Booting Linux and Windows NT/2000" later in this chapter for more information.

In addition to booting Linux, LILO can boot other operating systems, such as MS-DOS, Windows 95/98, or OS/2. During installation, the major Linux distributions provide the opportunity to install LILO; it can also be installed later if necessary. LILO can be installed on the master boot record (MBR) of your hard drive or as a secondary boot loader on the Linux partition. LILO consists of several pieces, including the boot loader itself, a configuration file (*/etc/lilo.conf*), a map file (*/boot/map*) containing the location of the kernel, and the **lilo** command (*/sbin/lilo*), which reads the configuration file and uses the information to create or update the map file and to install the files LILO needs.

If LILO is installed on the MBR, it replaces the MS-DOS boot loader. If you have problems with your installation or you simply want to uninstall LILO and restore the original boot loader, you can do one of the following:

- Boot Linux from a floppy disk and restore the backed-up boot sector:

  `% /sbin/lilo -u`

- Boot to DOS and run a special version of the **fdisk** command that rebuilds the MBR:

  `C:> fdisk /mbr`

One thing to remember about LILO is that it has two aspects: the boot loader and the **lilo** command. The **lilo** command configures and installs the boot loader and updates it as necessary. The boot loader is the code that executes at system boot time and boots Linux or another operating system.

## The LILO Configuration File

The **lilo** command reads the LILO configuration file, */etc/lilo.conf,* to get the information it needs to install LILO. Among other things, it builds a map file containing the locations of all disk sectors needed for booting.

Note that any time you change */etc/lilo.conf* or rebuild or move a kernel image, you need to rerun **lilo** to rebuild the map file and update LILO.

The configuration file starts with a section of global options, described in the next section. Global options are those that apply to every system boot, regardless of what operating system you are booting. Here is an example of a global section (a hash sign, #, begins a comment):

```
boot = /dev/hda          # The boot device is /dev/hda
map = /boot/map          # Save the map file as /boot/map
install = /boot/boot.b    # The file to install as the new boot sector
prompt                   # Always display the boot prompt
timeout = 30             # Set a 3-second (30 tenths of a second) timeout
```

Following the global section, there is one section of options for each Linux kernel and for each non-Linux operating system that you want LILO to be able to boot. Each of those sections is referred to as an *image* section, because each boots a different kernel image (shorthand for a binary file containing a kernel) or another operating system. Each Linux image section begins with an **image=** line.

```
image = /boot/vmlinuz      # Linux image file
   label = linux           # Label that appears at the boot prompt
   root = /dev/hda2        # Location of the root filesystem
   vga = ask               # Always prompt the user for VGA mode
   read-only               # Mount read-only to run fsck for a filesystem check
```

The equivalent section for a non-Linux operating system begins with **other=** instead of **image=**. For example:

```
other = /dev/hda1          # Location of the partition
   label = dos
   table = /dev/hda        # Location of the partition table
```

Put LILO configuration options that apply to all images into the global section of */etc/lilo.conf* and options that apply to a particular image into the section for that image. If an option is specified in both the global section and an image section, the setting in the image section overrides the global setting for that image.

Here is an example of a complete */etc/lilo.conf* file for a system that has the Linux partition on */dev/hda2*:

```
## Global section
boot=/dev/hda2
map=/boot/map
delay=30
timeout=50
prompt
vga=ask

## Image section: For regular Linux
image=/boot/vmlinuz
   label=linux
   root=/dev/hda2
   install=/boot/boot.b
   map=/boot/map
   read-only

## Image section: For testing a new Linux kernel
image=/testvmlinuz
   label=testlinux
   root=/dev/hda2
   install=/boot/boot.b
   map=/boot/map
   read-only
   optional                # Omit image if not available when map is built

## Image section: For booting DOS
other=/dev/hda1
   label=dos
   loader=/boot/chain.b
   table=/dev/hda          # The current partition table

## Image section: For booting Windows 95
other=/dev/hda1
   label=win95
   loader=/boot/chain.b
   table=/dev/hda
```

## Global options

In addition to the options listed here, the kernel options **append**, **read-only**, **read-write**, **root**, and **vga** (described in the section "Kernel options'later) also can be set as global options.

**backup=***backup-file*

> Copies the original boot sector to *backup-file* instead of to the file */boot/boot.nnnn*, where *nnnn* is a number that depends on the disk device type.

**boot=***boot-device*

> Sets the name of the device that contains the boot sector. **boot** defaults to the device currently mounted as root, such as */dev/hda2*. Specifying a device such as */dev/hda* (without a number) indicates that LILO should be installed in the master boot record; the alternative is to set it up on a particular partition such as */dev/hda2*.

**compact**

> Merges read requests for adjacent disk sectors to speed up booting. Use of **compact** is particularly recommended when booting from a floppy disk. Use of **compact** may conflict with **linear**.

**default=***name*

> Uses the image *name* as the default boot image. If **default** is omitted, the first image specified in the configuration file is used.

**delay=***tsecs*

> Specifies, in tenths of a second, how long the boot loader should wait before booting the default image. If **serial** is set, **delay** is set to 20 at a minimum. The default is to not wait.

**disk=***device-name*

> Defines parameters for the disk specified by *device-name* if LILO can't figure them out. Normally, LILO can determine the disk parameters itself and this option isn't needed. When **disk** is specified, it is followed by one or more parameter lines, such as:

```
disk=/dev/sda
  bios= 0x80       # First disk is usually 0x80, second is usually 0x81
  sectors= ...
  heads= ...
```

> Note that this option is not the same as the disk geometry parameters you can specify with the **hd** boot command-line option. With **disk**, the information is given to LILO; with **hd**, it is passed to the kernel. The parameters that can be specified with **disk** are listed briefly here. They are described in detail in the LILO User's Guide, which comes with the LILO distribution.

> **bios=***bios-device-code*
>
> > The number the BIOS uses to refer to the device. See the previous example.

**cylinders=***cylinders*

> The number of cylinders on the disk.

**heads=***heads*

> The number of heads on the disk.

**inaccessible**

> Tells LILO that the BIOS can't read the disk; used to prevent the system from becoming unbootable if LILO thinks the BIOS can read it.

**partition=***partition-device*

> Starts a new section for a partition. The section contains one variable, **start=***partition-offset*, which specifies the zero-based number of the first sector of the partition:

```
partition=/dev/sda1
   start=2048
```

**sectors=***sectors*

> The number of sectors per track.

**disktab=***disktab-file*

> This option has been superseded by the **disk=** option.

**fix-table**

> If set, allows **lilo** to adjust 3D addresses (addresses specified as sector/head/cylinder) in partition tables. This is sometimes necessary if a partition isn't track-aligned and another operating system such as MS-DOS is on the same disk. See the *lilo.conf* manpage for details.

**force-backup=***backup-file*

> Like **backup** but overwrites an old backup copy if one exists.

**ignore-table**

> Tells **lilo** to ignore corrupt partition tables.

**install=***boot-sector*

> Installs the specified file as the new boot sector. If **install** is omitted, the boot sector defaults to */boot/boot.b*.

**lba32**

> Generates 32-bit Logical Block Addresses instead of sector/head/cylinder addresses, allowing booting from any partition on hard disks greater than 8.4GB (i.e., it removes the 1024-cylinder limit). Requires BIOS support for the EDD packet call interface* and at least LILO Version 21-4.

**linear**

> Generates linear sector addresses, which do not depend on disk geometry, instead of 3D (sector/head/cylinder) addresses. If LILO can't determine your disk's geometry itself, you can try using **linear**; if that doesn't work, then you need to specify the geometry with **disk=**. Note, however, that **linear** sometimes doesn't work with floppy disks, and it may conflict with **compact**.

---

\* If your BIOS is dated after 1998, it should include EDD packet call interface support.

**lock**

Tells LILO to record the boot command line and use it as the default for future boots until it is overridden by a new boot command line. **lock** is useful if there is a set of options that you need to enter on the boot command line every time you boot the system.

**map=***map-file*

Specifies the location of the map file. Defaults to */boot/map*.

**message=***message-file*

Specifies a file containing a message to be displayed before the boot prompt. The message can include a formfeed character (Ctrl-L) to clear the screen. The map file must be rebuilt by rerunning the **lilo** command if the message file is changed or moved. The maximum length of the file is 65,535 bytes.

**nowarn**

Disables warning messages.

**optional**

Specifies that any image that is not available when the map is created should be omitted and not offered as an option at the boot prompt. Like the per-image option **optional** but applies to all images.

**password=***password*

Specifies a password that the user is prompted to enter when trying to load an image. The password is not encrypted in the configuration file, so if passwords are used, permissions should be set so that only the superuser is able to read the file. This option is like the per-image version, except that all images are password-protected and they all have the same password.

**prompt**

Automatically displays the boot prompt without waiting for the user to press the Shift, Alt, or Scroll Lock key. Note that setting **prompt** without also setting **timeout** prevents unattended reboots.

**restricted**

Can be used with **password** to indicate that a password needs to be entered only if the user specifies parameters on the command line. Like the per-image **restricted** option but applies to all images.

**serial=***parameters*

Allows the boot loader to accept input from a serial line as well as from the keyboard. Sending a break on the serial line corresponds to pressing a Shift key on the console to get the boot loader's attention. All boot images should be password-protected if serial access is insecure (e.g., if the line is connected to a modem). Setting **serial** automatically raises the value of **delay** to 20 (i.e., 2 seconds) if it is less than that. The parameter string *parameters* has the following syntax:

```
port[,bps[parity[bits]]]
```

For example, to initialize COM1 with the default parameters:

```
serial=0,2400n8
```

The parameters are:

*port*
> The port number of the serial port. The default is 0, which corresponds to COM1 (*/dev/ttys0*). The value can be one of 0 through 3, for the four possible COM ports.

*bps* The baud rate of the serial port. Possible values of *bps* are 110, 300, 1200, 2400, 4800, 9600, 19200, and 38400. The default is 2400 bps.

*parity*
> The parity used on the serial line. Parity is specified as: *n* or *N* for no parity, *e* or *E* for even parity, and *o* or *O* for odd parity. However, the boot loader ignores input parity and strips the 8th bit.

*bits* Specifies whether a character contains 7 or 8 bits. Default is 8 with no parity and 7 otherwise.

**timeout=***tsecs*
> Sets a timeout (specified in tenths of a second) for keyboard input. If no key has been pressed after the specified time, the default image is booted automatically. **timeout** is also used to determine when to stop waiting for password input. The default timeout is infinite.

**verbose=***level*
> Turns on verbose output, where higher values of *level* produce more output. If −v is also specified on the **lilo** command line, the level is incremented by 1 for each occurrence of −v. The maximum verbosity level is 5.

## Image options

The following options are specified for a particular image.

**alias=***name*
> Provides an alternate name for the image that can be used instead of the name specified with the **label** option.

**image=***pathname*
> Specifies the file or device containing the boot image of a bootable Linux kernel. Each per-image section that specifies a bootable Linux kernel starts with an **image** option. See also the **range** option.

**label=***name*
> Specifies the name that is used for the image at the boot prompt. Defaults to the filename of the image file (without the path).

**loader=***chain-loader*
> For a non-Linux operating system, specifies the chain loader to which LILO should pass control for booting that operating system. The default is */boot/chain.b*. If the system will be booted from a drive that is neither the first hard disk or a floppy, the chain loader must be specified.

**lock**

> Like **lock** as described in the global options section; it can also be specified in an image section.

**optional**

> Specifies that the image should be omitted if it is not available when the map is created by the **lilo** command. Useful for specifying test kernels that are not always present.

**password=***password*

> Specifies that the image is password-protected and provides the password that the user is prompted for when booting. The password is not encrypted in the configuration file, so if passwords are used, only the superuser should be able to read the file.

**range=***sectors*

> Used with the **image** option, when the image is specified as a device (e.g., **image=**/*dev/fd0*), to indicate the range of sectors to be mapped into the map file. *sectors* can be given as the range *start-end* or as *start+number,* where *start* and *end* are zero-based sector numbers and *number* is the increment beyond *start* to include. If only *start* is specified, only that one sector is mapped. For example:

```
image = /dev/fd0
range = 1+512   # take 512 sectors, starting with sector 1
```

**restricted**

> Specifies that a password is required for booting the image only if boot parameters are specified on the command line.

**table=***device*

> Specifies, for a non-Linux operating system, the device that contains the partition table. If **table** is omitted, the boot loader does not pass partition information to the operating system being booted. Note that */sbin/lilo* must be rerun if the partition table is modified. This option cannot be used with **unsafe**.

**unsafe**

> Can be used in the per-image section for a non-Linux operating system to indicate that the boot sector should not be accessed when the map is created. If **unsafe** is specified, then some checking isn't done, but the option can be useful for running the **lilo** command without having to insert a floppy disk when the boot sector is on a fixed-format floppy disk device. This option cannot be used with **table**.

## Kernel options

The following kernel options can be specified in */etc/lilo.conf* as well as on the boot command line:

**append=***string*

> Appends the options specified in *string* to the parameter line passed to the kernel. This typically is used to specify certain hardware parameters. For

example, if your system has more than 64 MB of memory (i.e., more than your BIOS can recognize), you can use **append**:

```
append = "mem=128M"
```

initrd=*filename*
> Specifies the file to load into */dev/initrd* when booting with a RAM disk. See also the options **load_ramdisk** (in the later section "Boot-time Kernel Options"), **prompt_ramdisk**, **ramdisk_size**, and **ramdisk_start** (in the later section "initrd: Using a RAM Disk").

literal=*string*
> Like **append** but replaces all other kernel boot options.

noinitrd
> Preserves the contents of */dev/initrd* so they can be read once after the kernel is booted.

prompt_ramdisk=*n*
> Specifies whether the kernel should prompt you to insert the floppy disk that contains the RAM disk image, for use during Linux installation. Values of *n* are:

> 0    Don't prompt. Usually used for an installation in which the kernel and the RAM disk image both fit on one floppy.

> 1    Prompt. This is the default.

ramdisk=*size*
> Obsolete; use only with kernels older than Version 1.3.48. For newer kernels, see the option **load_ramdisk** in the later section "Boot-time Kernel Options" as well as **prompt_ramdisk**, **ramdisk_size**, and **ramdisk_start**, elsewhere in this section.

ramdisk_size=*n*
> Specifies the amount of memory, in kilobytes, to be allocated for the RAM disk. The default is 4096, which allocates 4 megabytes.

ramdisk_start=*offset*
> Used for a Linux installation in which both the kernel and the RAM disk image are on the same floppy. *offset* indicates the offset on the floppy where the RAM disk image begins; it is specified in kilobytes.

root=*root-device*
> Specifies the device that should be mounted as root. If the special name **current** is used as the value, the root device is set to the device on which the root filesystem currently is mounted. Defaults to the root-device setting contained in the kernel image.

vga=*mode*
> Specifies the VGA text mode that should be selected when booting. *mode* defaults to the VGA mode setting in the kernel image. The values are case-insensitive. They are:

**ask**  Prompts the user for the text mode. Pressing Ènter in response to the prompt displays a list of the available modes.

**extended** (or **ext**)
Selects 80x50 text mode.

**normal**
Selects normal 80x25 text mode.

*number*
Use the text mode that corresponds to *number*. A list of available modes for your video card can be obtained by booting with **vga=ask** and pressing Enter.

## The lilo Command

You need to run the **lilo** command to install the LILO boot loader and to update it whenever the kernel changes or to reflect changes to */etc/lilo.conf.*

The path to the **lilo** command is usually */sbin/lilo.* The syntax of the command is:

```
lilo [options]
```

Some of the options correspond to */etc/lilo.conf* keywords:

| Configuration Keyword | Command Option |
|---|---|
| boot=*bootdev* | −b *bootdev* |
| compact | −c |
| delay=*tsecs* | −d *tsecs* |
| default=*label* | −D *label* |
| disktab=*file* | −f *file* |
| install=*bootsector* | −i *bootsector* |
| lba32 | −L |
| linear | −l |
| map=*mapfile* | −m *mapfile* |
| fix-table | −P fix |
| ignore-table | −P ignore |
| backup=*file* | −s *file* |
| force-backup=*file* | −S *file* |
| verbose=*level* | −v |

These options should be put in the configuration file whenever possible; putting them on the **lilo** command line instead of in */etc/lilo.conf* is now deprecated. The next section describes those options that can be given only on the **lilo** command line; the others are described earlier in this section.

## lilo Command Options

The following list describes those **lilo** command options that are available only on the command line. Multiple options are given separately:

```
% lilo -q -v
```

**–C** *config-file*

Specifies an alternative to the default configuration file (*/etc/lilo.conf*). **lilo** uses the configuration file to determine what files to map when it installs LILO.

**–I** *label*

Prints the path to the kernel specified by *label* to standard output or an error message if no matching label is found. For example:

```
% lilo -I linux
/boot/vmlinuz-2.0.34-0.6
```

**–q** Lists the currently mapped files. **lilo** maintains a file (by default */boot/map*), containing the name and location of the kernel(s) to boot. Running **lilo** with this option prints the names of the files in the map file to standard output, as in this example (in which the asterisk indicates that **linux** is the default):

```
% lilo -q
linux      *
test
```

**–r** *root-directory*

Specifies that before doing anything else, **lilo** should **chroot** to the indicated directory. Used for repairing a setup from a boot floppy—you can boot from a floppy but have **lilo** use the boot files from the hard drive. For example, if you issue the following commands, **lilo** will get the files it needs from the hard drive:

```
% mount /dev/hda2 /mnt
% lilo -r /mnt
```

**–R** *command-line*

Sets the default command for the boot loader the next time it executes. The command executes once and then is removed by the boot loader. This option typically is used in reboot scripts, just before calling **shutdown –r**.

**–t** Indicates that this is a test. Does not really write a new boot sector or map file. Can be used with **–v** to find out what **lilo** would do during a normal run.

**–u** *device-name*

Uninstalls **lilo** by restoring the saved boot sector from */boot/boot.nnnn*, after validating it against a timestamp. *device-name* is the name of the device on which LILO is installed, such as */dev/hda2*.

**–U** *device-name*

Like **–u** but does not check the timestamp.

**–V** Prints the **lilo** version number.

# Loadlin: Booting from MS-DOS

Loadlin is a Linux boot loader that you run from within a bootable MS-DOS partition; the system must be in real DOS mode, not in an MS-DOS window running under Windows. No installation is required; you just need to copy the executable file *loadlin.exe* from the Loadlin distribution to your MS-DOS partition.* You also need a compressed Linux kernel (e.g., *vmlinuz*), which you can load from a floppy, from the DOS partition, or from a RAM disk. For example:

```
C:> loadlin c:\vmlinuz root=/dev/hda2
```

This example loads the Linux kernel image *vmlinuz*, passing it the boot parameter **root=/dev/hda2**, telling the kernel that the Linux root partition is */dev/hda2*. (If you are using a RAM disk, see the section "initrd: Using a RAM Disk" later in this chapter.)

If you want to use Loadlin with Windows 95/98, see the Loadlin User Guide and the Loadlin+Win95 mini-HOWTO for how to do that. Note that if your disk uses the FAT32 filesystem, the standard techniques for using Loadlin and Windows 95 won't work; if this is the case or if you aren't sure whether you have FAT16 or FAT32, it's important to read the mini-HOWTO before you proceed.

Loadlin can be run directly from the DOS prompt, as in the example, or it can be invoked from CONFIG.SYS or AUTOEXEC.BAT. Like LILO, Loadlin takes both options that direct its operation and options (also referred to as *parameters*) that it passes to the kernel.

There are two forms of the Loadlin syntax:

```
LOADLIN @params
LOADLIN [zimage_file] [options] [boot_params]
```

## Using a Parameter File

In the first form of the preceding syntax, *params* is a DOS file that contains the options you want Loadlin to run with. The Loadlin distribution comes with a sample parameter file, *test.par*, that you can use as a basis for creating your own. Each line in a parameter file contains one parameter. If you want to specify the name of the Linux kernel to use (the **image=** parameter), it must be the first entry in the

---

\* If Loadlin didn't come with your Linux distribution, you can download it from any of the major Linux sites, such as the Metalab site at *http://metalab.unc.edu/pub/Linux*.

file. Comments start with a hash sign (#). The entries in the parameter file can be overridden or appended on the command line. For example, to override the value of **vga** set in the parameter file:

```
C:> LOADLIN @myparam vga=normal
```

### Putting Parameters on the Command Line

In the second form of the preceding Loadlin syntax, *zimage_file* is the name of a Linux kernel to run, followed by a list of Loadlin options and/or boot options. Specifying **LOADLIN** with no parameters gives a help message listing the Loadlin options and some of the possible kernel boot options. The message is long enough that you probably want to pipe the output through a pager like **more**:

```
C:> LOADLIN | more
```

The Loadlin options are:

**–clone**
> Bypasses certain checks—read the LOADLIN User Guide that comes with the Loadlin distribution before using.

**–d** *file*
> Debug mode. Like **–t** but sends output to *file* as well as to standard output.

**–dskreset**
> Causes disks to be reset after loading but before booting Linux.

**–noheap**
> For use by serious Linux hackers only; disables use of the setup heap.

**–t**  Test mode. Goes through the loading process but doesn't actually start Linux. Also sets **–v**.

**–txmode**
> Sets the screen to text mode (80x25) on startup.

**–v**  Verbose. Prints parameter and configuration information to standard output.

**–wait=***nn*
> After loading, waits *nn* (DOS) ticks before booting Linux.

In addition to these Loadlin options, the help message prints a number of kernel boot options that you can specify. The boot options that it prints are only a few of the many available boot options. See also the BootPrompt-HOWTO for a more complete list.

## Dual Booting Linux and Windows NT/2000

As we said earlier, when you run Windows NT, its boot loader expects to be the one in charge; therefore, the normal way to dual boot Windows NT and Linux is to add Linux as an option on the NT boot menu. The information in this section also applies to Windows 2000, which uses the NT loader.

To accomplish this, you need to provide the NT loader with a copy of the Linux boot sector. Here's how you do that on a computer running Windows NT with an NTFS filesystem (note that Windows NT should be installed on your system already). See the NT OS Loader+Linux mini-HOWTO for more information and other alternatives.

You should have a Linux boot floppy available so that, if necessary, you can boot Linux before the NT boot loader has been modified. You also should have a DOS-formatted floppy to transfer the boot sector to the Windows NT partition. If LILO is already installed, you may need to modify */etc/lilo.conf* as described later. Otherwise, you'll either install LILO as part of the Linux installation, or you can install it with the *QuickInst* script that comes with LILO. Once LILO is installed, and you have a configuration file, you can set up the system for dual booting.

Note that the following instructions assume your Linux partition is on */dev/hda2*. If Linux is on another partition, be sure to replace */dev/hda2* in the following examples with the correct partition.

1.  Specify the Linux root partition as your boot device. If you are editing */etc/ lilo.conf* manually, your entry will look like this:

    ```
    boot=/dev/hda2
    ```

    and will be the same as the **root=** entry.

2.  Run the **lilo** command to install LILO on the Linux root partition.

3.  At this point, if you need to reboot Linux, you'll have to use the boot floppy, because the NT loader hasn't been set up yet to boot Linux.

4.  From Linux, run the **dd** command to make a copy of the Linux boot sector:

    ```
    % dd if=/dev/hda2 of=/bootsect.lnx bs=512 count=1
    ```

    This command copies one block, with a blocksize of 512 bytes, from the input file */dev/hda2* to the output file */bootsect.lnx*. (The output filename can be whatever makes sense to you; it doesn't have to be *bootsect.lnx*.)

5.  Copy *bootsect.lnx* to a DOS-formatted floppy disk:

    ```
    % mount -t msdos /dev/fd0 /mnt
    % cp /bootsect.lnx /mnt
    % umount /mnt
    ```

6.  Reboot the system to Windows NT and copy the boot sector from the floppy disk to the hard disk. For example, using the command line to copy the file:

    ```
    C:> copy a:\bootsect.lnx c:\bootsect.lnx
    ```

    It doesn't matter where on the hard drive you put the file because you'll tell the NT loader where to find it in step 8.

7. Modify the attributes of the file *boot.ini** to remove the system and read-only attributes so you can edit it:

```
C:> attrib -s -r c:\boot.ini
```

8. Edit *boot.ini* with a text editor to add the line:

```
C:\bootsect.lnx="Linux"
```

This line adds Linux to the boot menu and tells the Windows NT boot loader where to find the Linux boot sector. You can insert the line anywhere in the **[operating systems]** section of the file. Its position in the file determines where it will show up on the boot menu when you reboot your computer. Adding it at the end, for example, results in a *boot.ini* file that looks something like this (the second **multi(0)** entry is wrapped to fit in the margins of this page):

```
[boot loader]
timeout=30
default=multi(0)disk(0)rdisk(0)partition(1)\WINNT
[operating systems]
multi(0)disk(0)rdisk(0)partition(1)\WINNT="Windows NT Server Version 4.00"
multi(0)disk(0)rdisk(0)partition(1)\WINNT="Windows NT Server Version 4.00
  [VGA mode]" /basevideo /sos
C:\bootsect.lnx="Linux"
```

If you want Linux to be the default operating system, modify the `default=` line to say:

```
default=C:\bootsect.lnx
```

9. Rerun **attrib** to restore the system and read-only attributes:

```
C:> attrib +s +r c:\boot.ini
```

Now you can shut down Windows NT and reboot; NT will prompt you with a menu that looks something like this:

```
OS Loader V4.00

Please select the operating system to start:

Windows NT Workstation Version 4.00
Windows NT Workstation Version 4.00 [VGA mode]
Linux
```

Select Linux, and the NT loader reads the Linux boot sector and transfers control to LILO, on the Linux partition.

If you later modify */etc/lilo.conf* or rebuild the kernel, you need to rerun the **lilo** command, create a new *bootsect.lnx* file, and replace the version of *bootsect.lnx* on the Windows NT partition with the new version. That is, you need to rerun steps 2–6.

---

\* *boot.ini* is the Windows NT counterpart to */etc/lilo.conf*. It defines what operating systems the NT loader can boot.

If you have any problems or you simply want to remove LILO later, you can reverse the installation procedure: boot to Windows NT, change the system and read-only attributes on *boot.ini*, reedit *boot.ini* to remove the Linux entry, save the file, restore the system and read-only attributes, and remove the Linux boot sector from the NT partition.

## Boot-time Kernel Options

The Loadlin and LILO sections of this chapter described some of the options you can specify when you boot Linux. There are many more options that can be specified. This section touches on the ways to pass options to the kernel and then describes some of the kinds of parameters you might want to use. The parameters in this section affect the kernel and therefore apply regardless of which boot loader you use.

As always with Unix systems, there are a number of choices for the boot process itself. If you are using Loadlin, you can pass parameters to the kernel on the command line or in a file.

If LILO is your boot loader, you can add to or override the parameters specified in */etc/lilo.conf* during the boot process as follows:

- If **prompt** is set in */etc/lilo.conf,* LILO always presents the boot prompt and waits for input. At the prompt, you can choose the operating system to be booted. If you choose Linux, you also can specify parameters.

- If **prompt** isn't set, when the word "LILO" appears, press Control, Shift, or Alt, and the boot prompt appears. You also can press the Scroll Lock key before LILO is printed and not have to wait poised over the keyboard for the right moment.

- At the boot prompt, specify the system you want to boot or press Tab to get a list of the available choices. You then can enter the name of the image to boot. For example:

```
LILO boot: <press Tab>
linux   test   dos
boot: linux
```

You also can add boot command options:

```
boot: linux single
```

- If you don't provide any input, LILO waits the amount of time specified in the **delay** parameter and then boots the default operating system with the default parameters as set in */etc/lilo.conf.*

Some of the boot parameters have been mentioned earlier. Many of the others are hardware-specific and are too numerous to mention here. For a complete list of parameters and a discussion of the booting process, see the BootPrompt-HOWTO.

Some of the parameters not shown earlier that you might find useful are listed next; many more are covered in the HOWTO. Most of the following parameters are used to provide information or instructions for the kernel, rather than to LILO.

**debug**

Prints all kernel messages to the console.

**hd=***cylinders,heads,sectors*

Specifies the hard drive geometry to the kernel. Useful if Linux has trouble recognizing the geometry of your drive, especially if it's an IDE drive with more than 1024 cylinders.

**load_ramdisk=***n*

Tells the kernel whether to load a RAM disk image for use during Linux installation. Values of *n* are:

0    Don't try to load the image. This is the default.

1    Load the image from a floppy disk to the RAM disk.

**mem=***size*

Specifies the amount of system memory installed. Useful if your BIOS reports memory only up to 64 MB and your system has more memory installed. Specify as a number with **M** or **k** (case-insensitive) appended:

```
mem=128M
```

Because **mem** would have to be included on the command line for every boot, it often is specified on a command line saved with **lock** or with **append** to be added to the parameters passed to the kernel.

**noinitrd**

When set, disables the two-stage boot and preserves the contents of */dev/initrd* so the data is available after the kernel has booted. */dev/initrd* can be read only once, and then its contents are returned to the system.

**number**

Starts Linux at the runlevel specified by *number*. A runlevel is an operating state that the system can be booted to, such as a multiuser system or a system configuration running the X Window System. A runlevel is generally one of the numbers from 1 to 6; the default usually is 3. The runlevels and their corresponding states are defined in the file */etc/inittab*. See the manpage for */etc/inittab* for more information.

ro   Mounts the root filesystem read-only. Used for doing system maintenance, such as checking the filesystem integrity, when you don't want anything written to the filesystem.

rw   Mounts the root filesystem read-write. If neither **ro** nor **rw** is specified, the default value (usually **rw**) stored in the kernel image is used.

**single**

Starts Linux in single-user mode. This option is used for system administration and recovery. It gives you a root prompt as soon as the system boots, with minimal initialization. No other logins are allowed.

# initrd: Using a RAM Disk

Modern Linux distributions use a modular kernel, which allows modules to be added without requiring that the kernel be rebuilt. If your root filesystem is on a device whose driver is a module, as is frequently true of SCSI disks, you can use the **initrd** facility, which provides a two-stage boot process, to first set up a temporary root filesystem in a RAM disk containing the modules you need to add (e.g., the SCSI driver) and then load the modules and mount the real root filesystem. The RAM disk containing the temporary filesystem is the special device file */dev/ initrd*.

Before you can use **initrd**, both RAM disk support (CONFIG_BLK_DEV_RAM=y) and initial RAM disk support (CONFIG_BLK_DEV_INITRD=y) must be compiled into the Linux kernel. Then you need to prepare the normal root filesystem and create the RAM disk image. Your Linux distribution may have utilities to do some of the setup for you; for example, the Red Hat distribution comes with the **mkinitrd** command, which builds the **initrd** image. For detailed information, see the **initrd** manpage and the file *initrd.txt* (the path may vary but is usually something like */usr/src/linux/Documentation/initrd.txt*).

Once your Linux system has been set up for **initrd**, you can do one of the following, depending on which boot loader you are using:

- If LILO is your boot loader, add the **initrd** option to the appropriate image section:

```
image = /vmlinuz
  initrd = /boot/initrd  # The file to load as the contents of /dev/initrd
  ...
```

  Run the **/sbin/lilo** command, and you can reboot with **initrd**.

- If you are using Loadlin, add the **initrd** option to the command line:

```
loadlin c:\linux\vmlinuz initrd=c:\linux\initrd
```

CHAPTER 5

# Red Hat and Debian Package Managers

This chapter describes the two major Linux packaging systems, the Red Hat Package Manager (RPM) and the Debian GNU/Linux Package Manager.

When you want to install applications on your Linux system, most often you'll find a binary or a source package containing the application you want, instead of (or in addition to) a *.tar.gz* file. A package is a file containing the files necessary to install an application. But note that while the package contains the files you need for installation, the application might require the presence of other files or packages that are not included, such as particular libraries (and even specific versions of the libraries), in order to be able to run. Such requirements are known as *dependencies*.

Package management systems offer many benefits. As a user, you may find you want to query the package database to find out what packages are installed on the system and their versions. As a system administrator, you need tools to install and manage the packages on your system. And, if you are also a developer, you need to know how to build a package for distribution.

Among other things, package managers:

- Provide tools for installing, updating, removing, and managing the software on your system.

- Let you install new or upgraded software directly across a network.

- Tell you what software package a particular file belongs to or what files a package contains.

- Maintain a database of packages on the system and their state, so you can find out what packages or versions are installed on your system.

- Provide dependency checking, so you don't mess up your system with incompatible software.

- Provide PGP, MD5, or other signature verification tools.

- Provide tools for building packages.

Any user can list or query packages. However, installing, upgrading, or removing packages generally requires superuser privileges. This is because the packages normally are installed in systemwide directories that are writable only by root. Sometimes you can specify an alternate directory, to install, for example, a package into your home directory or into a project directory where you have write permission.

Both RPM and the Debian Package Manager back up old files before installing an updated package. Not only does this let you go back if there is a problem, but also if you've made changes (to configuration files, for example), they aren't completely lost.

## The Red Hat Package Manager

The Red Hat Package Manager (RPM) is a freely available packaging system for software distribution and installation. In addition to Red Hat and Red Hat-based distributions, both SuSE and Caldera are among the Linux distributions that use RPM.

Using RPM is straightforward. A single command, **rpm**, has options to perform all the package functions. For example, to find out if the Emacs editor is installed on your system, you could say:

```
% rpm -q emacs
emacs-20.4-4
```

In addition, the GNOME-RPM program provides an X-based graphical frontend to RPM (that can be run even if you are not running GNOME). This section describes the **rpm** command and then the **gnorpm** command that runs GNOME-RPM.

### The rpm Command

RPM packages are built, installed, and queried with the **rpm** command. RPM package names usually end with a *.rpm* extension. **rpm** has a set of modes, each with its own options. The format of the **rpm** command is:

```
rpm [options] [packages]
```

With a few exceptions, as noted in the lists of options that follow, the first option specifies the **rpm** mode (e.g., install, query, update, build, etc.), and any remaining options affect that mode.

In the option descriptions that refer to packages, you'll sometimes see them specified as *package-name* and sometimes as *package-file*. The package name is the name of the program or application, such as **gif2png**. The package file is the name of the RPM file: *gif2png-2.2.5-1.i386.rpm*.

RPM provides a configuration file for specifying frequently used options. The system configuration file is usually */etc/rpmrc*, and users can set up their own

$HOME/.rpmrc file. You can use the **--showrc** option to show the values RPM will use for all the options that may be set in an *rpmrc* file:

```
rpm --showrc
```

The **rpm** command includes FTP and HTTP clients, so you can specify an *ftp://* or *http://* URL to install or query a package across the Internet. You can use an FTP or HTTP URL wherever *package-file* is specified in the commands presented here.

Any user can query the RPM database. Most of the other functions require super-user privileges.

### General options

The following options can be used with all modes:

**--dbpath** *path*
> Use *path* as the path to the RPM database.

**--ftpport** *port*
> Use *port* as the FTP port.

**--ftpproxy** *host*
> Use *host* as a proxy server for all transfers. Specified if you are FTPing through a firewall system that uses a proxy.

**--help**
> Print a long usage message (running **rpm** with no options gives a shorter usage message).

**--justdb**
> Update only the database; don't change any files.

**--pipe** *command*
> Pipe the **rpm** output to *command*.

**--quiet**
> Display only error messages.

**--rcfile** *filename*
> Use *filename* as the configuration file instead of the system configuration file */etc/rpmrc* or *$HOME/.rpmrc*.

**--root** *dir*
> Perform all operations within directory *dir*.

**--version**
> Print the version number of **rpm**.

**-vv**
> Print debugging information.

## Install, upgrade, and freshen options

Install or upgrade an RPM package. The syntax of the **install** command is:

```
rpm -i [install-options] package_file ...
rpm --install [install-options] package_file ...
```

To install a new version of a package and remove an existing version at the same time, use the **upgrade** command instead:

```
rpm -U [install-options] package_file ...
rpm --upgrade [install-options] package_file ...
```

One feature of **-U** is that if the package doesn't already exist on the system, it acts like **-i** and installs it. To prevent that behavior, you can **freshen** a package instead; in that case, **rpm** upgrades the package only if an earlier version is already installed. The **freshen** syntax is:

```
rpm -F [install-options] package_file ...
rpm --freshen [install-options] package_file ...
```

Installation and upgrade options are:

**--allfiles**
Install or upgrade all files.

**--badreloc**
Used with **--relocate** to force relocation even if the package is not relocatable.

**--excludedocs**
Don't install any documentation files.

**--excludepath** *path*
Don't install any file whose filename begins with *path*.

**--force**
Force the installation. Equivalent to using **--replacepkgs**, **--replacefiles**, and **--oldpackage**.

**-h, --hash**
Print 50 hash marks as the package archive is unpacked. Use with **--version** for a nicer display.

**--ignorearch**
Install even if the binary package is intended for a different architecture.

**--ignoreos**
Install binary package even if the operating systems don't match.

**--ignoresize**
Don't check disk space availability before installing.

**--includedocs**
Install documentation files. This is needed only if **excludedocs: 1** is specified in an *rpmrc* file.

**--nodeps**

Don't check whether this package depends on the presence of other packages.

**--noorder**

Don't reorder packages to satisfy dependencies before installing.

**--noscripts**

Don't execute any preinstall or postinstall scripts.

**--notriggers**

Don't execute any scripts triggered by package installation.

**--oldpackage**

Allow an upgrade to replace a newer package with an older one.

**--percent**

Print percent-completion messages as files are unpacked.

**--prefix** *path*

Set the installation prefix to *path* for relocatable packages.

**--replacefiles**

Install the packages even if they replace files from other installed packages.

**--replacepkgs**

Install the packages even if some of them are already installed.

**--test**

Go through the installation to see what it would do, but don't actually install the package.

## Query options

The syntax for the **query** command is:

```
rpm -q[information-options] [package-options]
rpm --query[information-options] [package-options]
```

There are two subsets of query options: *package selection* options that determine what packages to query and *information selection* options that determine what information to provide.

## Package selection options

*package_name*

Query the installed package *package_name*.

**-a, --all**

Query all installed packages.

**-f** *file*, **--file** *file*

Find out what package owns *file*.

**–g** *group*, **––group** *group*

Find out what packages have group *group*.

**–p** *package_file*

Query the uninstalled package *package_file*.

**––querybynumber** *num*

Query the *num*th database entry. Primarily useful for debugging.

**–qf, ––queryformat** *num*

Specify the format for displaying the query output, using tags to represent different types of data (e.g., NAME, FILENAME, DISTRIBUTION). The format specification is a variation of the standard **printf** formatting. (Use **––querytags** in the section "Miscellaneous options" to view a list of available tags.

**––specfile** *specfile*

Query *specfile* as if it were a package.

**––triggeredby** *pkg*

List packages that trigger installation of package *pkg*.

**––whatrequires** *capability*

List packages that require the given capability to function.

**––whatprovides** *capability*

List packages that provide the given capability.

## Information selection options

**–c, ––configfiles**

List configuration files in the package.

**––changelog**

Display the log of change information for the package.

**–d, ––docfiles**

List documentation files in the package.

**––dump**

Dump information for each file in the package. This option must be used with at least one of –l, –c, or –d. The output includes the following information in this order:

```
path size mtime md5sum mode owner group isconfig isdoc rdev symlink
```

**––filesbypkg**

List all files in each package.

**–i**   Display package information, including the name, version, and description.

**–l, ––list**

List all files in the package.

**––last**

List packages by install time, with the latest packages listed first.

**--provides**

List the capabilities this package provides.

**-R, --requires**

List any packages this package depends on.

**-s, --state**

List each file in the package and its state. The possible states are **normal, not installed,** or **replaced.**

**--scripts**

List any package-specific shell scripts used during installation and uninstallation of the package.

### Uninstall options

The syntax for the **uninstall** command is:

```
rpm -e package_name
rpm --erase package_name
```

The uninstall options are:

**--allmatches**

Remove all versions of the package. Only one package should be specified; otherwise, an error results.

**--nodeps**

Don't check dependencies before uninstalling the package.

**--noscripts**

Don't execute any preuninstall or postuninstall scripts.

**--notriggers**

Don't execute any scripts triggered by the removal of this package.

**--test**

Don't really uninstall anything; just go through the motions.

### Verify options

The syntax for the **verify** command is:

```
rpm -V|-y|--verify[package-selection-options]
```

Verify mode compares information about the installed files in a package with information about the files that came in the original package and displays any discrepancies. The information compared includes the size, MD5 sum, permissions, type, owner, and group of each file. Uninstalled files are ignored.

The package selection options include those available for query mode, as well as the following:

**--nofiles**
   Ignore missing files.

**--nomd5**
   Ignore MD5 checksum errors.

**--nopgp**
   Ignore PGP checking errors.

The output is formatted as an eight-character string, possibly followed by a "c" to indicate a configuration file, and then the filename. Each of the eight characters in the string represents the result of comparing one file attribute to the value of that attribute from the RPM database. A period (.) indicates that the file passed that test. The following characters indicate failure of the corresponding test:

5    MD5 sum
D    Device
G    Group
L    Symlink
M    Mode (includes permissions and file type)
S    File size
T    Mtime
U    User

### Database rebuild options

The syntax of the command to rebuild the RPM database is:

`rpm --rebuilddb [options]`

You also can build a new database:

`rpm --initdb [options]`

The options available with the database rebuild mode are the **--dbpath** and **--root** options described earlier under "General options."

### Signature check options

RPM packages may have a PGP signature built into them. PGP configuration information is read from */etc/rpmrc*. The syntax of the signature-check mode is:

`rpm --checksig package_file...`
`rpm -K package_file...`

The signature-checking options are:

**--nogpg**
   Don't check any GPG signatures.

**--nomd5**

    Don't check any MD5 signatures.

**--nopgp**

    Don't check any PGP signatures.

Two other options let you add signatures to packages:

**--addsign** *binary-pkgfile*...

    Generate and append new signatures to those that already exist in the specified binary packages.

**--resign** *binary-pkgfile*...

    Generate and insert new signatures in the specified binary packages, removing any existing signatures.

## Miscellaneous options

Several additional **rpm** options are available:

**--querytags**

    Print the tags available for use with the **--queryformat** option in query mode.

**--setgids** *packages*

    Set file owner and group of the specified packages to those in the database.

**--setperms** *packages*

    Set file permissions of the specified packages to those in the database.

**--showrc**

    Show the values **rpm** will use for all options that can be set in an *.rpmrc* file.

## FTP/HTTP options

The following options are available for use with *ftp://* and *http://* URLs in install, update, and query modes:

**--ftpport** *port*

    Use *port* for making an FTP connection on the proxy FTP server instead of the default port. Same as specifying the macro **_ftpport**.

**--ftpproxy** *host*

    Use *host* as the proxy server for FTP transfers through a firewall that uses a proxy. Same as specifying the macro **_ftpproxy**.

**--httpport** *port*

    Use *port* for making an HTTP connection on the proxy HTTP server instead of the default port. Same as specifying the macro **_httpport**.

**--httpproxy** *host*

    Use *host* as a proxy server for HTTP transfers. Same as specifying the macro **_httpproxy**.

## Build options

The syntax for the build options is:

```
rpm -[b|t]step [build-options] spec-file ...
```

Specify –b to build a package directly from a spec file or –t to open a tarred gzipped file and use its spec file. Both forms take the following single-character **step** arguments:

p    Perform the prep stage, unpacking source files and applying patches.

l    Do a list check, expanding macros in the files section of the spec file and verifying that each file exists.

c    Perform the build stage. Done after the prep stage; generally equivalent to doing a **make**.

i    Perform the install stage. Done after the prep and build stages; generally equivalent to doing a **make install**.

b    Build a binary package. Done after prep, build, and install.

s    Build a source package. Done after prep, build, and install.

a    Build both binary and source packages. Done after prep, build, and install.

The following additional options can be used when building an **rpm** file:

**––buildarch** *arch*
**––buildos** *os*
> For use with pre-3.0 versions of RPM. Build the package for architecture *arch* or the operating system *os*. Replaced in 3.0 with **––target**.

**––buildroot** *dir*
> Override the **BuildRoot** tag with *dir* when building the package.

**––clean**
> Clean up (remove) the build files after the package has been made.

**––rmsource**
> Remove the source files and the spec file when the build is done. Can be used as a standalone option with **rpm** to clean up files separately from creating the packages.

**––short-circuit**
> Can be used with –bc and –bi to skip previous stages.

**––sign**
> Add a PGP signature to the package.

**––target** *platform*
> When building the package, set the macros **_target**, **_target_arch**, and **_target_os** to the value indicated by *platform*.

**--test**

Go through the motions, but don't execute any build stages. Used for testing spec files.

**--timecheck**

Set the timecheck age (the maximum age in seconds of a file being packaged). Set to 0 to disable.

Two other options can be used standalone with **rpm** to recompile or rebuild a package:

**--rebuild** *source-pkgfile...*

Like **--recompile**, but also build a new binary package. Remove the build directory, the source files, and the spec file once the build is complete.

**--recompile** *source-pkgfile...*

Install the named source package, and prep, compile, and install the package.

### RPM examples

Query the RPM database to find Emacs-related packages:

```
% rpm -q -a | grep emacs
```

Query an uninstalled package, printing information about the package, and list the files it contains:

```
% rpm -qpil ~/downloads/bash2-doc-2.03-8.i386.rpm
```

Install a package (assumes superuser privileges):

```
% rpm -i sudo-1.5.3-6.i386.rpm
```

## GNOME-RPM

GNOME-RPM is a graphical user frontend to **rpm** that runs under X. You can run **gnorpm** even if you are not running GNOME. When you run **gnorpm**, it opens a window that lets you manage your **rpm** packages via a graphical interface. The format of the **gnorpm** command is:

```
gnorpm [options]
```

### gnorpm options

The **gnorpm** options are:

**--geometry=**geom

Specify the geometry of the main window in standard X geometry format (i.e., $w \times h + x + y$).

**-i** *pkgfiles*, **--install** *pkgfiles*

Install the specified packages.

**−p** *pkgs*, **−−packages** *pkgs*

The packages are in files, not in the **rpm** database (i.e., they haven't been installed yet).

**−q** *pkgs*, **−−query** *pkgs*

Display a query window for the specified installed packages.

**−qp** *pkgfiles*, **−−query −−packages** *pkgfiles*

Display a query window for the specified package files. This is the same as specifying the −q and −p options.

**−U** *pkgfiles*, **−−upgrade** *pkgfiles*

Upgrade the specified packages.

**−K** *pkgfiles*, **−−checksig** *pkgfiles*

Check the signatures on the specified packages.

**−y** *pkgs*, **−−verify** *pkgs*

Verify the specified packages.

**−?**, **−−help**

Display a help message and exit.

**−−root=***dir*

Specify the filesystem root to use.

**−−usage**

Display a brief usage message and exit.

## *The GNOME-RPM window*

The GNOME-RPM main window has five parts. At the top is a menu bar with three buttons:

*Packages*

Menu options are Query, Uninstall, and Verify.

*Operations*

Menu options are Find, Web find, Install, and Preferences.

*Help*

Provides online help for GNOME-RPM.

Below the menu bar is a toolbar, with buttons to Install, Unselect, Uninstall, Query, Verify, Find, and Web find. At the very bottom of the window is a status bar.

The rest of the window is the main panel. On the left is the package panel, which displays package folders in a tree structure. Clicking on a folder selects it; double-click to display the contents of the folder (i.e., the packages in that folder) on the righthand panel. Clicking on a package selects it; you then can use the menus and the toolbar buttons to operate on the package. You can select several packages at the same time and operate on them as a group. Right-clicking on a package icon selects the package if it isn't already and presents a menu with Query, Uninstall, and Verify options.

See the GNOME-RPM documentation and online help for full details.

# The Debian Package Manager

Debian GNU/Linux provides several package management tools, primarily intended to facilitate the building, installation, and management of binary packages. Debian package names generally end in *.deb*. The Debian package management tools include:

**dpkg**
> Until recently, the most important of the Debian packaging tools and still the primary package management program. Used to install or uninstall packages or as a frontend to **dpkg-deb**.

**dpkg-deb**
> Lower-level packaging tool. Used to create and manage the Debian package archives. Accepts and executes commands from **dpkg** or can be called directly.

**dselect**
> An interactive frontend to **dpkg**.

**apt-get**
> The currently available piece of the Advanced Package Tool (APT), which is still being developed and is intended to be a modern, user-friendly package management tool. Can be run from the command line or selected as a method from **dselect**. One of the features of **apt-get** is that you can use it to get and install packages across the Internet by specifying an *ftp://* or *http://* URL. Another feature is that you can use it to upgrade all packages currently installed on your system in a single operation.

## Files

Some important files used by the Debian package management tools are:

*control*
> Comes with each package; documents dependencies; contains the name and version of the package, a description, maintainer, installed size, and so on.

*conffiles*
> Comes with each package and contains a list of the configuration files associated with the package.

*preinst, postinst, prerm, postrm*
> Scripts that can be included in a package to be run before installation, after installation, before removal, or after removal of the package.

*/var/lib/dpkg/available*
> Contains information about packages available on the system.

*/var/lib/dpkg/status*

Contains information about the status of packages available on the system.

*/etc/apt/sources.list*

A list for APT of package sources, used to locate packages. The sources are listed one per line, in order of preference.

*/etc/apt/apt.conf*

The main APT configuration file.

## Package States and Selection States

The possible states that a package can be in are:

**config-files**

Only the configuration files for the package are present on the system.

**half-configured**

The package is unpacked and configuration was started but not completed.

**half-installed**

Installation was started but not completed.

**installed**

The package is unpacked and configured.

**not-installed**

The package is not installed.

**unpacked**

The package is unpacked but not configured.

The possible package selection states are:

**deinstall**

The package has been selected for deinstallation (i.e., for removal of everything but configuration files).

**install**

The package has been selected for installation.

**purge**

The package has been selected to be purged (i.e., for removal of everything including the configuration files).

## Package Flags

There are two possible package flags that can be set for a package. They are:

**hold**

The package is not to be handled by **dpkg**, unless forced with the **−−force-hold** option.

**reinst-required**
> The package is broken and needs to be reinstalled. Such a package cannot be removed, unless forced with the – –force-reinstreq option.

## Scripts

In addition to the commands described in the next subsection, several shell and Perl scripts are included with the package manager for use in building packages:

**dpkg-buildpackage**
> Help automate package building. Shell script.

**dpkg-distaddfile**
> Add an entry for a file to *debian/files*. Perl script.

**dpkg-genchanges**
> Generate an upload control file from the information in an unpacked, built, source tree and the files it has generated. Perl script.

**dpkg-gencontrol**
> Read information from an unpacked source tree and display a binary package control file on standard output. Perl script.

**dpkg-name**
> Rename Debian packages to their full package names. Shell script.

**dpkg-parsechangelog**
> Read and parse the changelog from an unpacked source tree and write the information to standard output in machine-readable form. Perl script.

**dpkg-scanpackages**
> Create a *Packages* file from a tree of binary packages. The *Packages* file is used by **dselect** to provide a list of packages available for installation. Perl script.

**dpkg-shlibdeps**
> Calculate shared library dependencies for named executables. Perl script.

**dpkg-source**
> Pack and unpack Debian source archives. Perl script.

## Debian Package Manager Command Summary

| apt-cdrom | apt-cdrom [*options*] *command* |
|---|---|
| | Add a new CD-ROM to APT's list of available sources. Currently, the only command is **add**, which is required (except with the – –**help** option). The database of CD-ROM IDs that APT maintains is */var/state/apt/cdroms.list*. |

Options can be specified on the command line or they may be set
in the configuration file. Boolean options set in the configuration
file can be overridden on the command line in a number of different ways, a couple of which are **--no-***opt* and *-opt*=**no**, where *opt*
is the single-character or full name of the option.

**-a, --thorough**
Do a thorough package scan. May be needed with some old
Debian CD-ROMs.

**-c, --config-file**
Specify a configuration file to be read after the default configuration file.

**-d, --cdrom**
Specify the CD-ROM mount point, which must be listed in */etc/
fstab*. The configuration option is Acquire::cdrom::mount.

**-f, --fast**
Do a fast copy, assuming the files are valid and don't all need
checking. Specify this only if this disk has been run before
without error. The configuration option is APT::CDROM::Fast.

**-h, --help**
Print help message and exit.

**-m, --no-mount**
Don't mount or unmount the mount point. The configuration
option is APT::CDROM::NoMount.

**-n, --just-print, --recon, --no-act**
Check everything, but don't actually make any changes. The
configuration option is APT::CDROM::NoAct.

**-o, --option**
Set a configuration option. Syntax is **-o** *group::tool=option*
(e.g., APT::CDROM=Fast).

**-r, --rename**
Prompt for a new label and rename the disk to the new value.
The configuration option is APT::CDROM::Rename.

**-v, --version**
Print the version information and exit.

---

**apt-get** [*options*] *command* [*package*...]

A command-line tool for handling packages. Will eventually be a
backend to APT.

→

| apt-get ← | **Commands** |

**autoclean**

Like **clean**, but remove only package files that can no longer be downloaded.

**clean**

Clear the local repository of retrieved package files.

**check**

Update the package cache and check for broken packages.

**dist-upgrade**

Like **upgrade** but also handle dependencies intelligently.

**dselect-upgrade**

Used together with **dselect**. Track the changes made by **dselect** to the **Status** field of available packages and take actions necessary to realize that status.

**install** *package*...

Install one or more packages. Specify the package name, not the full filename. Other required packages also are retrieved and installed. With a hyphen appended to the package name, the package is removed if it is already installed.

**remove** *package*...

Remove one or more packages. Specify the package name, not the full filename. With a plus sign appended to the name, the package is installed.

**source** *package*...

Find source packages and download them into the current directory. If specified with **−−compile**, the source packages are compiled into binary packages. With **−−download-only**, the source packages are not unpacked.

**update**

Resynchronize the package overview files from their sources. Must be done before an **upgrade** or **dist-upgrade**.

**upgrade**

Install the latest versions of all packages currently installed. Run **update** first.

**Options**

Options can be specified on the command line or they may be set in the configuration file. Boolean options set in the configuration file can be overridden on the command line in one of several ways, a couple of which are **−−no−***opt* and **−***opt***=no**, where *opt* is the single-character or full name of the option.

**–b, ––compile, ––build**

Compile source packages after download.

**–c, ––config-file**

Specify a configuration file to read after the default.

**–d, ––download-only**

Retrieve package files, but don't unpack or install them. The configuration option is APT::Get::Download-only.

**–f, ––fix-broken**

Try to fix a system with broken dependencies. Can be used alone or with a command. The configuration option is APT::Get::Fix-Broken.

**––force-yes**

Force yes. Causes APT to continue without prompting if it is doing something that could damage your system. Use with great caution and only if absolutely necessary. The configuration option is APT::Get::force-yes.

**–h, ––help**

Display a help message and exit.

**––ignore-hold**

Ignore a hold placed on a package. Use with **dist-upgrade** to override many undesired holds. The configuration option is APT::Get::Ignore-Hold.

**–m, ––ignore-missing, ––fix-missing**

Ignore missing or corrupted packages or packages that cannot be retrieved. Can cause problems when used with **–f**.

**––no-download**

Disable package downloading; use with **––ignore-missing** to force APT to use only the packages that have already been downloaded.

**––no-upgrade**

Do not upgrade packages. Use with **install** to prevent upgrade of packages that are already installed. The configuration option is APT::Get::no-upgrade.

**–o, ––option**

Set a configuration option. Syntax is **–o** *group::tool=option* (e.g., APT::Get=force-yes).

**––print-uris**

Print URIs of files instead of fetching them. Print path, destination filename, size, and expected MD5 hash. The configuration option is APT::Get::Print-URIs.

$\rightarrow$

| | |
|---|---|
| **apt-get**<br>← | **−q, −−quiet**<br>Quiet. Omit progress indicators, produce only logging output. Add a **q** to make even quieter.<br><br>**−s, −−simulate, −−just-print, −−dry-run, −−recon, −−no-act**<br>Go through the motions, but don't actually make any changes to the system. The configuration option is APT::Get::Simulate.<br><br>**−u, −−show-upgraded**<br>Print a list of all packages to be upgraded. The configuration option is APT::Get::Show-Upgraded.<br><br>**−v, −−version**<br>Display the version and exit.<br><br>**−y, −−yes, −−assume-yes**<br>Automatically reply "yes" to prompts and run noninteractively. Abort if there is an error. The configuration option is APT::Get::Assume-Yes. |
| **dpkg** | **dpkg** [*options*] *action*<br><br>A tool for installing, managing, and building packages. Serves as a frontend to **dpkg-deb**.<br><br>***dpkg actions***<br><br>These actions are carried out by **dpkg** itself:<br><br>**−i** *pkgfile*, **−−install** *pkgfile*<br>Install the package specified as *pkgfile*. With **−R** or **−−recursive**, *pkgfile* must be a directory.<br><br>**−−unpack** *pkgfile*<br>Unpack the package, but don't configure it. With **−R** or **−−recursive**, *pkgfile* must be a directory.<br><br>**−−configure** [*packages* | **−a** | **−−pending**]<br>Reconfigure one or more unpacked *packages*. If **−a** or **−−pending** is given instead of *packages*, configure all packages that are unpacked but not configured.<br><br>**−r, −−remove** [*packages* | **−a** | **−−pending**]<br>**−−purge** [*packages* | **−a** | **−−pending**]<br>Remove or purge one or more installed *packages*. Removal gets rid of everything except the configuration files listed in *debian/conffiles*; purging also removes the configuration files. If **−a** or **−−pending** is given instead of *packages*, **dpkg** removes or purges all packages that are unpacked and marked (in */var/lib/dpkg/status*) for removing or purging. |

**--print-avail** *package*

Print the details about *package* from */var/lib/dpkg/available*.

**--update-avail** *pkgs-file*

**--merge-avail** *pkgs-file*

Update the record of available files kept in */var/lib/dpkg/available*. This information is used by **dpkg** and **dselect** to determine what packages are available. Update will replace the information with the contents of the *pkgs-file*, distributed as *Packages*. Merge combines the information from *Packages* with the existing information.

**–A** *pkgfile*, **--record-avail** *pkgfile*

Update the record of available files kept in */var/lib/dpkg/available* with information from *pkgfile*. This information is used by **dpkg** and **dselect** to determine what packages are available. With **–R** or **--recursive**, *pkgfile* must be a directory.

**--forget-old-unavail**

Forget about uninstalled unavailable packages.

**--clear-avail**

Remove existing information about what packages are available.

**–l**, **--list** [*pkg-name-pattern*]

List all packages whose names match the specified pattern. With no pattern, list all packages in */var/lib/dpkg/available*. The pattern can include standard shell wildcard characters and may have to be quoted to prevent the shell from doing file-name expansion.

**–s** *packages*, **--status** *packages*

Report the status of one or more *packages* by displaying the entry in the status database */var/lib/dpkg/status*.

**–C**, **--audit**

Search for partially installed packages and suggest how to get them working.

**--get-selections** [*pattern*]

Get list of package selections and write to standard output. With *pattern* specified, write selections that match the pattern.

**--set-selections**

Set package selections based on input file read from standard input.

**--yet-to-unpack**

Search for uninstalled packages that have been selected for installation.

→

**dpkg**
←

−L *packages,* −−listfiles *packages*
> List installed files that came from the specified package or packages.

−S *filename-pattern,* −−search *filename-pattern*
> Search installed packages for a filename. The pattern can include standard shell wildcard characters and may have to be quoted to prevent the shell from doing filename expansion.

−−print-architecture
> Print target architecture.

−−print-gnu-build-architecture
> Print the GNU version of the target architecture.

−−print-installation-architecture
> Print host architecture for installation.

−−compare-versions *ver1 op ver2*
> Perform a binary comparison of two version numbers. The operators lt le eq ne ge gt treat a missing version as earlier. The operators lt-nl le-nl ge-nl gt-nl treat a missing version as later (where nl is "not later"). There is a third set of operators (< << <= = >= >> >) that is provided for compatibility with control-file syntax. **dpkg** returns zero for success (i.e., the condition is satisfied) and nonzero otherwise.

−−help
> Print help message and exit.

−−force-help
> Print help message about the −−force-*list* options and exit.

−Dh, −−debug=help
> Print debugging help message and exit.

−−license
> Print **dpkg** license information and exit. Accepts the spelling −−licence in addition to −−license.

−−version
> Print **dpkg** version information and exit.

*dpkg-deb actions*

The following actions can be specified for **dpkg** and are passed to **dpkg-deb** for execution. Also see **dpkg-deb**.

−b *dir* [*archive*], −−build *dir* [*archive*]
> Build a package.

**-c** *archive*, **--contents** *archive*
  List the contents of a package.

**-e**, **--control** *archive dir*
  Extract control information from a package.

**-f** *archive* [*control-fields*], **--field** *archive* [*control-fields*]
  Display the control field or fields of a package.

**-I** *archive* [*control-files*], **--info** *archive* [*control-files*]
  Show information about a package.

**--fsys-tarfile** *archive*
  Display the filesystem tar- file contained by a package.

**-x** *archive dir*, **--extract** *archive dir*
  Extract the files from a package.

**-X** *archive dir*, **--vextract** *archive dir*
  Extract and display the filenames from a package.

*Options*

**--abort-after=***num*
  Abort processing after *num* errors. Default is 50.

**-B**, **--auto-deconfigure**
  When a package is removed, automatically deconfigure any
  other package that depended on it.

**-D***octal*, **--debug=***octal*
  Turn on debugging, with the *octal* value specifying the desired
  level of debugging information. Use **-Dh** or **--debug=help** to
  display the possible values. You can OR the values to get the
  desired output.

**-E**, **--skip-same-version**
  Don't install the package if this version is already installed.

**--force-***list*, **--no-force-***list*, **--refuse-***list*
  Force or refuse to force an operation. *list* is specified as a
  comma-separated item of options. With **--force**, a warning is
  printed, but processing continues. **--refuse** and **--no-force**
  cause processing to stop with an error. The force/refuse
  options are:

  **architecture**
    Process even if intended for a different architecture.

  **auto-select**
    Select or deselect packages to install or remove them.
    Forced by default.

→

**bad-path**

Some programs are missing from the path.

**configure-any**

Configure any unconfigured package that the package depends on.

**conflicts**

Permit installation of conflicting packages. Can result in problems from files being overwritten.

**depends**

Turn dependency problems into warnings.

**depends-version**

Warn of version problems when checking dependencies, but otherwise ignore.

**downgrade**

Install even if a newer version is already installed. Forced by default.

**hold**

Process packages even if they are marked to be held.

**not-root**

Try to install or remove even when not logged on as root.

**overwrite**

Overwrite a file from one package with the same file from another package. Forced by default.

**overwrite-dir**

Overwrite one package's directory with a file from another package.

**overwrite-diverted**

Overwrite a diverted file with an undiverted version.

**remove-essential**

Remove an essential package. Note that this can cause your system to stop working.

**remove-reinstreq**

Remove packages that are broken and are marked to require reinstallation.

**−G** Don't install a package if a newer version is already installed. The same as **−−refuse-downgrade**.

**−−ignore-depends=***pkglist*

Dependency problems result only in a warning for the packages in *pkglist*.

**--largemem**

Specify that **dpkg** can use as much memory as it needs.

**--new**

New binary package format. This is a **dpkg-deb** option.

**--no-act**

Go through the motions, but don't actually write any changes. Used for testing. Be sure to specify before the action; otherwise changes might be written.

**--nocheck**

Ignore the contents of the control file when building a package. This is a **dpkg-deb** option.

**-O, --selected-only**

Process only packages that are marked as selected for installation.

**--old**

Old binary package format. This is a **dpkg-deb** option.

**-R, --recursive**

Recursively handle *.deb* files found in the directories specified with **-A**, **--install**, **--unpack**, and **--avail** and their subdirectories.

**-R, --root=***dir*, **--admindir=***dir*, **--instdir=***dir*

Change default directories. **admindir** contains administrative files with status and other information about packages; it defaults to */var/lib/dpkg*. **instdir** is the directory in which packages are installed and defaults to */*. Changing the **root** directory to *dir* automatically changes **instdir** to *dir* and **admindir** to */dir/var/lib/dpkg*.

**--smallmem**

Specify that **dpkg** should try to preserve memory.

---

**dpkg-deb** *action* [*options*]     dpkg-deb

Backend command for building and managing Debian package archives. Also see **dpkg**; you'll often want to use **dpkg** to pass commands through to **dpkg-deb**, rather than call **dpkg-deb** directly.

*Actions*

**-b** *dir* [*archive*], **--build** *dir* [*archive*]

Create an *archive* from the filesystem tree starting with directory *dir*. The directory must have a *DEBIAN* subdirectory containing the control file and any other control information. If *archive* is specified and is a filename, the package is written to

$\rightarrow$

that file; if no *archive* is specified, the package is written to *dir.deb*. If the archive already exists, it is replaced. If *archive* is the name of a directory, the **dpkg-deb** looks in the control file for the information it needs to generate the package name. (Note that for this reason, you cannot use **--no-check** with a directory name.)

**−c** *archive*, **--contents** *archive*
List the filesystem-tree portion of *archive*.

**−e**, **--control** *archive dir*
Extract control information from *archive* into the directory *dir*, which is created if it doesn't exist.

**−f** *archive* [*control-fields*], **--field** *archive* [*control-fields*]
Extract information about one or more fields in the control file for *archive*. If no fields are provided, print the entire control file.

**−h**, **--help**
Print help information and exit.

**−I** *archive* [*control-files*], **--info** *archive* [*control-files*]
Provide information about binary package *archive*. If no control files are provided, print a summary of the package contents; otherwise, print the control files in the order they were specified. An error message is printed to standard error for any missing components.

**--fsys-tarfile** *archive*
Extract the filesystem tree from *archive*, and send it to standard output in **tar** format. Can be used with **tar** to extract individual files from an archive.

**--license**
Print the license information and exit. Accepts the spelling **--licence** in addition to **--license**.

**--version**
Print the version number and exit.

**−x** *archive dir*, **--extract** *archive dir*
**−X** *archive dir*, **--vextract** *archive dir*
Extract the filesystem tree from *archive* into the specified directory, creating *dir* if it doesn't already exist. **−x** (**--extract**) works silently, while **−X** (**--vextract**) lists the files as it extracts them. Do not use this option to install packages; use **dpkg** instead.

*Options*

**dpkg-deb**

**-D**  Turn on debugging.

**--new**
> Build a new-style archive format (this is the default).

**--no-check**
> Don't check the control file before building an archive. This lets you build a broken archive.

**--old**
> Build an old-style archive format.

---

**dpkg-split** [*action*] [*options*]

**dpkg-split**

Split a binary package into smaller pieces and reassemble the pieces, manually or in automatic mode. The automatic mode maintains a queue of parts for reassembling. Useful for transferring to and from floppy disks.

*Actions*

**-a -o** *output part*, **--auto -o** *output part*
> Add *part* to the queue for automatic reassembly and if all the parts are available, reassemble the package as *output*.

**-d** [*packages*], **--discard** [*packages*]
> Discard parts from the automatic-assembly queue. If any *packages* are specified, discard only parts from those packages. Otherwise, empty the queue.

**-I** *parts*, **--info** *parts*
> Print information about the part file or files specified.

**-j** *parts*, **--join** *parts*
> Join the parts of a package file together from the *parts* specified. The default output file is *package-version.deb*.

**-l**, **--listq**
> List the contents of the queue of parts waiting for reassembly, giving the package name, the parts that are on the queue, and the number of bytes.

**-s** *full-package* [*prefix*], **--full-package** [*prefix*]
> Split the package *full-package* into parts, named *prefixNofM.deb*. The prefix defaults to the *full-package* name without the *.deb* extension.

$\rightarrow$

| | |
|---|---|
| **dpkg-split**<br>← | **–h, --help**<br>Print help message and exit.<br><br>**--license**<br>Print the license information and exit. Accepts the spelling **--licence** in addition to **--license**.<br><br>**--version**<br>Print the version information and exit.<br><br>*Options*<br><br>**--depotdir**<br>Specify an alternate directory *depotdir* for the queue of parts waiting for reassembly. Default is */var/lib/dpkg*.<br><br>**--msdos**<br>Force **--split** output filenames to be MS-DOS-compatible.<br><br>**–Q, --npquiet**<br>Do not print an error message for a part that doesn't belong to a binary package when doing automatic queuing or reassembly.<br><br>**–o** *output*, **--output** *output*<br>Use *output* as the filename for a reassembled package.<br><br>**–S** *num*, **--partsize** *num*<br>When splitting, specify the maximum part size (*num*) in kilobytes. Default is 450 KB. |
| **dselect** | **dselect** [*options*] [*action*]<br><br>A screen-oriented user frontend to **dpkg**. The primary user interface for installing and managing packages. See **dpkg** and **dpkg-deb** for information on building packages.<br><br>*Actions*<br><br>If **dselect** is run with no action specified on the command line, it displays the following menu:<br><br><pre>* 0. [A]ccess    Choose the access method to use.<br>  1. [U]pdate    Update list of available packages, if possible.<br>  2. [S]elect    Request which packages you want on your system.<br>  3. [I]nstall   Install and upgrade wanted packages.<br>  4. [C]onfig    Configure any packages that are unconfigured.<br>  5. [R]emove    Remove unwanted software.<br>  6. [Q]uit      Quit dselect.</pre><br>The asterisk (on the first line here) shows the currently selected option. Any of the menu items can be specified directly on the command line as an action (**access**, **update**, **select**, **install**, **config**, |

**remove, quit**) to go directly to the desired activity. For example:

```
% dselect access
```

If you enter **quit** on the command line, **dselect** exits immediately without doing anything. An additional command-line action is **menu**, which displays the menu and is equivalent to omitting the action.

*Options*

**--admindir** *dir*
> Change the directory that holds internal data files to *dir*. Default is */var/lib/dpkg*.

**-D** [*file*], **--debug** [*file*]
> Turn on debugging. Send output to *file* if specified.

**--help**
> Print help message and exit.

**--license**
> Print the license information and exit. Accepts the spelling **--licence** in addition to **--license**.

**--version**
> Print version information and exit.

*Package Managers*

# CHAPTER 6

# *The Linux Shells: An Overview*

The *shell* is a program that acts as a buffer between you and the operating system. In its role as a command interpreter, it should (for the most part) act invisibly. It also can be used for simple programming.

This section introduces three shells commonly used on Linux systems—the Bourne-Again shell (**bash**), the C shell (**csh**), and **csh**'s enhanced version, **tcsh**—and summarizes the major differences between them. Details on them are provided in Chapter 7, *bash: The Bourne-Again Shell*, and Chapter 8, *csh and tcsh*. (Some Linux distributions also offer the Korn shell, **ksh**, another popular version of the Bourne shell with some of the same features as **bash**.)

The following topics are presented in this chapter:

- Purpose of the shell
- Shell flavors
- Common features
- Differing features

## *Purpose of the Shell*

There are three main uses for the shell:

- Interactive use
- Customization of your Linux session
- Programming

## Interactive Use

When the shell is used interactively, it waits for you to issue commands, processes them (to interpret special characters, such as wildcards), and executes them. Shells also provide a set of commands, known as *built-ins*, to supplement Linux commands.

## Customization of Your Linux Session

A Linux shell defines variables, such as the locations of your home directory and mail spool, to control the behavior of your session. Some variables are preset by the system; you can define others in startup files that your shell reads when you log in. Startup files also can contain Linux or shell commands, for execution immediately after login.

## Programming

A series of individual commands (be they shell or other Linux commands available on the system) combined into one executable file is called a *shell script*. Batch files in MS-DOS are a similar concept. **bash** is considered a powerful programming shell, while scripting in **csh** is rumored to be hazardous to your health.

# Shell Flavors

Many different Linux shells are available. This book describes the three most popular shells:

- The Bourne-Again shell (**bash**), which is based on the Bourne shell (**sh**) and is standard for Linux

- The C shell (**csh**), which uses C syntax and has many conveniences

- **tcsh**, an extension of **csh** that appears instead of **csh** in many Linux distributions

Most systems have more than one shell, and people will often use one shell for writing shell scripts and another for interactive use.

When you log in, the system determines which shell to run by consulting your entry in */etc/passwd*. The last field of each entry calls a program to run as the default shell. For example:

| Program Name | Shell |
|---|---|
| */bin/sh* | Bourne-Again shell |
| */bin/bash* | Bourne-Again shell |
| */bin/csh* | C shell (or **tcsh**) |
| */bin/tcsh* | **tcsh** |

You can change to another shell by typing the program name at the command line. For example, to change from **bash** to **tcsh**, type:

```
$ exec tcsh
```

## Common Features

The following table is a sampling of features that are common to **bash**, **csh**, and **tcsh**. Note that **tcsh** is an enhanced version of **csh**; therefore, **tcsh** includes all features of **csh**, plus some others.

| Symbol/Command | Meaning/Action |
| --- | --- |
| > | Redirect output. |
| >> | Append output to file. |
| < | Redirect input. |
| << | "Here" document (redirect input). |
| \| | Pipe output. |
| & | Run process in background. |
| ; | Separate commands on same line. |
| * | Match any character(s) in filename. |
| ? | Match single character in filename. |
| !$n$ | Repeat command number $n$. |
| [ ] | Match any characters enclosed. |
| ( ) | Execute in subshell. |
| ` ` | Substitute output of enclosed command. |
| " " | Partial quote (allows variable and command expansion). |
| \ | Quote following character. |
| $var | Use value for variable. |
| $$ | Process ID. |
| $0 | Command name. |
| $n | $n$th argument ($0<n\leq9$). |
| $* | All arguments. |
| # | Begin comment. |
| bg | Background execution. |
| break | Break from loop statements. |
| cd | Change directories. |
| continue | Resume a program loop. |
| echo | Display output. |
| eval | Evaluate arguments. |
| exec | Execute a new shell or other program. |
| fg | Foreground execution. |
| jobs | Show active jobs. |
| kill | Terminate running jobs. |
| newgrp | Change to a new group. |
| shift | Shift positional parameters. |
| stop | Suspend a background job. |

| Symbol/Command | Meaning/Action |
|---|---|
| suspend | Suspend a foreground job. |
| umask | Set or list permissions on files to be created. |
| unset | Erase variable or function definitions. |
| wait | Wait for a background job to finish. |

## Differing Features

The following table is a sampling of features that are different among the three shells:

| Meaning/Action | bash | csh | tcsh |
|---|---|---|---|
| Default prompt. | $ | % | % |
| Force redirection. | >\| | >! | >! |
| Force append. | | >>! | >>! |
| Variable assignment. | var=val | set var=val | set var=val |
| Set environment variable. | export var=val | setenv var val | setenv var val |
| Number of arguments. | $# | $#argv | $#argv |
| Exit status. | $? | $status | $? |
| Execute commands in *file*. | . file | source file | source file |
| End a loop statement. | done | end | end |
| End case or switch. | esac | endsw | endsw |
| Loop through variables. | for/do | foreach | foreach |
| Sample if statement. | if [ $i -eq 5 ] | if ($i=5) | if ($i==5) |
| End if statement. | fi | endif | endif |
| Set resource limits. | ulimit | limit | limit |
| Read from terminal. | read | $< | $< |
| Make a variable read-only. | readonly | | set -r |
| File inquiry operator; tests for nonzero size. | | -s | |
| Complete current word. | Tab | | Tab |
| Ignore interrupts. | trap 2 | onintr | onintr |
| Begin until loop. | until/do | until | until |
| Begin while loop. | while/do | while | while |

CHAPTER 7

# *bash: The Bourne-Again Shell*

This chapter presents the following topics:

- Overview of features

- Invoking the shell

- Syntax

- Variables

- Arithmetic expressions

- Command history

- Built-in commands

- Job control

## *Overview of Features*

**bash** is the GNU version of the standard Bourne shell—the original Unix shell—and incorporates many popular features from other shells such as **csh**, **tcsh**, and the Korn shell (**ksh**). Both **tcsh**, which is described in the following chapter, and **ksh**, which offers many of the features in this chapter, also are available on most distributions of Linux. But **bash** is the standard Linux shell, loaded by default when most user accounts are created.

If executed as part of the user's login, **bash** starts by executing any commands found in */etc/profile*. Then it executes the commands found in *˜/.bash_profile*, *˜/.bash_login*, or *˜/.profile* (searching for each file only if the previous file is not found). Many distributions change shell defaults in */etc/profile* for all users, even changing the behavior of common commands like **ls**.

In addition, every time it starts (as a subshell or a login shell), **bash** looks for a file named ˜/.*bashrc*. Many system administration utilities create a small ˜/.*bashrc* automatically, and many users create quite large startup files. Any commands that can be executed from the shell can be included. A small sample file may look like this; each feature can be found either in this chapter or in Chapter 3, *Linux Commands*:

```
# Set bash variable to keep 50 commands in history.
HSTSIZE=50
#
# Set prompt to show current working directory and history number of command.
PS1='\w: Command \!$ '
#
# Set path to search for commands in my personal directories, then standard ones.
PATH=~/bin:~/scripts:$PATH
#
# Keep group and others from writing my newly created files.
umask 022
#
# Show color-coded file types.
alias ls='ls --color=yes'
#
# Make executable and .o files ugly yellow so I can find and delete them.
export LS_COLORS="ex=43:*.o=43"
#
# Quick and dirty test of a single-file program.
function gtst () {
    g++ -o $1 $1.C && ./$1
}
#
# Remove .o files.
alias clean='find ~ -name \*.o -exec rm {} \;'
```

**bash** provides the following features:

- Input/output redirection

- Wildcard characters (metacharacters) for filename abbreviation

- Shell variables for customizing your environment

- Powerful programming capabilities

- Command-line editing (using **vi**- or Emacs-style editing commands)

- Access to previous commands (command history)

- Integer arithmetic

- Arithmetic expressions

- Command name abbreviation (aliasing)

- Job control

- Integrated programming features

- Control structures

**bash**

- Directory stacking (using **pushd** and **popd**)

- Brace/tilde expansion

- Key bindings

## *Invoking the Shell*

The command interpreter for **bash** can be invoked as follows:

    **bash** [*options*] [*arguments*]

**bash** can execute commands from a terminal (when **−i** is specified), from a file (when the first *argument* is an executable script), or from standard input (if no arguments remain or if **−s** is specified).

### *Options*

Options that appear here with double hyphens also work when entered with single hyphens, but the double-hyphen versions are recommended because they are standard.

**−, −−**
> Treat all subsequent strings as arguments, not options.

**−−dump-po-strings**
> Same as **−−dump-strings** but uses a special "portable object" format suitable for scripting.

**−−dump-strings**
> For execution in non-English locales, dump all strings that **bash** translates.

**−c** *str*
> Read commands from string *str*.

**−i**   Create an interactive shell (prompt for input).

**−−help**
> Print information about which version of **bash** is installed, plus a list of options.

**−−login**
> Behave like a login shell; try to process */etc/profile* on startup. Then process ~/.*bash_profile*, ~/.*bash_login*, or ~/.*profile* (searching for each file only if the previous file is not found).

**−−nobraceexpansion**
> Disable brace expansion.

**−−noediting**
> Disable line editing with arrow and control keys.

**--noprofile**

Do not process */etc/profile,* ˜*/.bash_profile,* ˜*/.bash_login,* or ˜*/.profile* on startup.

**--norc**

Do not process ˜*/.bashrc* on startup.

**-p**  Start up as a privileged user; don't process *$HOME/.profile.*

**--posix**

Conform to POSIX standard.

**-r**  Restrict users to a very secure, limited environment; for instance, they cannot change out of the startup directory or use the **>** sign to redirect output.

**--rcfile** *file*

Substitute *file* for *.bashrc* on startup.

**--restricted**

Same as **-r**.

**-s**  Read commands from standard input; output from built-in commands goes to file descriptor 1; all other shell output goes to file descriptor 2.

**-v**  Print each line as it is executed (useful for tracing scripts).

**--verbose**

Same as **-v**.

**--version**

Print information about which version of **bash** is installed.

**-x**  Turn on debugging, as described under the **-x** option to the **set** built-in command.

**-D**  For execution in non-English locales, dump all strings that **bash** translates.

The remaining options to **bash** are listed under the **set** built-in command.

## *Arguments*

Arguments are assigned, in order, to the positional parameters **$1**, **$2**, and so forth. If the first argument is an executable script, commands are read from it and remaining arguments are assigned to **$1**, **$2**, and so on.

## *Syntax*

This subsection describes the many symbols peculiar to **bash**. The topics are arranged as follows:

- Special files

- Filename metacharacters

- Command-line editing

- Quoting

- Command forms

- Redirection forms

- Coprocesses

## Special Files

| File | Purpose |
| --- | --- |
| /etc/profile | Executed automatically at login |
| $HOME/.bash_profile | Executed automatically at login |
| $HOME/.bashrc | Executed automatically at shell startup |
| $HOME/.bash_logout | Executed automatically at logout |
| $HOME/.bash_history | Record of last session's commands |
| /etc/passwd | Source of home directories for ~name abbreviations |

## Filename Metacharacters

| Characters | Meaning |
| --- | --- |
| * | Match any string of zero or more characters. |
| ? | Match any single character. |
| [abc . . . ] | Match any one of the enclosed characters; a hyphen can be used to specify a range (e.g., a–z, A–Z, 0–9). |
| [!abc . . . ] | Match any character *not* among the enclosed characters. |
| {str1, . . . } | Brace expansion: match any of the enclosed strings. |
| ~name | HOME directory of user *name*. |
| ~+ | Current working directory (PWD). |
| ~− | Previous working directory from directory stack (OLDPWD, see also the **pushd** built-in command). |
| ~+n | The *n*th entry in the directory stack, counting from the start of the list with the first entry being 0. |
| ~−n | The *n*th entry in the directory stack, counting from the end of the list with the last entry being 0. |

Patterns can be a sequence of patterns separated by |; if any of the subpatterns match, the entire sequence is considered matching. This extended syntax resembles that available to **egrep** and **awk**.

### Examples

```
$ ls new*        List new and new.1
$ cat ch?        Match ch9 but not ch10
$ vi [D-R]*      Match files that begin with uppercase D through R
```

## Command-line Editing

Command lines can be edited like lines in either Emacs or vi. Emacs is the default. See the section called "Line-Edit Mode" later in this chapter for more information.

vi mode has two submodes, insert mode and command mode. The default mode is insert; you can go to command mode by pressing Esc. In command mode, typing a (append) or i (insert) will return you to insert mode.

Some users discover that the Del or Backspace key on the terminal does not delete the character before the cursor, as it should. Sometimes the problem can be solved by issuing one of the following commands (or placing it in your *.bashrc* file):

```
stty erase ^?
stty erase ^H
```

See the **stty** command in Chapter 3 for more information. On the X Window System, an alternative solution is to use the **xmodmap** command, but this cannot be described easily here because it requires you to do some research about your terminal.

Tables 7-1 through 7-14 show various Emacs and **vi** commands.

*Table 7–1. Basic Emacs-Mode Commands*

| Command | Description |
|---------|-------------|
| Ctrl-B | Move backward one character (without deleting). |
| Ctrl-F | Move forward one character. |
| Del | Delete one character backward. |
| Ctrl-D | Delete one character forward. |

*Table 7–2. Emacs-Mode Word Commands*

| Command | Description |
|---------|-------------|
| Esc b | Move one word backward. |
| Esc f | Move one word forward. |
| Esc Del | Kill one word backward. |
| Esc d | Kill one word forward. |
| Ctrl-Y | Retrieve (yank) last item killed. |

*Table 7–3. Emacs-Mode Line Commands*

| Command | Description |
|---------|-------------|
| Ctrl-A | Move to beginning of line. |
| Ctrl-E | Move to end of line. |
| Ctrl-K | Kill forward to end of line. |

bash

*Table 7-4. Emacs-Mode Commands for Moving Through the History File*

| Command | Description |
|---------|-------------|
| Ctrl-P | Move to previous line. |
| Ctrl-N | Move to next line. |
| Ctrl-R | Search backward. |
| Esc < | Move to first line of history file. |
| Esc > | Move to last line of history file. |

*Table 7-5. Completion Commands*

| Command | Description |
|---------|-------------|
| Tab | Attempt to perform general completion of the text. |
| Esc ? | List the possible completions. |
| Esc / | Attempt filename completion. |
| Ctrl-X / | List the possible filename completions. |
| Esc ~ | Attempt username completion. |
| Ctrl-X ~ | List the possible username completions. |
| Esc $ | Attempt variable completion. |
| Ctrl-X $ | List the possible variable completions. |
| Esc @ | Attempt hostname completion. |
| Ctrl-X @ | List the possible hostname completions. |
| Esc ! | Attempt command completion. |
| Ctrl-X ! | List the possible command completions. |
| Esc Tab | Attempt completion from previous commands in the history list. |

*Table 7-6. Emacs-Mode Miscellaneous Commands*

| Command | Description |
|---------|-------------|
| Ctrl-J | Same as Return. |
| Ctrl-L | Clear the screen, placing the current line at the top of the screen. |
| Ctrl-M | Same as Return. |
| Ctrl-O | Same as Return, then display next line in command history. |
| Ctrl-T | Transpose character left of and under the cursor. |
| Ctrl-U | Kill the line from the beginning to point. |
| Ctrl-V | Insert keypress instead of interpreting it as a command. |
| Ctrl-[ | Same as Esc (most keyboards). |
| Esc c | Capitalize word under or after cursor. |
| Esc u | Change word under or after cursor to all capital letters. |

*Table 7–6. Emacs-Mode Miscellaneous Commands (continued)*

| | |
|---|---|
| Esc l | Change word under or after cursor to all lowercase letters. |
| Esc . | Insert last word in previous command line after point. |
| Esc _ | Same as Esc. |

*Table 7–7. Editing Commands in vi Input Mode*

| Command | Description |
|---|---|
| Del | Delete previous character. |
| Ctrl-W | Erase previous word (i.e., erase until a blank). |
| Ctrl-V | Insert keypress instead of interpreting it as a command. |
| Esc | Enter control mode (see Table 7-8). |

*Table 7–8. Basic vi Control Mode Commands*

| Command | Description |
|---|---|
| h | Move left one character. |
| l | Move right one character. |
| b | Move left one word. |
| w | Move right one word. |
| B | Move to beginning of preceding nonblank word. |
| W | Move to beginning of next nonblank word. |
| e | Move to end of current word. |
| E | Move to end of current nonblank word. |
| 0 | Move to beginning of line. |
| ^ | Move to first nonblank character in line. |
| $ | Move to end of line. |

*Table 7–9. Commands for Entering vi Input Mode*

| Command | Description |
|---|---|
| i | Insert text before current character (insert). |
| a | Insert text after current character (append). |
| I | Insert text at beginning of line. |
| A | Insert text at end of line. |
| r | Replace current character with this text. |
| R | Overwrite existing text. |

**bash**

*Table 7-10. Some vi-Mode Deletion Commands*

| Command | Description |
|---------|-------------|
| dh | Delete one character backward. |
| dl | Delete one character forward. |
| db | Delete one word backward. |
| dw | Delete one word forward. |
| dB | Delete one nonblank word backward. |
| dW | Delete one nonblank word forward. |
| d$ | Delete to end-of-line. |
| d0 | Delete to beginning of line. |

*Table 7-11. Abbreviations for vi-Mode Delete Commands*

| Command | Description |
|---------|-------------|
| D | Delete to end of line (equivalent to **d$**). |
| dd | Delete entire line (equivalent to **0d$**). |
| C | Delete to end of line; enter input mode (equivalent to **c$**). |
| cc | Delete entire line; enter input mode (equivalent to **0c$**). |
| X | Delete character backward (equivalent to **dl**). |
| x | Delete character forward (equivalent to **dh**). |

*Table 7-12. vi Control Mode Commands for Searching the Command History*

| Command | Description |
|---------|-------------|
| k or − | Move backward one line. |
| j or + | Move forward one line. |
| G | Move to line given by repeat count. |
| /string | Search backward for *string*. |
| ?string | Search forward for *string*. |
| n | Repeat search in same direction as previous. |
| N | Repeat search in opposite direction of previous. |

*Table 7-13. vi-Mode Character-Finding Commands*

| Command | Description |
|---------|-------------|
| f*x* | Move right to next occurrence of *x*. |
| F*x* | Move left to previous occurrence of *x*. |
| t*x* | Move right to next occurrence of *x*, then back one space. |
| T*x* | Move left to previous occurrence of *x*, then forward one space. |

*Table 7–13. vi-Mode Character-Finding Commands (continued)*

| | |
|---|---|
| ; | Redo last character-finding command. |
| , | Redo last character-finding command in opposite direction. |

*Table 7–14. Miscellaneous vi-Mode Commands*

| Command | Description |
|---|---|
| ~ | Invert (toggle) case of current character(s). |
| – | Append last word of previous command; enter input mode. |
| Ctrl-L | Clear the screen and redraw the current line on it; good for when your screen becomes garbled. |
| # | Prepend # (comment character) to the line and send it to the history file; useful for saving a command to be executed later, without having to retype it. |

## Quoting

Quoting disables a character's special meaning and allows it to be used literally, as itself. The following characters have special meaning to **bash**:

| Character | Meaning |
|---|---|
| ; | Command separator |
| & | Background execution |
| ( ) | Command grouping (enter a subshell) |
| { } | Command block |
| \| | Pipe |
| > < & | Redirection symbols |
| * ? [ ] ~ ! | Filename metacharacters |
| " ' \ | Used in quoting other characters |
| ` | Command substitution |
| $ | Variable substitution (or command substitution) |
| newline space tab | Word separators |
| # | Comment |

The following characters can be used for quoting:

| Character | Action |
|---|---|
| " " | Everything between " and " is taken literally, except for the following characters that keep their special meaning:<br><br>$      Variable substitution will occur.<br>`      Command substitution will occur.<br>"      This marks the end of the double quote. |

| Character | Action |
|-----------|--------|
| ` ' ' ` | Everything between ' and ' is taken literally, except for another '. |
| `\` | The character following a \ is taken literally. Use within " " to escape ", $, and `. Often used to escape itself, spaces, or newlines. |

## Examples

```
$ echo 'Single quotes "protect" double quotes'
Single quotes "protect" double quotes

$ echo "Well, isn't that \"special\"?"
Well, isn't that "special"?

$ echo "You have `ls|wc -l` files in `pwd`"
You have  43 files in /home/bob

$ echo "The value of \$x is $x"
The value of $x is 100
```

## Command Forms

| Syntax | Effect |
|--------|--------|
| `cmd &` | Execute *cmd* in background. |
| `cmd1 ; cmd2` | Command sequence; execute multiple *cmd*s on the same line. |
| `(cmd1 ; cmd2)` | Subshell; treat *cmd1* and *cmd2* as a command group. |
| `cmd1 | cmd2` | Pipe; use output from *cmd1* as input to *cmd2*. |
| `cmd1 `cmd2`` | Command substitution; use *cmd2* output as arguments to *cmd1*. |
| `cmd1 $(cmd2)` | Command substitution; nesting is allowed. |
| `cmd1 && cmd2` | AND; execute *cmd2* only if *cmd1* succeeds. |
| `cmd1 || cmd2` | OR; execute *cmd2* only if *cmd1* fails. |
| `{ cmd1 ; cmd2 }` | Execute commands in the current shell. |

## Examples

| | |
|---|---|
| `$ nroff file &` | *Format in the background* |
| `$ cd; ls` | *Execute sequentially* |
| `$ (date; who; pwd) > logfile` | *All output is redirected* |
| `$ sort file | pr -3 | lp` | *Sort file, page output, then print* |
| `$ vi `grep -l ifdef *.c`` | *Edit files found by grep* |
| `$ egrep '(yes|no)' `cat list`` | *Specify a list of files to search* |
| `$ egrep '(yes|no)' $(cat list)` | *Same as previous using bash command substitution* |
| `$ egrep '(yes|no)' $(<list)` | *Same, but faster* |
| `$ grep XX file && lp file` | *Print file if it contains the pattern* |
| `$ grep XX file || echo "XX not found"` | *Echo an error message if the pattern is not found* |

## Redirection Forms

| File Descriptor | Name | Common Abbreviation | Typical Default |
|---|---|---|---|
| 0 | Standard input | stdin | Keyboard |
| 1 | Standard output | stdout | Screen |
| 2 | Standard error | stderr | Screen |

The usual input source or output destination can be changed as shown in Table 7-15.

*Table 7–15. I/O Redirectors*

| Redirector | Function |
|---|---|
| > *file* | Direct standard output to *file*. |
| < *file* | Take standard input from *file*. |
| *cmd1* \| *cmd2* | Pipe; take standard output of *cmd1* as standard input to *cmd2*. |
| >> *file* | Direct standard output to *file*; append to *file* if it already exists. |
| >\| *file* | Force standard output to *file* even if **noclobber** is set. |
| *n*>\| *file* | Force output from the file descriptor *n* to *file* even if **noclobber** is set. |
| <> *file* | Use *file* as both standard input and standard output. |
| << *text* | Read standard input up to a line identical to *text* (*text* can be stored in a shell variable). Input is usually typed on the screen or in the shell program. Commands that typically use this syntax include **cat**, **echo**, **ex**, and **sed**. If *text* is enclosed in quotes, standard input will not undergo variable substitution, command substitution, etc. |
| *n*> *file* | Direct file descriptor *n* to *file*. |
| *n*< *file* | Set *file* as file descriptor *n*. |
| >&*n* | Duplicate standard output to file descriptor *n*. |
| <&*n* | Duplicate standard input from file descriptor *n*. |
| &>*file* | Direct standard output and standard error to *file*. |
| <&– | Close the standard input. |
| >&– | Close the standard output. |
| *n*>&– | Close the output from file descriptor *n*. |
| *n*<&– | Close the input from file descriptor *n*. |

## Examples

```
$ cat part1 > book
$ cat part2 part3 >> book
$ mail tim < report
$ grep Chapter part* 2> error_file
```

```
$ sed 's/^/XX /' << END_ARCHIVE
> This is often how a shell archive is "wrapped",
> bundling text for distribution. You would normally
> run sed from a shell program, not from the command line.
> END_ARCHIVE
XX This is often how a shell archive is "wrapped",
XX bundling text for distribution. You would normally
XX run sed from a shell program, not from the command line.
```

To redirect standard output to standard error:

```
$ echo "Usage error: see administrator" 1>&2
```

The following command sends output (files found) to *filelist* and sends error messages (inaccessible files) to file *no_access*:

```
$ find / -print > filelist 2>no_access
```

## Coprocesses

Coprocesses are a feature of **bash** and do not appear in other shells.

| Syntax | Effect |
|---|---|
| *cmd1* \| *cmd2* \|**&** | Coprocess; execute the pipeline in the background. The shell sets up a two-way pipe, allowing redirection of both standard input and standard output. |
| **read -p** *var* | Read coprocess input into variable *var*. |
| **print -p** *string* | Write *string* to the coprocess. |
| *cmd* **<&p** | Take input for *cmd* from the coprocess. |
| *cmd* **>&p** | Send output of *cmd* to the coprocess. |

### Examples

| | |
|---|---|
| `cat memo` | *Print contents of file* |
| `Sufficient unto the day is` | |
| `A word to the wise.` | |
| `ed - memo |&` | *Start coprocess* |
| `print -p /word/` | *Send* **ed** *command to coprocess* |
| `read -p search` | *Read output of* **ed** *command into variable search* |
| `print "$search"` | *Show the line on standard output* |
| `A word to the wise.` | |

## Variables

Variables are prefaced by a dollar sign ($) and optionally enclosed in braces ({}). You can assign a value to a variable through an equals sign (=); no whitespace can appear on either side of the equals sign:

```
$ TMP=temp.file
```

By default, variables are seen only within the shell itself; to pass variables to other programs invoked within the shell, see the **export** built-in command.

---

If subscripted by brackets ([]), the variable is considered an array variable. For instance:

```
$ DIR_LIST[0]=src
$ DIR_LIST[1]=headers
$ ls ${DIR_LIST[1]}
```

The contents of *headers* are listed. Many substitutions and commands in this chapter handle arrays by operating on each element separately.

This subsection describes:

- Variable substitution
- Built-in shell variables

## Variable Substitution

In the following substitutions, braces ({}) are optional, except when needed to separate a variable name from following characters that would otherwise be considered part of the name.

| Variable | Meaning |
|---|---|
| ${var} | The value of variable *var*. |
| $0 | Name of the program. |
| ${n} | Individual arguments on command line (positional parameters); $1 \leq n \leq 9$. |
| $# | Number of arguments on command line. |
| $* | All arguments on command line. |
| $@ | Same as $* but contents are split into words when the variable is enclosed in double quotes. |
| $$ | Process number of current shell; useful as part of a filename for creating temporary files with unique names. |
| $? | Exit status of last command (normally 0 for success). |
| $! | Process number of most recently issued background command. |
| $- | Current execution options (see the **set** built-in command). By default, **hB** for scripts and **himBH** for interactive shells. |
| $_ | Initially set to name of file invoked for this shell, then set for each command to the last word of the previous command. |

Table 7-16 through Table 7-18 show various types of operators that can be used with **bash** variables.

*Table 7-16. Substitution Operators*

| Operator | Substitution |
|---|---|
| ${*varname*:-*word*} | If *varname* exists and isn't null, return its value; otherwise, return *word*. |
| **Purpose**: | Returning a default value if the variable is undefined. |
| **Example**: | ${count:-0} evaluates to 0 if **count** is undefined. |

*Table 7-16. Substitution Operators (continued)*

| Operator | Substitution |
|---|---|
| ${*varname*:=*word*} | If *varname* exists and isn't null, return its value; otherwise set it to *word* and then return its value. Positional and special parameters cannot be assigned this way. |
| Purpose: | Setting a variable to a default value if it is undefined. |
| Example: | ${count:=0} sets **count** to 0 if it is undefined. |
| ${*varname*:?*message*} | If *varname* exists and isn't null, return its value; otherwise, print *varname*: followed by *message*, and abort the current command or script (noninteractive shells only). Omitting *message* produces the default message "parameter null or not set." |
| Purpose: | Catching errors that result from variables being undefined. |
| Example: | {count:?"undefined!"} prints "count: undefined!" and exits if **count** is undefined. |
| ${*varname*:+*word*} | If *varname* exists and isn't null, return *word*; otherwise, return null. |
| Purpose: | Testing for the existence of a variable. |
| Example: | ${count:+1} returns 1 (which could mean **true**) if **count** is defined. |
| ${#*varname*} | Return the number of characters in *varname*. |
| Purpose: | Preparing for substitution or extraction of substrings. |
| Example: | If ${USER} currently expands to **root**, ${#USER} expands to 4. |

*Table 7-17. Pattern-Matching Operators*

| Operator | Meaning |
|---|---|
| ${*variable*#*pattern*} | If the pattern matches the beginning of the variable's value, delete the shortest part that matches and return the rest. |
| ${*variable*##*pattern*} | If the pattern matches the beginning of the variable's value, delete the longest part that matches and return the rest. |
| ${*variable*%*pattern*} | If the pattern matches the end of the variable's value, delete the shortest part that matches and return the rest. |
| ${*variable*%%*pattern*} | If the pattern matches the end of the variable's value, delete the longest part that matches and return the rest. |

*Table 7-17. Pattern-Matching Operators (continued)*

| Operator | Meaning |
|----------|---------|
| ${var/pat/sub} | Return *var* with the first occurrence of *pat* replaced by *sub*. Can be applied to $* or $@, in which case each word is treated separately. If *pat* starts with # it can match only the start of *var*; if *pat* ends with % it can match only the end of *var*. |
| ${var//pat/sub} | Return *var* with the every occurrence of *pat* replaced by *sub*. |
| ${variable:n} | Truncate the beginning of the variable and return the part starting with character number *n*, where the first character is 0. |
| ${variable:n:l} | Starting with character number *n*, where the first character is 0, return a substring of length *l* from the variable. |

*Table 7-18. Expression Evaluation*

| Operator | Meaning |
|----------|---------|
| $((arithmetic-expression)) | Return the result of the expression. Arithmetic operators are described under "Arithmetic Expressions." |
| **Example:** | TODAY='date +%-d' ; echo $(($TODAY+7)) stores the number of the current day in **$TODAY** and then prints that number plus 7 (the number of the same day next week). |
| [[$condition]] | Return 1 if *condition* is true and 0 if it is false. Conditions are described under the **test** built-in command. |

## Built-in Shell Variables

Built-in variables are set automatically by the shell and typically are used inside shell scripts. Built-in variables can make use of the variable substitution patterns already shown earlier. When setting variables, you do not include dollar signs, but when referencing their values later, the dollar signs are necessary.

Tables 7-19 through 7-22 show the commonly used built-in variables in **bash**.

*Table 7-19. Behavior-Altering Variables*

| Variable | Meaning |
|---|---|
| auto_resume | Allows a background job to be brought to the foreground simply by entering a substring of the job's command line; values can be **substring** (resume if the user's string matches part of the command); **exact** (string must exactly match command); or another value (string must match at beginning of command). |
| BASH_ENV | Startup file of commands to execute, if **bash** is invoked to run a script. |
| CDPATH | Colon-separated list of directories to search for the directory passed in a **cd** command. |
| EDITOR | Pathname of your preferred text editor. |
| IFS | Word separator; used by shell to parse commands into their elements. |
| IGNOREEOF | If nonzero, don't allow use of a single **Ctrl-D** (the end-of-file or EOF character) to log off; use the **exit** command to log off. |
| PATH | Colon-separated list of directories to search for each command. |
| PROMPT_COMMAND | Command that **bash** executes before issuing a prompt for a new command. |
| PS1 | Prompt displayed before each new command; see the later section "Variables in Prompt" for ways to introduce dynamically changing information such as the current working directory or command history number into the prompt. |
| PS2 | Prompt displayed before a new line if a command is not finished. |
| PS3 | Prompt displayed by **select** built-in command. |
| PS4 | Prompt displayed by **-x** debugging (see the earlier section "Invoking the Shell"). and the **set** built-in command). |

*Table 7-20. History Variables*

| Variable | Meaning |
|---|---|
| FCEDIT | Pathname of editor to use with the **fc** command. |
| HISTCMD | The history number of the current command. |

*Table 7–20. History Variables (continued)*

| Variable | Meaning |
|---|---|
| HISTCONTROL | If HISTCONTROL is set to the value of **ignorespace**, lines beginning with a space are not entered into the history list. If set to **ignoredups**, lines matching the last history line are not entered. Setting it to **ignoreboth** enables both options. |
| HISTFILE | Name of history file, on which the editing modes operate. |
| HISTFILESIZE | The maximum number of lines to store in the history file. The default is 500. |
| HISTSIZE | The maximum number of commands to remember in the command history. The default is 500. |

*Table 7–21. Mail Variables*

| Variable | Meaning |
|---|---|
| MAIL | Name of file to check for incoming mail. |
| MAILCHECK | How often, in seconds, to check for new mail (default is 60 seconds). |
| MAILPATH | List of filenames, separated by colons (:), to check for incoming mail. |

*Table 7–22. Status Variables*

| Variable | Meaning |
|---|---|
| BASH | Pathname of this instance of the shell you are running. |
| BASH_VERSION | The version number of the shell you are running. |
| COLUMNS | The number of columns your display has. |
| DIRSTACK | List of directories manipulated by **pushd** and **popd** commands. |
| EUID | Effective user ID of process running this shell, in the form of the number recognized by the system. |
| GROUPS | Groups to which user belongs, in the form of the numbers recognized by the system. |
| HOME | Name of your home (login) directory. |
| HOSTNAME | Host the shell is running on. |
| HOSTTYPE | Short name indicating the type of machine the shell is running on; for instance, i486. |
| LINES | The number of lines your display has. |
| MACHTYPE | Long string indicating the machine the shell is running on; for instance, **i486-pc-linux-gnu**. |
| OLDPWD | Previous directory before the last **cd** command. |

*Table 7-22. Status Variables (continued)*

| | |
|---|---|
| OSTYPE | Short string indicating the operating system; for instance, "linux-gnu." |
| PPID | Process ID of parent process that invoked this shell. |
| PWD | Current directory. |
| SECONDS | Number of seconds since the shell was invoked. |
| SHELL | Pathname of the shell you are running. |
| SHLVL | Depth to which running shells are nested. |
| TERM | The type of terminal that you are using. |
| UID | Real user ID of process running this shell, in the form of the number recognized by the system. |

# Arithmetic Expressions

The **let** command performs integer arithmetic. **bash** provides a way to substitute integer values (for use as command arguments or in variables); base conversion is also possible:

| Expression | Meaning |
|---|---|
| $(( expr)) | Use the value of the enclosed arithmetic expression. |

## Operators

**bash** uses arithmetic operators from the C programming language; the following list is in decreasing order of precedence. Use parentheses to override precedence.

| Operator | Meaning |
|---|---|
| − | Unary minus |
| ! ~ | Logical negation; binary inversion (one's complement) |
| * / % | Multiplication; division; modulus (remainder) |
| + - | Addition; subtraction |
| << >> | Bitwise left shift; bitwise right shift |
| <= >= | Less than or equal to; greater than or equal to |
| < > | Less than; greater than |
| == != | Equality; inequality (both evaluated left to right) |
| & | Bitwise AND |
| ^ | Bitwise exclusive OR |
| \| | Bitwise OR |
| && | Logical AND |
| \|\| | Logical OR |
| = | Assign value. |
| += -= | Reassign after addition/subtraction |

| Operator | Meaning |
|---|---|
| *= /= %= | Reassign after multiplication/division/remainder |
| &= ^= \|= | Reassign after bitwise AND/XOR/OR |
| <<= >>= | Reassign after bitwise shift left/right |

## Examples

See the **let** built-in command for more information and examples.

```
let "count=0" "i = i + 1"    Assign i and count
let "num % 2"                Test for an even number
```

# Command History

**bash** lets you display or modify previous commands. This is similar to the C shell's history mechanism. Commands in the history list can be modified using:

- Line-edit mode

- The **fc** command

In addition, the command substitutions described in Chapter 8, *csh and tcsh*, also work in **bash**.

## Line-Edit Mode

Line-edit mode lets you emulate many features of the **vi** or Emacs editors. The history list is treated like a file. When the editor is invoked, you type editing keystrokes to move to the command line you want to execute. Arrow keys work on most terminals in both Emacs mode and **vi** command mode. You also can change the line before executing it. See Table 7-23 for some examples of common line-edit commands. When you're ready to issue the command, press Return.

The default line-edit mode is Emacs. To enable **vi** mode, enter:

```
$ set -o vi
```

Note that **vi** starts in input mode; to type a **vi** command, press Esc first.

The mode you use for editing **bash** commands is an entirely separate choice from the editor that is invoked for you automatically within many commands (for instance, the editor mail readers invoke when you ask them to create a new mail message). To change the default editor, set the VISUAL or EDITOR variable to the filename or full pathname of your favorite editor:

```
$ export EDITOR=emacs
```

*bash*

*Table 7-23. Common Editing Keystrokes*

| vi | Emacs | Result |
|---|---|---|
| k | Ctrl-P | Get previous command. |
| j | Ctrl-N | Get next command. |
| /string | Ctrl-R string | Get previous command containing *string*. |
| h | Ctrl-B | Move back one character. |
| l | Ctrl-F | Move forward one character. |
| b | Esc B | Move back one word. |
| w | Esc F | Move forward one word. |
| X | Del | Delete previous character. |
| x | Ctrl-D | Delete one character. |
| dw | Esc D | Delete word forward. |
| db | Esc H | Delete word back. |
| xp | Ctrl-T | Transpose two characters. |

## The fc Command

Use fc −l to list history commands and fc −e to edit them. See the entry under built-in commands for more information.

### Examples

```
$ history           List the last 16 commands
$ fc -l 20 30       List commands 20 through 30
$ fc -l -5          List the last five commands
$ fc -l cat         List the last command beginning with cat
$ fc -ln 5 > doit   Save command 5 to file doit
$ fc -e vi 5 20     Edit commands 5 through 20 using vi
$ fc -e emacs       Edit previous command using Emacs
$ !!                Reexecute previous command
$ !cat              Reexecute last cat command
$ !cat foo-file     Reexecute last command, adding foo-file to the end of the argument list
```

## Command Substitution

| Syntax | Meaning |
|---|---|
| ! | Begin a history substitution. |
| !! | Previous command. |
| !N | Command number *N* in history list. |
| !−N | *N*th command back from current command. |
| !string | Most recent command that starts with *string*. |
| !?string? | Most recent command that contains *string*. |
| !?string?% | Most recent command argument that contains *string*. |
| !$ | Last argument of previous command. |

| Syntax | Meaning |
|--------|---------|
| !# | The current command up to this point. |
| !!*string* | Previous command, then append *string*. |
| !*N string* | Command *N*, then append *string*. |
| !{*s1*}*s2* | Most recent command starting with string *s1*, then append string *s2*. |
| ^*old*^*new*^ | Quick substitution; change string *old* to *new* in previous command; execute modified command. |

## Variables in Prompt

Using the following variables, you can display information about the current state of the shell or the system in your **bash** prompt. Set the PS1 variable to a string including the desired variables. For instance, the following command sets PS1 to a string that includes the \w variable in order to display the current working directory and the \! variable in order to display the number of the current command. The next line is the prompt displayed by the change.

```
$ PS1='\w: Command \!$ '
~/book/linux: Command 504$
```

Some of the prompt variables are relatively new, such as \j and \l, so they may not be supported in your version of **bash**.

| Variable | Meaning |
|----------|---------|
| \a | Alarm (bell) |
| \d | Date in the format "Mon May  8" |
| \e | Escape character (terminal escape, not backslash) |
| \h | Hostname |
| \j | Number of background jobs (active or stopped) |
| \l | Current terminal name |
| \n | Newline inserted in the prompt |
| \r | Carriage return inserted in the prompt |
| \s | Current shell |
| \t | Time in 24-hour format, where 3:30 p.m. appears as 15:30:00 |
| \u | User's account name |
| \v | Version and release of **bash** |
| \w | Current working directory |
| \H | Like \h |
| \T | Time in 12-hour format, where 3:30 p.m. appears as 03:30:00 |
| \V | Version, release, and patch level of **bash** |
| \W | Last element (following last slash) of current working directory |
| \\ | Single backslash inserted in the prompt |
| \! | Number of current command in the command history |
| \# | Number of current command, where numbers started at 1 when the shell started |
| \@ | Time in 12-hour format, where 3:30 P.M. appears as 03:30 p.m. |

**bash**

| Variable | Meaning |
|---|---|
| \\$ | Indicates whether you are **root**: displays # for **root**, $ for other users |
| \\[ | Starts a sequence of nonprinting characters, to be ended by \\] |
| \\] | Ends the sequence of nonprinting characters started by \\[ |
| \\*nnn* | The character in the ASCII set corresponding to the octal number *nnn* inserted into the prompt |

## Built-in Commands

Examples to be entered as a command line are shown with the $ prompt. Otherwise, examples should be treated as code fragments that might be included in a shell script. For convenience, some of the reserved words used by multiline commands also are included.

| | |
|---|---|
| # | # |
| | Ignore all text that follows on the same line. # is used in shell scripts as the comment character and is not really a command. |

| | |
|---|---|
| #! | #!*shell* |
| | Used as the first line of a script to invoke the named *shell* (with optional arguments). Some older, non-Linux systems do not support scripts starting with this line. For example: |
| | `#!/bin/bash` |

| | |
|---|---|
| : | : |
| | Null command. Returns an exit status of 0. Sometimes used as the first character in a file to denote a **bash** script. Shell variables can be placed after the : to expand them to their values. |

*Example*

Check whether someone is logged in:

```
if who | grep $1 > /dev/null
then :    # do nothing
    # if pattern is found
else echo "User $1 is not logged in"
fi
```

*. file [arguments]*

Same as **source**.

---

**alias** [-p] [*name*[=' *cmd*' ]]

Assign a shorthand *name* as a synonym for *cmd*. If =' *cmd* ' is omitted, print the alias for *name*; if *name* also is omitted or if [-p] is specified, print all aliases. See also **unalias**.

---

**bg** [*jobIDs*]

Put current job or *jobIDs* in the background. See "Job Control" later in this chapter.

---

**bind** [*options*]
**bind** [*options*] *key:function*

Print or set the bindings that allow keys to invoke functions such as cursor movement and line editing. Typical syntax choices for *keys* are "\C-t" for Ctrl-T and "\M-t" or "\et" for Esc T (quoting is needed to escape the sequences from the shell). Function names can be seen though the –l option.

*Options*

-f *filename*
Consult *filename* for bindings, which should be in the same format as on the **bind** command line.

-l    Print all Readline functions, which are functions that can be bound to keys.

-m *keymap*
Specify a keymap for this and further bindings. Possible keymaps are **emacs**, **emacs-standard**, **emacs-meta**, **emacs-ctlx**, **vi**, **vi-move**, **vi-command**, and **vi-insert**.

-p    Display all functions and the keys that invoke them, in the format by which keys can be set.

-q *function*
Display the key bindings that invoke *function*.

-r *key*
Remove the binding attached to *key*, so it no longer works.

→

| | |
|---|---|
| bind<br>← | **-s** Display all macros and the keys that invoke them, in the format by which keys can be set.<br><br>**-u** *function*<br>Remove all the bindings attached to *function*, so no keys will invoke it.<br><br>**-v** Display all Readline variables (settings that affect history and line editing) and their current settings, in the format by which variables can be set.<br><br>**-x** *key*:*command*<br>Bind key to a shell command (recent; not in all **bash** versions in common use).<br><br>**-P** Display all bound keys and the functions they invoke.<br><br>**-S** Display all macros and the keys that invoke them.<br><br>**-V** Display all Readline variables (settings that affect history and line editing) and their current settings.<br><br>*Example*<br><br>Bind Ctrl-T to **copy-forward-word**, the function that copies the part of the word following the cursor so it can be repasted:<br><br>`$ bind "\C-t":copy-forward-word` |
| break | **break** [*n*]<br><br>Exit from the innermost (most deeply nested) **for**, **while**, or **until** loop, or from the *n* innermost levels of the loop. Also exits from a **select** list. |
| builtin | **builtin** *command* [*arguments*]<br><br>Execute *command*, which must be a shell built-in. Useful for invoking built-ins within scripts of the same name. |

case *string*
  in
    *regex*)
      *commands*
      ;;
     . . .
    esac

If *string* matches regular expression *regex*, perform the following *commands*. Proceed down the list of regular expressions until one is found (to catch all remaining strings, use * as *regex* at the end).

---

cd [*dir&*]

With no arguments, change to home directory of user. Otherwise, change working directory to *dir*. If *dir* is a relative pathname but is not in the current directory, then the CDPATH variable is searched.

---

command [*options*] *command* [*arguments*]

Execute *command*; do not perform function look-up (i.e., refuse to run any command that is neither in PATH nor a built-in). Set exit status to that returned by *command*, unless *command* cannot be found, in which case exit with a status of 127.

-p  Search default path, ignoring the PATH variable's value.

--  Treat everything that follows as an argument, not an option.

---

continue [*n*]

Skip remaining commands in a **for**, **while**, or **until** loop, resuming with the next iteration of the loop (or skipping *n* loops).

---

declare [*options*] [*name*[=*value*]]
typeset [*options*] [*name*[=*value*]]

Print or set variables. Options prefaced by + instead of − are inverted in meaning.

-a  Treat the following names as array variables.

-f  Treat the following names as functions.

→

| | |
|---|---|
| declare<br>← | **-i** Expect variable to be an integer, and evaluate its assigned value. |
| | **-p** Print names and settings of all shell variables and functions; take no other action. |
| | **-r** Do not allow variables to be reset later. |
| | **-x** Mark variables for subsequent export. |
| | **-F** Print names of all shell functions; take no other action. |

| | |
|---|---|
| dirs | **dirs** [*options*] |
| | Print directories currently remembered for **pushd/popd** operations. |
| | *Options* |
| | +*entry*<br>    Print *entry*th entry (list starts at 0). |
| | -*entry*<br>    Print *entry*th entry from end of list. |
| | **-l** Long listing. |

| | |
|---|---|
| disown | **disown** [*options*] [*jobIDs*] |
| | Let job run, but disassociate it from the shell. By default, do not even list the job as an active job; commands like **jobs** and **fg** will no longer recognize it. When **-h** is specified, the job is recognized but simply is kept from being killed when the shell dies. |
| | *Options* |
| | **-a** Act on all jobs. |
| | **-h** Do not pass a SIGHUP signal received by the shell on to the job. |

| | |
|---|---|
| echo | **echo** [*options*] [*string*] |
| | Write *string* to standard output, terminated by a newline. If no *string* is supplied, echo a newline. In **bash**, **echo** is just an alias for **print –**. (See also **echo** in Chapter 3). |

**-e**  Enable interpretation of escape characters:

    \a   Audible alert

    \b   Backspace

    \c   Suppress the terminating newline (same as **-n**)

    \f   Form feed

    \n   Newline

    \r   Carriage return

    \t   Horizontal tab

    \v   Vertical tab

    \\   Backslash

    \\*nnn*
        The character in the ASCII set corresponding to the octal number *nnn*.

    \x*nnn*
        The character in the ASCII set corresponding to the hexadecimal number *nnn*.

**-n**  Do not append a newline to the output.

**-E**  Disable interpretation of escape characters.

---

### enable [*options*] [*built-in* ...]

Enable (or when **-n** is specified, disable) built-in shell commands. Without *built-in* argument or with **-p** option, print enabled built-ins. With **-a**, print the status of all built-ins. You can disable shell commands in order to define your own functions with the same names.

#### Options

**-a**  Display all built-ins, both enabled and disabled.

**-n** *builtin*
    Disable *builtin*.

**-p**  Display enabled built-ins.

**-s**  Restrict display to special built-ins defined by POSIX standard.

**echo**

**enable**

bash

| | |
|---|---|
| **eval** | **eval** [*command args . . .*]<br><br>Perform *command*, passing *args*. |
| **exec** | **exec** [*options*] [*command*]<br><br>Execute *command* in place of the current process (instead of creating a new process). **exec** also is useful for opening, closing, or copying file descriptors.<br><br>*Options*<br><br>**-a** *name*<br>    Tell *command* that it was invoked as *name*.<br><br>**-c**  Remove all environment variables from the process when the new command runs.<br><br>**-l**  Treat the new process as if the user were logging in.<br><br>*Examples*<br><br>`$ trap 'exec 2>&-' 0`   *Close standard error when*<br>                                     *shell script exits (signal 0)*<br>`$ exec /bin/tcsh`      *Replace current shell with extended C shell*<br>`$ exec < infile`       *Reassign standard input to infile* |
| **exit** | **exit** [*n*]<br><br>Exit a shell script with status *n* (e.g., **exit 1**). *n* can be zero (success) or nonzero (failure). If *n* is not given, exit status will be that of the most recent command. **exit** can be issued at the command line to close a window (log out).<br><br>*Example*<br><br>`if [ $# -eq 0 ]; then`<br>    `echo "Usage: $0 [-c] [-d] file(s)"`<br>    `exit 1     # Error status`<br>`fi` |
| **export** | **export** [*options*] [*variables*]<br>**export** [*options*] [*name=[value]*] . . .<br><br>Pass (export) the value of one or more shell *variables*, giving global meaning to the variables (which are local by default). For example, a variable defined in one shell script must be exported if its value will be used in other programs called by the script. If no *variables* are given, **export** lists the variables exported by the current shell. If *name* and *value* are specified, assign *value* to a variable *name*. |

## Options

-- Treat all subsequent strings as arguments, not options.

-f  Expect *variables* to be functions.

-n  Unexport variable.

-p  List variables exported by current shell.

---

**fc** [*options*] [*first*] [*last*]
**fc** −e − [*old=new*] [*command*]

Display or edit commands in the history list. (Use only one of −l or −e.) **fc** provides capabilities similar to the C shell's **history** and ! syntax. *first* and *last* are numbers or strings specifying the range of commands to display or edit. If *last* is omitted, **fc** applies to a single command (specified by *first*). If both *first* and *last* are omitted, **fc** edits the previous command or lists the last 16. The second form of **fc** takes a history *command*, replaces *old* string with *new* string, and executes the modified command. If no strings are specified, *command* is just reexecuted. If no *command* is given either, the previous command is reexecuted. *command* is a number or string like *first*. See examples under the preceding section "Command History."

## Options

-e [*editor*]
    Invoke *editor* to edit the specified history commands. The default *editor* is set by the shell variable FCEDIT.

-l [*first last*]
    List the specified command or range of commands, or list the last 16.

-n  Suppress command numbering from the −l listing.

-r  Reverse the order of the −l listing.

-s *pattern*=newpattern
    Edit command(s), replacing all occurrences of *pattern* with *newpattern*. Then reexecute.

**bash**

| | |
|---|---|
| **fg** | **fg** [ *jobIDs*]<br><br>Bring current job or *jobIDs* to the foreground. See the later section "Job Control." |
| **for** | **for** *x* [in *list*]<br>  **do**<br>    *commands*<br>  **done**<br><br>Assign each word in list to *x* in turn and execute commands. If *list* is omitted, **$@** (positional parameters) is assumed.<br><br>***Examples***<br><br>Paginate all files in the current directory; save each result:<br><br>```<br>for file in *<br>do<br>    pr $file > $file.tmp<br>done<br>```<br><br>Search chapters for a list of words (like **fgrep −f**):<br><br>```<br>for item in `cat program_list`<br>do<br>    echo "Checking chapters for"<br>    echo "references to program $item..."<br>    grep -c "$item.[co]" chap*<br>done<br>``` |
| **function** | function *command*<br>{<br>  . . .<br>}<br><br>Define a function. Refer to arguments the same way as positional parameters in a shell script (**$1**, etc.) and terminate with }. |
| **getopts** | **getopts** *string name* [*args*]<br><br>Process command-line arguments (or *args*, if specified) and check for legal options. **getopts** is used in shell script loops and is intended to ensure standard syntax for command-line options. *string* contains the option letters to be recognized by **getopts** when running the |

shell script. Valid options are processed in turn and stored in the shell variable *name*. If an option letter is followed by a colon, the option must be followed by one or more arguments.

## hash [-r] [*commands*]

Search for *commands* and remember the directory in which each command resides. Hashing causes the shell to remember the association between a "name" and the absolute pathname of an executable, so that future executions don't require a search of PATH. With no arguments, **hash** lists the current hashed commands. The display shows *hits* (the number of times the command is called by the shell) and *command* (the full pathname).

## help [-s] [*string*]

Print help text on all built-in commands or those matching *string*. With -s, display only brief syntax, otherwise display summary paragraph also.

## history [*options*]
## history [*lines*]

Print a numbered command history, denoting modified commands with a *. Include commands from previous sessions. You may specify how many lines of history to print.

*Options*

-a [*file*]
> **bash** maintains a file called *.bash_history* in the user's home directory, a record of previous sessions' commands. Ask **bash** to append the current session's commands to *.bash_history* or to *file*.

-c Clear history list: remove all previously entered commands from the list remembered by the shell.

-n [*file*]
> Append to the history list those lines in the *.bash_history* file or in *file* that have not yet been included.

-r [*file*]
> Use *.bash_history* or *file* as the history list, instead of the working history list.

→

| | |
|---|---|
| history<br>← | **-s** *command*<br>    Add *command* to working history list without executing it.<br><br>**-w** [*file*]<br>    Overwrite .*bash_history* or *file* with working history list. |

| | |
|---|---|
| if | **if** *test-cmds*<br><br>Begin a conditional statement. Possible formats are: |

```
if test-cmds    if test-cmds    if test-cmds
then            then            then
    cmds1           cmds1           cmds1
fi              else            elif test-cmds
                    cmds2       then
                fi                  cmds2
                                ...
                                else
                                    cmdsn
                                fi
```

Usually, the initial **if** and any **elif** lines execute one **test** or [] command (although any series of commands is permitted). When **if** succeeds (that is, the last of its *test-cmds* returns 0), *cmds1* are performed; otherwise each succeeding **elif** or **else** line is tried.

| | |
|---|---|
| jobs | **jobs** [*options*] [*jobIDs*]<br><br>List all running or stopped jobs, or those specified by *jobIDs*. For example, you can check whether a long compilation or text format is still running. Also useful before logging out. See also "Job Control" later in this chapter.<br><br>Options<br><br>**-l**   List job IDs and process group IDs.<br><br>**-n**   List only jobs whose status changed since last notification.<br><br>**-p**   List process group IDs only.<br><br>**-r**   List active, running jobs only.<br><br>**-s**   List stopped jobs only.<br><br>**-x** *command* [*arguments*]<br>    Execute *command*. If *jobIDs* are specified, replace them with *command*. |

**kill** [*options*] *IDs*

Terminate each specified process *ID* or job *ID*. You must own the process or be a privileged user. See also the later section "Job Control."

*Options*

−*signal*
> The signal number (from **ps −f**) or name (from **kill −l**). With a signal number of 9, the kill cannot be caught. The default is TERM.

−− Consider all subsequent strings to be arguments, not options.

−l   List the signal names. (Used by itself.)

−s *signal*
> Specify *signal*. May be a name.

---

**let** *expressions*

Perform arithmetic as specified by one or more integer *expressions*. *expressions* consist of numbers, operators, and shell variables (which don't need a preceding $). Expressions must be quoted if they contain spaces or other special characters. For more information and examples, see "Arithmetic Expressions" earlier in this chapter. See also **expr** in Chapter 3.

*Examples*

Both of the following examples add 1 to variable **i**:

```
let i=i+1
let "i = i + 1"
```

**bash**

---

**local** [*options*] [*variable*[=*value*]] [*variable2*[=*value*]] . . .

Without arguments, print all local variables. Otherwise, create (and set, if specified) one or more local variables. See the **declare** built-in command for options.

| | |
|---|---|
| logout | **logout** [*status*]<br><br>Exit the shell, returning *status* as exit status to invoking program if specified. Can be used only in a login shell. Otherwise, use **exit**. |
| popd | **popd** [*options*]<br><br>Manipulate the directory stack. By default, remove the top directory and **cd** to it.<br><br>***Options***<br><br>**+***n*  Remove the *n*th directory in the stack, counting from 0.<br><br>**-***n*  Remove *n*th entry from the bottom of the stack, counting from 0. |
| printf | **printf** *string* [*arguments*]<br><br>Format a string like the C library **printf** function. Standard percent-sign formats are recognized in *string*, such as %i for integer. Escape sequences such as **\n** can be included in *string* and are automatically recognized; if you want to include them in *arguments*, specify a *string* of %b. You can escape characters in *arguments* to output a string suitable for input to other commands by specifying a *string* of %q.<br><br>***Examples***<br><br>```$ printf "Previous command: %i\n" "$(($HISTCMD-1))"```<br>`Previous command: 534`<br>`$ echo $PAGER`<br>`less -E`<br>`$ printf "%q\n" "\t$PAGER"`<br>`\\tless\ -E`<br><br>The last command probably would be used to record a setting in a file where it could be read and assigned by another shell script. |
| pushd | **pushd** *directory*<br>**pushd** [*options*]<br><br>By default, switch top two directories on stack. If specified, add a new directory to the top of the stack instead, and **cd** to it. |

+*n*   Rotate the stack to place the *n*th (counting from 0) directory at the top.

-*n*   Rotate the stack to place the *n*th directory from the bottom of the stack at the top.

---

## pwd [-P]

Display the current working directory's absolute pathname. By default, any symbolic directories used when reaching the current directory are displayed, but with the -**P** option the real names are displayed instead.

---

## read [*options*] *variable1* [*variable2* ...]

Read one line of standard input, and assign each word (as defined by IFS) to the corresponding *variable*, with all leftover words assigned to the last variable. If only one variable is specified, the entire line will be assigned to that variable. The return status is 0 unless *EOF* is reached, a distinction that is useful for running loops over input files. If no variable names are provided, read the entire string into the environment variable REPLY.

*Options*

-**a** *var*
    Read each word into an element of *var*, which is treated as an array variable.

-**d** *char*
    Stop reading the line at *char* instead of at the newline.

-**e**   Line editing and command history are enabled during input.

-**n** *num*
    Read only *num* characters from the line.

-**p** *string*
    Display the prompt *string* to the user before reading each line, if input is interactive.

-**r**   Raw mode; ignore \ as a line continuation character.

-**s**   Do not echo the characters entered by the user (useful for reading a password).

**bash**

→

| | |
|---|---|
| **read**<br>← | **-t** *seconds*<br>    Time out and return without setting any variables if input is interactive and no input has been entered for *seconds* seconds.<br><br>*Examples*<br><br>```<br>$ read first last address<br>Sarah Caldwell 123 Main Street<br>$ echo "$last, $first\n$address"<br>Caldwell, Sarah<br>123 Main Street<br>```<br><br>The following commands, which read a password into the variable **$user_pw** and then display its value, use recently added options that are not in all versions of **bash** in current use.<br><br>```<br>$ read -sp "Enter password (will not appear on screen)" user_pw<br>Enter password (will not appear on screen)<br>$ echo $user_pw<br>You weren't supposed to know!<br>```<br><br>The following script reads input from the system's password file, which uses colons to delimit fields (making it a popular subject for examples of input parsing).<br><br>```<br>IFS=:<br>cat /etc/passwd |<br>while<br>read account pw user group gecos home shell<br>do<br>echo "Account name $account has user info: $gecos"<br>done<br>``` |
| **readonly** | **readonly** [*options*] [*variable1 variable2* ...]<br><br>Prevent the specified shell variables from being assigned new values. Variables can be accessed (read) but not overwritten. In **bash**, the syntax *variable=value* can be used to assign a new value that cannot be changed.<br><br>*Options*<br><br>**-a**  Treat the following names as array variables.<br><br>**-f**  Treat the following names as functions, and set them read-only so that they cannot be changed.<br><br>**-p**  Display all read-only variables (default). |

**return [*n*]**                                                                    return

Used inside a function definition. Exit the function with status *n* or
with the exit status of the previously executed command.

---

**select** *name* [ **in** *wordlist* ; ]                                          select
  **do**
    *commands*
  **done**

Choose a value for *name* by displaying the words in *wordlist* to the
user and prompting for a choice. Store user input in the variable
REPLY and the chosen word in *name*. Then execute *commands*
repeatedly until they execute a **break** or **return**. Default prompt can
be changed by setting the PS3 shell variable.

---

**set** [*options*] [*arg1 arg2* . . .]                                            set

With no arguments, **set** prints the values of all variables known to
the current shell. Options can be enabled (*-option*) or disabled
(*+option*). Options also can be set when the shell is invoked, via
**bash**. Arguments are assigned in order to **$1**, **$2**, and so on.

*Options*

-    Turn off −v and −x, and turn off option processing.

−−  Used as the last option; −− turns off option processing so that
    arguments beginning with − are not misinterpreted as options.
    (For example, you can set **$1** to −1.) If no arguments are given
    after −−, unset the positional parameters.

-a  From now on, automatically mark variables for export after
    defining or changing them.

-b  Report background job status at termination, instead of waiting
    for next shell prompt.

-e  Exit if a command yields a nonzero exit status.

-f  Do not expand filename metacharacters (e.g., * ? [ ]). Wildcard
    expansion is sometimes called *globbing*.

-h  Locate commands as they are defined, and remember them.

-k  Assignment of environment variables (*var=value*) will take
    effect regardless of where they appear on the command line.
    Normally, assignments must precede the command name.

*bash*

→

**-m**   Monitor mode. Enable job control; background jobs executes in a separate process group. **-m** usually is set automatically.

**-n**   Read commands, but don't execute. Useful for checking errors, particularly for shell scripts.

**-o** [*m*]

List shell modes, or turn on mode *m*. Many modes can be set by other options. The modes can be turned off through the **+o** option. Modes are:

**allexport**
Same as **-a**.

**braceexpand**
Same as **-B**.

**emacs**
Enter Emacs editing mode (on by default).

**errexit**
Same as **-e**.

**hashall**
Same as **-h**.

**histexpand**
Same as **-H**.

**history**
Default. Preserve command history.

**ignoreeof**
Don't allow use of a single **Ctrl-D** (the end-of-file or EOF character) to log off; use the **exit** command to log off. This has the same effect as setting the shell variable IGNOREEOF=1.

**interactive-comments**
Treat all words beginning with #, and all subsequent words, as comments.

**keyword**
Same as **-k**.

**monitor**
Same as **-m**.

**noclobber**
Same as **-C**.

**noexec**
Same as **-n**.

noglob
> Same as −f.

notify
> Same as −b.

nounset
> Same as −u.

onecmd
> Same as −t.

physical
> Same as −P.

posix
> Match POSIX standard.

privileged
> Same as −p.

verbose
> Same as −v.

vi   Enable vi-style command-line editing.

xtrace
> Same as −x.

+o [*m*]
> Display modes or turn off mode *m*. See the −o option for a list of modes.

−p   Start up as a privileged user; don't process *$HOME/.profile*.

−t   Exit after one command is executed.

−u   Indicate an error when user tries to use a variable that is undefined.

−v   Show each shell command line when read.

−x   Show commands and arguments when executed, preceded by a + or the prompt defined by the PS4 shell variable. This provides step-by-step debugging of shell scripts. (Same as −o **xtrace**.)

−B   Default. Enable brace expansion.

−C   Don't allow output redirection (>) to overwrite an existing file.

−H   Default. Enable ! and !! commands.

−P   Print absolute pathnames in response to **pwd**. By default, **bash** includes symbolic links in its response to **pwd**.

**bash**

→

| | |
|---|---|
| set<br>← | **Examples**<br><br>`set -- "$num" -20 -30`   *Set $1 to $num, $2 to –20, $3 to –30*<br>`set -vx`                     *Read each command line; show it;*<br>                              *execute it; show it again (with arguments)*<br>`set +x`                      *Stop command tracing*<br>`set -o noclobber`            *Prevent file overwriting*<br>`set +o noclobber`            *Allow file overwriting again* |

---

**shift**

shift [*n*]

Shift positional arguments (e.g., **$2** becomes **$1**). If *n* is given, shift to the left *n* places.

---

**source**

source *file* [*arguments*]

Read and execute lines in *file*. *file* does not have to be executable but must reside in a directory searched by PATH.

---

**suspend**

suspend [–f]

Same as **Ctrl-Z**. Often used to stop an **su** command.

*Option*

–f   Force suspend, even if shell is a login shell.

---

**test**

test *condition*
or
[ *condition* ]

Evaluate a *condition* and, if its value is true, return a zero exit status; otherwise, return a nonzero exit status. An alternate form of the command uses [ ] rather than the word *test*. *condition* is constructed using the following expressions. Conditions are true if the description holds true.

*File conditions*

–a *file*
    *file* exists.

–b *file*
    *file* is a block special file.

–c *file*
    *file* is a character special file.

**-d** *file*
> *file* is a directory.

**-e** *file*
> *file* exists.

**-f** *file*
> *file* is a regular file.

**-g** *file*
> *file* has the set-group-ID bit set.

**-h** *file*
> *file* is a symbolic link.

**-k** *file*
> *file* has its sticky bit (no longer used) set.

**-p** *file*
> *file* is a named pipe (FIFO).

**-r** *file*
> *file* is readable.

**-s** *file*
> *file* has a size greater than 0.

**-t** [*n*]
> The open file descriptor *n* is associated with a terminal device; default *n* is 1.

**-u** *file*
> *file* has its set-user-ID bit set.

**-w** *file*
> *file* is writable.

**-x** *file*
> *file* is executable.

**-G** *file*
> *file*'s group is the process's effective group ID.

**-L** *file*
> *file* is a symbolic link.

**-N** *file*
> *file* has been modified since its last time of access.

**-O** *file*
> *file*'s owner is the process's effective user ID.

**-S** *file*
> *file* is a socket.

bash

→

**test**
←

$f1$  **-ef** $f2$
> Files $f1$ and $f2$ are linked (refer to same file through a hard link).

$f1$  **-nt** $f2$
> File $f1$ is newer than $f2$.

$f1$  **-ot** $f2$
> File $f1$ is older than $f2$.

### String conditions

**-n** $s1$
> String $s1$ has nonzero length.

**-o** $s1$
> Shell option $s1$ is set. Shell options are described under the **set** built-in command.

**-z** $s1$
> String $s1$ has 0 length.

$s1 = s2$
> Strings $s1$ and $s2$ are identical.

$s1 == s2$
> Strings $s1$ and $s2$ are identical.

$s1 != s2$
> Strings $s1$ and $s2$ are not identical.

$s1 < s2$
> String $s1$ is lower in the alphabet (or other sort in use) than $s2$. By default, the check is performed character-by-character against the ASCII character set.

$s1 > s2$
> String $s1$ is higher in the alphabet (or other sort in use) than $s2$.

*string*
> *string* is not null.

### Integer comparisons

$n1$  **-eq** $n2$
> $n1$ equals $n2$.

$n1$  **-ge** $n2$
> $n1$ is greater than or equal to $n2$.

$n1$  **-gt** $n2$
> $n1$ is greater than $n2$.

*n1* **-le** *n2*
> *n1* is less than or equal to *n2*.

*n1* **-lt** *n2*
> *n1* is less than *n2*.

*n1* **-ne** *n2*
> *n1* does not equal *n2*.

### Combined forms

**!** *condition*
> True if *condition* is false.

*condition1* **-a** *condition2*
> True if both conditions are true.

*condition1* **-o** *condition2*
> True if either condition is true.

### Examples

Each of the following examples shows the first line of various statements that might use a test condition:

```
while test $# -gt 0          While there are arguments . . .
while [ -n "$1" ]            While the first argument is nonempty . . .
if [ $count -lt 10 ]        If $count is less than 10 . . .
if [ -d RCS ]               If the RCS directory exists . . .
if [ "$answer" != "y" ]     If the answer is not y . . .
if [ ! -r "$1" -o ! -f "$1" ]   If the first argument is not a
                                readable file or a regular file . . .
```

---

## times

Print accumulated process times for user and system.

---

## trap [–l] [ [*commands*] *signals*]

Execute *commands* if any of *signals* is received. Common signals include 0, 1, 2, and 15. Multiple commands should be quoted as a group and separated by semicolons internally. If *commands* is the null string (i.e., **trap** " "*signals*), then *signals* will be ignored by the shell. If *commands* is omitted entirely, reset processing of specified signals to the default action. If both *commands* and *signals* are omitted, list current trap assignments. See examples at the end of this entry and under **exec**.

### Option

$\rightarrow$

| trap | -l | List signals. |
| ← | | |

**Signals**

Signals are listed along with what triggers them.

|  |  |
| --- | --- |
| 0 | Exit from shell (usually when shell script finishes). |
| 1 | Hang up (usually logout). |
| 2 | Interrupt (usually through **Ctrl-C**). |
| 3 | Quit. |
| 4 | Illegal instruction. |
| 5 | Trace trap. |
| 6 | Abort. |
| 7 | Unused. |
| 8 | Floating-point exception. |
| 9 | Termination. |
| 10 | User-defined. |
| 11 | Reference to invalid memory. |
| 12 | User-defined. |
| 13 | Write to a pipe without a process to read it. |
| 14 | Alarm timeout. |
| 15 | Software termination (usually via **kill**). |
| 16 | Unused. |
| 17 | Termination of child process. |
| 18 | Continue (if stopped). |
| 19 | Stop process. |
| 20 | Process suspended (usually through **Ctrl-Z**). |
| 21 | Background process has tty input. |
| 22 | Background process has tty output. |
| 23 | Unused. |
| 24 | Unused. |
| 25 | Unused. |

26 Unused.

27 Unused.

28 Unused.

29 I/O possible on a channel.

### Examples

```
trap "" 2        Ignore signal 2 (interrupts)
trap 2           Obey interrupts again
```

Remove a $tmp file when the shell program exits or if the user logs out, presses Ctrl-C, or does a kill:

```
trap "rm -f $tmp; exit" 0 1 2 15
```

---

## type [options] commands

Report absolute pathname of programs invoked for *commands* and whether or not they are hashed.

-- Consider all subsequent strings to be arguments, not options.

-a, -all
:    Print all occurrences of *command*, not just that which would be invoked.

-p, -path
:    Print the hashed value of *command*, which may differ from the first appearance of *command* in the PATH.

-t, -type
:    Determine and state if *command* is an alias, keyword, function, built-in, or file.

### Example

```
$ type mv read
mv is /bin/mv
read is a shell built-in
```

---

## typeset

See declare.

---

## ulimit [options] [n]

Print the value of one or more resource limits, or, if *n* is specified, set a resource limit to *n*. Resource limits can be either hard (-H) or soft (-S). By default, ulimit sets both limits or prints the soft limit.

→

*bash*

| | |
|---|---|
| ulimit<br>← | The options determine which resource is acted on. |
| | **Options** |
| | — — Consider all subsequent strings to be arguments, not options. |
| | -a   Print all current limits. |
| | -H   Hard resource limit. |
| | -S   Soft resource limit. |
| | **Specific limits** |
| | These options limit specific resource sizes. |
| | -c   Core files. |
| | -d   Size of processes' data segments. |
| | -f    Size of shell-created files. |
| | -l    Size of memory that the process can lock. |
| | -m   Resident set size. |
| | -n   Number of file descriptors. On many systems, this cannot be set. |
| | -p   Pipe size, measured in blocks of 512 bytes. |
| | -s    Stack size. |
| | -t    Amount of CPU time, counted in seconds. |
| | -u   Number of processes per user. |
| | -v   Virtual memory used by shell. |
| umask | umask [*nnn*]<br>umask [-p] [-S] |
| | Display file creation mask or set file creation mask to octal value *nnn*. The file creation mask determines which permission bits are turned off (e.g., **umask 002** produces **rw–rw–r– –**). |
| | **Options** |
| | -p   Display mask within an **umask** command so that a caller can read and execute it. |
| | -S   Display **umask** symbolically, rather than in octal. |

**unalias [-a]** *names*

Remove *names* from the alias list. See also **alias**.

*Option*

-a   Remove all aliases.

---

**unset** [*options*] *names*

Erase definitions of functions or variables listed in *names*.

*Options*

-f   Expect *name* to refer to a function.

-v   Expect *name* to refer to a variable (default).

---

**until**
   *test-commands*
**do**
   *commands*
**done**

Execute *test-commands* (usually a **test** or **[]** command), and if the exit status is nonzero (that is, the test fails), perform *commands*; repeat.

---

**wait** [*ID*]

Pause in execution until all background jobs complete (exit status 0 will be returned), or pause until the specified background process *ID* or job *ID* completes (exit status of *ID* is returned). Note that the shell variable $! contains the process ID of the most recent background process. If job control is not in effect, *ID* can be only a process ID number. See the next section "Job Control."

*Example*

wait $!   *Wait for last background process to finish*

**bash**

---

**while**
   *test-commands*

$\rightarrow$

| while<br>← | do<br>    *commands*<br>done |
|---|---|
| | Execute *test-commands* (usually a **test** or [] command) and if the exit status is 0, perform *commands*; repeat. |

## *Job Control*

Job control lets you place foreground jobs in the background, bring background jobs to the foreground, or suspend (temporarily stop) running jobs. Job control is enabled by default. Once disabled, it can be reenabled by any of the following commands:

```
bash -m -i
set -m
set -o monitor
```

Many job control commands take *jobID* as an argument. This argument can be specified as follows:

%*n*  Job number *n*

%*s*  Job whose command line starts with string *s*

%?*s* Job whose command line contains string *s*

%%  Current job

%+  Current job (same as preceding)

%–  Previous job

**bash** provides the following job control commands. For more information on these commands, see "Built-in Commands" earlier in this chapter.

**bg**  Put a job in the background.

**fg**  Put a job in the foreground.

**jobs**
    List active jobs.

**kill** Terminate a job.

**stop**
    Suspend a background job.

**stty tostop**
    Stop background jobs if they try to send output to the terminal.

**wait**
    Wait for background jobs to finish.

**Ctrl-Z**

Suspend a foreground job. Then use **bg** or **fg** to restart it in the background or foreground. (Your terminal may use something other than Ctrl-Z as the suspend character.)

# CHAPTER 8

# *csh and tcsh*

This chapter describes the C shell and its enhancement, **tcsh**. On some versions of Linux, **tcsh** is used as the C shell; in that case, the **tcsh** features described in this chapter work even when you run **csh**. The C shell was so named because many of its programming constructs and symbols resemble those of the C programming language.

The default shell on Linux systems is **bash**. If you want to use **csh** or **tcsh**, you first need to change your default. Each user's shell preference is kept in the password table. If you are creating an account, you can set the default shell when you add the user. If the account already exists, use the **chsh** command to change the shell (see the command descriptions in Chapter 3, *Linux Commands*).

The following topics are presented in this chapter:

- Overview of features

- Invoking the shell

- Syntax

- Variables

- Expressions

- Command history

- Command-line manipulation

- Job control

- Built-in commands

# Overview of Features

Features of the C shell include:

- Input/output redirection

- Wildcard characters (metacharacters) for filename abbreviation

- Shell variables for customizing your environment

- Integer arithmetic

- Access to previous commands (command history)

- Command-name abbreviation (aliasing)

- A built-in command set for writing shell programs

- Job control

The **tcsh** shell includes all of the C shell features. In addition, it includes the following extensions to the C shell:

- Command-line editing and editor commands

- Word completion (tab completion)

- Spell checking

- Extended history commands

- Extended handling of directory manipulation

- Scheduled events—such as logout or terminal locking after a set idle period and delayed commands

- Additional shell built-ins

- Additional shell variables and environment variables

- New formatting sequences for the prompt string, as well as two new prompts (in loops and spelling correction)

- Read-only variables

# Invoking the Shell

A shell command interpreter can be invoked as follows:

    csh [options] [arguments]
    tcsh [options] [arguments]

csh and tcsh use syntax resembling C and execute commands from a terminal or a file. Options **-n**, **-v**, and **-x** are useful when debugging scripts.

## Options

-b   Allow the remaining command-line options to be interpreted as options to a specified command, rather than as options to **csh** itself.

-c   Execute command specified following the argument.

-d   Load directory stack from *~/.cshdirs* even if not a login shell. (**tcsh**)

-e   Exit if a command produces errors.

-f   Fast startup; start without executing *.cshrc* or *.tcshrc*.

-i   Invoke interactive shell (prompt for input).

-l   Login shell (must be the only option specified).

-m   Load *~/.tcshrc* even if effective user is not the owner of the file. (**tcsh**)

-n   Parse commands, but do not execute.

-s   Read commands from the standard input.

-t   Exit after executing one command.

-v   Display commands before executing them; expand history substitutions, but not other substitutions (e.g., filename, variable, and command). Same as setting **verbose**.

-V   Same as **-v**, but also display *.cshrc*.

-x   Display commands before executing them, but expand all substitutions. Same as setting **echo**.

-X   Same as **-x**, but also display *.cshrc*.

## Arguments

Arguments are assigned, in order, to the positional parameters **$1**, **$2**, and so on. If the first argument is an executable script, commands are read from it, and remaining arguments are assigned to **$1**, **$2**, and so forth.

## Syntax

This section describes the many symbols peculiar to **csh** and **tcsh**. The topics are arranged as follows:

* Special files

* Filename metacharacters

- Quoting

- Command forms

- Redirection forms

## Special Files

| Filename | Description |
|----------|-------------|
| ˜/.cshrc or ˜/.tcshrc | Executed at each instance of shell startup. For **tcsh**, if no ˜/.tcshrc, uses ˜/.cshrc if present. |
| ˜/.login | Executed by login shell after .cshrc at login. |
| ˜/.cshdirs | Executed by login shell after .login (**tcsh**). |
| ˜/.logout | Executed by login shell at logout. |
| /etc/passwd | Source of home directories for ˜name abbreviations. |

## Filename Metacharacters

| Characters | Meaning |
|------------|---------|
| * | Match any string of 0 or more characters. |
| ? | Match any single character. |
| [abc...] | Match any one of the enclosed characters; a hyphen can be used to specify a range (e.g., a–z, A–Z, 0–9). |
| {abc,xxx,...} | Expand each comma-separated string inside braces. |
| ˜ | Home directory for the current user. |
| ˜name | Home directory of user name. |

### Examples

```
% ls new*       Match new and new.1
% cat ch?       Match ch9 but not ch10
% vi [D-R]*     Match files that begin with uppercase D through R
% ls {ch,app}?  Expand, then match ch1, ch2, app1, app2
% cd ~tom       Change to tom's home directory
```

## Quoting

Quoting disables a character's special meaning and allows it to be used literally, as itself. The following characters have special meaning to the C shell:

| Characters | Description |
|------------|-------------|
| ; | Command separator |
| & | Background execution |
| ( ) | Command grouping |
| \| | Pipe |
| * ? [ ] ˜ | Filename metacharacters |

| Characters | Description |
| --- | --- |
| { } | String expansion characters (usually don't require quoting) |
| > < & ! | Redirection symbols |
| ! ^ | History substitution, quick substitution |
| " ' \ | Used in quoting other characters |
| ` | Command substitution |
| $ | Variable substitution |
| newline space tab | Word separators |

The characters that follow can be used for quoting:

" " Everything between " and " is taken literally, except for the following characters, which keep their special meaning:

$ Variable substitution will occur.

` Command substitution will occur.

" This marks the end of the double quote.

\ Escape next character.

! The history character.

*newline*
  The newline character.

' ' Everything between ' and ' is taken literally except for ! (history) and another ', and newline.

\ The character following a \ is taken literally. Use within " " to escape ", $, and `. Often used to escape itself, spaces, or newlines. Always needed to escape a history character (usually !).

## *Examples*

```
% echo 'Single quotes "protect" double quotes'
Single quotes "protect" double quotes

% echo "Well, isn't that "\""special?"\"
Well, isn't that "special"?

% echo "You have `ls|wc -l` files in `pwd`"
You have 43 files in /home/bob

% echo The value of \$x is $x
The value of $x is 100
```

## Command Forms

| Command | Action |
|---------|--------|
| *cmd* & | Execute *cmd* in background. |
| *cmd1* ; *cmd2* | Command sequence; execute multiple *cmd*s on the same line. |
| ( *cmd1* ; *cmd2* ) | Subshell; treat *cmd1* and *cmd2* as a command group. |
| *cmd1* \| *cmd2* | Pipe; use output from *cmd1* as input to *cmd2*. |
| *cmd1* `cmd2` | Command substitution; run *cmd2* first and use its output as arguments to *cmd1*. |
| *cmd1* \|\| *cmd2* | OR; execute either *cmd1* or (if *cmd1* fails) *cmd2*. |
| *cmd1* && *cmd2* | AND; execute *cmd1* and then (if *cmd1* succeeds) *cmd2*. |

### Examples

| | |
|---|---|
| `% nroff file > output &` | *Format in the background* |
| `% cd; ls` | *Execute sequentially* |
| `% (date; who; pwd) > logfile` | *All output is redirected* |
| `% sort file | pr -3 | lp` | *Sort file, page output, then print* |
| `% vi `grep -l ifdef *.c`` | *Edit files found by* grep |
| `% egrep '(yes|no)' `cat list`` | *Specify a list of files to search* |
| `% grep XX file && lp file` | *Print file if it contains the pattern* |
| `% grep XX file || echo XX not found` | *Echo an error message if* XX *not found* |

## Redirection Forms

| File Descriptor | Name | Common Abbreviation | Typical Default |
|-----------------|------|---------------------|-----------------|
| 0 | Standard input | stdin | Keyboard |
| 1 | Standard output | stdout | Screen |
| 2 | Standard error | stderr | Screen |

The usual input source or output destination can be changed with redirection commands listed in the following sections.

### Simple redirection

| Command | Action |
|---------|--------|
| *cmd* > *file* | Send output of *cmd* to *file* (overwrite). |
| *cmd* >! *file* | Same as preceding, even if **noclobber** is set. |
| *cmd* >> *file* | Send output of *cmd* to *file* (append). |
| *cmd*>>! *file* | Same as preceding, even if **noclobber** is set. |
| *cmd* < *file* | Take input for *cmd* from *file*. |

*csh and tcsh*

| Command | Action |
|---|---|
| cmd << text | Read standard input up to a line identical to text (text can be stored in a shell variable). Input usually is typed on the screen or in the shell program. Commands that typically use this syntax include **cat**, **echo**, **ex**, and **sed**. If text is enclosed in quotes, standard input will not undergo variable substitution, command substitution, etc. |

### Multiple redirection

| Command | Action |
|---|---|
| cmd >& file | Send both standard output and standard error to file. |
| cmd >&! file | Same as preceding, even if **noclobber** is set. |
| cmd >>& file | Append standard output and standard error to end of file. |
| cmd >>&! file | Same as preceding, even if **noclobber** is set. |
| cmd1 \|& cmd2 | Pipe standard error together with standard output. |
| (cmd> f1) >& f2 | Send standard output to file f1 and standard error to file f2. |
| cmd \| **tee** files | Send output of cmd to standard output (usually the screen) and to files. (See the example in Chapter 3 under **tee**.) |

### Examples

```
% cat part1 > book                          Copy part1 to book
% cat part2 part3 >> book                   Append parts 2 and 3 to same file as part1
% mail tim < report                         Take input to message from report
% cc calc.c >& error_out                    Store all messages, including errors
% cc newcalc.c >&! error_out                Overwrite old file
% grep Unix ch* |& pr                       Pipe all messages, including errors
% (find / -print > filelist) >& no_access   Separate error messages from list of files
% sed 's/^/XX /' << "END_ARCHIVE"           Supply text right after command
This is often how a shell archive is "wrapped",
bundling text for distribution. You would normally
run sed from a shell program, not from the command line.
"END_ARCHIVE"
```

# Variables

This subsection describes the following:

- Variable substitution

- Variable modifiers

- Predefined shell variables

- Formatting for the *prompt* variable

- Sample *.cshrc* file

- Environment variables

## Variable Substitution

In the following substitutions, braces ({}) are optional, except when needed to separate a variable name from following characters that would otherwise be considered part of the name:

| Variable | Description |
|---|---|
| `${var}` | The value of variable *var*. |
| `${var[i]}` | Select word or words in position *i* of *var*. *i* can be a single number, a range m–n, a range –n (missing m implies 1), a range m– (missing n implies all remaining words), or * (select all words). *i* also can be a variable that expands to one of these values. |
| `${#var}` | The number of words in *var*. |
| `${#argv}` | The number of arguments. |
| `$0` | Name of the program. |
| `${argv[n]}` | Individual arguments on command line (positional parameters); 1 ≤ *n* ≤ 9. |
| `${n}` | Same as `${argv[n]}`. |
| `${argv[*]}` | All arguments on command line. |
| `$*` | Same as `{$argv[*]}`. |
| `$argv[$#argv]` | The last argument. |
| `${?var}` | Return 1 if *var* is set, 0 if *var* is not set. |
| `$$` | Process number of current shell; useful as part of a filename for creating temporary files with unique names. |
| `${?name}` | Return 1 if *name* is set, 0 if not. |
| `$?0` | Return 1 if input filename is known, 0 if not. |

### Examples

Sort the third through last arguments and save the output in a file whose name is unique to this process:

```
sort $argv[3-] > tmp.$$
```

Process *.cshrc* commands only if the shell is interactive (i.e., the **prompt** variable must be set):

```
if ($?prompt) then
    set commands,
    alias commands,
    etc.
endif
```

## Variable Modifiers

Except for $?*var*, $$, and $?0, the variable substitutions in the preceding section may be followed by one of these modifiers (when braces are used, the modifier goes inside them):

:r   Return the variable's root (the portion before the last dot).

:e   Return the variable's extension.

:h   Return the variable's header (the directory portion).

:t   Return the variable's tail (the portion after the last slash).

:gr  Return all roots.

:ge  Return all extensions.

:gh  Return all headers.

:gt  Return all tails.

:q   Quote a wordlist variable, keeping the items separate. Useful when the variable contains filename metacharacters that should not be expanded.

:x   Quote a pattern, expanding it into a wordlist.

### Examples using pathname modifiers

The following table shows the use of pathname modifiers on the following variable:

```
set aa=(/progs/num.c /book/chap.ps)
```

| Variable Portion | Specification | Output Result |
| --- | --- | --- |
| Normal variable | echo $aa | /progs/num.c /book/chap.ps |
| Second root | echo $aa[2]:r | /book/chap |
| Second header | echo $aa[2]:h | /book |
| Second tail | echo $aa[2]:t | chap.ps |
| Second extension | echo $aa[2]:e | ps |
| Root | echo $aa:r | /progs/num /book/chap.ps |
| Global root | echo $aa:gr | /progs/num /book/chap |
| Header | echo $aa:h | /progs /book/chap.ps |
| Global header | echo $aa:gh | /progs /book |
| Tail | echo $aa:t | num.c /book/chap.ps |
| Global tail | echo $aa:gt | num.c chap.ps |
| Extension | echo $aa:e | c /book/chap.ps |
| Global extension | echo $aa:ge | c ps |

*Examples using quoting modifiers*

Unless quoted, the shell expands variables to represent files in the current directory:

```
% set a="[a-z]*" A="[A-Z]*"
% echo "$a" "$A"
[a-z]* [A-Z]*

% echo $a $A
at cc m4 Book Doc

% echo $a:x $A
[a-z]* Book Doc

% set d=($a:q $A:q)
% echo $d
at cc m4 Book Doc

% echo $d:q
[a-z]* [A-Z]*

% echo $d[1] +++ $d[2]
at cc m4 +++ Book Doc

% echo $d[1]:q
[a-z]*
```

# Predefined Shell Variables

Variables can be set in one of two ways, by assigning a value:

```
set var=value
```

or by simply turning the variable on:

```
set var
```

In the following list, variables that accept values are shown with the equals sign followed by the type of value they accept; the value then is described. (Note, however, that variables such as **argv**, **cwd**, or **status** are never explicitly assigned.) For variables that are turned on or off, the table describes what they do when set. tcsh automatically sets (and, in some cases, updates) the variables **addsuffix**, **argv**, **autologout**, **cwd**, **dirstack**, **echo-style**, **edit**, **gid**, **home**, **loginsh**, **logout**, **oid**, **owd**, **path**, **prompt**, **prompt2**, **prompt3**, **shell**, **shlvl**, **status**, **tcsh**, **term**, **tty**, **uid**, **user**, and **version**. Variables in italics are specific to **tcsh**.

| Variable | Description |
|---|---|
| *addsuffix* | Append / to directories and a space to files during tab completion to indicate a precise match. |
| *ampm* | Display all times in 12-hour format. |
| **argv**=(*args*) | List of arguments passed to current command; default is (). |

| Variable | Description |
|---|---|
| *autocorrect* | Check spelling before attempting to complete commands. |
| *autoexpand* | Expand history (such as ! references) during command completion. |
| *autolist*[=**ambiguous**] | Print possible completions when correct one is ambiguous. If **ambiguous** is specified, print possible completions only when completion adds no new characters. |
| *autologout*=*logout-minutes* [*locking-minutes*] | Log out after *logout-minutes* of idle time. Lock the terminal after *locking-minutes* of idle time, requiring a password before continuing. Not used if the DISPLAY environment variable is set. |
| *backslash_quote* | Always allow backslashes to quote \, ', and ". |
| **cdpath**=*dirs* | List of alternate directories to search when locating arguments for **cd**, **popd**, or **pushd**. |
| *color* | Turn on color for **ls-F**, **ls**, or both. Setting to nothing is equivalent to setting for both. |
| *command* | If set, holds the command passed to the shell with the −**c** option. |
| *complete*=**enhance** | When **enhance**, ignore case in completion, treat ., −, and _ as word separators, and consider _ and − to be the same. |
| *correct*={**cmd**|**complete**|**all**} | When **cmd**, spellcheck commands. When **complete**, complete commands. When **all**, spellcheck whole command line. |
| **cwd**=*dir* | Full pathname of current directory. |
| *dextract* | When set, the **pushd** command extracts the desired directory and puts it at the top of the stack, instead of rotating the stack. |
| *dirsfile*=*file* | History file consulted by **dirs −S** and **dirs −L**. Default is ˜/.cshdirs. |
| *dirstack* | Directory stack, in array format. **dirstack[0]** is always equivalent to **cwd**. The other elements can be artificially changed. |
| *dspmbyte*=*code* | Enable use of multibyte code; for use with Kanji. See the **tcsh** manpage for details. |
| *dunique* | Make sure that each directory exists only once in the stack. |
| **echo** | Redisplay each command line before execution; same as **csh −x** command. |
| *echo_style*={**bsd**|**sysv**|**both**|**none**} | Don't echo a newline with −**n** option (**bsd**) | parse escaped characters (**sysv**) | do both | do neither. |
| *edit* | Enable command-line editor. |
| *ellipsis* | For use with **prompt** variable. Represent skipped directories with .... |

| Variable | Description |
|----------|-------------|
| *fignore=chars* | List of filename suffixes to ignore during file-name completion (see **filec**). |
| **filec** | If set, a filename that is partially typed on the command line can be expanded to its full name when Esc is pressed. If more than one filename would match, type EOF to list possible completions. Ignored in **tcsh**. |
| *gid* | User's group ID. |
| *group* | User's group name. |
| **histchars=ab** | A two-character string that sets the characters to use in history-substitution and quick-substitution (default is !^). |
| *histdup=*{**all**\|**prev**} | Maintain a record only of unique history events (**all**), or do not enter new event when it is the same as the previous one (**prev**). |
| *histfile=file* | History file consulted by **history –S** and **history –L**. Default is `˜/.history`. |
| *histlit* | Do not expand history lines when recalling them. |
| **history=**n *format* | The first word indicates the number of commands to save in the history list. The second indicates the format with which to display that list (**tcsh** only; see the prompt section for possible formats). |
| **home=**dir | Home directory of user, initialized from HOME. The ˜ character is shorthand for this value. |
| **ignoreeof** | Ignore an end-of-file (EOF) from terminals; prevents accidental logout. |
| *implicitcd* | If directory name is entered as a command, **cd** to that directory. Can be set to **verbose** to echo the **cd** to standard output. |
| *inputmode=*{**insert**\|**overwrite**} | Control editor's mode. |
| *listflags=flags* | One or more of the **x**, **a**, or **A** options for the **ls-F** built-in command. Second word can be set to path for **ls** command. |
| *listjobs=***long** | When a job is suspended, list all jobs (in long format, if specified). |
| *listlinks* | In **ls –F** command, include type of file to which links point. |
| *listmax=num* | Do not allow **list-choices** to print more than *num* choices before prompting. |
| *listmaxrows=num* | Do not allow **list-choices** to print more than *num* rows of choices before prompting. |
| *loginsh* | Set if shell is a login shell. |
| *logout* | Indicates status of an imminent logout (**normal**, **automatic**, or **hangup**). |

csh and tcsh

| Variable | Description |
|---|---|
| mail=(*n files*) | One or more files checked for new mail every 5 minutes or (if *n* is supplied) every *n* seconds. |
| *match-beep*={never\|nomatch\|ambiguous\|notunique} | Specifies circumstances under which completion should beep: never, if no match exists, if multiple matches exist, or if multiple matches exist and one is exact. |
| *nobeep* | Disable beeping. |
| noclobber | Don't redirect output to an existing file; prevents accidental destruction of files. |
| noglob | Turn off filename expansion; useful in shell scripts. |
| *nokanji* | Disable Kanji (if supported). |
| nonomatch | Treat filename metacharacters as literal characters, if no match exists (e.g., **vi ch**✳ creates new file **ch**✳ instead of printing "No match"). |
| *nostat=directory-list* | Do not stat *directory-list* during completion. |
| notify | Declare job completions when they occur. |
| *owd* | Old working directory. |
| path=(*dirs*) | List of pathnames in which to search for commands to execute. Initialized from PATH; the default is: . **/usr/ucb /usr/bin** |
| *printexitvalue* | Print all nonzero exit values. |
| prompt='*str*' | String that prompts for interactive input; default is %. See the section "Formatting for the Prompt Variable" later in this chapter for formatting information. |
| *prompt2*='*str*' | String that prompts for interactive input in **foreach** and **while** loops and continued lines (those with escaped newlines). See "Formatting for the Prompt Variable" for formatting information. |
| *prompt3*='*str*' | String that prompts for interactive input in automatic spelling correction. See "Formatting for the Prompt Variable" for formatting information. |
| *promptchars=cc* | Use the two characters specified as *cc* with the %# **prompt** sequence to indicate normal users and the superuser, respectively. |
| *pushdsilent* | Do not print directory stack when **pushd** and **popd** are invoked. |
| *pushdtohome* | Change to home directory when **pushd** is invoked without arguments. |
| *recexact* | Consider completion to be concluded on first exact match. |
| *recognize_only_executables* | When command completion is invoked, print only executable files. |
| *rmstar* | Prompt before executing the command **rm** ✳. |

| Variable | Description |
|---|---|
| *rprompt=string* | The string to print on the right side of the screen while the prompt is displayed on the left. Specify as for **prompt**. |
| *savedirs* | Execute **dirs -S** before exiting. |
| **savehist=***max* [merge] | Execute **history -S** before exiting. Save no more than *max* lines of history. If specified, merge those lines with previous history saves, and sort by time. |
| *sched=string* | Format for **sched**'s printing of events. See "Formatting for the Prompt Variable" for formatting information. |
| **shell=***file* | Pathname of the shell program currently in use; default is */bin/csh*. |
| *shlvl* | Number of nested shells. |
| **status=***n* | Exit status of last command. Built-in commands return 0 (success) or 1 (failure). |
| *symlinks*= {chase\|ignore\|expand} | Specify manner in which to deal with symbolic links. Expand them to real directory name in *cwd* (**chase**), treat them as real directories (**ignore**), or expand arguments that resemble pathnames (**expand**). |
| *tcsh* | Version of **tcsh**. |
| **term** | Terminal type. |
| **time=**'*n* %*c*' | If command execution takes more than *n* CPU seconds, report user time, system time, elapsed time, and CPU percentage. Supply optional %*c* flags to show other data. |
| *tperiod* | Number of minutes between executions of **periodic** alias. |
| *tty* | Name of tty, if applicable. |
| *uid* | User ID. |
| **user** | Username. |
| **verbose** | Display a command after history substitution; same as the command **csh -v**. |
| *version* | Shell's version and additional information, including options set at compile time. |
| *visiblebell* | Flash screen instead of beeping. |
| *watch*=( [*n*] *user terminal* . . . ) | Watch for *user* logging in at *terminal*, where *terminal* can be a tty name or **any**. Check every *n* minutes or 10 by default. |
| *who=string* | Specify information to be printed by **watch**. |
| *wordchars=chars* | List of all nonalphanumeric characters that may be part of a word. Default is *?_-.[]~=. |

## Formatting for the Prompt Variable

tcsh provides a list of substitutions that can be used in formatting the prompt. (csh allows only plain-string prompts and the ! history substitution shown in the following list.) The list of available substitutions includes:

%% Literal %

%/ The present working directory

%~ The present working directory, in ~ notation

%# # for the superuser, > for others

%? Previous command's exit status

%b End boldfacing

%c[[0]n], %.[[0]n]
    The last *n* (default 1) components of the present working directory; if 0 is specified, replace removed components with **/&lt;skipped&gt;**

%d Day of the week (e.g., Mon, Tue)

%h, %!, !
    Number of current history event

%l Current tty

%m
    First component of hostname

%n Username

%p Current time, with seconds (12-hour mode)

%s End standout mode (reverse video)

%t, %@
    Current time (12-hour format)

%u End underlining

%w Month (e.g., Jan, Feb)

%y Year (e.g., 99, 00)

%B Begin boldfacing

%C Similar to %c, but uses full pathnames instead of ~ notation

%D Day of month (e.g., 09, 10)

%M Fully qualified hostname

%P Current time, with seconds (24-hour format)

%S  Begin standout mode (reverse video)

%T  Current time (24-hour format)

%U  Begin underlining

%W

　　Month (e.g., 09, 10)

%Y  Year (e.g., 1999, 2000)

## Sample .cshrc File

```
# PREDEFINED VARIABLES

set path=(~ ~/bin /usr/ucb /bin /usr/bin . )
set mail=(/usr/mail/tom)

if ($?prompt) then              # settings for interactive use
  set echo
  set noclobber ignoreeof

  set cdpath=(/usr/lib /usr/spool/uucp)
# Now I can type cd macros
# instead of cd /usr/lib/macros

  set history=100
  set prompt='tom \!% '         # includes history number
  set time=3

# MY VARIABLES

  set man1="/usr/man/man1"      # lets me do   cd $man1, ls $man1
  set a="[a-z]*"                # lets me do   vi $a
  set A="[A-Z]*"                # or           grep string $A

# ALIASES

  alias c "clear; dirs"         # use quotes to protect ; or |
  alias h "history|more"
  alias j jobs -l
  alias ls ls -sFC              # redefine ls command
  alias del 'mv \!* ~/tmp_dir'  # a safe alternative to rm
endif
```

## Environment Variables

The C shell maintains a set of *environment variables*, which are distinct from shell variables and aren't really part of the C shell. Shell variables are meaningful only within the current shell, but environment variables are exported automatically, making them available globally. For example, C-shell variables are accessible only to a particular script in which they're defined, whereas environment variables can be used by any shell scripts, mail utilities, or editors you might invoke.

Environment variables are assigned as follows:

```
setenv VAR value
```

By convention, environment variable names are all uppercase. You can create your own environment variables, or you can use the predefined environment variables that follow.

The following environment variables have corresponding C-shell variables. When either one changes, the value is copied to the other (italics means the variable is specific to **tcsh**):

*GROUP*

> User's group name; same as **group**.

**HOME**

> Home directory; same as **home**.

**PATH**

> Search path for commands; same as **path**.

*SHLVL*

> Number of nested shell levels; same as **shlvl**.

**TERM**

> Terminal type; same as **term**.

**USER**

> User's login name; same as **user**.

Other environment variables, which do not have corresponding shell variables, include the following (italics means the variable is specific to **tcsh**):

**COLUMNS**

> Number of columns on terminal.

**DISPLAY**

> Identifies user's display for the X Window System. If set, the shell doesn't set **autologout**.

**EDITOR**

> Pathname to default editor. See also **VISUAL**.

*HOST*

> Name of machine.

*HOSTTYPE*

> Type of machine. Obsolete; will be removed eventually.

*HPATH*

> Colon-separated list of directories to search for documentation.

**LANG**

> Preferred language. Used for native language support.

**LC_CTYPE**

The locale, as it affects character handling. Used for native language support.

**LINES**

Number of lines on the screen.

**LOGNAME**

Another name for the USER variable.

*MACHTYPE*

Type of machine.

**MAIL**

The file that holds mail. Used by mail programs. This is not the same as the C-shell **mail** variable, which only checks for new mail.

*NOREBIND*

Printable characters not rebound. Used for native language support.

*OSTYPE*

Operating system.

**PWD**

The current directory; the value is copied from **cwd**.

*REMOTEHOST*

Machine name of remote host.

**SHELL**

Undefined by default; once initialized to **shell**, the two are identical.

**TERMCAP**

The file that holds the cursor-positioning codes for your terminal type. Default is */etc/termcap*.

**VENDOR**

The system vendor.

**VISUAL**

Pathname to default full-screen editor. See also **EDITOR**.

# *Expressions*

Expressions are used in @, **if**, and **while** statements to perform arithmetic, string comparisons, file testing, and so on. **exit** and **set** also specify expressions, as can the **tcsh** built-in command **filetest**. Expressions are formed by combining variables and constants with operators that resemble those in the C programming language. Operator precedence is the same as in C but can be remembered as follows:

1. * / %

2. + -

Group all other expressions inside parentheses. Parentheses are required if the expression contains <, >, &, or | .

## Operators

Operators can be one of the following types:

### Assignment operators

| Operator | Description |
|---|---|
| = | Assign value. |
| += -= | Reassign after addition/subtraction. |
| *= /= %= | Reassign after multiplication/division/remainder. |
| &= ^= \|= | Reassign after bitwise AND/XOR/OR. |
| ++ | Increment. |
| -- | Decrement. |

### Arithmetic operators

| Operator | Description |
|---|---|
| * / % | Multiplication; integer division; modulus (remainder) |
| + - | Addition; subtraction |

### Bitwise and logical operators

| Operator | Description |
|---|---|
| ~ | Binary inversion (one's complement). |
| ! | Logical negation. |
| << >> | Bitwise left shift; bitwise right shift. |
| & | Bitwise AND. |
| ^ | Bitwise exclusive OR. |
| \| | Bitwise OR. |
| && | Logical AND. |
| \|\| | Logical OR. |
| { command } | Return 1 if command is successful, 0 otherwise. Note that this is the opposite of *command*'s normal return code. The **$status** variable may be more practical. |

### Comparison operators

| Operator | Description |
|---|---|
| == != | Equality; inequality |
| <= >= | Less than or equal to; greater than or equal to |
| < > | Less than; greater than |

## File inquiry operators

Command substitution and filename expansion are performed on *file* before the test is performed. **tcsh** permits operators to be combined (e.g., **–ef**). The following is a list of the valid file inquiry operators:

| Operator | Description |
|---|---|
| -d *file* | The file is a directory. |
| -e *file* | The file exists. |
| -f *file* | The file is a plain file. |
| -o *file* | The user owns the file. |
| -r *file* | The user has read permission. |
| -w *file* | The user has write permission. |
| -x *file* | The user has execute permission. |
| -z *file* | The file has 0 size. |
| ! | Reverse the sense of any preceding inquiry. |

Some additional operators specific to **tcsh** are:

| Operator | Description |
|---|---|
| -b *file* | The file is a block special file. |
| -c *file* | The file is a character special file. |
| -g *file* | The file's set-group-ID bit is set. |
| -k *file* | The file's sticky bit is set. |
| -l *file* | The file is a symbolic link. |
| -L *file* | Apply any remaining operators to symbolic link, not the file it points to. |
| -p *file* | The file is a named pipe (FIFO). |
| -s *file* | The file has nonzero size. |
| -S *file* | The file is a socket special file. |
| -t *file* | *file* is a digit and is an open file descriptor for a terminal device. |
| -u *file* | The file's set-user-ID bit is set. |
| -X *file* | The file is executable and is in the path or is a shell built-in. |

Finally, **tcsh** provides the following operators, which return other kinds of information:

| Operator | Description |
|---|---|
| -A[:] *file* | Last time file was accessed, as the number of seconds since the Epoch. With a colon (:), the result is in timestamp format. |
| -C[:] *file* | Last time inode was modified. With a colon (:), the result is in timestamp format. |
| -D *file* | Device number. |
| -F *file* | Composite file identifier, in the form *device:inode*. |
| -G[:] *file* | Numeric group ID for the file. With a colon (:), the result is the group name if known; otherwise, the numeric group ID. |
| -I *file* | Inode number. |

| Operator | Description |
|---|---|
| -L *file* | The name of the file pointed to by symbolic link *file*. |
| -M[:] *file* | Last time file was modified. With a colon (:), the result is in timestamp format. |
| -N *file* | Number of hard links. |
| -P[:] *file* | Permissions in octal, without leading 0. With a colon (:), the result includes a leading 0. |
| -P*mode* [:] *file* | Equivalent to -P *file* ANDed to *mode*. With a colon (:), the result includes a leading 0. |
| -U[:] *file* | Numeric user ID of the file's owner. With a colon (:), the result is the username if known, otherwise the numeric user ID. |
| -Z *file* | The file's size, in bytes. |

## Examples

The following examples show @ commands and assume n = 4:

| Expression | Value of $x |
|---|---|
| @ x = ($n > 10 \|\| $n < 5) | 1 |
| @ x = ($n >= 0 && $n < 3) | 0 |
| @ x = ($n << 2) | 16 |
| @ x = ($n >> 2) | 1 |
| @ x = $n % 2 | 0 |
| @ x = $n % 3 | 1 |

The following examples show the first line of **if** or **while** statements:

| Expression | Meaning |
|---|---|
| while ($#argv != 0) | While there are arguments . . . |
| if ($today[1] == "Fri") | If the first word is "Fri". . . |
| if (-f $argv[1]) | If the first argument is a plain file. . . |
| if (! -d $tmpdir) | If tmpdir is not a directory. . . |

## Command History

Previously executed commands are stored in a history list. The C shell lets you access this list so you can verify commands, repeat them, or execute modified versions of them. The **history** built-in command displays the history list; the predefined variables **histchars** and **history** also affect the history mechanism. There are four ways to use the history list:

- Rerun a previous command

- Make command substitutions

- Make argument substitutions (replace specific words in a command)

- Extract or replace parts of a command or word

The following subsections describe the **csh** tools for editing and rerunning commands. If you are running **tcsh**, you can use any of these features. In addition, you can use the arrow keys to move around in the command line and then use the editing features described in the later section "Command-Line Editing with tcsh" to modify the command. The **tcsh** arrow keys are:

| Key | Description |
|---|---|
| Up arrow | Previous command. |
| Down arrow | Next command. |
| Left arrow | Move left in command line. |
| Right arrow | Move right in command line. |

## Command Substitution

| Command | Description |
|---|---|
| ! | Begin a history substitution. |
| !! | Previous command. |
| !*N* | Command number *N* in history list. |
| !*-N* | *N*th command back from current command. |
| !*string* | Most recent command that starts with *string*. |
| !?*string*? | Most recent command that contains *string*. |
| !?*string*?% | Most recent command argument that contains *string*. |
| !$ | Last argument of previous command. |
| !!*string* | Previous command, then append *string*. |
| !*N string* | Command *N*, then append *string*. |
| !{*s1*}*s2* | Most recent command starting with string *s1*, then append string *s2*. |
| ^*old*^*new*^ | Quick substitution; change string *old* to *new* in previous command; execute modified command. |

## Command Substitution Examples

The following command is assumed:

```
%3 vi cprogs/01.c ch002 ch03
```

| Event Number | Command Typed | Command Executed |
|---|---|---|
| 4 | ^00^0 | vi cprogs/01.c ch02 ch03 |
| 5 | nroff !* | nroff cprogs/01.c ch02 ch03 |
| 6 | nroff !$ | nroff ch03 |
| 7 | !vi | vi cprogs/01.c ch02 ch03 |
| 8 | !6 | nroff ch03 |

| Event Number | Command Typed | Command Executed |
|---|---|---|
| 9 | !?01 | vi cprogs/01.c ch02 ch03 |
| 10 | !{nr}.new | nroff ch03.new |
| 11 | !!\|lp | nroff ch03.new \| lp |
| 12 | more !?pr?% | more cprogs/01.c |

## Word Substitution

Colons may precede any word specifier.

| Specifier | Description |
|---|---|
| :0 | Command name |
| :n | Argument number *n* |
| ^ | First argument |
| $ | Last argument |
| :n-m | Arguments *n* through *m* |
| -m | Words 0 through *m* same as :0-*m* |
| :n- | Arguments *n* through next-to-last |
| :n* | Arguments *n* through last; same as *n*-$ |
| * | All arguments; same as ^-$ or 1-$ |
| # | Current command line up to this point; fairly useless |

## Word Substitution Examples

The following command is assumed:

```
%13 cat ch01 ch02 ch03 biblio back
```

| Event Number | Command Typed | Command Executed |
|---|---|---|
| 14 | ls !13^ | ls ch01 |
| 15 | sort !13:* | sort ch01 ch02 ch03 biblio back |
| 16 | lp !cat:3* | more ch03 biblio back |
| 17 | !cat:0-3 | cat ch01 ch02 ch03 |
| 18 | vi !-5:4 | vi biblio |

## History Modifiers

Command and word substitutions can be modified by one or more of the following modifiers:

## Printing, substitution, and quoting

| Modifier | Description |
|---|---|
| :p | Display command, but don't execute. |
| :s/*old*/*new* | Substitute string *new* for *old*, first instance only. |
| :gs/*old*/*new* | Substitute string *new* for *old*, all instances. |
| :& | Repeat previous substitution (:s or ^ command), first instance only. |
| :g& | Repeat previous substitution, all instances. |
| :q | Quote a wordlist. |
| :x | Quote separate words. |

## Truncation

| Modifier | Description |
|---|---|
| :r | Extract the first available pathname root (the portion before the last period). |
| :gr | Extract all pathname roots. |
| :e | Extract the first available pathname extension (the portion after the last period). |
| :ge | Extract all pathname extensions. |
| :h | Extract the first available pathname header (the portion before the last slash). |
| :gh | Extract all pathname headers. |
| :t | Extract the first available pathname tail (the portion after the last slash). |
| :gt | Extract all pathname tails. |
| :u | Make first lowercase letter uppercase (**tcsh** only). |
| :l | Make first uppercase letter lowercase (**tcsh** only). |
| :a | Apply modifier(s) following **a** as many times as possible to a word. If used with **g**, **a** is applied to all words (**tcsh** only). |

# History Modifier Examples

From the preceding, command number 17 is:

```
%17 cat ch01 ch02 ch03
```

| Event Number | Command Typed | Command Executed |
|---|---|---|
| 19 | !17:s/ch/CH/ | cat CH01 ch02 ch03 |
| 20 | !17g& | cat CH01 CH02 CH03 |
| 21 | !more:p | more cprogs/01.c *(displayed only)* |
| 22 | cd !$:h | cd cprogs |
| 23 | vi !mo:$:t | vi 01.c |
| 24 | grep stdio !$ | grep stdio 01.c |
| 25 | ^stdio^include stdio^:q | grep "include stdio" 01.c |

| Event Number | Command Typed | Command Executed |
|---|---|---|
| 26 | nroff !21:t:p | nroff 01.c *(is that what I wanted?)* |
| 27 | !! | nroff 01.c *(execute it)* |

### Special Aliases in tcsh

Certain special aliases can be set in **tcsh**. The aliases are initially undefined. Once set, they are executed when specific events occur. The following is a list of the special aliases:

**beepcmd**
> At beep.

**cwdcmd**
> When the current working directory changes.

**periodic**
> Every few minutes. The exact amount of time is set by the *tperiod* shell variable.

**precmd**
> Before printing a new prompt.

**shell** *shell*
> If a script does not specify a shell, interpret it with *shell*, which should be a full pathname.

# Command-Line Manipulation

**csh** and **tcsh** offer a certain amount of functionality in manipulating the command line. Both shells offer word or command completion, and **tcsh** allows you to edit a command line.

### Completion

Both **tcsh** and **csh** provide word completion. **tcsh** automatically completes words and commands when the Tab key is hit; **csh** does so only when the *filec* variable is set, after the Esc key is hit. If the completion is ambiguous (i.e., more than one file matches the provided string), the shell completes as much as possible and beeps to notify you that the completion is not finished. You may request a list of possible completions with Ctrl-D. **tcsh** also notifies you when a completion is finished by appending a space to complete filenames or commands and a / to complete directories.

Both **csh** and **tcsh** recognize ~ notation for home directories. The shells assume that words at the beginning of a line and subsequent to |, &, ;, | |, or && are commands and modify their search paths appropriately. Completion can be done midword; only the letters to the left of the prompt are checked for completion.

## Related Shell Variables

- autolist

- fignore

- listmax

- listmaxrows

## Related Command-Line Editor Commands

- complete-word-back

- complete-word-forward

- expand-glob

- list-glob

## Related Shell Built-ins

- complete

- uncomplete

## Command-Line Editing with tcsh

tcsh lets you move your cursor around in the command line, editing the line as you type. There are two main modes for editing the command line, based on the two most common text editors: Emacs and **vi**. Emacs mode is the default; you can switch between the modes with:

```
bindkey -e      Select Emacs bindings
bindkey -v      Select vi bindings
```

The main difference between the Emacs and **vi** bindings is that the Emacs bindings are modeless (i.e., they always work). With the **vi** bindings, you must switch between insert and command modes; different commands are useful in each mode. Additionally:

- Emacs mode is simpler; **vi** mode allows finer control.

- Emacs mode allows you to yank cut text and set a mark; **vi** mode does not.

- The command-history-searching capabilities differ.

### Emacs mode

Tables 8-1 through 8-3 describe the various editing keystrokes available in Emacs mode.

*Table 8–1. Cursor Positioning Commands (Emacs Mode)*

| Command | Description |
|---------|-------------|
| Ctrl-B | Move cursor back (left) one character. |
| Ctrl-F | Move cursor forward (right) one character. |
| Esc b | Move cursor back one word. |
| Esc f | Move cursor forward one word. |
| Ctrl-A | Move cursor to beginning of line. |
| Ctrl-E | Move cursor to end of line. |

*Table 8–2. Text Deletion Commands (Emacs Mode)*

| Command | Description |
|---------|-------------|
| Del or Ctrl-H | Delete character to left of cursor. |
| Ctrl-D | Delete character under cursor. |
| Esc d | Delete word. |
| Esc Del or Esc Ctrl-H | Delete word backward. |
| Ctrl-K | Delete from cursor to end-of-line. |
| Ctrl-U | Delete entire line. |

*Table 8–3. Command Control (Emacs Mode)*

| Command | Description |
|---------|-------------|
| Ctrl-P | Previous command. |
| Ctrl-N | Next command. |
| Up arrow | Previous command. |
| Down arrow | Next command. |
| *cmd-fragment* Esc p | Search history for *cmd-fragment*, which must be the beginning of a command. |
| *cmd-fragment* Esc n | Like Esc p, but search forward. |
| Esc *num* | Repeat next command *num* times. |
| Ctrl-Y | Yank previously deleted string. |

## *vi mode*

vi mode has two submodes, insert mode and command mode. The default mode is insert. You can toggle modes by pressing Esc; alternatively, in command mode, typing **a** (append) or **i** (insert) will return you to insert mode.

Tables 8-4 through 8-10 describe the editing keystrokes available in vi mode.

*Table 8–4. Commands Available (vi's Insert and Command Mode)*

| Command | Description |
|---------|-------------|
| Ctrl-P | Previous command |
| Ctrl-N | Next command |
| Up arrow | Previous command |
| Down arrow | Next command |
| Esc | Toggle mode |

*Table 8–5. Editing Commands (vi Insert Mode)*

| Command | Description |
|---------|-------------|
| Ctrl-B | Move cursor back (left) one character. |
| Ctrl-F | Move cursor forward (right) one character. |
| Ctrl-A | Move cursor to beginning of line. |
| Ctrl-E | Move cursor to end-of-line. |
| DEL or Ctrl-H | Delete character to left of cursor. |
| Ctrl-W | Delete word backward. |
| Ctrl-U | Delete from beginning of line to cursor. |
| Ctrl-K | Delete from cursor to end-of-line. |

*Table 8–6. Cursor Positioning Commands (vi Command Mode)*

| Command | Description |
|---------|-------------|
| h or Ctrl-H | Move cursor back (left) one character. |
| l or SPACE | Move cursor forward (right) one character. |
| w | Move cursor forward (right) one word. |
| b | Move cursor back (left) one word. |
| e | Move cursor to next word ending. |
| W, B, E | Like **w**, **b**, and **e**, but treat just whitespace as word separator instead of any non-alphanumeric character. |
| ^ or Ctrl-A | Move cursor to beginning of line (first nonwhitespace character). |
| 0 | Move cursor to beginning of line. |
| $ or Ctrl-E | Move cursor to end-of-line. |

csh and
tcsh

*Table 8–7. Text Insertion Commands (vi Command Mode)*

| Command | Description |
|---|---|
| a | Append new text after cursor until **Esc**. |
| i | Insert new text before cursor until **Esc**. |
| A | Append new text after end of line until **Esc**. |
| I | Insert new text before beginning of line until **Esc**. |

*Table 8–8. Text Deletion Commands (vi Command Mode)*

| Command | Description |
|---|---|
| x | Delete character under cursor. |
| X or **Del** | Delete character to left of cursor. |
| d*m* | Delete from cursor to end of motion command *m*. |
| D | Same as **d$**. |
| **Ctrl-W** | Delete word backward. |
| **Ctrl-U** | Delete from beginning of line to cursor. |
| **Ctrl-K** | Delete from cursor to end of line. |

*Table 8–9. Text Replacement Commands (vi Command Mode)*

| Command | Description |
|---|---|
| c*m* | Change characters from cursor to end of motion command *m* until **Esc**. |
| C | Same as **c$**. |
| r*c* | Replace character under cursor with character *c*. |
| R | Replace multiple characters until **Esc**. |
| s | Substitute character under cursor with characters typed until **Esc**. |

*Table 8–10. Character-Seeking Motion Commands (vi Command Mode)*

| Command | Description |
|---|---|
| f*c* | Move cursor to next instance of *c* in line. |
| F*c* | Move cursor to previous instance of *c* in line. |
| t*c* | Move cursor just before next instance of *c* in line. |
| T*c* | Move cursor just after previous instance of *c* in line. |
| ; | Repeat previous **f** or **F** command. |
| , | Repeat previous **f** or **F** command in opposite direction. |

## Job Control

Job control lets you place foreground jobs in the background, bring background jobs to the foreground, or suspend (temporarily stop) running jobs. The C shell provides the following commands for job control. For more information on these commands, see the next section, "Built-in csh and tcsh Commands."

**bg**   Put a job in the background.

**fg**   Put a job in the foreground.

**jobs**
>   List active jobs.

**kill**   Terminate a job.

**notify**
>   Notify when a background job finishes.

**stop**
>   Suspend a background job.

**Ctrl-Z**
>   Suspend the foreground job.

Many job control commands take *jobID* as an argument. This argument can be specified as follows:

*%n*   Job number *n*.

*%s*   Job whose command line starts with string *s*.

*%?s*   Job whose command line contains string *s*.

*%%*   Current job.

*%*    Current job (same as preceding).

*%+*   Current job (same as preceding).

*%-*   Previous job.

## Built-in csh and tcsh Commands

---

**@** [*variable*[*n*]=*expression*]                                    **@**

Assign the value of the arithmetic *expression* to *variable* or to the *n*th element of *variable* if the index *n* is specified. With no *variable* or *expression* specified, print the values of all shell variables (same as **set**). Expression operators as well as examples are listed under "Expressions," earlier in this chapter. Two special forms also are valid:

→

---

| | |
|---|---|
| @ <br> ← | @ *variable*++    Increment *variable* by 1. <br><br> @ *variable*−−    Decrement *variable* by 1. |

---

**#**

#

Ignore all text that follows on the same line. # is used in shell scripts as the comment character and is not really a command.

---

**#!**

#!*shell*

Used as the first line of a script to invoke the named *shell* (with optional arguments). Not supported in all shells. For example:

```
#!/bin/csh -f
```

---

**:**

:

Null command. Returns an exit status of 0. The colon command often is put as the first character of a Bourne- or Korn-shell script to act as a place-holder to keep a # (hash) from accidentally becoming the first character.

---

**alias**

alias [*name* [*command*]]

Assign *name* as the shorthand name, or alias, for *command*. If *command* is omitted, print the alias for *name*; if *name* also is omitted, print all aliases. Aliases can be defined on the command line, but more often they are stored in *.cshrc* so that they take effect upon logging in. (See the sample *.cshrc* file earlier in this chapter.) Alias definitions can reference command-line arguments, much like the history list. Use \!* to refer to all command-line arguments, \!^ for the first argument, \!\!:2 for the second, \!$ for the last, and so on. An alias *name* can be any valid Unix command; however, you lose the original command's meaning unless you type \*name*. See also **unalias** and the "Special Aliases in tcsh" section.

*Examples*

Set the size for **xterm** windows under the X Window System:

```
alias R 'set noglob; eval `resize` unset noglob'
```

Show aliases that contain the string **ls**:

```
alias | grep ls
```

Run **nroff** on all command-line arguments:

```
alias ms 'nroff -ms \!*'
```

Copy the file that is named as the first argument:

```
alias back 'cp \!^ \!^.old'
```

Use the regular **ls**, not its alias:

```
% \ls
```

alias

---

**alloc**

Print totals of used and free memory.

alloc

---

**bg** [*jobIDs*]

Put the current job or the *jobIDs* in the background.

### Example

To place a time-consuming process in the background, you might begin with:

```
4% nroff -ms report Ctrl-Z
```

and then issue any one of the following:

```
5% bg
5% bg %        Current job
5% bg %1       Job number 1
5% bg %nr      Match initial string nroff
5% % &
```

bg

---

**bindkey** [*options*] [*key*] [*command*]

**tcsh** only. Display all key bindings, or bind a key to a command.

### Options

−a  List standard and alternate key bindings.

−b *key*
   Expect *key* to be one of the following: a control character (in hat notation—e.g., ^B—or C notation—e.g., C−B); a metacharacter (e.g., M−B); a function key (e.g., F−*string*); or an extended prefix key (e.g., X−B).

−c *command*
   Interpret *command* as a shell, not editor, command.

bindkey

csh and<br>tcsh

→

| | |
|---|---|
| bindkey<br>← | **−d** *key*<br>Bind key to its original binding.<br><br>**−e** Bind to standard Emacs bindings.<br><br>**−k** *key*<br>Expect *key* to refer to an arrow (**left**, **right**, **up**, or **down**).<br><br>**−l** List and describe all editor commands.<br><br>**−r** *key*<br>Completely unbind *key*.<br><br>**−s** Interpret *command* as a literal string and treat as terminal input.<br><br>**−u** Print usage message.<br><br>**−v** Bind to standard **vi** bindings. |
| break | **break**<br><br>Resume execution following the **end** command of the nearest enclosing **while** or **foreach**. |
| breaksw | **breaksw**<br><br>Break from a **switch**; continue execution after the **endsw**. |
| built-ins | **built-ins**<br><br>tcsh only. Print all built-in shell commands. |
| bye | **bye**<br><br>tcsh only. Same as **logout**. |
| case | **case** *pattern* :<br><br>Identify a *pattern* in a **switch**. |
| cd | **cd** [*dir*]<br><br>Change working directory to *dir*. Default is user's home directory. If *dir* is a relative pathname but is not in the current directory, the **cdpath** variable is searched. See the sample *.cshrc* file earlier in this chapter. tcsh includes some options for **cd**: |

*tcsh options*

    –    Change to previous directory.

    –l  Explicitly expand ˜ notation.

    –n  Wrap entries before end-of-line; implies **–p**.

    -p  Print directory stack.

    –v  Print entries one per line; implies **–p**.

**chdir** [*dir*]

Same as **cd**. Useful if you are redefining **cd**.

**complete** [*string* [*word/pattern/list*[*:select*]/[*suffix*]]]

tcsh only. List all completions, or, if specified, all completions for *string* (which may be a pattern). Further options can be/p specified.

*Options for word*

c    Complete current word only and without referring to *pattern*.

C    Complete current word only, referring to *pattern*.

n    Complete previous word.

N    Complete word before previous word.

p    Expect *pattern* to be a range of numbers. Perform completion within that range.

*Options for list*

Various *list*s of strings can be searched for possible completions. Some *list* options include:

(*string*)
    Members of the list *string*

$*variable*
    Words from *variable*

`command`
    Output from *command*

a    Aliases

cd

chdir

complete

csh and tcsh

→

| complete ← | b | Bindings |
|---|---|---|
| | c | Commands |
| | C | External (not built-in) commands |
| | d | Directories |
| | D | Directories whose names begin with *string* |
| | e | Environment variables |
| | f | Filenames |
| | F | Filenames that begin with *string* |
| | g | Groups |
| | j | Jobs |
| | l | Limits |
| | n | Nothing |
| | s | Shell variables |
| | S | Signals |
| | t | Text files |
| | T | Text files whose names begin with *string* |
| | u | Users |
| | v | Any variables |
| | x | Like **n** but prints *select* as an explanation with the editor command **list-choices** |
| | X | Completions |

*select*

*select* should be a glob pattern. Completions are limited to words that match this pattern. *suffix* is appended to all completions.

---

| continue | **continue** |
|---|---|
| | Resume execution of nearest enclosing **while** or **foreach**. |

---

| default | **default :** |
|---|---|
| | Label the default case (typically last) in a **switch**. |

**dirs** [*options*]

Print the directory stack, showing the current directory first. See also **popd** and **pushd**. All options except −l, −n, and −v are **tcsh** extensions.

*Options*

−c  Clear the directory stack.

−l  Expand the home directory symbol (˜) to the actual directory name.

−n  Wrap output.

−v  Print one directory per line.

−L *file*
   Re-create stack from *file*, which should have been created by **dirs** −S *file*.

−S *file*
   Print to *file* a series of **pushd** and **popd** commands, that can be invoked to replicate the stack.

dirs

---

**echo** [−n] *string*

Write *string* to standard output; if −n is specified, the output is not terminated by a newline. Unlike the Unix version (*/bin/echo*) and the Bourne-shell version, the C shell's **echo** doesn't support escape characters. See also **echo** in Chapter 3, and Chapter 7, *bash: The Bourne-Again Shell*.

echo

---

**echotc** [*options*] *arguments*

**tcsh** only. Display terminal capabilities, or move cursor on screen, depending on the argument.

*Options*

−s  Return empty string, not error, if capability doesn't exist.

−v  Display verbose messages.

*Arguments*

**baud**
   Display current baud.

echotc

**csh and tcsh**

→

| | |
|---|---|
| echotc<br>← | cols<br>    Display current column.<br><br>cm *column row*<br>    Move cursor to specified coordinates.<br><br>home<br>    Move cursor to home position.<br><br>lines<br>    Print number of lines per screen.<br><br>meta<br>    Does this terminal have meta capacity (usually the Alt key)?<br><br>tabs<br>    Does this terminal have tab capacity? |
| else | else<br><br>Reserved word for interior of **if** ... **endif** statement. |
| end | end<br><br>Reserved word that ends a **foreach** or **switch** statement. |
| endif | endif<br><br>Reserved word that ends an **if** statement. |
| endsw | endsw<br><br>Reserved word that ends a **switch** statement. |
| eval | eval *args*<br><br>Typically, **eval** is used in shell scripts, and *args* is a line of code that may contain shell variables. **eval** forces variable expansion to happen first and then runs the resulting command. This "double scanning" is useful any time shell variables contain input/output redirection symbols, aliases, or other shell variables. (For example, redirection normally happens before variable expansion, so a variable containing redirection symbols must be expanded first using **eval**; otherwise, the redirection symbols remain uninterpreted.) |

*Examples*

The following line can be placed in the .**login** file to set up terminal characteristics:

```
set noglob eval `tset -s xterm` unset noglob
```

The following commands show the effect of **eval**:

```
% set b='$a'
% set a=hello
% echo $b        Read the command line once
$a
% eval echo $b   Read the command line twice
hello
```

Another example of **eval** can be found under **alias**.

---

**exec** *command*

Execute *command* in place of current shell. This terminates the current shell, rather than create a new process under it.

---

**exit** [(*expr*)]

Exit a shell script with the status given by *expr*. A status of zero means success; nonzero means failure. If *expr* is not specified, the exit value is that of the **status** variable. **exit** can be issued at the command line to close a window (log out).

---

**fg** [*jobIDs*]

Bring the current job or the *jobIDs* to the foreground. *jobID* can be %*job-number*.

Example

If you suspend a **vi** editing session (by pressing **Ctrl-Z**), you might resume **vi** using any of these commands:

```
% %
% fg
% fg %
% fg %vi      Match initial string
```

*csh and tcsh*

| | |
|---|---|
| **filetest** | **filetest** *-op files* |
| | tcsh only. Apply *op* file-test operator to *files*. Print results in a list. See the earlier section "File inquiry operators" for the list of file-test operators. |
| **foreach** | **foreach** *name* (*wordlist*)<br>    *commands*<br>**end** |
| | Assign variable *name* to each value in *wordlist* and execute *commands* between **foreach** and **end**. You can use **foreach** as a multi-line command issued at the C-shell prompt (first of the following examples), or you can use it in a shell script (second example). |
| | *Examples* |
| | Rename all files that begin with a capital letter: |
| | ```
% foreach i ([A-Z]*)
? mv $i $i.new
? end
``` |
| | Check whether each command-line argument is an option or not: |
| | ```
foreach arg ($argv)
   # does it begin with - ?
   if ("$arg" =~ -*) then
      echo "Argument is an option"
   else
      echo "Argument is a filename"
   endif
end
``` |
| **glob** | **glob** *wordlist* |
| | Do filename, variable, and history substitutions on *wordlist*. No \ escapes are recognized in its expansion, and words are delimited by null characters. **glob** typically is used in shell scripts to hard-code a value so that it remains the same for the rest of the script. |
| **goto** | **goto** *string* |
| | Skip to a line whose first nonblank character is *string* followed by a colon and continue execution below that line. On the **goto** line, *string* can be a variable or filename pattern, but the label branched to must be a literal, expanded value and must not occur within a **foreach** or **while**. |

**hashstat**

Display statistics that show the hash table's level of success at locating commands via the **path** variable.

**history** [*options*]

Display the list of history events. (History syntax is discussed earlier, in "Command History.")

*Options*

−c  **tcsh** only. Clear history list.

−h  Print history list without event numbers.

−r  Print in reverse order; show oldest commands last.

*n*  Display only the last *n* history commands, instead of the number set by the **history** shell variable.

−L *file*

    **tcsh** only. Load series of **pushd** and **popd** commands from *file* in order to re-create a saved stack.

−M *file*

    **tcsh** only. Merge the current directory stack and the stack saved in *file*. Save both, sorted by time, in *file*, as a series of **pushd** and **popd** commands.

−S *file*

    **tcsh** only. Print to *file* a series of **pushd** and **popd** commands that can be invoked to replicate the stack.

*Example*

To save and execute the last five commands:

```
history -h 5 > do_it
source do_it
```

**hup** [*command*]

**tcsh** only. Start *command* but make it exit when sent a hangup signal, which is sent when shell exits. By default, configure shell script to exit on hangup signal.

| | |
|---|---|
| **if** | **if**

Begin a conditional statement. The simple format is:

```
if (expr) cmd
```

There are three other possible formats, shown side-by-side:

```
if (expr) then    if (expr) then    if (expr) then
   cmds               cmds1             cmds1
endif               else            else if (expr) then
                       cmds2             cmds2
                    endif           else
                                       cmds3
                                    endif
```

In the simplest form, execute *cmd* if *expr* is true; otherwise do nothing (redirection still occurs; this is a bug). In the other forms, execute one or more commands. If *expr* is true, continue with the commands after **then**; if *expr* is false, branch to the commands after **else** (or branch to after the **else if** and continue checking). For more examples, see "Expressions" earlier in this chapter, **shift**, or **while**.

*Example*

Take a default action if no command-line arguments are given:

```
if ($#argv == 0) then
    echo "No filename given. Sending to Report."
    set outfile = Report
else
    set outfile = $argv[1]
endif
```

|
| **jobs** | **jobs** [−l]

List all running or stopped jobs; −l includes process IDs. For example, you can check whether a long compilation or text format is still running. Also useful before logging out.

|
| **kill** | **kill** [*options*] *ID*

Terminate each specified process *ID* or job *ID*. You must own the process or be a privileged user. This built-in is similar to */bin/kill* described in Chapter 3 but also allows symbolic job names. Stubborn processes can be killed using signal 9.

|

*Options*

−l    List the signal names. (Used by itself.)

−*signal*

>The signal number or name, without the SIG prefix (e.g., HUP, not SIGHUP). The command **kill −l** prints a list of the available signal names. The list varies by system architecture; for a PC-based system, it looks like this:

```
% kill -l
HUP INT QUIT ILL TRAP ABRT BUS FPE KILL USR1 SEGV USR2
PIPE ALRM TERM STKFLT CHLD CONT STOP TSTP TTIN TTOU URG
XCPU XFSZ VTALRM PROF WINCH POLL PWR UNUSED
```

>The signals and their numbers are defined in */usr/include/ asm/signal.h*; look in that file to find the signals that apply to your system.

*Examples*

If you've issued the following command:

```
44% nroff -ms report &
```

you can terminate it in any of the following ways:

```
45% kill 19536      Process ID
45% kill %          Current job
45% kill %1         Job number 1
45% kill %nr        Initial string
45% kill %?report   Matching string
```

---

limit [−h] [*resource* [*limit*]]

Display limits or set a *limit* on resources used by the current process and by each process it creates. If no *limit* is given, the current limit is printed for *resource*. If *resource* also is omitted, all limits are printed. By default, the current limits are shown or set; with −h, hard limits are used. A hard limit imposes an absolute limit that can't be exceeded. Only a privileged user may raise it. See also **unlimit**.

*Option*

−h    Use hard, not current, limits.

*Resource*

cputime

>Maximum number of seconds the CPU can spend; can be abbreviated as **cpu**.

csh and tcsh

→

| | |
|---|---|
| limit<br>← | **filesize**<br>    Maximum size of any one file.<br><br>**datasize**<br>    Maximum size of data (including stack).<br><br>**stacksize**<br>    Maximum size of stack.<br><br>**coredumpsize**<br>    Maximum size of a core dump file.<br><br>*Limit*<br><br>A number followed by an optional character (a unit specifier).<br><br>For **cputime**:　　*n***h** (for *n* hours)<br>　　　　　　　　*n***m** (for *n* minutes)<br>　　　　　　　　*mm:ss* (minutes and seconds)<br>For others:　　　*n***k** (for *n* kilobytes, the default)<br>　　　　　　　　*n***m** (for *n* megabytes) |
| log | **log**<br><br>**tcsh** only. Consult the **watch** variable for list of users being watched. Print list of those who are presently logged in. If - is entered as an option, reset environment as if user had logged in with new group. |
| login | **login** [*user* \| **−p**]<br><br>Replace *user*'s login shell with */bin/login*. **−p** is used to preserve environment variables. |
| logout | **logout**<br><br>Terminate the login shell. |
| ls−F | **ls−F** [*options*] [*files*]<br><br>**tcsh** only. Faster alternative to **ls −F**. If given any options, invokes **ls**. |
| newgrp | **newgrp** [-] [*group*]<br><br>**tcsh** only. Change user's group ID to specified group ID, or, if none is specified, to original group ID. If - is entered as an |

| | |
|---|---|
| option, reset environment as if user had logged in with new group. Must have been compiled into the shell; see the **version** variable. | newgrp |

**nice** [+*n*] *command*                                                         nice

Change the execution priority for *command*, or, if none is given, change priority for the current shell. (See also **nice** in Chapter 3.) The priority range is −20 to 20, with a default of 4. The range seems backward: −20 gives the highest priority (fastest execution); 20 gives the lowest. Only a privileged user may specify a negative number.

+*n*   Add *n* to the priority value (lower job priority).

−*n*   Subtract *n* from the priority value (raise job priority). Privileged users only.

**nohup** [*command*]                                                         nohup

"No hangup signals." Do not terminate *command* after terminal line is closed (i.e., when you hang up from a phone or log out). Use without *command* in shell scripts to keep script from being terminated. (See also **nohup** in Chapter 3.)

**notify** [*jobID*]                                                         notify

Report immediately when a background job finishes (instead of waiting for you to exit a long editing session, for example). If no *jobID* is given, the current background job is assumed.

**onintr** *label*                                                         onintr
**onintr** −
**onintr**

"On interrupt." Used in shell scripts to handle interrupt signals (similar to **bash**'s **trap 2** and **trap "" 2** commands). The first form is like a **goto** *label*. The script will branch to *label*: if it catches an interrupt signal (e.g., **Ctrl-C**). The second form lets the script ignore interrupts. This is useful at the beginning of a script or before any code segment that needs to run unhindered (e.g., when moving files). The third form restores interrupt handling that was previously disabled with **onintr** −.

**csh and tcsh**

→

| | |
|---|---|
| onintr<br>← | *Example*<br><br>`onintr cleanup`  *Go to "cleanup" on interrupt*<br>   .<br>   .              *Shell* script commands<br>   .<br><br>`cleanup:`        *Label for interrupts*<br>  `onintr -`     *Ignore additional interrupts*<br>  `rm -f $tmpfiles` *Remove any files created*<br>  `exit 2`       *Exit with an error status* |
| popd | **popd** [*options*]<br><br>Remove the current entry from the directory stack, or remove the *n*th entry from the stack and print the stack that remains. The current entry has number 0 and appears on the left. See also **dirs** and **pushd**.<br><br>*Options*<br><br>+*n*  Specify *n*th entry.<br><br>−l  Expand ~ notation.<br><br>−n  Wrap long lines.<br><br>−p  Override the **pushdsilent** shell variable, which otherwise prevents the printing of the final stack.<br><br>−v  Print precisely one directory per line. |
| printenv | **printenv** [*variable*]<br><br>Print all (or one specified) environment variables and their values. |
| pushd | **pushd** *name*<br>**pushd** [*options*]<br>**pushd**<br><br>The first form changes the working directory to *name* and adds it to the directory stack. The second form rotates the *n*th entry to the beginning, making it the working directory. (Entry numbers begin at 0.) With no arguments, **pushd** switches the first two entries and changes to the new current directory. The +*n*, −l, −n, and −v options behave the same as in **popd**. See also **dirs** and **popd**. |

## Examples

```
% dirs
/home/bob /usr
% pushd /etc                Add /etc to directory stack
/etc /home/bob /usr
% pushd +2                  Switch to third directory
/usr /etc /home/bob
% pushd                     Switch top two directories
/etc /usr /home/bob
% popd                      Discard current entry; go to next
/usr /home/bob  ·
```

## rehash

Recompute the internal hash table for the PATH variable. Use **rehash** whenever a new command is created during the current session. This allows the PATH variable to locate and execute the command. (If the new command resides in a directory not listed in PATH, add this directory to PATH before rehashing.) See also **unhash**.

## repeat *n command*

Execute *n* instances of *command*.

### Examples

Print three copies of **memo**:

```
% repeat 3 pr memo | lp
```

Read 10 lines from the terminal and store in **item_list**:

```
% repeat 10 line > item_list
```

Append 50 boilerplate files to **report**:

```
% repeat 50 cat template >> report
```

## sched [*options*]
## sched *time command*

**tcsh** only. Without options, print all scheduled events. The second form schedules an event.

*time* should be specified in *hh:mm* form (e.g., 13:00).

$\rightarrow$

| | |
|---|---|
| sched<br>← | *Options*<br><br>+*hh:mm*<br>    Schedule event to take place *hh:mm* from now.<br><br>−*n*  Remove *n*th item from schedule. |

| | |
|---|---|
| set | set *variable*=*value*<br>set [*option*] *variable*[*n*]=*value*<br>set<br><br>Set *variable* to *value*, or if multiple values are specified, set the variable to the list of words in the value list. If an index *n* is specified, set the *n*th word in the variable to *value*. (The variable must already contain at least that number of words.) With no arguments, display the names and values of all set variables. See also "Predefined Shell Variables" earlier in this chapter.<br><br>*Option*<br><br>−r  tcsh only. List only read-only variables, or set specified variable to read-only.<br><br>*Examples* |

| | |
|---|---|
| `% set list=(yes no maybe)` | *Assign a wordlist* |
| `% set list[3]=maybe` | *Assign an item in existing wordlist* |
| `% set quote="Make my day"` | *Assign a variable* |
| `% set x=5 y=10 history=100` | *Assign several variables* |
| `% set blank` | *Assign a null value to* blank |

| | |
|---|---|
| setenv | setenv [*name* [*value*]]<br><br>Assign a *value* to an environment variable *name*. By convention, *name* is uppercase. *value* can be a single word or a quoted string. If no *value* is given, the null value is assigned. With no arguments, display the names and values of all environment variables. **setenv** is not necessary for the PATH variable, which is automatically exported from **path**. |

| | |
|---|---|
| settc | settc *capability value*<br><br>tcsh only. Set terminal *capability* to *value*. |

| | |
|---|---|
| setty | setty [*options*] [+ | -*mode*]<br><br>tcsh only. Do not allow shell to change specified tty modes. By default, act on the execute set. |

+*mode*

> Without arguments, list all modes in specified set that are on. Otherwise, set specified mode to on.

−*mode*

> Without arguments, list all modes in specified set that are off. Otherwise, set specified mode to on.

−a  List all modes in specified set.

−d  Act on the edit set of modes (used when editing commands).

−q  Act on the quote set of modes (used when entering characters verbatim).

−x  Act on the execute set of modes (default) (used when executing examples).

---

shift [*variable*]　　　　　　　　　　　　　　　　　　　　shift

If *variable* is given, shift the words in a wordlist variable (i.e., *name*[2] becomes *name*[1]). With no argument, shift the positional parameters (command-line arguments) (i.e., **$2** becomes **$1**). **shift** is typically used in a **while** loop. See additional example under **while**.

*Example*

```
while ($#argv)          While there are arguments
    if (-f $argv[1])
        wc -1 $argv[1]
    else
        echo "$argv[1] is not a regular file"
    endif
    shift               Get the next argument
end
```

---

source [−h] *script* [*args*]　　　　　　　　　　　　　　source

Read and execute commands from a C-shell script. With −h, the commands are added to the history list but aren't executed. For **tcsh** only, arguments can be passed to the script and are put in **argv**.

*Example*

```
source ~/.cshrc
```

**csh and
tcsh**

| | |
|---|---|
| stop | stop [*jobIDs*]<br><br>Suspend the current background jobs or the background jobs specified by *jobIDs*; this is the complement of **Ctrl-Z** or **suspend**. |
| suspend | **suspend**<br><br>Suspend the current foreground job; same as **Ctrl-Z**. Often used to stop an **su** command. |
| switch | **switch** |

Process commands depending on the value of a variable. When you need to handle more than three choices, **switch** is a useful alternative to an **if-then-else** statement. If the *string* variable matches *pattern1*, the first set of *commands* is executed; if *string* matches *pattern2*, the second set of *commands* is executed; and so on. If no patterns match, execute commands under the **default** case. *string* can be specified using command substitution, variable substitution, or filename expansion. Patterns can be specified using the pattern-matching symbols *, ?, and [ ]. **breaksw** is used to exit the **switch**. If **breaksw** is omitted (which is rarely done), the **switch** continues to execute another set of commands until it reaches a **breaksw** or **endsw**. Following is the general syntax of **switch**, side-by-side with an example that processes the first command-line argument:

```
switch (string)              switch ($argv[1])
   case pattern1:               case -[nN]:
      commands                     nroff $file | lp
      breaksw                      breaksw
   case pattern2:               case -[Pp]:
      commands                     pr $file | lp
      breaksw                      breaksw
   case pattern3:               case -[Mm]:
      commands                     more $file
      breaksw                      breaksw
         .                      case -[Ss]:
         .                         sort $file
         .                         breaksw
   default:                     default:
      commands                     echo "Error-no such option"
                                   exit 1
      breaksw                      breaksw
endsw                        endsw
```

| | |
|---|---|
| **telltc** | telltc |
| tcsh only. Print all terminal capabilities and their values. | |
| **time** [*command*] | time |
| Execute a *command* and show how much time it uses. With no argument, **time** can be used in a shell script to time the script. | |
| **umask** [*nnn*] | umask |
| Display file creation mask or set file creation mask to octal *nnn*. The file creation mask determines which permission bits are turned off. With no *nnn*, print the current mask. | |
| **unalias** *pattern* | unalias |
| Remove all aliases whose names match *pattern* from the alias list. See **alias** for more information. | |
| **uncomplete** *pattern* | uncomplete |
| tcsh only. Remove completions (specified by **complete**) whose names match *pattern*. | |
| **unhash** | unhash |
| Remove internal hash table. The shell stops using hashed values and searches the **path** directories to locate a command. See also **rehash**. | |
| **unlimit** [–h] [*resource*] | unlimit |
| Remove the allocation limits on *resource*. If *resource* is not specified, remove limits for all resources. See **limit** for more information. With –h, remove hard limits. This command can be run only by a privileged user. | |
| **unset** *variables* | unset |
| Remove one or more *variables*. Variable names may be specified as a pattern, using filename metacharacters. Does not remove | |
| | → |

*csh and tcsh*

| | |
|---|---|
| unset<br>← | read-only variables. See **set**. |
| unsetenv | **unsetenv** *variable*<br><br>Remove an environment variable. Filename matching is not valid. See **setenv**. |
| wait | **wait**<br><br>Pause in execution until all child processes complete, or until an interrupt signal is received. |
| watchlog | **watchlog**<br><br>tcsh only. Same as **log**. Must have been compiled into the shell; see the **version** shell variable. |
| where | **where** *command*<br><br>tcsh only. Display all aliases, built-ins, and executables named *command*. |
| which | **which** *command*<br><br>tcsh only. Report which version of command will be executed. Same as the executable **which**, but faster, and checks **tcsh** built-ins. |
| while | **while** (*expression*)<br>   *commands*<br>**end**<br><br>As long as *expression* is true (evaluates to nonzero), evaluate *commands* between **while** and **end**. **break** and **continue** can be used to terminate or continue the loop.<br><br>*Example*<br><br>```<br>set user = (alice bob carol ted)<br>while ($argv[1] != $user[1])    Cycle through each user, checking for a match<br>  shift user                    If we cycled through with no match...<br>  if ($#user == 0) then<br>    echo "$argv[1] is not on the list of users"<br>    exit 1<br>  endif<br>end<br>``` |

# CHAPTER 9

# *Pattern Matching*

A number of Linux text-editing utilities let you search for and, in some cases change, text patterns rather than fixed strings. These utilities include the editing programs **ed**, **ex**, **vi**, and **sed**; the **awk** scripting language; and the commands **grep** and **egrep**. Text patterns (also called *regular expressions*) contain normal characters mixed with special characters (also called *metacharacters*).

Perl's regular expression support is so rich that it does not fit into the tables in this chapter; you can find a description in the O'Reilly books *Perl in a Nutshell*, *Perl 5 Pocket Reference*, or *Programming Perl*. The Emacs editor also provides regular expressions similar to those shown in this chapter.

**ed** and **ex** are hardly ever used as standalone, interactive editors nowadays. But **ed** can be found as a batch processor invoked from shell scripts, and **ex** commands often are invoked within **vi** through the colon (:) command. We use **vi** in this chapter to refer to the regular expression features supported by both **vi** and the **ex** editor on which it is based.

**sed** and **awk** are widely used in shell scripts and elsewhere as filters to alter text.

This chapter presents the following information:

- Filenames versus patterns
- List of metacharacters available to each program
- Description of metacharacters
- Examples

A thorough guide to pattern matching can be found in the Nutshell handbook *Mastering Regular Expressions* by Jeffrey E. F. Friedl.

# Filenames Versus Patterns

Metacharacters used in pattern matching are different from those used for filename expansion. When you issue a command on the command line, special characters are seen first by the shell, then by the program; therefore, unquoted metacharacters are interpreted by the shell for filename expansion. The command:

```
$ grep [A-Z]* chap[12]
```

could, for example, be interpreted by the shell as:

```
$ grep Array.c Bug.c Comp.c chap1 chap2
```

and **grep** then would try to find the pattern "Array.c" in files *Bug.c*, *Comp.c*, *chap1*, and *chap2*. To bypass the shell and pass the special characters to **grep**, use quotes:

```
$ grep "[A-Z]*" chap[12]
```

Double quotes suffice in most cases, but single quotes are the safest bet.

Note also that * and ? have subtly different meanings in pattern matching and filename expansion.

# Metacharacters, Listed by Linux Program

Some metacharacters are valid for one program but not for another. Those that are available to a given program are marked by a bullet (•) in the following table. Notes are provided after the table, and full descriptions of metacharacters are in the following section.

| Symbol | ed | vi | sed | awk | grep | egrep | Action |
|--------|----|----|-----|-----|------|-------|--------|
| . | • | • | • | • | • | • | Match any character (can match newline in **gawk**). |
| * | • | • | • | • | • | • | Match zero or more preceding. |
| ^ | • | • | • | • | • | • | Match beginning of line or string. |
| $ | • | • | • | • | • | • | Match end of line or string. |
| \ | • | • | • | • | • | • | Escape character following. |
| [ ] | • | • | • | • | • | • | Match one from a list or range. |
| \( \) | • | • | • | | | | Store pattern for later replay. |
| \n | • | • | • | | | | Reuse matched text stored in *n*th \( \). |
| { } | | | | • | | | Match a range of instances. |
| \{ \} | • | • | • | | • | | Match a range of instances. |

| Symbol | ed | vi | sed | awk | grep | egrep | Action |
|--------|-----|-----|-----|-----|------|-------|--------|
| \< \> | | • | | | | | Match word's beginning or end. |
| + | | | | • | • | • | Match one or more preceding. |
| ? | | | | • | • | • | Match zero or one preceding. |
| \| | | | | • | | • | Separate choices to match. |
| ( ) | | | | • | | • | Group expressions to match. |

On some Linux systems, **grep** is a link to **egrep**, so whenever you run **grep** you actually get **egrep** behavior.

In **ed**, **vi**, and **sed**, when you perform a search-and-replace (substitute) operation, the metacharacters in this table apply to the pattern you are searching for but not to the string replacing it.

In **awk**, { } is specified in the POSIX standard and is supported by **gawk** if you run it with the **–Wre-interval** option.

In **ed**, **vi**, and **sed**, the following additional metacharacters are valid only in a replacement pattern:

| Symbol | ex | sed | ed | Action |
|--------|-----|-----|-----|--------|
| \ | • | • | • | Escape character following. |
| \n | • | • | • | Reuse matched text stored in nth \( \). |
| & | • | • | | Reuse previous search pattern. |
| ~ | • | | | Reuse previous replacement pattern. |
| \e | • | | | Turn off previous \L or \U. |
| \E | • | | | Turn off previous \L or \U. |
| \l | • | | | Change single following character to lowercase. |
| \L | • | | | Change following characters to lowercase until \E encountered. |
| \u | • | | | Change single following character to uppercase. |
| \U | • | | | Change following characters to uppercase until \E encountered. |

## Metacharacters

The following characters have special meaning in search patterns:

| Character | Meaning |
|-----------|---------|
| . | Match any *single* character except newline. |
| * | Match any number (or none) of the single character that immediately precedes it. The preceding character also can be a regular expression (e.g., since . (dot) means any character, .* means *match any number of any character*—except newlines). |
| ^ | Match the beginning of the line or string. |

Pattern Matching

| Character | Meaning |
|---|---|
| $ | Match the end of the line or string. |
| [ ] | Match any *one* of the enclosed characters. A hyphen (-) indicates a range of consecutive characters. A circumflex (^) as the first character in the brackets reverses the sense: it matches any one character *not* in the list. A hyphen or close bracket ( ] ) as the first character is treated as a member of the list. All other metacharacters are treated as members of the list. |
| [^ ] | Match anything except enclosed characters. |
| \{n,m\} | Match a range of occurrences of the single character that immediately precedes it. The preceding character also can be a regular expression. \{n\} matches exactly *n* occurrences, \{n,\} matches at least *n* occurrences, and \{n,m\} matches any number of occurrences between *n* and *m*. |
| {n,m} | Like \{n,m\}. Available in **grep** by default and in **gawk** with the –Wre-interval option. |
| \ | Turn off the special meaning of the character that follows. |
| \( \) | Save the matched text enclosed between \( and \) in a special holding space. Up to nine patterns can be saved on a single line. They can be "replayed" in the same pattern or within substitutions by the escape sequences \1 to \9. |
| \n | Reuse matched text stored in *n*th \( \). |
| ( ) | In **egrep** and **gawk**, save the matched text enclosed between \( and \) in a holding space to be replayed in substitutions by the escape sequences \1 to \9. |
| \< \> | Match the beginning (\<) or end (\>) of a word. |
| + | Match one or more instances of preceding regular expression. |
| ? | Match zero or one instance of preceding regular expression. |
| | | Match the regular expression specified before or after. |
| ( ) | Group regular expressions. |

Many utilities support POSIX character lists, which are useful for matching non-ASCII characters in languages other than English. These lists are recognized only within [ ] ranges. A typical use would be [[:lower:]], which in English is the same as [a-z].

The following table lists POSIX character lists:

| Notation | Action |
|---|---|
| [:alnum:] | Alphanumeric characters |
| [:alpha:] | Alphabetic characters, uppercase and lowercase |
| [:blank:] | Printable whitespace: spaces and tabs but not control characters |
| [:cntrl:] | Control characters, such as ^A through ^Z |
| [:digit:] | Decimal digits |
| [:graph:] | Printable characters, excluding whitespace |
| [:lower:] | Lowercase alphabetic characters |
| [:print:] | Printable characters, including whitespace but not control characters |
| [:punct:] | Punctuation, a subclass of printable characters |

| Notation | Action |
|---|---|
| [:space:] | Whitespace, including spaces, tabs, and some control characters |
| [:upper:] | Uppercase alphabetic characters |
| [:xdigit:] | Hexadecimal digits |

The following characters have special meaning in replacement patterns:

| Character | Meaning |
|---|---|
| \ | Turn off the special meaning of the character that follows. |
| \n | Restore the *n*th pattern previously saved by \( and \). *n* is a number from 1 to 9, matching the patterns searched sequentially from left to right. |
| & | Reuse the search pattern as part of the replacement pattern. |
| ~ | Reuse the previous replacement pattern in the current replacement pattern. |
| \e | End replacement pattern started by \L or \U. |
| \E | End replacement pattern started by \L or \U. |
| \l | Convert first character of replacement pattern to lowercase. |
| \L | Convert replacement pattern to lowercase. |
| \u | Convert first character of replacement pattern to uppercase. |
| \U | Convert replacement pattern to uppercase. |

# Examples of Searching

When used with **grep** or **egrep**, regular expressions normally are surrounded by quotes to avoid interpretation by the shell. (If the pattern contains a $, you must use single quotes, as in `'$200'`, or escape the $, as in `"\$200"`.) When used with **ed**, **vi**, **sed**, and **awk**, regular expressions usually are surrounded by / (although any delimiter works). Here are some sample patterns:

| Pattern | What does it match? |
|---|---|
| bag | The string *bag*. |
| ^bag | "bag" at beginning of line or string. |
| bag$ | "bag" at end of line or string. |
| ^bag$ | "bag" as the only text on line. |
| [Bb]ag | "Bag" or "bag." |
| b[aeiou]g | Second character is a vowel. |
| b[^aeiou]g | Second character is not a vowel. |
| b.g | Second character is any character except newline. |
| ^...$ | Any line containing exactly three characters. |
| ^\. | Any line that begins with a dot. |
| ^\.[a-z][a-z] | Same, followed by two lowercase letters (e.g., troff requests). |
| ^\.[a-z]\{2\} | Same as previous, **grep** or **sed** only. |
| ^[^.] | Any line that doesn't begin with a dot. |
| bugs* | "bug," "bugs", "bugss", etc. |

| | |
|---|---|
| "word" | A word in quotes. |
| "*word"* | A word, with or without quotes. |
| [A-Z][A-Z]* | One or more uppercase letters. |
| [A-Z]+ | Same, **egrep** or **awk** only. |
| [A-Z].* | An uppercase letter, followed by zero or more characters. |
| [A-Z]* | Zero or more uppercase letters. |
| [a-zA-Z] | Any letter. |
| [0-9A-Za-z]+ | Any alphanumeric sequence. |

| egrep or awk pattern | What does it match? |
|---|---|
| [567] | One of the numbers *5*, *6*, or *7* |
| five\|six\|seven | One of the words *five*, *six*, or *seven* |
| 80[23]?86 | *8086*, *80286*, or *80386* |
| compan(y\|ies) | *company* or *companies* |

| vi pattern | What does it match? |
|---|---|
| \<the | Words like *theater* or *the* |
| the\> | Words like *breathe* or *the* |
| \<the\> | The word *the* |

| sed or grep pattern | What does it match? |
|---|---|
| 0\{5,\} | Five or more zeros in a row |
| [0-9]\{3\}-[0-9]\{2\}-[0-9]\{4\} | Social security number (*nnn-nn-nnnn*) |

## Examples of Searching and Replacing

The following examples show the metacharacters available to **sed** and **vi**. We have shown **vi** commands with an initial colon because that is how they are invoked within **vi**. A space is marked by a □; a tab is marked by *tab*.

| Command | Result |
|---|---|
| s/.*/(&)/ | Reproduce the entire line, but add parentheses. |
| s/.*/mv & &.old/ | Change a wordlist (one word per line) into **mv** commands. |
| /^$/d | Delete blank lines. |
| :g/^$/d | Same as previous, in **vi** editor. |
| /^[□*tab*]*$/d | Delete blank lines, plus lines containing spaces or tabs. |
| :g/^[□*tab*]*$/d | Same as previous, in **vi** editor. |
| s/□□*/□/g | Turn one or more spaces into one space. |
| :%s/□□*/□/g | Same as previous, in **vi** editor. |
| :s/[0-9]/Item &:/ | Turn a number into an item label (on the current line). |
| :s | Repeat the substitution on the first occurrence. |
| :& | Same as previous. |
| :sg | Same, but for all occurrences on the line. |
| :&g | Same as previous. |

| Command | Result |
|---------|--------|
| :%&g | Repeat the substitution globally. |
| :.,$s/Fortran/\U&/g | Change word to uppercase, on current line to last line. |
| :%s/.*/\L&/ | Lowercase entire file. |
| :s/\<./\u&/g | Uppercase first letter of each word on current line. (Useful for titles.) |
| :%s/yes/No/g | Globally change a word (**yes**) to another word (**No**). |
| :%s/Yes/~/g | Globally change a different word to **No** (previous replacement). |

Finally, here are some **sed** examples for transposing words. A simple transposition of two words might look like this:

```
s/die or do/do or die/          Transpose words
```

The real trick is to use hold buffers to transpose variable patterns. For example:

```
s/\([Dd]ie\) or \([Dd]o\)/\2 or \1/      Transpose, using hold buffers
```

# CHAPTER 10

# *The Emacs Editor*

This chapter presents the following topics:

- Introduction
- Typical problems
- Summary of Emacs commands by group
- Summary of Emacs commands by key
- Summary of Emacs commands by name

## *Introduction*

Although Emacs is not part of Linux, this text editor is found on many Unix systems because it is a popular alternative to **vi**. Many versions are available. This book documents GNU Emacs, which is available from the Free Software Foundation in Cambridge, Massachusetts. For more information, see the O'Reilly book *Learning GNU Emacs*, 2d ed., by Debra Cameron, Bill Rosenblatt, and Eric Raymond.

To start an Emacs editing session, type:

**emacs** [*file*]

## *Typical Problems*

A very common problem is that the Del or Backspace key on the terminal does not delete the character before the cursor, as it should. Instead, it invokes a help prompt. This problem is caused by an incompatible terminal.

A fairly robust fix is to create a file named *.emacs* in your home directory (or edit one that's already there) and add the following lines:

```
(keyboard-translate ?\C-h ?\C-?)
(keyboard-translate ?\C-\\ ?\C-h)
```

Now the Del or Backspace kill should work, and you can invoke help by pressing C-\ (an arbitrarily chosen key sequence).

Another potential problem is that on some systems, C-s causes the terminal to hang. This is due to an old-fashioned handshake protocol between the terminal and the system. You can restart the terminal by pressing C-q, but that doesn't help you enter commands that contain the sequence C-s. The solution (aside from using a more modern dial-in protocol) is to create new key bindings that replace C-s or to enter those commands as M-x *command-name*.

## Notes on the Tables

Emacs commands use the Ctrl key and the Meta key. Most modern terminals provide a key named Alt that functions as a Meta key. In this section, the notation C- indicates that you should hold down the Ctrl key and press the character that follows, while M- indicates that the Meta or Alt key is pressed in the same way, along with the character that follows. As an alternative to Meta or Alt, you can press the Esc key, release it, and press the character. You might want to do this if you have any problems with controlling windows capturing the Alt key (which sometimes happens).

In the command tables that follow, the first column lists the keystroke and the last column describes it. When there is a middle column, it lists the command name. The command can be executed by typing M-x followed by the command name; you have to do this when the binding is listed as "(none)." If you're unsure of the full command name, you can type a space or a carriage return, and Emacs will list possible completions of what you've typed so far.

Because Emacs is such a comprehensive editor, containing hundreds of commands, some commands must be omitted for the sake of preserving a "quick" reference. You can browse the command set by typing C-h (for help) and then b to get a list of the key bindings* or M-x followed by a space or Tab to get the command names.

## Modes

One of the features that makes Emacs popular is its editing modes. The modes set up an environment designed for the type of editing you are doing, with features like having appropriate key bindings available and automatically indenting according to standard conventions for that type of document. There are modes for various programming languages like C or Perl, for text processing (e.g., SGML or even straight text), and many more. One particularly useful mode is Dired (Directory Editor), which has commands that let you manage directories. For a full discussion

---

\* If you want to learn to create your own key bindings, see *Learning GNU Emacs* (O'Reilly).

of modes, see *Learning GNU Emacs*, mentioned at the beginning of this chapter, or the Emacs Info documentation system (C-h i).

## Absolutely Essential Commands

If you're just getting started with Emacs, here's a short list of the most important commands to know:

| Binding | Action |
|---|---|
| C-h | Enter the online help system. |
| C-x C-s | Save the file. |
| C-x C-c | Exit Emacs. |
| C-x u | Undo last edit (can be repeated). |
| C-g | Get out of current command operation. |
| C-p | Up by one line. |
| C-n | Down by one line. |
| C-f | Forward by one character. |
| C-b | Back by one character. |
| C-v | Forward by one screen. |
| M-v | Backward by one screen. |
| C-s | Search forward for characters. |
| C-r | Search backward for characters. |
| C-d | Delete current character. |
| Del | Delete previous character. |
| Backspace | Delete previous character. |

# Summary of Commands by Group

Reminder: Tables list keystrokes, command name, and description. C- indicates the Control key; M- indicates the Meta key.

## File-Handling Commands

| Binding | Command | Action |
|---|---|---|
| C-x C-f | find-file | Find file and read it. |
| C-x C-v | find-alternate-file | Read another file; replace the one read currently in the buffer. |
| C-x i | insert-file | Insert file at cursor position. |
| C-x C-s | save-buffer | Save file. (If terminal hangs, C-q restarts.) |
| C-x C-w | write-file | Write buffer contents to file. |
| C-x C-c | save-buffers-kill-emacs | Exit Emacs. |
| C-z | suspend-emacs | Suspend Emacs (use **exit** or **fg** to restart). |

## Cursor Movement Commands

Some words are emphasized in the **Action** column to help you remember the binding for the command.

| Binding | Command | Action |
|---------|---------|--------|
| C-f | forward-char | Move *forward* one character (right). |
| C-b | backward-char | Move *backward* one character (left). |
| C-p | previous-line | Move to *previous* line (up). |
| C-n | next-line | Move to *next* line (down). |
| M-f | forward-word | Move one word *forward*. |
| M-b | backward-word | Move one word *backward*. |
| C-a | beginning-of-line | Move to beginning of line. |
| C-e | end-of-line | Move to *end* of line. |
| M-a | backward-sentence | Move backward one sentence. |
| M-e | forward-sentence | Move forward one sentence. |
| M-{ | backward-paragraph | Move backward one paragraph. |
| M-} | forward-paragraph | Move forward one paragraph. |
| C-v | scroll-up | Move forward one screen. |
| M-v | scroll-down | Move backward one screen. |
| C-x [ | backward-page | Move backward one page. |
| C-x ] | forward-page | Move forward one page. |
| M-> | end-of-buffer | Move to end-of-file. |
| M-< | beginning-of-buffer | Move to beginning of file. |
| (none) | goto-line | Go to line *n* of file. |
| (none) | goto-char | Go to character *n* of file. |
| C-l | recenter | Redraw screen with current line in the center. |
| M-*n* | digit-argument | Repeat the next command *n* times. |
| C-u *n* | universal-argument | Repeat the next command *n* times. |

## Deletion Commands

| Binding | Command | Action |
|---------|---------|--------|
| Del | backward-delete-char | Delete previous character. |
| C-d | delete-char | Delete character under cursor. |
| M-Del | backward-kill-word | Delete previous word. |
| M-d | kill-word | Delete the word the cursor is on. |
| C-k | kill-line | Delete from cursor to end-of-line. |
| M-k | kill-sentence | Delete sentence the cursor is on. |
| C-x Del | backward-kill-sentence | Delete previous sentence. |
| C-y | yank | Restore what you've deleted. |
| C-w | kill-region | Delete a marked region (see the next section, "Paragraphs and Regions"). |

| Binding | Command | Action |
| --- | --- | --- |
| (none) | backward-kill-paragraph | Delete previous paragraph. |
| (none) | kill-paragraph | Delete from the cursor to the end of the paragraph. |

## Paragraphs and Regions

| Binding | Command | Action |
| --- | --- | --- |
| C-@ | set-mark-command | Mark the beginning (or end) of a region. |
| C-Space | (Same as preceding) | (Same as preceding) |
| C-x C-p | mark-page | Mark page. |
| C-x C-x | exchange-point-and-mark | Exchange location of cursor and mark. |
| C-x h | mark-whole-buffer | Mark buffer. |
| M-q | fill-paragraph | Reformat paragraph. |
| (none) | fill-region | Reformat individual paragraphs within a region. |
| M-h | mark-paragraph | Mark paragraph. |
| M-{ | backward-paragraph | Move backward one paragraph. |
| M-} | forward-paragraph | Move forward one paragraph. |
| (none) | backward-kill-paragraph | Delete previous paragraph. |
| (none) | kill-paragraph | Delete from the cursor to the end of the paragraph. |

## Stopping and Undoing Commands

| Binding | Command | Action |
| --- | --- | --- |
| C-g | keyboard-quit | Abort current command. |
| C-x u | advertised-undo | Undo last edit (can be done repeatedly). |
| (none) | revert-buffer | Restore buffer to the state it was in when the file was last saved (or auto-saved). |

## Transposition Commands

| Binding | Command | Action |
| --- | --- | --- |
| C-t | transpose-chars | Transpose two letters. |
| M-t | transpose-words | Transpose two words. |
| C-x C-t | transpose-lines | Transpose two lines. |
| (none) | transpose-sentences | Transpose two sentences. |
| (none) | transpose-paragraphs | Transpose two paragraphs. |

## Capitalization Commands

| Binding | Command | Action |
|---------|---------|--------|
| M-c | capitalize-word | Capitalize first letter of word. |
| M-u | upcase-word | Uppercase word. |
| M-l | downcase-word | Lowercase word. |
| M- – M-c | negative-argument; capitalize-word | Capitalize previous word. |
| M- – M-u | negative-argument; upcase-word | Uppercase previous word. |
| M- – M-l | negative-argument; downcase-word | Lowercase previous word. |
| (none) | capitalize-region | Capitalize initial letters in region. |
| C-x C-u | upcase-region | Uppercase region. |
| C-x C-l | downcase-region | Lowercase region. |

## Incremental Search Commands

| Binding | Command | Action |
|---------|---------|--------|
| C-s | isearch-forward | Start or repeat incremental search forward. |
| C-r | isearch-backward | Start or repeat incremental search backward. |
| Return | (none) | Exit a successful search. |
| C-g | keyboard-quit | Cancel incremental search; return to starting point. |
| Del | (none) | Delete incorrect character of search string. |
| M-C-r | isearch-backward-regexp | Incremental search backward for regular expression. |
| M-C-s | isearch-forward-regexp | Incremental search forward for regular expression. |

## Word Abbreviation Commands

| Binding | Command | Action |
|---------|---------|--------|
| (none) | abbrev-mode | Enter (or exit) word abbreviation mode. |
| C-x a – | inverse-add-global-abbrev | Define previous word as global (mode-independent) abbreviation. |
| C-x a i l | inverse-add-mode-abbrev | Define previous word as mode-specific abbreviation. |
| (none) | unexpand-abbrev | Undo the last word abbreviation. |
| (none) | write-abbrev-file | Write the word abbreviation file. |
| (none) | edit-abbrevs | Edit the word abbreviations. |

| Binding | Command | Action |
|---------|---------|--------|
| (none) | list-abbrevs | View the word abbreviations. |
| (none) | kill-all-abbrevs | Kill abbreviations for this session. |

## Buffer Manipulation Commands

| Binding | Command | Action |
|---------|---------|--------|
| C-x b | switch-to-buffer | Move to specified buffer. |
| C-x C-b | list-buffers | Display buffer list. |
| C-x k | kill-buffer | Delete specified buffer. |
| (none) | kill-some-buffers | Ask about deleting each buffer. |
| (none) | rename-buffer | Change buffer name to specified name. |
| C-x s | save-some-buffers | Ask whether to save each modified buffer. |

## Window Commands

| Binding | Command | Action |
|---------|---------|--------|
| C-x 2 | split-window-vertically | Divide the current window in two vertically, resulting in one window on top of the other. |
| C-x 3 | split-window-horizontally | Divide the current window in two horizontally, resulting in two side-by-side windows. |
| C-x > | scroll-right | Scroll the window right. |
| C-x < | scroll-left | Scroll the window left. |
| C-x o | other-window | Move to the other window. |
| C-x 0 | delete-window | Delete current window. |
| C-x 1 | delete-other-windows | Delete all windows but this one. |
| (none) | delete-windows-on | Delete all windows on a given buffer. |
| C-x ^ | enlarge-window | Make window taller. |
| (none) | shrink-window | Make window shorter. |
| C-x } | enlarge-window-horizontally | Make window wider. |
| C-x { | shrink-window-horizontally | Make window narrower. |
| M-C-v | scroll-other-window | Scroll other window. |
| C-x 4 f | find-file-other-window | Find a file in the other window. |
| C-x 4 b | switch-to-buffer-other-window | Select a buffer in the other window. |
| C-x 5 f | find-file-other-frame | Find a file in a new frame. |
| C-x 5 b | switch-to-buffer-other-frame | Select a buffer in another frame. |
| (none) | compare-windows | Compare two buffers; show first difference. |

## Special Shell Mode Characters

| Binding | Command | Action |
|---------|---------|--------|
| C-c C-c | interrupt-shell-subjob | Terminate the current job. |
| C-c C-d | shell-send-eof | End-of-file character. |
| C-c C-u | kill-shell-input | Erase current line. |
| C-c C-w | backward-kill-word | Erase the previous word. |
| C-c C-z | stop-shell-subjob | Suspend the current job. |

## Indentation Commands

| Binding | Command | Action |
|---------|---------|--------|
| C-x . | set-fill-prefix | Prepend each line in paragraph with characters from beginning of line up to cursor column; cancel prefix by typing this command in column 1. |
| (none) | indented-text-mode | Major mode: each tab defines a new indent for subsequent lines. |
| (none) | text-mode | Exit indented text mode; return to text mode. |
| M-C-\ | indent-region | Indent a region to match first line in region. |
| M-m | back-to-indentation | Move cursor to first character on line. |
| M-^ | delete-indentation | Join this line to the previous line. |
| M-C-o | split-line | Split line at cursor; indent to column of cursor. |
| (none) | fill-individual-paragraphs | Reformat indented paragraphs, keeping indentation. |

## Centering Commands

| Binding | Command | Action |
|---------|---------|--------|
| (none) | center-line | Center line that cursor is on. |
| (none) | center-paragraph | Center paragraph that cursor is on. |
| (none) | center-region | Center currently defined region. |

## Macro Commands

| Binding | Command | Action |
|---------|---------|--------|
| C-x ( | start-kbd-macro | Start macro definition. |
| C-x ) | end-kbd-macro | End macro definition. |
| C-x e | call-last-kbd-macro | Execute last macro defined. |
| M-$n$ C-x e | digit-argument and call-last-kbd-macro | Execute last macro defined $n$ times. |
| C-u C-x ( | start-kbd-macro | Execute last macro defined, then add keystrokes. |

| Binding | Command | Action |
|---|---|---|
| (none) | name-last-kbd-macro | Name last macro you created (before saving it). |
| (none) | insert-last-keyboard-macro | Insert the macro you named into a file. |
| (none) | load-file | Load macro files you've saved. |
| (none) | *macroname* | Execute a keyboard macro you've saved. |
| C-x q | kbd-macro-query | Insert a query in a macro definition. |
| C-u C-x q | (none) | Insert a recursive edit in a macro definition. |
| M-C-c | exit-recursive-edit | Exit a recursive edit. |

## Detail Information Help Commands

| Binding | Command | Action |
|---|---|---|
| C-h a | command-apropos | What commands involve this concept? |
| (none) | apropos | What commands, functions, and variables involve this concept? |
| C-h c | describe-key-briefly | What command does this keystroke sequence run? |
| C-h b | describe-bindings | What are all the key bindings for this buffer? |
| C-h k | describe-key | What command does this keystroke sequence run, and what does it do? |
| C-h l | view-lossage | What are the last 100 characters I typed? |
| C-h w | where-is | What is the key binding for this command? |
| C-h f | describe-function | What does this function do? |
| C-h v | describe-variable | What does this variable mean, and what is its value? |
| C-h m | describe-mode | Tell me about the mode the current buffer is in. |
| C-h s | describe-syntax | What is the syntax table for this buffer? |

## Help Commands

| Binding | Command | Action |
|---|---|---|
| C-h t | help-with-tutorial | Run the Emacs tutorial. |
| C-h i | info | Start the Info documentation reader. |
| C-h n | view-emacs-news | View news about updates to Emacs. |
| C-h C-c | describe-copying | View the Emacs General Public License. |
| C-h C-d | describe-distribution | View information on ordering Emacs from the FSF. |
| C-h C-w | describe-no-warranty | View the (non)warranty for Emacs. |

# Summary of Commands by Key

Emacs commands are presented next in two alphabetical lists. Tables list keystrokes, command name, and description. C- indicates the Ctrl key; M- indicates the Meta key.

## Control-Key Sequences

| Binding | Command | Action |
|---------|---------|--------|
| C-@ | set-mark-command | Mark the beginning (or end) of a region. |
| C-Space | (Same as preceding) | (Same as preceding) |
| C-] | abort-recursive-edit | Exit recursive edit and exit query-replace. |
| C-a | beginning-of-line | Move to beginning of line. |
| C-b | backward-char | Move *backward* one character (left). |
| C-c C-c | interrupt-shell-subjob | Terminate the current job. |
| C-c C-d | shell-send-eof | End-of-file character. |
| C-c C-u | kill-shell-input | Erase current line. |
| C-c C-w | backward-kill-word | Erase the previous word. |
| C-c C-z | stop-shell-subjob | Suspend the current job. |
| C-d | delete-char | Delete character under cursor. |
| C-e | end-of-line | Move to *end* of line. |
| C-f | forward-char | Move *forward* one character (right). |
| C-g | keyboard-quit | Abort current command. |
| C-h | help-command | Enter the online help system. |
| C-h a | command-apropos | What commands involve this concept? |
| C-h b | describe-bindings | What are all the key bindings for this buffer? |
| C-h c | describe-key-briefly | What command does this keystroke sequence run? |
| C-h C-c | describe-copying | View the Emacs General Public License. |
| C-h C-d | describe-distribution | View information on ordering Emacs from the FSF. |
| C-h C-w | describe-no-warranty | View the (non)warranty for Emacs. |
| C-h f | describe-function | What does this function do? |
| C-h i | info | Start the Info documentation reader. |
| C-h k | describe-key | What command does this keystroke sequence run, and what does it do? |
| C-h l | view-lossage | What are the last 100 characters I typed? |
| C-h m | describe-mode | Tell me about the mode the current buffer is in. |
| C-h n | view-emacs-news | View news about updates to Emacs. |
| C-h s | describe-syntax | What is the syntax table for this buffer? |
| C-h t | help-with-tutorial | Run the Emacs tutorial. |
| C-h v | describe-variable | What does this variable mean, and what is its value? |
| C-h w | where-is | What is the key binding for this command? |

| Binding | Command | Action |
| --- | --- | --- |
| C-k | kill-line | Delete from cursor to end-of-line. |
| C-l | recenter | Redraw screen with current line in the center. |
| C-n | next-line | Move to *next* line (down). |
| C-p | previous-line | Move to *previous* line (up). |
| C-q | quoted-insert | Insert next character typed. Useful for inserting a control character. |
| C-r | isearch-backward | Start or repeat nonincremental search backward. |
| C-r | (none) | Enter recursive edit (during query replace). |
| C-s | isearch-forward | Start or repeat nonincremental search forward. |
| C-t | transpose-chars | Transpose two letters. |
| C-u $n$ | universal-argument | Repeat the next command $n$ times. |
| C-u C-x ( | start-kbd-macro | Execute last macro defined, then add keystrokes. |
| C-u C-x q | (none) | Insert recursive edit in a macro definition. |
| C-v | scroll-up | Move forward one screen. |
| C-w | kill-region | Delete a marked region. |
| C-x ( | start-kbd-macro | Start macro definition. |
| C-x ) | end-kbd-macro | End macro definition. |
| C-x [ | backward-page | Move backward one page. |
| C-x ] | forward-page | Move forward one page. |
| C-x ^ | enlarge-window | Make window taller. |
| C-x { | shrink-window-horizontally | Make window narrower. |
| C-x } | enlarge-window-horizontally | Make window wider. |
| C-x < | scroll-left | Scroll the window left. |
| C-x > | scroll-right | Scroll the window right. |
| C-x . | set-fill-prefix | Prepend each line in paragraph with characters from beginning of line up to cursor column; cancel prefix by typing this command in column 1. |
| C-x 0 | delete-window | Delete current window. |
| C-x 1 | delete-other-windows | Delete all windows but this one. |
| C-x 2 | split-window-vertically | Divide current window in two vertically, resulting in one window on top of the other. |
| C-x 3 | split-window-horizontally | Divide current window in two horizontally, resulting in two side-by-side windows. |
| C-x 4 b | switch-to-buffer-other-window | Select a buffer in the other window. |
| C-x 4 f | find-file-other-window | Find a file in the other window. |
| C-x 5 b | switch-to-buffer-other-frame | Select a buffer in another frame. |

| Binding | Command | Action |
| --- | --- | --- |
| C-x 5 f | find-file-other-frame | Find a file in a new frame. |
| C-x a - | inverse-add-global-abbrev | Define previous word as global (mode-independent) abbreviation. |
| C-x a i l | inverse-add-mode-abbrev | Define previous word as mode-specific abbreviation. |
| C-x b | switch-to-buffer | Move to the buffer specified. |
| C-x C-b | list-buffers | Display the buffer list. |
| C-x C-c | save-buffers-kill-emacs | Exit Emacs. |
| C-x C-f | find-file | Find file and read it. |
| C-x C-l | downcase-region | Lowercase region. |
| C-x C-p | mark-page | Place cursor and mark around whole page. |
| C-x C-q | (none) | Toggle read-only status of buffer. |
| C-x C-s | save-buffer | Save file. (If terminal hangs, C-q restarts.) |
| C-x C-t | transpose-lines | Transpose two lines. |
| C-x C-u | upcase-region | Uppercase region. |
| C-x C-v | find-alternate-file | Read an alternate file, replacing the one currently in the buffer. |
| C-x C-w | write-file | Write buffer contents to file. |
| C-x C-x | exchange-point-and-mark | Exchange location of cursor and mark. |
| C-x Del | backward-kill-sentence | Delete previous sentence. |
| C-x e | call-last-kbd-macro | Execute last macro defined. |
| C-x h | mark-whole-buffer | Place cursor and mark around whole buffer. |
| C-x i | insert-file | Insert file at cursor position. |
| C-x k | kill-buffer | Delete the buffer specified. |
| C-x o | other-window | Move to the other window. |
| C-x q | kbd-macro-query | Insert a query in a macro definition. |
| C-x s | save-some-buffers | Ask whether to save each modified buffer. |
| C-x u | advertised-undo | Undo last edit (can be done repeatedly). |
| C-y | yank | Restore what you've deleted. |
| C-z | suspend-emacs | Suspend Emacs (use **exit** or **fg** to restart). |

## *Meta-Key Sequences*

| Binding | Command | Action |
| --- | --- | --- |
| M-- M-c | negative-argument; capitalize-word | Capitalize previous word. |
| M-- M-l | negative-argument; downcase-word | Lowercase previous word. |
| M-- M-u | negative-argument; upcase-word | Uppercase previous word. |
| M-$ | spell-word | Check spelling of word after cursor. |

| Binding | Command | Action |
|---------|---------|--------|
| M-< | beginning-of-buffer | Move to beginning of file. |
| M-> | end-of-buffer | Move to end-of-file. |
| M-{ | backward-paragraph | Move backward one paragraph. |
| M-} | forward-paragraph | Move forward one paragraph. |
| M-^ | delete-indentation | Join this line to the previous one. |
| M-$n$ | digit-argument | Repeat the next command $n$ times. |
| M-$n$ C-x e | digit-argument; call-last-kbd-macro | Execute the last defined macro $n$ times. |
| M-a | backward-sentence | Move backward one sentence. |
| M-b | backward-word | Move one word *backward*. |
| M-c | capitalize-word | Capitalize first letter of word. |
| M-C-\ | indent-region | Indent a region to match first line in region. |
| M-C-c | exit-recursive-edit | Exit a recursive edit. |
| M-C-o | split-line | Split line at cursor; indent to column of cursor. |
| M-C-r | isearch-backward-regexp | Incremental search backward for regular expression. |
| M-C-s | isearch-forward-regexp | Incremental search forward for regular expression. |
| M-C-v | scroll-other-window | Scroll other window. |
| M-d | kill-word | Delete word that cursor is on. |
| M-Del | backward-kill-word | Delete previous word. |
| M-e | forward-sentence | Move forward one sentence. |
| M-f | forward-word | Move one word *forward*. |
| (none) | fill-region | Reformat individual paragraphs within a region. |
| M-h | mark-paragraph | Place cursor and mark around whole paragraph. |
| M-k | kill-sentence | Delete sentence the cursor is on. |
| M-l | downcase-word | Lowercase word. |
| M-m | back-to-indentation | Move cursor to first nonblank character on line. |
| M-q | fill-paragraph | Reformat paragraph. |
| M-t | transpose-words | Transpose two words. |
| M-u | upcase-word | Uppercase word. |
| M-v | scroll-down | Move backward one screen. |
| M-x | (none) | Execute a command by typing its name. |

## Summary of Commands by Name

The following Emacs commands are presented alphabetically by command name. Use M-x to access the command name. Tables list command name, keystroke, and description. C- indicates the Ctrl key; M- indicates the Meta key.

| Command | Binding | Action |
|---------|---------|--------|
| *macroname* | (none) | Execute a keyboard macro you've saved. |
| abbrev-mode | (none) | Enter (or exit) word abbreviation mode. |
| abort-recursive-edit | C-] | Exit recursive edit and exit query-replace. |
| advertised-undo | C-x u | Undo last edit (can be done repeatedly). |
| apropos | (none) | What functions and variables involve this concept? |
| back-to-indentation | M-m | Move cursor to first nonblank character on line. |
| backward-char | C-b | Move backward one character (left). |
| backward-delete-char | Del | Delete previous character. |
| backward-kill-paragraph | (none) | Delete previous paragraph. |
| backward-kill-sentence | C-x Del | Delete previous sentence. |
| backward-kill-word | C-c C-w | Erase previous word. |
| backward-kill-word | M-Del | Delete previous word. |
| backward-page | C-x [ | Move backward one page. |
| backward-paragraph | M-{ | Move backward one paragraph. |
| backward-sentence | M-a | Move backward one sentence. |
| backward-word | M-b | Move backward one word. |
| beginning-of-buffer | M-< | Move to beginning of file. |
| beginning-of-line | C-a | Move to beginning of line. |
| call-last-kbd-macro | C-x e | Execute last macro defined. |
| capitalize-region | (none) | Capitalize region. |
| capitalize-word | M-c | Capitalize first letter of word. |
| center-line | (none) | Center line that cursor is on. |
| center-paragraph | (none) | Center paragraph that cursor is on. |
| center-region | (none) | Center currently defined region. |
| command-apropos | C-h a | What commands involve this concept? |
| compare-windows | (none) | Compare two buffers; show first difference. |
| delete-char | C-d | Delete character under cursor. |
| delete-indentation | M-^ | Join this line to previous one. |
| delete-other-windows | C-x 1 | Delete all windows but this one. |
| delete-window | C-x 0 | Delete current window. |
| delete-windows-on | (none) | Delete all windows on a given buffer. |
| describe-bindings | C-h b | What are all the key bindings for in this buffer? |
| describe-copying | C-h C-c | View the Emacs General Public License. |

| Command | Binding | Action |
|---|---|---|
| describe-distribution | C-h C-d | View information on ordering Emacs from the FSF. |
| describe-function | C-h f | What does this function do? |
| describe-key | C-h k | What command does this keystroke sequence run, and what does it do? |
| describe-key-briefly | C-h c | What command does this keystroke sequence run? |
| describe-mode | C-h m | Tell me about the mode the current buffer is in. |
| describe-no-warranty | C-h C-w | View the (non)warranty for Emacs. |
| describe-syntax | C-h s | What is the syntax table for this buffer? |
| describe-variable | C-h v | What does this variable mean, and what is its value? |
| digit-argument | M-$n$ | Repeat next command $n$ times. |
| downcase-region | C-x C-l | Lowercase region. |
| downcase-word | M-l | Lowercase word. |
| edit-abbrevs | (none) | Edit word abbreviations. |
| end-kbd-macro | C-x ) | End macro definition. |
| end-of-buffer | M-> | Move to end-of-file. |
| end-of-line | C-e | Move to end-of-line. |
| enlarge-window | C-x ^ | Make window taller. |
| enlarge-window-horizontally | C-x } | Make window wider. |
| exchange-point-and-mark | C-x C-x | Exchange location of cursor and mark. |
| exit-recursive-edit | M-C-c | Exit a recursive edit. |
| fill-individual-paragraphs | (none) | Reformat indented paragraphs, keeping indentation. |
| fill-paragraph | M-q | Reformat paragraph. |
| fill-region | (none) | Reformat individual paragraphs within a region. |
| find-alternate-file | C-x C-v | Read an alternate file, replacing the one currently in the buffer. |
| find-file | C-x C-f | Find file and read it. |
| find-file-other-frame | C-x 5 f | Find a file in a new frame. |
| find-file-other-window | C-x 4 f | Find a file in the other window. |
| forward-char | C-f | Move forward one character (right). |
| forward-page | C-x ] | Move forward one page. |
| forward-paragraph | M-} | Move forward one paragraph. |
| forward-sentence | M-e | Move forward one sentence. |
| forward-word | M-f | Move forward one word. |
| goto-char | (none) | Go to character $n$ of file. |
| goto-line | (none) | Go to line $n$ of file. |
| help-command | C-h | Enter the online help system. |
| help-with-tutorial | C-h t | Run the Emacs tutorial. |

| Command | Binding | Action |
|---|---|---|
| indent-region | M-C-\ | Indent a region to match first line in region. |
| indented-text-mode | (none) | Major mode: each tab defines a new indent for subsequent lines. |
| info | C-h i | Start the Info documentation reader. |
| insert-file | C-x i | Insert file at cursor position. |
| insert-last-keyboard-macro | (none) | Insert the macro you named into a file. |
| interrupt-shell-subjob | C-c C-c | Terminate the current job (shell mode). |
| inverse-add-global-abbrev | C-x a - | Define previous word as global (mode-independent) abbreviation. |
| inverse-add-mode-abbrev | C-x a i l | Define previous word as mode-specific abbreviation. |
| isearch-backward | C-r | Start incremental search backward. |
| isearch-backward-regexp | M-C-r | Same, but search for regular expression. |
| isearch-forward | C-s | Start incremental search forward. |
| isearch-forward-regexp | M-C-s | Same, but search for regular expression. |
| kbd-macro-query | C-x q | Insert a query in a macro definition. |
| keyboard-quit | C-g | Abort current command. |
| kill-all-abbrevs | (none) | Kill abbreviations for this session. |
| kill-buffer | C-x k | Delete the buffer specified. |
| kill-line | C-k | Delete from cursor to end-of-line. |
| kill-paragraph | (none) | Delete from cursor to end of paragraph. |
| kill-region | C-w | Delete a marked region. |
| kill-sentence | M-k | Delete sentence the cursor is on. |
| kill-shell-input | C-c C-u | Erase current line. |
| kill-some-buffers | (none) | Ask about deleting each buffer. |
| kill-word | M-d | Delete word the cursor is on. |
| list-abbrevs | (none) | View word abbreviations. |
| list-buffers | C-x C-b | Display buffer list. |
| load-file | (none) | Load macro files you've saved. |
| mark-page | C-x C-p | Place cursor and mark around whole page. |
| mark-paragraph | M-h | Place cursor and mark around whole paragraph. |
| mark-whole-buffer | C-x h | Place cursor and mark around whole buffer. |
| name-last-kbd-macro | (none) | Name last macro you created (before saving it). |
| negative-argument; capitalize-word | M-- M-c | Capitalize previous word. |

| Command | Binding | Action |
|---------|---------|--------|
| negative-argument; downcase-word | M-- M-l | Lowercase previous word. |
| negative-argument; upcase-word | M-- M-u | Uppercase previous word. |
| next-line | C-n | Move to next line (down). |
| other-window | C-x o | Move to the other window. |
| previous-line | C-p | Move to previous line (up). |
| query-replace-regexp | (none) | Query-replace a regular expression. |
| quoted-insert | C-q | Insert next character typed. Useful for inserting a control character. |
| recenter | C-l | Redraw screen, with current line in center. |
| rename-buffer | (none) | Change buffer name to specified name. |
| replace-regexp | (none) | Replace a regular expression unconditionally. |
| re-search-backward | (none) | Simple regular-expression search backward. |
| re-search-forward | (none) | Simple regular-expression search forward. |
| revert-buffer | (none) | Restore buffer to the state it was in when the file was last saved (or auto-saved). |
| save-buffer | C-x C-s | Save file. (If terminal hangs, C-q restarts.) |
| save-buffers-kill-emacs | C-x C-c | Exit Emacs. |
| save-some-buffers | C-x s | Ask whether to save each modified buffer. |
| scroll-down | M-v | Move backward one screen. |
| scroll-left | C-x < | Scroll the window left. |
| scroll-other-window | M-C-v | Scroll other window. |
| scroll-right | C-x > | Scroll the window right. |
| scroll-up | C-v | Move forward one screen. |
| set-fill-prefix | C-x . | Prepend each line in paragraph with characters from beginning of line up to cursor column; cancel prefix by typing this command in column 1. |
| set-mark-command | C-@ or C-Space | Mark the beginning (or end) of a region. |
| shell-send-eof | C-c C-d | End-of-file character (shell mode). |
| shrink-window | (none) | Make window shorter. |
| shrink-window-horizontally | C-x { | Make window narrower. |
| spell-buffer | (none) | Check spelling of current buffer. |
| spell-region | (none) | Check spelling of current region. |
| spell-string | (none) | Check spelling of string typed in minibuffer. |

| Command | Binding | Action |
|---|---|---|
| spell-word | M-$ | Check spelling of word after cursor. |
| split-line | M-C-o | Split line at cursor; indent to column of cursor. |
| split-window-horizontally | C-x 3 | Divide current window horizontally into two. |
| split-window-vertically | C-x 2 | Divide current window vertically into two. |
| start-kbd-macro | C-x ( | Start macro definition. |
| stop-shell-subjob | C-c C-z | Suspend current job. |
| suspend-emacs | C-z | Suspend Emacs (use **fg** to restart). |
| switch-to-buffer | C-x b | Move to the buffer specified. |
| switch-to-buffer-other-frame | C-x 5 b | Select a buffer in another frame. |
| switch-to-buffer-other-window | C-x 4 b | Select a buffer in the other window. |
| text-mode | (none) | Enter text mode. |
| transpose-chars | C-t | Transpose two letters. |
| transpose-lines | C-x C-t | Transpose two lines. |
| transpose-paragraphs | (none) | Transpose two paragraphs. |
| transpose-sentences | (none) | Transpose two sentences. |
| transpose-words | M-t | Transpose two words. |
| unexpand-abbrev | (none) | Undo the last word abbreviation. |
| universal-argument | C-u $n$ | Repeat the next command $n$ times. |
| upcase-region | C-x C-u | Uppercase region. |
| upcase-word | M-u | Uppercase word. |
| view-emacs-news | C-h n | View news about updates to Emacs. |
| view-lossage | C-h l | What are the last 100 characters I typed? |
| where-is | C-h w | What is the key binding for this command? |
| write-abbrev-file | (none) | Write the word abbreviation file. |
| write-file | C-x C-w | Write buffer contents to file. |
| yank | C-y | Restore what you've deleted. |

# CHAPTER 11

# *The vi Editor*

**vi** is the classic screen-editing program for Unix. A number of enhanced versions exist, including **nvi**, **vim**, **vile**, and **elvis**. On Linux, the **vi** command is usually a link to one of these programs.

**vi** is based on an older line editor called **ex**. Powerful editing capabilities can be invoked within **vi** by pressing the colon (:), entering an **ex** command, and pressing the Return key. Furthermore, you can place **ex** commands in a startup file called *~/.exrc*, which **vi** reads at the beginning of your editing session. Because **ex** commands are still an important part of **vi**, they also are described in this chapter. On Linux, **ex** is sometimes called **hex**.

This chapter, which essentially covers standard **vi** but reflects **nvi** extensions, presents the following topics:

- Review of **vi** operations
- **vi** command-line options
- **ex** command-line options
- Movement commands
- Edit commands
- Saving and exiting
- Accessing multiple files
- Interacting with the shell
- Macros
- Miscellaneous commands

- Alphabetical list of keys in command mode

- Syntax of **ex** commands

- Alphabetical summary of **ex** commands

- **vi** configuration (setting options at startup)

For more information, see the O'Reilly book *Learning the vi Editor* by Linda Lamb and Arnold Robbins.

# Review of vi Operations

This section provides a review of the following:

- Command-line options

- **vi** modes

- Syntax of **vi** commands

- Status-line commands

## Command Mode

Once the file is opened, you are in command mode. From command mode, you can:

- Invoke insert mode

- Issue editing commands

- Move the cursor to a different position in the file

- Invoke **ex** commands

- Invoke a Linux shell

- Save or exit the current version of the file

## Insert Mode

In insert mode, you can enter new text in the file. Press the Esc or Ctrl-[ keys to exit insert mode and return to command mode. The following commands invoke insert mode:

**a**    Append after cursor

**A**    Append at end-of-line

**c**    Begin change operation (must be followed by a movement command)

**C**    Change to end-of-line

| | |
|---|---|
| i | Insert before cursor |
| I | Insert at beginning of line |
| o | Open a line below current line |
| O | Open a line above current line |
| R | Begin overwriting text |
| s | Substitute a character |
| S | Substitute entire line |

## Syntax of vi Commands

In **vi**, commands have the following general form:

> [*n*] *operator* [*m*] *object*

The basic editing *operators* are:

| | |
|---|---|
| c | Begin a change |
| d | Begin a deletion |
| y | Begin a yank (or copy) |

If the current line is the object of the operation, then the operator is the same as the object: **cc**, **dd**, **yy**. Otherwise, the editing operators act on objects specified by cursor-movement commands or pattern-matching commands. *n* and *m* are the number of times the operation is performed or the number of objects the operation is performed on. If both *n* and *m* are specified, the effect is *n* × *m*.

An object can represent any of the following text blocks:

*word*
> Includes characters up to a space or punctuation mark. A capitalized object is a variant form that recognizes only blank spaces.

*sentence*
> Extends to ., !, ? followed by two spaces.

*paragraph*
> Extends to next blank line or **nroff/troff** paragraph macro (defined by **para=** option).

*section*
> Extends to next **nroff/troff** section heading (defined by **sect=** option).

### Examples

**2cw** Change the next two words

**d}** Delete up to next paragraph

**d^** Delete back to beginning of line

**5yy** Copy the next five lines into temporary buffer (for future pasting)

**y]]** Copy up to the next section into temporary buffer (for future pasting)

## Status-Line Commands

Most commands are not echoed on the screen as you input them. However, the status line at the bottom of the screen is used to echo input for the following commands:

**/**    Search forward for a pattern

**?**    Search backward for a pattern

**:**    Invoke an **ex** command

**!**    Pipe the text indicated by a subsequent movement command through the following shell command, and replace the text with the output of the shell command

Commands that are input on the status line must be entered by pressing the Return key. In addition, error messages and output from the **Ctrl-G** command are displayed on the status line.

# • *vi Command-Line Options*

The three most common ways of starting a **vi** session are:

```
vi file
vi + n file
vi +/ pattern file
```

You can open *file* for editing, optionally at line *n* or at the first line matching *pattern*. If no *file* is specified, **vi** opens with an empty buffer. The command-line options that can be used with **vi** are:

+[*num*]

Start editing at line number *num*, or the last line of the file if *num* is omitted.

+/*pattern*

Start editing at the first line matching *pattern*. (Fails if **nowrapscan** is set in your *.exrc* startup file.)

−c *command*

Run the given **vi** command upon startup. Only one −c option is permitted. **ex** commands can be invoked by prefixing them with a :. An older form of this option, +*command*, is still supported.

**-e**  Run as **ex** (line editing rather than full-screen mode).

**-l**  Enter LISP mode for running LISP programs (not supported in all versions).

**-r** [*file*]

> Recover and resume editing on *file* after an aborted editor session or system crash. Without *file*, list files available for recovery.

**-t** *tag*

> Edit the file containing *tag* and position the cursor at its definition (see **ctags** in Chapter 3, *Linux Commands* for more information).

**-v**  Run in full-screen mode (default).

**-w** *rows*

> Set the window size so *rows* lines at a time are displayed; useful when editing over a slow dial-up line.

**-x**  Prompt for a key that will be used to try to encrypt or decrypt a file using **crypt** (not supported in all versions).

**-C**  Same as **-x**, but assume the file is encrypted already (not supported in all versions).

**-L**  List files that were saved due to an aborted editor session or system crash (not supported in all versions).

**-R**  Edit files read-only.

## ex Command-Line Options

While most people know **ex** commands only by their use within **vi**, the editor exists also as a separate program and can be invoked from the shell (for instance, to edit files as part of a script). Within **ex**, you can enter the **vi** or **visual** command to start **vi**. Similarly, within **vi**, you can enter **Q** to quit the **vi** editor and enter **ex**.

If you invoke **ex** as a standalone editor, you can include the following options:

**+**[*num*]

> Start editing at line number *num*, or the last line of the file if *num* is omitted.

**+/**pattern

> Start editing at the first line matching *pattern*. (Fails if **nowrapscan** is set in your *.exrc* start-up file.)

**-c** *command*

> Run the given **ex** command upon start-up. Only one **-c** option is permitted. An older form of this option, **+**command, is still supported.

**-e**  Run as a line editor rather than full-screen **vi** mode (default).

**-l**  Enter LISP mode for running LISP programs (not supported in all versions).

**−r** [*file*]

Recover and resume editing on *file* after an aborted editor session or system crash. Without *file*, list files available for recovery.

**−s**  Silent; do not display prompts. Useful when running a script. This behavior also can be set through the older − option.

**−t** *tag*

Edit the file containing *tag* and position the cursor at its definition (see **ctags** in Chapter 3 for more information).

**−v**  Run in full-screen mode (same as invoking **vi**).

**−w** *rows*

Set the window size so *rows* lines at a time are displayed; useful when editing by a slow dial-up line.

**−x**  Prompt for a key that will be used to try to encrypt or decrypt a file using **crypt** (not supported in all versions).

**−C**  Same as **−x**, but assume the file is encrypted already (not supported in all versions).

**−L**  List files that were saved due to an editor of system crash (not supported in all versions).

**−R**  Edit files read-only; do not allow changes to be saved.

You can exit **ex** in several ways:

**:x**  Exit (save changes and quit).

**:q!**  Quit without saving changes.

**:vi**  Enter the **vi** editor.

## Movement Commands

A number preceding a command repeats the movement. Movement commands are also objects for change, delete, and yank operations.

### Character

| Command | Action |
|---|---|
| **h, j, k, l** | Left, down, up, right (←, ↓, ↑, →) |
| **Spacebar** | Right |
| **Backspace** | Left |
| **Ctrl-H** | Left |

## Text

| Command | Action |
|---|---|
| w, b | Forward, backward by word (treating punctuation marks as words). |
| W, B | Forward, backward by word (recognizing only whitespace, not punctuation, as separators). |
| e | End of word (treating a punctuation mark as the end of a word). |
| E | End of word (recognizing only whitespace as the end of a word). |
| ), ( | Beginning of next, current sentence. |
| }, { | Beginning of next, current paragraph. |
| ]], [[ | Beginning of next, current section. |
| Ctrl-D | Move to previous tab setting. |
| Ctrl-T | Move to next tab setting. |
| Ctrl-W | Move back one word. |

## Lines

| Command | Action |
|---|---|
| 0, $ | First, last position of current line. |
| ^, _ | First nonblank character of current line. |
| +, − | First character of next, previous line. |
| Return | First nonblank character of next line. |
| n\| | Column n of current line. |
| H | Top line of screen. |
| M | Middle line of screen. |
| L | Last line of screen. |
| nH | n lines after top line. |
| nL | n lines before last line. |
| Ctrl-J | Move down one line. |
| Ctrl-M | Move to first nonblank character of next line. |

## Screens

| Command | Action |
|---|---|
| Ctrl-F, Ctrl-B | Scroll forward, backward one screen. |
| Ctrl-D, Ctrl-U | Scroll down, up one-half screen. |
| Ctrl-E, Ctrl-Y | Show one more line at bottom, top of window. |
| z Return | Reposition line with cursor to top of screen. |
| z . | Reposition line with cursor to middle of screen. |
| z − | Reposition line with cursor to bottom of screen. |
| Ctrl-L, Ctrl-R | Redraw screen (without scrolling). |

## Searches

| Command | Action |
|---|---|
| /*pattern* | Search forward for *pattern*. |
| / | Repeat previous search forward. |
| /*pattern*/+n | Go to line *n* after *pattern*. |
| ?*pattern* | Search backward for *pattern*. |
| ? | Repeat previous search backward. |
| ?*pattern*?−n | Go to line *n* before *pattern*. |
| n | Repeat previous search. |
| N | Repeat previous search in opposite direction. |
| % | Find match of current parenthesis, brace, or bracket. |
| f*x* | Move forward to *x* on current line. |
| F*x* | Move backward to *x* on current line. |
| t*x* | Move forward to just before *x* in current line. |
| T*x* | Move back to just after *x* in current line. |
| , | Reverse search direction of last **f**, **F**, **t**, or **T**. |
| ; | Repeat last character search (**f**, **F**, **t**, or **T**). |

## Line numbering

| Command | Action |
|---|---|
| Ctrl-G | Display current filename and line number. |
| *n*G | Move to line number *n*. |
| G | Move to last line in file. |
| :*n* | Move to line number *n*. |

## Marking position

| Command | Action |
|---|---|
| m*x* | Mark current position with character *x*. |
| `*x* | (backquote) Move cursor to mark *x*. |
| '*x* | (apostrophe) Move to start of line containing *x*. |
| `` | (backquotes) Return to previous mark (or location prior to search). |
| '' | (apostrophes) Like preceding, but return to start of line. |

# Edit Commands

Recall that **c**, **d**, and **y** are the basic editing operators.

## Inserting New Text

| Command | Action |
|---------|--------|
| a | Append after cursor. |
| A | Append to end of line. |
| i | Insert before cursor. |
| I | Insert at beginning of line. |
| o | Open a line below cursor. |
| O | Open a line above cursor. |
| Esc | Terminate insert mode. |
| Tab | Insert a tab. |
| Backspace | Delete previous character (in insert mode). |
| Ctrl-I | Insert a tab. |
| Ctrl-U | Delete current line. |
| Ctrl-V | Insert next character verbatim. |
| Ctrl-[ | Terminate insert mode. |

Some of the control characters listed in the previous table are set by **stty**. Your terminal settings may differ.

## Changing and Deleting Text

The following table is not exhaustive but illustrates the most common operations.

| Command | Action |
|---------|--------|
| cw | Change through end of current word. |
| cc | Change line. |
| c$ | Change text from current position to end-of-line. |
| c | Same as **c$**. |
| dd | Delete current line. |
| d$ | Delete remainder of line. |
| D | Same as **d$**. |
| ndd | Delete n lines. |
| dw | Delete a word. |
| d} | Delete up to next paragraph. |
| d^ | Delete back to beginning of line. |
| d/pattern | Delete up to first occurrence of pattern. |
| dn | Delete up to next occurrence of pattern. |
| dfa | Delete up to and including a on current line. |
| dta | Delete up to (not including) a on current line. |
| dL | Delete up to last line on screen. |
| dG | Delete to end-of-file. |
| p | Insert last deleted text after cursor. |
| P | Insert last deleted text before cursor. |
| rx | Replace character with x. |

| Command | Action |
|---------|--------|
| Rtext | Replace *text* beginning at cursor. |
| s | Substitute character. |
| *n*s | Substitute *n* characters. |
| S | Substitute entire line. |
| u | Undo last change. |
| U | Restore current line. |
| x | Delete current character. |
| X | Delete back one character. |
| *n*X | Delete previous *n* characters. |
| . | Repeat last change. |
| ~ | Reverse case. |
| & | Repeat last substitution. |
| Y | Copy (yank) current line to temporary buffer. |
| yy | Same as **Y**. |
| "*x*yy | Copy current line to buffer *x*. |
| ye | Copy text to end of word into temporary buffer. |
| yw | Same as **ye**. |
| y$ | Copy rest of line into temporary buffer. |
| "*x*dd | Delete current line into buffer *x*. |
| "*X*dd | Delete current line and append to buffer *x*. |
| "*x*p | Put contents of buffer *x*. |
| J | Join previous line to current line. |
| :j! | Same as **J**. |

## Saving and Exiting

Writing a file means saving the edits and updating the file's modification time.

| Command | Action |
|---------|--------|
| ZZ | Quit **vi**, writing the file only if changes were made. |
| :x | Same as **ZZ**. |
| :wq | Write and quit file. |
| :w | Write file. |
| :w *file* | Save copy to *file*. |
| :*n1,n2*w *file* | Write lines *n1* to *n2* to new *file*. |
| :*n1,n2*w >> *file* | Append lines *n1* to *n2* to existing *file*. |
| :w! | Write file (overriding protection). |
| :w! *file* | Overwrite *file* with current buffer. |
| :w %.*new* | Write current buffer named *file* as *file.new*. |
| :q | Quit file. |
| :q! | Quit file (discarding edits). |
| Q | Quit **vi** and invoke **ex**. |
| :vi | Return to **vi** after **Q** command. |

| Command | Action |
|---|---|
| % | Current filename. |
| # | Alternate filename. |

## Accessing Multiple Files

| Command | Action |
|---|---|
| :e file | Edit another *file*; current file becomes alternate. |
| :e! | Restore last saved version of current file. |
| :e+ file | Begin editing at end of new *file*. |
| :e+ n file | Open new *file* at line *n*. |
| :e# | Open to previous position in alternate file. |
| :ta tag | Edit file containing *tag* at the location of the tag. |
| :n | Edit next file. |
| :n! | Force next file into buffer (don't save changes to current file). |
| :n files | Specify new list of *files*. |
| :args | Display multiple files to be edited. |
| :rew | Rewind list of multiple files to top. |

## Interacting with the Shell

| Command | Action |
|---|---|
| :r file | Read in contents of *file* after cursor. |
| :r !command | Read in output from *command* after current line. |
| :nr !command | Like preceding, but place after line *n* (0 for top of file). |
| :!command | Run *command*, then return. |
| !object command | Send *object*, indicated by a movement command, as input to shell command *command*; replace *object* with command output. |
| :n1,n2! command | Send lines *n1* through *n2* to *command*; replace with output. |
| n!!command | Send *n* lines to *command*; replace with output. |
| !! | Repeat last system command. |
| !!command | Replace current line with output of *command*. |
| :sh | Create subshell; return to file with EOF. |
| Ctrl-Z | Suspend editor, resume with **fg**. |
| :so file | Read and execute **ex** commands from *file*. |

# Macros

| Command | Action |
|---|---|
| **:ab** *in out* | Use *in* as abbreviation for *out.* |
| **:unab** *in* | Remove abbreviation for *in.* |
| **:ab** | List abbreviations. |
| **:map** *c sequence* | Map character *c* as *sequence* of commands. |
| **:unmap** *c* | Disable map for character *c.* |
| **:map** | List characters that are mapped. |
| **:map!** *c sequence* | Map character *c* to input mode *sequence.* |
| **:unmap!** *c* | Disable input mode map (you may need to quote the character with **Ctrl-V**). |
| **:map!** | List characters that are mapped to input mode. |

The following characters are unused in command mode and can be mapped as user-defined commands:

*Letters:*
> g K q V v

*Control keys:*
> ^K ^O ^T ^W ^X

*Symbols:*
> _ * \ =

The = is used by **vi** if LISP mode is set. Different versions of **vi** may use some of these characters, so test them before using them.

# Miscellaneous Commands

| Command | Action |
|---|---|
| < | Shift line left to position indicated by following movement command. |
| > | Shift line right to position indicated by following movement command. |
| << | Shift line left one shift width (default is 8 spaces). |
| >> | Shift line right one shift width (default is 8 spaces). |
| >} | Shift right to end of paragraph. |
| <% | Shift left until matching parenthesis, brace, bracket, etc. (Cursor must be on the matching symbol.) |
| ^[ | Abort command or end input mode. |
| ^] | Perform a tag look-up on the text under the cursor. |
| ^\ | Enter **ex** line-editing mode. |
| ^^ | (Caret key with Ctrl key pressed) Return to previously edited file. |

# Alphabetical List of Keys in Command Mode

For brevity, control characters are marked by ^.

| Command | Action |
|---------|--------|
| a | Append text after cursor. |
| A | Append text at end-of-line. |
| ^A | Search for next occurrence of word under cursor. |
| b | Back up to beginning of word in current line. |
| B | Back up one word, treating punctuation marks as words. |
| ^B | Scroll backward one window. |
| c | Change text up to target of next movement command. |
| C | Change to end of current line. |
| ^C | End insert mode; interrupts a long operation. |
| d | Delete up to target of next movement command. |
| D | Delete to end of current line. |
| ^D | Scroll down half-window; in insert mode, unindent to **shiftwidth** if **autoindent** is set. |
| e | Move to end of word. |
| E | Move to end of word, treating punctuation as part of word. |
| ^E | Show one more line at bottom of window. |
| f | Find next character typed forward on current line. |
| F | Find next character typed backward on current line. |
| ^F | Scroll forward one window. |
| g | Unused. |
| G | Go to specified line or end-of-file. |
| ^G | Print information about file on status line. |
| h | Left arrow cursor key. |
| H | Move cursor to home position. |
| ^H | Left arrow cursor key; Backspace key in insert mode. |
| i | Insert text before cursor. |
| I | Insert text before first nonblank character on line. |
| ^I | Unused in command mode; in insert mode, same as Tab key. |
| j | Down arrow cursor key. |
| J | Join previous line to current line. |
| ^J | Down arrow cursor key; in insert mode, move down a line. |
| k | Up arrow cursor key. |
| K | Unused. |
| ^K | Unused. |
| l | Right arrow cursor key. |
| L | Move cursor to last position in window. |
| ^L | Redraw screen. |
| m | Mark the current cursor position in register (a-z). |
| M | Move cursor to middle position in window. |

| Command | Action |
|---------|--------|
| ^M | Move to beginning of next line. |
| n | Repeat the last search command. |
| N | Repeat the last search command in reverse direction. |
| ^N | Down arrow cursor key. |
| o | Open line below current line. |
| O | Open line above current line. |
| ^O | Unused. |
| p | Put yanked or deleted text after or below cursor. |
| P | Put yanked or deleted text before or above cursor. |
| ^P | Up arrow cursor key. |
| q | Unused. |
| Q | Quit **vi** and enter **ex** line-editing mode. |
| ^Q | Unused. (On some terminals, resume data flow.) |
| r | Replace character at cursor with the next character you type. |
| R | Replace characters. |
| ^R | Redraw the screen. |
| s | Change the character under the cursor to typed characters. |
| S | Change entire line. |
| ^S | Unused. (On some terminals, stop data flow.) |
| t | Find next character typed forward on current line and position cursor before it. |
| T | Find next character typed backward on current line and position cursor after it. |
| ^T | Unused in command mode; in insert mode, move to next tab setting. |
| u | Undo the last change made. |
| U | Restore current line, discarding changes. |
| ^U | Scroll the screen upward a half-window. |
| v | Unused. |
| V | Unused. |
| ^V | Unused in command mode; in insert mode, insert next character verbatim. |
| w | Move to beginning of next word. |
| W | Move to beginning of next word, treating punctuation marks as words. |
| ^W | Unused in command mode; in insert mode, back up to beginning of word. |
| x | Delete character under cursor. |
| X | Delete character before cursor. |
| ^X | Unused. |
| y | Yank or copy text up to target of following movement command into temporary buffer. |
| Y | Make copy of current line. |
| ^Y | Show one more line at top of window. |

| Command | Action |
|---------|--------|
| **z** | Reposition line containing cursor. **z** must be followed by Return (reposition line to top of screen), . (reposition line to middle of screen), or − (reposition line to bottom of screen). |
| **zz** | Exit the editor, saving changes. |

## Syntax of ex Commands

To enter an **ex** command from **vi**, type:

> :[*address*] *command* [*options*]

An initial : indicates an **ex** command. As you type the command, it is echoed on the status line. Enter the command by pressing Return. *address* is the line number or range of lines that are the object of *command*. *options* and *addresses* are described in the following sections. **ex** commands are described in the alphabetical summary.

### Options

! Indicates a variant command form, overriding the normal behavior.

*count*
> The number of times the command is to be repeated. Unlike **vi** commands, **ex** commands cannot be preceded by *count*, because a number preceding an **ex** command is treated as a line address. For example, **d3** deletes 3 lines beginning with the current line; **3d** deletes line 3.

*file* The name of a file that is affected by the command. % stands for current file; # stands for previous file.

### Addresses

If no address is given, the current line is the object of the command. If the address specifies a range of lines, the format is:

> *x,y*

where *x* and *y* are the first and last addressed lines (*x* must precede *y* in the buffer). *x* and *y* may be line numbers or symbols. Using ; instead of , sets the current line to *x* before interpreting *y*. The notation **1,$** addresses all lines in the file, as does %.

## Address Symbols

| Symbol | Meaning |
|---|---|
| **1,$** | All lines in the file |
| **%** | All lines; same as **1,$** |
| ***x,y*** | Lines *x* through *y* |
| ***x;y*** | Lines *x* through *y*, with current line reset to *x* |
| **0** | Top of file |
| **.** | Current line |
| *n* | Absolute line number *n* |
| **$** | Last line |
| ***x-n*** | *n* lines before *x* |
| ***x+n*** | *n* lines after *x* |
| **-[*n*]** | One or *n* lines previous |
| **+[*n*]** | One or *n* lines ahead |
| **'*x*** | Line marked with *x* |
| **' '** | Previous mark |
| **/*pattern*/** | Forward to line matching *pattern* |
| **?*pattern*?** | Backward to line matching *pattern* |

See Chapter 9, *Pattern Matching*, for more information on using patterns.

# Alphabetical Summary of ex Commands

**ex** commands can be entered by specifying any unique abbreviation. In this listing, the full name appears in the margin, and the shortest possible abbreviation is used in the syntax line. Examples are assumed to be typed from **vi**, so they include the : prompt.

---

**ab** [*string text*]                                                         **abbrev**

Define *string* when typed to be translated into *text*. If *string* and *text* are not specified, list all current abbreviations.

Examples

Note: ^M appears when you type **Ctrl-V** followed by Return.

```
:ab ora O'Reilly & Associates, Inc.
:ab id Name:^MRank:^MPhone:
```

| | |
|---|---|
| append | [*address*] a[!]<br>*text*<br><br>.<br><br>Append *text* at specified *address*, or at present address if none is specified. Add a ! to switch the **autoindent** setting that will be used during input (e.g., if **autoindent** was enabled, ! disables it). Terminate input by entering a line consisting of just a period. |
| args | **ar**<br><br>Print filename arguments (the list of files to edit). The current argument is shown in brackets ([ ]). |
| cd | **cd** *dir*<br>**chdir** *dir*<br><br>Change current directory within the editor to *dir.* |
| change | [*address*] c[!]<br>*text*<br><br>.<br><br>Replace the specified lines with *text.* Add a ! to switch the **autoindent** setting during input of *text.* Terminate input by entering a line consisting of just a period. |
| copy | [*address*] co *destination*<br><br>Copy the lines included in *address* to the specified *destination* address. The command **t** is the same as **copy**.<br><br>***Example***<br><br>`:1,10 co 50`    *Copy first 10 lines to just after line 50* |
| delete | [*address*] d [*buffer*]<br><br>Delete the lines included in *address*. If *buffer* is specified, save or append the text to the named buffer.<br><br>Examples<br><br>`:/Part I/,/Part II/-1d`    *Delete to line above "Part II"*<br>`:/main/+d`    *Delete line below "main"*<br>`:.,$d`    *Delete from this line to last line* |

## e[!] [+n] [*file*]

edit

Begin editing *file*. Add a ! to discard any changes to the current file. If no *file* is given, edit another copy of the current file. With the +*n* argument, begin editing on line *n*.

### Examples

```
:e file
:e#       Return to editing the previous file
:e!       Discard edits since last save
```

## exu [*command*]

exusage

Print a brief usage message describing *command*, or a list of available commands if *command* is omitted.

## f [*filename*]

file

Change the name of the current file to *filename*, which is considered "not edited." If no *filename* is specified, print the current status of the file.

### Example

```
:f %.new
```

## [*address*] g[!]/*pattern*//[*commands*]

global

Execute *commands* on all lines that contain *pattern* or, if *address* is specified, on all lines within that range. If *commands* are not specified, print all such lines. If ! is used, execute *commands* on all lines that don't contain *pattern*. See **v**.

### Examples

```
:g/Unix/p            Print all lines containing "Unix"
:g/Name:/s/tom/Tom/  Change "tom" to "Tom" on all lines
                     containing "Name:"
```

## h

help

Print a brief help message. Information on particular commands can be obtained through the **exusage** and **viusage** commands.

| insert | *address* i[!]<br>*text*<br>. |
|---|---|
| | Insert *text* at line before the specified *address*, or at present address if none is specified. Add a ! to switch the **autoindent** setting during input of *text*. Terminate input by entering a line consisting of just a period. |
| join | [*address*] j[!] [*count*] |
| | Place the text in the specified *address* on one line, with whitespace adjusted to provide two blank characters after a period (.), no blank characters after a ), and one blank character otherwise. Add a ! to prevent whitespace adjustment.<br><br>**Example**<br><br>`:1,5j!`     *Join first five lines, preserving whitespace* |
| k | [*address*] k *char* |
| | Mark the given *address* with *char*. Return later to the line with ' *char*. |
| list | [*address*] l [*count*] |
| | Print the specified lines so that tabs display as ^I, and the ends of lines display as $. l is a temporary version of :**set list**. |
| map | map[!] [*char commands*] |
| | Define a keyboard macro named *char* as the specified sequence of *commands*. *char* is usually a single character, or the sequence #*n*, representing a function key on the keyboard. Use a ! to create a macro for input mode. With no arguments, list the currently defined macros.<br><br>Examples<br><br>`:map K dwwP`     *Transpose two words*<br>`:map q :w^M:n^M`     *Write current file; go to next*<br>`:map! + ^[bi(^[ea)`     *Enclose previous word in parentheses* |

*[address]* **ma** *char* | mark

Mark the specified line with *char*, a single lowercase letter. Return later to the line with **'** *char*. Same as **k**.

---

**mk**[!] *file* | mkexrc

Create an *.exrc* file containing a **set** command for every **ex** option, set to defaults.

---

*[address]* **m** *destination* | move

Move the lines specified by *address* to the *destination* address.

**Example**

`:.,/Note/m /END/`        *Move text block after line containing "END"*

---

**n**[!] [[+*command*] *filelist*] | next

Edit the next file from the command-line argument list. Use **args** to list these files. If *filelist* is provided, replace the current argument list with *filelist* and begin editing on the first file; if *command* is given (containing no spaces), execute *command* after editing the first such file. Add a ! to discard any changes to the current file.

**Example**

`:n chap*`        *Start editing all "chapter" files*

---

*[address]* **nu** *[count]* | number

Print each line specified by *address*, preceded by its buffer line number. Use **#** as an alternate abbreviation for **number**. *count* specifies the number of lines to show, starting with *address*.

---

*[address]* **o** *[/pattern/]* | open

Enter **vi**'s open mode at the lines specified by *address* or at the lines matching *pattern*. Enter and exit open mode with **Q**. Open mode lets you use the regular **vi** commands, but only one line at a time. May be useful on slow dial-up lines.

| preserve | **pre** |
|---|---|
| | Save the current editor buffer as though the system had crashed. |

| previous | **prev[!]** |
|---|---|
| | Edit the previous file from the command-line argument list. |

| print | *[address]* **p** *[count]*<br>*[address]* **P** *[count]* |
|---|---|
| | Print the lines specified by *address*. *count* specifies the number of lines to print, starting with *address*. Add a ! to discard any changes to the current file.<br><br>***Example***<br><br>`:100;+5p`    *Show line 100 and the next 5 lines* |

| put | *[address]* **pu** *[char]* |
|---|---|
| | Restore the lines that were previously deleted or yanked from named buffer *char*, and put them after the line specified by *address*. If *char* is not specified, restore the last deleted or yanked text. |

| quit | **q[!]** |
|---|---|
| | Terminate current editing session. Use ! to discard changes made since the last save. If the editing session includes additional files in the argument list that were never accessed, quit by typing **q!** or by typing **q** twice. |

| read | *[address]* **r** *file* |
|---|---|
| | Copy in the text from *file* on the line below the specified *address*. If *file* is not specified, the current filename is used.<br><br>***Example***<br><br>`:0r $HOME/data`    *Read file in at top of current file* |

| read | *[address]* **r** *!command* |
|---|---|
| | Read the output of Linux *command* into the text after the line specified by *address*. |

| | |
|---|---|
| *Example* | read |
| :$r !cal     *Place a calendar at end-of-file* | |

---

**rec** [*file*]

Recover *file* from system save area.

recover

---

**rew**[!]

Rewind argument list and begin editing the first file in the list. The ! flag rewinds, discarding any changes to the current file that haven't been saved.

rewind

---

**sc**[!] [*file*]

Create a new shell in a buffer that can be saved, optionally specifying *file* where the buffer can be saved. Can be used only in **vi**.

script

---

**se** *parameter1 parameter2* ...

Set a value to an option with each *parameter*, or if no *parameter* is supplied, print all options that have been changed from their defaults. For Boolean-valued options, each *parameter* can be phrased as *option* or **no***option*; other options can be assigned with the syntax *option=value*. Specify **all** to list current settings.

*Examples*

```
:set nows wm=10
:set all
```

set

---

**sh**

Create a new shell. Resume editing when the shell is terminated.

shell

---

**so** *file*

Read and execute **ex** commands from *file*.

*Example*

```
:so $HOME/.exrc
```

source

---

| | |
|---|---|
| stop | **st** |
| | Suspend the editing session. Same as **Ctrl-Z**. Use **fg** to resume session. |
| substitute | [*address*] **s** [/*pattern*/*replacement*/] [*options*] [*count*] |
| | Replace each instance of *pattern* on the specified lines with *replacement*. If *pattern* and *replacement* are omitted, repeat last substitution. *count* specifies the number of lines on which to substitute, starting with *address*. When preceded by the **global** (**g**) or **v** command, this command can be specified with a blank *pattern*, in which case the pattern from the **g** or **v** command is then used. For more examples, see "Examples of Searching and Replacing" in Chapter 9. |

*Options*

c   Prompt for confirmation before each change.

g   Substitute all instances of *pattern* on each line.

p   Print the last line on which a substitution was made.

*Examples*

| | |
|---|---|
| `:1,10s/yes/no/g` | *Substitute on first 10 lines* |
| `:%s/[Hh]ello/Hi/gc` | *Confirm global substitutions* |
| `:s/Fortran/\U&/ 3` | *Uppercase first instance of "Fortran" on next three lines* |
| `:g/^[0-9][0-9]*/s//Line &:/` | *For every line beginning with one or more digits, add the "Line" and a colon* |

| | |
|---|---|
| suspend | **su** |
| | Suspend the editing session. Same as **Ctrl-Z**. Use **fg** to resume session. |
| t | [*address*] **t** *destination* |
| | Copy the lines included in *address* to the specified *destination* address. **t** is an alias for **copy**. |

*Example*

| | |
|---|---|
| `:%t$` | *Copy the file and add it to the end* |

| [*address*] ta[!] *tag* | tag |
|---|---|

Switch the editing session to the file containing *tag*.

*Example*

Run **ctags**, then switch to the file containing *myfunction*:

```
:!ctags *.c
:tag myfunction
```

| tagn[!] | tagnext |
|---|---|

Find the next occurrence of the current tag.

| tagp[!] | tagpop |
|---|---|

Forget the current tag and return to the last position of the previous tag found.

| tagpr[!] | tagprev |
|---|---|

Return to the previous occurrence of the current tag.

| tagt[!] | tagtop |
|---|---|

Return to the first tag searched for and forget about all tags.

| una *word* | unabbreviate |
|---|---|

Remove *word* from the list of abbreviations.

| u | undo |
|---|---|

Reverse the changes made by the last editing command.

| unm[!] *char* | unmap |
|---|---|

Remove *char* from the list of keyboard macros. Use ! to remove a macro for input mode.

| | |
|---|---|
| v | [*address*] v/*pattern*/[*commands*] |
| | Execute *commands* on all lines *not* containing *pattern*. If *commands* are not specified, print all such lines. v is equivalent to g!. See **global**. |
| | ***Example*** |
| | `:v/#include/d`    *Delete all lines except "#include" lines* |
| **version** | ve |
| | Print the editor's current version number. |
| **vi** | vi [+*n*] *file* |
| | Begin editing *file*, optionally at line *n*. Can be used only in **vi**. |
| **visual** | [*address*] vi [*type*] [*count*] |
| | Enter visual mode (vi) at the line specified by *address*. Exit with Q. *type* can be one of −, ^, or . (See the z command.) *count* specifies an initial window size. |
| **viusage** | viu [*key*] |
| | Print a brief usage message describing the operation of *key*, or a list of defined keys if *key* is omitted. |
| **wq** | wq[!] |
| | Write and quit the file in one command. The ! flag forces the editor to write over any current contents of *file*. |
| **write** | [*address*] w[!] [[>>] *file* |
| | Write lines specified by *address* to *file*, or write full contents of buffer if *address* is not specified. If *file* also is omitted, save the contents of the buffer to the current filename. If >>*file* is used, write contents to the end of an existing *file*. The ! flag forces the editor to write over any current contents of *file*. |

| | |
|---|---|
| [*address*] **w** !*command* | write |

Write lines specified by *address* to *command*.

**Examples**

```
:1,10w name_list        Copy first 10 lines to name_list
:50w >> name_list       Now append line 50
```

| | |
|---|---|
| **x** | xit |

Write the file if it was changed since the last write, then quit.

| | |
|---|---|
| [*address*] **ya** [*char*] [*count*] | yank |

Place lines specified by *address* in named buffer *char*. If no *char* is given, place lines in general buffer. *count* specifies the number of lines to yank, starting with *address*.

**Example**

```
:101,200 ya a
```

| | |
|---|---|
| [*address*] **z** [*type*] [*count*] | z |

Print a window of text, with the line specified by *address* at the top. *count* specifies the number of lines to be displayed.

**Type**

+    Place specified line at top of window (the default).

–    Place specified line at bottom of window.

.    Place specified line in center of window.

ˆ    Move up one window.

=    Place specified line in center of window, and leave this line as the current line.

| | |
|---|---|
| [*address*] !*command* | ! |

Execute Linux *command* in a shell. If *address* is specified, apply the lines contained in *address* as standard input to *command*, and replace the lines with the output.

→

| | |
|---|---|
| !<br>← | **Examples**<br><br>`:!ls`  *List files in the current directory*<br>`:11,20!sort -f`  *Sort lines 11–20 of current file* |
| = | *[address]* =<br><br>Print the line number of the next line matching *address*. If no address is given, print the number of the last line. |
| < > | *[address]* < *[count]*<br>*[address]* > *[count]*<br><br>Shift lines specified by *address* either left (<) or right (>). Only blanks and tabs are removed in a left shift. *count* specifies the number of lines to shift, starting with *address*. |
| *address* | *address*<br><br>Print the line specified in *address*. |
| **Return** | *Return*<br><br>Print the next line in the file. |
| & | *&* *[options]* *[count]*<br><br>Repeat the previous substitution (s) command. *count* specifies the number of lines on which to substitute, starting with *address*.<br><br>**Examples**<br><br>`:s/Overdue/Paid/`  *Substitute once on current line*<br>`:g/Status/&`  *Redo substitution on all "Status" lines* |
| ~ | *[address]* ~ *[count]*<br><br>Replace the previous regular expression with the previous replacement pattern from a **substitute** (s) command. |

| ^D | ^D |
|---|---|
| Scroll through the file. | |
| ^Z | ^Z |
| Suspend the editing session. Use **fg** to resume session. | |

# *vi Configuration*

This section describes the following:

- The :**set** command
- Options available with :**set**
- Sample *ˆ/.exrc* file

## *The :set Command*

The :**set** command lets you specify options that change characteristics of your editing environment. Options may be put in the *ˆ/.exrc* file or set during a **vi** session.

The colon should not be typed if the command is put in *ˆ/.exrc*.

| Command | Action |
|---|---|
| :**set** *x* | Enable option *x*. |
| :**set no***x* | Disable option *x*. |
| :**set** *x=val* | Give *value* to option *x*. |
| :**set** | Show changed options. |
| :**set all** | Show all options. |
| :**set** *x?* | Show value of option *x*. |

## *Options Used by :set*

The following table describes the options to :**set**. The first column includes the optional abbreviation, if there is one, and uses an equals sign to show that the option takes a value. The second column gives the default, and the third column describes the behavior of the enabled option.

| Option | Default | Description |
|---|---|---|
| autoindent (ai) | noai | In insert mode, indent each line to the same level as the line above or below. Use with **shiftwidth** option. |

| Option | Default | Description |
|--------|---------|-------------|
| autoprint (ap) | ap | Display changes after each editor command. (For global replacement, display last replacement.) |
| autowrite (aw) | noaw | Automatically write (save) file if changed, before opening another file with :n or before giving Linux command with :!. |
| beautify (bf) | nobf | Ignore all control characters during input (except tab, newline, or form-feed). |
| directory= (dir) | /tmp | Name the directory in which **ex** stores buffer files. (Directory must be writable.) |
| edcompatible | noed-compatible | Use **ed**-like features on substitute commands. |
| errorbells (eb) | errorbells | Sound bell when an error occurs. |
| exrc (ex) | noexrc | Allow the execution of ˜/.exrc files that reside outside the user's home directory. |
| hardtabs= (ht) | 8 | Define boundaries for terminal hardware tabs. |
| ignorecase (ic) | noic | Disregard case during a search. |
| lisp | nolisp | Insert indents in appropriate LISP format. ( ), { }, [[, and ]] are modified to have meaning for LISP. |
| list | nolist | Print tabs as ^I; mark ends of lines with $. (Use **list** to tell if end character is a tab or a space.) |
| magic | magic | Wildcard characters . (dot), * (asterisk), and [ ] (brackets) have special meaning in patterns. |
| mesg | mesg | Permit system messages to display on terminal while editing in **vi**. |
| number (nu) | nonu | Display line numbers on left of screen during editing session. |
| open | open | Allow entry to open mode from **ex**. |
| optimize (opt) | noopt | Abolish carriage returns at the ends of lines when printing multiple lines; speeds output on dumb terminals when printing lines with leading whitespace (blanks or tabs). |
| paragraphs= (para) | IPLPPPQPLI pplpipbp | Define paragraph delimiters for movement by { or }. The pairs of characters in the value are the names of **nroff/troff** macros that begin paragraphs. |

| Option | Default | Description |
|---|---|---|
| prompt | prompt | Display the **ex** prompt (:) when vi's Q command is given. |
| readonly (ro) | noro | Any writes (saves) of a file will fail unless you use ! after the write (works with **w**, **ZZ**, or **autowrite**). |
| redraw (re) | noredraw | Terminal redraws screen whenever edits are made (in other words, insert mode pushes over existing characters, and deleted lines immediately close up). Default depends on line speed and terminal type. **noredraw** is useful at slow speeds on a dumb terminal: deleted lines show up as @, and inserted text appears to overwrite existing text until you press Esc. |
| remap | remap | Allow nested map sequences. |
| report= | 5 | Display a message on the prompt line whenever you make an edit that affects at least a certain number of lines. For example, **6dd** reports the message "6 lines deleted." |
| scroll= | <1/2 window> | Amount of screen to scroll. |
| sections= (sect) | **SHNHH HU** | Define section delimiters for [[ ]] movement. The pairs of characters in the value are the names of **nroff/troff** macros that begin sections. |
| shell= (sh) | /bin/sh | Pathname of shell used for shell escape (:!) and shell command (:sh). Default value is derived from SHELL variable. |
| shiftwidth= (sw) | 8 | Define number of spaces used by the indent commands (^T, ^D, >>, and <<). |
| showmatch (sm) | nosm | In **vi**, when ) or } is entered, cursor moves briefly to matching ( or {. (If the match is not on the screen, rings the error message bell.) Very useful for programming. |
| showmode | noshowmode | In insert mode, displays a message on the prompt line indicating the type of insert you are making, such as "Open Mode" or "Append Mode." |
| slowopen (slow) | | Hold off display during insert. Default depends on line speed and terminal type. |
| tabstop= (ts) | 8 | Define number of spaces that a tab indents during editing session. (Printer still uses system tab of 8.) |

| Option | Default | Description |
|--------|---------|-------------|
| taglength= (tl) | 0 | Define number of characters that are significant for tags. Default (0) means that all characters are significant. |
| tags= | tags /usr/lib/tags | Define pathname of files containing tags (see the **ctags** command in Chapter 3). By default, the system looks for files **tags** (in the current directory) and */usr/lib/tags*. |
| term= | | Set terminal type. |
| terse | noterse | Display shorter error messages. |
| timeout (to) | timeout | Keyboard maps timeout after 1 second. |
| ttytype= | | Set terminal type. Default is inherited from TERM environment variable. |
| warn | warn | Display the message, "No write since last change." |
| window= (w) | | Show a certain number of lines of the file on the screen. Default depends on line speed and terminal type. |
| wrapmargin= (wm) | 0 | Define right margin. If greater than 0, automatically insert carriage returns to break lines. |
| wrapscan (ws) | ws | Searches wrap around either end of file. |
| writeany (wa) | nowa | Allow saving to any file. |

## Sample ~/.exrc File

The following lines of code are an example of a customized *.exrc* file:

```
set nowrapscan wrapmargin=7
set sections=SeAhBhChDh nomesg
map q :w^M:n^M
map v dwElp
ab ORA O'Reilly & Associates, Inc.
```

CHAPTER 12

# *The sed Editor*

This chapter presents the following topics:

- Conceptual overview of **sed**

- Command-line syntax

- Syntax of **sed** commands

- Group summary of **sed** commands

- Alphabetical summary of **sed** commands

For more information, see the O'Reilly book *sed & awk*, 2d ed., by Dale Dougherty and Arnold Robbins.

## *Conceptual Overview*

**sed** is a noninteractive, or stream-oriented, editor. It interprets a script and performs the actions in the script. **sed** is stream-oriented, because, as with many Unix programs, input flows through the program and is directed to standard output. For example, **sort** is stream-oriented; **vi** is not. **sed**'s input typically comes from a file but can be directed from the keyboard. Output goes to the screen by default but can be captured in a file instead.

Typical uses of **sed** include:

- Editing one or more files automatically

- Simplifying repetitive edits to multiple files

- Writing conversion programs

**sed** operates as follows:

- Each line of input is copied into a pattern space.

- All editing commands in a **sed** script are applied in order to each line of input.

- Editing commands are applied to all lines (globally) unless line addressing restricts the lines affected.

- If a command changes the input, subsequent commands are applied to the changed line, not to the original input line.

- The original input file is unchanged, because the editing commands modify a copy of the original input line. The copy is sent to standard output (but can be redirected to a file).

## Command-Line Syntax

The syntax for invoking **sed** has two forms:

> **sed** [*options*] '*command*' *file(s)*
> **sed** [*options*] –f *scriptfile file(s)*

The first form allows you to specify an editing command on the command line, surrounded by single quotes. The second form allows you to specify a *scriptfile*, a file containing **sed** commands. If no files are specified, **sed** reads from standard input.

The following *options* are recognized:

**-e** *cmd*
> Next argument is an editing command; not needed unless specifying two or more editing commands.

**-f** *scriptfile*
> Next argument is a file containing editing commands.

**-n**  Suppress the default output; **sed** displays only those lines specified with the **p** command or with the **p** flag of the **s** command.

**-V**  Display version number.

**--quiet**
> Same as **-n**.

**--expression=***cmd*
> Same as **-e**.

**--file=***file*
> Same as **-f**.

**--help**
> Display brief help message with command-line options.

**--silent**

> Same as **-n**.

**--version**

> Same as **-V**.

# Syntax of sed Commands

**sed** commands have the general form:

> [*address*[, *address*]][!]*command* [*arguments*]

**sed** commands consist of *addresses* and editing *commands*. *commands* consist of a single letter or symbol; they are described later, alphabetically and by group. *arguments* include the label supplied to **b** or **t**, the filename supplied to **r** or **w**, and the substitution flags for **s**. *addresses* are described in the next section.

## Pattern Addressing

A **sed** command can specify zero, one, or two addresses. An address can be a line number, the symbol **$** (for last line), or a regular expression enclosed in slashes (*/pattern/*). Regular expressions are described in Chapter 9, *Pattern Matching*. Additionally, \n can be used to match any newline in the pattern space (resulting from the N command) but not the newline at the end of the pattern space.

| If the Command Specifies | Then the Command Is Applied To |
|---|---|
| No address | Each input line. |
| One address | Any line matching the address. Some commands (**a**, **i**, **r**, **q**, and **=**) accept only one address. |
| Two comma-separated addresses | First matching line and all succeeding lines up to and including a line matching the second address. |
| An address followed by **!** | All lines that do *not* match the address. |

### Examples

```
s/xx/yy/g                   Substitute on all lines (all occurrences)
/BSD/d                      Delete lines containing BSD
/^BEGIN/,/^END/p            Print between BEGIN and END, inclusive
/SAVE/!d                    Delete any line that doesn't contain SAVE
/BEGIN/,/END/!s/xx/yy/g     Substitute on all lines, except between BEGIN and END
```

Braces ({}) are used in **sed** to nest one address inside another or to apply multiple commands at the same address:

> [*/address/*[,*/address/*]]{
> *command1*
> *command2*
> }

The opening curly brace must end a line, and the closing curly brace must be on a line by itself. Be sure there are no blank spaces after the braces.

# Group Summary of sed Commands

In the following tables, the **sed** commands are grouped by function and are described tersely. Full descriptions, including syntax and examples, can be found afterward in the alphabetical summary.

## Basic Editing

| Command | Action |
|---------|--------|
| a\ | Append text after a line. |
| c\ | Replace text (usually a text block). |
| i\ | Insert text before a line. |
| d | Delete lines. |
| s | Make substitutions. |
| y | Translate characters (like **tr** in Chapter 3, *Linux Commands*). |

## Line Information

| Command | Action |
|---------|--------|
| = | Display line number of a line. |
| l | Display control characters in ASCII. |
| p | Display the line. |

## Input/Output Processing

| Command | Action |
|---------|--------|
| n | Skip current line and go to line below. |
| r | Read another file's contents into the input. |
| w | Write input lines to another file. |
| q | Quit the **sed** script (no further output). |

## Yanking and Putting

| Command | Action |
|---------|--------|
| h | Copy pattern space into hold space; wipe out what's there. |
| H | Copy pattern space into hold space; append to what's there. |
| g | Get the hold space back; wipe out the pattern space. |
| G | Get the hold space back; append to pattern space. |
| x | Exchange contents of hold space and pattern space. |

## Branching Commands

| Command | Action |
|---------|--------|
| **b** | Branch to *label* or to end of script. |
| **t** | Same as **b**, but branch only after substitution. |
| **:***label* | Label branched to by **t** or **b**. |

## Multiline Input Processing

| Command | Action |
|---------|--------|
| **N** | Read another line of input (creates embedded newline). |
| **D** | Delete up to the embedded newline. |
| **P** | Print up to the embedded newline. |

# Alphabetical Summary of sed Commands

**#**

Begin a comment in a **sed** script. Valid only as the first character of the first line. (Some versions of **sed**, including the GNU version on Linux, allow comments anywhere, but it is better not to rely on this.) If the first line of the script is **#n**, **sed** behaves as if **–n** had been specified.

**#**

---

*:label*

Label a line in the script for the transfer of control by **b** or **t**. *label* may contain up to seven characters.

**:**

---

[*/pattern/*]**=**

Write to standard output the line number of each line containing *pattern*.

**=**

---

[*address*]**a\**
*text*

Append *text* following each line matched by *address*. If *text* goes over more than one line, newlines must be "hidden" by preceding them with a backslash. The *text* will be terminated by the first newline that is not hidden in this way. The *text* is not available in the pattern space, and subsequent commands cannot be applied to it. The results of this command are sent to standard output when the list of editing commands is finished, regardless of what happens to the current line in the pattern space.

**a**

$\rightarrow$

| | |
|---|---|
| a ← | *Example*<br><br>```<br>$a\<br>This goes after the last line in the file\<br>(marked by $). This text is escaped at the\<br>end of each line, except for the last one.<br>``` |

---

| | |
|---|---|
| b | [*address1*[,*address2*]]b[*label*]<br><br>Transfer control unconditionally to :*label* elsewhere in script. That is, the command following the *label* is the next command applied to the current line. If no *label* is specified, control falls through to the end of the script, so no more commands are applied to the current line.<br><br>*Example*<br><br>Ignore lines between .**TS** and .**TE**; resume script after .**TE**:<br><br>```<br>/^\.TS/,/^\.TE/b<br>``` |

---

| | |
|---|---|
| c | [*address1*[,*address2*]]c\<br>*text*<br><br>Replace the lines selected by the address with *text*. When a range of lines is specified, all lines as a group are replaced by a single copy of *text*. The newline following each line of *text* must be escaped by a backslash, except the last line. The contents of the pattern space are, in effect, deleted, and no subsequent editing commands can be applied.<br><br>*Example*<br><br>Replace first 100 lines in a file:<br><br>```<br>1,100c\<br>\<br><First 100 names to be supplied><br>``` |

---

| | |
|---|---|
| d | [*address1*[,*address2*]]d<br><br>Delete the addressed line (or lines) from the pattern space. Thus, the line is not passed to standard output. A new line of input is read, and editing resumes with the first command in the script.<br><br>*Example*<br><br>Delete all blank lines:<br><br>```<br>/^$/d<br>``` |

---

[*address1*[,*address2*]]**D**

**D**

Delete first part (up to embedded newline) of multiline pattern space created by **N** command, and resume editing with first command in script. If this command empties the pattern space, then a new line of input is read, as if the **d** had been executed.

*Example*

Strip multiple blank lines, leaving only one:

```
/^$/{
N
/^\n$/D
}
```

[*address1*[,*address2*]]**g**

**g**

Paste the contents of the hold space (see **h** or **H** command) back into the pattern space, wiping out the previous contents of the pattern space. The example shows a simple way to copy lines.

*Example*

This script collects all lines containing the word *Item:* and copies them to a place marker later in the file. The place marker is overwritten.

```
/Item:/H
/<Replace this line with the item list>/g
```

[*address1*[,*address2*]]**G**

**G**

Same as **g**, except that the hold space is pasted below the address instead of overwriting it. The example shows a simple way to cut and paste lines.

*Example*

This script collects all lines containing the word *Item:* and moves them after a place marker later in the file. The original *Item:* lines are deleted.

```
/Item:/{
H
d
}
/Summary of items:/G
```

[*address1*[,*address2*]]**h**

**h**

Copy the pattern space into the hold space, a special temporary buffer. The previous contents of the hold space are obliterated. You can use **h** to

→

| | |
|---|---|
| h<br>← | save a line before editing it.<br><br>*Example*<br><br>```<br># Edit a line; print the change; replay the original<br>/Linux/{<br>h<br>s/.* Linux \(.*\) .*/\1:/<br>p<br>x<br>}<br>```<br><br>Sample input:<br><br>```<br>This describes the Linux ls command.<br>This describes the Linux cp command.<br>```<br><br>Sample output:<br><br>```<br>ls:<br>This describes the Linux ls command.<br>cp:<br>This describes the Linux cp command.<br>``` |
| H | [*address1*[,*address2*]]H<br><br>Append the contents of the pattern space (preceded by a newline) to the contents of the hold space. Even if the hold space is empty, H still appends a newline. H is like an incremental copy. See examples under **g** and **G**. |
| i | [*address1*]i\<br>*text*<br><br>Insert *text* before each line matched by *address*. (See **a** for details on *text*.)<br><br>*Example*<br><br>```<br>/Item 1/i\<br>The five items are listed below:<br>``` |
| l | [*address1*[,*address2*]]l<br><br>List the contents of the pattern space, showing nonprinting characters as ASCII codes. Long lines are wrapped. |
| n | [*address1*[,*address2*]]n<br><br>Read next line of input into pattern space. The current line is sent to standard output, and the next line becomes the current line. Control passes to the command following **n** instead of resuming at the top of the script. |

*Example*

In the **ms** macros, a section header occurs on the line below an .NH macro. To print all lines of header text, invoke this script with **sed −n**:

```
/^\.NH/{
n
p
}
```

---

[*address1*[,*address2*]]N

Append next input line to contents of pattern space; the two lines are separated by an embedded newline. (This command is designed to allow pattern matches across two lines.) Using **\n** to match the embedded newline, you can match patterns across multiple lines. See example at **D**.

*Examples*

Like previous example, but print .NH line as well as header title:

```
/^\.NH/{
N
p
}
```

Join two lines (replace newline with space):

```
/^\.NH/{
N
s/\n/ /
p
}
```

---

[*address1*[,*address2*]]p

Print the addressed lines. Unless the **−n** command-line option is used, this command causes duplicate lines to be output. Also, it typically is used before commands that change flow control (**d**, **N**, **b**) and that might prevent the current line from being output. See examples at **h**, **n**, and **N**.

---

[*address1*[,*address2*]]P

Print first part (up to embedded newline) of multiline pattern created by **N** command. Same as **p** if **N** has not been applied to a line.

---

[*address*]q

Quit when *address* is encountered. The addressed line first is written to output (if default output is not suppressed), along with any text appended

→

| | |
|---|---|
| q<br>← | to it by previous **a** or **r** commands.<br><br>*Examples*<br><br>Delete everything after the addressed line:<br><br>`/Garbled text follows:/q`<br><br>Print only the first 50 lines of a file:<br><br>`50q` |
| r | *[address]***r** *file*<br><br>Read contents of *file* and append after the contents of the pattern space. Exactly one space must be put between the **r** and the filename.<br><br>*Example*<br><br>`/The list of items follows:/r item_file` |
| s | *[address1[,address2]]***s/***pattern***/***replacement***/***[flags]*<br><br>Substitute *replacement* for *pattern* on each addressed line. If pattern addresses are used, the pattern // represents the last pattern address specified. The following flags can be specified:<br><br>*n*    Replace *n*th instance of */pattern/* on each addressed line. *n* is any number in the range 1 to 512; the default is 1.<br><br>**g**    Replace all instances of */pattern/* on each addressed line, not just the first instance.<br><br>**p**    Print the line if a successful substitution is done. If several successful substitutions are done, multiple copies of the line will be printed.<br><br>**w** *file*<br>    Write the line to a *file* if a replacement was done.<br><br>*Examples*<br><br>Here are some short, commented scripts:<br><br>`# Change third and fourth quote to ( and ):`<br>`/function/{`<br>`s/"/(/3`<br>`s/")/4`<br>`}`<br><br>`# Remove all quotes on a given line:`<br>`/Title/s/"//g`<br><br>`# Remove first colon or all quotes; print resulting lines:`<br>`s/://p` |

```
s/"//gp
```

```
# Change first "if" but leave "ifdef" alone:
/ifdef/!s/if/    if/
```

## [*address1*[,*address2*]]t [*label*]

Test if any substitutions have been made on addressed lines, and if so, branch to line marked by :*label*. (See b and :.) If *label* is not specified, control falls through to bottom of script. The t command is like a case statement in the C programming language or the shell programming languages. You test each case; when it's true, you exit the construct.

### Example

Suppose you want to fill empty fields of a database. You have this:

```
ID: 1    Name: greg    Rate: 45
ID: 2    Name: dale
ID: 3
```

You want this:

```
ID: 1    Name: greg    Rate: 45    Phone: ??
ID: 2    Name: dale    Rate: ??    Phone: ??
ID: 3    Name: ????    Rate: ??    Phone: ??
```

You need to test the number of fields already there. Here's the script (fields are tab-separated):

```
/ID/{
s/ID: .* Name: .* Rate: .*/&    Phone: ??/p
t
s/ID: .* Name: .*/&    Rate: ??  Phone: ??/p
t
s/ID: .*/&    Name: ??    Rate: ??  Phone: ??/p
}
```

## [*address1*[,*address2*]]w *file*

Append contents of pattern space to *file*. This action occurs when the command is encountered, rather than when the pattern space is output. Exactly one space must separate the w and the filename. This command will create the file if it does not exist; if the file exists, its contents will be overwritten each time the script is executed. Multiple write commands that direct output to the same file append to the end of the file.

### Example

```
# Store tbl and eqn blocks in a file:
/^\.TS/,/^\.TE/w troff_stuff
/^\.EQ/,/^\.EN/w troff_stuff
```

| x | [*address1*[,*address2*]]x |
|---|---|
| | Exchange contents of the pattern space with the contents of the hold space. See **h** for an example. |
| y | [*address1*[,*address2*]]y/*abc*/*xyz*/ |
| | Translate characters. Change every instance of *a* to *x*, *b* to *y*, *c* to *z*, etc. |
| | *Example* |
| | ``` |
| | # Change item 1, 2, 3 to Item A, B, C ... |
| | /^item [1-9]/y/123456789/ABCDEFGHI/ |
| | ``` |

## CHAPTER 13

# *The gawk Scripting Language*

**gawk** is the GNU version of **awk**, a powerful pattern-matching program for processing text files that may be composed of fixed or variable length records separated by some delineator (by default, a newline character). **gawk** may be used from the command line or in **gawk** scripts. Normally you should be able to invoke this utility using either **awk** or **gawk** on the shell command line.

This chapter presents the following topics:

- Conceptual overview

- Command-line syntax

- Patterns and procedures

- System variables

- Operators

- Variable and array assignment

- Group listing of commands

- Alphabetical summary of commands

For more information, see the O'Reilly book *sed & awk*, 2d ed., by Dale Dougherty and Arnold Robbins.

## *Conceptual Overview*

With **gawk**, you can:

- Conveniently process a text file as though it were made up of records and fields in a textual database.

- Use variables to change the database.

- Execute shell commands from a script.

- Perform arithmetic and string operations.

- Use programming constructs such as loops and conditionals.

- Define your own functions.

- Process the result of shell commands.

- Process command-line arguments more gracefully.

- Produce formatted reports.

## Command-Line Syntax

**gawk**'s syntax has two forms:

> **gawk** [*options*] '*script*' *var=value file(s)*
> **gawk** [*options*] −**f** *scriptfile var=value file(s)*

You can specify a *script* directly on the command line, or you can store a script in a *scriptfile* and specify it with −**f**. Multiple −**f** options are allowed; **awk** concatenates the files. This feature is useful for including libraries.

**gawk** operates on one or more input *files*. If none are specified (or if − is specified), **gawk** reads from the standard input.

Variables can be assigned a value on the command line. The *value* assigned to a variable can be a literal, a shell variable (**$**name), or a command substitution (`cmd`), but the value is available only after a line of input is read (i.e., after the **BEGIN** statement).

For example, to print the first three (colon-separated) fields of the password file, use −**F** to set the field separator to a colon:

```
gawk -F: '{print $1; print $2; print $3}' /etc/passwd
```

Numerous examples are shown later in this section under "Patterns and Procedures."

## Options

All options exist in both traditional POSIX (one-letter) format and GNU-style (long) format. Some recognized *options* are:

−− Treat all subsequent text as commands or filenames, not options.

−**f** *scriptfile*, −−**file**=*scriptfile*
    Read **gawk** commands from *scriptfile* instead of command line.

**−v** *var=value,* **−−assign**=*var=value*

Assign a *value* to variable *var*. This allows assignment before the script begins execution.

**−F**c, **−−field-separator**=*c*

Set the field separator to character *c*. This is the same as setting the variable **FS**. *c* may be a regular expression. Each input line, or record, is divided into fields by whitespace (blanks or tabs) or by some other user-definable record separator. Fields are referred to by the variables **$1**, **$2**, . . . , **$**n. **$0** refers to the entire record.

**−W** *option*

All **−W** options are specific to **gawk**, as opposed to **awk**. An alternate syntax is *−−option* (i.e., *−−***compat**). *option* may be one of:

**compat**

Same as **traditional**.

**copyleft**

Print copyleft notice and exit.

**copyright**

Same as **copyleft**.

**help**

Print syntax and list of options, then exit.

**lint** Warn about commands that might not port to other versions of **awk** or that **gawk** considers problematic.

**lint-old**

Like **lint** but compares to an older version of **awk**.

**posix**

Expect exact compatibility with POSIX; additionally, ignore \x escape sequences, **\*\***, and **\*\***=.

**re-interval**

Allow use of {*n,m*} intervals in regular expressions.

**source**=*script*

Treat *script* as **gawk** commands. Like the '*script*' argument but lets you mix commands from files (using **−f** options) with commands on the **gawk** command line.

**traditional**

Behave exactly like traditional (non-GNU) **awk**.

**usage**

Same as **help**.

**version**

Print version information and exit.

# Patterns and Procedures

**gawk** scripts consist of patterns and procedures:

> *pattern* {*procedure*}

Both are optional. If *pattern* is missing, {*procedure*} is applied to all records. If {*procedure*} is missing, the matched record is printed. By default, each line of input is a record, but you can specify a different record separator through the **RS** variable.

## Patterns

A pattern can be any of the following:

> /*regular expression*/
> *relational expression*
> *pattern-matching expression*
> *pattern,pattern*
> **BEGIN**
> **END**

Some rules regarding patterns include:

- Expressions can be composed of quoted strings, numbers, operators, functions, defined variables, or any of the predefined variables described later under "gawk System Variables."

- Regular expressions use the extended set of metacharacters and are described in Chapter 9, *Pattern Matching*.

- In addition, ^ and $ can be used to refer to the beginning and end of a field, respectively, rather than the beginning and end of a record.

- Relational expressions use the relational operators listed under "Operators" later in this chapter. Comparisons can be either string or numeric. For example, $2 > $1 selects lines for which the second field is greater than the first.

- Pattern-matching expressions use the operators ~ (match) and !~ (don't match). See "Operators" later in this chapter.

- The **BEGIN** pattern lets you specify procedures that take place *before* the first input record is processed. (Generally, you set global variables here.)

- The **END** pattern lets you specify procedures that take place *after* the last input record is read.

- If there are multiple **BEGIN** or **END** patterns, their associated actions are taken in the order in which they appear in the script.

- *pattern,pattern* specifies a range of lines. This syntax cannot include **BEGIN** or **END** as a pattern.

Except for **BEGIN** and **END**, patterns can be combined with the Boolean operators || (OR), && (AND), and ! (NOT).

---

In addition to other regular-expression operators, GNU **awk** supports POSIX character lists, which are useful for matching non-ASCII characters in languages other than English. These lists are recognized only within [ ] ranges. A typical use would be [[:**lower**:]], which in English is the same as [a–z]. See Chapter 9 for a complete list of POSIX character lists.

## Procedures

Procedures consist of one or more commands, functions, or variable assignments, separated by newlines or semicolons and contained within curly braces. Commands fall into four groups:

- Variable or array assignments

- Printing commands

- Built-in functions

- Control-flow commands

## Simple Pattern-Procedure Examples

1. Print first field of each line (no pattern specified):

   `{ print $1 }`

2. Print all lines that contain "Linux":

   `/Linux/`

3. Print first field of lines that contain "Linux":

   `/Linux/{ print $1 }`

4. Print records containing more than two fields:

   `NF > 2`

5. Interpret each group of lines up to a blank line as a single input record:

   `BEGIN { FS = "\n"; RS = "" }`

6. Print fields 2 and 3 in switched order but only on lines whose first field matches the string "URGENT":

   `$1 ~ /URGENT/ { print $3, $2 }`

7. Count and print the number of instances of "ERR" found:

   `/ERR/ { ++x }; END { print x }`

8. Add numbers in second column and print total:

   `{total += $2 }; END { print "column total is", total}`

9.  Print lines that contain fewer than 20 characters:

    ```
    length() < 20
    ```

10. Print each line that begins with "Name:" and that contains exactly seven fields:

    ```
    NF == 7 && /^Name:/
    ```

11. Reverse the order of fields:

    ```
    { for (i = NF; i >= 1; i--) print $i }
    ```

## *gawk System Variables*

| Variable | Description |
|---|---|
| $n | nth field in current record; fields are separated by **FS** |
| $0 | Entire input record |
| ARGC | Number of arguments on command line |
| ARGIND | Current file's place in command line (starting with 0) |
| ARGV | An array containing the command-line arguments |
| CONVFMT | Conversion format for numbers (default is %.**6g**) |
| ENVIRON | An associative array of environment variables |
| ERRNO | Description of last system error |
| FIELDWIDTHS | List of field widths (whitespace-separated) |
| FILENAME | Current filename |
| FNR | Like **NR**, but relative to the current file |
| FS | Field separator (default is any whitespace; null string separates into individual characters) |
| IGNORECASE | If true, make case-insensitive matches |
| NF | Number of fields in current record |
| NR | Number of the current record |
| OFMT | Output format for numbers (default is %.**6g**) |
| OFS | Output field separator (default is a blank) |
| ORS | Output record separator (default is a newline) |
| RLENGTH | Length of the string matched by **match** function |
| RS | Record separator (default is a newline) |
| RSTART | First position in the string matched by **match** function |
| SUBSEP | Separator character for array subscripts (default is \ 034) |

## Operators

The following table lists the operators, in order of increasing precedence, that are available in **gawk**.

| Symbol | Meaning |
| --- | --- |
| `= += -= *= /= %= ^= **=` | Assignment |
| `?:` | C conditional expression |
| `||` | Logical OR |
| `&&` | Logical AND |
| `~ !~` | Match regular expression and negation |
| `< <= > >= != ==` | Relational operators |
| (blank) | Concatenation |
| `+ -` | Addition, subtraction |
| `* / %` | Multiplication, division, and modulus |
| `+ - !` | Unary plus and minus and logical negation |
| `^ **` | Exponentiation |
| `++ --` | Increment and decrement, either prefix or postfix |
| `$` | Field reference |
| `in` | Array membership (see **for** command) |

## Variable and Array Assignments

Variables can be assigned a value with an equals sign. For example:

```
FS = ","
```

Expressions using the operators +, −, /, and % (modulo) can be assigned to variables.

Arrays can be created with the **split** function (see the listing in the "Alphabetical Summary of Commands"), or they can simply be named in an assignment statement. Array elements can be subscripted with numbers (*array*[1]) or with names. For example, to count the number of occurrences of a pattern, you could use the following script:

```
/pattern/ { array["/pattern/"]++ }
END { print array["/pattern/"] }
```

In **gawk**, variables need not be declared previous to their use, nor do arrays need to be dimensioned; they are activated upon first reference. All variables are stored as strings but may be used either as strings or numbers. **gawk** will use the program script context to determine whether to treat a variable as a string or a number, but the distinction also can be forced by the user. To force a variable to be treated as a string, catenate a null to the variable:

```
var ""
```

To force a variable to be treated as a number, add 0 to it:

```
var + 0
```

## Group Listing of gawk Commands

gawk commands may be classified as follows:

| Arithmetic Functions | String Functions | Control Flow Statements | Input/Output Processing | Time Functions | Misc. |
|---|---|---|---|---|---|
| atan2 | gensub | break | close | strftime | delete |
| cos | gsub | continue | fflush | systime | function |
| exp | index | do/while | getline | | system |
| int | length | exit | next | | |
| log | match | for | nextfile | | |
| rand | split | if | print | | |
| sin | sub | return | printf | | |
| sqrt | substr | | sprintf | | |
| srand | tolower | | while | | |
| | toupper | | | | |

## Alphabetical Summary of Commands

The following alphabetical list of statements and functions includes all that are available in **gawk** in Linux.

| atan2 | atan2 ($y,x$) |
|---|---|
| | Return the arctangent of $y/x$ in radians. |

| break | **break** |
|---|---|
| | Exit from a **while** or **for** loop. |

| close | close (*filename-expr*) <br> close (*command-expr*) |
|---|---|
| | Close a file read by a **getline** command or a pipe; takes as an argument the same expression that opened the pipe or file. |

| | |
|---|---|
| **continue** | continue |

Begin next iteration of **while** or **for** loop without reaching the bottom.

| | |
|---|---|
| **cos** (*x*) | cos |

Return the cosine of *x*, an angle in radians.

| | |
|---|---|
| **delete** *array*[*element*]<br>**delete** *array* | delete |

Delete *element* of *array*. If no element is specified, all elements are deleted.

| | |
|---|---|
| **do**<br>    *body*<br>**while** (*expr*) | do |

Looping statement. Execute statements in *body*, then evaluate *expr*. If *expr* is true, execute *body* again.

| | |
|---|---|
| **exit** | exit |

Do not execute remaining instruction, and read no new input. **END** procedures will be executed.

| | |
|---|---|
| **exp** (*arg*) | exp |

Return the natural exponent of *arg* (the inverse of **log**).

| | |
|---|---|
| **fflush** (*filename*) | fflush |

Flushes output to *filename*; default is the standard output.

| | |
|---|---|
| **for** (*i=lower* ; *i<=upper* ; *i++*)<br>    *command* | for |

While the value of variable *i* is in the range between *lower* and *upper*, do *command*. A series of commands must be put within

→

| | |
|---|---|
| for<br>← | braces. <= or any relational operator can be used; ++ or − − can be used to increment or decrement the variable. |
| for | for (*item* **in** *array*)<br>    *command*<br><br>For each *item* in an associative *array*, do *command*. Multiple commands must be put inside braces. Refer to each element of the array as *array*[ *item* ]. Elements of **gawk** arrays are stored in an order that enables access of any element in essentially equivalent time. This order may appear to be indiscriminate; if the output is desired in sorted order, you must pipe it through the **sort** command. |
| function | function *name* (*parameter-list*) {<br>    *statements*<br>}<br><br>Create *name* as a user-defined function consisting of **gawk** *statements* that apply to the specified list of parameters. |
| gensub | **gensub** (*r, s, n, t*)<br><br>Substitute *s* for the *n*th match of regular expression *r* in the string *t*. Leave *t* unchanged, but return new string as the result. If *n* is "g" or "G" change all matches. If *t* is not supplied, it defaults to **$0**. |
| getline | **getline** [*var*hairsp;] [<*file*]<br>*command* \| **getline** [*var*]<br><br>The first form reads input from *file* or the next file on the command line, and the second form reads the output of *command*. Both forms read one line at a time, and each time the statement is executed it gets the next line of input. The line of input is assigned to **$0** and is parsed into fields, setting **NF**, **NR**, and **FNR**. If *var* is specified, the result is assigned to *var*, and neither **$0** nor **NF** is changed. Thus, if the result is assigned to a variable, the current line does not change. **getline** is actually a function, and it returns 1 if it reads a record successfully, 0 at *EOF*, and −1 if for some reason it is otherwise unsuccessful. |

**gsub** (*r, s, t*)                                                      gsub

Globally substitute *s* for each match of the regular expression *r* in
the string *t*. Return the number of substitutions. If *t* is not supplied,
it defaults to $0.

---

**if** (*condition*)                                                        if
    *command1*
[**else**
    *command2*]

If *condition* is true, do *command1*; otherwise, do *command2*. Condition can be an expression using any of the relational operators <,
<=, ==, !=, >=, or >, as well as the pattern-matching operator ˜. A
series of commands must be put within braces.

### Example

The following lines determine whether the first word in each line
starts with A, uppercase or lowercase:

```
if ($1 ˜ /[Aa]*/)
    ...Begins with A or a
```

---

**index** (*substr,str*)                                                 index

Return the position of a substring in a string. Returns 0 if *substr* is
not contained in *str*.

---

**int** (*arg*)                                                            int

Return the integer part of *arg*.

---

**length** (*arg*)                                                      length

Return the length of *arg*. If *arg* is not supplied, $0 is assumed.

---

**log** (*arg*)                                                            log

Return the natural logarithm of *arg* (the inverse of **exp**).

| | |
|---|---|
| match | match $(s, r)$ |
| | Return position in $s$ where regular expression $r$ first matches or 0 if no occurrences are found. Sets the value of **RSTART** and **RLENGTH**. |
| next | next |
| | Read next input line and start new cycle through pattern/procedures statements. |
| nextfile | nextfile |
| | Skip to the next file on the **gawk** command line and start new cycle through pattern/procedures statements. |
| print | print [*args*] [*destination*] |
| | Print *args* on output. Literal strings must be quoted. Fields are printed in the order they are listed. If separated by commas in the argument list, they are separated in the output by the character specified by **OFS**. If separated by spaces, they are concatenated in the output. *destination* is a shell redirection or pipe expression (e.g., > *file*) that redirects the default output. |
| printf | printf [*format* [, *expressions*]] |
| | Formatted **print** statement. Expressions or variables can be formatted according to instructions in the *format* argument. The number of *expressions* must correspond to the number specified in the format sections. |
| | *format* follows the conventions of the C-language **printf** statement. Here are a few of the most common formats: |
| | %s  A string. |
| | %d  A decimal number. |
| | %$n.m$f |
| | A floating point number. $n$ = total number of digits; $m$ = number of digits after decimal point. |
| | %[–]$nc$ |
| | $n$ specifies minimum field length for format type $c$, while – left-justifies value in field; otherwise, value is right-justified. |
| | Field widths are adjustable. For example, %**3.2f** limits a floating-point number to a total width of three digits, with two digits after |

the decimal point.

*format* also can contain embedded escape sequences, \n (newline) and \t (tab) being the most common. Spaces and literal text can be placed in the *format* argument by quoting the entire argument. If there are multiple expressions to be printed, multiple formats should be specified.

### Example

Using the script:

```
{printf ("The sum on line %s is %d.\n", NR, $1+$2)}
```

the following input line:

```
5    5
```

produces this output, followed by a newline:

```
The sum on line 1 is 10.
```

## rand ()

Generate a random number between 0 and 1. This function returns the same series of numbers each time the script is executed, unless the random number generator is seeded using the **srand** function.

## return [*expr*]

Used at end of user-defined functions to exit function, returning the value of *expr.*

## sin (*x*)

Return the sine of *x*, an angle in radians.

## split (*string,array*[,*sep*])

Split *string* into elements of array *array*[1], . . . ,*array*[*n*]. The string is split at each occurrence of separator *sep*. If *sep* is not specified, **FS** is used. If *sep* is a null string, a split is performed on every character. The number of array elements created is returned.

| | |
|---|---|
| **sprintf** | **sprintf** [*format* [, *expression(s)*]] |
| | Return the value of one or more *expressions*, using the specified *format* (see **printf**). Data is formatted but not printed. |
| **sqrt** | **sqrt** (*arg*) |
| | Return square root of *arg*. |
| **srand** | **srand** (*expr*) |
| | Use *expr* to set a new seed for random number generator. Default is time of day. |
| **strftime** | **strftime**([*format* [, *timestamp*]]) |
| | Format *timestamp* according to *format*. Return the formatted string. The *timestamp* is a time-of-day value in seconds since midnight, January 1, 1970, UTC. The *format* string is similar to that of **sprintf**. (See the example for **systime**.) If *timestamp* is omitted, it defaults to the current time. If *format* is omitted, it defaults to a value that produces output similar to that of **date**. |
| **sub** | **sub** (*r,s,t*) |
| | Substitute *s* for first match of the regular expression *r* in the string *t*. Return 1 if successful; 0 otherwise. If *t* is not supplied, the default is $0. |
| **substr** | **substr** (*string,m*[,*n*]) |
| | Return substring of *string* beginning at character position *m* and consisting of the next *n* characters. If *n* is omitted, include all characters to the end of string. |
| **system** | **system** (*command*) |
| | Execute the specified shell *command* and return its status. The status of the command that is executed typically indicates its success (1), completion (0), or unexpected error (–1). The output of the command is not available for processing within the **gawk** script. |

| | |
|---|---|
| **systime ( )** | systime |

Return number of seconds since midnight UTC, January 1, 1970.

*Example*

Log the start and end times of a data-processing program:

```
BEGIN {
        now = systime()
        mesg = strftime("Started at %m/%d/%Y %H:%M:%S", now)
        print mesg
}
process data ...
END {
        now = systime()
        mesg = strftime("Ended at %m/%d/%Y %H:%M:%S", now)
        print mesg
}
```

| | |
|---|---|
| **tolower** (*str*) | tolower |

Translate all uppercase characters in *str* to lowercase and return the new string.

| | |
|---|---|
| **toupper** (*str*) | toupper |

Translate all lowercase characters in *str* to uppercase and return the new string.

| | |
|---|---|
| **while** (*condition*)<br>  *command* | while |

Do *command* while *condition* is true (see **if** for a description of allowable conditions). A series of commands must be put within braces.

CHAPTER 14

# CVS and RCS

CVS, and the older RCS, offer *version control* (or *revision control*), the practice of maintaining information about a project's evolution so that prior versions may be retrieved, changes tracked, and, most importantly, the efforts of a team of developers coordinated.

## Basic Concepts

RCS (Revision Control System) works within a single directory. To accommodate large projects using a hierarchy of several directories, CVS creates two new concepts called the *repository* and the *sandbox*.

The repository (also called an *archive*) is the centralized storage area, managed by the version control system and the repository administrator, which stores the projects' files. The repository contains information required to reconstruct historical versions of the files in a project. An administrator sets up and controls the repository using the procedures and commands in the later section "CVS Administrator Reference."

A *sandbox* (also called a *working directory*) contains copies of versions of files from the repository. New development occurs in sandboxes, and any number of sandboxes may be created from a single repository. The sandboxes are independent of one another and may contain files from different stages of the development of the same project. Users set up and control sandboxes using the procedures and commands found in the "CVS User Reference," later in this chapter.

In a typical interaction with the version control system, a developer checks out the most current code from the repository, makes changes, tests the results, and then commits those changes back to the repository when they are deemed satisfactory.

## Locking and Merging

Some systems, including RCS, use a *locking model* to coordinate the efforts of multiple developers by serializing file modifications. Before making changes to a file, a developer must not only obtain a copy of it, but he must also request and obtain a lock on it from the system. This lock serves to prevent (really dissuade) multiple developers from working on the same file at the same time. When the changes are committed, the developer unlocks the file, permitting other developers to gain access to it.

The locking model is pessimistic: it assumes that conflicts *must* be avoided. Serialization of file modifications through locks prevents conflicts. But it is cumbersome to have to lock files for editing when bug-hunting. Often, developers will circumvent the lock mechanism to keep working, which is an invitation to trouble.

Unlike RCS and SCCS, CVS uses a *merging model* which allows everyone to have access to the files at all times and supports concurrent development. The merging model is optimistic: it assumes that conflicts are not common and that when they do occur, it *usually* isn't difficult to resolve them.

CVS is capable of operating under a locking model via the –L and –l options to the **admin** command. Also, CVS has special commands (**edit** and **watch**) for those who want additional development coordination support. CVS uses locks internally to prevent corruption when multiple people are accessing the repository simultaneously, but this is different from the user-visible locks of the locking model discussed here.

## Conflicts and Merging

In the event that two developers commit changes to the same version of a file, CVS automatically defers the commit of the second committer's file. The second developer then issues the **cvs update** command, which merges the first developer's changes into the local file. In many cases, the changes will be in different areas of the file, and the merge is successful. However, if both developers have made changes to the same area of the file, the second to commit will have to resolve the conflict. This involves examination of the problematic area(s) of the file and selection among the multiple versions or making changes that resolve the conflict.

CVS only detects textual conflicts, but conflict resolution is concerned with keeping the project as a whole logically consistent. Therefore, conflict resolution sometimes involves changing files other than the one about which CVS complained.

For example, if one developer adds a parameter to a function definition, it may be necessary for all the calls to that function to be modified to pass the additional parameter. This is a logical conflict, so its detection and resolution is the job of the developers (with support from tools like compilers and debuggers); CVS won't notice the problem.

In any merge situation, whether or not there was a conflict, the second developer to commit will often want to retest the resulting version of the project because it has changed since the original commit. Once it passes, the developer will need to recommit the file.

## Tagging

CVS tracks file versions by revision number, which can be used to retrieve a particular revision from the repository. In addition, it is possible to create symbolic tags so that a group of files (or an entire project) can be referred to by a single identifier even when the revision numbers of the files are not the same (which is most often the case). This capability is often used to keep track of released versions or other important project milestones.

For example, the symbolic tag hello-1_0 might refer to revision number 1.3 of *hello.c* and revision number 1.1 of *Makefile* (symbolic tags are created with the **tag** and **rtag** commands).

## Branching

The simplest form of development is *linear*, in which there is a succession of revisions to a file, each derived from the prior revision. Many projects can get by with a completely linear development process, but larger projects (as measured by number of files, number of developers, and/or the size of the user community) often run into maintenance issues that require additional capabilities. Sometimes, it is desirable to do some speculative development while the main line of development continues uninterrupted. Other times, bugs in the currently released version must be fixed while work on the next version is underway. In both of these cases, the solution is to create a branch (*fork*) from an appropriate point in the development of the project. If at a future point some or all of the changes on the branch are needed back on the main line of development (or elsewhere), they can be merged in (*joined*).

Branches are forked with the **tag −b** command; they are joined with the **update −j** command.

# *The CVS Utility*

This section offers general background about CVS.

## CVS Command Format

CVS commands are of the form:

```
cvs global_options command command_options
```

For example, here is a simple sequence of commands showing both kinds of options in the context of creating a repository, importing existing files, and performing a few common operations on them:

```
user@localhost$ cvs -d /usr/local/cvsrep init
user@localhost$ cd ~/work/hello
user@localhost$ cvs -d /usr/local/cvsrep import -m 'Import' hello vendor start
user@localhost$ cd ..
user@localhost$ mv hello hello.bak
user@localhost$ cvs -d /usr/local/cvsrep checkout hello
user@localhost$ cd hello
```

```
user@localhost$ vi hello
user@localhost$ cvs commit -m 'Fixed a typo'
user@localhost$ cvs tag hello-1_0
user@localhost$ cvs remove -f Makefile
user@localhost$ cvs commit -m 'Removed old Makefile'
user@localhost$ cvs upd -r hello-1_0
user@localhost$ cvs upd -A
```

Some global options are common to both user and administrator commands, and some are specific to each of these. The common global options are described in the next section, and the user and administrator options are described in the "CVS User Reference" and "CVS Administrator Reference" sections, respectively.

## Common Global Options

Table 14-1 lists the global options that apply to both user and administrator commands.

*Table 14-1. Common Global Options*

| Option | Description |
|--------|-------------|
| **-b** *bindir* | Location of external RCS programs. This option is obsolete, having been deprecated at CVS versions above 1.9.18. |
| **-T** *tempdir* | Absolute path for temporary files. Overrides the setting of $TMPDIR. |
| **-v**<br>**-version** | Display version and copyright information. |

## Gotchas

This section clarifies a few aspects of CVS that can sometimes cause confusion.

*CVS's file orientation*
> While directories are supported, they are not versioned in the same way as traditional files. This is particularly important in the early evolutionary stages of a project, when the structure may be in flux. Also, if the project is undergoing major changes, the structure is likely to change. See the later section "Hacking the Repository."

*CVS's text-orientation*
> There is no equivalent to **diff** for binary files, although CVS's support for binary files is usually sufficient. Use **admin -kb** to tell CVS a file is binary.

*CVS's line-orientation*
> Moving a segment of code from one place in a file to another is seen as one delete (from the old location) and an unrelated add (to the new location).

*CVS is not syntax-aware*
> As far as CVS is concerned, small formatting changes are equivalent to sweeping logic changes in the same line ranges.

## RCS anachronisms

CVS was originally built on top of RCS, but now all the RCS-related functionality is internal to CVS itself. RCS still shows up in the name of the $RCSBIN environment variable and the description of the **-b** option, which are now obsolete.

# CVS Administrator Reference

This section provides details on creating and configuring repositories and performing other CVS administrative tasks. A single computer can run multiple copies of the CVS server, and each server can serve multiple repositories.

## Creating a Repository

Select a directory that will contain the repository files (*/usr/local/cvsrep* is used in the following examples). Use the **init** command to initialize the repository. Either set the $CVSROOT environment variable first:

```
user@localhost$ export CVSROOT=/usr/local/cvsrep
user@localhost$ cvs init
```

or use the **-d** option to specify the repository location:

```
user@localhost$ cvs -d /usr/local/cvsrep init
```

For information on importing code, see the "CVS User Reference," especially the "import" and "add" sections.

### Setting up the password server

If you want users to access the repository from other computers, then configure the pserver by doing the following as root:

- Make sure there is an entry in */etc/services* similar to the following:

  ```
  cvspserver 2401/tcp
  ```

- If you are not using tcpwrappers, then place a line like this in */etc/inetd.conf*:

  ```
  cvspserver stream tcp nowait root /usr/bin/cvs cvs
  --allow-root=/usr/local/cvsroot pserver
  ```

- Or, if you *are* using tcpwrappers, then use a line like this:

  ```
  cvspserver stream tcp nowait root /usr/sbin/tcpd /usr/bin/cvs
  --allow-root=/usr/local/cvsroot pserver
  ```

- Once these changes are in place, restart **inetd** (or send it the appropriate signal to cause it to re-read *inetd.conf*).

## Security Issues

The following are security issues that need to be considered when working with CVS:

- The contents of files will be transmitted in the open over the network with pserver and **rsh**. With pserver, passwords are transmitted in the open as well.

- When using a local repository (i.e., when CVS is not being used in client/server mode), developers need write access to the repository, which means they can hack it.

- The CVS server runs as root briefly before changing its user ID.

- The ˜/.cvspass file must be kept unreadable by all users except the owner to prevent passwords from being accessible.

- A user who has authority to make changes to the files in the *CVSROOT* module can run arbitrary programs.

- Some of the options to the **admin** command are very dangerous, so it is advisable to restrict its use. This can be accomplished by creating a user group named cvsadmin. If this user group exists, then only users in that group can run the **admin** command (except **admin –k***kflag*, which is available to everyone).

## Repository Structure

The CVS repository is implemented as a normal directory with special contents. This section describes the contents of the repository directory.

### The CVSROOT directory

The *CVSROOT* directory contains the administrative files for the repository; other directories in the repository contain the modules. The administrative files permit (and ignore) blank lines and comment lines in addition to the lines with real configuration information on them. Comment lines start with a hash mark ('#').

Some of the administrative files contain filename patterns to match file and directory names. These patterns are regular expressions like those used in GNU Emacs. Table 14-2 contains the special constructions used most often.

*Table 14–2. Filename Pattern Special Constructions*

| Construction | Description |
|---|---|
| ^ | Match the beginning of the string. |
| $ | Match the end of the string. |
| . | Match any single character. |
| * | Modify the preceding construct to match zero or more repetitions. |

CVS will perform a few important expansions in the contents of the administrative files before interpreting the results. First, the typical shell syntax for referring to a home directory is ~/, which expands to the home directory of the user running CVS; and ~user expands to the home directory of the specified user.

In addition, CVS provides a mechanism similar to the shell's environment variable expansion capability. Constructs such as ${variable} will be replaced by the value of the named variable. Variable names start with letters and consist entirely of letters, numbers, and underscores. Curly brackets may be omitted if the character immediately following the variable reference is not a valid variable name character. While this construct looks like a shell environment variable reference, the full environment is not available. Table 14-3 contains the built-in variables.

*Table 14-3. Administrative File Variables*

| Variable | Description |
| --- | --- |
| CVSEDITOR<br>EDITOR<br>VISUAL | The editor CVS uses for log file editing. |
| CVSROOT | The repository locator in use. |
| USER | The name of the user (on the server, if using a remote repository) running CVS. |
| =var | The value of a user-defined variable named var. Values for these variables are provided by the global **−s** option. |

In order to edit these files, check out the *CVSROOT* module from the repository, edit the files, and commit them back to the repository. You must commit the changes for them to affect CVS's behavior.

Table 14-4 describes the administrative files and their functions.

*Table 14-4. CVSROOT Files*

| File | Description |
| --- | --- |
| *checkoutlist* | Extra files to be maintained in *CVSROOT* |
| *commitinfo* | Specifications for commit governors |
| *config* | Settings to affect the behavior of CVS |
| *cvsignore* | Filename patterns of files to ignore |
| *cvswrappers* | Specifications for **checkout** and **commit** filters |
| *editinfo* | Specifications for log editors (obsolete) |
| *history* | Log information for the **history** command |
| *loginfo* | Specify **commit** notifier program(s) |
| *modules* | Module definitions |
| *notify* | Notification processing specifications |
| *passwd* | A list of users and their CVS-specific passwords |
| *rcsinfo* | Template form for log messages |

*Table 14–4. CVSROOT Files (continued)*

| File | Description |
|------|-------------|
| *readers* | A list of users having read-only access |
| *taginfo* | Tag processing specifications |
| *users* | Alternate user email addresses for use with *notify* |
| *verifymsg* | Specify log message evaluator program |
| *writers* | A list of users having read/write access |

Since the *editinfo* file is obsolete, use the $EDITOR environment variable (or the –e option) to specify the editor and the *verifymsg* file to specify an evaluator.

Each line of the *taginfo* file contains a filename pattern and a command line to execute when files with matching names are tagged.

### The checkoutlist file

Whenever changes to files in the *CVSROOT* module are committed, CVS prints the message:

```
cvs commit: Rebuilding administrative file database
```

to inform you that the checked-out copy in the repository has been updated to reflect any changes just committed. As with any other module directory in the repository, the *CVSROOT* directory contains RCS (*\*,v*) files that retain the history of the files. But to use the files, CVS needs a copy of the latest revision. So, when CVS prints this message, it is checking out the latest revisions of the administrative files.

If you have added files to the *CVSROOT* module (such as scripts to be called via entries in the *loginfo* file), you will need to list them in the *checkoutlist* file. This makes CVS treat them the same way as it treats the standard set of *CVSROOT* files.

Each line in this file consists of a filename and an optional error message that is displayed in case there is trouble checking out the file.

### The commitinfo file

Whenever a **commit** is being processed, CVS consults this file to determine whether or not any precommit checking of the file is required. Each line of the file contains a directory name pattern, followed by the path of a program to invoke when files are commited in directories with matching names.

Aside from the usual filename-pattern syntax, there are two special patterns:

ALL If this pattern is present in the file, then all files are passed to the specified checking program. CVS then looks for a pattern that matches the name of each particular file and runs the additional checks found, if any.

DEFAULT

If this pattern is present in the file, all files for which there was no pattern match are sent to the specified checking program. The automatic match of every file to the ALL entry, if any, does not count as a match when determining whether or not to send the file to the DEFAULT checking program.

CVS constructs the command line for the checking program by appending the full path to the directory within the repository and the list of files being committed (this means you can specify the first few command-line arguments to the program, if necessary). If the checking program exits with a nonzero status, the **commit** is aborted.

The programs that run via this mechanism run on the server computer when a remote repository is used. Here is an example of a *commitinfo* file:

```
ALL $CVSROOT/CVSROOT/commit-ALL.pl
DEFAULT $CVSROOT/CVSROOT/commit-DEFAULT.pl
CVSROOT$ $CVSROOT/CVSROOT/commit-CVSROOT.pl
```

This example assumes you will create the script files in the *CVSROOT* module and add them to the *checkoutlist* file.

## The config file

Repository configuration is specified in the *config* administrative file.

LockDir=*dir*

Directs CVS to put its lock files in the alternate directory given instead of in the repository itself, allowing users without write access to the repository (but with write access to *dir*) to read from the repository.

Version 1.10 doesn't support alternate directories for lock files and reports an error if this option is set. Older versions of CVS (1.9 and older) don't support this option either and will not report an error. Do not mix versions that support alternate directories for lock files with versions that don't, since lock files in both places defeat the purpose of having them.

RCSBIN=*dir*

Obsolete (used in versions 1.9.12 to 1.9.18). This option used to tell CVS where to find RCS programs. Since all RCS-related functions are now handled internally, this option does nothing.

SystemAuth=*value*

CVS tries to authenticate users via the *CVSROOT/passwd* file first, and if that fails and this option is set to yes, CVS tries to authenticate via the system's user database. This option is used with the password server. The default is yes.

TopLevelAdmin=*value*

If this option is set to yes, an additional *CVS* directory is created at the top-level directory when **checkout** is run. This allows the client software to detect the repository locator in that directory (see "Repository Locators). The default is no.

This option is useful if you check out multiple modules to the same sandbox directory. If it is enabled, you won't have to provide a repository locator after the first checkout; CVS infers it from the information in the top-level *CVS* directory created during the first checkout.

### The cvsignore file

The *cvsignore* administrative file contains a list of filename patterns to ignore, just like the *.cvsignore* files that can appear in sandboxes and user home directories. Unlike the filename patterns in other administrative files, these patterns are in **sh** syntax; they are not GNU Emacs–style regular expressions. There can be multiple patterns on a line, separated by whitespace (consequently, the patterns themselves cannot contain whitespace).

Table 14-5 shows the most commonly used sh-style pattern constructs.

*Table 14–5. Filename Patterns for cvsignore*

| Construct | Description |
| --- | --- |
| ? | Any one character. |
| * | Any sequence of zero or more characters. |

Again, diverging from the standards used by the rest of the administrative files, the *cvsignore* file does not support comments.

### The cvswrappers file

While the *cvsignore* file allows CVS to ignore certain files, the *cvswrappers* file allows you to give CVS default options for commands that work with files. Lines in this file consist of a sh-style filename pattern followed by a –k (keyword substitution mode) option and/or an –m (update method) option. The legal values for –k are described in Table 14-19. The legal values for –m are COPY and MERGE.

If –m COPY is specified, CVS will not attempt to merge the files. Instead, it presents the user with conflicting versions of the file, and he can choose one or the other or resolve the conflict manually.

For example, to treat all files ending in *.exe* as binary, add this line to the file:

```
*.exe -k b
```

### The history file

If this file exists, CVS inserts records of activity against the repository. This information produces displays of the **cvs history** command. The history file is not intended for direct reading or writing by programs other than CVS.

A repository set up with **cvs init** automatically has a *history* file.

## The loginfo file

The *loginfo* administrative file works much like the *commitinfo* file and can use the special patterns ALL and DEFAULT. This file allows you to do something with **commit** log messages and related information.

The programs called during *loginfo* processing receive the log message on standard input. Table 14-6 shows the three codes that can pass additional information to the called programs via command-line arguments.

*Table 14-6. Special loginfo Variables*

| Variable | Description |
| --- | --- |
| s | Filename |
| V | Pre-commit revision number |
| v | Post-commit revision number |

If a percent sign (%) followed by the desired variable is placed after the command path, CVS inserts the corresponding information as a whitespace-separated list with one entry for each file, preceded by the repository path (as with *commitinfo*). There can be only one percent sign on the command line, so if you want information from more than one variable, place the variable names inside curly brackets: %{...}. In this case, each file-specific entry has one field for each variable, separated by commas. For example, the code %{sVv} expands into a list like this:

```
/usr/local/cvsrep/hello Makefile,1.1,1.2 hello.c,1.8,1.9
```

It can be helpful to send email notifications each time someone commits a file to the repository. Developers can monitor this stream of notices to determine when they should pull the latest development code into their private sandboxes. For example, consider a developer doing some preparatory work in his sandbox while he awaits stabilization and addition of another developer's new library. As soon as the new library is added and committed, email notification goes out, and the waiting developer sees the code is ready to use. So, he runs **cvs upd −d** in the appropriate directory to pull in the new library code and then sets about integrating it with his work.

It is simple to set up this kind of notification. Just add a line like this to the *CVSROOT/loginfo* file:

```
DEFAULT mail -s %s developers@company.com
```

Often, the email address is a mailing list, which has all the interested parties (developers or otherwise) on the distribution list. If you want to send messages to multiple email addresses, you can write a script to do that and have that script called via this file. Alternatively, you can use the *log.pl* program that comes as part of the CVS source distribution (located at */usr/local/src/cvs-1.10.8/contrib/log.pl*, assuming CVS was unpacked into */usr/local/src*). Instructions for its use are provided as comments in the file.

### The modules file

The top-level directories in a repository are called *modules*. In addition to these physical modules, CVS provides a mechanism to create logical modules through the *modules* administrative file. Here are the three kinds of logical modules:

*Alias*
> Alias modules are defined by lines of the form:
>
> ```
> module_name -a alias_module ...
> ```
>
> You can use the alias module name in CVS commands in the same way you use the modules named after the −a option.

*Regular*
> Regular modules are defined by lines of the form:
>
> ```
> module_name [options] directory file ...
> ```
>
> Checking out *module_name* results in the specified files from *directory* being checked out into a directory named *module_name*. The intervening directories (if any) are not reflected in the sandbox.

*Ampersand*
> Ampersand modules are defined by lines of the form:
>
> ```
> module_name [options] &other_module ...
> ```
>
> Checking out such a module results in a directory named *module_name*, which in turn contains copies of the *other_module* modules.

Table 14-7 shows the options that can define modules.

*Table 14-7. Module Options*

| Option | Description |
|---|---|
| −d *name* | Overrides the default working directory name for the module |
| −e *prog* | Runs the program *prog* when files are exported from the module; the module name is passed to *prog* as the sole argument |
| −i *prog* | Runs the program *prog* when files are committed to the module; the repository directory of the committed files is passed in to *prog* as the sole argument |
| −i *prog* | Runs the program *prog* when files are checked out from the module; the module name is passed in to *prog* as the sole argument |
| −s *status* | Assigns a status descriptor to the module |
| −t *prog* | Runs the program *prog* when files are tagged in the module using **rtag**; the module name and the symbolic tag are passed to *prog* |

*Table 14–7. Module Options (continued)*

| Option | Description |
|--------|-------------|
| **–u** *prog* | Runs the program *prog* when files are updated in the module's top-level directory; the full path to the module within the repository is passed to *prog* as the sole argument |

Alias modules provide alternative names for other modules or shortcuts for referring to collections or subdirectories of other modules. Alias module definitions function like macro definitions in that they cause commands to run as if the expanded list of modules and directories was on the command line. Alias modules do not cause the modules of their definition to be grouped together under the alias name (use ampersand modules for that). For example, the definition:

```
h -a hello
```

makes the name *h* a synonym for the *hello* module. This definition:

```
project -a library client server
```

allows you to check out all three modules of the project as a unit. If an entry in the definition of an alias module is preceded by an exclamation point (!), then the named directory is excluded from the module.

Regular modules allow you to create modules that are subsets of other modules. For example, the definition:

```
header library library.h
```

creates a module that just contains the header file from the *library* module.

Ampersand modules are true logical modules. There are no top-level directories for them in the repository, but you can check them out to sandboxes, and directories with their names will then appear. The modules listed in the definition are below that directory. For example:

```
project &library &client &server
```

is almost the same as the alias module example given earlier, except that the sub-modules are checked out inside a subdirectory named *project*.

In this file, long definitions may be split across multiple lines by terminating all but the last line with backslashes (\).

### The notify file

This file is used in conjunction with the **watch** command. When notifications are appropriate, this file is consulted to determine how to do the notification.

Each line of the *notify* file contains a filename pattern and a command line. CVS's notification mechanism uses the command line specified to perform notifications for files having names that match the corresponding pattern.

There is a single special-purpose variable, %s, that can appear in the command specification. When the command is executed, the name of the user to notify replaces the variable name. If the *users* administrative file exists, the user names are looked up there, and the resulting values are used for %s instead. This allows emails to be sent to accounts other than those on the local machine. Details are sent to the notification program via standard input.

Typical usage of this feature is the single entry:

```
ALL mail %s -s "CVS notification"
```

In fact, this entry is present in the default *notify* file created when you run **cvs init** to create a repository (although it is initially commented out).

### The passwd file

If you access the repository via a *pserver* repository locator (see "Repository Locators"), then CVS can have its own private authentication information, separate from the system's user database. This information is stored in the *CVSROOT/passwd* administrative file.

This feature provides anonymous CVS access over the Internet. By creating an entry for a public user (usually *anoncvs* or *anonymous*), the *pserver* can be used by many people sharing the public account. If you don't want to create a system user with the same name as the public user, or if you have such a user but it has a different purpose, you can employ a user alias to map it to something else:

```
anonymous:TY7QWpLw8bvus:cvsnoname
```

Then, make sure you create the cvsnoname user on the system. You can use */bin/false* as the login shell and the repository's root directory as the home directory for the user.

To restrict the public user to read-only access, list it in the *CVSROOT/readers* administrative file.

Additionally, CVS's private user database is useful even if you don't want to set up anonymous CVS access. You can restrict access to a subset of the system's users, provide remote access to users who don't have general system access, or prevent a user's normal system password from being transmitted in the clear over the network (see "Security Issues).

There is no **cvs passwd** command for setting CVS-specific passwords (located in the repository file *CVSROOT/passwd*). CVS-specific user and password management are manual tasks.

### The rcsinfo file

CVS consults this file when doing a **commit** or **import** to determine the log message editor template. Each entry in the file consists of a filename pattern and the name of the file to use as the template for module directories with matching names.

The ALL and DEFAULT special patterns apply to this file.

### The readers file

If this file exists, users listed in it have read-only access.

### The taginfo file

CVS consults this file whenever the **tag** or **rtag** commands are used. Entries in this file are filename patterns and program specifications. The ALL special pattern applies to this file.

The *taginfo* file is called with the tag, the operation being performed, the module directory name (relative to the repository root), and the filename and revision number for each affected file. The valid operations are: add (for **tag**), del (for **tag** −d), and mov (for **tag** −F).

If the *taginfo* program returns a nonzero status, the **tag** or **rtag** command that caused its execution is aborted.

### The users file

If this file exists, it is consulted during processing of the *notify* administrative file's contents. Entries in this file consist of two colon-separated fields on a single line. The first field is the name of a user, and the second field is a value (normally the user's email address on another machine). For example:

```
john:john@somecompany.com
jane:jane@anothercompany.com
```

### The verifymsg file

CVS consults this file to determine if log messages should be validated. If the program returns a nonzero status, the commit is aborted. The *verifymsg* file is called with the full path to a file containing the log message to be verified.

The ALL special pattern is not supported for this file, although DEFAULT is. If more than one pattern matches, the first match is used.

### The writers file

If this file exists, users listed in it have read/write access (unless they are also listed in the *readers* file, in which case they have read-only access).

## Hacking the Repository

Since the repository is a normal directory, albeit one with special contents, it is possible to **cd** into the directory and examine its contents and/or make changes to the files and directories there. For each file that has been added there will be a file with the same name followed by *,v* in a corresponding directory in the repository. These are RCS (the format, not the program) files that contain multiple versions of the file.

Since the activities discussed in this section involve making changes directly to the repository instead of working through CVS commands, you should exercise extreme caution and have current backups when following these instructions.

### Restructuring a project

Restructuring the project by moving files and directories around (and possibly renaming them) in the repository will allow the files to retain their history. The standard way to rename a file when using CVS is to rename the file in the sandbox and do a **cvs remove** on the old name and a **cvs add** on the new name. This results in the file being disconnected from its history under the new name, so sometimes it is better to do the renaming directly in the repository, although doing this while people have active sandboxes is dangerous, since the sandboxes will contain information about a file that is no longer in the repository.

### Bulk importing

When importing an entire project, all of the project's files will be added to the repository. But, if some of these files shouldn't have been added, you'll want to remove them. Doing a **cvs remove** will accomplish this, but copies of those files will remain in the repository's *.Attic* directory forever. To avoid this, you can delete the files from the repository directly before checking out sandboxes from it.

## Importing

If you have an existing code base, you'll want to import it into CVS in a way that preserves the most historical information. This section provides instructions for importing projects into CVS from code snapshots or other version control systems. All of these, except the code snapshot import procedure, are based upon conversion to RCS files, followed by placing the RCS files in the proper location in the CVS repository.

### Importing code snapshots

If you have maintained project history archives manually by taking periodic snapshots of the code, you can import the first snapshot, tag it with the date or version number, and then successively overlay the updated files from later archives. Each set can then be committed and tagged in order to bootstrap a repository that maintains the prior history.

For example, first unpack the distributions (this assumes they unpack to directories containing the version numbers):

```
user@localhost$ tar xvzf foo-1.0.tar.gz
user@localhost$ tar xvzf foo-1.1.tar.gz
user@localhost$ tar xvzf foo-2.0.tar.gz
```

Next, make a copy of the first version, import it into the CVS repository, check it out to make a sandbox (since importing doesn't convert the source directory into a sandbox), and use **cvs tag** to give it a symbolic name reflecting the project version:

```
user@localhost$ mkdir foo
user@localhost$ cp -R -p foo-1.0/* foo
user@localhost$ cd foo
user@localhost$ cvs import -m 'Imported version 1.0' foo vendor start
user@localhost$ cd ..
user@localhost$ mv foo foo.bak
user@localhost$ cvs checkout foo
user@localhost$ cd foo
user@localhost$ cvs tag foo-1_0
user@localhost$ cd ..
```

Now, apply the differences between version 1.0 and 1.1 to the sandbox, commit the changes, and create a tag:

```
user@localhost$ diff -Naur foo-1.0 foo-1.1 | (cd foo; patch -Np1)
user@localhost$ cd foo
user@localhost$ cvs commit -m 'Imported version 1.1'
user@localhost$ cvs tag foo-1_1
user@localhost$ cd ..
```

Now, apply the differences between version 1.1 and 2.0 to the sandbox, commit the changes, and create a tag:

```
user@localhost$ diff -Naur foo-1.1 foo-2.0 | (cd foo; patch -Np1)
user@localhost$ cd foo
user@localhost$ cvs commit -m 'Imported version 2.0'
user@localhost$ cvs tag foo-2_0
```

Now, you can use the **log** command to view the history of the files, browse past versions of the files, and continue development under version control.

### Importing from RCS

If you are migrating from RCS to CVS, following these instructions will result in a usable CVS repository. This procedure involves direct modification of the CVS repository, so it should be undertaken with caution.

Before beginning, make sure none of the files to be imported into CVS are locked by RCS. Then, create a new CVS repository and module (or a new module within an existing repository). Next, create directories in the CVS repository to mirror the project's directory structure. Finally, copy all the version files (*,v*) from the project (which may be in *RCS* subdirectories) into the appropriate directories in the repository (without *RCS* subdirectories).

For example, first move aside the directory under RCS control, create an empty directory to build the new CVS structure, import the directory, and then check it out to make a sandbox:

```
user@localhost$ mv foo foo-rcs
user@localhost$ mkdir foo
user@localhost$ cd foo
user@localhost$ cvs import -m 'New empty project' foo vendor start
user@localhost$ cd ..
```

---

```
user@localhost$ mv foo foo.bak
user@localhost$ cvs checkout foo
```

Next, make directories and add them to the repository to match the structure in
the RCS project:

```
user@localhost$ cd foo
user@localhost$ mkdir dir
user@localhost$ cvs add dir
user@localhost$ cd ..
```

Now, copy the *,v* files from the RCS project into the *repository* for the CVS
project:

```
user@localhost$ cp -p foo-rcs/*,v $CVSROOT/foo
user@localhost$ cp -p foo-rcs/dir/*,v $CVSROOT/foo/dir
```

Finally, issue the **cvs update** command in the sandbox directory to bring in the latest versions of all the files:

```
user@localhost$ cd foo
user@localhost$ cvs upd
```

### Importing from SCCS

To import from SCCS, use the *sccs2rcs* script located in the *contrib* directory of the
CVS distribution to convert the files to RCS format, and then follow the preceding
RCS procedure. You must have both CVS and SCCS installed for this to work. The
script's comments contain additional instructions.

### Importing from PVCS

To import from PVCS, use the *pvcs_to_rcs* script located in the *contrib* directory of
the CVS distribution to convert the files to RCS format, and then follow the previous RCS procedure. You must have both CVS and PVCS installed for this to work.
The script's comments contain additional instructions.

## Using an Interim Shared Sandbox

Sometimes projects will develop unintended environmental dependencies over
time, especially when there is no pressure for the code to be relocatable. A project
developed outside version control may even be initially developed in place (at its
intended installation location). While these practices are not recommended, they
do occur in real-world situations; CVS can be helpful in improving the situation,
by encouraging relocatability from the beginning of a project.

The default mode of operation for CVS is multiple independent sandboxes, all
coordinated with a central shared repository. Code that runs in this environment is
necessarily (at least partially) relocatable. So, using CVS from the beginning of a
project helps ensure flexibility.

However, if a project is already well underway, an interim approach can be used.
For example, you could convert the development area to a single shared sandbox
by importing the code into CVS and checking it back out again:

```
user@localhost$ cd /usr/local/bar
user@localhost$ cvs import bar vendor start
user@localhost$ cd ..
user@localhost$ mv bar bar.bak
user@localhost$ cvs checkout bar
```

Chances are good that this approach is too aggressive and will check in more files than absolutely necessary. You can either go back and hack the repository to remove the files that shouldn't be there or just issue the **cvs remove** command to delete them as you discover them.

In addition, there will probably be some binary files in the sandbox that were imported as text files. Wherever you see a binary file that needs to remain in the repository, you should issue the command **cvs admin –kb** *file*, then make a fresh copy from the project backup. Finally, issue the command **cvs commit** *file* to commit the fixed file back to the repository.

Having version control in place before making flexibility enhancements is a good idea, since it makes it easier to find (and possibly reverse) changes that cause trouble.

The repository locator (see the later section "Repository Locators") is specified via the -d option or the $CVSROOT environment variable. It is stored in the various sandbox *CVS/root* files. If you are using the password server (**pserver**), the user ID of the person checking out the sandbox will be remembered. If more than one person is working with a particular sandbox, they will have to share an account for CVS access.

One way to do this is to have a neutral user account, with a password known by everyone with CVS access. Everyone can then issue the **cvs login** command with the same user ID and password and have access to the repository. Once you are no longer using a shared sandbox, this workaround won't be necessary. However, during the time you are using a shared sandbox, it is important that the developers type their real user IDs into their log messages, since all the changes will appear to be made by the common user.

## Global Server Option

The server has one global option: –**allow-root=***rootdir*. This option is used to tell the CVS server to accept and process requests for the specified repository.

## Administrator Commands

Table 14-8 lists the commands that CVS administrators can use to manage their repositories.

*Table 14-8. Administrator Commands*

| Command | Description |
|---|---|
| admin<br>adm<br>rcs | Perform administrative functions |
| init | Create a new repository |
| server | Run in server mode |

### admin

```
admin
  [ -b[rev] ]
  [ -cstring ]
  [ -kkflag ]
  [ -l[rev] ]
  [ -L ]
  [ -mrev:msg ]
  [ -nname[:[rev]] ]
  [ -Nname[:[rev]] ]
  [ -orange ]
  [ -q ]
  [ -sstate[:rev] ]
  [ -t[file] ]
  [ -t-string ]
  [ -u[rev] ]
  [ -U ]
  [ files ... ]
```

The **admin** is used to perform administrative functions. If a *cvsadmin* user group exists, then only those users in that group will be able to run **admin** with options other than **–k**. Additional options that may be used with the **admin** command are listed in Table 14-9.

*Table 14-9. admin Options*

| Option | Description |
|---|---|
| –b[*rev*] | Set the default branch. |
| –c*string* | Obsolete. Set the comment leader. |
| –k*kflag* | Set the default keyword substitution mode. |
| –l[*rev*] | Lock the specified revision. |
| –L | Enable strict locking. |
| –m*rev:msg* | Change the revision's log message. |
| –n*name*[:[*rev*]] | Give the branch or revision specified the symbolic name *name*. |
| –N*name*[:[*rev*]] | The same as **–n**, except that if *name* is already in use, it is moved. |
| –o*range* | Delete revisions permanently. |
| –q | Don't print diagnostics. |

*Table 14–9. admin Options (continued)*

| Option | Description |
|---|---|
| −s*state*[:*rev*] | Change the state of a revision. |
| −t[*file*] | Set the descriptive text in the RCS file. |
| −t-*string* | Set the descriptive text in the RCS file to *string*. |
| −u[*rev*] | Unlock the specified revision. |
| −U | Disable strict locking. |

If the revision specified for −l is a branch, the latest revision on that branch will be used. If no revision is given, the latest revision on the default branch is used.

If the name given for −n is already in use, an error is generated. You can use −N to move a tag (change the revision associated with the tag); however, you should usually use **cvs tag** or **cvs rtag** instead.

The −o option is very dangerous and results in a permanent loss of information from the repository. Use it with extreme caution and only after careful consideration. See Table 14-10 for the various ways to specify ranges. There must not be any branches or locks on the revisions to be removed. Beware of interactions between this command and symbolic names.

If no *file* is specified to the −t option, CVS reads from standard input until it reaches the end of the file or a period on a line by itself.

The determination of the target revision for the −u option is the same as for −l.

*Table 14–10. Range Formats*

| Format | Description |
|---|---|
| *rev1*::*rev2* | Eliminate versions between *rev1* and *rev2*, retaining only enough information to go directly from *rev1* to *rev2*. The two specified versions are retained. |
| ::*rev* | The same as *rev1::rev2*, except the first revision is the branchpoint revision. |
| *rev*:: | The same as *rev1::rev2*, except the second revision is the end of the branch, and it is deleted instead of retained. |
| *rev* | Delete the specified revision. |
| *rev1*:*rev2* | The same as *rev1::rev2*, except the two named revisions are deleted as well. |
| :*rev* | The same as ::*rev2*, except the named revision is deleted as well. |
| *rev*: | The same as *rev1::*, except the named revision is deleted as well. |

The options in Table 14-11 are present in CVS for historical reasons and should not be used (using these options may corrupt the repository).

*Table 14-11. Obsolete admin Options*

| Option | Description |
|---|---|
| **-a***logins* | Append the logins to the RCS file's access list. |
| **-A***oldfile* | Append the access list of *oldfile* to the access list of the RCS file. |
| **-e**[*logins*] | Erases logins from the RCS file's access list, or erases all if a list is not provided. |
| **-i** | Create and initialize a new RCS file. Don't use this option. Instead, use **add** to add files to a CVS repository. |
| **-I** | Run interactively. This option doesn't work with client/server CVS and is likely to be removed in a future version. |
| **-V***n* | Obsolete. This option was used to specify that the RCS files used by CVS should be made compatible with a specific version of RCS. |
| **-x***suffixes* | This option used to be described as determining the filename suffix for RCS files, but CVS has always only used *,v* as the RCS file suffix. |

### *init*

    init

Initializes the repository. Use the global **-d** option to specify the repository's directory if $CVSROOT isn't set appropriately.

The newly initialized repository will contain a *CVSROOT* module, but nothing else. Once the repository is initialized, use other CVS commands to add files to it or to check out the *CVSROOT* module to make changes to the administrative files.

### *pserver*

    pserver

Operate as a server, providing access to the repositories specified before the command with the **-allow-root** option. This command is used in the *inetd.conf* file, not on the command line. Another global option frequently used with this command is **-T** (see Table 14-1).

# *CVS User Reference*

This section provides details on connecting to a repository, the structure of sandboxes, and using the CVS commands.

## *Repository Locators*

CVS currently supports five methods for the client to access the repository: local, external, a password server, a GSS-API (Generic Security Services API) server, and a Kerberos 4 server (most Kerberos users will want to use GSS-API). Table 14-12 describes the various repository locator types and their respective access methods.

*Table 14-12. Repository Access Types and Methods*

| Method | Locator Format | Description |
|--------|----------------|-------------|
| Local | `path` | If the repository directory is local to the computer from which you will access it (or appears local, such as an NFS or Samba mounted filesystem), the repository string is just the pathname of the repository directory, such as */usr/local/cvsrep.* |
| External | `:ext:`*user@host:path* | External repositories are accessed via a remote shell utility, usually **rsh** (the default) or **ssh**. The environment variable $CVS_RSH is used to specify the remote shell program. |
| Password server | `:pserver:`*user@host:path* | Password server repositories require authentication to a user account before allowing use of the repository. Public CVS servers are commonly configured this way so they can provide anonymous CVS access. See "The passwd file," earlier in this chapter, for more information on anonymous CVS. |

*Table 14-12. Repository Access Types and Methods (continued)*

| Method | Locator Format | Description |
|---|---|---|
| GSS-API server | `:gserver:` | This locator type is used for servers accessible via Kerberos 5 or other authentication mechanisms supported by GSS-API. |
| Kerberos server | `:kserver:` | This locator type is used for servers accessible via Kerberos 4. |

## Configuring CVS

CVS's behavior can be influenced by two classes of settings other than the command-line arguments: the *environment variables* (see Table 14-13) and *special files* (see Table 14-14).

*Table 14-13. Environment Variables*

| Variable | Description |
|---|---|
| $COMSPEC | Command interpreter on OS/2, if not *cmd.exe*. |
| $CVS_CLIENT_LOG | Client-side debugging file specification for client/server connections.<br><br>$CVS_CLIENT_LOG is the basename for the *$CVS_CLIENT_LOG.in* and *$CVS_CLIENT_LOG.out* files, which will be written in the current working directory at the time a command is executed. |
| $CVS_CLIENT_PORT | The port number for :kserver: locators.<br><br>$CVS_CLIENT_PORT doesn't need to be set if the **kserver** is listening on port 1999 (the default). |
| $CVS_IGNORE_REMOTE_ROOT | According to the *ChangeLog*, this variable was removed from CVS with Version 1.10.3. |
| $CVS_PASSFILE | Password file for :PSERVER: locators. This variable must be set before issuing the **cvs login** to have the desired effect. Defaults to *$HOME/.cvspass*. |

*Table 14–13. Environment Variables (continued)*

| Variable | Description |
|---|---|
| $CVS_RCMD_PORT | For non-Unix clients, the port for connecting to the server's **rcmd** daemon. |
| $CVS_RSH | Remote shell for :ext: locators, if not **rsh**. |
| $CVS_SERVER | Remote server program for :ext: locators, if not **cvs**. |
| $CVS_SERVER_SLEEP | Server-side execution delay (in seconds) to allow time to attach a debugger. |
| $CVSEDITOR | Editor used for log messages; overrides $EDITOR. |
| $CVSIGNORE | A list of filename patterns to ignore, separated by white space. (See also *cvsignore* in Table 14-4 and *.cvsignore* in Table 14-14.) |
| $CVSREAD | Determines read-only (if the variable is set) or read/write (if the variable is not set) for **checkout** and **update**. |
| $CVSROOT | Default repository locator. |
| $CVSUMASK | Used to determine permissions for (local) repository files. |
| $CVSWRAPPERS | A list of filename patterns for the *cvswrappers* function. See also the earlier section "Repository Structure." |
| $EDITOR | Specifies the editor to use for log messages; see notes for $CVSEDITOR earlier in this table. |
| $HOME | On Unix, used to find the *.cvsrc* file. |
| $HOMEDRIVE | On Windows NT, used to find the *.cvsrc* file. |
| $HOMEPATH | On Windows NT, used to find the *.cvsrc* file. |
| $PATH | Used to locate programs to run. |
| $RCSBIN | Used to locate RCS programs to run. This variable is obsolete. |
| $TEMP $TMP $TMPDIR | Location for temporary files. $TMPDIR is used by the server. On Unix, */tmp* (and TMP on Windows NT) may not be overridden for some functions of CVS due to reliance on the system's tmpnam() function. |

Despite the similarity in names, the $CVSROOT environment variable and the *CVSROOT* directory in a repository are not related to each other.

The "RSH" in the name of the $CVS_RSH environment variable doesn't refer to the particular program (**rsh**), but rather to the program CVS is supposed to use for creating remote shell connections (which could be some program other than **rsh**, such as **ssh**).

Since there is only one way to specify the remote shell program to use ($CVS_RSH), and since this is a global setting, users that commonly access multiple repositories may need to pay close attention to which repository they are using. If one repository requires one setting of this variable and another requires a different setting, then you will have to change this variable between accesses to repositories requiring different settings. This aspect of the repository access method is not stored in the *CVS/Root* file in the sandbox (see "CVS directories," later in this chapter). For example, if you access some repositories via **rsh** and some via **ssh**, then you can create the following two utility aliases (**bash** syntax):

```
user@localhost$ alias cvs="export CVS_RSH=ssh; cvs"
user@localhost$ alias cvr="export CVS_RSH=rsh; cvs"
```

Table 14-14 shows the files used by the CVS command-line client for server connection and client configuration information. These files reside in the user's home directory.

*Table 14-14. Client Configuration Files*

| Option | Description |
|---|---|
| ~/.cvsignore | Filename patterns of files to ignore |
| ~/.cvspass | Passwords cached by **cvs login** |
| ~/.cvsrc | Default command options |
| ~/.cvswrappers | User-specific **checkout** and **commit** filters |

The ~/.cvspass file is really an operational file, not a configuration file. It is used by the **cvs** client program to store the repository user account password between **cvs login** and **cvs logoff**.

Some common .cvsrc settings are:

update −dP
    Brings in new directories and prunes empty directories on **cvs update**.

diff −c
    Give output in context **diff** format.

## Creating a Sandbox

In order to use CVS, you must create a sandbox or have one created for you. This section describes sandbox creation, assuming there is already a module in the repository you want to work with. See the later section "import" for information on importing a new module into the repository.

1. Determine the repository locator. Talk to the repository administrator if you need help finding the repository or getting the locator syntax right.

2. If this will be the main repository you use, set $CVSROOT; otherwise, use the −d option when running CVS commands that don't infer the repository from the sandbox files.

3. Pick a module to check out.

4. Pick a sandbox location, and **cd** to the parent directory.

5. If the repository requires login, do **cvs login**.

6. Run **cvs checkout** *module*.

For example:

```
export CVSROOT=/usr/local/cvsroot
cd ~/work
cvs checkout hello
```

## Sandbox Structure

This section describes the files and directories that may be encountered in sandboxes.

### .cvsignore files

Sandboxes may contain *.cvsignore* files. These files specify filename patterns for files that may exist in the sandbox but which normally won't be checked into CVS. This is commonly used to cause CVS to bypass derived files.

### .cvswrappers files

Sandboxes may contain *.cvswrappers* files, which provide directory-specific file handling information like that in the repository configuration file *cvswrappers* (see "The cvswrappers file," earlier in this chapter).

### CVS directories

Each directory in a sandbox contains a *CVS* directory. The files in this directory (see Table 14-15) contain metadata used by CVS to locate the repository and track which file versions have been copied into the sandbox.

*Table 14-15. Files in the CVS Directories*

| File | Description |
|------|-------------|
| Base<br>Baserev<br>Baserev.tmp | The *Base* directory stores copies of files when the **edit** command is in use. The *Baserev* file contains the revision numbers of the files in *Base*. The *Baserev.tmp* file is used in updating the *Baserev* file. |

*Table 14–15. Files in the CVS Directories (continued)*

| File | Description |
|------|-------------|
| *Checkin.prog*<br>*Update.prog* | The programs specified in the modules file for options –i and –u, respectively (if any). |
| *Entries* | Version numbers and timestamps for the files as they were copied from the repository when checked out or updated. |
| *Entries.Backup*<br>*Entries.Log*<br>*Entries.Static* | These are temporary and intermediate files used by CVS. |
| *Notify*<br>*Notify.tmp* | These are temporary files used by CVS for dealing with notifications for commands like **edit** and **unedit**. |
| *Repository* | The name by which the directory is known in the repository. |
| *Root* | The repository locator in effect when the sandbox was created (via **cvs checkout**). |
| *Tag* | Information about sticky tags and dates for files in the directory. |
| *Template* | Used to store the contents of the *rcsinfo* administrative file from the repository for remote repositories. |

Since each sandbox directory has one *CVS/Root* file, a sandbox directory corresponds to exactly one repository. You cannot check out some files from one repository and some from another into a single sandbox directory.

## Client Global Options

Table 14-16 lists the global options that control the operation of the CVS client program.

*Table 14–16. Client Global Options*

| Option | Description |
|--------|-------------|
| –a | Authenticate (**gserver** only). |
| –d root | Locate the repository. Overrides the setting of $CVSROOT. |
| –e editor | Specify message editor. Overrides the settings of $CVSEDITOR and $EDITOR. |
| –f | Don't read ~/.cvsrc. Useful when you have .cvsrc settings that you want to forgo for a particular command. |
| –H [command]<br>–help [command] | Display help. If no command is specified, general CVS help, including a list of other help options, is displayed. |

*Table 14-16. Client Global Options (continued)*

| Option | Description |
|--------|-------------|
| −l | Don't log command in history. |
| −n | Don't change any files. Useful when you want to know ahead of time which files will be affected by a particular command. |
| −q | Be quiet. |
| −Q | Be very quiet. Print messages only for serious problems. |
| −r | Make new working files read-only. |
| −s variable=value | Set the value of a user variable to a given value. User variables can be used in the contents of administrative files. |
| −t | Trace execution. Helpful in debugging remote repository connection problems and, in conjunction with −n, in determining the effect of an unfamiliar command. |
| −w | Make new working files read/write. Overrides $CVSREAD. Files are read/write unless $CVSREAD is set or −r is specified. |
| −x | Encrypt. (Introduced in Version 1.10.) |
| −z gzip_level | Set the compression level. Useful when using CVS in client/ server mode across slow connections. |

## *Common Client Options*

Table 14-17 and Table 14-18 describe the options that are common to many CVS commands. Table 14-17 lists the common options with a description of their function, while Table 14-18 lists which options can be used with the user commands. In the sections that follow, details will be provided only for options that are not listed here and for those that do not function as described here.

*Table 14-17. Common Options*

| Option | Description |
|--------|-------------|
| −D date | Use the most recent revision no later than *date*. |
| −f | For commands that involve tags (via −r) or dates (via −D), include files not tagged with the specified tag or not present on the specified date. The most recent revision will be included. |
| −k kflag | Determine how keyword substitution will be performed. The space between −k and *kflag* is optional. See Table 14-19 for the list of keyword substitution modes. |
| −l | Do not recurse into subdirectories. |
| −n | Don't run module programs. |

*Table 14–17. Common Options (continued)*

| Option | Description |
|---|---|
| –R | Do recurse into subdirectories (the default). |
| –r rev | Use a particular revision number or symbolic tag. |

Table 14-18 shows which common options are applicable to each user command.

*Table 14–18. Client Common Option Applicability*

| User Command | –D | –f | –k | –l | –n | –R | –r |
|---|---|---|---|---|---|---|---|
| add | | | • | | | | |
| annotate | • | • | | • | | • | • |
| checkout | • | • | • | • | • | • | • |
| commit | | | | • | • | • | • |
| diff | • | | • | • | | • | • |
| edit | | | | • | | • | |
| editors | | | | • | | • | |
| export | • | • | • | • | • | • | • |
| help | | | | | | | |
| history | • | | | | | | • |
| import | | | • | | | | |
| log | | | | • | | • | |
| login | | | | | | | |
| logout | | | | | | | |
| rdiff | • | • | | • | | • | • |
| release | | | | | | | |
| remove | | | | • | | • | |
| rtag | • | • | | • | | • | • |
| status | | | | • | | • | |
| tag | | | | • | | • | |
| unedit | | | | • | | • | |
| update | • | • | • | • | | • | • |

*Table 14-18. Client Common Option Applicability (continued)*

| User Command | –D | –f | –k | –l | –n | –R | –r |
|---|---|---|---|---|---|---|---|
| watch | | | | • | | • | |
| watchers | | | | • | | • | |

## Date formats

CVS can understand dates in a wide variety of formats, including:

*ISO standard*
> The preferred format is `YYYY-MM-DD HH:MM`, which would read as `2000-05-17`, or `2000-05-17 22:00`. The technical details of the format are defined in the ISO 8601 standard.

*Email standard*
> `17 May 2000`. The technical details of the format are defined in the RFC 822 and RFC 1123 standards.

*Relative*
> `10 days ago`, `4 years ago`.

*Common*
> *month/day/year*. This form can cause confusion because not all cultures use the first two fields in this order (`1/2/2000` would be ambiguous).

*Other*
> Other formats are accepted, including `YYYY/MM/DD` and those omitting the year (which is assumed to be the current year).

## Keyword substitutions

Table 14-19 describes the keyword substitution modes that can be selected with the **–k** option. CVS uses keyword substitutions to insert revision information into files when they are checked out or updated.

*Table 14-19. Keyword Substitution Modes*

| Mode | Description |
|---|---|
| b | Binary mode. Treat the file the same as with mode o, but also avoid newline conversion. |
| k | Keyword-only mode. Flatten all keywords to just the keyword name. Use this mode if you want to compare two revisions of a file without seeing the keyword substitution differences. |
| kv | Keyword-value mode. The keyword and the corresponding value are substituted. This is the default mode. |

*Table 14–19. Keyword Substitution Modes (continued)*

| Mode | Description |
|------|-------------|
| kvl | Keyword-value-locker mode. This mode is the same as **kv** mode, except it always adds the lock holder's user ID if the revision is locked. The lock is obtained via the **cvs admin –l** command. |
| o | Old-contents mode. Use the keyword values as they appear in the repository rather than generate new values. |
| v | Value-only mode. Substitute the value of each keyword for the entire keyword field, omitting even the $ delimiters. This mode destroys the field in the process, so use it cautiously. |

Keyword substitution fields are strings of the form $*Keyword* . . .$. The valid keywords are:

**Author**
> The user ID of the person who committed the revision.

**Date**
> The date and time (in standard UTC format) the revision was committed.

**Header**
> The full path of the repository RCS file, the revision number, the commit date, time, and user ID, the file's state, and the lock holder's user ID if the file is locked.

**Id** A shorter form of **Header**, omitting the leading directory name(s) from the RCS file's path, leaving only the filename.

**Name**
> The tag name used to retrieve the file, or empty if the no explicit tag was given when the file was retrieved.

**Locker**
> The user ID of the user holding a lock on the file, or empty if the file is not locked.

**Log**
> The RCS filename. In addition to keyword expansion in the keyword field, each commit adds additional lines in the file immediately following the line containing this keyword. The first such line contains the revision number, the commit date, time, and user ID. Subsequent lines are the contents of the commit log message. The result over time is a reverse-chronological list of log entries for the file. Each of the additional lines is preceded by the same characters that precede the keyword field on its line. This allows the log information to be formatted in a comment for most languages. For example:

```
#
# foo.pl
#
# $Log: foo.pl,v $
```

```
# Revision 1.2  2000/06/09 22:10:23  me
# Fixed the new bug introduced when the last one was fixed.
#
# Revision 1.1  2000/06/09 18:07:51  me
# Fixed the last remaining bug in the system.
#
```

Be sure that you don't place any keyword fields in your log messages if you use this keyword, since they will get expanded if you do.

RCSfile

> The name of the RCS file (without any leading directories).

Revision

> The revision number of the file.

Source

> The full path of the RCS file.

State

> The file's state, as assigned by **cvs admin −s** (if you don't set the state explicitly, it will be **Exp** by default).

## User Commands

The CVS client program provides the user commands defined in Table 14-20.

*Table 14–20. User Commands*

| Command | Description |
|---------|-------------|
| ad add new | Indicate that files/directories should be added to the repository. |
| ann annotate | Display contents of the head revision of a file, annotated with the revision number, user, and date of the last change for each line. |
| checkout co get | Create a sandbox for a module. |
| ci com commit | Commit changes from the sandbox back to the repository. |
| di dif diff | View differences between file versions. |
| edit | Prepare to edit files. This is used for enhanced developer coordination. |

*Table 14-20. User Commands (continued)*

| Command | Description |
|---|---|
| editors | Display a list of users working on the files. This is used for enhanced developer coordination. |
| ex<br>exp<br>export | Retrieve a module, but don't make the result a sandbox. |
| help | Get help. |
| hi<br>his<br>history | Display the log information for files. |
| im<br>imp<br>import | Import new modules into the repository. |
| lgn<br>login<br>logon | Log in to (cache the password for) a remote CVS server. |
| lo<br>log<br>rlog | Show the activity log for the file(s). |
| logout | Log off from (flush the password for) a remote CVS server. |
| pa<br>patch<br>rdiff | Release **diff**. The output is the format of input to Larry Wall's **patch** command. Does not have to be run from within a sandbox. |
| re<br>rel<br>release | p Perform a logged delete on a sandbox. |
| remove<br>rm<br>delete | Remove a file or directory from the repository. |
| rt<br>rtag<br>rfreeze | Tag a particular revision. |

*Table 14-20. User Commands (continued)*

| Command | Description |
|---|---|
| st<br>stat<br>status | Show detailed status for files. |
| ta<br>tag<br>freeze | Attach a tag to files in the repository. |
| unedit | Abandon file modifications and make read-only again. |
| up<br>upd<br>update | Synchronize sandbox to repository. |
| watch | Manage the watch settings. This is used for enhanced developer coordination. |
| watchers | Display the list of users watching for changes to the files. This is used for enhanced developer coordination. |

## add

```
add
  [ -k kflag ]
  [ -m message ]
  file ...
```

Indicate that files/directories should be added to the repository. They are not actually added until they are committed via **cvs commit**. This command is also used to resurrect files that have been deleted with **cvs remove**.

The standard meaning of the common client option **–k** applies. There is only one additional option that can be used with the **add** command: **–m** *message*. This option is used to provide a description of the file (which appears in the output of the **log** command).

## annotate

```
annotate
  [ [ -D date | -r rev ] -f ]
  [ -l | -R ]
  file ...
```

CVS prints a report showing each line of the specified file. Each line is prefixed by information about the most recent change to the line, including the revision number, the user, and the date. If no revision is specified, then the head of the trunk is used.

The standard meanings of the common client options –D, –f, –l, –r, and –R apply.

## *checkout*

```
checkout
  [ -A ]
  [ -c | -s ]
  [ -d dir [ -N ] ]
  [ [ -D date | -r rev ] -f ]
  [ -j rev1 [ -j rev2 ] ]
  [ -k kflag ]
  [ -l | -R ]
  [ -n ]
  [ -p ]
  [ -P ]
  module ...
```

Copy files from the repository to the sandbox.

The standard meanings of the common client options –D, –f, –k, –l, –r, and –R apply. Additional options are listed in Table 14-21.

*Table 14–21. Checkout Options*

| Option | Description |
|--------|-------------|
| –A | Reset any sticky tags or dates. |
| –c | Copy the *module* file to standard output. |
| –d *dir* | Override the default directory name. |
| –j *rev* | Join branches together. |
| –N | Don't shorten module paths. |
| –p | Pipe the files to standard output, with header lines between them showing the filename, RCS filename, and version. |
| –P | Prune empty directories. |
| –s | Show status for each module from the *modules* file. |

## *commit*

```
commit
  [ -f | [ -l | -R ] ]
  [ -F file | -m message ]
  [ -n ]
  [ -r revision ]
  [ files ... ]
```

Commit the changes made to files in the sandbox to the repository.

The standard meanings of the common client options –l, –n, –r, and –R apply. Additional options are listed in Table 14-22.

*Table 14–22. commit Options*

| Option | Description |
|--------|-------------|
| –f | Force commit, even if no changes were made. |
| –F *file* | Use the contents of the file as the message. |
| –m *message* | Use the message specified. |

Use of the –r option causes the revision to be sticky, requiring the use of **admin** –A to continue to use the sandbox.

## *diff*

```
diff
  [ -k kflag ]
  [ -l | -R ]
  [ format ]
  [ [ -r rev1 | -D date1 ] [ -r rev2 | -D date2 ] ]
  [ file ... ]
```

The **diff** command compares two versions of a file and displays the differences in a format determined by the options. By default, the sandbox version of the file will be compared to the repository version it was originally copied from.

The standard meanings of the common client options –D, –k, –l, –r, and –R apply. All options for the **diff** command in Chapter 3, *Linux Commands* can also be used.

## *edit*

```
edit
  [ -a action ]
  [ -l | -R ]
  [ file ... ]
```

The **edit** command is used in conjunction with **watch** to permit a more coordinated (serialized) development process. It makes the file writable and sends out an advisory to any users who have requested them. A temporary **watch** is established and will be removed automatically when either the **unedit** or the **commit** command is issued.

The standard meanings of the common client options –l and –R apply. There is only one additional option that can be used with the **edit** command: –a *actions*. This option is used to specify the actions to watch. The legal values for actions are described in the entry for the **watch** command.

## *editors*

```
editors
  [ -l | -R ]
  [ file ... ]
```

Display a list of users working on the files specified. This is determined by checking which users have run the **edit** command on those files. If the **edit** command has not been used, no results will be displayed.

The standard meanings of the common client options −l and −R apply.

See also the later section on **watch**.

## export

```
export
  [ -d dir [ -N ] ]
  [ -D date | -r rev ]
  [ -f ]
  [ -k kflag ]
  [ -l | -R ]
  [ -n ]
  [ -P ]
  module ...
```

Export files from the repository, much like the **checkout** command, except that the result is not a sandbox (i.e., *CVS* subdirectories are not created). This can be used to prepare a directory for distribution. For example:

```
user@localhost$ cvs export -r foo-1_0 -d foo-1.0 foo
user@localhost$ tar czf foo-1.0.tar.gz foo-1.0
```

The standard meanings of the common client options −D, −f, −k, −l, −n, −r, and −R apply. Additional options are listed in Table 14-23.

*Table 14-23. export Options*

| Option | Description |
| --- | --- |
| −d *dir* | Use *dir* as the directory name instead of using the module name. |
| −n | Don't run any checkout programs. |
| −N | Don't shorten paths. |

When checking out a single file located one or more directories down in a module's directory structure, the −N option can be used with −d to prevent the creation of intermediate directories.

## help

help

Display helpful information about using the **cvs** program.

## history

```
history
  [ -a | -u user ]
  [ -b string ]
  [ -c ]
```

```
[ -D date ]
[ -e | -x type ]
[ -f file | -m module | -n module | -p repository ]...
[ -l ]
[ -o ]
[ -r rev ]
[ -t tag ]
[ -T ]
[ -w ]
[ -z zone ]
[ file ... ]
```

Display historical information. To use the **history** command, you must first set up the *history* file in the repository. See the earlier section "Repository Structure" for more information on this file.

 When used with the **history** command, the functions of **–f**, **–l**, **–n**, and **–p** are not the same as elsewhere in CVS.

The standard meanings of the common client options **–D**, and **–r** apply. History is reported for activity subsequent to the date or revision indicated. Additional options are listed in Table 14-24.

*Table 14–24. history Options*

| Option | Description |
|---|---|
| **–a** | Show history for all users (default is current user). |
| **–b** str | Show history back to the first record containing *str* in the module name, filename, or repository path. |
| **–c** | Report each **commit**. |
| **–e** | Report everything. |
| **–f** file | Show the most recent event for *file*. |
| **–l** | Show last event only. |
| **–m** module | Produce a full report on *module*. |
| **–n** module | Report the last event for *module*. |
| **–o** | Report on modules that have been checked out. |
| **–p** repository | Show history for a particular repository directory. |
| **–t** tag | Show history since the tag *tag* was last added to the history file. |
| **–T** | Report on all tags. |
| **–u** name | Show history for a particular user. |
| **–w** | Show history only for the current working directory. |

*Table 14-24. history Options (continued)*

| Option | Description |
|--------|-------------|
| **-w** *zone* | Display times according to the time zone *zone*. |
| **-x** *type* | Report on specific types of activity. See Table 14-25. |

The **-p** option should limit the **history** report to entries for the directory or directories (if multiple **-p** options are specified) given, but as of Version 1.10.8, it doesn't seem to affect the output. For example, to report history for the *CVSROOT* and *hello* modules, run the command:

```
cvs history -p CVSROOT -p hello
```

Using **-t** is faster than using **-r** because it only needs to search through the history file, not all of the RCS files.

The record types shown in Table 14-25 are generated by **update** commands.

*Table 14-25. Update-Related history Record Types*

| Type | Description |
|------|-------------|
| C | Merge was necessary, but conflicts requiring manual intervention occurred. |
| G | Successful automatic merge. |
| U | Working file copied from repository. |
| W | Working copy deleted. |

The record types shown in Table 14-26 are generated by **commit** commands:

*Table 14-26. Commit-Related history Record Types*

| Type | Description |
|------|-------------|
| A | Added for the first time |
| M | Modified |
| R | Removed |

Each of the record types shown in Table 14-27 is generated by a different command.

*Table 14-27. Other history Record Types*

| Type | Command |
|------|---------|
| E | **export** |
| F | **release** |
| O | **checkout** |
| T | **rtag** |

## import

```
import
   [ -b branch ]
   [ -d ]
   [ -I pattern ]
   [ -k kflag ]
   [ -m message ]
   [ -W spec ]
   module
   vendor_tag
   release_tag ...
```

Import an entire directory into the repository as a new module. Used to incorporate code from outside sources or other code that was initially created outside the control of the CVS repository. More than one *release_tag* may be specified, in which case multiple symbolic tags will be created for the initial revision.

The standard meaning of the common client option **–k** applies. Additional options are listed in Table 14-28.

*Table 14–28. import Options*

| Option | Description |
|---|---|
| **–b** *branch* | Import to a vendor branch. |
| **–d** | Use the modification date and time of the file instead of the current date and time as the import date and time. For local repository locators only. |
| **–I** *pattern* | Filename patterns for files to ignore. |
| **–m** *message* | Use *message* as the log message instead of invoking the editor. |
| **–W** *spec* | Wrapper specification. |

The **–k** setting will apply only to those files imported during this execution of the command. The keyword substitution modes of files already in the repository are not modified.

When used with **–W**, the *spec* variable is in the same format as entries in the *cvswrappers* administrative file (see the previous section "The cvswrappers file").

Table 14-29 describes the status codes displayed by the **import** command.

*Table 14–29. import Status Codes*

| Status | Description |
|---|---|
| C | Changed. The file is in the repository, and the sandbox version is different; a merge is required. |
| I | Ignored. The *.cvsignore* file is causing CVS to ignore the file. |
| L | Link. Symbolic links are ignored by CVS. |

*Table 14–29. import Status Codes (continued)*

| Status | Description |
|--------|-------------|
| N | New. The file is new. It has been added to the repository. |
| U | Update. The file is in the repository, and the sandbox version is not different. |

## *log*

```
log
  [ -b ]
  [ -d dates ]
  [ -h ]
  [ -N ]
  [ -rrevisions ]
  [ -R ]
  [ -s state ]
  [ -t ]
  [ -wlogins ]
  [ file ... ]
```

Print an activity log for the files.

The standard meaning of the common client option –l applies. Additional options are listed in Table 14-30.

*Table 14–30. log Options*

| Option | Description |
|--------|-------------|
| –b | List revisions on default branch. |
| –d *dates* | Report on these dates. |
| –h | Print header only. |
| –N | Don't print tags. |
| –r[*revisions*] | Report on the listed revisions. There is no space between –r and its argument. Without an argument, the latest revision of the default branch is used. |
| –R | Print RCS filename only. The usage of –R here is different than elsewhere in CVS (–R usually causes CVS to operate recursively). |
| –s *state* | Print only those revisions having the specified state. |
| –t | Print only header and descriptive text. |
| –w*logins* | Report on checkins by the listed logins. There is no space between –w and its argument. |

For –d, use the date specifications in Table 14-31. Multiple specifications separated by semicolons may be provided.

*Table 14-31. log Date Range Specifications*

| Specification | Description |
|---|---|
| *d1<d2*, or *d2>d1* | The revisions dated between *d1* and *d2*, exclusive |
| *d1<=d2*, or *d2>=d1* | The revisions dated between *d1* and *d2*, inclusive |
| *<d*, or *d>* | The revisions dated before *d* |
| *<=d*, or *d>=* | The revisions dated on or before *d* |
| *d<*, or *>d* | The revisions dated after *d* |
| *d<=*, or *>=d* | The revisions dated on or after *d* |
| *d* | The most recent revision dated *d* or earlier |

For **−r**, use the revision specifications in Table 14-32.

*Table 14-32. log Revision Specifications*

| Specification | Description |
|---|---|
| *rev1: rev2* | The revisions between *rev1* and *rev2*, inclusive. |
| *:rev* | The revisions from the beginning of the branch to *rev*, inclusive. |
| *rev:* | The revisions from *rev* to the end of the branch, inclusive. |
| *branch* | All revisions on the branch. |
| *branch1: branch2* | All revisions on all branches between *branch1* and *branch2* inclusive. |
| *branch*. | The latest revision on the branch. |

For *rev1:rev2*, it is an error if the revisions are not on the same branch.

## login

```
login
```

This command is used to log in to remote repositories. The password entered will be cached in the `~/.cvspass` file, since a connection to the server is not maintained across invocations.

## logout

```
logout
```

This command logs out of a remote repository. The password cached in the `~/.cvspass` file will be deleted.

## rdiff

```
rdiff
 [ -c | -s | -u ]
 [ { { -D date1 | -r rev1 } [ -D date2 | -r rev2 ] } | -t ]
 [ -f ]
 [ -l | -R ]
 [-V vn]
 file ...
```

The **rdiff** command creates a **patch** file that can be used to convert a directory containing one release into a different release.

The standard meanings of the common client options –D, –f, –l, –r, and –R apply. Additional options are listed in Table 14-33.

*Table 14-33. rdiff Options*

| Option | Description |
|---|---|
| –c | Use **context diff** format (the default). |
| –s | Output a summary of changed files instead of a **patch** file. |
| –t | Show the differences between the two most recent revisions. |
| –u | Use **unidiff format**. |
| –V *rcsver* | Obsolete. Used to specify version of RCS to emulate for keyword expansion. (Keyword expansion emulates RCS Version 5.) |

## release

```
release
 [ -d ]
 directory ...
```

Sandboxes can be abandoned or deleted without using **cvs release** if desired; using the **release** command will log an entry to the history file (if this mechanism is configured) about the sandbox being destroyed. In addition, it will check the disposition (recursively) of each of the sandbox files before deleting anything. This can help prevent destroying work that has not yet been committed.

There is only one option that can be used with the **release** command, –d. The –d option will delete the sandbox copy if no uncommitted changes are present.

New directories (including any files in them) in the sandbox will be deleted if the –d option is used with **release**.

The status codes listed in Table 14-34 are used to describe the disposition of each file encountered in the repository and the sandbox.

*Table 14-34. release Status Codes.*

| Status | Description |
|--------|-------------|
| A | The sandbox file has been added (the file was created and **cvs add** was run), but the addition has not been committed. |
| M | The sandbox copy of the file has been modified. |
| P U | Update available. There is a newer version of the file in the repository, and the copy in the sandbox has not been modified. |
| R | The sandbox copy was removed (the file was deleted and **cvs remove** was run), but the removal was not committed. |
| ? | The file is present in the sandbox but not in the repository. |

## *remove*

```
remove
  [ -f ]
  [ -l | -R ]
  [ file ... ]
```

Indicate that files should be removed from the repository. The files will not actually be removed until they are committed. Use **cvs add** to resurrect files that have been removed if you change your mind later.

The standard meanings of the common client options −l and −R apply. Only one other option may be used with the **remove** command, −f. When used, −f will delete the file from the sandbox first.

## *rtag*

```
rtag
  [ -a ]
  [ -b ]
  [ -d ]
  [ -D date | -r rev ]
  [ -f ]
  [ -F ]
  [ -l | - R ]
  [ -n ]
  tag
  file ...
```

Assign a tag to a particular revision of a set of files. If the file already uses the tag for a different revision, **cvs rtag** will complain unless the −F option is used. This command does not refer to the sandbox file revisions (use **cvs tag** for that), so it can be run outside of a sandbox, if desired.

The standard meanings of the common client options −D, −f, −l, −r, and −R apply. Additional options are listed in Table 14-35.

*Table 14–35. rtag Options*

| Option | Description |
|--------|-------------|
| –a | Search the *Attic* for removed files containing the tag. |
| –b | Make it a branch tag. |
| –d | Delete the tag. |
| –F | Force. Move the tag from its current revision to the one specified. |
| –n | Don't run any tag program from the *modules* file. |

### status

```
status
  [ -l | -R ]
  [ -v ]
  [ file ... ]
```

Display the status of the files.

The standard meanings of the common client options –l and –R apply. The other option that can be used with the status command, –v, may be used to include tag information.

### tag

```
tag
  [ -b ]
  [ -c ]
  [ -d ]
  [ -D date | -r rev ]
  [ -f ]
  [ -F ]
  [ -l | R ]
  tag
  [ file ... ]
```

Assign a tag to the sandbox revisions of a set of files. You can use the **status –v** command to list the existing tags for a file.

The *tag* must start with a letter and must consist entirely of letters, numbers, dashes (–) and underscores (_). Therefore, while you might want to tag your *hello* project with 1.0 when you release Version 1.0, you'll need to tag it with something like hello-1_0 instead.

The standard meanings of the common client options –D, –f, –l, –r, and –R apply. Additional options are listed in Table 14-36.

*Table 14-36. tag Options*

| Option | Description |
|--------|-------------|
| **–b** | Make a branch. |
| **–c** | Check for changes. Make sure the files are not locally modified before tagging. |
| **–d** | Delete the tag. |
| **–F** | Force. Move the tag from its current revision to the one specified. |

Since the **–d** option throws away information that might be important, it is recommended that you use it only when absolutely necessary. It is usually better to create a different tag with a similar name.

### unedit

```
unedit
  [ -l | -R ]
  [ file ... ]
```

Abandon file modifications and make the file read-only again. Watchers will be notified.

The standard meanings of the common client options **–l** and **–R** apply.

### update

```
update
  [ -A ]
  [ -d ]
  [ -D date | -r rev ]
  [ -f ]
  [ -I pattern ]
  [ -j rev1 [ -j rev2 ] ]
  [ -k kflag ]
  [ -l | -R ]
  [ -p ]
  [ -P ]
  [ -W spec ]
  [ file ... ]
```

Update the sandbox, merging in any changes from the repository. For example:

```
cvs -n -q update -AdP
```

can be used to do a quick status check of the current sandbox versus the head of the trunk of development.

The standard meanings of the common client options **–D**, **–f**, **–k**, **–l**, **–r**, and **–R** apply. Additional options are listed in Table 14-37.

*Table 14-37. update Options*

| Option | Description |
|--------|-------------|
| –A | Reset sticky tags. |
| –d | Create and update new directories. |
| –I *pattern* | Provide filename patterns for files to ignore. |
| –j *revision* | Merge in changes between two revisions. Mnemonic: *join*. |
| –p | Check out files to standard output. |
| –P | Prune empty directories. |
| –W *spec* | Provide wrapper specification. |

Using –D or –r results in sticky dates or tags, respectively, on the affected files (using –p along with these prevents stickiness). Use –A to reset any sticky tags or dates.

If two –j specifications are made, the differences between them are computed and applied to the current file. If only one is given, then the common ancestor of the sandbox revision and the specified revision is used as a basis for computing differences to be merged.

For example, suppose a project has an experimental branch, and important changes to the file *foo.c* were introduced between revisions 1.2.2.1 and 1.2.2.2. Once those changes have proven stable, you want them reflected in the main line of development. From a sandbox with the head revisions checked out, we run:

```
user@localhost$ cvs update -j 1.2.2.1 -j 1.2.2.2 foo.c
```

CVS finds the differences between the two revisions and applies those differences to the file in our sandbox.

The *spec* used with –W is in the same format as entries in the *cvswrappers* administrative file (see the previous section, "The cvswrappers file").

The status codes listed in Table 14-38 are used to describe the action taken on each file encountered in the repository and the sandbox.

*Table 14-38. update Status Codes*

| Status Code | Description |
|-------------|-------------|
| A | Added. Server took no action because there was no repository file. Indicates that **cvs add**, but not **cvs commit**, has been run. |
| C | Conflict. Sandbox copy is modified (it has been edited since it was checked out or last committed). There was a new revision in the repository, and there were conflicts when CVS merged its changes into the sandbox version. |

*Table 14–38. update Status Codes (continued)*

| Status Code | Description |
|---|---|
| M | Modified. Sandbox copy is modified (it has been edited since it was checked out or last committed). If there was a new revision in the repository, its changes were successfully merged into the file (no conflicts). |
| P | Patched. Same as U but indicates the server used a **patch**. |
| R | Removed. Server took no action. Indicates that **cvs remove**, but not **cvs commit**, has been run. |
| U | Updated. The file was brought up-to-date. |
| ? | File is present in sandbox but not in repository. |

### *watch*

```
watch
  { { on | off } | { add | remove } [ -a action ] }
  [ -l | -R ]
  file ...
```

The **watch** command controls CVS's edit-tracking mechanism. By default, CVS operates in its concurrent development mode, allowing any user to edit any file at any time. CVS includes this **watch** mechanism to support developers who would rather be notified of edits made by others proactively than discover them when doing an **update**.

The *CVSROOT/notify* file determines how notifications are performed.

Table 14-39 shows the **watch** sub-commands and their uses.

*Table 14–39. watch Sub-commands*

| Sub-command | Description |
|---|---|
| **add** | Start watching files. |
| **off** | Turn off watching. |
| **on** | Turn on watching. |
| **remove** | Stop watching files. |

The standard meanings of the common client options −l and −R apply. The only other option that can be used with the **watch** command is −a *action*. The −a option is used in conjunction with one of the actions listed in Table 14-40.

*Table 14–40. watch Actions*

| Action | Description |
|--------|-------------|
| all | All of the following. |
| commit | A user has committed changes. |
| edit | A user ran **cvs edit**. |
| none | Don't watch. Used by the **edit** command. |
| unedit | A user ran **cvs unedit**, **cvs release**, or deleted the file and ran **cvs update**, re-creating it. |

See also the descriptions of the **edit**, **editors**, **unedit**, and **watchers** commands.

### *watchers*

```
watchers
  [ -l | -R ]
  [ file ... ]
```

Display a list of users watching the specified files. This is determined by checking which users have run the **watch** command on a particular file (or set of files). If the **watch** command has not been used, no results will be displayed.

The standard meanings of the common client options **–l** and **–R** apply.

See also **watch**.

# The RCS Utility

The Revision Control System (RCS) is designed to keep track of multiple file revisions, thereby reducing the amount of storage space needed. With RCS you can automatically store and retrieve revisions, merge or compare revisions, keep a complete history (or log) of changes, and identify revisions using symbolic keywords. This chapter describes Version 5.7 but notes differences from earlier versions.

# Overview of RCS Commands

The three most important RCS commands are:

**ci**   Check in revisions (put a file under RCS control).

**co**   Check out revisions.

**rcs**  Set up or change attributes of RCS files.

Two additional commands provide information about RCS files:

**ident**
> Extract keyword values from an RCS file.

**rlog**
> Display a summary (log) about the revisions in an RCS file.

You can compare RCS files with these commands:

**rcsdiff**
> Report differences between revisions.

**rcsmerge**
> Incorporate changes from two RCS files into a third RCS file.

The following command helps with configuration management:

**rcsclean**
> Remove working files that have not been changed.

## Basic RCS Operations

Normally, you maintain RCS files in a subdirectory called **RCS**, so the first step in using RCS should be:

`mkdir RCS`

Next, you place an existing file (or files) under RCS control by running the check-in command:

`ci` *file*

This creates a file called *file,v* in directory **RCS**. *file,v* is called an *RCS file*, and it will store all future revisions of *file*. When you run **ci** on a file for the first time, you are prompted to describe the contents. **ci** then deposits *file* into the RCS file as revision 1.1.

To edit a new revision, check out a copy:

`co -l` *file*

This causes RCS to extract a copy of *file* from the RCS file. You must lock the file with –l to make it writable by you. This copy is called a working file. When you're done editing, you can record the changes by checking the working file back in again:

`ci` *file*

This time, you are prompted to enter a log of the changes made, and the file is deposited as revision 1.2. Note that a checkin normally removes the working file. To retrieve a read-only copy, do a checkout without a lock:

**co** *file*

This is useful when you need to keep a copy on hand for compiling or searching. As a shortcut to the previous **ci**/**co**, you could type:

**ci -u** *file*

This checks in the file but immediately checks out a read-only copy. To compare changes between a working file and its latest revision, you can type:

**rcsdiff** *file*

Another useful command is **rlog**, which shows a summary of log messages.

System administrators can use the **rcs** command to set up default behavior for RCS.

# General RCS Specifications

This section discusses:

- Keyword substitution
- Revision numbering
- Specifying the date
- Specifying states
- Standard options and environment variables

## Keyword Substitution

RCS lets you place keyword variables in your working files. These variables are later expanded into revision notes. You can then use the notes either as embedded comments in the input file or as text strings that appear when the output is printed. To create revision notes via keyword substitution, follow this procedure:

1. In your working file, type any of the keywords listed in the next section.

2. Check the file in.

3. Check the file out again. Upon checkout, the **co** command expands each keyword to include its value. That is, **co** replaces instances of:

   *$keyword$*

   with:

   *$keyword:value$*

4. Subsequent checkin and checkout of a file will update any existing keyword values. Unless otherwise noted later, existing values are replaced by new values.

Note: Many RCS commands have a **-k** option that provides more flexibility during keyword substitution.

## *Keywords*

**$Author$**

Username of person who checked in revision.

**$Date$**

Date and time of checkin.

**$Header$**

A title that includes the RCS file's full pathname, revision number, date, author, state, and (if locked) the person who locked the file.

**$Id$**

Same as **$Header$**, but exclude the full pathname of the RCS file.

**$Locker$**

Username of person who locked the revision. If the file isn't locked, this value is empty.

**$Log$**

The message that was typed during checkin to describe the file, preceded by the RCS filename, revision number, author, and date. Log messages accumulate rather than being overwritten.

**$RCSfile$**

The RCS filename, without its pathname.

**$Revision$**

The assigned revision number.

**$Source$**

The RCS filename, including its pathname.

**$State$**

The state assigned by the **-s** option of **ci** or **rcs**.

## *Example values*

Let's assume that the file */projects/new/chapter3* has been checked in and out by a user named *daniel*. Here's what keyword substitution would produce for each keyword, for the second revision of the file:

```
$Author: daniel $

$Date: 2000/02/25 18:21:10 $

$Header: /projects/new/chapter3,v 1.2 2000/02/25 18:21:10 daniel \
    Exp Locker: daniel $
```

```
$Id: chapter3,v 1.2 2000/02/25 18:21:10 daniel Exp Locker: daniel $

$Locker: daniel $

$Log: chapter3,v $
# Revision 1.2  2000/02/25  18:21:10  daniel
# Added section on error-handling
#
# Revision 1.1  2000/02/25  16:49:59  daniel
# Initial revision
#

$RCSfile: chapter3,v $

$Revision: 1.2 $

$Source: /projects/new/chapter3,v $

$State: Exp $
```

## *Revision Numbering*

Unless told otherwise, RCS commands typically operate on the latest revision. Some commands have an **−r** option that is used to specify a revision number. In addition, many options accept a revision number as an optional argument. (In the command summary, this argument is shown as [*R*].) Revision numbers consist of up to four fields, release, level, branch, and sequence, but most revisions consist of only the release and level.

For example, you can check out revision 1.4 as follows:

```
co -l -r1.4 ch01
```

When you check it in again, the new revision will be marked as 1.5. But suppose the edited copy needs to be checked in as the next release. You would type:

```
ci -r2 ch01
```

This creates revision 2.1. You can also create a branch from an earlier revision. The following command creates revision 1.4.1.1:

```
ci -r1.4.1 ch01
```

Numbers are not the only way to specify revisions, though. You can assign a text label as a revision name, using the **−n** option of **ci** or **rcs**. You can also specify this name in any option that accepts a revision number for an argument. For example, you could check in each of your C programs, using the same label regardless of the current revision number:

```
ci -u -nPrototype *.c
```

In addition, beginning with RCS Version 5.6, you can specify a **$**, which means the revision number is extracted from the keywords of a working file. For example:

```
rcsdiff -r$ ch01
```

compares *ch01* to the revision that is checked in. You can also combine names and symbols. The command:

```
rcs -nDraft:$ ch*
```

assigns a name to the revision numbers associated with several chapter files.

## Specifying the Date

Revisions are timestamped by time and date of checkin. Several keyword strings include the date in their values. Dates can be supplied in options to **ci**, **co**, and **rlog**. RCS uses the following date format as its default:

```
1999/10/16 02:00:00    (year/month/day time)
```

The default time zone is Greenwich Mean Time (GMT), which is also referred to as Coordinated Universal Time (UTC). Dates can be supplied in free format. This lets you specify many different styles. Here are some of the more common ones, which show the same time as in the preceding example:

```
6:00 pm lt          (assuming today is Oct. 16, 1999)
2:00 AM, Oct. 16, 1999
Sat Oct 16 18:00:00 1999 LT
Sat Oct 16 18:00:00 PST 1999
```

The uppercase or lowercase *lt* indicates local time (here, Pacific Standard Time). The third line shows **ctime** format (plus the *LT*); the fourth line is the **date** command format.

## Specifying States

In some situations, particularly programming environments, you want to know the status of a set of revisions. RCS files are marked by a text string that describes their *state*. The default state is **Exp** (experimental). Other common choices include **Stab** (stable) or **Rel** (released). These words are user-defined and have no special internal meaning. Several keyword strings include the state in their values. In addition, states can be supplied in options to **ci**, **co**, **rcs**, and **rlog**.

## Standard Options and Environment Variables

RCS defines the environment variable RCSINIT, which is used to set up default options for RCS commands. If you set RCSINIT to a space-separated list of options, they will be prepended to the command-line options you supply to any RCS command. Three options are useful to include in RCSINIT: **−q**, **−V**, and **−x**. They can be thought of as standard options because most RCS commands accept them. Note that **−V** was new in RCS Version 5 and that **−x** was new in Version 5.6.

−q[*R*]
    Quiet mode; don't show diagnostic output. *R* specifies a file revision.

**−V[*n*]**

Emulate version *n* of RCS; useful when trading files between systems that run different versions. *n* can be 3, 4, or 5. If *n* is omitted, the command prints the version number of this version of RCS.

**−x*suffixes***

Specify an alternate list of *suffixes* for RCS files. Each suffix is separated by a /. On Unix systems, RCS files normally end with the characters *,v*. The **−x** option provides a workaround for systems that don't allow a comma (,) character in filenames.

**−z[*zone*]**

Specify the format of the date in keyword substitution. If empty, the default is to output the UTC time with no zone indication. With an argument of *LT*, the local time zone will be used to output an ISO 8601 format, with an indication of the separation from UTC. You may also specify a numeric UTC offset. For example, **−z+4:30** would output a string such as: 1998-11-24 02:30:00+4:30.

For example, when depositing a working file into an RCS file, the command:

```
ci -x,v/ ch01        (second suffix is blank)
```

searches in order for the RCS filenames:

```
RCS/ch01,v
ch01,v
RCS/ch01
```

## Alphabetical Summary of RCS Commands

For details on the syntax of keywords, revision numbers, dates, states, and standard options, refer to the previous discussions.

---

ci [*options*] *files*                                                                    ci

Check in revisions. **ci** stores the contents of the specified working *files* into their corresponding RCS files. Normally, **ci** deletes the working file after storing it. If no RCS file exists, then the working file is an initial revision. In this case, the RCS file is created and you are prompted to enter a description of the file. If an RCS file exists, **ci** increments the revision number and prompts you to enter a message that logs the changes made. Starting with RCS Version 5.6, if a working file is checked in without changes, the file reverts to the previous revision. In older RCS versions, you may end up having to check in a new revision that contains no changes.

The mutually exclusive options **−u**, **−l**, and **−r** are the most common. Use **−u** to keep a read-only copy of the working file (for example, so that the file can be compiled or searched). Use **−l** to update a revision and then immediately check it out again with a lock. This allows you to save intermediate changes but continue editing (for example, during a long editing session). Use **−r** to check in a file with a

$\rightarrow$

---

different release number. **ci** accepts the standard options **−q**, **−V**, **−x**, and **−z**.

*Options*

**−d**[*date*]
Check the file in with a timestamp of *date* or, if no date is specified, with the time of last modification.

**−f**[*R*]
Force a checkin even if there are no differences.

**−I**[*R*]
Interactive mode; prompt user even when standard input is not a terminal (e.g., when **ci** is part of a command pipeline). **−I** was new in RCS Version 5.

**−i**[*R*]
Create (initialize) an RCS file and check it in. A warning is reported if the RCS file already exists.

**−j**[*R*]
Check in a file without initializing. Will report an error if file does not already exist.

**−k**[*R*]
Assign a revision number, creation date, state, and author from keyword values that were placed in the working file, instead of computing the revision information from the local environment. **−k** is useful for software distribution: the preset keywords serve as a timestamp shared by all distribution sites.

**−l**[*R*]
Do a **co** **−l** after checking in. This leaves a locked copy of the next revision.

**−m***msg*
Use the *msg* string as the log message for all files checked in. When checking in multiple files, **ci** normally prompts whether to reuse the log message of the previous file. **−m** bypasses this prompting.

**−M**[*R*]
Set the working file's modification time to that of the retrieved version. Use of **−M** can confuse **make** and should be used with care. (This was new in RCS Version 5.6.)

**−n***name*
Associate a text *name* with the new revision number.

**−N***name*
Same as **−n**, but override a previous *name*.

**−r**[*R*]

> Check the file in as revision *R*.

**−r** By itself, reverts to default behavior when releasing a lock and removing the working file. This option overrides any **−l** or **−u** options that have been initialized by shell aliases or scripts. This behavior for **−r** is specific to **ci**.

**−s***state*

> Set the *state* of the checked-in revision.

**−T** Set the RCS file's modification time to the time of the latest revision if the RCS file's time precedes the new revision.

**−t***file*

> Replace RCS file description with contents of *file*. As of Version 5, this works only for initial checkin.

**−t−***string*

> Replace RCS file description with *string*. As of Version 5, this works only for initial checkin.

**−u**[*R*]

> Do a **co −u** after checking in. This leaves a read-only copy.

**−w***user*

> Set the author field to *user* in the checked-in revision.

### Examples

Check in chapter files using the same log message:

```
ci -m'First round edits' chap*
```

Check in edits to **prog.c**, leaving a read-only copy:

```
ci -u prog.c
```

Start revision level 2; refer to revision 2.1 as "Prototype":

```
ci -r2 -nPrototype prog.c
```

---

## co [*options*] *files*

Retrieve a previously checked-in revision, and place it in the corresponding working file (or print to standard output if **−p** is specified). If you intend to edit the working file and check it in again, specify **−l** to lock the file. **co** accepts the standard options **−q**, **−V**, and **−x**.

→

*Options*

**–d***date*

Retrieve latest revision whose checkin timestamp is on or before *date*.

**–f**[*R*]

Force the working file to be overwritten.

**–I**[*R*]

Interactive mode; prompt user even when standard input is not a terminal. (New in RCS Version 5.)

**–j***R2:R3*

This works like **rcsmerge**. *R2* and *R3* specify two revisions whose changes are merged into a third file: either the corresponding working file or a third revision (any *R* specified by other **co** options).

**–k***c*

Expand keyword symbols according to flag *c*. *c* can be:

b   Like o, but performs its operations in binary mode, generating the previous revision's keywords and values in binary.

k   Expand symbols to keywords only (no values). This is useful for ignoring trivial differences during file comparison.

kv  Expand symbols to keyword and value (the default). Insert the locker's name only during a **ci** –l or **co** –l.

kvl Like **kv**, but always insert the locker's name.

o   Expand symbols to keyword and value present in previous revision. This is useful for binary files that don't allow substring changes.

v   Expand symbols to values only (no keywords). This prevents further keyword substitution and is not recommended.

**–l**[*R*]

Same as **–r**, but also lock the retrieved revision.

**–M**[*R*]

Set the working file's modification time to that of the retrieved version. Use of **–M** can confuse **make** and should be used with care. (This was new in RCS Version 5.6.)

**–p**[*R*]

Send retrieved revision to standard output instead of to a working file. Useful for output redirection or filtering.

**−r**[*R*]
>Retrieve the latest revision or, if *R* is given, retrieve the latest revision that is equal to or lower than *R*.

**−s***state*
>Retrieve the latest revision having the given *state*.

**−T**  Preserve the modification time of the RCS file even if a lock is added or removed.

**−u**[*R*]
>Same as **−r**, but also unlock the retrieved revision if you locked it previously.

**−w**[*user*]
>Retrieve the latest revision that was checked in either by the invoking user or by the specified *user*.

### Examples

Sort the latest stored version of *file*:

```
co -p file | sort
```

Check out (and lock) all uppercase filenames for editing:

```
co -l [A-Z]*
```

Note that filename expansion fails unless a working copy resides in the current directory. Therefore, this example works only if the files were previously checked in via **ci −u**. Finally, here are some different ways to extract the working files for a set of RCS files (in the current directory):

```
co -r3 *,v              Latest revisions of release 3
co -r3 -wjim *,v        Same, but only if checked in by jim
co -d'May 5, 2 pm LT' *,v   Latest revisions that were modified on or before the date
co -rPrototype *,v      Latest revisions named Prototype
```

---

### ident [*option*] [*files*]                                                 ident

Extract keyword/value symbols from *files*. *files* can be text files, object files, or dumps.

### Option

**−q**  Suppress warning message when no keyword patterns are found.

### Examples

If file **prog.c** is compiled, and it contains this line of code:

```
char rcsID[] = "$Author: george $";
```

→

*Alphabetical Summary of RCS Commands − ident*  693

| | |
|---|---|
| **ident**<br>← | then the following output is produced:<br><br>```<br>% ident prog.c prog.o<br>prog.c:<br>        $Author: george $<br>prog.o:<br>        $Author: george $<br>```<br><br>Show keywords for all RCS files (suppress warnings):<br><br>```<br>co -p RCS/*,v | ident -q<br>``` |
| **rcs** | **rcs** [*options*] <*files*<br><br>An administrative command for setting up or changing the default attributes of RCS files. Among other things, **rcs** lets you set strict locking (−L), delete revisions (−o), and override locks set by **co** (−l and −u). RCS files have an access list (created via −a); anyone whose username is on the list can run **rcs**. The access list is often empty, meaning that **rcs** is available to everyone. In addition, you can always invoke **rcs** if you own the file, if you're a privileged user, or if you run **rcs** with −i. **rcs** accepts the standard options −q, −V, −x, and −z.<br><br>*Options*<br><br>−a*users*<br>    Append the comma-separated list of *users* to the access list.<br><br>−A*otherfile*<br>    Append *otherfile*'s access list to the access list of *files*.<br><br>−b[*R*]<br>    Set the default branch to *R* or, if *R* is omitted, to the highest branch on the trunk.<br><br>−c'*s*'<br>    The comment character for **$Log** keywords is set to string *s*. By default, **co** expands embedded **$Log** keywords into comments preceded by #. You could, for example, set *s* to .\" for **troff** files or set *s* to * for C programs. (You would need to manually insert an enclosing /* and */ before and after **$Log**.)<br><br>−e[*users*]<br>    Erase everyone (or only the specified *users*) from the access list.<br><br>−i    Create (initialize) an RCS file, but don't deposit a revision.<br><br>−I    Interactive mode; prompt user even when standard input is not a terminal. (New in RCS Version 5.) |

**−k***c*

Use *c* as the default style for keyword substitution. (See **co** for values of *c*.) **−kkv** restores the default substitution style; all other styles create incompatibilities with RCS Version 4 or earlier.

**−l** [*R*]

Lock revision *R* or the latest revision. **−l** "retroactively locks" a file and is useful if you checked out a file incorrectly by typing **co** instead of **co −l**.

**−L** Turn on strict locking (the default). This means that everyone, including the owner of the RCS file, must use **co −l** to edit files. Strict locking is recommended when files are to be shared. (See **−U**.)

**−m***R*:*msg*

Use the *msg* string to replace the log message of revision *R*. (This was new in RCS Version 5.6.)

**−M** Disable email notification when breaking a lock on a file with **rcs −u**. This should only be used when there is another means to warn users that their files have been unlocked.

**−n***flags*

Add or delete an association between a revision and a name. *flags* can be:

*name*:*R*

Associate *name* with revision *R*.

*name*:

Associate *name* with latest revision.

*name*

Remove association of *name*.

**−N***flags*

Same as **−n**, but overwrite existing *names*.

**−o***R_list*

Delete (outdate) revisions listed in *R_list*. *R_list* can be specified as *R1*, *R1−R2*, *R1−*, or *−R2*. When a branch is given, **−o** deletes only the latest revision on it. RCS Version 5.6 changed the range separator character to :, although − is still valid.

**−s***state*[:*R*]

Set the state of revision *R* (or the latest revision) to the word *state*.

**−t** [*file*]

Replace RCS file description with contents of *file* or, if no file is given, with standard output.

→

CVS and
RCS

**rcs**
←

−t−*string*
> Replace RCS file description with *string*. Preserves the time of modification on an RCS file unless a revision is removed.

−T Preserve the modification time of the RCS file.

−u[*R*]
> The complement of −l: unlock a revision that was previously checked out via co −l. If someone else did the checkout, you are prompted to state the reason for breaking the lock. This message is mailed to the original locker.

−U Turn on nonstrict locking. Everyone except the file owner must use co −l to edit files. (See −L.)

−V Print the RCS version number.

−z*zone*
> Set the default time zone for timestamp options performed by the ci and co commands.

### Examples

Associate the label **To_customer** with the latest revision of all RCS files:

```
rcs -nTo_customer: RCS/*
```

Add three users to the access list of file **beatle_deals**:

```
rcs -ageorge,paul,ringo beatle_deals
```

Delete revisions 1.2 through 1.5:

```
rcs -o1.2-1.5 doc
```

Replace an RCS file description with the contents of a variable:

```
echo "$description" | rcs -t file
```

---

**rcsclean**

rcsclean [*options*] [*files*]

Compare checked-out files against the corresponding latest revision or revision *R* (as given by the options). If no differences are found, the working file is removed. (Use **rcsdiff** to find differences.) **rcsclean** is useful in makefiles. For example, you could specify a "clean-up" target to update your directories. **rcsclean** is also useful prior to running **rcsfreeze**. **rcsclean** accepts the standard options −q, −V, −x, and −z.

*Options*

**−k***c*

   When comparing revisions, expand keywords using style *c*. (See co for values of *c*.)

**−n**[*R*]

   Show what would happen, but don't actually execute.

**−r**[*R*]

   Compare against revision *R*. *R* can be supplied as arguments to other options, so **−r** is redundant.

**−T**   Preserve the modification time of the RCS file even if a lock is added or removed.

**−u**[*R*]

   Unlock the revision if it's the same as the working file.

*Examples*

Remove unchanged copies of program and header files:

```
rcsclean *.c *.h
```

---

**rcsdiff** [*options*] [*diff_options*] *files*

Compare revisions via **diff**. Specify revisions using **−r** as follows:

| Number of Revisions Specified: | Comparison Made: |
|---|---|
| None | Working file against latest revision |
| One | Working file against specified revision |
| Two | One revision against the other |

**rcsdiff** accepts the standard options **−q**, **−T**, **−V**, **−x**, and **−z**, as well as *diff_options*, which can be any valid **diff** option. **rcsdiff** exits with a status of 0 (no differences), 1 (some differences), or 2 (unknown problem).

*Options*

**−k***c*

   When comparing revisions, expand keywords using style *c*. (See co for values of *c*.)

**−r***R1*

   Use revision *R1* in the comparison.

**−r***R2*

   Use revision *R2* in the comparison. (**−r***R1* must also be specified.)

| | |
|---|---|
| rcsmerge | **rcsmerge** [*options*] *file* |

Perform a three-way merge of file revisions, taking two differing versions and incorporating the changes into the working *file*. You must provide either one or two revisions to merge (typically with **−r**). Overlaps are handled the same as with **merge**, by placing warnings in the resulting file. **rcsmerge** accepts the standard options **−q**, **−V**, **−x**, and **−z**. **rcsmerge** exits with a status of 0 (no overlaps), 1 (some overlaps), or 2 (unknown problem).

*Options*

**−k***c*

When comparing revisions, expand keywords using style *c*. (See co for values of *c*.)

**−p** [*R*]

Send merged version to standard output instead of overwriting *file*.

**−r** [*R*]

Merge revision *R* or, if no *R* is given, merge the latest revision.

*Examples*

Suppose you need to add updates to an old revision (1.3) of *prog.c*, but the current file is already at revision 1.6. To incorporate the changes:

```
co -l prog.c
```
*(edit latest revision by adding revision 1.3 updates, then:)*
```
rcsmerge -p -r1.3 -r1.6 prog.c > prog.updated.c
```

Undo changes between revisions 3.5 and 3.2, and overwrite the working file:

```
rcsmerge -r3.5 -r3.2 chap08
```

| | |
|---|---|
| rlog | **rlog** [*options*] *files* |

Display identification information for RCS *files*, including the log message associated with each revision, the number of lines added or removed, date of last checkin, and so on. With no options, **rlog** displays all information. Use options to display specific items. **rlog** accepts the standard options **−T**, **−V**, **−x**, and **−z**.

**−b** Prune the display; print only about the default branch.

**−d***dates*

Display information for revisions whose checkin timestamp falls in the range of *dates* (a list separated by semicolons). Be sure to use quotes. Each date can be specified as:

*date1 < date2*

Select revisions between *date1* and *date2*, inclusive.

*date1 <*

Select revisions made on or after *date1*.

*date1*

Select revisions made on or before *date1*.

**−h** Display the beginning of the normal **rlog** listing.

**−l**[*users*]

Display information only about locked revisions or, if *lockers* is specified, only revisions locked by the list of *users*.

**−L** Skip files that aren't locked.

**−N** Don't display symbolic names.

**−r**[*list*]

Display information for revisions in the comma-separated *list* of revision numbers. If no *list* is given, the latest revision is used. Items can be specified as:

*R1* Select revision *R1*. If *R1* is a branch, select all revisions on it.

*R1 .*

If *R1* is a branch, select its latest revision.

*R1−R2*

Select revisions *R1* through *R2*.

*−R1*

Select revisions from beginning of branch through *R1*.

*R1−*

Select revisions from *R1* through end of branch.

RCS Version 5.6 changed the range separator character to :, although − is still valid.

**−R** Display only the name of the RCS file.

→

−s*states*
> Display information for revisions whose state matches one from the comma-separated list of *states*.

−t   Same as −h, but also display the file's description.

−w [*users*]
> Display information for revisions checked in by anyone in the comma-separated list of *users*. If no *users* are supplied, assume the name of the invoking user.

### Examples

Display a file's revision history:

```
rlog RCS/*,v | more
```

Display names of RCS files that are locked by user *daniel*:

```
rlog -R -L -ldaniel RCS/*
```

Display the "title" portion (no revision history) of a working file:

```
rlog -t calc.c
```

# CHAPTER 15

# *GNOME*

GNOME stands for the GNU Network Object Model Environment. It is a user-friendly, graphically driven environment that controls the look and feel of your desktop and provides a consistent method of interaction and cooperation between applications. GNOME is one of two popular desktop environments used with Linux. It is standard with Red Hat, Debian, and other popular distributions. The other popular Linux environment is called KDE, which is discussed in Chapter 16, *KDE*.

GNOME is not a window manager. As a graphical environment, it provides users with a highly customizable user interface and consistent functionality of common GUI features such as menus, toolbars, and buttons. As a user environment, GNOME utilizes a growing set of native applications to create a productive computing system.

One of GNOME's most attractive features is its CORBA-based architecture, which allows interaction among applications through the sharing and embedding of component objects. CORBA stands for Common Object Request Broker Architecture. It specifies methods that software objects use to interact with each other through an ORB (object request broker). The ORB package currently used by GNOME is the ORBit package (*http://www.labs.redhat.com/orbit*). ORBit allows similar functionality to Window's COM and OLE. For example, a spreadsheet created by **gnumeric** (a GNOME spreadsheet program) can be placed as an object into an AbiWord document.

GNOME does rely on a window manager to handle the particulars of the X Window System environment. The window manager controls the placement, movement, and graphical style of the windows on your screen. You can use GNOME with many different window managers, but they must be compliant with GNOME in order to utilize features such as drag-and-drop. Sawfish and Enlightenment are commonly used window managers and are fully compliant with the GNOME environment. Other window managers that can be used are IceWM, WindowMaker, and AfterStep.

## Desktop Overview

Figure 15-1 shows the default GNOME desktop. The left side of the screen contains icons that are shortcuts to open applications. The top icon is a symbolic link to the user's home folder, and when double-clicked, opens the GNOME file manager displaying that folder. The other icons include shortcuts to the floppy drive and CD-ROM and links to web pages. Desktop icons can be used to launch any program on your system, invoke the appropriate application for a data file or view a directory or URL.

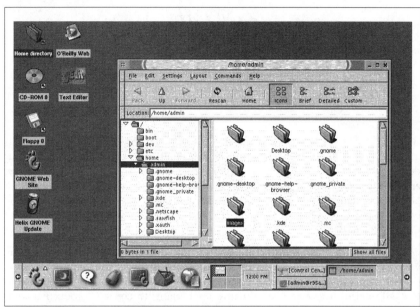

*Figure 15-1. The GNOME desktop*

The bar across the bottom of the screen is the GNOME panel. It is your primary means of finding and opening applications and managing your desktop. The panel contains launcher buttons for the main menu, help and configuration tools, and the Netscape browser. You can add buttons to the control panel to launch any application on your system.

The panel also runs two special programs (called *applets*) that help you get around your desktop. The Desk Guide applet displays your desktop workspace. Many window managers allow you to divide your workspace into a number of different screens (called *virtual desktops* or *viewports*). Desk Guide provides a small display of the available desktops and outlines of the windows they contain. Clicking on an area of the display will switch your desktop view.

The Tasklist applet lets you keep track of open windows. It displays a button on the panel for each window you have open. Clicking on a button in the tasklist will bring focus to its window or reopen it if it was minimized.

GNOME allows you an enormous number of configuration options for your desktop environment. You can right-click on just about anything and get a pop-up menu (called a *context menu*) containing specific actions for that item and a way to configure its properties. General configuration settings are contained in the GNOME Control Center. You can access this tool in the following ways: click the toolbox button on the panel to open the Control Center window, or from the main menu, select Settings, then GNOME Control Center (individual configuration applications also are accessible from this menu).

## Adding Desktop Icons

Desktop icons offer you convenient double-click access to your most important files, applications, and links. The items displayed on your desktop exist as files in the *.gnome-desktop* directory of your home directory. Anything you add to that directory will appear on the desktop.

The desktop context menu contains a New submenu that allows you to add different types of items to your desktop.

To add an icon that launches an application, select New→Launcher. This opens the Desktop Entry Properties dialog box shown in Figure 15-2. Provide the name of the launcher (this will be the text displayed underneath the icon), a comment (this will be the tooltip that appears when the pointer is over the icon), and the command used to run the application. After you click OK, the new launcher icon appears on your desktop.

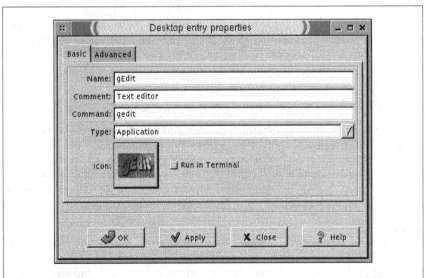

*Figure 15-2. Desktop entry properties*

To add a desktop icon that opens a directory, select New→Directory from the desktop context menu. Provide the name of a directory in the dialog box. If you specify a full pathname, the desktop icon will be created as a symbolic link. If it is not a full pathname, the new directory will be created in `~/.gnome-desktop`.

To add a URL link to the desktop, select New→URL Link from the desktop context menu. This will open a dialog box that asks you for the URL you wish to open and a caption to use as the icon's text label. Click OK, and the icon appears on your desktop. You also can click and drag any link displayed in the Netscape browser to the desktop to create a link.

A convenient use of desktop icons is to have shortcuts to frequently used files or folders. Adding shortcuts is easiest from the file manager (*gmc*). If you click on an item in the file manager and drag it to the desktop, you will create a launcher icon for it. This action actually moves the item to the ˜/.gnome-desktop folder. If you press the Ctrl key while selecting and dragging the item, you will only copy the item to the desktop. If you middle-click or press Alt while selecting and dragging an item, a small pop-up window will ask you if you want to move, copy, or link the file. Selecting Link Here will create a symbolic link on the desktop that points to the original location of the item. For most files and folders, you may find this a best option.

## *The Panel*

The GNOME panel can contain several different types of objects. The most obvious are the buttons for the menu and application launchers. You also can use a button to open a drawer, which is like a subpanel containing additional launchers. There are a few special types of buttons used for logging out of the session and locking the screen. Finally, small programs called applets can be run on the panel. The Desk Guide and the clock are examples of panel applets.

Settings for the panel are found in the Panel menu on the main menu or by right-clicking on the panel. This menu offers options to add new launchers or applets to the panel; adjust the style, size, and display of the panel; or create new panels on the desktop.

### *Additional Panels*

You can create more than one panel on your desktop. This is useful if you have different sets of applications used for specific but common tasks. For example, if you do a lot of work on graphics, you can dedicate a panel to launch your favorite graphics tools. To create a new panel, right-click on the default panel and select Add New Panel. Or from the main menu, select Panel→Add New Panel. There are five different types of panels available from the submenu:

*edge panel*
> The style of the default panel. It stretches across one entire edge of the screen. Arrow buttons on each end of the panel are used to collapse the panel to the side of a screen. Clicking on the remaining visible arrow button of a collapsed panel will cause the panel to appear again in full.

*aligned panel*
> A similar panel that is effectively anchored to one corner of the screen and extends just enough to fit the buttons and applets it contains. An aligned panel can be hidden by clicking the arrow button that is at the edge of the

screen. The arrow button farthest from the edge will anchor an aligned panel on the opposite side of the screen.

*sliding panel*

Like an aligned panel except that it can be placed anywhere along the edge of the screen. It is not anchored to a corner.

*floating panel*

As you'd suspect, a panel that can be placed anywhere on the screen.

*menu panel*

A special type of panel that stretches along the top of the screen. It is a thin bar that contains drop-down menus for the Programs, Favorites, Settings, and Desktop menus found in the main menu.

All of the panels except the menu panel can be moved by middle-clicking (or clicking the left and right buttons simultaneously) and dragging the panel to another part of the screen where it can be placed.

Each panel can be configured individually from the Panel menu in its context (right-click) menu. Right-click and select Panel→Properties. Here you can choose from several different menu options. The Type submenu changes the panel's type (although a menu panel cannot be changed to another type of panel). The Hiding Policy submenu has settings for Explicit Hide, where you click one of the arrow buttons to collapse the panel to the side of the screen; or Auto Hide, where the panel automatically reduces when not in use. The Hide Buttons submenu allows you to show or hide the arrow and hide buttons of a panel. The Size submenu sets the size of the panel from tiny to huge. The Background Type submenu lets you set the background of a panel to either a color or a pixmap image.

To access all of the panel's properties in one dialog, select All Properties from this menu. Global property settings are found in the GNOME Control Center. They are described later in this chapter.

## Adding an Application Launcher to the Panel

One of the conveniences of the panel is creating launcher icons that allow you one-click access to frequently used applications. To add an application, right-click the panel and select Add New Launcher. You also can right-click on an application in the main menu and choose Add This Launcher to Panel.

In each case, the Create Launcher Applet dialog will appear. Provide a name for the application, a comment to be used as a tooltip, and the command used to open the application. Click on the icon button to select the image to be used for the button on the panel. If the application is to be run in a Terminal, click the Run in Terminal button.

The drag-and-drop functionality of GNOME allows you to place applications on the panel in a number of ways. For example, you can click on an application file in the file manager and drag it to the panel. This will open the Add New Launcher dialog and create a new launcher button on the panel. You also can drag a desktop icon to the panel.

You can configure a launcher's properties by right-clicking it and selecting Properties. This opens the Launcher Properties window, where you can change the name, comment, command, application type, and icon used for the launcher.

Launcher buttons can be placed in any position and order you want on the panel. To move a launcher button, right-click it and select Move. The mouse pointer will change, allowing you to drag the button to another position. Click to set the new position of the button.

## The Main Menu

By default, the GNOME panel contains one menu—the main menu. It is displayed using the first button on the right with the GNOME foot icon on it (sometimes it is called the *foot menu*). The default main menu offers a number of items and submenus divided into sections:

- The System menu contains items for installed GNOME applications and utilities, separated into additional submenus by categories, such as Graphics, Utilities, Internet, and so on. Two items are included at the bottom of the System menu: Help opens the GNOME help browser, and Run Command opens the single command-line prompt window. The System menu can be changed only by a user with **root** access, and this action will change it for all users.

- The User menu is empty by default. Individual users can add their own items to the User menu section.

- If other packages, like KDE or AnotherLevel, are installed on your system, their default menus also may be included in the main menu.

- The Panel menu contains actions and configuration shortcuts for the panel. The items in this menu also are found in the pop-up menu accessed by right-clicking on the panel.

- The four items at the bottom of the menu allow you to lock the screen (requiring the user's password to reenter the desktop), view version information for the panel, and log out.

You will notice that the top entry for each menu section and each submenu is not an actionable item. It is the titlebar for the menu. Right-clicking a titlebar opens a pop-up menu containing a couple of options:

*Add this as drawer to panel*
> Takes the current submenu and converts it to a drawer on the panel.

*Add this as menu to panel*
> Copies the menu to a new menu launcher on the panel. Keep in mind that the submenu from the main menu and the menu on the panel are the same. You can edit the submenu in the menu editor, and the changes will occur in the Panel menu.

*Add this to personal menu*
    Copies the menu to the User menu.

The default configuration of the main menu makes it a bit difficult to customize. Since the System menus are set and cannot be altered (unless you are **root**), you can initially configure only the User menu section.

The best way to make a fully customizable main menu (other than being **root** all the time) is to copy the desired parts of the System menu to your User menu. Once you have done this, you can edit the User menu in the menu editor to your liking.

## Menu Display Properties

You can choose which menus are displayed by using the menu properties. Right-click the menu button and choose Properties to open this dialog. The Menu Properties window contains display settings for the System menu, User menu, and any other default menus you have installed. You can choose to display each menu as either fully listed, in a submenu, or not displayed at all.

## Editing the Menu

The Menu Editor, shown in Figure 15-3, lets you add and remove items from your menu and move them around. To open the menu editor, select Settings, then Menu Editor from the main menu.

The menu editor is divided into two sections: the left window displays the hierarchy of the User and System menus and the items they contain. You can reorder menu items or move them to other submenus by clicking and dragging them in the left window. The right window shows the properties of an item selected in the left window.

The buttons on the toolbar provide you with the following actions on a selected menu item: add a new submenu, add a new item, delete the selection, move it up or down, and sort a submenu.

To add a new submenu, select the menu in which you want to place it in the menu tree and click the New Submenu button. Provide the name of the submenu in the right window and click OK.

To add a new item to the menu, select its location in the menu tree and click the New Item button. The right window displays the properties settings for the item. Type in the name for the item, a comment for the tooltip, the command to launch the item, and its application type. Click OK to add the item to the menu.

# The GNOME Control Center

The GNOME Control Center (Figure 15-4) is where most customization and configuration of your desktop environment takes place. Open the Control Center using the toolbox button on the panel, or from Utilities on the main menu. The Control Center contains a number of configuration applications, called *capplets*, that allow

GNOME

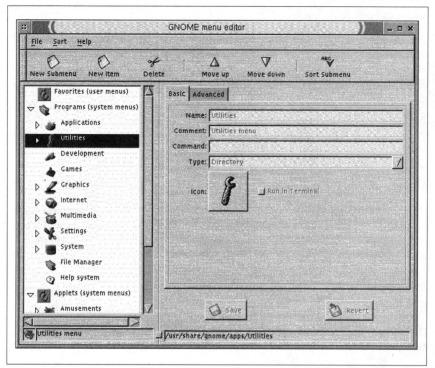

*Figure 15-3. The Menu Editor*

you to change various GNOME settings. The capplets are listed in the left pane of the Control Center window, and clicking on a name opens the capplet in the right pane.

## Desktop Settings

These sections provide settings for the overall look of your desktop by letting you choose the background, screensaver, theme, and window manager.

### Background

Here's where you set your desktop background. You can choose to use an image for wallpaper or colors. In the wallpaper section, click the Browse button to select an image file from the filesystem. You can choose to have the image tiled on the background, centered, or scaled. In the color section, select to use either a solid, single color, or a horizontal or vertical gradient of two colors. Click the boxes for primary color and secondary color to pick the color.

This capplet sets the background via GNOME. Window managers also can set the background and can sometimes conflict with the GNOME setting. To ensure that GNOME sets the background, check the box labeled Use GNOME to Set Background at the bottom of the window.

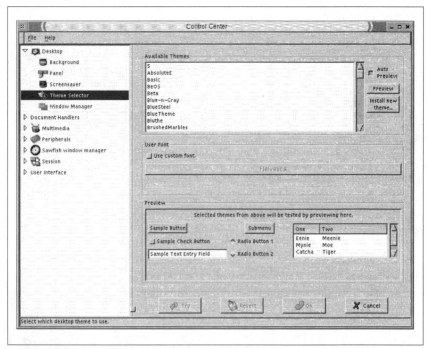

*Figure 15–4. GNOME Control Center*

## Screensaver

Contains settings for the screensaver. You can choose from a list of available screensavers (including a random setting). Input the number of minutes of inactivity before the screensaver starts and whether you, the user, will be required to give your password before going back to the desktop. Power management settings are available here if your system is configured for them.

## Theme selector

Themes provide a consistent overall style to the many widgets and components used by GNOME. A number of basic themes are included with the *gtk-engines* package, and you can download and install additional themes from *http://gtk.themes.org*.

Any themes that are installed on your system are listed in the Theme Selector. You can select one and preview it in the lower section of the window. If you click Auto Preview, a theme will preview automatically when you click on it. Otherwise, click the Preview button to see how it looks.

If you have downloaded a theme and wish to install it, click the Install New Theme button. Provide the name and location of the *.tar.gz* or *.tgz* file and click OK. The new theme will be installed in the */usr/share/themes* directory and be available for you to use on your desktop.

### Window manager

This section allows you to select the window manager that GNOME will use and configure its properties if it has a configuration tool. By default, GNOME runs with the Enlightenment window manager. Other window managers may be used, but make sure that they are compliant with the GNOME architecture so as not to create problems for your applications.

The listing shows installed window managers that you can use. You can add a new window manager to the list by clicking the Add button. Type the window manager's name in the dialog box. If it has its own configuration tool, supply the tool name and location, too. A button underneath the list will be enabled stating Run the Configuration Tool for *wm-name*. Clicking this button will open the configuration application for that window manager.

## Panel

Panels can be configured individually or globally. For individual configuration, right-click on the panel and select This Panel's Properties.

Most of the panel settings are made in the global panel configuration tool shown in Figure 15-5. To open this tool, select Global Preferences from the Panel menu.

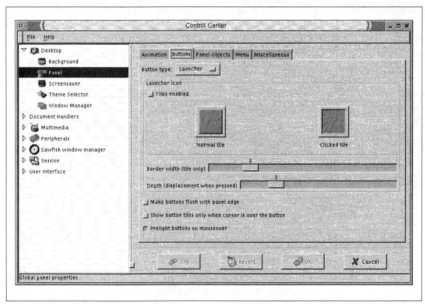

*Figure 15-5. Panel configuration settings*

The global panel configuration section of the Control Center opens. It contains the following sections:

## Animation

This tab controls the animated movements of the panel, such as when the panel is hidden or a drawer is opened. At the top of the tab is a radio button to enable or disable animation entirely. The rest of the settings are done with slider bars. The first two sliders to determine how fast or slow the panel will collapse when it minimizes under autohide and when you explicitly hide the panel with the arrow buttons. The next slider sets the speed of the opening and closing of drawers. For autohide panels, there are additional sliders for the amount of time before the panel minimizes and the size (in pixels) of the hidden panel.

## Buttons

This tab controls the look of the various types of buttons on a panel (See Figure 15-5). Select which type of button you want to configure from the drop-down box.

Tiles provide a square background for a panel icon instead of the icon being displayed directly on the panel background. If you enable tiles (using the radio button at the top), you can select an image to use for the background of all buttons on the menu. Tiles also are used to create 3D-style buttons on the panel. You can choose the images for the up position and the down position (i.e., on a mouse-down). To select the image files, click the tile images, and the image file selection dialog opens for you to choose from.

Two slider controls allow you to set the number of pixels used for the border width around tiles and the depth of the icon when pressed.

The following additional settings are available:

*Make buttons flush with panel edge*
This setting causes buttons to be placed at the edges of the panel. There is no visible space between the button and the desktop background, although there is still spacing between panel buttons.

*Show button tiles only when cursor is over them*
This setting causes tiles to be unseen until the mouse pointer is over the button.

*Prelight buttons on mouse-over*
This setting causes buttons to "light up" when the pointer is over them.

## Panel objects

This tab allows you to select among three methods of icon placement: Switched Movement makes icons switch places with the icon you are moving. This is the default behavior. Free Movement locks the current icons in place as you move another icon. Icons can be moved only to empty areas of the panel when this method is selected. Push Movement causes moving icons to push the others around but not move over them.

The Padding slider sets the amount of space (in pixels) separating objects on the panel.

## Menu

This tab contains the global menu settings.

The first radio button enables large icons to be used for each menu item, indicating whether it is a folder, file, or application.

The second radio button, Show ... Buttons, toggles the cascading display of submenus off and on. If this button is selected, buttons containing ... are displayed for each menu item that contains a submenu. The submenu is displayed only when you press the ... button. Automatic display of cascading menus is used if this button is *not* selected.

The Show Pop-Up Menus Outside of Panels button controls the relative placement of pop-up menus to the panel. If this is enabled, pop-up menus are displayed on the desktop so that they don't overlap the panel. The Keep Menus in Memory button allows you to cache recently opened menus in memory, providing faster response from your desktop environment.

The remainder of this tab configures which sections of the menu you want to display. You have a choice of placing the sections directly on the main menu, placing them in a submenu, or not showing the sections.

### Miscellaneous

The Miscellaneous tab provides a number of panel configuration settings:

*Tooltips enabled*
Enables tooltips to be displayed for launcher icons.

*Close drawer if launcher inside it is pressed*
Causes a drawer to close after one of its items is selected. Otherwise, it will remain open until you click on its closing arrow.

*Raise panels on mouse-over*
Causes the panel to come to the foreground on mouse-over if it is covered by another window.

*Keep panel below windows*
Allows GNOME-compliant applications to display over the panel (normally they would not cover the panel).

*Confirm the removal of panels with a dialog*
A pop-up window will ask you if you really want to remove a panel.

## Document Handlers

This section configures the default programs used to run specific files based on their content type or URL.

### Default editor

This section sets the text editor to be used by default when you open an editable file or choose the Edit menu command on a file within the file manager. A drop-down list of available editors is displayed. Click the Run in Terminal Window button if your chosen editor must be run in a terminal.

### Mime types

This section allows you to set or edit mime types. Click the Add button to add a new type. A dialog will open asking for the category/type listing for the mime type and the extensions to associate with it. Optionally, you can supply up to two regular expressions to identify the mime type. To edit a mime type, select it in the listing and click the Edit button. You will see a dialog box in which you can choose an icon to be used for the file type, add or remove file extensions, and supply commands that will open, view, and edit this type of file. To delete a type, select it from the list and click the Delete button.

### URL handlers

This page allows you to adjust the settings for special URL launchers used by the GNOME help system. The defaults for protocols such as HTTP, FTP, and Mail are already set and likely handled by your default web browser (for example, Netscape). The special URLs are *ghelp*, *info*, and *man*, corresponding to GNOME help files, command *info* files, and *man* files. The defaults use the help browser for these types of files. It is best to leave these settings as they are.

## Multimedia

This section adjusts the settings for system sounds.

### Sound

This page sets up a sound scheme for various actions. You can enable or disable all sounds on the General tab. The Sound Events tab displays a listing of available events and the sound files used for them. Select an event from the listing and click Play to hear its assigned sound. Use the textbox to input the name of the sound file to assign to an action, or use the Browse button to locate a sound file on the filesystem.

## Peripherals

This section provides configuration settings for the keyboard and mouse.

### Keyboard

Contains settings for keyboard autorepeat and sounds. You can set the repeat rate of a pressed key and the delay before it starts. You also can enable keyboard clicks and their volume. Settings can be previewed by typing in the Test Settings textbox.

Three sliders adjust the volume, pitch, and duration of the keyboard bell. Click the Test button to hear the the bell's new settings.

## Mouse

Lets you set the mouse to be configured for either a righthanded user or a left-handed user. You also can set the acceleration and threshold (sensitivity) of the mouse.

## Session

This section contains settings for programs loaded at the start of each session.

### Startup hint

The Startup Hint is a program that displays a message every time you log in. Hints can provide a useful tip for a GNOME function that the user might not yet know about. You also can use this program to display a fortune or a message of the day.

### Startup programs

Since GNOME is session-aware, applications that are open when you log off are remembered and reopened the next time you log in. Not all applications are compliant with the GNOME session state, however. If you would like to set up programs to automatically start at login, you can configure them here. You can add, edit, or delete startup programs and view the currently running programs.

At the top of the window, there is an option button to show the splash screen on login. Two additional buttons give you the option either to be prompted to save session changes on logout or to automatically save the changes.

## User Interface

This section sets various properties for application window components such as menus, toolbars, status bars, and dialog boxes.

### Applications

The settings available in the applications section control the behavior of menus, toolbars, and status bars for GNOME applications.

Menu bars in GNOME applications can be detached from windows and placed anywhere on the desktop. This is the default behavior.

A detachable menu will have a small bar placed on its left edge. Click on this bar and drag to move the menu bar to another part of the desktop. To redock the menu bar, drag it back to the titlebar of its application window, and it will reattach.

For unmovable menu bars, unselect the the radio button labeled Can Detach and Move Menus.

The same detachable functionality is applied to submenus by default. To disable this behavior, unselect the radio button labeled Submenus Can Be Torn Off.

Three settings allow you to display menus, toolbars, and buttons on toolbars with a relieved border. The relieved border gives a three-dimensional visual appearance to the components; otherwise, they appear very flat.

Two options are available for status bars displayed at the bottom of windows. If a progress meter is used in a status bar, you can configure it to always appear on the right side of the statusbar. If this setting is disabled, the application will determine the progress meter placement.

Some statusbars may have user functionality defined by the application. You can enable statusbar interactivity with the supplied setting.

### Dialogs

This page is divided into sections for the look of dialog windows and the positioning of dialog windows.

The Dialog Layout section allows you to configure the position of dialog buttons with the following options: Default, Spread Buttons Out, Put Buttons on Edges, Left-justify Buttons, and Right-justify Buttons. You also can enable or disable icons for dialog buttons and choose to use a window's statusbar instead of a dialog, when possible.

The Dialog Behavior section allows you to set the position of dialog windows with the following options: Let Window Manager Decide, Center of the Screen, and At the Mouse Pointer. You also can configure dialog hints and enable the automatic placement of a dialog over the application window from which it was launched.

### MDI

MDI (Multiple Document Interface) describes the way multiple open documents are displayed in an application window. There are three styles available: Modal, Toplevel, and Notebook. Modal is the default setting. If you choose the Notebook style, you can set the document tab position to either left, right, top, or bottom.

## Sawfish Window Manager Configuration

The Sawfish window manager is the default window manager used by the Helix GNOME Desktop used in the figures in this chapter. Sawfish is GNOME-compliant, working well not to overlap the GNOME desktop settings. The Helix version of the GNOME Control Center integrates the Sawfish configuration settings instead of using a separate configuration tool. The Sawfish section of the Control Center is shown in Figure 15-6.

The following sections describe the Sawfish configuration settings contained in the Helix GNOME Control Center.

### Appearance

This section sets the default appearance of windows, including the style of the window frame, fonts, and movement style.

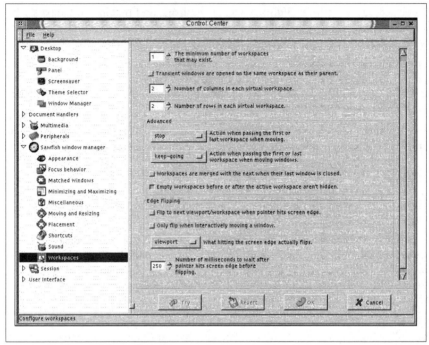

*Figure 15–6. Sawfish configuration settings*

The drop-down box contains a list of frame styles. The frame style determines how the titlebars of windows are displayed by customizing the buttons and background of the title.

Some pop-up windows are configured to be displayed without the window titlebar. To force the display of the title bar for all windows, click the button labeled Decorate Transient Windows Similarly to Top-level Windows.

The default window animation mode determines the display of windows when they are being minimized. You can choose from solid or wireframe modes or None for no animation.

The font button allows you to select the default desktop font. The default font is set by the GNOME desktop theme and Sawfish is aware of the setting so that they match.

### Focus behavior

This section contains settings that determine how windows receive the input focus.

The selection box at the top determines how the mouse pointer sets focus. The default is to focus when the mouse clicks on the window. The other choices are to focus only when the pointer is in the window ("enter-exit") and focus stays with the last window entered ("enter-only").

Three checkboxes are used to enable the following focus policies: focus each window when first displayed, transient windows inherit focus from their parent, and raise windows when they are focused. You can set the delay (in milliseconds) between focus and the time the window is raised (brought to the foreground).

The advanced section contains the following additional settings:

- Give focus to windows even when they haven't asked for it.

- Offset from left window edge when warping.

- Offset from top window edge when warping.

- Does click-to-focus mode pass the click through to the window?

The Shade Hover section contains settings for the behavior of shaded windows. A shaded window is effectively rolled up, like a window shade, into its titlebar, usually by double-clicking on the titlebar. If you check the button to enable shade hover, a shaded window will temporarily unshade when the mouse pointer is placed on its titlebar. The next box allows you to select the delay (in milliseconds) before unshading occurs. The final setting in this section enables windows to be raised automatically when they are unshaded.

### Minimizing and maximizing

This window contains settings for minimizing and maximizing windows. The settings for minimizing windows are as follows:

*Windows are uniconified onto the current workspace*
Minimized windows are opened on the current desktop workspace when they are clicked in the tasklist. You will usually have only one workspace in GNOME, which is divided into a grid of separate screens called viewports.

*Windows are raised after being uniconified*
Minimized windows are opened in the foreground when they are clicked in the tasklist.

*Windows are focused after being uniconified*
Minimized windows receive keyboard focus when they are clicked in the tasklist.

*Iconifying a window that's a member of a group removes the whole group*
If you minimize a window that is part of a group (e.g., an application may spawn several child windows from the main window), the whole group of windows will be minimized.

*Uniconifying a window that's a member of a group restarts the whole group*
In conjunction with the previous setting, a minimized window group will reopen if one of its members is raised.

*Windows are uniconified to the current viewport*
Minimized windows will reopen in the current screen, regardless of where they were before. In Sawfish, each screen of a desktop is referred to as a viewport.

The settings for maximizing windows are as follows:

*Maximizing a window dimension always increases the size of that dimension*
A window maximized vertically or horizontally will increase to that size even if it fills the screen.

*Raise windows when they're maximized*
Maximized windows automatically come to the foreground and receive focus.

*Let ignored windows be overlapped when filling windows*
If a window is set to be ignored (via the window menu), it will be overlapped by a fill command.

*Lock window geometry while the window is maximized*
No resizing of a window can occur if it is maximized.

### Miscellaneous

This section contains some miscellaneous window settings, including settings for the display of tooltips.

*Windows selected (normally by the Windows menu) are raised*
A selected window, either by keyboard shortcut or the desktop window menu, will be raised with focus.

*Unshade selected windows*
If a shaded window is selected, it will automatically unshade.

*Warp the mouse pointer to selected windows*
The pointer is automatically moved to a selected window.

*Keep transient windows stacked above*
This listbox selects how transient windows are placed. Choose from None, Parents, or All.

*Update all windows when the default frame style is changed*
If you change the window frame style, all windows will be automatically updated.

*Automatically reload themes when they are updated*
If a theme is edited, the changes are made immediately.

*Group transient windows with their parents*
Transient windows such as dialogs are automatically placed in the window group of their parents.

*Raise windows when they are unshaded*
Windows receive focus and come to the top when unshaded.

To enable window manager tooltips, click the button labeled Display Tooltips for Window Frames.

Tooltips will be displayed until the pointer leaves the item. You can set them to automatically disappear by enabling Remove Tooltips After a Period of Time. The amount of time before displaying and before removing tooltips is set by two input boxes.

You also can set the font used in tooltips, as well as the background and foreground colors.

### Moving and resizing

The method for drawing windows when they are being moved can be set to opaque or box. The same options are available for the drawing of windows being resized.

You also can toggle the following settings:

• Raise windows being moved or resized interactively.

• Show the current position while moving windows interactively.

• Show the current dimensions while resizing windows interactively.

### Placement

This section contains settings for the default placement of new windows. There are placement policy options for both normal windows and transient windows. Each setting contains a listbox with the following options:

• Randomly (transient default)

• Interactively

• Centered

• Centered-on-parent

• Under-pointer

• None

• First-fit

• Best-fit (window default)

• First-fit-or-interactive

If you don't want to allow applications any control over placement, check the box Ignore Program-specific Window Positions. This setting is disabled by default.

For a first-fit or best-fit policy, you can set an amount of space in pixels to leave between window edges.

### Workspaces

Sawfish manages the desktop work area by creating workspaces that can be divided into a number of different viewable screens, referred to by the GNOME Desk Guide applet as *viewports*. Workspaces can be thought of as desktops stacked on top of one another. Viewports are configured by a grid of rows and columns.

The first option in this window sets the number of workspaces. To define the grid of viewports, select the numbers of columns and rows you want each workspace divided into from the available settings.

By default, transient (pop-up) windows will be opened in the same workspace as the window that spawned them.

The Advanced section contains settings for moving between workspaces. When moving through workspaces or moving a window, choose the following options for movement at the ends of workspaces: stop, wrap around, or keep going.

The easiest way to move among viewports is by using the Desk Guide applet in the GNOME panel. If you would like to move through screens when moving the pointer on the screen, you can enable edge flipping. Two checkbox options set up edge flipping:

- Flip to next viewport/workspace when pointer hits screen edge.

- Flip only when interactively moving a window.

You can specify whether edge flipping takes you to the next viewport (the default) or the next workspace. If you want to set a delay for edge flipping when the pointer hits the screen edge, input a number in milliseconds.

## Configuring the Enlightenment Window Manager

The Enlightenment window manager is the most common window manager used with GNOME. Configuring the window manager allows you to adjust the most general behavior of the desktop, such as mouse behavior, window placement, border styles, and the number of virtual desktops. You can access the Enlightenment configuration editor from the GNOME Control Center. Go to the window manager page, select Enlightenment from the list, and click the Run Configuration Tool for Enlightenment button. This opens the configuration window shown in Figure 15-7. The Enlightenment configuration tool is composed of the following sections:

### Basic options

The options on this page set styles of window movement and window focus.

*Move methods*
These buttons select how the window is drawn when it is moved. The following styles are available: Opaque, Lined, Box, Shaded, Semi-Solid, and Translucent.

*Resize methods*
These buttons select how the window is drawn when it is resized. The following styles are available: Opaque, Lined, Box, Shaded, and Semi-Solid.

*Keyboard focus follows*
These buttons determine how "focus" is selected by the actions of the mouse. The available settings are Mouse Pointer (focus follows mouse), Sloppy Pointer (focus follows mouse after a delay), and Pointer Clicks (focus is given to window on which a mouse clicks).

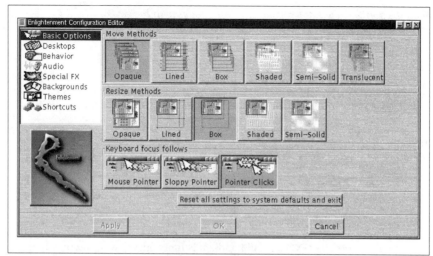

*Figure 15–7. Enlightenment configuration tool*

### Desktops

This section configures your desktop space. You can create a number of virtual desktops, each using its own screen and switch from one to another as needed. Two sliders allow you to create the column and row grid of a virtual desktop. Enabling Edge Flip will cause you to move to the adjacent desktop when the pointer moves across the edge of the current screen. The delay for the edge flip can be set in milliseconds. The Separate Desktops setting allows you to set a number of layered desktops (instead of multiscreen panes). Note that the GNOME Desk Guide applet does not support layered desktops.

### Behavior

This section contains options for setting additional keyboard focus properties on new windows and miscellaneous options such as tooltips and placement of pop-up windows. The Advanced Focus tab contains the following settings:

*All new windows that appear get the keyboard focus*
New windows automatically receive the keyboard focus.

*All new pop-up windows get the keyboard focus*
New pop-ups automatically receive the keyboard focus.

*Only new pop-up windows whose owner is focused get the keyboard focus*
Only pop-ups generated by the window with the current focus receive the keyboard focus.

*Raise windows when switching focus with keyboard*
Minimized windows open when receiving focus.

*Send the pointer to windows when switching focus with the keyboard*
Mouse pointer moves automatically to windows that receive keyboard focus.

The Miscellaneous tab contains the following settings:

*Tooltips*
Click the Enable button to allow tooltips to appear when the pointer is over an icon. You can set the amount of time in seconds for the tooltip to display with the slider control.

*Transient pop-up windows appear together with leader*
Displays additional pop-up windows with the window that generated them.

*Switch to where pop-up window appears*
Automatically switches to the desktop screen where a new pop-up appears.

*Display icons when windows are iconified*
Displays a small icon on the screen when a window is minimized. Leave this option disabled as GNOME will handle this functionality with the panel.

*Place windows manually*
When a new window is opened, the pointer is automatically switched to the activated move bar of the window. Move the window to the desired location and click to place it.

### Audio

This page is used to enable sounds in Enlightenment. Sounds for specific actions can be set manually or set as a group from a theme.

### Special FX

This section contains settings for the motion of desktop components, with the following options:

*Window Sliding Methods*
The same window drawing options as on the Basic Options page appear here for sliding window animations, in addition to the following settings:

—Windows slide in when they appear.

—Windows slide about during window cleanup.

—Desktops slide in when changing desktops.

—Window shading speed (pixels/sec).

*Drag bar*
Click the button to enable, and set the location to left, right, top, or bottom.

*Animate menus*
Select this button to enable sliding menu animation.

*Reduce Refresh*

Select this button to reduce the rate at which the contents of the desktop are refreshed.

## Backgrounds

This section lets you set the background for each virtual desktop you have. Select the specific desktop and then choose an image file from the list of available images. You also have an option button to select No Background. To add an image to the background list, click the Add New . . . button and specify the file.

The High Quality Rendering for Background button enables background images to be displayed at the full resolution and color depth that your display is set to.

Background for desktops that have not recently been viewed can be removed from memory by enabling the Minutes After Which to Expunge Unviewed Backgrounds from Memory button. Set the number of minutes to keep them in memory with the slider.

Note that setting a background image in Enlightenment will override the background settings you have made with GNOME.

## Themes

This section allows you to select a theme to apply to the window manager. Themes create a distinctive and consistent look for windowing components and the background. Enlightenment themes are installed in the */usr/share/enlightenment/themes* directory. You can download any number of user-created themes from *http://e.themes.org*. If you use a desktop theme in GNOME, use a basic window manager theme so you don't create any unwanted conflicts in your desktop style.

## Shortcuts

This section allows you to set up keyboard shortcuts for Enlightenment functions. This section displays a list of predefined shortcuts. You can edit a shortcut by selecting it in the list, choosing a key modifier, and clicking the Change . . . button. A pop-up will ask you to press the key button to use for the shortcut.

# CHAPTER 16

# *KDE*

KDE, the K Desktop Environment, is an open source software project that aims at providing a consistent, user-friendly, contemporary desktop for Unix and Linux systems. KDE is not simply a window manager like **fvwm** but a whole desktop system that integrates the window manager functions into its own graphical configuration. The KDE interface makes full use of drag-and-drop functionality, so you can grab an icon for a text file in the file manager and drag it to a text editor window to open it. Full network integration of KDE applications allows you to transparently access files from other computers or FTP sites and manipulate them as if they were local.

KDE also implements a standard help system based on HTML. Applications that display a Help button can open a specific help file in the help viewer.

One goal of KDE is to provide the user with system information and configuration through easy-to-use graphical interfaces of the desktop. The KDE Control Center is a central utility for desktop and application configuration, as well as a source of information for important system components. The Information module of the Control Center can retrieve and display status information for your processor, memory, PCI bus, and network devices.

A wide variety of applications have been developed to take advantage of KDE's features and provide the user with a wealth of productive applications. The base package comes with programs such as a mail client, a calendar and organizer, a CD player, image viewers, chat programs, and many more.

Most Linux distributions ship with KDE and allow you to set it up as the default session environment when you install the operating system. If you are installing KDE separately, download and install the KDE packages (you can find them at *ftp://ftp.kde.org*, among other places).

To set KDE as your desktop environment, look for the X initialization files in your home directory. Depending on your distribution, look for either *.xinitrc*, *.xsession*, or *.Xclients* in your home directory. If none of these files exist, create a new

*.xinitrc* file. Edit the file to remove any window manager references that may exist and add **startkde** on a line at the end of the file. Make sure to put the KDE directories in your path. The default package installation is */opt/kde*. Note that some distributions will use a different KDE path, but it will be configured by the default setup.

## Desktop Overview

Figure 16-1 shows a typical KDE desktop. The bar across the top edge of the screen is the taskbar. It is used to keep track of application windows running on the desktop. The panel is at the bottom of the screen. The panel contains buttons for the main menu, the window list, and the desktop pager as well as other buttons used to launch applications.

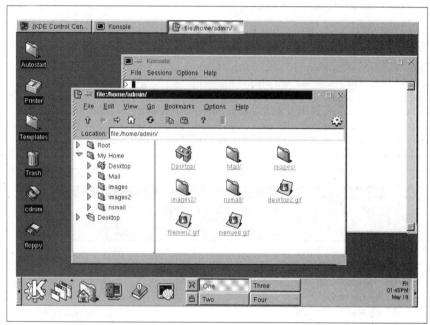

*Figure 16-1. The KDE desktop*

The desktop displays open application windows and contains icons that can be used to launch applications with a single click. A number of icons are placed on the desktop by default. There are two folder icons. One opens the Templates folder, which contains a set of generic files used to create desktop links. The Autostart folder contains links to applications that are started automatically every time you log in. The Trash icon is a link to a special desktop folder to which you can drag files that you want to delete. There are also icons that link to mounted CD-ROM and floppy drives.

## Application Windows

Each KDE window has a titlebar with common buttons on the right for minimize, maximize, and close. On the left side of the titlebar, there is a small icon (or a dash, if an icon isn't specified by the application) and a button that looks like a pushpin. The icon opens the window menu that contains a number of different functions you can apply to the window, such as sending it to another desktop. The push pin button is used to stick or unstick the window to the screen. If you click on the pushpin, the window will be sticky and appear on all of the virtual desktops. The button appears pushed in when a window is sticky. Click the button again to unstick a window.

The window menu contains standard window commands: Maximize, Iconify, Move, Resize, Sticky, and Close. There is also a command that lets you send the window to another virtual desktop.

## kfm — the KDE File Manager

One of the most important KDE applications is **kfm**. **kfm** is a graphical file manager and Internet browser and also controls the workings of the KDE desktop and the icons it contains. Anytime you click a folder icon, such as the Home folder button on the panel or the Autostart icon on the desktop, a **kfm** window opens displaying the contents of the directory. Figure 16-2 shows a **kfm** window displaying a home directory. Files and directories are shown as icons by default, but you can use the View menu to view contents with more detail.

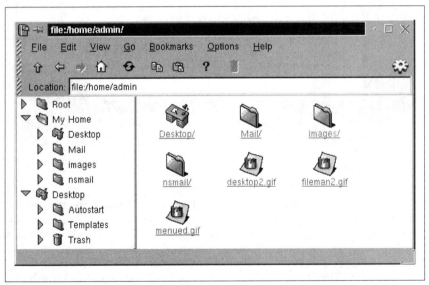

*Figure 16-2. kfm, the KDE file manager*

The **kfm** interface has its roots in web browsers. The toolbar contains back and forward buttons for stepping through your selection history, a home button, reload, and stop. The Location bar uses URL addressing for both network addresses and local filesystems. HTML rendering is well-supported in **kfm**, although not as robust as commercial browsers. If you don't like the bells and whistles of advanced features such as Java applets and scripting, **kfm** makes a perfect, simple web browser. You can even save addresses as bookmarks and use HTTP cookies.

In addition to file management, **kfm** is responsible for the functioning of the desktop. When you log into a KDE session, **kfm** reads the contents of the Desktop directory. Any files or folders will be represented as icon links on the desktop. Items contained in the Autostart folder will be launched as well. **kfm** uses text files ending in *.kdelnk* to configure desktop links. These files are described later.

## Adding a Link to the Desktop

There are a couple of ways to add a desktop link. The simplest way is to right-click on the background and select the New submenu in the pop-up menu. The New menu offers a number of choices for the type of link to create: Folder, File System Device, FTP URL, Mime Type, Application, Internet Address, and WWW URL. When you make a selection, a default icon for that type will appear on the desktop, and the properties window will appear for the link.

The properties window varies slightly for the type of link, but for all links you need to specify a name for the link file, the label for the icon, and the executable command or file location. You can also set the permissions for the link file and select a new icon.

The following example shows how to create an application desktop link that opens the Kedit text editor. First right-click on the desktop and select New→Application. A new icon appears on the screen with the default KDE "gear" graphic and labeled "Application," and the properties window opens.

The General tab, shown in Figure 16-3, shows the default name of the *kdelnk* file and other file information. Change the name of the file to reflect the purpose of the link; in this example, it is *Kedit.kdelnk*.

Since you created the link file, the permissions allow you to use it. If you want to adjust the permissions, go to the Permissions tab. The next step is to supply the command used to open the application. On the Execute tab (Figure 16-4), type in the command, or click the Browse button to locate the file. Here you can change the icon for the link by clicking the button showing the current icon. This opens a window that displays a set of default KDE icons found on your system. Pick the one you like and click OK.

The final step is to supply the name for the link and a tooltip comment. Fill in the Comment box on the Application tab (Figure 16-5) with a description of the application. Supply the name of the link (the label that appears under the icon on the desktop) in the Name box. Click the OK button to finish the configuration.

For URL or Internet address settings, the properties windows are all the same except for the default names and icons. These type of links require you to supply the URL address on the URL tab (Figure 16-6).

**KDE**

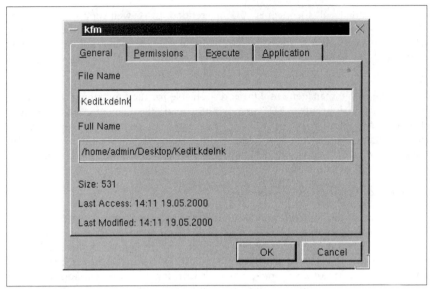

*Figure 16–3. General tab of desktop link properties*

For a new device link, set the link name and permissions if needed. On the Device tab, supply the location of the device, such as */dev/fd3* and the mount point. Specify the filesystem type in the Filesystems box (e.g., default, msdos, etc.).

You can also add a link to the desktop by dragging an item from a file manager window. You can do this with any file or directory. After you drag the item to the desktop, a small pop-up window asks you whether you want to copy, move, or link the item. Copy simply makes a copy of the item in the Desktop directory. Move will remove the item from its original location and place it in the Desktop directory. If you choose link, the desktop icon will contain a symbolic link that points to the item's current location.

## The Desktop Folder and kdelnk Files

Everything that is shown on the desktop exists in the *~/Desktop* folder. If you open this folder in the file manager, you will see directories for Templates and Autostart, as well as *.kdelnk* files for the CD-ROM and floppy drive and any other links you have set. When KDE starts, it scans the contents of the Desktop directory and creates icons for each item.

Desktop links that launch applications, URLs, or files are configured in the background by *.kdelnk* files. These are simple text files that contain all the information that you set for a link in the link properties dialog boxes. Although all the configuration of desktop links is handled thoroughly by the configuration pop-up windows, the content of *.kdelnk* files may be of interest to advanced users. The following example shows the *.kdelnk* file for a link to the Kedit text editor:

```
# KDE Config File
[KDE Desktop Entry]
Name[]=Kedit
```

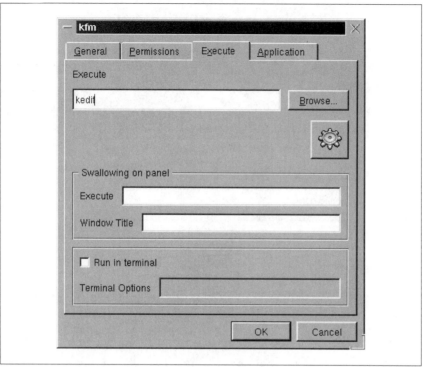

*Figure 16–4. Execute tab of desktop link properties*

```
Exec=kedit
Type=Application
Comment[]=Text editor
BinaryPattern=kedit;Kedit
Icon=exec.xpm
TerminalOptions=
Path=
Terminal=0
MimeType=
SwallowExec=
SwallowTitle=
Name[fi]=Sovellus
Name[hr]=Program
Name[sl]=Uporabniki program
Name[pl]=Aplikacja
...
```

As you can see, the syntax is simple and straightforward. The items filled in on the
properties windows are listed on each line of the file. The Type line identifies the
kind of link file. In this example, Kedit is an application. Type=URL would indicate
an Internet address link file. The Name line lists the name of the application, Exec
lists the command, Icon identifies the icon image file, and so on. Unspecified
options have empty values. The additional Names lines are set in the template files
and provide alternate names for other languages should you switch the default
language setting for your environment.

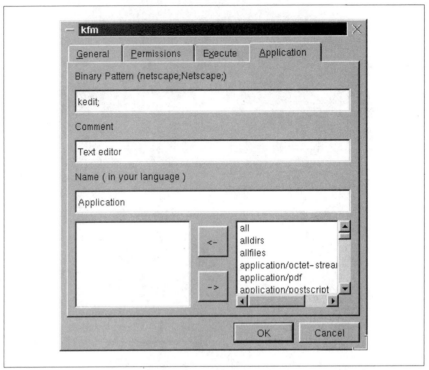

*Figure 16–5. Application tab of desktop link properties*

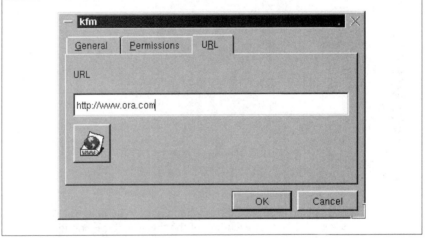

*Figure 16–6. URL tab of desktop link properties*

## The Panel and Taskbar

The **kpanel** program runs the panel and the taskbar. The panel is the control bar across the bottom of the screen. The panel is used to find and launch applications and navigate among windows and desktops. It contains the menu, which organizes the installed KDE applications into submenus; the disk navigator, which provides a menu-driven display of filesystem contents; and the desktop pager. Additional buttons that open applications, directories, and URLs can be added to the panel.

## The Desktop Pager and Window List

Like most window managers, **kwm** (KDE's window manager) can divide your workspace into multiple desktops. Different application windows can be open on each desktop, reducing the amount of clutter on your screen. You can switch among desktops by using the desktop buttons on the panel or by using the window list. The panel displays a grid of buttons, one for each virtual desktop, and their names (One, Two, Three, etc., by default). Clicking on a button will switch your screen to the corresponding desktop.

If you click the window list icon, it displays a menu divided into sections for each desktop and items for each window they contain. (The window list is also accessible by middle-clicking on the desktop background.) For example, if desktop two contains an open file manager window, you can click on it in the window list, and you will switch to desktop two and activate the file manager window.

You can configure the number of virtual desktops and their names in the Desktops section of the Panel configuration module in the Control Center.

## The Taskbar

The taskbar runs across the top of your screen and helps you keep track of running applications. The taskbar contains buttons to identify each open application window. If the button for an application is clicked, it is the current active window. When you iconify a window, you can raise it again by clicking its button on the toolbar. If a window has been iconified, its taskbar button contains a parenthesized text label.

Whenever you use the arrow buttons to hide the panel, the toolbar displays buttons to access the main menu, the disk navigator, and the window list. These buttons will disappear when you show the panel again.

In the panel settings module of the Control Center, you can adjust the positioning of the taskbar on the screen or choose not to display it at all. You can also set it to autohide so that it reduces when you aren't using it.

## Adding an Application Link to the Panel

The simplest way to add an application button to the panel is by dragging an icon from the desktop to the panel. This will copy the link from the desktop. Any application listed on the main menu can be easily added to the panel. From the main menu, choose Panel→Add Application, then select from submenus or items that are listed. The choices you have are the same items that appear on the main menu.

KDE

If you don't want to display some of the default panel buttons, you can use the Panel menu to turn them off (or on again). The window list and the disk navigator items on the Panel menu toggle the display of the buttons on the panel. If the item's menu icon appears clicked, the Panel buttons are enabled. Select it again from the menu to disable the Panel buttons.

## Running an Application on the Panel

A swallowed application is a program that you run on the panel instead of in a desktop window. A swallowed application can be a small utility that monitors network activity or provides mail notification, for example. In the Execute tab of the properties window, type in the Swallowing on Panel section with the command to execute and the title that appears in the titlebar of the application's window. The panel identifies the application to "swallow" by its window title.

# The KDE Control Center

The KDE Control Center contains a number of configuration tools, called *modules*, that allow you to configure and view information about your system. You can configure the desktop, the window manager, input devices, and any other important part of your system here. The Control Center is split into two windows: the left window shows a hierarchical list of installed modules, and the right window displays them when they are selected. (You also have the option to display each module in its own window. Go to the Options menu and click the Swallow Modules entry, which is checked by default, to unselect it.)

## Applications

The Applications modules set preferences for important KDE components, such as the login manager, **kfm**, and the panel.

### Login manager (root only)

The KDE login manager is the program that controls the graphical login screen. This module lets you configure the graphical style of the login screen, as well as set some default display options, such as prelisted users and available session environments.

The Appearance tab lets you edit the greeting string displayed on the login screen and choose a logo. A drop-down box offers you a choice of the GUI style of the login screen: either Windows or a Motif style. The Language option on this tab lets you select the default character encoding for the login manager.

The Fonts tab lets you choose the font style and size for the Greeting, Fail, and Standard screen messages. Select which type you want to configure from the drop-down list and click the Change Font button. The pop-up window shows a list of available fonts and lets you set the point size. Click the OK button to close the pop-up window. The font you have chosen is displayed in the Example area of the tab.

The Background tab lets you select the background for the login screen. Like the desktop background, you can choose a color or wallpaper to use.

The Users tab allows you to show a list of users on the login screen. The users are listed by username with a logo above the login boxes. A user can simply click her logo to automatically enter her name into the login box, but she still must supply her password. The tab contains listings for all users, selected users, and no-show users. You can select names from the lists and use the arrow buttons to move them from one box to another. Two options are available for who to display on the login screen. You can place names in the selected users list and click the Show Only Selected Users button. Or, you can edit the all users list and click the Show All Users But No-Show Users button. No-show users are user IDs that are used to control access-restricted system resources (e.g., **root**, **news**, and **nobody**).

The Sessions tab configures session settings. The drop-down list at the top sets who is allowed to shut down the system. You have the choices None, All, Root Only, and Console Only. The Commands section allows you to set the commands used for shutdown and restart. The Session Types section configures the list of session types that a user can log into from the login screen. The Default list contains the various environments that are installed on your system such as KDE and GNOME. You can add a new type or remove a type from the listing.

### File manager

This module contains configuration settings for **kfm**, the KDE file manager and browser. The first tab contains the font settings. Set the font size used in the file manager to either small, medium, or large by selecting the corresponding button. You can set the font styles used for displayed files or web pages with the Standard Font and Fixed Font settings. You can also set the character set to use.

The Color tab allows you to set the colors used for background, text, and links. You can set two colors for URL links: one for new links and one for links that have already been followed (as recorded by the URL history). There are also settings to change the cursor when it is over a link, underline links, and override HTML-specified colors with the default colors set on this tab.

The Other tab allows you to enable URL-specific settings. If you have set certain properties to view a certain URL or local directory, like menu bar display or the view settings, you can have them saved for the next time you visit that URL. The Tree View Follows Navigation button causes the directory tree in the left pane of the file manager to match the current open folders in the right pane. The final settings on this page allow you to select the default programs the file manager uses for a terminal when you use Open Terminal from the File Menu and the editor used to view the source of documents.

### Web browser

This module configures settings used for **kfm**'s web browsing functionality.

If your system is behind a firewall, you may need to use a proxy server for HTTP and FTP services. The Proxy tabs lets you enable the use of a proxy and configure it. Check the Use Proxy box, and supply the hostname or IP address for the proxy server and the port number to use. Some sites may not work properly when accessing them through a proxy server. The No Proxy For: box lets you specify a list of hostnames and domains that will not be accessed via the proxy server.

The HTTP tab sets a few of the parameters sent in HTTP requests by the browser. The Accept Languages box contains a list of two-letter abbreviations used to indicate the language that the browser can accept. The abbreviations, like *en* for English and *fr* for French, can be comma-or-space separated. The order of the list determines the preference of language. The Accept-Language HTTP request header is configured with this setting.

The Accept Character Sets box contains a list of character sets that the browser is capable of receiving. (This sets the Accept-Charset HTTP request header.) The list can accept the standardized character set strings, separated by spaces or commas. The Assume HTML button tells the browser to render as HTML documents whose type is not fully specified from the server response header.

The User Agent tab allows you to specify the user-agent string reported by the browser for sites that may not recognize **kfm**, or anything that's not a major commercial web browser. The user-agent string contains the name and version number of the client program making the request. The default for **kfm** at the time of this writing is "Konqueror/1.1.2". To set a different string for a specific server, type the server name in the On Server box and supply the user-agent string in the Login As box. Click Add to save this setting. All settings will be listed in the Known Bindings box. If you want to remove a setting, select it from the list, and click the Delete button.

The Cookies tab configures how **kfm** will manage cookies. Cookies are not used at all unless you check the Enable Cookies box at the top of the tab. You should set the default cookie policy to either accept all cookies, reject all cookies, or prompt for action each time a cookie is received. You can specify the policy for individual domains as well. Type the domain into the Change Domain Accept Policy box, and specify Accept, Ask, or Reject for the policy. Click the Change button, and the setting is saved. You will see it listed in the Domain Specific Settings list. If you would like to remove a setting, select it from the list and click the Delete button.

## Panel

The panel configuration module controls the panel, the toolbar, virtual desktops, and the disk navigator.

The Panel tab contains settings for the location of the panel. You can choose to place it at the top, bottom, left side, or right side of the screen by clicking the appropriate radio button. Three settings are available to set the size of the panel to either Tiny, Normal, or Large. You also have choices for how the taskbar is displayed. If you do not want the taskbar to be displayed at all, click the Hidden radio button. If you want the taskbar displayed fully across the top or bottom of the screen, click either the Top or Bottom button. If you choose the Bottom option, the taskbar will appear just above the panel. Finally, the Top/Left option displays the taskbar at the top-left corner of your screen, with window buttons stacked on top of each other.

The Options tab, shown in Figure 16-7, is divided into three sections. The Menu Tooltips section contains a button to enable tooltips to be shown on menu items. You can use the slider to set the amount of time that the pointer is held over the item before the tooltip appears. The Visuals section allows you to set the panel and taskbar to autohide (i.e., disappear when not being used). Enable these settings by clicking the Auto Hide Panel and Auto Hide Taskbar buttons. Each option has two slider settings if autohide is enabled. The Delay slider sets the amount of time after use (after the pointer has left the panel/taskbar) that the panel will reduce. The Speed slider sets how fast or slow the panel or taskbar will open and hide. The Animate Show/Hide setting enables the panel to use a sliding visual effect when you show or hide it with its side arrow buttons. The slider sets the speed of this animation.

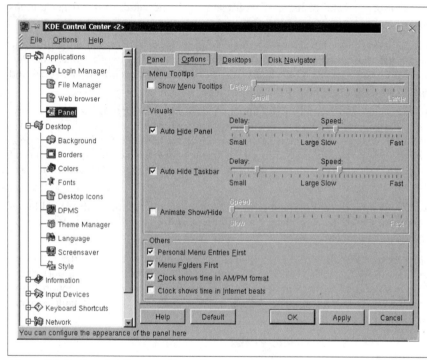

*Figure 16–7. Panel options configuration*

The Options tab contains the following additional settings:

*Personal Menu Entries First*

Check this box to display your personal menu section instead of the default system menu at the top of the main menu. The system menus will be contained in the default submenu.

*Menu Folders First*

Check this box if you want folders to appear at the top of your personal menu, above individual items. This setting can be overridden by customizing the menu order with the menu editor.

*Clock Shows Time in AM/PM Format*

This option enables AM/PM designation on your panel clock. Otherwise, the hour listing will range from 00 to 24.

*Clock Shows Time in Internet Beats*

This option allows you to have the panel clock display the Swatch-created time format, which divides a day into 1000 beats, in the GMT+1 time zone.

The Desktops tab sets the number of virtual desktops you can divide your workspace into. The default is 4, and you can use up to 8. The Visible slider selects the number of desktops (you can choose only even numbers). The desktops are listed, numbered 1 through 8. If enabled, the desktop listing has a usable textbox next to it. You can type in a label for the desktop that will be used in the pager display on the panel. The Width slider sets the width of the pager buttons shown on the panel.

The Disk Navigator tab allows you to configure the disk navigator shown on the menu and the taskbar. The History section of this tab has two buttons: Edit Personal and Edit Shared, which allow you to edit the contents of the Personal and Shared sections of the disk navigator from the file manager.

The Edit Personal button opens **kfm** in the ~/.kde/share/apps/kdisknav directory. This folder in the user's home directory contains *kdelnk* files for the items displayed in the Personal section of the disk navigator. The Edit Shared button opens */usr/share/apps/kdisknav* in **kfm**, which contains *kdelnk* files for the contents of the Shared section. This directory can be edited only by **root**; other users will have this button disabled.

Additional options set the number of folder entries and file entries displayed in the Recent section of the disk navigator and the maximum number of files that can be displayed in a folder.

The Options section of the Disk Navigator tab contains buttons for the following settings: Show Dot Files (which shows the hidden files that start with a dot), Show Shared Section, Show Recent Section, Show Personal Section, Show Option Entry, and Ignore Case When Sorting. There is also a selection for the default terminal application to use.

## Desktop

The Desktop modules set preferences for the visual display of your environment. You can individually set the background, fonts, or window colors or use the Theme Manager to configure all of the settings from an installed package.

### Background

This module sets the desktop background. It allows you to specify a background for each virtual desktop or just one for all of them. Select the desktop you want to configure from the list, or check the Common Background box. You can use colors or a wallpaper image for your background. The One Color setting applies a solid color to the background. The Two Color setting lets you choose a blend of two colors. Select the colors you desire by clicking on the color bars. The Setup button opens a dialog box for two-color settings. You can select to blend the colors vertically, horizontally, or with a pattern.

If you would like to use an image file as wallpaper on the background, select it from the drop-down list, or click the Browse button to look for the image on the filesystem. The Arrangement setting determines how the image file is laid out. You can choose from the basic tiling layout to such effects as symmetrical mirroring. You can also choose a random background. A new image file and settings will be used every session.

### Borders

This module sets up border properties for windows and the screen. Active desktop borders enable you to switch between desktops by moving the mouse pointer to an adjacent screen edge. Check the box to enable this setting. The Desktop switch-delay slider sets a delay time for the switch to the adjacent desktop. Set this time to a comfortable setting that doesn't cause an unwanted desktop switch every time you move the pointer to the screen edge. Check the Move Pointer Towards Center After Switch box if you want the pointer to go to the center of the screen when you switch desktops.

Magic Borders sets up "snap-to" zones around windows and at the edge of screens. You can set the width of zones, in pixels, in which moved windows will be placed.

### Colors

The Colors module allows you to select the colors for the various window widgets, the components used to build windows. You can select the colors based on a scheme installed on your system. Available schemes are listed. Select one from the list, and click Add to change the color scheme. You can also set colors for individual components. The top of the tab shows sample windows components. Click on the component you want to configure, such as the active titlebar or window background to select it. You can also select a component from the widget color list. Click the color bar under the list to open the color selector dialog box and choose your color. You can also set the contrast of the component with the Contrast slider.

### Fonts

The Fonts module sets the default fonts used in your display. You can set the font for the following listed selections: the general font, fixed-width font, window titles, panel buttons, and the panel clock. You can set the typeface of the font from the drop-down list and choose if you want it either bold or italic. Select the point size of the font, and optionally change the character set used. A sample of the selected font is displayed at the bottom of the window.

### Desktop icons

This module controls the display of icons on the desktop. Icons are placed along invisible grid lines on the desktop. The grid spacing sets the number of pixels surrounding each icon. Two controls allow you to set the horizontal grid spacing and the vertical grid spacing.

Labels for icons are displayed with transparent backgrounds, allowing the background to be visible underneath them by default. Uncheck the Transparent Text for Desktop Icons box if you would like to view the background box of the label. You can set the color of text labels by clicking the Icon Foreground Color button. If backgrounds are nontransparent, you can choose their color by clicking the Icon Background Color button.

The final setting on this tab allows you to show hidden files (files that begin with a dot) on the desktop.

### DPMS

DPMS stands for Display Power Management System. If your hardware supports power management, you can enable it by clicking the DPMS enabled button. Now you can set the amount of idle time before the system goes to standby mode, then suspend mode, and finally turns off.

### Theme manager

Themes provide an overall visual style to your desktop, instead of you having to configure items individually. A theme can determine the color scheme of windows, the font styles, icons, the background, and even sound events for your desktop. A couple of themes are installed by default with KDE, and many more are available for downloading at *http://kde.themes.org*.

The Installer tab, shown in Figure 16-8, lists the themes you have installed on your system. These include global themes, which are stored in the */share/apps/kthememgr/Themes* directory of your default KDE directory, and local themes, stored in *˜/.kde/share/apps/kthememgr/Themes* in your home directory. Local themes are themes that are installed or customized by the user and stored in his home directory. The user is able to edit and save local themes. Global themes cannot be altered by individual users.

If you select a theme from the list, a sample desktop image using the theme is displayed on the tab, with a short text description. If you would like to apply a new theme, select from the list and click the Apply button. The selected theme will be copied to the user's theme manager work directory (*˜/.kde/share/apps/kthememgr/Work*).

You can also manage installed themes on the Installer tab. To install a new theme that you have downloaded, click the Add button. Specify the filename and location of the theme's *.tgz* file in the pop-up dialog box and click OK. The Save button lets you save the currently configured theme as local or save a global theme as local. The Save As button saves the currently configured theme as a separate local package without altering the original theme. The Create button works similarly, allowing you to copy your current working theme as a new local theme package. The Remove button deletes a local theme or inactivates a global theme.

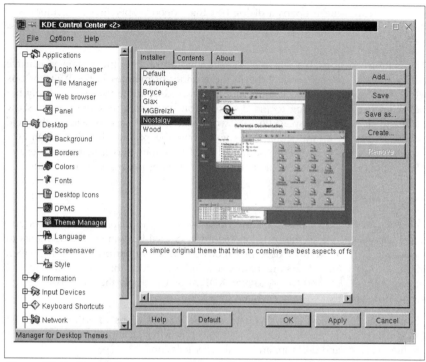

*Figure 16–8. Theme Manager installer*

The Contents tab shows the components that are configured by a theme. A theme may not have settings available for all the listed components. If a theme configures a specific component, it is listed as available. Otherwise, the component is listed as empty. Use the checkboxes to select which theme components you want to use. If you choose to not activate a specific component, information on that component from a previous theme will be used if its information is still in the theme manager work directory. If you don't want this to happen, activate the component, even if it is listed as empty, and default settings will be used.

The About tab shows you author and version information for a selected theme.

## Language

The Language module sets the preferred locale (language) settings for your programs. The drop-down lists allow you to choose first, second, and third choices for the language, if programs make them available.

## Screensaver

This module sets up your screensaver. A list of available screensavers is shown with a preview window. If you do not want to use the screensaver, select No Screensaver from the top of the list. Otherwise, select the screensaver you want to use. The Setup button opens a dialog box that contains specific configuration settings for each screensaver. For a full-screen test of the screensaver, click the Test button.

The Settings section allows you to set the amount of time the system is inactive before the screensaver starts. Type in the number of minutes in the Wait For box to set this time. If you check the Require Password box, the user must supply her password before returning to the desktop. You can also check the box to Show Password as Stars to display the password text as asterisks, instead of the field being blank. The Priority control lets you adjust the priority that the screensaver process has when it is run. If you have lots of important server activity, for example, set the priority to low so the performance of other programs will not suffer.

### Style

The Style module contains a couple of settings for the display of windows and icons. Draw Widgets in the Style of Windows 95 enables window components to have a similar look to those used in Windows. The Menu bar on Top of the Screen in the Style of MacOS setting places a window's menu bar across the top of screen. Apply Fonts and Colors to Non-KDE Apps will apply the styles you've chosen to programs that were not written for KDE.

The Icon Style section allows you to set the size of icons to either Normal or Large. You can set the size for icons in the following locations: on the panel, in the file manager and desktop, and at all other locations.

## Information

The Information modules allow you to view status information about various system components. There are no configuration settings here, but if you need to see information about your processor or what PCI devices you have installed, use these modules. Information is provided for the following system components:

- Devices

- DMA-Channels

- Interrupts

- IO-Ports

- Memory

- Partitions

- PCI

- Processor

- SCSI

- Samba Status

- Sound

- X-Server

## Input Devices

The modules here control the configuration of the keyboard and mouse.

### Keyboard

This module configures keyboard repeat. Select the On option to enable keyboard repeat, and use the slider to set the volume of keyclicks. If you don't want keyclicks, set the slider to 0.

### Mouse

This module configures the movement and button layout of your mouse. The Acceleration slider sets the speed at which the pointer moves on your screen when you move your mouse. The Threshold slider set the distance (in pixels) that the mouse must move before pointer movement occurs. The Button Mapping options let you choose if you use the mouse with your right hand or left hand.

## Keyboard Shortcuts

You can choose the scheme used for shortcuts by selecting the KDE defaults or the current scheme if you have customized the shortcuts. The bottom section of the tab allows you to edit the selected keyboard shortcut. You can choose no key for the action, the default key, or a custom key. If you want to customize a key, check the box for the modifier you want to use (Shift, Ctrl, or Alt), or unselect all of them if you don't want a modifier. Then click the key button and press the key on the keyboard that you want to use. Click the Save Changes button if you want to save the change to the current scheme.

### Global keys

The following table lists the keyboard combinations that cause global window events:

| Keys | Action |
|------|--------|
| Alt-Esc, Ctrl-Esc | Displays a list of currently running applications |
| Alt-Tab, Alt-Shift-Tab | Switches among windows on the desktop |
| Ctrl-Tab, Ctrl-Shift-Tab | Switches among virtual desktops |
| Alt-F2 | Opens the single-command-line utility |
| Alt-F3 | Opens the control menu of the current window |
| Alt-F4 | Closes the current window |
| Ctrl-F[1..8] | Switches to the correspondingly numbered virtual desktop |
| Ctrl-Alt-Esc | Kills the current window |

*KDE*

## Standard keys

The standard key mappings are shortcuts to common actions that you would find in most KDE programs like the file manager or graphical text editor.

| Keys | Actions |
|------|---------|
| Ctrl-W | Close |
| Ctrl-C | Copy |
| Ctrl-X | Cut |
| Ctrl-End | End |
| Ctrl-F | Find |
| F1 | Help |
| Ctrl-Home | Home |
| Ctrl-Insert | Insert |
| Ctrl-N | New |
| PageDown | Next |
| Ctrl-O | Open |
| Ctrl-V | Paste |
| Ctrl-P | Print |
| PageUp | Prior (or Previous) |
| Ctrl-Q | Quit |
| Ctrl-R | Replace |
| Ctrl-S | Save |
| Ctrl-Z | Undo |

# Sound

The modules contained in this section configure the keyboard bell and other system sounds.

## Bell

This module configures the system bell.

The Volume slider sets the volume of the bell. The Pitch slider sets the tone of the slider in Hz. You can set the duration of the system bell with the Duration slider control. To listen to your settings, click the Test button.

## System Sounds

Desktop themes can set .*wav* audio files to play for specific events, such as raising a window or clicking a dialog button. This module allows you to enable and configure sound events. Check the Enable System Sounds checkbox to enable sound events.

The tab contains two panes. The left pane contains the Event list of the available actions that you can apply a sound to. The right pane contains a list of .*wav* files that you can assign to actions. Selecting an event will highlight its currently assigned sound in the Sounds list. To set a sound event, select an action from the Events list, then select a sound file from the Sounds list. The Test button allows you to listen to a selected sound. Click the Apply button to save your settings.

## Window Behavior

The modules contained in this section allow you to set the look and functions of window titlebars, mouse button actions, and focus and placement policy.

### Advanced

The Keyboard and Mouse section of the Advanced tab contains the following settings:

*Ctrl-Tab walks through desktops*
> This checkbox sets the Ctrl-Tab key combination to switch through your virtual desktops. It is checked by default.

*Alt-Tab is limited to current desktop*
> This checkbox restricts the action of the Alt-Tab key combination to switch through windows on the current desktop only. It is checked by default.

*Alt-Tab mode*
> This setting describes the style of using Alt-Tab to switch through windows. The KDE setting uses a graphical style. When you press Alt-Tab, a window appears indicating the current window and other available windows. The CDE setting switches directly without a graphic.

*Grab the Right Mouse Button*
> This setting is on by default. It sets the control of the right mouse button to KDE by default. Some non-KDE applications require control over the right mouse button. If you need control for these applications, unselect this setting.

The Filters section of the Advanced tab contains settings that let you customize window styles or functions for application windows based on their titles or classes. The drop-down box contains a list of settings that you can define for a filtered window. After the Windows Will label, you can choose the following settings:

- Have tiny decorations

- Have no decorations

- Never gain focus

- Start as sticky

- Be excluded from session management

Select a setting, then define the window in the next section, which begins with If They Match the Following. Here you have two boxes, Titles and Classes. You can define one or both properties. Put the title of the application window in the Title box and the application's class name in the Classes box. (This is usually the capitalized name of the application, preceded by an X, for example, XEmacs for an Emacs window.) You can specify more than one title or class for a window setting.

### Buttons

This module configures the layout of buttons that appear on the titlebars of windows. There are five buttons: minimize (dot), maximize (square), sticky (pushpin), close (X), and menu (dash or application-specified icon). Each button has three placement options, specified by radio buttons: left, right, or off. You can place no more than three buttons on one side of the titlebar.

### Mouse

This module configures the actions of mouse buttons on the various window components. Drop-down boxes contain several options, such as raise or lower, for the left, middle, and right buttons, as shown in Figure 16-9. Select from the following options in each category:

*For active titlebars and frames*
    Raise

    Lower

    Operations menu

    Toggle raise and lower

*For inactive titlebars and frames*
    Activate

    Activate and raise

    Activate and lower

*For an inactive inner window*
    Activate, raise, and pass click

    Activate and pass click

    Activate

    Activate and raise

*For titlebars and frames of inner windows*
    Move

    Toggle raise and lower

    Resize

    Raise

    Lower

    Nothing

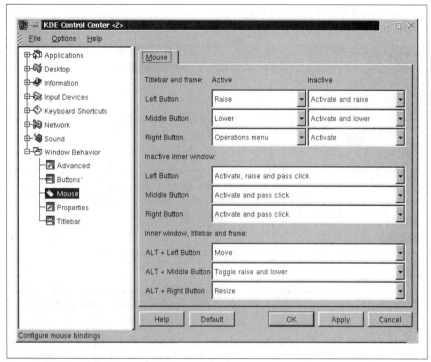

*Figure 16–9. Mouse button configuration settings*

## Properties

This tab sets windows options and the placement and focus policy. The Windows section of the tab has three settings:

*Vertical maximization only by default*
Check this box to cause the maximize window command to expand a window only to the full screen height, but leaving its width unchanged.

*Display content in moving windows*
Check this box to enable the display of window contents when the window is moved.

*Display content in resizing window*
Check this box to enable the display of window contents when the window is resized.

*Resize animation*
This slider controls the animation of windows that are maximized or minimized. Setting the slider all the way to the left (None), disables animation, and windows will maximize or minimize instantly. You can set the speed of the animation faster by setting the slider farther to the right.

The Placement Policy section of the tab contains a drop-down box with five options for determining the initial placement of new windows on the desktop:

*Smart (default)*
> This setting uses a placement scheme that attempts to keep windows as uncluttered as possible.

*Cascade*
> This setting attempts to place windows in a cascaded pattern, with a set of offset positions available on each desktop.

*Interactive*
> This setting enables the "allowed overlap" setting. If a window can be placed on the desktop without overlapping another by the specified percentage, it will be placed automatically. If the overlap exceeds the setting, you will be given manual control of the window placement.

*Random*
> This setting randomly places a new window on the desktop.

*Manual*
> This setting opens a window with the mouse pointer activated in move mode on the titlebar. Move the window to the desired position and click once to place the window.

The Focus Policy section sets the policy for giving a window keyboard focus and an active titlebar. The drop-down box contains four focus styles. The default is Click to Focus, which gives a window the keyboard focus and brings it to the foreground only when you click on it. The remaining settings follow the mouse and activate the Auto Raise and Click Raise options.

*Click to focus*
> The default focus policy requires a mouseclick in a window to give it focus and raise it (bring it to the foreground). This setting uses a graphical Alt-Tab style to switch through windows on a desktop.

*Focus follows mouse*
> This setting causes a window to receive focus when the mouse pointer enters it. The window will not come to the foreground unless the Auto Raise button is checked. The window will maintain focus until the pointer enters another window.

*Classic focus follows mouse*
> This setting is similar to the Focus Follows Mouse setting, except that the window loses focus when the mouse pointer moves out of it. If the pointer is not in a window, no window has focus. Also, Alt-Tab switches directly among windows, without showing the graphical listing of windows.

*Classic sloppy focus*
> This setting is similar to Focus Follows Mouse, with focus remaining in a window even when a mouse pointer leaves it. The only difference is that the nongraphical Alt-Tab style is used.

For any of the nondefault settings, you need to check either the Auto Raise or Click Raise boxes to be able to raise windows to the foreground. Click Raise raises a window when you click on it. Auto Raise raises a window after a short delay, which you can set with the Delay slider.

## Titlebar

This tab contains many settings for the appearance and action of window titlebars. The Title Alignment sets the positioning of the window title in the titlebar to either Left, Middle, or Right.

The Appearance settings adjust the graphical decoration of the titlebar:

*Shaded Vertically*
Uses a two-color background in a top-to-bottom gradient.

*Shaded Horizontally*
Uses a two-color background in a left-to-right gradient.

*Plain*
Uses a solid color for the background.

*Pixmap*
Uses a pixmap image for the titlebar background. This enables the Pixmap settings, which allow you to choose images for both active and inactive title-bars. If you don't want the image to appear under the window title text for better clarity, check the box labeled No Pixmap Under Text.

The checkbox labeled Active Title has Shaded Frame gives a shadowed, 3D appearance to active titlebars.

The Mouse Action options specify the action of double-clicking on a window title-bar. The available options are (Un)Shade (the default), (Un)Maximize, Iconify, (Un)Sticky, and Close. The settings identified with (Un) are toggle settings.

Title animation can be enabled to display a sliding titlebar animation when a title is too long for the display area. The slider sets the speed of the back-and-forth motion.

**KDE**

CHAPTER 17

# An Alternative Window Manager: fvwm2

Among the more appealing characteristics of a Linux system are its flexibility, its independence from industry-dominating standards, and the degree of control a user has over his own working environment. Most flavors of Linux come with a default desktop environment replete with handy tools and menus and a consistent look and feel. The most widely used of these desktop environments are GNOME and KDE, the customization of which are detailed in Chapter 15, *GNOME*, and Chapter 16, *KDE*, respectively.

Both of these environments put a PC-like wrapper around what is basically a no-frills Unix-based system suitable for personal computers. For some people this is a good thing. But if you don't want a lot of dialog boxes cluttering up the screen, and you're comfortable editing configuration files to customize your environment, you might instead try the **fvwm2** window manager.

**fvwm2** is the latest generation of a window manager called **fvwm**, but in neither case has it been entirely clear what *fv* stands for. *Virtual* seems a reasonable guess for the *v*. **fvwm** predates both GNOME and KDE as a program that can provide multiple virtual screens to expand your desktop real estate. But the meaning of the *f* in **fvwm** has led to much speculation. In fact, among the latest group of the program's developers are a number of cat lovers who claim the *f* stands for *feline*.

The first important concept you should understand in order to work with **fvwm** is that your desktop can be larger than the area of your screen. In fact, **fvwm2** can let you have acres of desktop real estate in the form of virtual screens, or pages. In a typical default environment, you might have a single desktop composed of four virtual screens/pages arranged in a two-by-two grid.

You can run applications on any of the screen pages you want and navigate the entire desktop in a variety of ways. And if the default environment doesn't suit you, well, you can specify a grid of any size you like. How about three screens across and two down? No problem.

And if that isn't enough space for you, you can also have multiple desktops, each composed of multiple pages! You might use separate desktops for different applications or different projects, whatever you like. **fvwm2** provides the tools for you to navigate whatever space you design.

**fvwm2** is also customizable in a vast number of other ways, some of the more significant of which this chapter will summarize. What it all boils down to is maximum workspace and maximum flexibility.

## Running fvwm2

Most flavors of Linux will come with some reasonably current version of **fvwm2**. If you're running GNOME or KDE, the easiest way to switch over to **fvwm2** is to:

1.  Invoke the window manager in your X client's startup file. (Depending on your environment, this file may be called *.xinitrc*, *.startx*, *.xsession*, or *.Xclients*.)

2.  Then restart X.

Here is an excerpt from a simple startup file that has been edited to run **fvwm2**:

```
xterm -geometry +50+0 &
xterm -geometry -0+0&
fvwm2 &
xterm -title login -iconic
```

Although hypothetically you can run **fvwm2** along with GNOME or KDE, they provide greatly overlapping functionality. What you get is an ugly hybrid and not **fvwm** at all.

## Configuration Files

The key to how **fvwm2** works is the configuration file it reads at startup or restart. The systemwide configuration file is called *system.fvwm2rc* and usually lives in the directory */etc/X11/fvwm2*.

The typical *system.fvwm2rc* file that gets distributed should create a simple but perfectly workable environment. We'll take a look at one in the next section. There's no guarantee that the file on your system will create the same layout, but you'll get the idea.

If you want to customize **fvwm2** to suit your needs, you need to make a copy of *system.fvwm2rc* called *.fvwm2rc* and put it in your home directory. This personal configuration file takes precedence over the systemwide file. You edit your *.fvwm2rc* file to adapt the window manager to your needs.

There are a few simple rules in editing your *.fvwm2rc* file. First, any line that begins with a pound sign (#) is a comment (i.e., it is not interpreted as part of the window manager definition). Second, a plus sign (+) at the beginning of a line means to repeat the first terms from the previous line. The section "Making the FvwmWinList Part of Your Default Environment," later in this chapter, illustrates the use of this syntax. The final thing to keep in mind is that it will make life simpler if you weave your own definitions into the file, respecting its current contents and their order. So, for instance, if you decide to define some function keys, put your new lines in the section of the file that already deals with keys.

In terms of **fvwm2** customization, there's some good news and some bad news. The good news is that you can make an extraordinary number of changes to the way **fvwm2** looks and operates. That's also the bad news. The window manager has dozens of configuration options, many very handy and easy to use, others complex and even arcane. The sum total can make the configuration file syntax daunting to anyone who isn't accustomed to serious tinkering. In fact, you could get dizzy considering the possibilities.

The **fvwm2** manpage gives all of the configuration options and illustrates their use; you may also want to consult the manpages for the so-called **fvwm2** modules, introduced in the next section. The web site *http://www.fvwm.org* is the definitive source for window manager documentation, news, source code, and updates.

This chapter should help you cut to the chase in performing some of the more basic and useful customizations, as well as some tricky but handy upgrades.

## *A Modular Approach*

**fvwm2** has been designed to allow the interested programmer or programmer wanna-be to devise new components, known to insiders as *modules*. A typical module is the Pager (FvwmPager), which provides a map of the desktop space and a way to navigate it, as we'll see a little later in the chapter. The Pager is a default module in just about any environment.

The FvwmWinList is another useful module. Though not as ubiquitous as the Pager, it is just as useful. The FvwmWinList is a small window that provides a list of all the windows running on all pages of all desktops. The WinList is another navigation tool, allowing you to switch the pointer focus to any application you have running and to switch the screen view so that you can use that application. More about this later.

A module is actually a separate program from **fvwm2** but works in concert with it, passing commands to be executed to the window manager. Many configurations of **fvwm2** have a Root menu with an FvwmModules submenu from which you can start certain of these programs. (Naturally the list of modules on the menu is configurable.) You might also edit your *fvwm2rc* file to run modules in other ways (when you type certain keys, when other events happen, etc.).

Since a module is a separate program, users can write their own modules without adversely affecting **fvwm2**. Note, however, that you must configure **fvwm2** to start the module process; you cannot start one from the command line. Note that while some modules, like the Pager, are intended to be used for the entire session, others simply perform a function and exit (e.g., RefreshWindow). Since modules are programs in their own right, many of them have their own manpages too.

# How to Implement Window Manager Customizations

If you edit your *.fvwm2rc* file, simply restart **fvwm2** to have the changes implemented. In most environments, there will be a menu item that restarts the window manager. The vanilla setup we started with offers the item Exit **fvwm2** on the Root menu. If you select that item, you'll get a submenu titled Really quit fvwm? and several items including Restart **fvwm2**. When you select Restart **fvwm2**, your configuration changes should be implemented. A slower but just as effective way is to quit the X session and start it again (presuming your session startup file includes **fvwm2**).

# A Quick Tour of the fvwm Environment

In any desktop environment with multiple virtual screens/pages, you can work on only a single screenful at a time. But **fvwm2** makes it easy to switch the view between pages, run applications on different pages, and move applications between them. If you refer to a particular window all the time, you can even arrange for it to appear on every page of every desktop. (We'll come back to this concept of "sticky" windows.) And you're not limited to viewing a page proper or keeping a window entirely on a single page.

Notice the long horizontal box in the bottom right corner of our sample environment (Figure 17-1). This box is the **FvwmButtons** module (also called the *button bar*). FvwmButtons is generally used to house a number of tools and applications to which the user needs frequent access. Often these are other **fvwm** modules.

In our sample configuration, FvwmButtons contains two other modules: the Icon Manager (FvwmIconMan) on the left side of the box and to its right, the Pager (FvwmPager). At the far right of FvwmButtons you'll also see three small application windows: **xbiff** (a mailbox that indicates when you have new messages), **xclock**, and **xload** (a graphic representation of your system's workload).

The Icon Manager and the Pager are tools that let you both monitor what's happening in your environment and manipulate the windows running there. The Icon Manager shows an entry for every conventional window currently on your display. If that window is iconified, the Icon Manager entry is preceded by a square that has a three-dimensional appearance. You can iconify and deiconify any window on the current page by clicking the first pointer button on the corresponding entry in the Icon Manager. (The Icon Manager always shows the windows on the current page; for a similar tool that reflects what's running on every page on every desktop, check out the FvwmWinList, described later in this chapter.)

Think of the Pager as a tiny mirror of your entire desktop(s). In a typical default environment of a single desktop composed of two-by-two screen pages, the Pager shows a small grid of four partitions separated by dotted lines. These partitions correspond to the desktop's four virtual screen pages. (If you configure for multiple desktops, a solid line is used to show the border between desktops. The section "Having Multiple Desktops," later in this chapter, tells you how to set this up.)

```
                              xterm
[val@dhcp-254-105 ~]$ ftp ruby
Connected to ruby.ora.com.
220 ruby.ora.com FTP server (Version wu-2.6.0(1) Fri Apr 28 15:38:08 EDT 2000) r
eady.
Name (ruby:val):
331 Password required for val.
Password:
230 User val logged in.
Remote system type is UNIX.
Using binary mode to transfer files.
ftp> put 17-1.xwd
local: 17-1.xwd remote: 17-1.xwd
200 PORT command successful.
150 Opening BINARY mode data connection for 17-1.xwd.
226 Transfer complete.
960875 bytes sent in 1.29 secs (7.3e+02 Kbytes/sec)
ftp> bye
221-You have transferred 960875 bytes in 1 files.
221-Total traffic for this session was 961286 bytes in 1 transfers.
221-Thank you for using the FTP service on ruby.ora.com.
221 Goodbye.
[val@dhcp-254-105 ~]$ xsetroot -solid gray
[val@dhcp-254-105 ~]$ xwd -root > 17-2.xwd
```

*Figure 17–1. A typical fvwm2 environment*

Each application you run appears in miniature in the Pager window. Applications with small windows are fairly hard to spot in miniature, but a blip representing them is there if you look closely. The miniature version of a larger client, like *xterm*, should have a readable label.

Whatever operations you perform on windows on the desktop—e.g., move, iconify, resize, and so on—are mirrored in the Pager. But the Pager is more than a monitor of activity; it's also a tool. Thus, you can move the miniature versions, and the actual windows will be moved. The Pager can also help you move windows between pages and desktops and select the area to be displayed on your monitor (which does not have to correspond to a page proper).

In addition to the desktop tools, **fvwm2** is commonly configured to provide a slew of cascading menus beginning with the Root menu. Clicking the first pointer button on the root window should reveal this menu. The Root menu is usually a good way to start a new terminal emulator window. If you start with the default environment for your system, the Root menu is likely to have submenus like Fvwm Modules, Fvwm Window Ops (which offers items like moving, resizing, and closing windows), Fvwm Simple Config Ops (for changing focus policies, how paging works, etc.), and Exit Fvwm (for restarting or exiting the window manager, starting another one, etc.).

This chapter assumes you know how to perform basic window manager operations. We're not going to teach you how to use the Pager or all the menu items. But we will show you how to change the number of desktops the Pager shows, add menu items, configure keyboard shortcuts, and make useful customizations.

## *Specifying Click-to-Type Focus*

Most versions of **fvwm2** are configured to use the pointer focus model (FocusFollowsMouse or MouseFocus in the configuration file). This means you need to move the pointer into a window in order to type in it, post an application menu, and so forth. However, **fvwm2** is somewhat more versatile than other window managers in this regard.

There are two other focus policies available: click-to-type focus (ClickToFocus), which requires you to click the pointer on the window in order to type in it, and the very handy SloppyFocus, which is like pointer focus with a twist—the focus does not leave the last window that had it until you move it into another window that takes over the focus. This can come in handy, particularly with terminal emulator windows like **xterm** and **rxvt**. You can actually move the pointer out of the way—accidentally or on purpose—and still continue to type in the window.

The best part of **fvwm2**'s way of handling focus policy is that you can mix and match what windows use what type of focus. All of the settings for focus policy are used as arguments to the Style variable. (Style takes several arguments that determine the appearance and behavior of a particular client or window manager component.)

In the following excerpt from a configuration file, the first line makes pointer focus the default for all applications (the asterisk is a wildcard). The subsequent lines specify the exceptions to this rule. The button bar works better with click-to-type focus, as do **xman** (the manpage viewer) and **xmag** (a magnification tool). The two terminal emulators benefit from sloppy focus.

```
Style "*"           FocusFollowsMouse
Style "FvwmButtons" Icon toolbox.xpm, ClickToFocus
Style "xman"        Icon xman.xpm, RandomPlacement, ClickToFocus
Style "xmag"        Icon mag_glass.xpm, RandomPlacement, ClickToFocus
Style "XTerm"       Icon xterm.xpm, SloppyFocus, IconBox -70 1 -1 -140
Style "rxvt"        Icon term.xpm, SloppyFocus, IconBox -70 1 -1 -140
```

(See Style on the **fvwm2** manpage for more information about this versatile option.)

In our sample configuration, the Simple Config Ops submenu of the Root menu offers three items that let you change the focus policy on the fly, just for the current window manager session:

- Sloppy Focus

- Click to Focus

- Focus Follows Mouse

*fvwm2*

Note, however, that these items supersede what's in your configuration file for all applications. If you want to recover the more specialized definitions in your configuration file, you'll have to restart the window manager.

## *Raising the Focus Window Automatically*

If you're using pointer focus (FocusFollowsMouse), you might want to consider also using the FvwmAuto module to automatically raise the focus window. If we add the following line to our *fvwm2rc* file, the focus window is automatically raised after the pointer has been in it for 200 milliseconds:

```
Module FvwmAuto 200
```

(That's one-fifth of a second to metric-resistant types.) The delay is important and makes FvwmAuto much more practical. Generally when pointer focus is in effect, an autoraise feature can make the display seem chaotic: when you move the pointer across the screen, the focus hits several windows and they are raised in a distracting shuffle. With an autoraise delay, you can avoid the shuffling by moving the pointer quickly to the window you want to focus on.

If you use ClickToFocus mode by default, the autoraise feature is built in and you don't have to make this modification.

Of course, those who adapt to using the FvwmWinList module to transfer focus will have their windows raised automatically, without having to edit their *fvwm2rc* file—or even move the pointer off the WinList.

One of your menus may also be configured to offer an item that turns on autoraise on the fly and another item that turns it off again. In some default setups, the Fvwm Modules menu features AutoRaise and Stop AutoRaise for these purposes.

## *Changing the Size of the Desktop*

Many default configuration files have a default desktop of two screen pages across (horizontal) by two screen pages down (vertical), which in the configuration file is defined using the line:

```
DeskTopSize 2x2
```

It's easy to change the size of your desktop by editing the dimensions of the grid. Thus, the following line creates a desktop of three pages across by two pages down:

```
DeskTopSize 3x2
```

You don't have to have multiple pages in both directions. You can have a desktop of one page above another above another:

```
DeskTopSize 1x3
```

You don't even have to have multiple pages at all:

```
DeskTopSize 1x1
```

But then why use **fvwm2**?

Of course, the number of pages you select will depend on your space needs and style of working and also on whether you will use more than one desktop (described in the next section). If you configure for multiple desktops, each one will have the same exact DeskTopSize. So if you want a desktop for work and one for play, you may not need each one to be many pages. Two desktops of three-by-three, for instance, would give you a total of 18 pages to get lost on. Yipes. However, graphical artists may welcome a larger workspace.

## Having Multiple Desktops

In order to work with multiple desktops, you simply have to configure the Pager to display the number of desktops you want. Each desktop will have the same number of pages, the number you've specified using DeskTopSize (see the preceding section, "Changing the Size of the Desktop").

In order to specify more than one desktop, you'll need to edit a line that looks something like this one:

```
*FvwmButtons(2x2 Frame 2 Swallow(UseOld) "FvwmPager" "Module FvwmPager 0 0")
```

This line incorporates the Pager into the FvwmButtons module (the button bar). The two numbers at the end of the definition line give the range of desktops visible. The first desktop is number 0, and in this case the last desktop is also number 0—i.e., there is only one.

If you want two desktops, change the final number to a 1:

```
*FvwmButtons(1x2 Frame 2 Swallow(UseOld) "FvwmPager" "Module FvwmPager 0 1")
```

The following line would create a Pager with four desktops, numbered through 3:

```
*FvwmButtons(1x2 Frame 2 Swallow(UseOld) "FvwmPager" "Module FvwmPager 0 3")
```

Few people will require this much space. But even if you add only a single desktop, keep in mind that you may have to change the overall dimensions of the Pager, and thus of the button bar that contains it, in order to have a reasonably sized view of your various desktops. You may also have to reallocate the space you have so that the Pager gets a large enough area.

There are a few relevant sizes you can tinker with to make room for a Pager that shows multiple desktops:

- The dimensions of the button bar (FvwmButtons module)

- The number of columns the button bar is divided into

- How many of those columns the Pager takes up

A typical FvwmButtons module might be 520 pixels wide and 100 pixels high:

```
*FvwmButtonsGeometry 520x100-1-1
```

*fvwm2*

And it might be configured as two rows and five columns (the sizes of which are entirely dependent on FvwmButton's geometry):

```
*FvwmButtons(Frame 2 Padding 2 2 Container(Rows 2 Columns 5 Frame 1 Padding 10 0))
```

In this particular setup, the Pager takes up a one-column by two-row section of the FvwmButtons module:

```
*FvwmButtons(1x2 Frame 2 Swallow(UseOld) "FvwmPager" "Module FvwmPager 0 1")
```

The Icon Manager takes up three columns:

```
*FvwmButtons(3x2 Frame 2 Swallow "FvwmIconMan" "Module FvwmIconMan")
```

And the remaining column is occupied by the desktop applications (e.g., **xbiff**, **xclock**, **xload**) that run within a Container in the FvwmButtons module:

```
*FvwmButtons(1x2 Frame 0 Container(Rows 2 Columns 2 Frame 0))
*FvwmButtons(Frame 2 Swallow(UseOld,NoHints,Respawn) "xbiff" 'Exec exec xbiff -bg
bisque3')
*FvwmButtons(Frame 3 Swallow(UseOld,NoHints,Respawn) "xclock" 'Exec exec xclock -bg
bisque3 -fg black -hd black -hl black -padding 0 update 1')
*FvwmButtons(2x1 Frame 2 Swallow(UseOld,NoHints,Respawn) "xload" 'Exec exec xload -bg
bisque3 -fg black -update 5 -nolabel')
```

Notice that the container is further subdivided into two rows and two columns so the applications can be laid out. But don't let this layer confuse you. (Parsing the configuration file can be exacting.)

Back to the issue of multiple desktops. If you want two desktops, first set that up by changing the number of the final desktop to a 1 at the end of this line:

```
*FvwmButtons(1x2 Frame 2 Swallow(UseOld) "FvwmPager" "Module FvwmPager 0 1")
```

Then to make the Pager big enough to display both desktops adequately, add some pixels to the width of the button bar. Here's an extra hundred from the 520 we started with:

```
*FvwmButtonsGeometry 620x100-1-1
```

And let's also reallocate the available five columns so that the icon manager takes up only two (rather than the three it started with), and give the extra column to the Pager. The section with the applications remains a single column wide:

```
*FvwmButtons(2x2 Frame 2 Swallow "FvwmIconMan" "Module FvwmIconMan")
*FvwmButtons(2x2 Frame 2 Swallow(UseOld) "FvwmPager" "Module FvwmPager 0 0")
*FvwmButtons(1x2 Frame 0 Container(Rows 2 Columns 2 Frame 0))
```

Figure 17-2 shows our new double desktop reflected in the updated button box. This is just one sample customization. With your individual needs and display specifics, you can imagine how complicated this can get. But it's easy to test your changes by simply restarting the window manager.

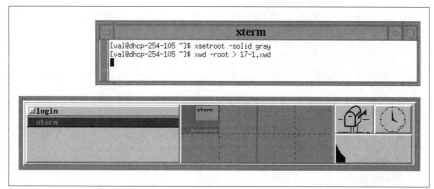

*Figure 17–2. The modified FvwmButtons module shows two desktops in the Pager*

# Making the Same Window Appear on Every Page

A window that appears on every virtual screen page is called a *sticky* window because it seems to stick to the glass. Some windows are designated as sticky in the *system.fvwm2rc* file, among them **xbiff**, programs ending in *lock* (e.g., clock programs such as **xclock** and **oclock**), and all of the **fvwm2** modules (because you need the button bar, Pager, etc., on every page).

If you want a window to appear on the desktop no matter what page you're viewing, you need to specify that in your *.fvwm2rc* file. The specification requires you to use the Style variable, followed by the client's name, and a hard-to-forget parameter, Sticky. The Style variable is used to set many different characteristics. Here are some lines you might see in a configuration file to establish that a window is sticky, among other things:

```
Style "xbiff"      NoTitle, Sticky, WindowListSkip, ClickToFocus
Style "*lock"      NoTitle, NoHandles, Sticky, WindowListSkip, ClickToFocus
Style "Fvwm*"      NoTitle,  Sticky, WindowListSkip
```

Notice that the Style variable can recognize a wildcard character (*) to widen the scope of the definition. Fvwm* would encompass all **fvwm2** modules.

Try adding the following line, which specifies that an application called **xpostit** will stick to the glass:

```
Style "xpostit"    Sticky
```

Practically speaking, you probably also want to specify that **xpostit** uses click-to-type focus and doesn't appear on the FvwmWinList, so this definition is better:

```
Style "xpostit"    Sticky, WindowListSkip, ClickToFocus
```

In most cases, you'll want only small windows that you run a single instance of (and that you use frequently) to be sticky. Having a terminal emulator like *xterm* appear on every page is not as practical; it would take up too much space. However, if you do want a client like *xterm* to follow you around, be sure to give that instance of the program a distinctive name using the **-name** option.

For example, in your X session startup file you could run an **xterm** you name **mailwindow**:

```
xterm -name mailwindow &
```

Then make that window appear on every page by adding the following line to your *.fvwm2rc* file:

```
Style "mailwindow"  Sticky
```

If you'd like to make a particular window sticky temporarily, look for an Fvwm Window Ops menu under your Root menu. Commonly you will find a toggle to (Un)Stick a Window. Or you can set up such a menu item yourself. See the section "Customizing Menus," later in this chapter.

## *Starting Windows on Different Desktops and Pages*

There's an obvious, low-tech way to start applications on different desktops and on different pages within a desktop: switch the view to the desktop and page you want (using the Pager, keyboard shortcuts, or whatever method you like), open a terminal emulator window (e.g., using the Root menu), then run any program you like. Voila. The application window opens on the current desktop and page.

But there are two automated ways to accomplish this same thing. In the first method, you specify in your *.fvwm2rc* file that certain programs will appear on certain desktops and/or pages automatically when you run them. You do this using **fvwm2**'s Style variable, which takes two relevant options: StartsOnPage and StartsOnDesk.

Here comes a confusing part. StartsOnPage takes up to three numeric arguments. If there is only one argument, it corresponds to the number of the desk on which to open the application. If there are three arguments, the second and third additionally identify the page, using an X,Y coordinate scheme. We'll come back to this in a moment. (Two arguments alone are interpreted as the X,Y coordinates of the page.)

And what about the closely associated StartsOnDesk variable? A little more confusion here. StartsOnDesk takes only one argument: the desk number. But since you can set this with StartsOnPage, along with the more specific page address, in practice there is no need to use StartsOnDesk at all. The only real reason to use StartsOnDesk is if you want your *.fvwm2rc* file definitions to be as obvious as possible.

Now back to desktop and page addressing. Let's consider the addressing scheme of a single two-by-two-page desktop. Just as the first desk is addressed as number 0, the first page on a desk is 0,0. The next page to the right is 1,0. The third page clockwise (the lower-right quadrant) is 1,1. And the fourth page clockwise (the lower-left quadrant) is 0,1.

Supposing there are at least two desktops of four pages each, the following definition says that when you run an **xterm** called "bigxterm" it will be opened in the lower-left quadrant (0,1) of the second desktop (number 1):

```
Style "bigxterm"    StartsOnPage 1 0 1
```

Once you make this update to your *fvwm2rc* file and restart the window manager, running the command:

```
xterm -name bigxterm &
```

will open the window where you want it.

You also have the option of accomplishing the same thing using X resource syntax on the command line. This strategy may even be a little more practical than putting the definitions in your *fvwm2rc* file because you won't have to define many different instances of the various programs (e.g., bigxterm, littlexterm, mailwindow, or whatever). The **-xrm** option (recognized by many X clients) lets you specify an X resource variable on the command line:

```
xterm -xrm '*Page: 1 0 1' &
```

You can even put a series of such lines in your X session startup file in order to open applications wherever you want them on your desktop(s) when you log in.

While it looks as if these two methods of opening windows on different desktops/pages (the Style variable with StartsOnPage or StartsOnDesk and the **-xrm** command-line option) produce identical results, there is actually a subtle difference in behavior. When you use Style with StartsOnPage (or StartsOnDesk) and you specify only the desktop number, the window is opened on the first page (0,0) of that desk. If you give the same information on the command line (using **-xrm**), the destination page of the new window is related to the page you're on when you run the command. The new window appears on the analogous page of the desktop you specify.

You have still one more alternative if you're interested in opening a window on a different page within the current desktop. Run a window with the **-geometry** option and supply large enough coordinates to place it on a particular page in the desktop. If you use a desktop three pages square, the following line places a window in the middle page (of the nine-page grid):

```
xterm -geometry +1200+1200 &
```

Keep in mind, however, that display-specific characteristics play a big part in gauging these distances, and they are not easy to guess.

## *If It's Too Hard (or Easy) to Move the Pointer Between Pages*

If you're trying to navigate the desktop by moving the pointer and you find it either too easy or too difficult to go from one page to the next, there's a configuration file variable you can customize. The aptly named EdgeResistance variable lets you adjust how easy it is to move the pointer beyond the perimeter of the current page.

The variable takes two parameters. The first is more relevant to the problem at hand: the number of milliseconds the pointer must be at the screen edge before you'll be moved onto the next page. The second parameter has to do with the way a window is moved between pages: it's the number of pixels over the edge of the screen a window's border must move before it moves partially off the screen. Typical default settings are:

```
EdgeResistance 250 10
```

Some people find the EdgeResistance they're working with is too low for them, the inconvenient result being that they inadvertently knock the pointer off of the current screen page. If this is your problem, you can increase the first parameter:

```
EdgeResistance 500 10
```

A first parameter between 500 and 1000 will greatly enhance the resistance. The maximum resistance is 10000, which actually makes it impossible to page over.

As it happens, if you have the opposite problem and have to bounce the mouse against what feels like a hard rubber wall in order to page over, try reducing the first number:

```
EdgeResistance 100 10
```

In a typical default configuration, **fvwm2** is set up to provide a number of menu options that let you change your paging options on the fly. A number of them are located on the Fvwm Simple Config Ops menu, a submenu of the Root menu. Thus, you can toggle the ability to page on and off with Full Paging On and All Paging Off.

All Paging Off does exactly what it sounds like—it limits you to keeping the pointer on the current page. You might prefer this if you're going to be working on that page for a while and you don't want to worry about knocking the pointer onto another page. You can toggle paging back on with the Full Paging On menu item.

There are other items to constrain paging in different ways (e.g., Horizontal Paging Only, Vertical Paging Only).

The Partial Paging item lets you move the pointer so that the view straddles two adjacent pages; the area you see will be highlighted in the Pager window.

The item Full Paging & Edge Wrap actually expands the range of paging possibilities. Normally when you reach the edge of a desktop, you can't move the pointer beyond. With this item selected, you can drag the pointer beyond the edge of the desktop, and it wraps around to the page on the other side (either horizontally or vertically). Thus, if you have the pointer in the upper-right page of a two-by-two desktop, and you drag the pointer off of the right edge, it will wrap around to the upper-left page of that desktop.

Underlying all of these menu items is the EdgeScroll variable. Here are the Edge-Scroll parameters that map to the various menu items:

```
Full Paging ON            EdgeScroll 100 100
All Paging OFF            EdgeScroll 0 0
Horizontal Paging Only   EdgeScroll 100 0
Vertical Paging Only     EdgeScroll 0 100
Partial Paging           EdgeScroll 50 50
Full Paging & Edge Wrap  EdgeScroll 100000 100000
```

EdgeScroll's two parameters specify the percentage of a page to scroll when you reach the border of the page. The first parameter is for horizontal moves, the second for vertical. If the horizontal and vertical percentages are multipled by 1000, scrolling will wrap around at the edge of the desktop. EdgeScroll 100000 100000 will wrap both for both horizontal and vertical moves.

Rather than rely on menu items like these, you could make any of these a default behavior by putting the EdgeScroll variable on its own line in your *fvwm2rc* file. See the **fvwm2** manpage and check out the *system.fvwm2rc* file for guidance.

Note that none of these variations will scroll you from one desktop to another. The next section shows how to configure some keyboard shortcuts to do just that.

# *Adding Keyboard Shortcuts*

The bare-bones *system.fvwmrc* file that we started with offers little in the way of keyboard shortcuts, or accelerators, for window management functions. But if you're one of those users who prefers to keep her hands on the keyboard and off the mouse as much as possible, within your *fvwm2rc* file you can easily define keys to perform a variety of functions.

## *Keyboard Shortcuts to Navigate the Desktop*

The Pager is a great tool for getting around one or more desktops. But many people hate using the mouse. You can configure a bunch of keys to let you move around in various ways.

Add the following lines to your *fvwm2rc* file to set up key combinations to scroll one page in any direction on the desktop using Ctrl plus an arrow key. The view scrolls in the direction of the arrow.

Each definition uses the Key variable followed by:

1. The name of the key

2. The context (location) in which it must be typed

3. Any modifying keys (that must also be held down)

4. The action initiated by the key or key combination

Thus, in the following example, the first definition line says that pressing the left arrow key in any "A" context, while also holding down the Ctrl "C" key will scroll the screen one page to the left on the current desktop:

```
# Press arrow + Control in any context
# to scroll by one page in the direction of the arrow
Key Left        A           C       Scroll -100 0
Key Right       A           C       Scroll +100 +0
Key Up          A           C       Scroll +0    -100
Key Down        A           C       Scroll +0    +100
```

*fvwm2*

Table 17-1 summarizes the functionality.

*Table 17–1. Key Combinations to Change the Page*

| Key Combination | Moves View |
|---|---|
| Control, right arrow key | One page to the right |
| Control, left arrow key | One page to the left |
| Control, up arrow key | One page up |
| Control, down arrow key | One page down |

The Scroll variable takes the same parameters as EdgeScroll, which are explained in the section "If It's Too Hard (or Easy) to Move the Pointer Between Pages," earlier in this chapter. See the **fvwm2** manpage for more information. Note that the key combinations we've defined let you get around a single desktop but won't let you advance to another desktop. We'll deal with that contingency later.

Here's another possible key binding. This one advances the view to every page in the desktop in order and finally wraps back to the first page. You use the Tab key while holding down Control, again in any context. The definition line looks like this:

```
# Press Tab + Control in any context to scroll
# by one page with wrap scrolling
Key Tab        A        C        Scroll 100000 0
```

Table 17-2 summarizes another page-changing combination.

*Table 17–2. Another Key Combination to Change the Page*

| Key Combination | Moves View |
|---|---|
| Control, Tab | To the next page in the desktop |

Since application windows can straddle pages, there may be times when you want the screen to display a screenful other than a page proper. (You might also want to look at windows on two different pages at once.) The following shortcuts scroll the view one-tenth of a page at a time. Instead of Control, these shortcuts use the so-called Meta key. This is a symbolic name—the actual key that serves the Meta function varies from keyboard to keyboard. In many cases, the key labeled Alt serves as the Meta key. Here are the configuration file definition lines:

```
## Press arrow + meta key in any context
## to scroll by 1/10 of a page in the direction of arrow
Key Left        A        M        Scroll -10 +0
Key Right       A        M        Scroll +10 +0
Key Up          A        M        Scroll +0   -10
Key Down        A        M        Scroll +0   +10
```

These lines establish the following functionality, outlined in Table 17-3.

*Table 17–3. Key Combinations to Scroll the Page by 1/10*

| Key Combination | Moves View |
|---|---|
| Meta, left arrow key | One-tenth page to the left |
| Meta, right arrow key | One-tenth page to the left |
| Meta, up arrow key | One-tenth page up |
| Meta, down arrow key | One-tenth page down |

If you have more than one desktop, you can also create shortcuts to move between those. The following two shortcuts are intended to let you go back and forth between desktops in a two-desktop environment:

```
## Press Control + Return in any context
## to scroll forward by 1 desktop
Key Return        A       C       Desk 1 1 1
## Press Shift + Control + Return in any context
## to scroll back by 1 desktop
Key Return        A       SC      Desk -1 0 0
```

Table 17-4 summarizes these shortcuts.

*Table 17–4. Key Combinations to Scroll to the Next Desktop*

| Key Combination | Moves View |
|---|---|
| Control + Return | One desktop ahead |
| Shift + Control + Return | One desktop back |

The second and third parameters to the Desk variable constrain the paging so that you can't page beyond the first or second desktops. (Hypothetically, you can page outside the view of the Pager!) If you have more than two desktops, you will need to edit these definitions. See the **fvwm2** manpage for more about the Desk variable.

## Moving the Pointer with Keystrokes

The previous section outlines some keyboard shortcuts you can define to scroll the page view. But you can also define shortcuts to move the position of the pointer on the screen. Admittedly this is for people who are downright mouse haters. But if you're someone who prefers to use the keyboard to the mouse, these shortcuts can come in handy. They employ the CursorMove variable, also described on the **fvwm2** manpage.

The keyboard accelerators in the first group move the cursor symbol one-tenth of a screen at a time. The first definition line says that pressing the left arrow key in any "A" context, while also holding down the Shift "S" and Meta "M" keys will move the cursor one-tenth of a page in the direction of the arrow:

```
## Press Shift + Meta + arrow in any context
## to move the pointer by 1/10 of a page in direction of arrow
Key Left          A       SM      CursorMove -10  +0
Key Right         A       SM      CursorMove +10  +0
```

```
Key Up            A         SM          CursorMove +0    -10
Key Down          A         SM          CursorMove +0    +10
```

Table 17-5 summarizes the commands.

*Table 17–5. Key Combinations to Move the Pointer by 1/10 of the Page*

| Key Combination | Moves Pointer |
| --- | --- |
| Meta, Shift, left arrow key | One-tenth of a page to the left |
| Meta, Shift, right arrow key | One-tenth of a page to the right |
| Meta, Shift, up arrow key | One-tenth of a page up |
| Meta, Shift, down arrow key | One-tenth of a page down |

If you want to have just about as much control moving the pointer with keystrokes as you do moving it by hand, you can specify shortcuts to move it a mere one percent of a page at a time:

```
## Press Shift + Control + arrow in any context
## to move the pointer by 1% of a page in direction of arrow
Key Left          A         SC          CursorMove -1 0
Key Right         A         SC          CursorMove +1 +0
Key Up            A         SC          CursorMove +0    -1
Key Down          A         SC          CursorMove +0    +1
```

Table 17-6 summarizes the commands.

*Table 17–6. Key Combinations to Move the Pointer by 1 Percent of the Page*

| Key Combination | Moves Pointer |
| --- | --- |
| Shift, Control, left arrow key | One percent of a page to the left |
| Shift, Control, right arrow key | One percent of a page to the right |
| Shift, Control, up arrow key | One percent of a page up |
| Shift, Control, down arrow key | One percent of a page down |

## *Keyboard Shortcuts for Menu and Window Manipulation*

So far we've limited our keyboard shortcuts to scrolling the view and moving the pointer. But you can create keyboard bindings for any window manager function.

Here are some sample bindings to perform simple window operations and to display a few menus:

```
# Keyboard accelerators
Key F1            A         M           Iconify
Key F2            A         M           Move
Key F3            A         M           Resize
Key F4            A         M           Popup "RootMenu"
Key F5            A         M           Popup "Misc-Ops"
Key F6            A         M           Popup "Utilities"
Key F7            A         M           Popup "Module-Popup"
```

```
Key F10        A      M        Restart fvwm2
Key F12        A      SM       Close
```

These are just sample bindings; you may want to set up your own keyboard short-cuts to do entirely different things. But these bindings will let us look at some of the possibilities, as well as potential problems.

In our sample definition lines, the first binding specifies that if you press the F1 function key while holding down the Meta "M" key, with the pointer in any "A" context, the focus window will be iconified (or deiconified). Meta+F2 lets you ini-tiate moving the focus window, while Meta+F3 starts a resize operation. (The Meta key is described in the section "Keyboard Shortcuts to Navigate the Desktop," ear-lier in this chapter.)

Note that if you've adopted the keyboard bindings to move the pointer (as described in the previous section), you can perform the move and resize opera-tions entirely with keystrokes. For example, use Meta+F2 to begin a move, then drag the window outline by moving the pointer symbol using the appropriate key-board shortcuts, then press the Return key to complete the operation.

In addition, we've set up function keys to pop-up four different menus, the con-tents of which are also defined in the *.fvwm2rc* file. Once a menu is popped up, you can use the up and down arrow keys to highlight items on the menu, right and left keys to move down and up through submenus (cascading menus), the Return key to select an item, and Esc to pop down the menu without making a selection.

Because we do a lot of tinkering with **fvwm2** customization, we have set up Meta+F10 to restart the window manager. This is much faster than bringing up menus.

We've also created a key combination to close the focus window: Shift+Meta+F12. Certainly it's handy to be able to get rid of a window with a keyboard shortcut, but you don't want it to be too easy or you may do it by mistake. Having an extra modifying key (Shift) and using the very last function key (F12) require you to act deliberately in closing a window using this method.

## Customizing Menus

Among the window manager features and functions defined in the configuration file are the contents of menus. The *system.fvwm2rc* file generally defines a number of menus intended to be useful to a large percentage of people. But what menus you have, if any, and what they offer, are basically up to you.

Typically the Root menu would be defined:

```
AddToMenu RootMenu    "Root Menu"          Title
+                     "XTerm"              Exec exec xterm
+                     "Rxvt"               Exec exec rxvt
+                     ""                   Nop
+                     "Remote Logins"      Popup Remote-Logins
+                     ""                   Nop
+                     "Utilities"          Popup Utilities
+                     ""                   Nop
```

| + | "Fvwm Modules" | Popup Module-Popup |
| + | "Fvwm Window Ops" | Popup Window-Ops |
| + | "Fvwm Simple Config Ops" | Popup Misc-Ops |
| + | "" | Nop |
| + | "Refresh Screen" | Refresh |
| + | "Recapture Screen" | Recapture |
| + | "" | Nop |
| + | "Exit Fvwm" | Popup Quit-Verify |

You use the AddToMenu variable to create a menu. The first parameter AddToMenu takes is the name of the menu, in this case RootMenu. The menu name is used to reference the menu elsewhere in the configuration file (e.g., to specify a key binding to pop-up the menu). (Note that the AddToMenu variable and the menu name are repeated on each line of the menu definition, as indicated by the plus sign.

Each line of the definition creates a line on the menu; that may be the menu title, a menu item proper, a blank line, or a separator. The third component of each line specifies the text that appears on that line. The fourth component specifies the window manager function to be performed.

The first line of our example specifies the menu title. Lines with empty text fields ("") and the Nop function (which specifies "No operation") are used to create divider lines on the menu.

The Pop-up function is worth looking at more closely. Pop-up specifies that a menu is displayed; the menu name is given as an argument to Pop-up. When Pop-up is invoked from another menu, it creates a submenu (or cascading menu). This sample Root Menu definition has six submenus, named Remote-Logins, Utilities, Module-Popup, Window-Ops, Misc-Ops, and Quit-Verify. These menus would also be defined using the AddToMenu command, elsewhere in the configuration file.

You can use the sample menus in the *system.fvwm2rc* file and the **fvwm2** man-page to modify the existing menus or create your own. It is simple to replace definition lines in the template menus and not much more difficult to write one from scratch.

You can also change how the menus are displayed. Perhaps you don't want a bunch of cascading menus off of the Root menu. In the previous section we set up some function keys to display certain menus. That's one option. You might instead specify pointer buttons to display various menus. In a typical default, the first pointer button displays the Root menu and the second displays the Window Ops menu. But since most Window Ops functions (e.g., Move, Resize; Iconify) are available using the pointer directly on parts of a window, you may instead choose to have the second pointer button display another menu (e.g., Utilities).

## *The FvwmWinList: Switching the Focus*

The FvwmWinList is an **fvwm2** module that lets you keep track of all the application windows on your many screen pages. Generally the WinList is configured to let you switch the focus to whatever window you want, but hypothetically you can set it up to perform other operations.

In many typical environments, you can start the FvwmWinList from an Fvwm Modules menu (often a submenu of the Root menu). If you'd instead like to configure **fvwm** to start the WinList automatically, see the next section, "Making the FvwmWinList Part of Your Default Environment." (You might also configure a keyboard shortcut to start the WinList module; see the earlier section "Adding Keyboard Shortcuts" for details.)

Some of FvwmWinList's appearance and behavior can be customized. We'll see some typical module definition lines in the next section. If you are using this configuration, FvwmWinList performs the following operations:

*First mouse button click:*
Switch the focus to the window in question. If the window is iconified, deiconify. Switch the screen view so that the page with the window is displayed.

*Second mouse button click:*
Iconify/deiconify window; the page displayed does not change.

*Third mouse button click:*
Display a pop-up box containing information about the window in question (e.g., dimensions in pixels, whether it is sticky, permanent or transient, etc.). Pop down the box by clicking any mouse button on it.

One of the interesting features of the WinList is that none of these commands moves the pointer to the focus window. Instead, the pointer stays on the entry in the WinList that corresponds to the focus window.

Hypothetically you could simply keep the pointer on the FvwmWinList and do all of your navigation from there—except when you want to work with the Fvwm-Buttons module or another of the windows that don't normally appear in the WinList.

## Using the FvwmWinList with Multiple Instances of the Same Window

The primary limitation of the FvwmWinList is that it's somewhat difficult to tell which window in the list is which. Each entry in the FvwmWinList gives the text that appears in the corresponding window's titlebar. (If the titlebar is suppressed, it gives the text that would normally appear.) If you tend to run the same program many times simultaneously—e.g., several **xterms**—on the FvwmWinList, they all look alike. (The one difference is that iconified windows have entries surrounded by parentheses.)

If you get attached to using the FvwmWinList, you should probably specify different titles for multiple instances of the same window. The standard X options **–title** or **–name** will do the trick. Note, however, that while **–title** changes only the text in the titlebar, **–name** literally changes the name of the application. Thus it affects how resources and configuration file parameters are assigned.

*fvwm2*

## Making the FvwmWinList Part of Your Default Environment

If you want to make FvwmWinList part of your default environment, edit your configuration file to have it run at both initialization and restart of the window manager. In the following example, we've added lines three and six for these purposes:

```
AddToFunc InitFunction    "I" Module FvwmButtons
+          "I" exec xsetroot -mod 2 2 -fg \#554055 -bg \#705070
+          "I" Module FvwmWinList

AddToFunc RestartFunction "I" Module FvwmButtons
+          "I" exec xsetroot -mod 2 2 -fg \#554055 -bg \#705070
+          "I" Module FvwmWinList
```

These lines specify that the FvwmWinList module is run whenever you start or restart the window manager. The window appears in the bottom left corner of the screen.

As an alternative, you might make the FvwmWinList appear as a pop-up menu. The following definition binds the module to the third pointer button when it is held down on the root window (this may not be as handy as having the module present all the time):

```
Mouse 3        R       A       Module FvwmWinList Transient
```

But running a module is different than specifying how it looks and behaves. Like a number of other modules (FvwmButtonBox, FvwmPager, etc.), the various characteristics of the FvwmWinList are defined elsewhere in the configuration file. Here are some typical definition lines:

```
##########################FvwmWinList#######################
*FvwmWinListBack #908090
*FvwmWinListFore Black
*FvwmWinListFont -adobe-helvetica-bold-r-*-*-10-*-*-*-*-*-*-*
*FvwmWinListAction Click1 Iconify -1,Focus
*FvwmWinListAction Click2 Iconify
*FvwmWinListAction Click3 Module "FvwmIdent" FvwmIdent
*FvwmWinListUseSkipList
*FvwmWinListGeometry +0-1
```

The first three lines specify the background color, foreground color, and text font used for the application. The next three define what actions first, second, and third mouse button clicks invoke when you do them within the WinList. UseSkipList tells the WinList not to list any windows that are assigned the Style classification WindowListSkip elsewhere in the configuration file. (Generally all module windows are classified thus and will not appear in the FvwmWinList.) The final line specifies the location at which the window should appear (bottom-left corner).

The WinList is also a sticky window; that is, it appears on every page on every desktop. But the configuration file can be confusing. This characteristic is specified elsewhere in the file, using the Style option:

```
Style "Fvwm*"     NoTitle, Sticky, WindowListSkip
```

This line specifies that all modules (including the WinList) have no titlebars, are sticky, and will not appear on the FvwmWinList. In the case of the FvwmWinList module, having it appear as an entry on itself would be more than a little confusing.

# *Index*

# S

s command (sed), 616

sandboxes, CVS (see CVS utility, sandboxes)

savehist variable (csh/tcsh), 513

saving, vi commands for, 585

Sawfish window manager
  focus behavior of windows, 716
  minimizing/maximizing windows, 717
  moving and resizing windows, 719
  placement of new windows, 719
  shaded windows, 717
  tooltips, displaying, 718
  updating windows, 718
  window appearance, setting, 715
  workspaces, 719

scale keyword, 41

SCCS, importing files from, 651

sched command (csh/tcsh), 545

sched variable (csh/tcsh), 513

screensavers, setting
  GNOME, 709
  KDE, 739

script command, 308-315

script command (ex), 597

scripts
  exiting, 478
  gawk for (see gawk scripting language)
  running all in directory, 306
  shell/Perl, 432

Scroll variable (fvwm2), 762

searching
  for bad blocks, 38
  for commands, 481
  commands for, 8
  Emacs commands for, 563
  file contents, 104, 153, 224, 393
  for files, 116-121, 220
  files contents, 115
  man pages, 32, 380
  metacharacters for, 553-557
  and replacing, 556-557
  vi commands for, 583

searching commands, 8

Second Extended Filesystem
  debugging a, 85
  e2fsck command and, 102

formatting device as, 254

tuning the parameters of, 366

sections
  of files, 76, 323
  man pages, 250

sectors, boot, 400

security
  administration commands for, 15
  firewalls and masquerading, 23-25
    ipchains and, 181-186
    ipfwadm and, 187-191
    iptables and, 192-201

sed editor, 308, 555, 607-618
  commands (by name), 611
  metacharacters for, 552

sed utility, 5

select command (bash), 487

semaphore files, 220

sendmail
  mailq command and, 240
  mailstats command and, 240
  makemap command and, 248
  praliases command and, 284

serial line communication, 22, 320

servers
  getting information on, 318
  NFS, 26-28
  NIS, 27-28
  rshd daemon, 306

set command (bash), 487-490

set command (csh/tcsh), 546

set command (ex), 597

:set command (vi), options, 603-606

setdprm command, 315

setenv command (csh/tcsh), 546

setsid command, 315

settc command (csh/tcsh), 546

setty command (tcsh), 546

sh command, 40

sh shell, 315

shar command, 315-318

shell command (ex), 597

shell programming commands, 9

shell programs, remote, 659

shell variable (csh/tcsh), 513

shell variables
  bash shell, 465-468
  exporting values of, 478

shells, 4, 446-449

# Z